Inclusive Education

A Systematic Perspective

Inclusive Education

A Systematic Perspective

Edited by

Aimee Howley
WordFarmers Associates

Cassondra M. Faiella
The University of Cincinnati

Stephen D. Kroeger
The University of Cincinnati

Barbara Hansen
Muskingum University

INFORMATION AGE PUBLISHING, INC.
Charlotte, NC • www.infoagepub.com

Library of Congress Cataloging-in-Publication Data

CIP record for this book is available from the Library of Congress
http://www.loc.gov

ISBNs: 978-1-64113-928-1(Paperback)

978-1-64113-929-8 (Hardcover)

978-1-64113-930-4 (ebook)

CONTENTS

SECTION VII INTRODUCTION:
STATE SUPPORT FOR INCLUSIVE PRACTICE

FOREWORD

INCLUSIVE PRACTICE

Challenging Exclusion in Educational Norms

Rodrick S. Lucero

In my work with many of the authors of chapters in this book, I have been overwhelmed with hope and excitement about the growth of our profession, and I am confident that readers will find this same sense of inspiration as they engage with the discourse that follows in the book's 27 chapters. As their work shows, the careers of these authors are a testament to the expertise offered by those in the field of education. Daily, they work with students and colleagues, consider and construct theoretical frameworks, look for implementation strategies that make a difference, and participate in the ongoing dialogue of the profession. These processes have informed their thinking and strengthened their determination to champion inclusive practices.

Readers will, I believe, consider themselves fortunate to engage with the authors concerning problems of practice as they read through the chapters. Their described intersections of problem and opportunity, need and resource are rich with nuance, creativity, and intellectual ingenuity in response to the challenge of making improvements to complex systems. Moreover, the authors remind us that the complexity of the systems and the implementation of inclusive practices are not separate; they coexist in many configurations, both in opposition and in support of each other.

Inclusive Education: A Systematic Perspective, pp. ix–xi
Copyright © 2020 by Information Age Publishing
All rights of reproduction in any form reserved.

Inclusivity holds great promise as educators work to eliminate the opportunity gap, ensure safety, and empower individuals and groups who have been marginalized. Inclusive practices promise to guide all students and support their development toward engaged citizenship in an informed society. Inclusive practices are at the heart of our commitment to being effective educators, and this deep commitment moves us to consider the challenge extended by this book for every educator to include every child in the educational opportunities common to all students in our public schools. This committed mindset provides room to maneuver within our current work, and to grow within it, for the good of all students within the system.

The authors of these chapters acknowledge and lay out the complexity of the task of creating inclusive schools. As professionals, they come with differing views and perspectives to address this complexity, by analyzing the difficulty and offering ideas that can empower us as educators to address our own biases as we make meaning and find solutions to our educational conundrums. Such journeys of self-discovery, difficult as they may be, allow educators the freedom to consider alternatives for learners, for classrooms, for systems, and for policy that can become more agile in addressing the needs of all learners.

The book offers practical solutions, not untried theory, identifying and addressing inherent barriers to success and inspiring scholars and practitioners to persist within their various contexts to achieve the goals of inclusive practice. Its chapters offer a range of recommendations useful for various levels of the educational system, some including recommendations for institutions of higher education—such as incorporating dual licensure into teacher preparation programs and incorporating concepts of inclusive leadership into the curriculum of principal preparation programs—and some examining practices within the PK–12 milieu and its need for ongoing inquiry and professional development for faculty and administrators and for time allocated to collaboration in support of inclusion. These recommendations distill down to one essential truth: all teachers must be prepared to meet the needs of every student, every day.

Pedagogy matters. It is our moral and practical imperative to provide tools, opportunities, settings, and skills to prepare every teacher to help students through these challenges. Every student will struggle in some ways, and every teacher must be prepared to meet those struggles with the confidence provided them in strong, pedagogically-based teacher preparation programs and through administrative support that enables them to make the best use of what they have learned. Persisting through these barriers is basic to the learning process and crucial not only to how students gain agency in their own learning beyond formal schooling but also to how teachers and administrators improve year after year.

As the lessons of this book argue eloquently, inherent in this equation is the need for PK–12 systems and university systems to work collaboratively, blurring traditional territorial lines for the sake of all learners. The AACTE Clinical Practice Commission position statement (2018)—so compatible with the work represented herein—through its set of proclamations and supporting tenets required for fidelity in the implementation of clinical practice, refocuses the purpose of education on the needs of learners, be they PK–12students or college students preparing to become teachers. The AACTE report complements the work presented by the authors here and reinforces their implicit and explicit recommendations. Both of these significant publications offer compelling evidence of the many educators engaged in the improvement of educational processes.

This work toward inclusion, along with the work of many others, sets the stage for renewal of our profession, a renewal that offers learners the best of what we know and understand. To be clear, this is not a work that advocates for reform simply for the sake of change. It is a call for *renewal* that offers a realistic charge: understand the past, know the present, and continually work to meet the needs of the learners as they present themselves in the classroom.

Finally, this work is a testament to the intellectual clarity held by the educational experts in our field. We live in a remarkable time, a time where challenges can no longer be ignored and should be met by those best qualified to address them. We, as professional educators, understand the skills necessary to weave pedagogy, content, relevance, and integrity together in ways that resonate with and engage students, community members, educators, and policy makers. Taken together, the chapters here offer a multitiered framework within which to effect change that promises a fertile learning environment for all involved. It is in this realm that these authors offer their best thinking for the ongoing renewal of educational practice, compassion for the needs of all learners, and evidence that full inclusion offers access to a world of possibility and a future filled with hope: a practice and an educational system that meet the Jeffersonian ideal of the free, public education that is requisite for citizens to build and sustain a free, democratic society. The book's implicit charge, to renew ourselves and our profession and enact fully inclusive practices for every student in the United States' public education system, is incumbent upon us, not just as a challenge, but as a moral imperative.

REFERENCE

AACTE Clinical Practice Commission. (2018). *A pivot toward clinical practice, its lexicon, and the renewal of educator preparation.* Washington, DC: American Association of Colleges for Teacher Education.

PREFACE

This collection of chapters weaves together ideas generated through work in Ohio to promote an effective, equitable, and inclusive education for all students. Not all of the chapters come from Ohio authors, however, because part of our effort has been to align our work with related efforts across the nation. We are indebted to and inspired by those efforts: The Collaboration for Effective Educator Development, Accountability and Reform (CEEDAR) Center; the Teachers College Inclusive Classrooms Project; and new work supported by the Council of Chief State School Officers (CCSSO) on inclusive leadership for principals, among others.

Ohio's work on equity and inclusive practice has benefited from these and other sources—but its heart and soul belong to Ohio educators and agencies with a compelling vision of what is fair and just. Our list of individual contributors to the work would be too long to include, but the foundation of the work and its ongoing support reside in the Ohio Department of Education and the Ohio Department of Higher Education (formerly the Ohio Board of Regents). Together, these agencies made possible the creation of the Ohio Deans Compact—a collaborative assembly of educator preparation and PK–12 leaders with a shared commitment to the work of preparing new and practicing educators to embrace inclusive practice on behalf of all learners, however diverse.

At the very heart of the Ohio Deans Compact is the collective and ongoing effort to increase inclusive models of teaching, educational leadership, and related services preparation so that everyone—all education

Inclusive Education: A Systematic Perspective, pp. xiii–xv
Copyright © 2020 by Information Age Publishing

professionals—are better able to teach and support all learners. With a singular focus on that commitment, coupled with a rich understanding of productive levers for strategic improvement, the Ohio Deans Compact has incentivized its partners to engage in new practices as well as to shift and change the way they do things through purposeful restructuring of programs and partnerships. Several chapters in the edited volume describe this work in detail.

Initial efforts at this renewal and deepening of inclusive practices also resulted in a number of studies that provided evidence that institutions were working to change and that their candidates were becoming stronger as a result of those efforts. As the community associated with the Ohio Deans Compact grew, so did the evidence that institutions and partners were continually reaching outside of their academic and school silos to learn from each other, and step across disciplines to benefit from the measures they were taking to build and support an inclusive culture of learning. To capture this new spirit of collaboration, marked by a humble acknowledgement that the work is too important to achieve it alone, leadership in the Compact invited members and partners to consider contributing essays documenting their work and collaboration. This book is the response to that invitation.

Throughout the book Ohio Deans Compact members and partners explore the social justice grounding of inclusive education in all of the complexity that such work entails from a systems perspective. Writing teams investigated the moral basis of the work as well as its practical challenges, ongoing dilemmas, and evident accomplishments. The collection intersperses theory, descriptions of institutional efforts, and research reports. Taken together, the collection shows how the force of a singular commitment can support generative and contextually situated efforts across an entire state.

Readers of this text should expect to learn about the wonderfully complex nature of collaborative work that is focused on inclusive practices. Deans and other university leaders will take heart at the potential to see faculty and staff working across the aisle to accomplish a common task. Principals and teachers will see greater potential for collaboration with universities and colleges. Preservice teachers will appreciate the nature of more focused, clinically based programs that ask them to think in new ways as they prepare to enter a profession in which matters of social justice are necessarily at stake.

As editors of this book we have learned that our collective wisdom is greater than our individual efforts. We could see how one institution's strength could support other institutions' needs. Institutions were changing in different ways along varying time lines. Each of these factors created opportunities to learn. It was obvious to Ohio Deans Compact leadership that the teams that entered the process of developing more inclusive preparation programs later in the evolution of the Compact's work avoided mistakes that were such hard-won insights on the part of institutions involves in the Compact's early efforts. Likewise, the later teams' activity drew support from the experiences of earlier cohorts. Even in the writing of the various chapters, we assisted one another in how we articulated our growth, challenging each other to use more current sources, or urging authors to paint stronger or clearer pictures of what was changing as a result of their work.

We hope you will find the content between these covers encouraging, inspiring, and all the while challenging. We want to provide a context for your own critical thinking about ways to increase broad and deep opportunities for equity and inclusive practice. Whether you read all of the chapters or concentrate on those most applicable to your work, we think you will find the argumentation compelling and the reports of improvement work illuminating and richly descriptive. Making systemic change on behalf of social justice is difficult and lonely work. By reading the chapters in this book, we hope you will find yourself less alone, bolstered in your resolve, and more fully armed for the struggles ahead.

We would especially like to thank the following people for their important roles in making this text possible: Brenda Haas, Brian McNulty, Kim Monachino, Deborah Telfer, Jo Hannah Ward, Rebecca Watts, and Sue Zake; and we also want to express our deep appreciation to reviewers Edwina Pendarvis, Rachel Quenemoen, and Martha Thurlow.

SECTION I INTRODUCTION

INCLUSIVE PRACTICE: MEANINGS AND SIGNIFICANCE

Section I presents a conceptual framework for understanding inclusive educational practices. Its three chapters share similar, but by no means identical, perspectives on inclusive practice—showing the depth and complexity of the ethical underpinnings and practical manifestations of inclusion.

The section begins with "Inclusive Practice: Pushing Against Persistent Structures and Comfortable Routines," in which Deborah Telfer and Aimee Howley propose that inclusive instructional practice requires significant changes in school and classroom structures and routines to which educators have become accustomed. Using illustrations from classroom visits in several school districts, the authors point to durable practices that are in need of change: ability grouping, unproductive co-teaching arrangements, and assigning paraprofessionals responsibilities that, in effect, place them in the role of teacher of the students with disabilities with whom they work.

Celia Oyler's "Inclusive Practices in Schools" considers the social justice implications of inclusive classrooms and schools—contrasting them with educational institutions that marginalize some students while privileging others. In calling attention to the ethical grounding of inclusive practice, her chapter helps to set the stage for the rest of the book.

In "What Inclusive Practice Means for Students From Marginalized Groups: Interview With Sue Zake, PhD," Sally Brannan and K. Ann Kaufman present their interview with Sue Zake, former Director of Ohio's Office for Exceptional Children. In the interview, Dr. Zake discusses inclusive practice not only as a moral imperative, but also as a critical response to social and

Inclusive Education: A Systematic Perspective, pp. 1–2
Copyright © 2020 by Information Age Publishing

educational inequities. In addition, she positions inclusive practice as a way to ensure quality instruction; high expectations; and safe, supportive learning environments. She also identifies some of the challenges associated with improvements that align with these imperatives across districts in large and diverse states such as Ohio. To address such challenges, she advises, the work of inclusion must be grounded in team-based inquiry and in collaboration between partners and stakeholders throughout a state's system of schooling.

CHAPTER 1

INCLUSIVE PRACTICE

Pushing Against Persistent Structures and Comfortable Routines

Deborah M. Telfer
University of Cincinnati

Aimee Howley
WordFarmers Associates

This chapter provides a brief conceptual discussion of what inclusive practice means and the conditions in schools that appear to support (or impede) it. Drawing on a communitarian foundation, it treats inclusive practice as a form of democratic education and therefore sees inclusive practice as a necessary and constitutive part of democracy (Tam, 1998). Dickson (2012) characterizes this perspective as follows:

> Communitarians regard the school as a community within a community. It is both a microcosm of the wider community and a place of transition from the family to the wider community. If school fills the intermediate space between family and society, it fills also the intermediate time between infancy and adulthood. It has the primary responsibility—above family, above

Inclusive Education: A Systematic Perspective, pp. 3–20
Copyright © 2020 by Information Age Publishing
All rights of reproduction in any form reserved.

neighbourhood, above church—for building citizens who are equipped to create a strong, free, democratic society. The school's responsibility is both explicit and implicit: to teach the practical and moral information students need to function as citizens; to model the structure and shape of democratic society. (p. 1097)

This view of democratic education fits better with what some political theorists call "strong democracy" (Barber, 1984) than with weaker alternatives—liberal or procedural democracy. The grounding for strong democracy is a shared (although not necessarily unitary) understanding of the common good along with the willingness to act on its behalf (Theobald, 1997). Strong democracy is participatory and deliberative, and some theorists argue that, to be strong, it must be inclusive (e.g., Fotopoulis, 1997). A more procedural approach, by contrast, grounds democracy in a set of rights and responsibilities that protects individuals, to the greatest extent possible, from the interference of their neighbors and even, for that matter, their governments (e.g., Berlin, 1969; Pabst, 2016).

A BROAD DEFINITION OF INCLUSIVE PRACTICE

With an eye toward the common good, many educators logically turn attention to the children and families that society rejects or deprives. Currently educators are likely to refer to these children and their families as "marginalized," but in earlier decades they might have called them "disadvantaged" or "underprivileged." Underlying these terms is the idea that society sponsors an unequal distribution of valued "goods" to people from different groups. Those goods might be care, opportunities, resources, voice, authority, or power.

In contrast to the idea that society allocates (or should allocate) goods to individuals is the idea that a "good society" sets aside (or should set aside) goods for everyone to use (Bellah, Madsen, Sullivan, Swidler, & Tipton, 1985). This notion of a *common good* suggests the importance in a democracy of defining a broad domain of shared benefit, understood in terms of shared resources (e.g., Stoll, 2017) and some approximation of equal power. In the reality of political life, educators observe few instances, other than the existence of a common system of schooling, in which citizens share benefit and strive to give everyone access to power. Even within the ostensibly *common* system of schooling, stark inequities often overtake rhetorical possibilities for equal benefit and equal opportunity to participate (e.g., Zhao, 2016).

Inclusive practice works deliberately to disrupt inequity by creating affordances intended to enable all children to receive high-quality and responsive education with peers from their communities. Arguably, of course, neighborhood segregation leads to segregated neighborhood schooling, resulting in schooling inputs, processes, and outcomes that vary based on race, income level, and other family characteristics (e.g., Johnson, 2014). Inclusive educational practice has limited capacity to redress all social ills, but inclusive educators (sometimes called "social justice" or "progressive" educators) do what they can to counter inequity and "create a new social order" (e.g., Counts, 1932; Lugg & Shoho, 2006). They use three broad strategies:

- giving all students access to a common curriculum,
- placing students in classrooms randomly to assure proportional representation, and
- reframing the curriculum to make room for multiple perspectives.

Of course, few inclusive educators make use of all three strategies simultaneously, and critics (e.g., McLaren & Farahmandpur, 2001) fault halfway measures (e.g., a limited version of multicultural education) as inadequate and sometimes even disingenuous. Furthermore, any of the strategies can fall victim to cooptation or to an "ends-means conversion." For instance, powerful neoliberals coopted progressive efforts to illuminate achievement gaps by shaping accountability testing and disclosure into a mechanism for attacking public schooling as an institution (e.g., Hursh, 2005), and many well-meaning educators responded defensively to accountability testing by choosing to teach to the test or even teach the test (e.g., Au, 2007).

The Problems With Narrow Definitions

In the United States, the term "inclusion" often refers narrowly to students with disabilities. Other similar terms—now not much in use—focus narrowly on students of African descent ("integration") and those who immigrated to the United States ("assimilation"). These have also been used in Europe to refer to the process by which countries respond to the arrival of newcomers from other places (Houtkamp, 2015). These terms all relate to the actions that "insiders" take in response to the arrival (or continued presence) of "outsiders." Worldwide, cross-national migration is on the rise (e.g., Doyle, 2004; United Nations, 2017), as are other population shifts, and these changes sometimes lead to discord and even violence (Dancygier & Laitin, 2014).

With increases in diversity across nations like the United States (Alba & Yrizar Barbosa, 2016), "insiders" find it tempting to distinguish between desirable and undesirable "outsiders" (e.g., Wu, 2015). The practice of creating a hierarchy of "outsider" groups, however, pits groups against one another, exacerbating inequities and legitimizing hegemonic rhetoric—for instance, rhetoric about racial differences in ability, rhetoric equating a free market to a meritocracy, and so on (Parsons, Walsemann, Jones, Knopf, & Blake, 2018). Describing this process in relationship to Asian Americans, Wu (2017) claimed that "the Asian American model minority status also served as a foil for other racialized groups in the U.S. context. Asian American 'success' affirmed the discourse of meritocracy in opposition to those who identified and protested against structural inequality" (p. 100).

Similarly, schools' efforts to include students from one marginalized group at a time (but not all marginalized groups at once) may provide temporary and partial correctives, but they skirt more systemic causes of inequity and injustice (e.g., Johnson, 2016). Furthermore, as in other arenas, efforts to offer inclusion selectively tend to reinforce the belief that some groups are worthy of becoming "insiders" while others must remain "outsiders" (e.g., McCann, 2012). In contrast to this exclusionary kind of inclusion, broad interpretations of "inclusion" make reference to a far-reaching equity and social justice agenda and support practices that expand access and equalize power.

PRACTICES THAT STAND IN
THE WAY OF EQUITY AND JUSTICE

As numerous analysts have pointed out, schooling in the United States responds to and embeds contradictory aims and practices (e.g., Kliebard, 1986; McMahon, 2013). Some aims and practices advance efforts to transform existing structures of economic and social power, and some seek to keep those structures intact. Furthermore, some are so vague that they encourage competing (even contradictory) interpretations. For instance, the intent to be accountable to the public (along with associated accountability practices) sometimes seems to reflect a democratic principle (as in, "consent of the governed"), while sometimes it seems to promote a free-market ethos (as in, "let the market decide"). This section of the chapter briefly describes four practices that tend to sustain prevailing relations of access and power. The subsequent section identifies practices that tend to promote democratic engagement by explicitly addressing issues of equity and social justice (see Structures and Partnerships that Promote Equity and Social Justice below).

Ability Grouping

Ability grouping of students takes various forms, some more exclusionary than others. For example, school districts that isolate their students with cognitive impairments or those with academic talents in separate buildings are using an extreme form of ability grouping. Classroom grouping of students by reading comprehension level for some reading lessons is less extreme. The underlying message is the same, however.

Ability grouping posits a hierarchy of performance that mirrors status hierarchies in society. Students are not merely seated with others; they are treated differently. As McGillicuddy and Devine (2018) reported, based on a mixed method study in Irish primary schools,

> Teachers in this study held higher expectations for pupils assigned to the higher ability groups, and lower expectations for those in the lower ability groups. More control was exercised over the time and space of children in the lower ability groups who were not afforded the opportunity to work independently. Furthermore, teachers in this study perceived classroom management to be more challenging when there were greater numbers of low ability and special educational needs (SEN) pupils present in the class. (pp. 97–98)

Furthermore, ability grouping reinforces the view that some students are more important than others because they perform better academically and ostensibly have more to offer society (e.g., Marks, 2014). This perspective accords with free-market ideologies, which frame educational purposes primarily in terms of human capital development and individual attainment within narrowly defined parameters of success (e.g., salary, occupational status).

Some researchers suggest that ability grouping persists because it helps teachers organize the types of instruction they believe are most beneficial (e.g., Maloch, Worthy, Hampton, Jordan, Hungerford-Kresser, & Semingson, 2013; Oakes, 1985). Teachers do not deliberately use a practice they know will harm some students or that will exclude them from equal participation in the life of the classroom. They fall back on ability grouping because it (a) fits with their foundational beliefs about the fixed nature of cognitive ability (Park & Datnow, 2017) and (b) seems like the logical way to structure the use of "evidence-based" practices, such as guided reading, carefully sequenced math instruction, and so on (e.g., Maloch et al., 2013).

Arguably, then, alternatives to ability grouping might best be framed in relationship to the evidence-based practices that teachers are learning to use in educator preparation and professional development programs. For instance, showing teachers how to scaffold guided reading by using universal design for learning might allow them to understand their grouping practices as distinct from their instructional practices rather than as necessary to (or facilitative of) them.

Unproductive Co-teaching

Co-teaching is a staffing approach with the ostensible aim of giving all students the benefit of high-quality instruction in general education classrooms by providing extra instructional support to those who need it (e.g., Friend, 2008). Although co-teaching has not been studied extensively (e.g., Cook, McDuffie-Landrum, Oshita, & Cook, 2011), it continues to be recommended as a scaffold to inclusion (Sweigart & Landrum, 2015). According to Sweigart and Landrum (2015), the purported benefits of co-teaching might be indirect, resulting from its facilitation of certain effective instructional practices that rely on support from more than one adult.

Nevertheless, as critics (e.g., Chitiyo, 2017) continue to argue, teachers may not know how to use these effective practices or how to collaborate in orchestrating complex instructional designs involving two or more adults. In fact, Sweigart and Landrum's (2015) study showed that, while some elementary school teachers leverage extra instructional personnel in classrooms to support high-quality instruction, middle and high school teachers rarely do.

Furthermore, observations of co-teaching show that its least disruptive and easiest-to-implement variant (i.e., the one teach-one assist model) is most often used. According to Isherwood, Barger-Anderson, and Erickson (2012),

> [The] co-teaching partnership[s] were unable to realize the total benefits of co-teaching and were mostly observed using the one teach-one assist model. There was a sense of stratification in the classroom between the teachers, and the students were observed in many situations treating the special education teacher like a para-educator. In the dysfunctional co-teaching partnership the special educators described themselves as becoming de-professionalized and reported feeling a sense of frustration. (p. 12)

Finally, other observers (e.g., Embury & Kroeger, 2012; Randhare Ashton, 2014) suggest that, in part because of power differentials between general and special educators, co-teaching may not be powerful enough to disrupt "ableist" beliefs and practices. In fact, observations of co-teaching teams confirm their tendency to reinforce prevailing distinctions between students who are general education "insiders" and those who remain general education "outsiders" (e.g., Naraian, 2010; Zindler, 2009). Randhare Ashton (2014) describes the preferred alternative in the following way:

> An inclusive co-taught classroom should not just be another place to educate students with disabilities. Rather, it needs to be a place where new professional identities are conceptualized in order to provide an appropri-

ate education to all students in the classroom, regardless of their status as a general or special education student. (p. 59)

Assigning Paraprofessional Educators as De Facto Teachers

Another staffing approach with problematic consequences is the use of paraprofessional educators to mediate instruction for students with disabilities or for those whose first language is not English. In its most extreme application, the assignment of a paraprofessional involves one-on-one attachment to a single student. The paraprofessional accompanies the student all day long, intervening not only with the student's schoolwork but also with his or her social interactions. According to Giangreco (2010), this approach interferes with inclusive practice by walling off some students from their peers. It marks them as less capable, reinforces their dependency on adult helpers, and buffers their involvement with the social life of the classroom. Simultaneously, it treats some students as less worthy than their classmates by entrusting their education to the adults in the school with the least preparation.

Giangreco (2010) considers the one-on-one assignment of a paraprofessional to be such a restrictive arrangement that he advises individualized education program (IEP) teams to consider a host of other options before considering that one:

> Prior to considering the use of a one-to-one paraprofessional, IEP teams should consider what other actions might allow a student with a disability to make meaningful progress in the general education classroom. A combination of possibilities can be considered, such as (a) assistive technology, (b) teacher training (e.g., teaching mixed-ability groups, facilitating social interactions), (c) teaching formats that are amenable to students pursuing different learning outcomes or progressing at varying rates (e.g., activity-based instruction), (d) use of existing schoolwide supports (e.g., learning laboratory), (e) use of a paraprofessional assigned to a class rather than an individual student, (f) different models of delivery (e.g., coteaching in the classroom), (g) positive behavior supports, and (h) peer supports. (p. 8)

The practices described above are examples of routines that reinforce and maintain separate educational subsystems for groups of children based on programmatic silos (e.g., special education, general education, Title I, gifted education, and so on), thus limiting access to relevant curricular content and instruction for many children. Instead of fostering shared responsibility and accountability on the part of *all* educators for the success of *all* children, these routines promote isolated and exclusionary practice.

While maintaining the status quo might be more comfortable for many adults, it does little to prepare children, particularly those with learning challenges or diverse learning needs, for success in life. The next section describes structures and practices that support educators in working differently in order to promote equity and social justice.

STRUCTURES AND PARTNERSHIPS THAT PROMOTE EQUITY AND SOCIAL JUSTICE

Some structures and practices already in place in certain schools and districts can be used to promote democratic engagement of all students by explicitly addressing issues of equity and social justice. These structures and practices do not automatically support equity, however. They can also be used to foster improvements of other sorts—improvements that increase overall school performance, for instance, without altering the way academic, social, or economic benefits are allocated to different groups of students in the school or district. Only when educators use these structures and practices explicitly to foster democratic and equitable opportunities to learn do they result in outcomes that promote social justice.

Even though these structures and practices already are used by some schools and districts in the United States, they require a different way of working from the siloed approach that exists in most U.S. school systems today. In these typical systems, teachers work primarily in isolation from one another, schools operate as autonomous entities within their districts, and central office personnel seldom play a supportive role in partnership with school leaders. These typical arrangements rarely encourage shared values supportive of social justice, nor do they support the sort of coherent strategies that are needed to make and sustain meaningful improvements on behalf of all students.

Nevertheless, the structures and practices that allow school districts to provide democratic and equitable opportunities to learn are not unfamiliar to educational leaders and policymakers. More than a decade ago, Fullan (2007) argued that in order for change to occur at the classroom level, other levels of the system (e.g., school, central office) also needed to change, noting that "the main reason that change fails to occur in the first place on any scale, and does not get sustained when it does, is that the infrastructure is weak, unhelpful, or working at cross purposes" (p. 18).

More recently, Bryk and associates (2017) described the importance of "seeing the system" (p. 58) in order to understand the outcomes it produces, describing systems as the product of interactions among the people engaged with them, the tools and materials they have at their disposal, and the processes through which these people and resources come together to do the work.

This section discusses the role of the district in setting the conditions for system-wide learning, describes structures that facilitate system-wide improvement on behalf of all students, and suggests partnerships that can facilitate equity and social justice.

The District Role

A commitment to improving learning outcomes for all students, including those who traditionally have been marginalized, requires personnel system-wide to work together in focused and intentional ways that foster high performance through equitable practice. District leadership (the superintendent and central office staff) creates the conditions for moving from autonomous practice to shared practice by thinking and working systemically. According to Barr (2012),

> Systems thinking is not one thing, but rather a set of habits or practices within a framework that is based on the belief that the component parts of a system can best be understood within the context of relationships with each other and with other systems, rather than in isolation. Systems thinking focuses on cyclical, rather than linear cause and effect, relationships. A functional system is built with a high degree of understanding of what is/is not working well and the inter-relatedness of all the component parts. The system is built to provide successful capacity at all levels, which assumes that no upper layer of the system can be successful if the layers beneath it are not also successful. (pp. 1–2)

In functional systems—systems that build the capacity for continuous improvement at all levels—district personnel (i.e., central office personnel such as superintendents; deputy/assistant superintendents; chief academic officers; special education directors/coordinators; curriculum, instruction, assessment directors/coordinators; and so on) work collaboratively and in a supportive role with the district's schools. Honig and associates' (2010) study of the role of central office personnel in districts that improved teaching and learning highlighted the importance of transforming the central office to focus on the educational core—a focus that involved shifting from delivering services to solving problems, even if those problems cut across multiple central office units (p. viii). It also involved supporting school principals through central office-principal partnerships and communicating with and building the capacity of all central office personnel to act on behalf of the district's theory of action (i.e., the big picture or rationale for why change was needed; Honig et al., 2010).

A study of 10 demographically different school districts in nine states across the country (a project known as *Moving Your Numbers*) also offered illustrations of functional systems, revealing commonalities in district/central office behavior that contributed to continuous district-wide improvement on behalf of all learners (see www.movingyournumbers.com). Each district used a common set of leadership practices, though applying them somewhat differently, to focus educator discourse and improvement efforts on teaching and learning, align the work between and across system components (e.g., between the central office and schools), and engage all personnel in improving outcomes for all students. In these districts, central office personnel worked to build the capacity of principals and teachers in each school, principals supported individual and collective teacher learning, and most personnel demonstrated a sense of shared responsibility for following through on districtwide priorities (Telfer, 2012a).

Inherent in the actions of district and central office leadership, moreover, was the belief that harnessing and building on the individual and varied expertise of educators at different levels of the system were essential to increasing the district's capacity to educate all children in effective and equitable ways. The superintendent of one district in the study described the district's commitment to reducing isolation among and across program areas and schools. "Breaking down isolated practice and raising the capacity of the entire system of 850 teachers through collaborative teaming is a substantial cost to the district, but one that is necessary for improving learning for all students" (Telfer, 2012b, p. 8). The superintendent went on to explain, "We ask staff, 'what is your collaboration capital?' We have to increase collaboration and reduce competition by encouraging every staff member to share his or her best ideas. If we do that, all ships will rise" (M. McCormick, personal communication, September 27, 2016).

In all the *Moving Your Numbers* districts studied, the district leadership took steps to change the ways in which instruction was delivered to all students by developing structures to support more collaborative learning among central office personnel, principals, teachers, and other staff members. Such structures, described in the next subsection, were used to foster coherence and consistency in implementing the district's core work (i.e., teaching and learning).

System-Wide Use of Improvement Teams

Bryk and associates (2017) describe the changes needed in order for improvements to be made as a learning-to-improve problem, suggesting that all improvement asks three fundamental questions: (a) "What specifically are we trying to accomplish?" (b) "What change might we introduce and why?" and (c) "How will we know that a change is actually an improve-ment?" (p. 114). According to the authors,

> The three questions scaffold a learning dynamic that involves making hy-potheses about change explicit, testing these hypotheses against evidence, revising one's change ideas based on what is learned through such tests, and testing again. Improvement research typically entails cycling through this process multiple times. (p. 114)

School districts like those mentioned above, which are committed to building system-wide capacity to teach students more effectively and equitably, engage all personnel through collaborative team structures that support continuous inquiry and learning. These team structures allow educators to undertake different kinds of inquiry processes, such as action research (e.g., Bryk et al., 2012), equity audits (e.g., View et al., 2016), and lesson study (e.g., Widjaja, Vale, Groves, & Doig, 2017).

Leadership teams, instructional improvement teams, data teams, teacher-based teams (TBTs), grade-level/content-area teams, and other similar groups are types of collaborative structures. When explicitly focused on the improvement and equitable practice of teaching and learning, such structures support the development of a common instructional vocabulary, provide a forum for selecting particular strategies or approaches to instruc-tion and then testing the effects of their implementation, and serve as a mechanism for engaging in shared inquiry and collective learning about how to facilitate deeper levels of learning for all students.

A growing body of evidence shows the impact of collaborative teams that use a structured inquiry-based process for improving learning (e.g., Hargreaves & Fullan, 2012; McNulty & Besser, 2014). Collaborative inquiry can promote shared responsibility for the success of all students, thereby focusing educators' attention on equity (Datnow & Park, 2015). Working together to examine relevant data, making evidence-based decisions about the use of instructional strategies, and evaluating the degree to which the implementation of such strategies is making a difference for all learners shifts the focus away from what certain groups of students should be taught to a focus on how to improve the design and delivery of instruction in ways that expand all students' opportunities to learn.

In Ohio, for example, aligned collaborative learning teams at the district, school, and teacher-team level support collaborative inquiry by groups of educators. District leadership teams—comprising central office personnel, principals, teachers, and others—set direction for and oversee improve-ment and social justice efforts district-wide. At the school level, building leadership teams align school goals with district goals, provide support to TBTs, and monitor the work of TBTs across the school. And, at the classroom level, TBTs match instructional strategies to students' needs by selecting and monitoring the team members' use of selected instructional strategies and then testing the efficacy of the strategies selected. More information about Ohio's approach to collaborative inquiry—including the structures, processes, and tools used to support improvement and learning—can be found on the Ohio Leadership Advisory Council website at www.ohioleadership.org (e.g., the module titled, *The Collaborative Process*).

Support Networks and Partnerships

The changes in instruction and associated educational structures that lead to inclusive practice are substantial. They disrupt long-standing traditions and counter widespread biases, whether espoused or implicit. Changes of this magnitude require support from distributed structures, not just local ones.

In improvement science terminology, these structures are referred to as *networked improvement communities* (NICs). These communities strengthen shared commitments and communicate what they learn broadly. They cultivate as well as depend on practices that distribute learning across an entire network. For instance, Level-A learning might involve what teachers are learning individually, Level-B learning might involve learning in school-based or district settings, and Level-C learning might involve learning across districts or other entities (Bryk et al., 2017, p. 142). According to Bryk and associates (2017), NICs are better able to identify "bright spots" or "positive deviants," places where unusually positive outcomes are occurring, and to discern what it is that these places have actually done. Part of the work of a NIC involves comparing results and learning from one another. Elaborating on this advantage, Bryk and associates (2017) explain,

> Within the safe collaborative environment of a NIC, two related processes become activated. First, comparing one's results to those of others can create a sense of moral urgency—if others can accomplish this, we can and should be able to do better too. This positive response stands in sharp contrast to the defensiveness that comparative data tend to generate in high-stakes accountability contexts. In the latter cases, the knee-jerk reaction is to discount the data, question their credibility, and explain away differences as others having better students or more support or better conditions, and so on. Second, when trusted colleagues are getting better outcomes in the same improvement system, participants are now more inclined to ask, "What exactly did you do to get those results?" Consequently, an explicit learning-to-improve opportunity is now created. (p. 148)

As with participation in networks that are focused on supporting members in reaching shared goals, school district partnership efforts (such as those involving district-community collaboration) can support districts in making the kind of system-wide improvements needed to better serve all students. Smith and Brazer's (2016) study of superintendents in districts that increased equitable opportunities to learn for all groups of students showed that partnerships with community organizations are an "important strategy that cuts across a number of the opportunity gaps on which they were working" (p. 123). The authors described one superintendent's efforts: "She and others demonstrated that it may be more effective to think about achievement gaps and opportunity gaps together and to address them with collaborations that cross boundaries between school districts and the communities in which they are embedded" (p. 123).

Personnel in organizations external to school districts (e.g., state support teams, intermediate units, higher education institutions) can serve as critical friends, offering a more impartial view that can help district and school personnel gain insight into needed improvements to teaching and learning. The Glossary of Educational Reform (Great Schools Partnership, 2013) defines critical friend this way:

> A critical friend is typically a colleague or other educational professional, such as a school coach, who is committed to helping an educator or school improve. A critical friend is someone who is encouraging and supportive, but who also provides honest and often candid feedback that may be uncomfortable or difficult to hear. In short, a critical friend is someone who agrees to speak truthfully, but constructively, about weaknesses, problems, and emotionally charged issues. (Great Schools Partnership, 2013, "Critical Friend," para. 1)

Inviting an outside perspective, initiating partnerships that extend beyond district boundaries, and participating in networks that augment and offer new perspectives on learning to improve are important ways that district and school personnel can support the use of inclusive practices that expand opportunities and improve outcomes for all students.

These collaborative efforts depend on educators' commitment to viewing improved performance and increased equity as critical conditions for the common good. They push against prevailing practices that isolate and stir dissent among education practitioners, schools, districts, and larger communities (e.g., Mascini & Braster, 2017; McTighe, 1999). Arguably, democratic aims of schooling—such as greater inclusiveness and more equitable performance—require educators to shape their work collaboratively in consideration of a shared vision of pluralism within a widening, but widely accessible community (e.g., Bickmore, 2005; Greene, 1993; Obenchain, Balkute, Vaughn, & White, 2016). The motive for this work, as Greene (1993) has argued, is the sense that our current circumstances do not serve well enough as an imaginative grounding for a better future:

> Publics, after all, take shape in response to unmet needs and broken promises. Human beings are prone to take action in response to the sense of injustice or to the imagination's capacity to look at things as if they could be otherwise. The democratic community, always a community in the making, depends not so much on what has been achieved and funded in the past. It is kept alive; it is energized and radiated by an awareness of future possibility. To develop a vision of such possibility, a vision of what might and ought to be, is very often to be made aware of present deficiencies and present flaws. (p. 17)

SUMMARY AND CONCLUSIONS

As noted earlier, schooling practices in the United States respond to incompatible pressures and accomplish contradictory aims. As a result, the practices themselves communicate contradictory messages. Certainly, some of the practices—including the serious work of educational teams— communicate the need to give all students access to meaningful learning opportunities in preparation for full participation as adults in a complex society. Other practices communicate the value of segregating students in preparation for their inevitable adult distribution across economic and social strata.

Arguably, a system mired in these contradictions is not the worst possibility. After all, some aims and practices in a contradictory system still provide a foothold for improving performance and equity. But, as Saltman (2014) suggests, market-driven reforms have considerably narrowed—and possibly obliterated—that foothold:

> The corporate reforms have succeeded in reframing public discourse about education: transforming public schooling into an individualized responsibility while upwardly redistributing educational resources, gutting public schooling for the poor, making kids into commodities by privatizing schools, and radically undermining the autonomy of teachers to link knowledge to public and critical issues and to help students theorize particular experiences and contexts in ways that would facilitate political agency and public life. (p. 252)

This chapter takes a less gloomy, but still sober view of the possibilities, recognizing that many educators still draw strength from their belief in a common system of schooling for all children (e.g., Glass, 2016). The districts studied through the *Moving Your Numbers* initiative acted on that belief through intentional and focused actions that were implemented across the school system. They demonstrated that dedicated public-school educators, working collaboratively to bring educational practices into line with inclusive aims, *can* and do make improvements that build on "the imagination's capacity to look at things as if they could be otherwise" (Greene, 1993, p. 17).

REFERENCES

Alba, R., & Yrizar Barbosa, G. (2016). Room at the top? Minority mobility and the transition to demographic diversity in the USA. *Ethnic & Racial Studies, 39*, 917–938. doi:10.1080/01419870.2015.1081966

Au, W. (2007). High-stakes testing and curricular control: A qualitative metasynthesis. *Educational Researcher, 36*, 258–267. doi:10.3102/0013189X07306523

Barber, B. R. (1984). *Strong democracy: Participatory politics for a new age.* Berkeley, CA: University of California Press.

Barr, S. L. (2012). *State education agencies: The critical role of SEAs in facilitating school district capacity to improve learning and achievement for students with disabilities.* Minneapolis, MN: University of Minnesota, National Center on Educational Outcomes.

Bellah, R. N., Madsen, R., Sullivan, W. M., Swidler, A., & Tipton, S. M. (1985). *Habits of the heart: Individualism and commitment in American life.* Berkeley, CA: University of California Press.

Berlin, I. (1969). *Four essays on liberty.* Oxford, England: Oxford University Press.

Bickmore, K. (2005). Teacher development for conflict participation: Facilitating learning for "difficult citizenship" education. *International Journal of Citizenship and Teacher Education, 1*(2), 1–16.

Bryk, A. S., Gomez, L. M., Grunow, A., & LeMahieu, P. G. (2017). *Learning to improve: How America's schools can get better at getting better.* Cambridge, MA: Harvard Education Press.

Chitiyo, J. (2017). Challenges to the use of co-teaching by teachers. *International Journal of Whole Schooling, 13*(3), 55–66.

Cook, B. G., McDuffie-Landrum, K. A., Oshita, L., & Cook, S. C. (2011). Co-teaching for students with disabilities. In J. M. Kauffman & D. P. Hallahan (Eds.), *Handbook of special education* (pp. 147–159). New York, NY: Routledge.

Counts, G. S. (1932). *Dare the school build a new social order?* New York, NY: John Day.

Dancygier, R. M., & Laitin, D. D. (2014). Immigration into Europe: Economic discrimination, violence, and public policy. *Annual Review of Political Science, 17*, 43–64.

Datnow, A., & Park, V. (2015). 5 (good) ways to talk about DATA. *Educational Leadership, 73*(3), 10–15.

Dickson, E. (2012). A communitarian theory of the education rights of students with disabilities. *Educational Philosophy and Theory, 44*, 1093–1109. doi:10.1111/j.1469-5812.2011.00788.x

Doyle, M. W. (2004). The challenge of worldwide migration. *Journal of International Affairs, 57*(2), 1–5.

Embury, D. C., & Kroeger, S. D. (2012). Let's ask the kids: Consumer constructions of co-teaching. *International Journal of Special Education, 27*, 102–112.

Fotopoulis, T. (1997). *Towards an inclusive democracy: The crisis of the growth economy and the need for a new liberatory project.* London, England: Cassell.

Friend, M. (2008). *Co-teach! A manual for creating and sustaining classroom partnerships in inclusive schools.* Greensboro, NC: Marilyn Friend.

Fullan, M. (2007). *The new meaning of educational change.* New York, NY: Teachers College Press.

Giangreco, M. F. (2010). One-to-one paraprofessionals for students with disabilities in inclusive classrooms: Is conventional wisdom wrong? *Intellectual and Developmental Disabilities, 48*(1), 1–13. doi:10.1352/1934-9556-48.1.1

Glass, G. (2016). *Advancing democratic education: Would Horace Mann tweet?* Retrieved from http://ed2worlds.blogspot.com/2016/02/would-horace-manntweet.html

Great Schools Partnership. (2013). Critical friend. In *Glossary of Education Reform.* Retrieved from: https://www.edglossary.org/critical-friend/

Greene, M. (1993). The passions of pluralism: Multiculturalism and the expanding community. *Educational Researcher, 22*, 13–18. doi:10.2307/1177301

Hargreaves, A., & Fullan, M. (2012). *Professional capital: Transforming teaching in every school.* New York, NY: Teachers College Press.

Honig, M. I., Copland, M. A., Rainey, L., Lorton, J. A., & Newton, M. (2010). *Central office transformation for district-wide teaching and learning improvement.* Seattle, WA: University of Washington, Center for the Study of Teaching and Policy.

Houtkamp, C. (2015). Beyond assimilation and integration: The shift to 'national' and 'transnational' inclusion. *Acta Universitatis Sapientiae: European and Regional Studies, 8*, 73–87. doi:10.1515/auseur-2015-0014

Hursh, D. (2005). Neo-liberalism, markets and accountability: Transforming education and undermining democracy in the United States and England. *Policy Futures in Education, 3*, 3–15. doi:10.2304/pfie.2005.3.1.6

Isherwood, R. S., Barger-Anderson, R., & Erickson, M. (2012). Examining co-teaching through a socio-technical systems lens. *Journal of Special Education Apprenticeship, 2*(2), 1–17.

Johnson, O. A. (2014). Still separate, still unequal: The relation of segregation in neighborhoods and schools to education inequality. *Journal of Negro Education, 83*, 199–215. doi:10.7709/jnegroeducation.83.3.0199

Johnson, O. A. (2016). Inclusion, exclusion, and the "new" economic inequality. *Texas Law Review, 94*, 1647–1665.

Kliebard, H. M. (1986). *The struggle for the American curriculum, 1893–1958.* Boston, MA: Routledge & Kegan Paul.

Lugg, C. A., & Shoho, A. R. (2006). Dare public school administrators build a new social order? Social justice and the possibly perilous politics of educational leadership. *Journal of Educational Administration, 44*, 196–208. https://doi.org/10.1108/09578230610664805

Maloch, B., Worthy, J., Hampton, A., Jordan, M., Hungerford-Kresser, H., & Semingson, P. (2013). Portraits of practice: A cross-case analysis of two first-grade teachers and their grouping practices. *Research in The Teaching of English, 47*, 277–312.

Marks, R. (2014). Educational triage and ability-grouping in primary mathematics: a case-study of the impacts on low-attaining pupils. *Research in Mathematics Education, 16*, 38–53. doi:10.1080/14794802.2013.874095

Mascini, P., & Braster, S. (2017). Choice and competition in education: Do they advance performance, voice and equality? *Public Administration, 95*, 482–497. https://doi.org/10.1111/padm.12308

McCann, M. W. (2012). Inclusion, exclusion, and the politics of rights mobilization: Reflections on the Asian American experience. *Seattle Journal for Social Justice, 11*, 115–126.

McGillicuddy, D. D., & Devine, D. (2018). "Turned off" or "ready to fly"—Ability grouping as an act of symbolic violence in primary school. *Teaching & Teacher Education, 70*, 88–99. https://doi.org/10.1016/j.tate.2017.11.008

McLaren, P., & Farahmandpur, R. (2001). Class, cultism, multiculturalism. *Multicultural Education, 8*(3), 2–14.

McMahon, B. J. (2013). Conflicting conceptions of the purposes of schooling in a democracy. *Journal of Thought, 48*, 17–32.

McNulty, B. A., & Besser, L. (2014). *Leaders make it happen! An administrator's guide to data teams.* Boston, MA: Houghton Mifflin Harcourt.

McTighe, J. (1999). Collaboration for the common good: An overture to cooperation in K–12 education. *Catholic Education: A Journal of Inquiry & Practice, 3*, 81–86. doi:10.15365/joce.0301092013

Naraian, S. (2010). General, special and … inclusive: Refiguring professional identities in a collaboratively taught classroom. *Teaching and Teacher Education, 26*, 1677–1686. https://doi.org/10.1016/j.tate.2010.06.020

Oakes, J. (1985). *Keeping track: How school systems structure inequality.* New Haven, CN: Yale University Press.

Obenchain, K. M., Balkute, A., Vaughn, E., & White, S. (2016). High school teachers' identities: Constructing civic selves. *High School Journal, 99*, 252–278. doi:10.1353/hsj.2016.0009

Pabst, A. (2016). Is liberal democracy sliding into "democratic despotism"? *Political Quarterly, 87*, 91–95. doi:10.1111/1467-923X.12209

Park, V., & Datnow, A. (2017). Ability grouping and differentiated instruction in an era of data-driven decision making. *American Journal of Education, 123*, 281–306. doi:10.1086/689930

Parsons, A. A., Walsemann, K. M., Jones, S. J., Knopf, H., & Blake, C. E. (2018). Parental involvement: Rhetoric of inclusion in an environment of exclusion. *Journal of Contemporary Ethnography, 47*, 113–139. doi:10.1177/0891241616676874

Randhare Ashton, J. (2014). Beneath the veneer: Marginalization and exclusion in an inclusive co-teaching context. *International Journal of Whole Schooling, 10*, 43–62.

Saltman, K. J. (2014). Neoliberalism and Corporate School Reform: "Failure" and "creative destruction." *Review of Education, Pedagogy & Cultural Studies, 36*, 249–259. doi:10.1080/10714413.2014.938564

Smith, R. S., & Brazer, S. D. (2016). *Striving for equity: District leadership for narrowing opportunity and achievement gaps.* Cambridge, MA: Harvard Education Press.

Stoll, S. (2017). *Ramp Hollow: The ordeal of Appalachia.* New York, NY: Hill and Wang.

Sweigart, C. A., & Landrum, T. J. (2015). The impact of number of adults on instruction: implications for co-teaching. *Preventing School Failure, 59*, 22–29. doi:10.1080/1045988X.2014.919139

Tam, H. (1998). *Communitarianism: A new agenda for politics and citizenship.* New York, NY: New York University Press.

Telfer, D. M. (2012a). *Moving your numbers. A synthesis of lessons learned: How districts used assessment and accountability to increase performance for students with disabilities as part of district-wide improvement.* Minneapolis, MN: University of Minnesota, National Center on Educational Outcomes.

Telfer, D. M. (2012b). *Moving your numbers. Val Verde Unified School District: Achievement profile. Using assessment and accountability to increase performance for students with disabilities as part of district-wide improvement.* Minneapolis, MN: University of Minnesota, National Center on Educational Outcomes.

Theobald, P. (1997). *Teaching the commons: Place, pride, and the renewal of community.* Boulder, CO: Westview.

United Nations. (2017). *Population facts.* Retrieved from http://www.un.org/en/development/desa/population/migration/publications/migrationreport/index.shtml

View, J., DeMulder, E., Stribling, S., Dodman, S., Ra, S., Hall, B., & Swalwell, K. (2016). Equity audit: A teacher leadership tool for nurturing teacher research. *Educational Forum, 80*, 380–393. doi:10.1080/00131725.2016.1206162

Widjaja, W., Vale, C., Groves, S., & Doig, B. (2017). Teachers' professional growth through engagement with lesson study. *Journal of Mathematics Teacher Education, 20*, 357–383. doi:10.1007/s10857-015-9341-8

Wu, E. D. (2015). *The color of success: Asian Americans and the origins of the model minority.* Princeton, NJ: Princeton University Press.

Wu, J. T. (2017). The origins of the model minority. *Journal of American Ethnic History, 36*, 99–101. doi:10.5406/jamerethnhist.36.2.0099

Zhao, Y. (2016). From deficiency to strength: Shifting the mindset about education inequality. *Journal of Social Issues, 72*, 720–739. doi:10.1111/josi.12191

Zindler, R. (2009). Trouble in paradise: A study of who is included in an inclusion classroom. *Teachers College Record, 111*, 1971–1996.

CHAPTER 2

INCLUSIVE PRACTICES IN SCHOOLS

Celia Oyler
Teachers College

Schools are places where status differentials often are keenly felt (Lawrence-Brown & Sapon-Shevin, 2015). These differentials relate to characteristics that define human diversity: body size, hair type, skin color, race/ethnicity, home language, religious affiliation or nonaffiliation, speed and accuracy with academic work, oral fluency, social skills, executive functions such as impulse control and organization of materials, and so on. Almost all human interactions showcase a myriad of intersecting human diversities.

As ubiquitous as human differences are, however, the values we attach to these differences are socially, culturally, and historically shaped (Holland, Lachicotte, Skinner, & Cain, 1998). Whether it is on the sports field, at the awards ceremony, or on a bulletin board filled with student work, schools are places where human differences are made public. Obviously, some differences are given high status, and others lower status, or even stigmas (Oliver, 1990). Some differences, like being left-handed, pose difficulties (e.g., finding an appropriate pair of scissors) but do not affect someone's status. Much more stigmatizing and isolating are differences such as not having a reliable means of communication (Rubin et al., 2001) or lacking positive peer connections (Collins, 2003).

Inclusive Education: A Systematic Perspective, pp. 21–39
Copyright © 2020 by Information Age Publishing

When working with educators on inclusive education, I often ask them to recall times in their own preschool through 12th-grade schooling when one or more of their characteristics made them feel conspicuous, self-conscious, embarrassed, or perhaps humiliated. People always have stories: stumbling and stuttering during round-robin reading; being chosen last for the kickball team; not having their art work put up on the bulletin board; being asked to line up by height; having unfashionable clothes that other children made fun of; bringing a lunch that classmates said was stinky; having to leave the room during the Halloween party due to their family's religion. The stories go on and on. Almost everyone has experienced isolation or embarrassment as a result of a personal characteristic, although individual experiences differ in terms of degree and frequency.

In addition to these unfortunate but transitory experiences are some that are more systematic. Historically, for instance, schools have marked for exile or exclusion students with specific human differences (Kliewer, 1998; Van der Klift & Kunc, 1994). As Joel Spring (1989) noted decades ago, schools—unless intentionally disrupted—function as sorting machines, with designated tracks based in large part on presumed competence or incompetence (Biklen & Burke, 2006).

Positioned to counter the common experience of exclusion and isolation, *inclusion* offers a viable framework for promoting equity in education for all (Ainscow, 2005). This chapter elaborates a view of inclusion, not just as a practice of bringing students with disabilities into general education classrooms, but as a practice for moving people from the margins into the mainstream—or center. It is a view of inclusion that fundamentally remakes what is considered "normal."

Rather than fearing differences, educators who take an inclusive stance value them. Such educators are particularly attuned to what human differences can teach us about ourselves, about human possibility, and about democratic community (Ainscow, Howes, Farrell, & Frankham, 2003). This version of *inclusion* might be called "critical inclusivity." The word "critical" in this phrase refers to a focus on power and positioning; it invites us to consider how life in schools can be examined for the ways we, as educators, structure and produce equality—or, too frequently, inequality.

In this chapter, I first define critical inclusivity in the context of discussing the dilemmas of dealing with human difference. Then, I provide a template for understanding how critical inclusivity works in schools in relationship to school structures, curricular and instructional practices, ideological framings, and attention to the affective dimensions of life in school. I show how taking up a stance of critical inclusivity depends in large part on rejecting "bell curve thinking" and problematizing the very conception of what is normal. This stance challenges some of the beliefs and practices that are of long standing in the field of special education. But it does so on behalf of a view of inclusion that values (rather than stigma-tizes) diversity along a range of dimensions: race, ethnicity, religion, social class, size, gender expression, sexuality, learning preferences, and so on. Examples for classroom practice are integrated throughout the chapter so as to connect the stance of critical inclusivity to everyday life in schools.

HUMAN DIFFERENCE AND CRITICAL INCLUSIVITY

Early practices of including students with disabilities in general educa-tion classrooms depended on the idea of mainstreaming, in which some students, with some disabilities, were allowed to participate sometimes—as their skill levels allowed—with more typically developing chronological peers (Allan, 1996). Some minor classroom changes were made to "accom-modate" these "mainstreamed" students, but the premise was that students who were "different" would need to fit in with age-peers so as not to cause disruption. The practices associated with mainstreaming persisted mostly intact even though its name eventually changed to "inclusion."

In contrast to mainstreaming and the conventional view of inclusion, critical inclusivity challenges fundamental assumptions about what is normal. According to Black feminist scholar, Patricia Hill Collins (2016), critical inclusivity requires us to shift what, and who, is at the center of our work by questioning whose knowledge and ways of knowing are (and ought to be) valued and normalized (see also Florian & Black-Hawkins, 2011). This perspective opens up the center to people who have previously been marginalized or "minoritized." Through this process, the center is transformed.

An analogy may be helpful here. Imagine we are hosting a dinner party and we are persuaded to invite people from different cultures than our own to share a meal with us. Mainstreaming would have us opening the door and inviting our guests to sit at the table, but we would not be making any special food for them; they could either take what was offered, or not eat at all. Inclusion (in its most basic form) would have us make a physical space for them at the table, perhaps get the menu translated, provide an interpreter, and even make a special dish from the guests' home cultures. Continuing the analogy further, a critically inclusive approach would encourage us to find out how and what our guests eat and to expand our own culinary horizons to experience the value of our guests' preferred foods. We might even remake the table to expand options based on a wider range of preferences. Perhaps, for instance, some of the attendees would be more comfortable sitting on the floor at a low table, in which case we might provide a variety of seating options from which all people could choose. Our stance of critical inclusivity does not merely admit people with different characteristics into the room to sit together at a traditional table. Rather, it asks us not only to reimagine the food available at the table, but to change our ways of sitting and eating together. Thus, a stance of critical inclusivity is not a project of assimilation, but of transformation.

Difference as Productive

Human differences are omnipresent. Indeed, it is our differences that create the possibilities for pluralism, for collaboration, for creativity, for social dynamism, and even for the survival of our species (hooks, 2003). Differences shape human endeavors, preferences, perception, and expression; they stimulate and guide sensory and intellectual exploration and learning.

To embrace a critically inclusive approach to schooling and classrooms does not mean we seek to eradicate difference (Sapon-Shevin, 2007). As African American professor Yolanda Sealey-Ruiz tells her students, "Please do not say you do not see my Blackness; if you do not see me as Black, you do not see me fully." Likewise, those of us committed to the project of critical inclusivity do not want to try to flatten or obscure differences that occur due to disability. Rather, the project of critical inclusivity proposes that we recognize and attend to matters of status inequality in schools, and that we work to design curriculum and pedagogy so that all students have equal access to all that school, community, and society have to offer.

The project of critical inclusivity changes schools into places of belonging by actively embracing human identities, especially those that have been historically marginalized (Emdin, 2007). In practice this means, for example, that adults and children work to make recess play accessible to all, including students who use wheelchairs. It means that students fasting during Ramadan are provided with options that keep them from having to watch others eat in the cafeteria (e.g., staying in the library) and choices of activities that expend less energy and generate less thirst (e.g., working on a computer project during recess). Schools can even make these activity options open to all students, and thus be more inclusive.

In addition to requiring our understanding of students' identities and disabilities, critical inclusivity also asks us to determine students' individual proclivities (Howley, Howley, & Pendarvis, 2017), for example identifying students who "learn verbal and mathematical concepts more rapidly than other children" (p.138). When we take students' proclivities and talents into account from the beginning of the educational planning process, we can provide intellectual and creative challenge to all. The practice of offering intellectual challenge (and support) to all students is at the heart of critical inclusivity (Oyler, 2001).

Supporting and challenging all learners requires that we think carefully about spaces in classrooms and schools, time allocated to various activities, and groupings (Naraian, 2017). For instance, in fostering critical inclusivity, we do not require that a child who has negative reactions to cacophony eat lunch in a loud cafeteria; we create a small, low-volume lunchroom for children who prefer a quieter atmosphere. Similarly, for students who learn rapidly, we do not require they stay all day with their age peers, but instead look across the school setting to find content that can challenge them offered at viable times and locations. In our work as critically inclusive pedagogues, we strive to integrate students' identities, their individual proclivities and talents, and their social-emotional needs into our curriculum, instruction, and school structures.

Critical inclusivity requires that we help students find ways to reach full actualization in the school community. Such self-actualization benefits the individual as well as the entire community. Classroom, school, workplace, town—every community is richer, more productive, and more powerful when everyone is contributing (Theobald, 1997). When communities are able to maximize all members' contributions; and individuals in those communities feel they belong and have full access to all that is offered, the communities are likely to be healthy, effective, and happy.

Admittedly, history is not on our side here, and the work of critical inclusivity must be understood as counter-hegemonic (Ohito & Oyler, 2017). As Italian anti-fascist activist and political prisoner Antonio Gramsci (1971) explained, capitalist society is permeated with a system of values, attitudes, beliefs, and morality that supports the status quo and limits people's ability to think and act outside it. To the extent that this prevailing consciousness is internalized by the population, it becomes part of what we all think of as "common sense." The philosophy, culture, and morality of the dominant center come to be regarded as the natural order of things.

What is normalized and naturalized, and thus hegemonic, in United States schools is a culture rooted in competition rather than cooperation and collaboration (Cohen, Brody, & Sapon-Shevin, 2004). Educators often use practices that reward individual success rather than using practices that demonstrate commitment to the collective, community, or common good (Oyler, 2006). Instruction is typically designed around a single lesson sequence and format, rather than allowing for multiple entry points and opportunities for engagement (Oyler, 2001). Classroom learning is most often assessed by single, predetermined correct answers rather than through complex, open-ended inquiry (Cazden, 2001). Most U.S. schools place a laser-like focus on academic learning, rather than endorsing a balanced approach that attends to (and thereby honors) the physical, emotional, social, cognitive, and aesthetic aspects of children's and adolescents' development (Peterson & Hittie, 2010).

A FRAMEWORK FOR CRITICAL INCLUSIVITY

In my recent work with colleagues on critical inclusivity (Watson, Oyler, Schlessinger, & Chako, 2012), we have been using a four-part framework to think through the complexity of applying critical inclusivity to widely different school contexts. Our approach involves looking at four intersecting dimensions to analyze how schools challenge or reproduce status inequalities:

- school structures, policies, and practices;
- curricular and instructional practices;
- ideological framing (beliefs, values), whether stated or not stated; and
- affects that circulate between and among all school members.

School Structures

School structures, policies, and practices that stand as barriers to inclusive practice vary in scope and pervasiveness across school systems (Hehir, 2012). They may include such things as school funding mechanisms; assessment, grading, report cards, and accountability testing; tracking; identification of student exceptionalities, and qualification for programs such as special education and gifted/talented education; behavior codes and discipline; treatment of religious and cultural holidays and celebrations (including school calendar decisions); school menus and food policies; school and classroom routines; ways in which school and classroom membership is formed (e.g., seating, teams, learning groups); means of communicating with families; and teacher evaluations. As we work with teachers on matters of curricular and pedagogical practices, they repeatedly point to school structures, policies, and practices as either facilitating or impeding their work of classroom inclusion.

Curricular and Instructional Practices

Curricular and instructional practices that teachers implement in classrooms create or inhibit opportunities for students to work directly with one another in social, emotional, physical, aesthetic, and cognitive ways (Henderson & Kesson, 2004). A first step in creating such opportunities is to design classroom spaces to maximize smooth student movement and organization of their materials and bodies (Kluth, 2010). In inclusive classrooms this sometimes complicated task is facilitated by involving the students actively in decision-making about how the classroom should operate (Schultz, 2008).

In all aspects of curricular and instructional decision-making we must ask:

- How can we maximize active participation by all?
- How can we help all students feel they truly belong and are valued members of the community?
- How can we work skillfully, reflectively, and collaboratively to attend to human differences in ways that support and encourage, rather than isolate and humiliate?

This type of work on curriculum and instruction is always in process (Allan, 2008). It is dynamic work, responsive to time and place as well as to the students for whom it is undertaken.

Although the mantra of inclusive education is to challenge and support all learners, human beings, including teachers, vary in their views and practices. Even when they support the overarching goal of inclusiveness, they are not likely to address it in every detail of daily educational practice. The process of implementing curricular and instructional practices that challenge and support all students is, in fact, complicated by the fact that we often do not actually know what is best for students—or what they are learning—at every point in time. For example, a student's "fooling around" behavior may actually be an important step in his or her effort to develop a network of natural peer supports—an outcome that is of great cognitive and emotional consequence to that student's future learning. As teachers, we need to remain open to multiple interpretations of what we are seeing in the classroom; but often the pace of classroom life gets in the way of this kind of openness.

Ideological Frames

School community members' ideological frames are also at play when we are working toward greater inclusivity (Ohito & Oyler, 2017). Our ideological frames can be thought of as lenses through which we filter meaning (and affect), specifically asking: What is right? What is good? What is true? What is meaningful? Of course, our ideological frames are themselves shaped by what we absorb from our home culture; the dominant culture; our professional education; our schooling; our life experiences; the media; and our teachers, friends, and associates. Moreover, much of our ideological framing is tacit and not frequently probed or uncovered in our daily practice as educators.

Although our ideological frames may operate largely beneath our consciousness, they nonetheless shape our values and decision making as we apply a critically inclusive approach to teaching. If, for example, we lack the ideological frame of disability rights, we might not notice that the practice of pulling out students to accommodate the schedule of related-service providers often removes students with individualized education programs (IEPs) from classroom activities that would be valuable to them or that create a sense of full classroom membership (Kliewer, 1998). Likewise, when teachers have an ideological commitment to antiracism, they look carefully at the ways that race and racism are addressed, or not addressed, in curricular and instructional acts and in interactions among students. Confronting the ways that racist, ableist, sexist, classist, and heterosexist ideas have taken up residence in our hearts and minds and are expressed in our curriculum and school structures is, without a doubt, an intensely challenging life-long project.

Affects

Affects are subjectively experienced feelings and sensations. As queer theorist Eve Sedgwick (2003) explains, affects "can be, and are, attached to things, people, ideas, sensations, relations, activities, ambitions, institutions, and any number of other things, including other affects" (p. 19). Affects continually move people and are moved by people, especially when they pertain to matters of belonging, exclusion, marginalization, popularity, affirmations, oppression, and sanctions. In thinking about affects from this viewpoint, we are not focusing only (or even mostly) on feelings and emotions, but more on the "non-conscious, non-cognitive, trans-personal, and non-representational processes, as well as the communicative capacities of bodies and matter 'beyond' discourse" (Lara et al., 2017, p. 31).

An example of affect might be the wave of pleasure that washes over us as we walk into a school in which students value one another and engage enthusiastically in their endeavors. On a recent school visit, I experienced this kind of pleasure when students energetically greeted me and explained what they were learning. Similarly, many of us also have felt blood rushing to our faces when we witnessed an unjust act in a classroom, such as a student being put on the spot or a student who erupts with great anger toward a teacher or peer.

From our work in schools and communities, we know that affects continually circulate in response to matters of importance such as power, knowledge, and belonging. They can be particularly salient when we engage in the demanding work of teaching and learning—the constant human interaction that schooling requires. Affects complicate our understanding of the dynamics that comprise and shape students' experiences of school, and they influence our efforts to address issues of inequality and inclusivity. Because affects function beyond our cognition and control, we can get caught up in their transmission even when our thoughts and values might encourage us to resist.

Integrating the Four Dimensions

Much of school reform in the current era of accountability and audit (Lipman, 2006) focuses on "best practices," and indeed, a significant amount of the work on inclusion in schools during the past three decades has centered on "best" practices for classroom teachers and schools to enact (Oyler, 2011). Unquestionably, educators have implemented successful curricula, interventions, instructional approaches, and school change projects. Yet, in many schools across the United States, we still struggle with status inequalities and exclusions (Sensoy & DiAngelo, 2017), as evidenced (for example) by an increased incidence of hate speech (Southern Poverty Law Center, 2017), lower graduation rates for students with disabilities and low-income students of color (Gorski, 2017), and racial disproportionality in discipline and placement of students of color in segregated settings (Annamma, Connor, & Ferri, 2013; Blanchett, Klinger, & Harry, 2009). In Ohio, the Kirwan Institute for the Study of Race and Ethnicity found that, in 2015:

> White students with disabilities received 3.1 times more disciplinary actions than Whites in the general education population did. However, when comparing across racial groups, it is clear that ability status alone is only a small piece of the puzzle. Though Black students with disabilities were disciplined at rates relatively similar to the non-disabled population of Black students (1.6 times more), Black students without disabilities were disciplined nearly 40 percent more than White students with disabilities, on average. The *intricate relationship between race and ability* [emphasis added] yields a wide continuum of discipline outcomes. In fact, when examining outcomes across the various intersections of both race and disability, discipline occurrences for every 100 Ohio students range from 5.7 to a startling 167.8 incidents. (Capatosto, 2015, p. 2)

This "intricate relationship between race and ability" (Capatosto, 2015, p. 2) provides a key insight to guide our examination and practice of critical inclusivity. Many other insights also can be productive, especially those that reveal dilemmas sufficiently poignant to limit some students' opportunities in life-altering ways.

Schools cannot keep students from confronting such dilemmas. By adopting a stance of critical inclusivity, we can help students see, understand, and navigate these challenges. Critical inclusivity helps us consider how school structures, people's ideologies, our curricular and instructional practices, and the attendant affects create and maintain, or challenge and interrupt, status inequalities and access to full participation and belonging.

CHALLENGING BELL CURVE THINKING

One of the most salient concepts that inform much of contemporary schooling is the idea of the "normal" (Dudley-Marling & Gurn, 2016). What is considered normal human behavior, appearance, intellect, and ability, and what is considered abnormal? Of course, our ideas about what is normal shift over time and across cultural groups. For instance, in the town of Chilmark, on the island of Martha's Vineyard, Massachusetts, in the 17th and 18th centuries so many people were deaf that everyone in the community used sign language in order to participate in community life. As Groce (1985) explains in her book on the subject, being Deaf was not considered to be a handicap; and Martha's Vineyard Sign Language belonged to the town, not just to the people who were Deaf.

A key construct that helps maintain the idea of normal is "bell curve thinking" (Fendler & Muzaffar, 2008), which undergirds the day-to-day instructional practices and structures of the vast majority of public schools in the United States. In *Troubling the Foundations of Special Education: Examining the Myth of the Normal Curve*, Dudley-Marley and Gurn (2010) explain how the "normal curve signifies a theory of human difference that has no empirical basis" (p. 17). This is a crucial fact: The normal curve distribution does not hold up under empirical scrutiny when looking at complex human characteristics and behaviors. As the authors state, "the normal curve applies only to truly random events" and "not to socially-mediated human behaviors" (p. 15). Yet—almost two centuries after Adolphe Quetelet first proposed the idea that the normal curve could be used to understand individual human differences in *A Treatise on Man and the Development of His Faculties* (as cited in Dudley-Marlin & Gurn, 2010)—we are still imprisoned by an idea that has no credible evidence supporting it.

"Bell curve thinking" sustains the construct of intelligence, which is theorized to be singular and stable. This view of intelligence supports tracking and other forms of (so called) "ability grouping." As Leonardo and Broderick (2011) explain,

> A substantial part of the ideological work of schooling constructs and
> constitutes some students as "smart," while simultaneously constructing
> and constituting other students as "not-so-smart"—that is, some students
> are taught their intellectual supremacy and concomitant entitlement to
> cultural capital, whereas others are taught their intellectual inferiority and
> concomitant lack of entitlement to both an identity as a "smart" person,
> and the cultural and material spoils that such an identity generally affords.
> (p. 2214)

I propose that it is our devotion to this myth of meritocracy that motivates
our exclusionary practices of ranking, sorting, and labeling. However, in
order to build schools that act on a commitment to equity and justice for
all learners, we must abandon bell curve thinking, reject the concept of
the normal, and strive to reposition those students (Collins, 2003) who are
viewed as inferior, categorized as abnormal, and/or excluded by socially-
constructed status inequalities.

The Normal Curve and Special Education

The infamous theorists who most stridently promoted bell curve
thinking were the eugenicists (Dudley-Marling & Gurn, 2010). In their
time, they were well-respected academics and social engineers. Indeed,
Edward Thorndike, a highly renowned Columbia University professor who
actively published works that used the term "eugenics," was instrumental in
creating the field of educational psychology and heavily promoted the use
of "intelligence" tests in schools. As Deborah Gallagher (2010) explains,
Thorndike, the author of *The Contribution of Psychology to Education*, avowed
that "the extent to which the intellectual and moral differences found in
human beings are the consequences of their *original* [emphasis added]
nature and determined by the *ancestry from which they spring* [emphasis
added], is a matter of fundamental importance for education" (as cited
in Gallagher, 2010, p. 32). Eugenics relied on the concept of White racial
and upper-class superiority, and it used statistics to buttress the belief that
to make social progress people who are on the lower end of the bell curve
and the darker end of the phenotype spectrum should not reproduce. Yet,
as we acknowledge a century later, the IQ tests that were developed to
measure differences in intelligence and on which judgments of superiority and inferiority were based have enormous cultural, linguistic, regional,
gender, and class bias (Au, 2009).
    Some decades after Thorndike, the field of special education came into
being. And despite its connection to civil rights legislation (i.e., Public
Law 94-142, The Education of All Handicapped Children Act of 1975),
paradoxically drew in large part on the concept of the normal (and the

abnormal) and operationalized this concept through the use of standardized tests. "Exceptional education," as it was often called in the 1970s, was based on the bell curve: Those thought to be far along the right tail of the bell curve were labeled gifted and those far along the left tail were labeled educable mentally retarded (EMR). Those even further along the left tail were labeled trainable mentally retarded (TMR). In the 1970s, many undergraduate special education majors took courses such as "Characteristics of the EMR" and "Methods for Teaching the EMR," and then similar courses for the TMR, learning disabled, and emotionally disturbed.

The 1970s was a burgeoning decade for special education, as PL 94-142 had a component called Child Find, which required all school districts across the United States to identify children with disabilities and bring them into full-time public education in the "least restrictive environment." At the same time, the deinstitutionalization movement was taking place (e.g., Taylor, Blatt, & Braddock, 1999), and children were being returned to home and community settings with the expectation that the public schools would provide them an education. Unfortunately, from a critically inclusive stance, many students with moderate and significant disabilities were not (and are still not) given an academic education in the public schools (Kluth, Straut, & Biklen, 2003). This failure to provide adequate education to students with disabilities can be traced to the large variability in state-level policies toward inclusion, mainstreaming, and integration. Ohio, for instance, in 2013 reported that approximately 16% of students with disabilities spent less than 40% of their school day with nondisabled peers (Ohio Department of Education, 2018).

Despite the well-intentioned premise of special education and its civil-rights legacy, it is a project based on conceptual flaws and fraught with enormous contradictions. Segregating students worsens these contradictions. In addition to the flawed premise of the normal curve, there are decades of evidence that—contrary to the best thinking of the last century—students with different "disabilities" do not require specialized instructional methods matched to those disabilities (Mitchell, 2014).

SCHOOLING AND TEACHER EDUCATION FOR CRITICAL INCLUSIVITY

Critically inclusive schooling asks us to reimagine the problem we are trying to solve. Rather than develop specialized services—often in a segregated location—for people for whom the system of mass schooling was not built (Gorski, 2017), critical inclusivity asks us to reconceive school structures and curricular and instructional practices using principles of accessible instruction (Oyler, 2001), cultural sustainability (Paris, 2012), and holistic democracy (Woods, 2017). The example of creating physical access for people who use wheelchairs can be helpful here. If we need to retrofit an old building that has barriers for people who use wheelchairs, we often put in stair lifts. These are clunky and slow, unreliable, and typically need keys to operate. On the other hand, when a new structure is built, architects and engineers can use universal design and make it accessible right from the start. The accessible design has obvious advantages: It can be constructed to be aesthetically pleasing with practical and reliable accessibility features built into the design. Furthermore, the features that support access for a person using a wheelchair also provide support for people who have limited mobility or decreased stair-climbing capability, who push baby strollers, and who use carts to deliver supplies or transport cleaning equipment.

We can use universal design to rethink schooling so that time and place are reimagined for all students. As Mara Sapon-Shevin (1996) aptly points out, students with significant disabilities serve as disclosing tablets,[1] making apparent to us the structures, policies, and practices that reduce inclusion for many students. Likewise, students and families who identify with any group that is not the predominant group in the community (depending on the community this might involve disability, gender expression, sexual orientation, religious affiliation or nonaffiliation, nationality, race, or ethnicity) help highlight what is missing for many other students. An example of this might be seen by doing a curriculum audit of the people featured in classroom or assigned texts, as in this experience in my own life: Upon examining the summer reading list issued by the school my Puerto Rican foster children attend, I noticed that not one single book was written by a person of color or had as the main protagonist a person of color. Not only does an all-White reading list do damage to a child of color, it mis-educates and undereducates the White students. How can we possibly prepare our young people to confidently navigate the world with all its diversities if we do not prepare them to encounter the perspectives and hear about the lives of people with these diversities?

What happens when the lives of people different from us are made invisible? In the preservice teacher preparation program in which I work, we ask student teachers to engage in critical autobiographical analysis. They examine their identities and ideologies and reflect on how they came to believe what they do, and how they came to know (or not know) what they do (or do not) about people who have different identities and different experiences from theirs. Specifically, we ask them to take stock of their own social location by examining racial, ethnic, linguistic, social class, religious/non-religious, immigration-status, gender/gender expression, dis/ability status, and sexual orientation identities and experiences.

One of our students, Barbara Wang wrote:

In elementary school, Bettina, my classmate was paralyzed from the waist down and used crutches to move around. She was also a child with significant intellectual disabilities. She did not spend much time in our classroom: never came to math, reading, writing or gym. She did not even lunch with the rest of the class. I remember during the first week of third grade wondering where Bettina disappeared to after 11:00 in the morning. She was part of our classroom for a few hours each day and then seemed to have vanished. When we asked where Bettina was, our teacher responded: "Don't worry about it. It doesn't concern you." I soon stopped wondering why Bettina didn't get to go on field trips or eat lunch with the rest of the class. I quickly learned that the correct response to difference was to turn the other way and avoid it at all costs. (Oyler & The Preservice Inclusion Study Group, 2006)

Many of us have been denied close contact with people who have significant disabilities, just as many White students have been denied close contact with People of Color. As Britt Hamre and I discovered from our research (Hamre & Oyler, 2004), our preservice teachers who are most invested in, and confident about, teaching students with disabilities are the ones who had a neighbor, friend, classmate, or relative with a disability. It is through relationships that we can come to know the day-to-day experiences of people who are different from ourselves. Of course, we should be cautious about overgeneralizing from the individual to the group; many people think because they have had one experience with a person who has a group identity different from their own, they have knowledge of all people with that identity. This is our job as educators: to help our students learn about other ways of being and thinking in the world, but not to overgeneralize from a limited amount of contact.

Fundamental to the work of critically inclusive pedagogues is a belief in the transformability (Hart, 2004) of our students and ourselves. As Florian (2013) explains in her research on successful teachers of all students, teachers who enact inclusive classroom pedagogies view students as unlimited in their potential for growth and learning (Florian & Black-Hawkins, 2011). These teachers believe they can teach all students and thus approach the difficulties that students demonstrate in acquiring knowledge as quandaries of *teaching* that are ripe for problem-solving rather than as evidence of inherent deficits in the learners. School practices that level and label students and sort them into categories such as "high flyers" and "low level kids" are replaced by more equitable practices. These practices are informed by the knowledge that all students "can make progress if the conditions are right" (Spratt & Florian, 2015, p. 92) and that a wide range of difference is always a part of the human condition. Moreover, the inclusive classroom pedagogies framework acknowledges that the work of welcoming all students into classrooms is supported by strong collaborations among educators, as complex learning dilemmas sometimes require "creative new ways of working with and through others" (Spratt & Florian, 2015, p. 92).

This work of redesigning PK–12 schools for critical inclusivity will always be retrofitting work if we do not simultaneously prepare new teachers for critical inclusivity. Our historic dual system of special education and general education initially served as a device to ensure special teachers were "trained" to educate students with disabilities (Blatt, Biklen, & Bogdan, 1977). Later, many university-based teacher educators created dual certification programs and separate programs for teachers of English as an additional language. As Pugach, Blanton, and Correa (2011) assert in their analysis of collaboration between general teacher educators and special education teacher educators, we can look at the practices, discourses, and relationships across the past 50 years and see that collaborative teacher preparation is no longer isolated in pockets but is a national trend. They contend,

> This overall reform context must be viewed as a unique, urgent, and qualitatively different opportunity than in the past to connect issues that are valued by special education with a broader consideration of how teacher educators prepare graduates to create productive learning communities within highly diverse classrooms and schools. (p. 195)

Meeting the divergent needs of learners requires a fundamental rethinking of teacher preparation, rather than just tinkering with required courses and content coverage (Florian & Linklater, 2010). By harnessing the advanced expertise from special education, the teaching of English as an additional language, and such areas as culturally sustaining pedagogy (Paris, 2012), we can "rethink the enterprise of what it means to teach within a diverse society" (Pugach et al., 2011, p. 196).

A stance of critical inclusivity can prompt us to imagine what it might look, sound, and feel like when the structures, policies, and practices of schooling work to promote collaboration rather than competition, belonging rather than segregation, and differentiation rather than standardization. We know that getting more than a few people together in any room results in a cascade of intersecting, and oft-times conflicting, differences. These differences enrich us all. When a critically inclusive perspective permeates, it contributes to affects that support solidarity across individuals and groups, shaping broad understanding and, at the same time, commitment to the common good. By prioritizing discussions about how our schooling and societal structures and practices position some students as insiders and others as squatters on the periphery (Kliewer, 1998), we can work to bring more and more students into the embrace of meaningful and connected learning on behalf of equality and democratic engagement.

NOTE

1. Disclosing tablets are used in dental hygiene education. Children brush their teeth and then chew on a red tablet. They then look in a mirror and the spots they fail to brush properly are red.

REFERENCES

Ainscow, M. (2005). Developing inclusive education systems: What are the levers for change? *Journal of Educational Change, 6*, 109–124. doi:10.1007/s10833-005-1298-4

Ainscow, M., Howes, A., Farrell, P., & Frankham, J. (2003). Making sense of the development of inclusive practices. *European Journal of Special Needs Education, 18*, 227–242. doi:10.1080/0885625032000079005

Allan, J. (1996). Foucault and special educational needs: A 'box of tools' for analysing children's experiences of mainstreaming. *Disability & Society, 11*, 219–234. doi:10.1080/09687599650023245

Allan, J. (2008). *Rethinking inclusive education: The philosophers of difference in practice.* The Netherlands: Springer.

Annamma, S. A., Connor, D., & Ferri, B. (2013). Dis/ability critical race studies (DisCrit): Theorizing at the intersections of race and dis/ability. *Race Ethnicity and Education, 16*, 1–31. doi:10.1080/13613324.2012.730511

Au, W. (2009). *Unequal by design: High-stakes testing and the standardization of inequality.* New York, New York: Routledge.

Blanchett, W. J., Klingner, J. K., & Harry, B. (2009). The intersection of race, culture, language, and disability: Implications for urban education. *Urban Education, 44*(4), 389–409. doi:10.1177/0042085909338686

Blatt, B., Biklen, D., & Bogdan, B. (1977). *An alternative textbook in special education.* Denver, CO: Love.

Biklen, D., & Burke, J. (2006). Presuming competence. *Equity & Excellence in Education, 39*, 166–175. doi:10.1080/10665680500540376

Capatosto, K. (2015). *Ohio discipline data: An analysis of ability and race.* Columbus, OH: The Kirwan Institute for the Study of Race and Ethnicity. Retrieved from http://kirwaninstitute.osu.edu/wp-content/uploads/2016/04/Ohio-Discipline-Data-An-Analysis-of-Ability-and-Race.pdf

Cazden, C. (2001). *Classroom discourse: The language of teaching and learning* (2nd ed.). Portsmouth, NH: Heinemann.

Cohen, E. G., Brody, C., & Sapon-Shevin, M. (Eds.). (2004). *Teaching cooperative learning: The challenge for teacher education.* Albany, NY: SUNY Press.

Collins, K. M. (2003). *Ability profiling and school failure: One child's struggle to be seen as competent*. London, England: Laurence Erlbaum.

Collins, P. H. (2016). Shifting the center: Race, class, and feminist theorizing about motherhood. In E. N, Glenn, G. Chang, & L. R. Forcey (Eds.), *Mothering: Ideology, experience and agency* (pp. 45–65). New York, NY: Routledge.

Dudley-Marling, C., & Gurn, A. (Eds.). (2010). *The myth of the normal curve*. New York, NY: Peter Lang.

Emdin, C. (2007). *For white folks who teach in the 'hood' and the rest of ya'll too: Reality pedagogy and urban education*. New York, NY: Beacon.

Fendler, L., & Muzaffar, I. (2008). The history of the bell curve: Sorting and the idea of normal. *Educational Theory, 58*, 63–82. doi:10.1111/j.1741-5446.2007.0276.x

Florian, L. (2013). Reimagining special education: Why new approaches are needed. In L. Florian (Ed.), *SAGE handbook of special education* (2nd ed., pp. 9-22). London, England: SAGE.

Florian, L., & Black-Hawkins, K. (2011). Exploring inclusive pedagogy. *British Educational Research Journal, 37*, 813–828. doi:10.1080/01411926.2010.501 096

Florian, L., & Linklater, H. (2010). Preparing teachers for inclusive education: Using inclusive pedagogy to enhance teaching and learning for all. *Cambridge Journal of Education, 40*, 369–386. doi:10.1080/0305764X.2010.526588

Gallagher, D. (2010). Educational researchers and the making of normal people. In C. Dudley-Marling & A. Gurn (Eds.), *The myth of the normal curve* (pp. 25–38). New York, NY: Peter Lang.

Gorski, P. C. (2017). *Reaching and teaching students in poverty: Strategies for erasing the opportunity gap* (2nd ed.). New York, NY: Teachers College Press.

Gramsci, A. (1971). *Selections from the prison notebooks of Antonio Gramsci* (Q. Hoare & G. N. Smith, Eds.). New York, NY: International Publishers.

Groce, N. E. (1985). *Everyone here spoke sign language*. Cambridge, MA: Harvard University Press.

Hamre, B., & Oyler, C. (2004). Preparing teachers for inclusive classrooms: Learning from a collaborative inquiry group. *Journal of Teacher Education, 55*, 154–163. doi:10.1177/0022487103261588

Hart, S. (2004). *Learning without limits*. London, England: McGraw-Hill Education.

Hehir, T. (2012). *Effective inclusive schools: Designing successful schoolwide programs*. San Francisco, CA: Jossey-Bass.

Henderson, J. G., & Kesson, K. (2003). *Curriculum wisdom: Educational wisdom in democratic societies*. New York, NY: Pearson.

Holland, D., Lachicotte, W., Skinner, D., & Cain, C. (1998). *Identity and agency in cultural worlds*. Cambridge, MA: Harvard University Press.

hooks, b. (2003). *Teaching community: A pedagogy of hope*. New York, NY: Routledge.

Howley, C. B., Howley, A., & Pendarvis, E. D. (2017). *Out of our minds: Turning the tide of anti-intellectualism in American schools* (2nd ed.). Waco, TX: Prufrock.

Kliewer, C. (1998). *Schooling children with Down syndrome: Toward an understanding of possibility*. New York, NY: Teachers College Press.

Kluth, P. (2010). *"You're gonna love this kid!": Teaching students with autism in the inclusive classroom* (2nd ed.). Baltimore, MD: Brookes.

Kluth, P., Straut, D. M., & Biklen, D. P. (Eds.). (2003). *Access to academics for all students: Critical approaches to inclusive curriculum, instruction, and policy*. New York, NY: Routledge.

van der Klift, E., & Kunc, N. (1994). Hell-bent on helping: Helping, benevolence, and the politics of help. In J. Thousand, R. Villa, & A. Nevin, (Eds.), *Creativity and collaborative learning: A practical guide to empowering students and teachers*. Baltimore, MD: Paul Brookes. Retrieved from https://www.broadreachtraining.com/van-der-klift-kunc-hellbent-on-helping-benevolence-friendship-and-the-politics-of-help/

Lara, A., Liu, W., Ashley, C. P., Nishida, A., Liebert, R. J., & Billies, M. (2017). Affect and subjectivity. *Subjectivity, 10*, 30–43. doi:10.1057/s41286-016-0020-8

Lawrence-Brown, D., & Sapon-Shevin, M. (2015). *Condition critical: Key principles for equitable and inclusive education*. New York, NY: Teachers College Press.

Leonardo, Z., & Broderick, A. (2011). Smartness as property: A critical exploration of intersections between whiteness and disability studies. *Teachers College Record, 113*, 2206–2232.

Lipman, P. (2006). The politics of education accountability in a post-9/11 world. *Cultural Studies Critical Methodologies, 6*, 52–72. doi:10.1177/1532708605282820

Mitchell, D. (2014). *What really works in special and inclusive education: Using evidence-based teaching strategies*. New York, NY: Routledge.

Naraian, S. (2017). *Teaching for inclusion: Eight principles for effective and equitable practice*. New York, NY: Teachers College Press.

Ohio Department of Education. (2018). *OH Part B FFY2014 State Performance Plan/Annual Performance Report*. Retrieved from http://education.ohio.gov/getattachment/Topics/Special-Education/State-Performance-Plan/Ohio-2014-2015-APR-with-OSEP-Responses-2-2.pdf.aspx

Ohito, E., & Oyler, C. (2017). Feeling our way toward counter-hegemonic pedagogies in teacher education. In L. Florian & N. Pantic (Eds.), *Teacher education for the changing demographics of schooling* (pp. 183–198). London, England: Springer.

Oliver, M. (1990). *The politics of disablement*. London, England: The Macmillan Press LTD.

Oyler, C. (2001). Democratic classrooms and accessible instruction. *Democracy and Education, 14*, 28–31.

Oyler, C. (2006). *Actions speak louder than words: Social action as curriculum*. New York, NY: Teachers College Press.

Oyler, C., and the Preservice Inclusion Study Group. (2006). *Learning to teach inclusively: Student teachers' classroom inquiries*. Mahwah, NJ: Lawrence Erlbaum.

Oyler, C. (2011). Teacher preparation for inclusive and critical (special) education. *Teacher Education and Special Education, 34*, 201–218. doi:10.1177/0888406411406745

Paris, D. (2012). Culturally sustaining pedagogy: A needed change in stance, terminology, and practice. *Educational Researcher, 41*, 93–97. doi:10.3102/0013189X12441244

Peterson, J. M., & Hittie, M. M. (2010). *Inclusive teaching: The journey towards effective school for all learners* (2nd ed.). Boston, MA: Pearson.

Pugach, M. C., Blanton, L. P., & Correa, V. I. (2011). A historical perspective on the role of collaboration in teacher education reform: Making good on the promise of teaching all students. *Teacher Education and Special Education, 34,* 183–200. doi:10.1177/0888406411406141

Rubin, S., Biklen, D., Kasa-Hendrickson, C., Kluth, P., Cardinal, D. N., & Broderick, A. (2001). Independence, participation, and the meaning of intellectual ability. *Disability & Society, 16,* 415–429. doi:10.1080/09687590120045969

Sapon-Shevin, M. (1996). Full inclusion as disclosing tablet: Revealing the flaws in our present system. *Theory into Practice, 35,* 35–41.

Sapon-Shevin, M. (2007). *Widening the circle: The power of inclusive classrooms.* New York, NY: Beacon.

Schultz, B. (2008). *Spectacular things happen along the way: Lessons from an urban classroom.* New York, NY: Teachers College Press.

Sedgwick, E. K. (2003). *Touching feeling: Affect, pedagogy, performativity.* Durham, NC: Duke University Press.

Sensoy, O., & DiAngelo, R. (2017). *Is everyone really equal?: An introduction to key concepts in social justice education* (2nd ed.). New York, NY: Teachers College Press.

Southern Poverty Law Center (2018). FBI: Hate crimes soar to 7,016 in 2017, third highest year since start of data collection. Retrieved from https://www.splcenter.org/hatewatch/2018/11/16/fbi-hate-crime-numbers-soar-7106-2017-third-worst-year-start-data-collection

Spratt, J., & Florian, L. (2015). Inclusive pedagogy: From learning to action. Supporting each individual in the context of "everybody". *Teaching and Teacher Education, 49,* 89–96. doi:10.1016/j.tate.2015.03.006

Spring, J. (1989). *The sorting machine revisited.* New York, NY: Longman.

Taylor, S. J., Blatt, S. D., & Braddock, D. L. (1999). *In search of the promised land: The collected papers of Burton Blatt.* Washington, DC: American Association on Mental Retardation.

Theobald, T. (1997). *Teaching the commons: Pride, place, and renewal of community.* Boulder: CO: Westview.

Watson, W., Oyler, C., Schlessinger, S., & Chako, M. (May, 2012). *Towards a praxis of critical inclusivity.* Presented at the Sixth Annual Critical Race Studies in Education Conference, NY, New York.

Woods, P. (2017). Researching holistic democracy in schools. *Democracy & Education, 25,* 1–6.

CHAPTER 3

WHAT INCLUSIVE PRACTICE MEANS FOR STUDENTS FROM MARGINALIZED GROUPS

Interview With Sue Zake, PhD

Sara A. Brannan
Wittenberg University

K. Ann Kaufman
Marietta College

INTRODUCTION

Creating an education system built upon inclusive practices and grounded in social justice has become a moral imperative for some educators; this chapter presents the views of one such educator—Sue Zake, PhD. We (the authors of this chapter) interviewed Zake and used transcribed passages from her interview to both characterize the importance of fostering social justice education and to explore some of the challenges facing those who take on this necessary work. The chapter's hybrid format—falling some-

Inclusive Education: A Systematic Perspective, pp. 41–58
Copyright © 2020 by Information Age Publishing

where between a synthetic essay and an interview transcript presented with commentary—uses Zake's comments at length, not only as source material for revealing the key issues mentioned above but also as a way to characterize the perspectives of an important leader in the field of inclusive education.

During her career, Zake has served in multiple leadership roles, enabling her to engage in sustained work to improve outcomes for all students. Most recently, she served as the director of the Office for Exceptional Children at the Ohio Department of Education. With respect to that role and her other positions, Zake considers herself primarily an advocate for students with special learning needs. In her various capacities, her aim has always been to work with state and local administrative teams to design, implement, and assess effective instructional programming to close the achievement gap for students with learning differences. From her early years as a teacher onward, she has held two central beliefs: (a) that all students can learn and (b) that students learn best when those with and those without disabilities receive instruction together.

This chapter begins with essential background on the continuing marginalization that occurs in the United States and considers social justice education as the foundation for inclusive educational practices. It then moves on to discuss inclusion as a strategy for promoting high achievement among all students. It describes certain features of inclusion as particularly salient: the focus on school climate, team-based approaches to learning, the emphasis on systemic change, and its reliance on evidence-based practices. The final sections of the chapter discuss the challenges that educators face as they work to make improvements to educational structures and practices. Throughout the chapter, excerpts from our interview with Dr. Zake serve as the vehicle for illuminating these major points.

Continued Marginalization

Despite advocacy and legislation on behalf of educational equity (e.g., No Child Left Behind Act of 2001, 2002), members of marginalized groups (e.g., English learners, low-income students, students with disabilities, and students of color) still face marginalization (Frattura & Capper, 2007). This section briefly discusses three examples of marginalization that continue to occur in the U.S. education system.

The first example relates to school discipline, explicitly the enactment of zero-tolerance policies (Wald & Losen, 2003). These policies, it appears, disproportionately harm students of color and those living in poverty, and they contribute to creating a school-to-prison pipeline. These policies, in fact, force students out of school and target them as criminals (Elias, 2013).

Research on school discipline consistently demonstrates that students of color and those living in poverty are given more stringent school punishments despite the fact that they are no more likely than other students to misbehave (Skiba, Michael, Carroll Nardo, & Peterson, 2002).

The second example involves disparities in educational opportunities and outcomes. In terms of racial disparities, the U.S. Government Accountability Office released a report stating that the number of Black and Latino students enrolled in low-income K–12 public schools has increased since the 2000–01 school year (U.S. Government Accountability Office, 2016). Compared to middle- and high-income families, students from low-income families are more likely to drop out before graduating from high school (Table 219.75; U.S. Department of Education, National Center for Education Statistics, 2018), less likely to attend college (U.S. Department of Education, National Center for Education Statistics, 2018; Table 302.30),[1] and are less likely to graduate when they do attend college because they are ill prepared for the demands of higher education (Oseguera, 2013; Tinto, 2006). For students with disabilities aged 14 to 21 years, the 2014–2015 school year dropout rate was 17.8% (Table 219.90; U.S. Department of Education, National Center for Education Statistics, 2018). Furthermore, students with disabilities accounted for only 19.4% of students enrolled in postsecondary education for an undergraduate degree in the 2015–2016 school year (Table 311.10; U.S. Department of Education, National Center for Education Statistics, 2018).

Lastly, initiatives to help members of marginalized groups through specialized instruction have resulted in further segregation (Frattura & Capper, 2007). In terms of time spent in an inclusive classroom, the reauthorization of the Individuals with Disabilities Education Act (1997) reaffirmed that children with disabilities need to be educated with their nondisabled peers to the "maximum extent appropriate." There are, however, different interpretations of what the "maximum extent appropriate" entails. Even in 2014, 39 years after the passage of the initial Education for All Handicapped Children Act (1975), 33.6% of students with disabilities are still educated in the regular classroom less than 80% of the time (Table 204.60; U.S. Department of Education, National Center for Education Statistics, 2017).

These statistics illustrate the problem, but they hardly describe it in an exhaustive way. Many other findings reveal the magnitude of the opportunity gaps that students from marginalized groups encounter when they try to navigate a system of schooling that, seemingly, is rigged against them.

Social Justice Education as the Foundation for Inclusive Education Practices

As a way to combat these persistent opportunity gaps, educator preparation programs have been helping preservice teachers learn to use more inclusive practices. Many school districts also use inclusive education to counter educational inequity (Pugach, Blanton, & Correa, 2011). Zake described these trends:

> Go back about 20 years to the time parents started to understand least restrictive environment provisions and, more specifically, what inclusion was meant to be and could be for their children. That movement helped move people forward in embracing the idea of inclusive education. As a field of special education, we reintroduced the continuum of least restrictive environment, redefining the possibilities within the continuum of learning environments and rallied around the concept of special education not being a place. We challenged one another to stay true to the intent of least restrictive environment and to have intentional discussions that started with how a learner with a disability can be educated in a general education classroom with their peers. (S. Zake, personal communication, January 19, 2018)[2]

The concept of least restrictive environment—language taken directly from the Individuals with Disabilities Education Act (1997)—underscores much current thinking on inclusive practice. Generally speaking, students should learn in the least restrictive environment possible or, to put it another way, they should spend as much time as possible in general education classrooms. Zake also elaborated on the role that higher education played (and continues to play) in establishing these new modes of thinking about inclusion.

> During this time, I think higher education played a major role in helping to drive what inclusive education practices could be as colleges of education prepared students to enter the field as novice teachers. We started to minimize the thinking of teachers restricted by past practice saying, "I have to do this," or "This is the only way it can be done," or special education teachers saying, "I still want to have my very own students." I think that all shifted as teacher preparation programs introduced inclusionary practice into well-designed co-teaching opportunities. This contributed and made a difference in understanding and embracing inclusion.

Salend and Garrick Duhaney (1999) described inclusive education as a push toward designing educational environments to meet the needs of all learners. They explained that inclusive education establishes communities of learners that both appreciate and grow from diversity. Indeed, Zake's vision of inclusion—drawing on her experiences observing and evaluating classroom environments, highlighting the aspects of inclusion that she has seen work for students—reflects these ideas and describes an ideal classroom environment.

> For me, what comes to mind when I think of inclusive education is that all learners are educated together for the entire day with the supports they need to be successful—however you define successful, because the definition of success is not the same for every child. It is that we, as educators, know our students and provide what they need, ensuring their growth and guiding their learning.

> I see an inclusive classroom as starting with the students as the focus as we educators get a sense of the diversity of our students and their needs. Then we weave in the course resources needed for student learning and growth. When I envision inclusion, I see technology; I see very dynamic groupings of students for learning. I see a variety of teachers guiding that learning, not just one individual. I also see the expertise in understanding ... the science or the craft of teaching ... so that teachers have the opportunity to learn their students well enough to know how to maximize learning by keeping them engaged and involved. And that, while we have standards, we don't hold so tightly to standards that teachers are fearful of straying, or do not understand how to stray in a constructive way while still meeting those standards.

> I remember early inclusive education practices as an evolving experience and practice. The mindset and experience of implementing inclusive education becomes a guide for how you solve problems and expand the practice. It takes processing time to think through the concept of inclusion and how to apply the principles to classroom and school structures and routines as well as specific situations.

Zake's perspective fits with the work of other educators who position inclusive education as an important way to promote social justice in schools (Celoria, 2016). In fact, Theoharis (2007) concluded that social justice *depends on* inclusive educational practices. Generalizing from Theoharis's (2007) definition of "social justice leadership" to an even broader conception of "social justice education," we concur that, with this approach, "[educators] make issues of race, class, gender, disability, sexual orientation, and other historically and currently marginalizing conditions in the United States central to their advocacy ... practice, and vision. This definition centers on addressing and eliminating marginalization in schools" (p. 223). Others (e.g., Hackman, 2005; Levitan, 2016) have described social justice education as education that enables students to think critically about oppression, observe and participate in models of social change, speak out on their own behalf, and experience camaraderie in a democratically governed environment. Clearly, as some educators argue, social justice education relies on inclusion, not just as an instructional principle, but as a moral imperative. Zake described this point of view:

> Morally there has to be a valuing of diversity, and of all types of diversity as the foundation. What follows or comes along with valuing of diversity is the belief that all children can learn. All children learn. Whether it is guided, intentional, or incidental is impacted by educators.

> In addition, it is imperative that we as educators believe that what we do makes a difference in the life of our students. It is not as individuals that we educate all student but rather as a team or community of educators here for the purpose of our students' learning.

INCLUSION AS THE WAY
TO PROMOTE HIGH ACHIEVEMENT

Inclusion depends on intentional efforts to create school and classroom structures and instructional practices that enable all students to learn important things alongside a diverse group of peers. Several strategies facilitate the creation of inclusive educational settings and, therefore, promote high achievement. As a first step, for example, educators must create a positive school climate—one that promotes high expectations, quality instruction, and a safe and healthy learning environment. Other steps include adopting new models like team-based learning, recognizing that successful change must occur system-wide, and using evidence-based instructional practices (i.e., those grounded in the relevant research). This section examines these four steps in greater detail.

School Climate

The first important component of the work to create more responsive, democratic, and humanistic learning environments involves simultaneous efforts to promote inclusive education and to improve school climate. Research demonstrates that school climate significantly impacts student performance (e.g., MacNeil, Prater, & Busch, 2009). Classrooms and schools in which students feel safe, engaged, and supported foster development, risk prevention, learning, academic achievement, and increased graduation rates (Thapa, Cohen, Higgens-D'Alessandro, & Guffey, 2012). Proponents of inclusive education believe that the best way for educators to create positive and supportive learning environments in their classrooms is to implement inclusive practices. The interconnected concepts of positive school climate and inclusion are necessary for effective instruction (Coulston & Smith, 2013). Zake attested to this synergy, recalling her observations of successful inclusive classrooms.

> I remember the excitement and the dynamic classroom structure when inclusive education worked for the benefit of all learners in a class. A diverse group of students in the classroom, committed and involved teachers, and everyone on the same page—knowing what the work was, where they were headed, and parents excited about what was happening for all students in the class. This was not always easy, but it was there.

Even though researchers have demonstrated the connection between positive learning environments and improved student outcomes, Zake believes that educators must continue to develop skills for creating such environments. She described the lag between developing an understanding of needs and then implementing the supports that meet those needs:

> Educators in Ohio work to provide quality instruction in safe, healthy, positive learning environments. I think more and more educators are understanding the importance of safe, healthy, positive learning environment. As I was exiting the Ohio Department of Education, we were starting to embrace and look at positive behavior supports as part of a safe and healthy learning environment. I believe this is where inclusion must start.

Team-Based Learning

A second component of the work to promote social justice education requires educators to ground their work in team-based learning and thereby challenge learning models that encourage isolation. At the student level, team-based learning constitutes group instruction, grounded in evidence, that focuses on students' preparation before class, in-class readiness testing, and application of what students learn (Team-Based Learning Collaborative, 2018). Zake expands team-based learning to include a focus on the school or district as a community, a perspective that holds all members of the community responsible for the learning of all students. Zake described such a team-based learning environment:

> In my mind's eye, I see a dynamic instructional environment where students work in whole group and fluid small groups based on interest or skill development. Technology plays a role in the classroom not as the teacher, but as a facilitator of learning along with the teacher. Adults floating in and

out of the environment based on the kinds of supports and interests of the children, and children float in and out of the environment based on their supports, interests, and needs.

Systemic Change

A third component of the work to promote inclusive education entails the recognition that change must occur across the entire education system (also referred to as systemic change; e.g., Holzman, 1993). This means that change occurs across levels, including K–12 classrooms, the district, the community, higher education institutions, and policy making bodies. Change cannot occur in isolation.

Zake contends that reforming teacher education and preparation will help to effect change at the higher education, K–12, and community levels. As she argued:

> We need more teacher preparation programs that lead to integrated licensure. I would say to teacher candidates that you are going to meet other educators that may not have the same values or understandings you do for inclusionary practice. As a new teacher, show your colleagues a new way to organize your classroom and teach. Lead them to inclusive education through your instructional practice. I worry that sometimes new teachers do what they think administrators and teacher colleagues want them to do. Teaching is not an invisible activity. The well-being and evidence of student learning will lead others. Support for inclusive education grows from student achievement and parent support as well as from the visibility of practice. A novice teacher's best base of support is the community of fellow teachers with experience in the design and implementation of inclusive education practices.

Regarding integrated licensure, Zake's comments recall efforts to reform educator preparation programs—like those underway in Ohio—so that graduates receive licensure in a general-education field of study (e.g., middle childhood education) as well as in special education. Such training would enable dual-licensure program graduates to work with their colleagues on issues related to inclusive practice—an approach that would deepen overall commitment to these important practices.

Furthermore, Zake explained that teachers need to feel supported when making the shift to inclusive educational practices.

> I think about situations I've been in when consulting in classrooms on behalf of individual students with disabilities where it is evident the teacher knows what a student needs but is hesitant because s/he or colleagues have

not traditionally differentiated or taught in a different way. Seeing this has led me to think inclusionary education practices are a belief system that guides how schools and classrooms are organized as well as how instruction is delivered. It can be scary for a teacher to step out on their own. Educators must be supported when trying new strategies or experimenting with techniques to better educate their students. There has to be a level of trust and educators must be encouraged to use their professional education, training, and experience on how to implement inclusive education practice and make it work for the students in their classrooms, schools, and districts.

Administrators, Zake elaborated, play a unique role in helping support the implementation of inclusive practices within their schools and districts.

Administrators have to set aside some of the traditional views of what a classroom should look like or what it's supposed to look like in a school. They have to lead in a manner that has accountability in place, in a very practical way for both students and teachers. Administrators play a significant role in being a part of solution finding, not for the purpose of saying "you're accountable" to such a degree that it becomes a punishment for the educator, but "you're accountable for looking for solutions and for seeking and using resources that will support your students." And for us as administrators, we must set the expectation and tone for inclusive education practices while taking responsibility to be a part of problem-solving and solution-finding.

This view of leadership, where administrators take on instructional responsibility and also share decision-making with teachers (a form of distributed leadership), is well established in current educational thinking and theory (see, e.g., Fullan, 2011). Indeed, programmatic solutions for educational improvement often stress lateral, collective (i.e., shared or distributed) leadership structures (see, e.g., Bryk, Gomez, Grunow, & LeMahieu, 2015).

Applying Evidence-Based Practices

A final component for deepening inclusion entails efforts to implement instructional practices that are supported by empirical research (IRIS Center, 2018). As with other components of the improvement agenda, Zake expressed concern about the lag between what research shows to be effective and what is actually implemented in the classroom. One example she recalled involves quality instruction, specifically focusing on the importance of differentiation.

I worry about quality instruction. There is a gap between what the science of learning and the research that supports it tells us and what gets delivered in

> classrooms. I think educators apply quality instruction and safe and positive learning environment principles to some students but haven't at times thought through the implications for all or each student. There is no consideration that applying the evidence-based practice may require adaptations for some individuals.

Just because academic research demonstrates the efficacy of a particular practice does not mean that it can be implemented for all learners without making adaptations. Frameworks such as Universal Design for Learning (UDL) provide concrete ways to operationalize differentiation without reducing instructional rigor.

Nevertheless, the disconnects between research, policy, and K–12 practice sometimes interfere with educators' ability to implement research-supported practices (e.g., Levin & Van Hoorn, 2016). For example, while research suggests that homework may not be helpful for young children, policy makers see homework as promoting rigor. Caught between the research and the policy, some teachers use whatever practices they prefer, and others feel obligated to comply with policy.

Using a similar example, Zake described a somewhat ironic situation that she observed toward the beginning of her career.

> While working as a regional special education consultant I observed inclusive practices born out of necessity in several rural school districts. They were implementing what we now refer to as inclusionary practices 30 plus years ago because they had few students, wanted to keep their students in their home school, and had limited access to special education teachers. I remember saying to them, "You are not complying with federal and state requirements" and thinking, "But look at this student, s/he is successfully learning with the services and specialized instruction being provided and s/he is an accepted friend to peers." We didn't call it inclusion then. We accepted the practice as meeting the needs of a learner with disabilities with the resources that were available. The district would identify the student as having a disability and then they wouldn't necessarily serve in a manner that any of us at that time would have defined as appropriate service given the standards of practice at that time. It is an interesting dichotomy to have then come forward 20 years to a point in my career where we are promoting inclusive education practices and some of the varied structures that were born out of necessity in some districts are now accepted as an innovative practice.

Driven by necessity, districts implemented practices that were out of touch with then current thinking in education; today, those same practices more closely approximate our understanding of what is needed to promote inclusive education for all students.

CHALLENGES WITH SUPPORTING IMPROVEMENTS

This section outlines several challenges associated with the work of supporting improvements that align with social justice imperatives. In particular,
the section distinguishes between two types of challenges that Zake identified: those relevant to all states and those specific to large, complex, and
diverse states such as Ohio.

Challenges Confronting All States

Zake identified two challenges that all states face when implementing
inclusive practices. Given their wide-ranging applicability, these challenges
tend to be broadly construed, perhaps even amorphous. The first of these
involves actually defining inclusionary practice.

> We have not fully defined inclusionary practice or maybe we are evolving
> into higher levels of understanding of what it is. For a long time, inclusion-
> ary practice has meant co-teaching, but it is not always about co-teaching.
> Do children with disabilities need someone called a special education inter-
> vention specialist? Or, is a general education teacher who is then trained in
> how to teach diverse learners needed? And so, I think the field of special
> education—and probably some people would say all of education is poised
> for the next evolution of what educating diverse learners needs to be. It is
> time for us as educators to understand who our students are and with open
> minds figure out the resources, techniques and supports needed for suc-
> cessful teaching and learning.

Indeed, this recognition underpins the aforementioned reform work being
carried out across Ohio, which is discussed at length elsewhere in this
volume. Ongoing efforts in the state are reforming educator preparation
programs to merge in ways leading to dual licensure (i.e., programs where
graduates receive licensure in general and special education). The process
of reforming educator preparation programs actually forces the essential
stakeholders in this work to reevaluate their definitions of inclusive practice. By necessity, this work includes not only faculty from these institutions
of higher education, but also personnel from partnering school districts
and regulatory agencies (e.g., the Ohio Department of Education, the Ohio
Department of Higher Education).

A second challenge confronting all states is how best to educate students
with multiple disabilities or low-incidence disabilities.

> When I was a director of special education for a school district, we had a
> lot of success with including students with multiple disabilities in regular

education classrooms due to wrapping supports and services. They were [also] very successful for the students with low-incidence disabilities in that district because they wrapped the supports and resources around the students. It often began that students received one-on-one supports in every classroom throughout their school day. Although the cost was high due to the number of paid professionals and paraprofessionals hired to support students with multiple disabilities, the approach was very successful. When people would point out that we were successfully implementing inclusive education practices for students with multiple disabilities and ask why not with other students with disabilities, it caused us to pause and think about next steps. The same principles that led us to provide inclusive education for one group of students, led us to use a similar mindset and strategies for others. It led us to ask, "What do our students need? What would make a difference in their lives? In their learning success? In their ability to be part of a bigger community than a special education classroom community or a separate facility community?" The planning conversation must be student focused and consider the services, resources, and tools needed as well as how we will monitor the impact and progress of the student and determine the fidelity and success of the educational program design.

Zake, moreover, acknowledged the critical balance between inclusive education and specialized instruction for individual students, especially those with complex needs.

I have always been an advocate for students with disabilities to be members of general education classes. This may require alignment of services and supports and individualizing curriculum requirements for some. I also understand that there are times you may have to provide one-on-one or small group instruction with the intent of taking the introduced skill or new content back to the general classroom. I am concerned about the application of inclusionary education practices for students with significant cognitive disabilities at the high school level. In some situations I don't think we fully understand what it means for such learners to be a part of high school course work with their non-disabled peers. It is not understood what is required of general education teachers and special education intervention specialists to design and implement a valuable learning experience for that student with significant cognitive disabilities, as well as the other students in the class. In addition, the expansion of our definition of inclusive education may need to look towards other types of educational services within the greater community depending on student needs and future planning. I'm not advocating removal of students; I am, however, saying that knowing a student's needs is only the first step in the process of designing and implementing an educational program. It is imperative that we are realistic and informed as to the growth and changing needs of students with special needs and all other diverse learners in a class.

Challenges Specific to Ohio

Zake identified three core challenges (and several smaller ones) with which Ohio continues to grapple as it works to improve inclusive practices statewide. While Zake discussed these in the context of Ohio specifically, they might well be applied to other similarly large and diverse states. The first challenge that she identified is the way in which Ohio defines student success.

> One challenge is the rigidity in understanding and defining high expectations as mastery of grade level or course specific academic content standards only. Our setback came when we started to evaluate teachers or when teachers became very worried and concerned about being evaluated based on their students' performance and achievement. I think if we want people to embrace diversity, we have got to grow them into it as opposed to saying, "Not only will you teach this diverse group of learners, you will be evaluated on what your students achieve." I understand the need to improve learning outcomes for students, but punitive accountability seems counterintuitive in the framework of social justice and meeting the needs of marginalized students.

This perspective, of course, echoes similar critiques about the overuse or misuse of educational standards writ large (see, e.g., Blacker, 2013; Egan, 2002). Indeed, state standards tied to high-stakes testing—as products of market-based educational reforms—often stand in the way of more equity-minded approaches to education (Peters & Oliver, 2009). This critique need not advocate the wholesale removal of such standards and accountability measures, but it does point to the fact that the use of standards and accountability measures as tools for compliance can get in the way of effective and inclusive practice.

A second challenge that Zake identified is rigidity within the education system. Zake argues that flexibility is a key component for effecting change.

> I am hopeful and encourage Ohio, and other states as well, to embrace experimental designs for educational programming. Key components should be identified for what must be within the design and then allow for flexibility in the design and delivery. One area for experimenting is determining whether a case management model for special education would allow for greater flexibility and focus by teachers (general and special education) on the design and implementation of instruction day to day. The case manager would be responsible for the coordination of special education requirements including paperwork, meetings, and reports. Further experimentation might look to students with disabilities receiving their special education service from general education teachers with dual licensure with support from a case manager to coordinate the logistics of special educa

tion, ensuring resources are available as needed and assisting with progress monitoring. We are at a point where there needs to be greater flexibility in the system of educating learners with disabilities and other marginalized learners.

I worry that, as a field, special education is being defined as our ability to write compliant IEPs as opposed to what is the specialized training in how to design and implement specialized instruction and supports. Are we preparing special education teachers on how to recognize and diagnose a reading disability as well as how to appropriately teach reading to a student for whom learning to read is a deficit area? Do we ensure understanding and experience on how to create a positive behavior intervention program for an individual student with autism or some other kind of emotional or mental health issue? I worry that we have lost some of that specialization in the field of special education. This is okay if it means that others are able to step in and address student needs, but there appears to be a gap in service delivery without the assistance of special educators.

Zake identified a third key challenge—the difficulty of implementing change across variable environments and contexts.

Another challenge, in Ohio, with our diverse population of students is that while we have been successful in implementing inclusive educational practices in certain environments, we haven't figured out how to translate implementation in varied environments even within the same school and district. For example, I know of an average-sized school district where inclusionary practice has become the standard of practice for all teachers and administrators and where time for collaborative teaming as well as needed supports are provided. In contrast, a nearby district lacks flexibility within their structures and bureaucracy to make arrangements and get resources where they need to be in order to support inclusionary educational practices.

The challenge of rigidity and the need to adapt to variable contexts appear often enough in the improvement literature. In the business world, the notion of agile processes informs improvement strategies (see, e.g., Kotter, 2014); in education, improvement work aims to create flexibility that promotes scaling up (see, e.g., Bryk et al., 2015).[3] In both cases, bureaucratic or institutional structures prohibit organizations (for our purposes—schools, districts, state education agencies) from experimenting with new ideas or adapting otherwise good ideas to the work within their specific contexts.

Lastly, Zake highlighted a number of other challenges that Ohio faces as a diverse state. These include issues like teacher burnout, prohibitive structures, and others.

I worry that there are teachers who we are asking too much of and that they are either on their way to burning out or have already left the field. In Ohio, inclusionary practice was voluntary at its inception. We said, "Find a teacher you want to pair with, and we will provide you with support, training and assistance and time for planning. In hindsight, I worry that we fell short in thinking that it was a choice as opposed to the way we go about the business of educating all students.

Another challenge is that we have novice teachers with the most current training and education available who are not getting to practice what they've learned because of some of the structures and situations they find themselves in, such as district cuts due to finances, reduction in resources or lack of a concerted effort to support novice teachers in implementation of research-based practices.

So, those are the kinds of challenges that I think about in our large diverse state. While acknowledging these challenges, it is also evident that Ohio has many outstanding educators with both the passion and expertise to lead and develop our next generation of students and educators.

As Zake outlined, there are a number of challenges involved with implementing inclusive educational practices. But, if the necessary stakeholders are provided with the right supports and flexibility, these challenges can be navigated, thereby improving educational structures, processes, and outcomes.

CONCLUSION

Sue Zake's insights and perspectives help communicate the importance of inclusive educational practices, grounded in social justice education, to support learning for all students. Implementing inclusive practices is integral in helping to combat the continued marginalization of students within the U.S. education system.

Our conversation with Zake revealed several important lessons related to the implementation of inclusive practices:

- Student needs must come first.
- Districts need to consider their perspective(s) regarding the least restrictive environment.
- Districts need to provide supports that aid teachers in taking risks and that bridge the gap between best practice research and its implementation in the classroom.

- Teacher preparation programs need to prepare general education teachers to support all learners and to consider integrating content area preparation with special education training.
- Districts and state education agencies need to allow flexibility especially at the district level, and teachers also need to respond flexibly to the learning challenges their students present.
- States need to consider redefining accountability for districts and teachers.
- States need to consider redefining student success.
- All components of the system must be involved in order for effective change to occur.

NOTES

1. The NCES statistics for 2015 and 2016 show a noteworthy exception that low-income students are enrolling at a slightly higher rate than middle-income students.
2. This excerpt and all subsequent quotes from Dr. Zake come from our interview with her on January 19, 2018.
3. The concept of "scaling up," however, is not without its detractors (see, e.g., Elmore, 2016).

REFERENCES

Blacker, D. J. (2013). *The falling rate of learning and the neoliberal endgame*. Alresford, England: Zero Books.

Bryk, A. S., Gomez, L. M., Grunow, A., & LeMahieu, P. G. (2015). *Learning to improve: How America's schools can get better at getting better*. Cambridge, MA: Harvard Education Press.

Celoria, D. (2016). The preparation of inclusive social justice education leaders. *Educational Leadership and Administration: Teaching and Program Development, 27*, 199–219.

Coulston, C., & Smith, K. (2013). School climate and inclusion. In T. Dary & T. Pickeral (Eds.), *School climate practices for implementation and sustainability* (A School Climate Practice Brief, Number 1). New York, NY: National School Climate Center.

Education for All Handicapped Children Act of 1975, 20 USC § 1401 (1975).

Egan, K. (2002). *Getting it wrong from the beginning: Our progressivist inheritance from Herbert Spencer, John Dewey, and Jean Piaget*. New Haven, CT: Yale University Press.

Elias, M. (2013). The school-to-prison pipeline: Policies and practices that favor incarceration over education do us all a grave injustice. *Teaching Tolerance, 43*, 39–40. Retrieved from https://www.tolerance.org/sites/default/files/2017-07/Teaching-Tolerance-Spring-2013.pdf

Elmore, R. F. (2016). "Getting to scale ..." it seemed like a good idea at the time. *Journal of Educational Change, 17*, 529–537. doi:10.1007/s10833-016-9290-8

Frattura, E. M., & Capper, C. A. (2007). *Leading for social justice: Transforming schools for all leaners.* Thousand Oaks, CA: Corwin Press.

Fullan, M. (2011). *Choosing the wrong drivers for whole system reform* (Seminar Series 204). Victoria, Australia: Center for Strategic Education. Retrieved from https://edsource.org/wp-content/uploads/old/Fullan-Wrong-Drivers11.pdf

Hackman, H. W. (2005). Five essential components for social justice education. *Equity & Excellence in Education, 38*, 103–109. doi:10.1080/10665680590935034

Holzman, M. (1993). What is systemic change? *Education Leadership, 51*(1), 18. Retrieved from http://www.ascd.org/publications/educational-leadership/sept93/vol51/num01/What-Is-Systemic-Change¢.aspx

Individuals with Disabilities Education Act Amendments of 1997, 20 U.S.C., §1400 *et seq.* (1997). Retrieved from https://www.congress.gov/105/plaws/publ17/PLAW-105publ17.pdf

IRIS Center. (2018). *Why educators should use EBPs.* Retrieved from https://iris.peabody.vanderbilt.edu/module/ebp_01/cresource/q1/p02/#content

Kotter, J. P. (2014). *Accelerate: Building strategic agility for a faster-moving world.* Boston, MA: Harvard Business Review Press.

Levin, D. E., & Van Hoorn, J. (2016). *Teachers speak out: How school reforms are failing low-income young children.* Jamaica Plain, MA: Defending the Early Years. Retrieved from https://www.deyproject.org/uploads/1/5/5/7/15571834/teachersspeakfinal_rgb.pdf

Levitan, J. (2016). The difference between educational equality, equity, and justice... and why it matters. *Forum of the American Journal of Education.* Retrieved from http://www.ajeforum.com/the-difference-between-educational-equality-equity-and-justice-and-why-it-matters-by-joseph-levitan/

MacNeil, A. J., Prater, D. L., & Busch, S. (2009). The effects of school culture and climate on student achievement. *International Journal of Leadership in Education, 12*(1), 73–84. doi:10.1080/13603120701576241

No Child Left Behind Act of 2001, P.L. 107-110, 20 U.S.C. § 6319 (2002).

Oseguera, L. (2013). *Importance of high school conditions for college access* (Research Brief). Los Angeles, CA: University of California ACCORD. Retrieved from http://pathways.gseis.ucla.edu/publications/201307_HSConditionsRB.pdf

Peters, S., & Oliver, L. A. (2009). Achieving quality and equity through inclusive education in an era of high-stakes testing. *Prospects: Comparative Journal of Curriculum, Learning, and Assessment, 39*, 265–279. doi:10.1007/s11125-009-9116-z

Pugach, M. C., Blanton, L. P., & Correa, V. I. (2011). A historical perspective on the role of collaboration in teacher education reform: Making good on the promise of teaching all students. *Teacher Education and Special Education: The Journal of the Teacher Education Division of the Council for Exceptional Children, 34*, 183–200. doi:10.1177/0888406411406141

Salend, S. J., & Garrick Duhaney, L. M. (1999). The impact of inclusion on students with and without disabilities and their educators. *Remedial and Special Education, 20*, 114–126. doi:10.1177/074193259902000209

Skiba, R. J., Michael, R. S., Nardo, A. C., & Peterson, R. L. (2002). The color of discipline: Sources of racial and gender disproportionality in school punishment. *The Urban Review, 34*, 317–342. doi:10.1023/A:1021320817372

Team-Based Learning Collaborative. (2018). *What is TBL?: Overview.* Retrieved from http://www.teambasedlearning.org/definition/

Thapa, A., Cohen, J., Higgens-D'Alessandro, A., & Guffey, S. (2012). *School climate research summary: August 2012* (School Climate Brief, No. 3). New York, NY: National School Climate Center.

Theoharis, G. (2007). Social justice educational leaders and resistance: Toward a theory of social justice leadership. *Educational Administration Quarterly, 43*, 221–258. doi:10.1177/0013161X06293717

Tinto, V. (2006). Research and practice of student retention: What next? *Journal of College Student Retention: Research, Theory & Practice, 8*, 1–19. doi:10.2190/4YNU-4TMB-22DJ-AN4W

U.S. Department of Education, Office for Civil Rights. (2018). *2015–2016 civil rights data collection: School climate and safety.* Washington, DC: Author. Retrieved from https://www2.ed.gov/about/offices/list/ocr/docs/school-climate-and-safety.pdf

U.S. Department of Education, National Center for Education Statistics. (2017). *The digest of education statistics, 2016.* Washington, DC: Author. Retrieved from https://nces.ed.gov/pubs2017/2017094.pdf

U.S. Department of Education, National Center for Education Statistics. (2018). *The digest of education statistics, 2017.* Washington, DC: Author. Retrieved from https://nces.ed.gov/programs/digest/2017menu_tables.asp

U.S. Government Accountability Office. (2016). *K–12 education: Better use of information could help agencies identify disparities and address racial discrimination* (GAO-16-345). Washington, DC: Author. Retrieved from https://www.gao.gov/products/GAO-16-345

Wald, J., & Losen, D. (2003). Defining and redirecting a school-to-prison pipeline. *New Directions for Youth Development, 99*, 9–15. doi:10.1002/yd.51

SECTION II INTRODUCTION

INCLUSIVE CLASSROOMS AND SCHOOLS

In Section I, the authors examined the social justice implications of inclusive classrooms and schools, contrasting them with the implications of maintaining educational institutions that marginalize some students while privileging others. Section II examines practical iterations of inclusion as seen in classrooms and schools. The chapters in this section seek to illuminate aspects of work to foster inclusive practice—work through which educators willingly questioned their assumptions and transformed their practice in the interest of constructing beneficial and meaningful educational programs.

In "Assessing the Included Classroom: The Included Classroom Characteristics Check Sheet," Catherine Lawless Frank and Victoria Zascavage review research-based practices that promote high-quality education for students in inclusive classrooms. They describe an instrument—keyed to research-based practices and dispositions—that measures the level of classroom implementation of inclusion. The assessment instrument, which can also serve as a stimulus to reflection and discussion about inclusive practices, includes items relating to differentiation, environment, teacher dispositions, delivery method, respect for cultural diversity, and lesson components.

Anne Bauer and Stephen Kroeger's "Helping Preservice Teachers Come to Terms with Unintended Biases" asserts that new teachers often bring unintentional biases to their understanding of the teaching role and that inclusive education requires them to counter occupational socialization that reinforces a tacit belief in the superiority of White ways of teaching and working. The authors note the importance of teachers' reflection on

Inclusive Education: A Systematic Perspective, pp. 59–60
Copyright © 2020 by Information Age Publishing
All rights of reproduction in any form reserved.

the ways race and class function as powerful interpretative filters in many classrooms. They also consider the critical need for teachers to learn to integrate professional knowledge with inclusive practice in order to move beyond survival strategies toward a reflective approach to teaching that advances a social justice agenda.

CHAPTER 4

ASSESSING THE INCLUDED CLASSROOM

The Included Classroom Characteristics Check Sheet

Catherine Lawless Frank
University of Dayton

Victoria Zascavage
Xavier University

Inclusion has become widely accepted as a process for providing all students with an education of high quality (Kricke & Neubert, 2017). Predicated on respect for differences among learners (Salend & Garrick Duhaney, 1999), this process is intended to offer individualized, meaningful, and appropriate instruction for all learners in the general education classroom (Downing, 2010). Providing effective instruction in an inclusive environment, however, is a continuous and complex enterprise requiring a curriculum that reflects academic priorities and a community learning environment that facilitates the academic, social, and behavioral success of all students (United Nations Educational, Scientific and Cultural Organization [UNESCO], 2006).

Inclusive Education: A Systematic Perspective, pp. 61–80
Copyright © 2020 by Information Age Publishing
All rights of reproduction in any form reserved.

In theory, inclusion can, through effective instruction with individualized academic and behavioral supports, provide students with disabilities access to the same general education curriculum that is provided to students without disabilities (Bui, Quirk, Almazan, & Valenti, 2010; Friend & Bursuck, 2015). In practice, learning environments fall short of this ideal (Kricke & Neubert, 2017) and often fall short even of legal mandates. Alter, Gottlieb, and Gottlieb (2018), for example, found that there is a gap between federally mandated policies for special education and implementation of those policies in public schools; and one area in which they noted this discrepancy was in including students with special needs in the least restrictive environment, most often considered to be the general education classroom.

Such gaps result from many factors, including educators' dispositions as well as their levels of professional knowledge and skill (e.g., Sharron, 2018). Whatever the cause, lack of success in creating a positive climate in the classroom can result in unfortunate experiences and outcomes for students with disabilities. For instance, such students may experience academic failure, or they may be experience discrimination and social isolation, as Wieringo (2015) found in his case study of students with disabilities who did not complete high school.

If an inclusive program is not well designed or is missing necessary supports for some students, the inclusive setting will not achieve the academic, behavioral, or social goals that it is positioned, under more conducive circumstances, to achieve (Kricke & Neubert, 2017; Pivik, McComas, & Laflamme, 2002). This chapter outlines the basic components of an effective included classroom and provides an informal tool to help assess how well classroom practices align with these components.

FIVE ESSENTIAL COMPONENTS
OF THE INCLUDED CLASSROOM

Effective instruction, based on ability and not on disability, provided within an inclusive environment depends on three types of integration: physical integration, social integration, and instructional integration. According to Friend and Bursuk (2015), physical integration prioritizes placement of students with disabilities in the same classroom as nondisabled peers; social integration fosters the development of interactive relationships within the inclusive environment; and instructional integration educates the majority of students in the standard curriculum by adjusting teaching and the measurement of learning to promote student success. To achieve the goals of a successful inclusive program, the "included" or "inclusive" classroom must embody the essential components that facilitate physical, social, and instructional integration. Research has identified five essential components that must be addressed in the inclusive classroom:

- differentiation (Santangelo & Tomlinson, 2012; Tomlinson, 2014);
- the classroom environment (Friend & Bursuck, 2015; Heward, 2018);
- teacher disposition (Koca, 2016);
- delivery method (Mercer, Mercer, & Pullen, 2011; Crockett & Kauffman, 2015); and
- lesson components (Downing, 2010; Mercer et al., 2011).

Differentiation

Differentiation is an approach to teaching that emphasizes instructional practices that are customizable to individual learners' needs (Mastrioperi & Scruggs, 2010). Differentiation includes a wide variety of instructional strategies and lesson adaptations that help teachers instruct students with diverse educational needs in the *same* learning environment ("Differentiation," 2013). A differentiated classroom extends beyond making basic accommodations (e.g., extra time on an assignment or preferential seating) or modifications (e.g., using fewer options on multiple-choice test questions or providing assignments at an easier reading level). Differentiation supports decisions for how to prioritize curriculum content by focusing on all students' interests and readiness, fairness, and high priority curricular outcomes (Friend & Bursuck, 2015; Center for Applied Special Technology [CAST], 2018b). True differentiation emphasizes Universal Design for Learning (UDL) and includes multisensory approaches (visual, auditory, and kinesthetic); appropriate assistive technology and software; and concrete and functional instructional material designed to meet students' needs (CAST, 2018a).

Universal Design for Learning

Whereas differentiation is the application of different learning techniques, UDL is a research-based framework that provides teachers with an understanding of how students learn and how various student needs and preferences influence learning. These understandings then help teachers identify ways to optimize instruction (CAST, 2018a). The principles of UDL inform differentiated instruction, providing insight into the methods, materials, and technology that maximize student learning by reducing barriers and creating accessibility to information. The framework of a UDL included classroom centers on curricula designed with high expectations for all learners and the use of technology and appropriate accommodations to enhance individual instruction and assessment (Zascavage & Winterman, 2009).

UDL is based on three principal guidelines (CAST, 2018b). The first guideline, Multiple Means of Representation, advises teachers to present learning material in a multitude of ways and in an adaptable format. For example, the display of information can vary perceptual features such as the size of text, the contrast between background and text, or the volume or rate of speech or sound (CAST, 2018b). The second guideline, Multiple Means of Action and Expression, advises teachers to allow students a variety of ways to demonstrate their knowledge through actions and expression that facilitate their strengths and overcome their barriers. For example, teachers might offer alternative ways for students to respond to assignments. Or they might provide various options for navigating assessments (e.g., by allowing for changes in the rate, timing, speed, or range of motor action required to interact with instructional materials, physical manipulatives, and technologies). The third guideline, Multiple Means of Engagement, outlines ways for teachers to enhance student motivation through options that recruit student interest, sustain student effort and persistence, and encourage student use of self-regulation strategies. In order to optimize individual choice and autonomy, the teacher provides learners with choices in areas such as level of perceived challenge, the design of class activities, types of rewards for progress, or timing for the completion of subcomponents of a task.

Multisensory Approaches

In a differentiated classroom, Multiple Means of Representation can be achieved through multisensory approaches to learning, which are used to guide the lesson and reduce barriers, making information approximately equally perceptible to all learners (CAST, 2018b). When multisensory approaches are applied, learners are given the opportunity to acquire the same information from a variety of sensory modalities, thereby increasing students' opportunities to learn in formats that suit their needs. For example, a lesson plan designed to teach the names, physical characteristics, and relative locations of the planets in our solar system might offer students a choice of engaging with information about the planets by using models of the planets that can be manipulated to form the solar system (kinesthetic mode), watching a video on the solar system (visual mode), or using an interactive computer program with the option for auditory cues to learn the names and order of the planet (auditory mode).

Assistive Technology

A variety of presentation options help teachers use multi-sensory approaches, but one noteworthy mechanism that aligns particularly well with UDL is assistive technology (AT). The use of AT can enhance student engagement and optimize learning through Multiple Means of Representation. It also allows students to demonstrate their knowledge in various ways through Multiple Means of Action and Expression. Benefits of using AT to differentiate instruction include encouraging generalization, enhancing motivation, and increasing students' on-task behavior (Zascavage & Winterman, 2009).

Concrete and Functional Instructional Material

Another approach to addressing UDL's Multiple Means of Representation guideline is to modify instructional materials to make them more concrete and functional (CAST, 2018b). Such accommodations include highlighting critical reading passages and incorporating tools such as graphic organizers and guided notes into the lesson to help organize student work (Glang et al., 2008) as well as providing manipulatives to teach abstract concepts. For example, when teaching the concept of negative and positive numbers, a number line drawn on the floor offers a concrete and functional model that allows students to engage physically with the concept of negative and positive numbers. When lessons are functional and valued by the student as authentic, there is potential to enhance student engagement (Burney, Zascavage & Matherly, 2017; CAST, 2018b).

Student Interest

Another means for addressing UDL's Multiple Means of Engagement is by accommodating and increasing student interest. Student interest is used to guide learning and enhance motivation in differentiated classrooms (CAST, 2018b). In these classrooms, educators engage students in a variety of learning activities that differ based on each individual's interests and needs (Berkeley Graduate Division, Graduate Student Instruction Teaching Resource Center, 2018). Teachers activate student interest by providing choice in materials (e.g., book selection, sequencing of activities, graphics, pacing), content (e.g., in-depth learning on a special topic), assessments (e.g., report, project, or presentation), and classroom management methods (e.g., class vote on activities, lesson sequencing, or methods of instruction; CAST, 2018). Several benefits result from using student interest to guide classroom choices. This practice fosters students' sense of ownership, it facilitates their sustained engagement, and it contributes to feelings of inclusion in the classroom community (Bucholz & Sheffler, 2009).

Readiness, Fairness, and High Priority Outcomes

Additional concepts associated with differentiation are readiness, fairness, and high priority outcomes. First, readiness in the included classroom refers to educators' determinations about whether a student has the prerequisite skills and knowledge necessary to learn the planned lesson (Tomlinson & Imbeau, 2010). In terms of student readiness, differentiation requires ongoing assessment to establish a readiness level in order to implement data-driven instruction (Muskin, 2017; Schifter, Natarajan, Ketelhut, & Kirchgessner, 2014). Components of readiness teaching include preteaching vocabulary, reviewing previous lessons, and providing background information (Berkeley Graduate Division, Graduate Student Instruction Teaching Resource Center, 2018).

Second, and similar to the concept of readiness, is the concept of classroom fairness. According to principles of UDL, every student is entitled to an individual assessment to gauge his or her academic, social, and behavioral baseline in an effort to determine the learning experiences that would be optimal (Downing, 2010; Muskin, 2017; Raymond, 2012). A key distinction to keep in mind is that fairness is based on need, not on identical treatment of students (PBS Video & Lavoie, 2004). Therefore, if everyone is doing the same thing at the same time with no variation, the educators may not be sufficiently attuned to the principle of fairness.

Differentiation guidelines suggest that teachers in the included classroom should first focus on high priority curriculum outcomes. A high priority curriculum begins with the decisions made by the teacher to present the essential knowledge students should master within a designated timeframe. Student proficiency is determined by assessments that guide sequenced lessons on essential content. Lesson ideas are determined by which part of the curriculum most warrants the attention of individual students, especially those with disabilities and other diverse learning needs (CAST, 2018b). This method of differentiation focuses learners' attention on essential components of a concept, components that are then reinforced and practiced. Students are offered the opportunity to move to a broader conceptual understanding with the possibility of additional instructional support. By focusing on the higher priority components of the lesson, such as those concepts or skills that are useful across academic disciplines, educators enable students to make greater overall progress (Friend & Bursuck, 2015; UNESCO, 2006).

The Classroom Environment

A second key component of an included classroom is the environment, and its importance cannot be overstated (Tomlinson & Imbeau, 2010). Environmental factors that foster social, academic, behavioral, and physical engagement in the classroom help create an inclusive culture that encompasses all students. Two key traits of the included classroom environment are (a) the productive relationships fostered by the teacher and (b) the teacher's commitment to providing structure, enhancing student engagement, and establishing a positive classroom culture accessible to all students (Bucholz & Sheffler, 2009).

To create an inclusive environment, teachers intentionally develop mutually respectful and caring relationships with every student (Koca, 2016). Such relationships support students' academic engagement and on-task behaviors (Ros-Voseles & Moss, 2007). Relationships that are authentic and responsive promote an atmosphere of trust and open communication that can lead to successful classroom outcomes and create a foundation for positive behavior (Hemmeter, Ostrosky, & Corso, 2012). Teachers demonstrate their caring through their commitment to providing supportive structure, enhancing student engagement, and establishing a positive learning culture (National Association of Special Education Teachers, 2005).

Academic support in a positive classroom culture depends upon careful analysis of students' learning needs and timely use of accommodations that promote academic achievement (Friend & Bursuck, 2015). Structural support for behavior is provided when clear rules, expectations, and routines are judiciously enforced. The ensuing sense of safety and security that comes from structural support allows learning to occur (National Association of Special Education Teachers, 2005). An atmosphere of clear expectations and consistency helps organize a supportive classroom that positively influences student engagement (CAST, 2018b). Environmental supports, such as posting lesson objectives and daily schedules, provide visual prompts that foster engagement (Friend & Bursuck, 2015). These visual supports help students regulate their own behavior and meet the behavioral and academic expectations needed to be successful (Rao & Gagie, 2006).

Teachers also offer opportunities for enhanced student engagement by incorporating lessons that supply real life and culturally relevant connections that are authentic, active, and meaningful to students (Burney, Zascavage, & Matherly, 2017; Friend & Bursuck, 2015). By providing these connections, teachers both demonstrate an academic and social awareness of their students and reinforce students' perception of the teacher's commitment to the teacher-student relationship. Additionally, in the included classroom, collaborative activities and heterogeneous grouping arrangements promote student-student relationships that have the potential to increase engagement (Friend & Bursuck, 2015; Marzano, Marzano, & Pickering, 2003).

Teachers committed to establishing and maintaining a positive classroom culture that is accessible to all students provide a classroom that is physically welcoming to all individuals including those facing challenges with mobility or communication (Lang, 2017). One way to welcome all students is through a user-friendly arrangement of furniture. For example, individuals who have visual or physical impairments should be able to access their seats easily and navigate to the board or learning stations for classroom activities (U.S. Department of Education, 2015). In an inclusive classroom culture, students with augmentative communication systems are afforded the chance to answer questions and to participate in discussions and group activities (Grandbois, 2012).

Teacher Disposition

Teacher disposition includes the set of professional beliefs that guide the teacher's daily conduct (Koca, 2016). In Koca's (2016) version of the concept, the term "disposition" relates more to teacher's actions than to what they say. Their actions in the classroom, in other words, provide proof of their beliefs. Teachers' attitudes, actions, and beliefs, moreover, have a critical influence on students' motivation (Mastrioperi & Scruggs, 2010). Research has shown that the disposition of a teacher and the teacher's ability to form relationships and motivate student engagement depend upon mutual respect and positive regard between the teacher and the student (Hallam, 2009).

Delivery Method

The fourth key component of an included classroom is delivery method, or presentation of material (CAST, 2018b). There is no single delivery method that is appropriate for all lessons and meets the needs of all students all of the time (CAST, 2018b). Whether teaching one-on-one, co-teaching, or team teaching, to be inclusive, teachers must vary their approaches to ensure that students are engaged and actively learning (CAST, 2018a). Approaches as different as guided inquiry and direct instruction have been successfully used by both general and special education teachers (Mercer et al., 2011); but to promote inclusion, instructional practices should emphasize modeling (e.g., video instruction, peer-supported instruction) and cooperative learning. Such practices promote social skills, teaming, and peer support for instruction (McMasters & Fuchs, 2002). Visible interactions in the classroom between teachers, peers, and students with special needs welcome all students to participate in academic and social activities (Crockett & Kauffman, 2015).

Some inclusive learning environments incorporate co-teaching or the use of paraprofessional support. Co-teaching can facilitate the use of several different instructional models as a way to provide a more effective flow of instruction: it need not rely on the general education teacher as the sole deliverer of instruction, nor should it relegate the special educator (or other service provider) to the role of a helper whose only role is to support small group instruction or police the classroom for children in distress (Friend & Bursuck, 2015; Friend, Cook, Hurley-Chamberlain, & Shamberger, 2010; Tomlinson, 2014).

Teaming is a form of co-teaching whereby two teachers present the same material to a large group of students in order to demonstrate different viewpoints, teaching methods, or approaches to solving a problem (Friend & Bursuck, 2015). Teaming can also be used across disciplines to pool teacher expertise (Plank, 2011).

Furthermore, when paraprofessionals are assigned to the included classroom they can work with students on the academic, social, and behavioral goals developed by the teacher, assist in providing focused instruction, and manage the physical components of the learning environment (Iqtadar, 2016; Morgan & Ashbaker, 2001). The important feature to note is that no matter the dynamic, teachers, specialists, and paraprofessionals work together to pursue academic success of all learners (Morgan & Ashbaker, 2001).

The Lesson Itself

The fifth key component of an included classroom is the lesson and its basic parts. In the included classroom, lesson plans and the accompanying expectations for students with disabilities are differentiated in accordance with a student's individualized education program (IEP). Data-driven instruction makes use of students' strengths and addresses their weaknesses by designing lessons that are responsive to their existing skills and evident needs (Dunn, Airola, Lo, & Garrison, 2013; Schifter et al., 2014). Differentiation is then provided through UDL and guided by accommodations, and, for some students, modifications (as determined by an IEP or 504 planning team) (Mastrioperi & Scruggs, 2010). Important lesson components are collaboration, informed instruction, and progress monitoring,

Collaboration between the general education teacher, the intervention specialist, and other service providers, such as occupational therapists, allows the instructional team to differentiate lesson plans in ways that maximize each student's learning (Heward, 2018). In cooperative teaming such as this, lessons are designed jointly to provide a frame of reference for instructional changes to meet each student's learning needs (Dunn et al., 2013). The entire team works toward planning and implementing cross-curricular lessons that facilitate the acquisition of new skills and the generalization of knowledge (Neuman, 2016).

When planning the lesson, student work, interests, background, and prior knowledge should inform instruction (Neuman, 2016). In order to capture student interest, the teacher designs lessons that contain student-led activities and discussions that focus on authentic learning experiences that have the potential to validate students' life experiences and cultural backgrounds.

In sum, the five components of the included classroom, with their key concepts and practices, are integral parts of a well-designed included classroom. Recognizing and identifying the specific practices associated with each component can be help educators improve the inclusiveness of their classrooms.

For example, teachers can reflect on their own classrooms to identify the inclusive practices already in place and those that might be added. Then they can decide on ways to strengthen their inclusive practice overall. Pre-service teachers can also benefit by taking note of the inclusive practices that are modeled in the classrooms they observe. This information can guide their learning about how to teach and how to create a classroom community. Principals can use the components, as well, to help identify the teaching practices that need to be strengthened in order to foster an inclusive school community and, through that process, enhance learning for all students.

The five components described in the chapter thus far are essential for building an included classroom. Assessing their use periodically can, therefore, help educators expand the inclusiveness of their classroom practice. The Included Classroom Characteristics Check Sheet (IC3S) is an informal tool that can assist educators in their efforts to recognize, identify, and strengthen inclusive practices in their classrooms, practicum placements, and buildings.

ASSESSING COMPONENTS OF THE INCLUDED CLASSROOM—THE IC3S

For an included school setting to function well, the principal and the teachers must be able to keep track of school-wide implementation of inclusive practices (Pont, Nusche, & Moorman, 2008). Informal assessments can be used for this purpose (Ginsberg & Murphy, 2002). Informal assessments are nonstandardized evaluations (e.g., checklists, reflections, rating scales, observations) used to monitor implementation, measure progress, and evaluate performance (British Council, n.d.). Using informal assessments in these ways to monitor the implementation of inclusive practices is endorsed in federal, state, and professional standards (e.g., Council of Chief State School Officers, Interstate Teacher Assessment and Support Consortium [InTASC], 2013; Council for the Accreditation of Educational Preparation [CAEP], 2015; Ohio Board of Education, 2005).

The IC3S provides a user-friendly assessment of practices associated with differentiation, the maintenance of a caring environment, positive teacher disposition, effective instructional delivery, and differentiated lesson components. The IC3S can be used by current and future educators as a way to learn about effective inclusion and as a way to reflect on the extent to which inclusive practices are evident in a classroom. A teacher might use the tool for self-evaluation, an administrator as a tool for school-wide continuous improvement, and a preservice teacher to enhance and facilitate learning in a classroom placement. Informal assessments, such as the IC3S, also reminds educators of the importance of aligning classroom priorities with school and district priorities as well as research evidence about effective teaching (Ohio Board of Education, 2005).

Development of the IC3S

Ohio, as is the case with other states in the United States, lacks consistent requirements for preparing school principals to supervise special education classrooms (DiPaola & Walther-Thomas, 2003). The IC3S was developed in 2015, when the Ohio Leadership Advisory Council recruited authors to develop an inclusion module to address the professional development needs of Ohio principals. The original IC3S was developed as part of the module, *What Every Principal Needs to Know about Inclusion* (Frank & Zascavage, 2015). The main focus of the module was to support principals' supervision of inclusive classrooms by reminding them of the practices that characterize effective inclusion. Since 2015, the IC3S has undergone several revisions for clarity and ease of use, and its purpose has expanded.

Currently, the IC3S is used in Ohio Teacher Education and Educational Leadership preparation programs at two universities.

The five key components identified on the IC3S were determined through a review of the literature on best practices for inclusive education—practices that are supported in federal, state, and professional standards (e.g., Council of Chief State School Officers, 2013). The assessment tool is a one-page checklist divided into five columns, one for each of the five components, with the corresponding inclusive classroom characteristics and teacher behaviors listed below the component (see the Appendix). The instrument is easy to use. It also includes definitions of key terminology in order to promote understanding. This tool can help not only principals, but teacher candidates, as well as novice teachers easily understand, recognize, and identify the presence of the specific classroom practices that foster inclusion.

The comprehensive understanding of inclusion involves a broad vision that is not included in the IC3S. Segregation and its resulting compartmentalization have the potential to interrupt the spirit of democratic participation (Kricke & Neubert, 2017). Ideally, the included classroom would incorporate democratic integration such that the lines of distinction that reflect racism, classism, sexism, ableism, and discrimination based on sexual orientation are not allowed to influence the classroom community's acceptance of any student nor the equality of opportunity afforded all students (Kricke & Neubert, 2017; Zascavage & Keefe, 2007). While this instrument addresses cultural awareness and the sensitivity of the teacher to the needs of the individual students, it does not specifically address these broad areas of possible discrimination and inequity.

Implementation of the IC3S

The IC3S, can be used as an informal assessment tool by preservice teachers and principals. For preservice teachers it can create a stronger connection between what is taught in the university classroom and what is observed in the field placement setting (Alemdag & Simsek, 2017). Principals can also benefit from using the IC3S in formal teacher observations and in informal classroom or school walkthroughs—brief classroom visits that allow principals to gain familiarity with classroom and building happenings (Hopkins, 2011). The IC3S can assist principals in gathering data and can support identification of which classroom practices are enhancing the inclusion of students with special needs. Walkthrough data can also be used to improve communication between school leaders, teachers, and other school personnel (Skretta, 2007).

Reliability and Validity of the IC3S

Although the IC3S items are grounded in relevant standards, the instrument has the same limitations as other informal tools that attempt to measure complex practices (e.g., Becker, Roberts, & Dumas, 2000). For this reason, it can be used only to gather formative data. It is not designed to be a comprehensive or summative assessment instrument. As with many informal assessments, the IC3S lacks the strong evidence for validity and reliability associated with most formal or comprehensive assessment instruments. Nevertheless, this tool has been used for three years by:

- more than 200 general education and special education teacher candidates and by a number of university professors to structure observation and discussion of field experiences.
- more than 100 general education and special education preservice teachers in their review of video case studies of included classroom instruction and follow-up discussions.
- more than 30 educators enrolled at a Midwestern university as part of field observation requirements for educational leadership.

At this point, efforts to expand the usability of the IC3S might involve formal studies to assess its construct validity as well as to develop procedures for ensuring interrater reliability.

SUMMARY

The IC3S is intended to structure informal observations of inclusive classrooms. Primarily used by principals and preservice teachers to date, this observation tool is designed to identify the presence or absence of specific practices that research has shown to promote successful inclusion. The tool can be used by principals to facilitate teacher observations and to assess a school's overall need for professional development. For preservice and novice teachers, the instrument can serve as a learning tool by helping them identify specific observable behaviors that contribute to an inclusive environment.

REFERENCES

Alemdag, E., & Simsek, P. O. (2017). Pre-service teachers' evaluation of their mentor teachers, school experiences, and theory-practice relationship. *International*

Journal of Progressive Education, 13, 165–179. Retrieved from https://files.eric. ed.gov/fulltext/EJ1145612.pdf

Alter, M., Gottlieb, M., & Gottlieb, J. (2018). Four ways schools fail special education students: Education for students with disabilities must be improved. Retrieved from https://www.edweek.org/ew/articles/2018/02/15/four-ways-schools-fail-special-education-students.html?print=1

Becker, H., Roberts, G., & Dumas, S. (2000). The Inclusion Inventory: A tool to assess perceptions of the implementation of inclusive educational practices. *Special Services in the Schools, 16*, 57–72. doi:10.1300/J008v16n01_04

Bucholz, J., & Sheffler, J. (2009). Creating a warm and inclusive environment: Planning for all children to feel welcome. *Electronic Journal for Inclusive Education, 2*, 1–13. Retrieved from https://corescholar.libraries.wright.edu/cgi/viewcontent.cgi?article=1102&context=ejie

Bui, X., Quirk, C., Almazan, S., & Valenti, M. (2010). *Inclusive education, research, and practice.* Hanover, MD: Coalition for Inclusive Education. Retrieved from http://www.mcie.org/usermedia/application/6/inclusion_works_final.pdf

Burney, L., Zascavage, V., & Matherly, M. (2017) Advancing research of teaching efficacy: Developing a scale to measure student attitudes towards active learning experiences. *The Journal of the OCPEA, 4*, 60–82.

Berkeley Graduate Division, Graduate Student Instruction Teaching Resource Center. (2018). *Cognitive constructivism.* Retrieved from http://gsi.berkeley. edu/gsi-guide-contents/learning-theory-research/cognitive-constructivism/

Council for the Accreditation of Educational Preparation [CAEP]. (2015). *Standard 2: Clinical partnerships and practice.* Retrieved from http://www.ncate.org/standards/standard-2

Center for Applied Special Technology [CAST]. (2018a). *About universal design for learning.* Retrieved from http://www.cast.org/our-work/about-udl.html#. W037pMInbIU

Center for Applied Special Technology [CAST]. (2018b). The *UDL guidelines.* Retrieved from http://udlguidelines.cast.org/?utm_medium=web&utm_campaign=none&utm_source=cast-about-udl

Council of Chief State School Officers. (2013). Interstate Teacher Assessment and Support Consortium In TASC *Model Core Teaching Standards and Learning Progressions for Teachers 1.0: A Resource for Ongoing Teacher Development.* Washington, DC: Author.

Crockett, J. B., & Kauffman, J. M. (1999). *The least restrictive environment: Origins and interpretations in special education.* New York, NY: Routledge.

Differentiation (2013). *The Glossary of Educational Reform.* Retrieved from https://www.edglossary.org/differentiation

DiPaola, M. F., & Walther-Thomas, C. (2003). *Principals and special education: The critical role of school leaders (COPPSE Document No. IB-7).* Gainesville, FL: University of Florida, Center on Personnel Studies in Special Education.

Downing, J. E. (2010). *Academic instruction for students with moderate and severe disabilities in inclusive classrooms.* Thousand Oaks, CA: Corwin Press.

Dunn, K. E., Airola, D. T., Lo, W., & Garrison, M. (2013). Becoming data driven: The influence of teachers' sense of efficacy on concerns related to data-driven decision making. *Journal of Experimental Education*, *81*, 222–241. doi:10.108 0/00220973.2012.699899

Frank, K., & Zascavage, V. (2015). *What every principal needs to know about special education: Online module*. Retrieved from https://education-human-services.wright.edu/sites/education-human-services.wright.edu/files/page/attachments/Inclusive-Classroom-Module.pdf

Friend, M., & Bursuck, W. (2015). *Including students with special needs*. Boston, MA: Pearson.

Friend, M., Cook, L., Hurley-Chamberlain, D., & Shamberger, C. (2010). Co-teaching: An illustration of the complexity of collaboration in special education. *Journal of Educational and Psychological Consultation, 20*, 9–27. doi:10.1080/10474410903535380

Ginsberg, M. B., & Murphy, D. (2002). How walkthroughs open doors. *Beyond Instructional Leadership, 59*, 34–36.

Glang, A., Ylvisaker, M., Stein, M., Ehlhard, L., Todis, B., & Tyler, J. (2008). Validated instructional practices: Application to students with traumatic brain injury. *Journal of Head Trauma Rehabilitation, 23*, 243–251. doi:10.1097/01. HTR.0000327256.46504.9f

Grandbois, K. (2012). Alternative communication: A webinar. *Autism Speaks*. Retrieved from https://www.autismspeaks.org/sites/default/files/augmentative_alternative_communication_webinar.pdf

Hallam, M. K. (2009). Another piece of the language learning puzzle: Why teacher's dispositions are a critical aspect of success. *The Language Educator*, 26–29. http://video.wallace.edu/pd/articles/2013/2013_TLE_Jan09_Article.pdf

Hemmeter, M. L., Ostrosky, M. M., & Corso, R. M. (2012). Preventing and addressing challenging behavior: Common questions and practical strategies. Young Exceptional Children, *15* (2), 32–46. doi:10.1177/1096250611427350

Heward, W.L. (2018). *Exceptional children: An introduction to special education*. Upper Saddle River, NJ: Prentice Hall.

Hopkins, G. (2011). *Walkthroughs are on the move*. Retrieved from https://www.educationworld.com/a_admin/admin/admin405.shtml

British Council (n.d.). *Informal assessment*. Retrieved from https://www.teachingenglish.org.uk/article/informal-assessment

Iqtadar, S. (2016). *Roles and responsibilities of paraprofessionals in creating inclusive communities: A three dimensional perspective*. Annual Graduate Student Symposium 36, Cedar Falls, IA. Retrieved from https://scholarworks.uni.edu/agss/2016/all/36

Koca, F. (2016). Motivation to learn and teacher student relationship. *Journal of International Education and Leadership, 6*, 1–20.

Kricke, M., & Neubert, S. (2017). Inclusive education as a democratic challenge. *Education Services, 7*, 1-14. doi:10.3390/educsci7010012

Lang, J. M. (2017). A welcoming classroom. *The Chronicle of Higher Education*. Retrieved from https:// www.chronicle.com/article/A-Welcoming -Classroom/241294

Marzano, R. J., Marzano, J. S., & Pickering, D. J. (2003). *Classroom management that works*. Alexandria, VA: ASCD.

Mastrioperi, M., & Scruggs, T. E. (2010). *The inclusive classroom: Strategies for effective differentiated instruction*. Upper Saddle, NJ: Merrill.

McMasters, K. N., & Fuchs, D. (2002). Effects of cooperative learning on the academic achievement of students with learning disabilities: An update of Tateyama-Sniezek's review. *Learning Disabilities Research and Practice, 17*, 107–117. doi:10.1111/1540-5826.00037

Mercer, C. D., Mercer, A. R., & Pullen, P. C. (2011). *Teaching students with learning problems.* Boston, MA: Pearson.

Morgan, J., & Ashbaker, B. (2001). *A teacher's guide to working with paraeducators and other classroom aides.* Alexandria, VA: Association for Supervision and Curriculum Development.

Muskin, J. A. (2017). *Continuous assessment for improved teaching and learning.* UNESCO International Bureau of Education. Retrieved from http://unesdoc.unesco.org/images/0025/002555/255511e.pdf

Neuman, S. B. (2016). Code red: The danger of data-driven instruction. *Educational Leadership, 74*(3), 24–29. Retrieved from http://www.ascd.org/publications/educational_leadership/nov16/vol74/num03/Code_Red@_The_Danger_of_Data-Driven_Instruction.aspx

Ohio Board of Education. (2005). *The Ohio standards for educators.* Retrieved from https://education.ohio.gov/getattachment/Topics/Teaching/Educator-Equity/Ohio-s-Educator-Standards/StandardsforEducators_revaug10.pdf.aspx

Pivik, J., McComas, J., & Laflamme, M. (2002). Barriers and facilitators to inclusive education. *Exceptional Children, 69*, 97–107. doi:10.1177/001440290206900107

Plank, K. M. (Ed.). (2011). *Team teaching: Across the disciplines, across the academy.* Sterling, VA: Stylus.

Pont, B., Nusche, D., & Moorman, H. (2008). *Improving school leadership—Volume 1: Policy and practice.* Paris, France: OECD.

National Association of Special Education Teachers. (2005). *Promoting positive social interactions in an inclusion setting for students with a learning disability.* Retrieved from faculty.uml.edu/darcus/01.505/NASET_social_inclusion.pdf

Rao, S. M., & Gagie, B. (2006). Learning through seeing and doing: Visual supports for children with autism. *Teaching Exceptional Children, 38*(6), 26–33. doi:10.1177/004005990603800604

Raymond, E. B. (2012). *Learners with mild disabilities: Characteristics approach* (4th ed.). Boston, MA: Pearson.

Ros-Voseles, D., & Moss, L. (2007). The role of dispositions in the education of future teachers. *Young Children, 62*(5), 90–98.

PBS Video (Producer) & Lavoie, R. D. (Director). (2004). *How difficult can this be?: Understanding learning disabilities: Frustration, anxiety, tension, the F.A.T. city workshop* [DVD]. United States and Canada: PBS.

Salend, S. J., & Garrick Duhaney, L. M. (1999). The impact of inclusion on students with and without disabilities and their educators. *Remedial and Special Education, 20*, 114–126. doi:10.1177/074193259902000209

Santangelo, T., & Tomlinson, C. (2012). Teacher educators' perceptions and use of differentiated instruction practices: An exploratory investigation. *Action in Teacher Education, 34*, 309–321. doi:10.1080/01626620.2012.717032

Schifter, C. C., Natarajan, U., Ketelhut, D. J., & Kirchgessner, A. (2014). Data-driven decision making: Facilitating teacher use of student data to inform classroom instruction. *Contemporary Issues in Technology and Teacher Education, 14*(4).

Retrieved from http://www.citejournal.org/volume-14/issue-4-14/science/data-driven-decision-making-facilitating-teacher-use-of-student-data-to-inform-classroom-instruction

Sharron, H. (2018) The limits of inclusion. *Imaginative Mind Group: Teaching Times.* Retrieved from https://www.teachingtimes.com/articles/limits-of-inclusion.htm

Skretta, J. (2007). Using walkthroughs to gather data for school improvement. *Principal Leadership*, 7(9), 16–23.

Tomlinson, C.A. (2014). *The differentiated classroom: Responding to the needs of all learners.* Alexandria, VA: Association for Supervision & Curriculum Development.

Tomlinson, C., & Imbeau, M. (2010). *Leading and managing a differentiated classroom.* Alexandria, VA: ASCD.

U.S. Department of Education. (2015). *ADA update: A primer for state and local governments.* Retrieved from https://www.ada.gov/regs2010/titleII_2010/titleII_primer.pdf

Wieringo, R. (2015). *A case study of the experiences of students with disabilities who did not complete high school* (Doctoral dissertation). Liberty University, Lynchburg, VA.

United Nations Educational, Scientific and Cultural Organization [UNESCO]. (2006). *Guidelines for inclusion: Ensuring access to education for all.* Retrieved from http://www.ibe.unesco.org/sites/default/files/Guidelines_for_Inclusion_UNESCO_2006.pdf

Zascavage, V., & Winterman, K. (2009). What Middle School educators should know about assistive technology and universal design for learning. *Middle School Journal. 40*(4), 46–52. doi:10.1080/00940771.2009.11461681

Zascavage, V., & Keefe, C. (2007). Students with severe speech and physical impairments: Reflections of models of social construct in educational decisions for literacy instruction. *Journal of Disability Policy Studies, 18*, 32–42. doi:10.1177/10442073070180010401

Table 4.1

The Included Classroom Characteristics Check Sheet

Differentiation	Environment	Dispositions	Delivery Method	Lesson Components
□ Multisensory approach to learning (i.e., visual, auditory, kinesthetic)	□ Clear rules and expectations	□ Flexible	□ Interactive strategies	□ Data-driven instruction
□ Differentiation based on student interest	□ Well-established routines	□ Develops authentic relationships with students that promotes trust, communication, and successful outcomes	□ Modeling	□ Lessons designed at multiple levels
□ Differentiation based on student readiness	□ Learning objective posted		□ Guided inquiry	□ Guided note/graphic organizer
□ Fairness—every student gets what they need	□ Schedule posted		□ Small groups/stations/cooperative learning	□ Guided practice/scaffolding/support
□ Appropriate use of assistive technology and software to support learning	□ Positive atmosphere focused on learning evident		□ Co teaching	□ Access prior knowledge or real-life situations
□ A universal design for learning—program calls for a full range of options for participation and assessment	□ Collaborative		□ Team teaching	□ Student-led discussion/activities/lessons
□ Instructional material modified to be concrete and functional (e.g., color coding)	□ Students on-task and engaged throughout lesson		□ Direct instructions	□ Accommodations supports individual student learning
□ High-priority curriculum outcomes guide modified learning goals	□ Connections made to real-life experiences		• Orientation to the lesson	□ Modifications follow IEP
□ Implementation of behavior intervention plans (BIPs)	□ Mutual respect		• Initial Instruction	□ Lesson design results from cooperative team planning between general education teachers, intervention specialists, and appropriate therapists (e.g., occupational therapists, physical therapists, orientation and mobility specialists, speech therapists)
	□ Culturally responsive		• Teacher-guided practice	
	□ Supportive of students who use augmentative/alternative communication device		• Independent practice	
	□ Accessible to students who use wheelchairs		• Check for understanding	
	□ Employing heterogeneous grouping arrangements		• Reteach	
			□ Para-educator support responds to teacher directives	

Note. This tool was developed by Victoria Zascavage and Catherine Lawless-Frank.

Teacher _____ Date _____ School _____ Grade Level _____ Subject _____ Conducted

by:

□ Copy to principal □ Original to teacher □ Conference requested (Date & Time) _____

Critical Terminology Reminder

Accommodations: Changes that provide access to participate in a course, standard, or test. An accommodation *DOES NOT fundamentally alter or lower the course/test standards or expectations.* Students with a disability addressed by a 504 Plan may have an accommodation; students with an individualized education program (IEP) may also have accommodations if there is an educational need for such. Accommodations include environmental adaptations, large print, guided notes, color coding, assistive technology, assignment reduction, testing adaptations, increased time, quiet setting, etc..

Assistive Technology: Any kind of technology that enhances functional independence, including anything from a low-tech device such as raised lines on paper, to a high-tech computerized communication system.

Augmented/Alternative Communication (AAC): Refers to a variety of communication alternatives including specialized materials (e.g., charts, pictures, books) or equipment to generate speech from a beginning communicator to one that creates its own messages. AAC also includes unaided systems such as signing and gestures that do not require special materials or equipment. AAC methods range from high- to low-tech strategies.

Behavior Intervention Plan (BIP): Takes the observations made in a functional behavior assessment and develops a plan to manage the students' behavior. Like an IEP, the BIP is a legal agreement and requires educators to follow guidelines for environmental accommodation or positive behavior reinforcement.

Collaborative: Interaction and planning between co-teachers, support personnel, service providers, and parents to determine the best possible educational outcome for the student.

Culturally Responsive: Implies sensitivity to the values, beliefs, social systems, and languages or communication styles unique to the culture of each student.

Differentiation: Tailoring instruction to meet the individual needs of students. Whether teachers differentiate content, process, products, or the learning environment, the use of ongoing assessment and flexible grouping makes this a successful approach to instruction (see C. A. Tomlinson, http://www.readingrockets.org/article/what-differentiated-instruction).

Heterogeneous Grouping: For group activities, it is the grouping of students such that all levels of knowledge and skills are represented in each group. If the purpose of the group learning activity is to help struggling students, then according to Marzano, Pickering, & Pollock (2001) in *Classroom Instruction that Works* heterogeneous groups may help most.

Individualized Education Plan (IEP): IEPs are mandated by IDEA. IEPs include (a) present levels of educational performance (PLEP), which is a description of current levels of performance; (b) weaknesses and strengths, (c) and how these learning issues affect ability to learn in general education curriculum. An IEP includes annual educational goals and how the progress towards those goals will be monitored.

Modification: Determined by an IEP, a modification outlines the changes in the normal expectations and/or other attribute which facilitates participation in a course, standard, or test. A modification DOES *fundamentally alter or lower the standard or expectation of the course, standard, or test.* Modifications are lower grade level curriculum, fewer problems to solve, different grade level of assessment, individualized test preparation, materials simplified, grading scales or criterion changed, testing measures lowered, and so forth.

CHAPTER 5

HELPING PRESERVICE TEACHERS COME TO TERMS WITH UNINTENDED BIASES

Anne M. Bauer
University of Cincinnati

Stephen D. Kroeger
University of Cincinnati

Put yourself in the shoes of a first semester, first year student in Educational Psychology. You are eighteen years old, from the suburbs of Cincinnati. You are much like your White middle- or manager-class peers. Your parents are concerned about the university because it sits in a "rough neighborhood." You've never been in a police station before, but you need a background check. Then you have to walk six blocks off campus to the public school's central office to have an ID badge made; your mom has specifically told you not to walk around the neighborhood. Armed with your new ID, you board a school bus to the projects in the highest poverty area of the city. There are empty factories, razor wire on fences, and the smell of sewage. As you enter the school, the smiling records clerk tells you to stay in the building or go outside in pairs. You walk down the hall, and all the students you see are Black, smiling and laughing. The noise and activity level are not like your school experience, and you wonder why someone doesn't take control. The school nurse welcomes you and talks to

Inclusive Education: A Systematic Perspective, pp. 81–92
Copyright © 2020 by Information Age Publishing
All rights of reproduction in any form reserved.

you about lice, skin mites, and bed bugs. You are assigned a seat to wait for your third-grade tutee to arrive and wonder about the schools in which you pictured yourself teaching.

(Authors' vignette)

The teacher workforce in the United States is not nearly as diverse as the student population. Over 80% of public school teachers are White (U.S. Department of Education, 2016), while the percentage of White children ages 5 to 17 is only about 50% (Musu-Gillette et al., 2017). This disparity between teacher diversity and student diversity is disturbing in view of research indicating that White teachers' experiences predispose them to a view of students of color that works against the students' academic progress and even against White teachers' earnest efforts to support the students' progress (Marx, 2006). White teachers are, for example, less likely than teachers of color to hold high expectations for students of color (Grissom & Redding, 2016), to serve as advocates for students of color, or to confront issues of racism (Villegas & Irvine, 2010).

As faculty members in the University of Cincinnati's teacher preparation program, our challenge is to prepare all our teacher candidates to work effectively with all students. Most of the teacher candidates with whom we work are White women who grew up with the privileges that Whiteness confers. Through field experiences working directly with children of color and through course content that includes dialogue and reflection about social justice, race, and poverty, we strive to disrupt the biases likely to inhibit our candidates' ability to provide effective instruction to all students. This chapter briefly describes these field experiences, which incorporate strategies identified by Sleeter (2008) as important to such efforts in teacher preparation: confronting tacit belief in the superiority of White ways of teaching and working, reflecting on race and class as filters of interpretation, and integrating professional knowledge with practice

The University of Cincinnati is located in a diverse neighborhood in an impoverished section of the city. In this neighborhood, local residents are losing housing options because of gentrification. Seventy-six percent of its residents are people of color, and 65% of its families with children under five live below the poverty level. The lives of our teacher candidates have been different in many ways from the lives of the youth who live in this neighborhood. Few of our teacher candidates grew up worrying about where they would eat or sleep, whether or not they would see a doctor if they were sick or hurt, or whether they would have adequate clothing. Like many college students, our candidates tend to view their relatively comfortable lives as resulting from their parents' hard work and their own efforts to do well in school and get into college. Failing to recognize the privilege that supports their own and their families' success, they believe that hard work is sufficient for anyone's success. Consequently, they may see those who are poor as lacking in "grit." This simplistic view of poverty and success fuels many biases teachers bring to their study of teaching and learning (Berliner, 2009).

DISRUPTING RACIAL AND CLASS BIAS

Even among well-intentioned educators, racial and class biases lead to inequitable practices that result in inequitable outcomes (Staats, 2016). To move toward better academic outcomes for students of color, many educators (e.g., Marx, 2006) argue, White teachers' prevailing beliefs about race must be disrupted. Buchanan's (2015) study found that preservice teachers' racial identities influenced their ideas about race and even whether they were inclined to talk about race. The preservice teachers in the study did not feel, however, that their experiences would influence their teaching and voiced few concerns about possible impacts of their Whiteness on students of color. Buchanan believes that these views and the related claim of being "colorblind" hinder preservice teachers' ability to make positive changes in their understanding of race and poverty. His research suggests that Whiteness is likely to affect White teacher candidates' interactions with their future students although the candidates have little recognition of the impact of their race on their instruction.

The programmatic efforts described in this chapter are based on the premise that, as Fasching-Varner (2013) argued, preservice teachers

> Develop a better understanding of how to productively and meaning-
> fully work with students who are different from them only when they can
> acknowledge their own limitations with race and be open to understanding
> the privileged mechanisms they use to discuss race. (p. 39)

In discussions of good teaching, our preservice teachers relate to their personal experiences in White majority classrooms with White female teachers. Not surprisingly, they judge these experiences as the norm and even as standards of good teaching, not realizing that, in some schools and classrooms, teaching and learning look very different from what they are used to seeing.

Fasching-Verner (2013) advocated providing experiences to educators that break through their biases and help them teach in effective, culturally responsive ways. Providing such experiences includes equipping preservice educators with a critique that recognizes social and economic inequality as arising from the economic structure rather than from individual or cultural traits (Gorski, 2016). In a study of preservice and in-service teachers, Robinson (2007) found that teachers who believed poverty is rooted in social structure were more apt to be present in and to persist in schools serving poor, highly diverse student populations. Through their commitment to serving students living in poverty, these teachers developed a "structurally mitigated sense of occupational competence" (p. 541). Their sense of competence allowed the teachers to understand the problems they encountered in the classroom in structural terms. Because of that different understanding, they were more satisfied with their job placements and more committed to staying.

Field Experiences for Teacher Candidates

Research suggests that early and frequent field experiences in diverse schools can demystify diversity and help preservice teachers understand and relate to students from marginalized groups (McKinney, Haberman, Stafford-Johnson, & Robinson, 2008; Miller & Mikulec, 2014). The University of Cincinnati's teacher preparation program, in cooperation with a partnering school district, uses field experiences to prepare teachers who will not only work effectively in diverse schools, but will "stick," that is, persist in their work there. These experiences and related activities help preservice teachers reflect on their current thinking about poverty and race. Through such reflection, we believe they develop deeper and more equitable understandings that lead to competence in providing effective instruction to all students. The effort toward developing this competence begins when our first-year preservice teachers ride through the projects to the school in which they will tutor.

For first-year university students from the mostly White suburbs of Cincinnati, a contextual shift such as that described in the authors' vignette at the beginning of this chapter may trigger discoveries that challenge their tacit beliefs, support their reflection on race and class as filters of interpretation; and instigate growth in their professional knowledge. Such discoveries, however, do not just happen. As Freire (1970) suggested, regardless of their commitment to social justice, members of the privileged class maintain some of the prejudices of their class, such as a lack of confidence in marginalized people's intelligence and ability to identify and work toward goals. Despite their good intentions, individuals from relatively privileged backgrounds run the risk of adopting ineffective strategies for interacting with students of color and those living in poverty. Because they do not trust the capabilities of people from marginalized groups, they may, for example, give directions to individuals from those groups rather than engaging in dialogue with them. This predilection is true for teachers at every level, including faculty at the university level, and it applies to our relations with students enrolled in teacher education courses, as it does to the teacher candidates' relations with their future students.

As faculty members in positions of privilege and power in relation to our students, how do we avoid making the kind of mistakes that Freire describes, underestimating our teacher candidates' ability to learn and change? Preservice teachers do not arrive at the university asking, "Can you help me uncover my concealed racism and privilege?" How do we simultaneously affirm student views and question them? How do we create conditions where we can together acknowledge that we are inscribed in the systems of domination implicit in our economic structure?

Lankshear (1997) suggested that dialogue is an existential necessity for social understanding. We conceive dialogical learning as a process of abstracting from the nearly impenetrable whole of experience, breaking the experience apart, finding new meaning and affirming student voices as we interrogate those perceptions that arise through dialogue. A large proportion of our curriculum focuses not only on race and class, but on other aspects of diversity as well. Neville, Poteat, Lewis, and Spanierman (2014) reported that preservice teachers who completed more coursework in which diversity was the focus of discussion had a greater increase in their understanding of and positive attitude toward diversity.

Dialogical education requires what Bronfenbrenner (1979) called *progressive accommodation* between an actively developing person and the changing properties of the immediate setting. In ways that involve preservice teachers' perceptions of what they are experiencing as well as the actions they take in a given setting, the candidates engage in activities that reveal possibilities for restructuring that environment. This kind of activity is what Freire (1970) referred to as *testing action*, where initial perceptions of something as fixed or immutable are questioned, leading to small action steps that are then interrogated for their limits and contradictions. As a result, alternative perspectives as well as tacit biases are more easily detected. In this process, we believe that our teacher candidates increasingly come to feel like masters of their own thinking; dialogue deepens; and the candidates participate more fully in their own education.

The First-Year Field Experience

We provide the first-year field experience to our teacher candidates in partnership with an elementary school near the university. The median household income in the school's neighborhood is $15,543. Twenty percent of the students who attend the school are homeless. There is no Wi-Fi in the housing projects in which many of the students live, and the nearest library is two miles away. We have been bringing first-year university students who plan to become teachers to this school since fall, 2011.

Currently about 60 students participate in this experience each semester. During eight of the 14 weeks of team-taught introductory coursework in exceptionalities and educational psychology, preservice teachers take an eight-minute bus ride to a substantially different world. Each Tuesday and Thursday these preservice teachers tutor for an hour and attend class for a second hour. In their tutoring sessions, the teacher candidates use materials and a tutoring program designed and monitored by the school's reading specialist. Our preservice teachers learn to interact with the students and their teachers in a neighborhood where hunger, violence, and unpredictability are often present, though the school itself is considered safe and "off limits" to gangs.

The purpose of this school and university partnership is shared benefit. Since the beginning of the program, we have worked to assess change not only in the perceptions and beliefs of the preservice teachers, but also in the performance of the students in this prekindergarten through sixth-grade school. Last year, all third graders were eligible for promotion, a first that the reading specialist attributed to the tutoring.

Since 2014, our teacher education program has used the short form of the *Teacher Efficacy Scale* (Tschannen-Moran & Woolfolk Hoy, 2001) to gather information about changes in our preservice teachers' perceptions. Each semester, about 60 students have completed the survey prior to and at the conclusion of this field experience. Having grown up with the mantra, "Work hard and you'll succeed," our preservice teachers struggle with the notion that success is elusive for some no matter how hard they work. Our primary concern has been teacher candidates' responses to survey items that indicate institutionalized blaming:

- The amount a student can learn is primarily related to family background.
- If students are not disciplined at home, they are not likely to accept any discipline.
- A teacher is very limited in what he/she can achieve because a student's home environment is a large influence on his/her achievement.
- If parents would do more for their children, I could do more.
- When it comes right down to it, a teacher really cannot do much because most of a student's motivation and performance depends on his or her home environment.

Comparison of candidates' survey results at the beginning and end of the experience showed decreased levels of agreement with these statements, though the full range of responses was still apparent. The group's mean changes on these items did not reach statistical significance; yet for some individual students there was greater change. In fact, for some students the decrease in the level of support for these biased statements was as much as three points on the 5-point Likert-type scale.

Considering the limited information from this brief survey, in fall 2017 we adopted the "Learning to Teach for Social Justice" scale (Enterline, Cochran-Smith, Ludlow, & Mitescue, 2008). This shift aligns with our growing understanding that efficacy is not enough; teachers must believe they can ameliorate effects of the institutionalized poverty and racism in which they and their students are enmeshed. Despite our interest in seeing if participation in the field experience might be associated with increased commitment to social justice, candidates' compliance in completing the survey at the end of the semester has been a problem. Whereas 98% of the 71 students completed the survey at the beginning of the semester, only 34% completed the survey at the end of the semester, making it difficult to draw valid conclusions about possible associations. The largest changes in survey responses at the beginning of the semester and responses on completion of the field experience were for the following items:

- Although teachers have to appreciate diversity, it is not their job to change society (20.3% increase in "disagree" or "strongly disagree" responses).
- An important part of learning to be a teacher is examining one's own attitudes and beliefs about race, class, gender, disabilities, and sexual orientation (15% increase in "agree" or "strongly agree" responses).
- Teachers should teach students to think critically about government positions and actions (11% increase in "agree" or "strongly agree" responses).
- Part of the responsibilities of the teacher is to challenge school arrangements that maintain societal inequities (8.5% increase in "agree" or "strongly agree" responses).

Because of low response rates at the conclusion of the field experience, we cannot assume that these levels of change occurred across all participating preservice teachers in the fall of 2017. In fact, we suspect that many preservice teachers did not make these sorts of changes in their beliefs. After all, these preservice teachers have had 12 years of education in a milieu that supported far different beliefs. Beginning next year, we will require all our candidates to complete this survey both at the beginning and end of the field experience in order to provide a more reliable measure that can help us determine the impact of our program.

Two Years Later—The Junior Field Experience

> As I walked into the High School building I could feel my stomach turning into knots and my face getting hot. I was so nervous to meet Reginald for the first time. So many questions ran through my head. What if he doesn't like me? What if the teachers don't want me there? What if he doesn't do any of the work I need him to do for my Monday night class? I took a depth breath as I told the Biology teacher why I was there and my nerves were calmed by how nice and welcoming the teacher was. I sat down as all of the students started walking in. They were very loud and rowdy, but the teacher calmed them down right before class begun. The teacher pointed out Reginald to me. He was very fidgety, talked a lot, and often was off task; however, he seemed really nice and got along with all of his classmates. With two minutes left of class, I finally got the courage to go up to his table to see if I could talk to him for a couple of minutes. He happily said "yes" and came with me to the back of the classroom. I then conducted a prepared interview and Reginald was more than willing to answer all of my questions. I learned more about him than I ever thought I would. I thanked him for answering my questions and he said, "You're welcome! Will you be back every Monday?" I said "yes" and a huge smile came across his face, as he walked away. All of a sudden, all of my nerves went away and I was truly happy to be there and come back every Monday.

Making a choice on a survey is easy; preservice teachers may choose what they assume is the "right" answer rather than disclosing beliefs that diverge from what faculty members seem to expect. Writing a thick description of an experience, by contrast, is more challenging and less easy to second-guess—as illustrated by the preceding paragraph, quoted verbatim from a thick description written by a junior in a required course, "Reading and Writing in the Content Areas."

Juniors in our program are placed in a partnering high-needs school—99% of the students' family income is below the poverty level, and the school has a history of low performance on the Ohio School Report Card. Approximately 35 preservice teachers participate in weekly three-hour tutoring experiences in the classroom for 14 weeks during the school year. As part of the clinical experience, the teacher candidates complete six thick descriptions of their experiences in the school.

According to Ponterotto (2006), thick description details and interprets social action within a particular context. In being asked to write a thick description, these preservice teachers are directed to assign purpose and intentionality to social actions through their understanding and account of the context. We ask that they attempt to capture their own thoughts and feelings and those of the public-school students as well as interpreting the complex web of relationships among the educators and students they observe. We position the juniors' recorded observations as data to be analyzed and discussed.

Thick descriptions lead readers to a sense that they can cognitively and emotionally situate themselves in context. As Geertz (1973) noted, when we look closely at the ordinary in places where an action takes unaccustomed forms, this inspection illuminates the degree to which an action's meaning varies according to the pattern of life by which it is informed.

After writing the thick descriptions, preservice teachers analyze their writing for themes and produce concept definition maps showing component concepts and their interrelations through a graphic organizer that clarifies the interrelationships (Schwartz, 1988). Finally, they produce a critical discourse analysis to develop a conceptual synthesis that links broader sociopolitical dynamics to everyday lived experience (Weiss & Wodak, 2007). In one synthesis statement a candidate observes, "Writing these thick descriptions has been very insightful for me. I have learned a lot about myself—whether I like it or not. By this, I mean that in some situations I found that I had racist thoughts." She continues, "This experience showed me that the typical stereotypes that I hear are so far from the truth. It also gave me a sense of relief to know that there wasn't a target on my back." She ends her reflection by telling us, "The thick descriptions have shown me my own thoughts that I didn't realize I was having during practicum observations. When you're in the field, you're so concentrated on getting the work done for classes that you do not realize what you can learn from these students and mentor teachers."

In writing these observations, preservice teachers learn not only to confront their own racism, but also to use boundary-crossing and other cultural competencies in productive ways (Aceves & Orosco, 2014). One candidate described the value of learning about her students' funds of knowledge:

> Knowing what skills and strengths your students have will help you be able to teach them easier and to see more progress in their schoolwork. Also, making connections to their life and their interests can help them become more interested in what is being taught and enjoy learning it more. Students thrive off of their passions and it can be beneficial to see how their interests can connect to their schoolwork.

Another candidate described the potential for learning that the junior-year field experience offers:

> Working in a setting and with a population of students that was differ-
> ent than my own educational experience was very different for me.... I
> personally would like to teach in a setting like this because I believe it could
> benefit me greatly working with a more diverse population than I have had
> myself.

In her synthesis, another candidate confronted a consistent theme among preservice teachers—that low-achieving students do not care about their education. Disrupting this kind of thinking is challenging; but the thick description work provides an opportunity for preservice teachers to confront their own assumptions. According to the candidate,

> This process has allowed me to realize that things aren't always exactly as
> they seem. I realize now that if a student is not volunteering answers or
> seems disengaged, you shouldn't assume this student just doesn't care and
> therefore can't be reached. There could be many reasons behind a student
> who seems to "not care." A student might be embarrassed because they
> don't know an answer, is unable to follow along with a reading passage,
> or might have experienced a difficult or traumatizing event that is caus-
> ing them to be reserved or even to act out. Being able to understand and
> encourage your students can help them get more engaged.

CONCLUSION

Although not every teacher candidate in the University of Cincinnati's teacher preparation program engages these opportunities at the same level, we see evidence that our efforts to immerse preservice teachers in contexts that enable them to confront and renounce preexisting stereotypes and biases can be transformative and empowering. Because we agree with Gorski (2016) that teachers' concepts of race and poverty influence their choice of instructional strategies to reduce race- and class-based disparities in the allocation of justice, power, and opportunity, we believe that such changes in teacher candidates' perspectives effect positive change in their approach to teaching and, consequently, in the achievement of all their students—regardless of race or class.

REFERENCES

Aceves, T. C., & Orosco, M. J. (2014). Culturally responsive teaching (Document No. IC-2). Retrieved from University of Florida, Collaboration for Effective Educator, Development, Accountability, and Reform Center. Retrieved from http://ceedar.education.ufl.edu/tools/innovation-configurations/

Berliner, D. C. (2009). *Poverty and potential: Out-of-school factors and school success.* Boulder, CO: Education and the Public Interest Center & Education Policy Research Unit. Retrieved from http://epicpolicy.org/publication/poverty-and-potential

Bronfenbrenner, U. (1979). *The ecology of human development: Experiments by nature and design.* Cambridge, MA: Harvard University Press.

Buchanan, L. B. (2015). "We make it controversial": Elementary preservice teachers' beliefs about race. *Teacher Education Quarterly, 42*(1), 3–26.

Enterline, S., Cochran-Smith, M., Ludlow, L. H., & Mitescue, E. (2008). Learning to teach for social justice: Measuring change in the beliefs of teacher preservice teachers. *The New Educator, 4,* 267–290. doi:10.1080/15476880802430361

Fasching-Verner, K. (2013). "Uh, you know, don't you?" White racial bonding in the narrative of white preservice teachers. *Educational Foundations, 27*(3/4), 21–41.

Freire, P. (1970). *Pedagogy of the oppressed.* New York, NY: Herder and Herder.

Geertz, C. (1973). *The interpretation of cultures.* New York, NY: Basic.

Gorski, P. (2016). Poverty and the ideological imperative: A call to unhook from deficit and grit ideology and strive for structural ideology in teacher education. *Journal of Education for Teaching, 42,* 378–386. doi:10.1080/0260 7476.2016.1215546

Grissom, J., & Redding, C. (2016). Discretion and disproportionality: Explaining the underrepresentation of high-achieving students of color in gifted programs. *AERA Open, 2,* 1–25. doi:10.1177/2332858415622175

Lankshear, C. (1997). *Changing literacies.* Philadelphia, PA: Open University Press.

McKinney, S., Haberman, M., Stafford-Johnson, D., & Robinson, J. (2008). Developing teachers for high-poverty schools: The role of the internship experience. *Urban Education, 43,* 68–82. doi:10.1177/0042085907305200

Marx, S. (2006). *Revealing the invisible: Confronting passive racism in teacher education.* New York, NY: Routledge.

Miller, P. C., & Mikulec, E. A. (2014). Pre-Service teachers confronting issues of diversity through a radical field experience. *Multicultural Education, 21*(2), 18–24.

Musu-Gillette, L., de Brey, C., McFarland, J., Hussar, W. Sonnenberg, W., & Wilkinson-Flicker, S. (2017). *Status and trends in the education of racial and ethnic groups 2017.* Washington, DC: National Center for Education Statistics. Retrieved from https://nces.ed.gov/pubs2017/2017051.pdf

Neville, H. A., Poteat, V. P., Lewis, J. A., & Spanierman, L. B. (2014). Changes in White college students' color-blind racial ideology over 4 years: Do diversity experiences make a difference? *Journal of Counseling Psychology, 61,* 179–190. doi:10.1037/a0035168

Ponterotto, J. G. (2006). Brief note on the origins, evolution, and meaning of the qualitative research concept "thick description." *The Qualitative Report, 11,* 538–549. Retrieved from http://www.nova.edu/ssss/QR/QR11-3/ponterotto.pdf

Robinson, J. G. (2007). Presence and persistence: Poverty ideology and inner-city teaching. *Urban Review, 39,* 541–464. doi:10.1007/s11256-007-0072-8

Schwartz, R. (1988). Learning to learn vocabulary in content area textbooks. *Journal of Reading, 32,* 108–117.

Sleeter, C. (2008). An invitation to support diverse students through teacher education. *Journal of Teacher Education, 59*, 212–219. doi:10.1177/0022487108317019

Staats, C. (2016). Understanding implicit bias: What educators should know. *American Educator, 39*, 29–43. Retrieved from https://www.aft.org/ae/winter2015-2016/staats

Tschannen-Moran, M., & Woolfolk Hoy, A. (2001). Teacher efficacy: Capturing and elusive construct. *Teaching and Teacher Education, 17*, 783–805. doi:10.1016/S0742-051X(01)00036-1

U.S. Department of Education, Office of Planning, Evaluation and Policy Development, Policy and Program Studies Service. (2016). *The state of racial diversity in the educator workforce*. Retrieved from http://www2.ed.gov/rschstat/eval/highered/racial-diversity/state-racial-diversityworkforce.pdf

Villegas, A. M., & Irvine, J. J. (2010). Diversifying the teaching force: An examination of major arguments. *Urban Review, 42*, 175–192. doi:10.1007/s11256-010-0150-1

Weiss, G., & Wodak, R. (2007). *Critical discourse analysis: Theory and interdisciplinarity*. New York, NY: Springer.

SECTION III INTRODUCTION

INCLUSIVE ASSESSMENT PRACTICES

The etymology of "assessment" identifies its Latin origin as combining *"ad"* (to, at) and *"sedere"* (sit), connoting sitting with or sitting beside. The origin connotes the presence of a guide to someone making a judgment. This meaning persists in that assessment in schools assists teachers, parents, students, administrators, and community members to judge the character and effects of instruction and to make decisions accordingly. Assessment guides change in instruction by creating the capacity to examine what worked and what did not, often offering insights into *why* an instructional activity failed or succeeded with some students, but not others. When assessment results are timely, specific, relevant, and translated into action, they offer a highly effective means of improving students' achievement. Well-designed formative and summative assessments can guide and support educators who are working to deploy inclusive educational practices.

Section III emphasizes inclusive assessment. In classrooms and schools, such assessment helps avoid the common opposing tendencies of ineffective instructional methods—on the one hand, activity-centered methods that are engaging but do not adequately support mastery of new concepts and skills, and, on the other hand, more passive methods, such as worksheets or lectures, that focus on mastery of new concepts and skills but fail to offer students meaningful engagement with those concepts and skills. In districts and states, inclusive assessment reveals inequities and helps inform goal setting, curriculum development, and improvement strategies that promote systemwide excellence and equity.

In "The Role of State Assessment in District-Wide Reform: Improving Results for all Students," Deborah Telfer, Aimee Howley, and Martha

Inclusive Education: A Systematic Perspective, pp. 93–96
Copyright © 2020 by Information Age Publishing
All rights of reproduction in any form reserved.

Thurlow report findings from a study of school districts identified as positive outliers because of the districts' success in promoting inclusive education and, as a consequence, improved achievement for students from marginalized groups. Findings from the study show that U.S. districts in different locales and with different demographics are able to use local adaptations of a relatively consistent set of practices to improve academic outcomes for students with disabilities and other students from marginalized groups.

In "Inclusive Assessment Practices: Using Formative Instructional Practices to Support the Needs of All Students," Kristall Graham-Day, Carolyn Shemwell Kaplan, Cheryl Irish, and Francis Troyan outline a cross-content assessment framework designed to support inclusion. The proposed framework affirms the importance of formative assessment as a mechanism for collecting the data necessary to gauge accurately the progress of all students within the general education curriculum.

CHAPTER 6

THE ROLE OF STATE ASSESSMENT IN DISTRICT-WIDE REFORM

Improving Results for All Students

Deborah M. Telfer
University of Cincinnati

Aimee Howley
WordFarmers Associates

Martha Thurlow
University of Minnesota

In this chapter, we report findings from a study of school districts that are positive outliers because of their success in promoting inclusive education and, as a consequence, improved achievement for students with disabilities and students from other marginalized groups. The study, fittingly called *Moving Your Numbers* (MYN), investigated district-wide strategies that led to significant improvements in performance outcomes. These strategies

Inclusive Education: A Systematic Perspective, pp. 95–133
Copyright © 2020 by Information Age Publishing
All rights of reproduction in any form reserved.

notably implicated attentiveness to data from accountability testing in generating improvement. Attention to these data, moreover, contributed to a sense of moral outrage—outrage that prompted district leaders to make decisions and take actions that initiated (and ultimately sustained) meaningful reform.

Several research questions guided the study: (a) What were the practices commonly used by districts that were approximating achievement equity for students with disabilities? (b) What were the special challenges encountered by school districts that were approximating achievement equity for students with disabilities? (c) How did district-wide goals and structures support and impede efforts to establish and sustain achievement equity for students with disabilities as well as for other marginalized students?

Before turning to the study, we begin with a brief theoretical consideration of how the related concepts of transparency and visibility as well as outrage contribute to reform. That discussion starts with an illustration that has obvious existential consequences (mortality rates), but it quickly moves to illustrations that have greater immediacy to educators—schooling outcomes. Arguably, schooling outcomes also have existential consequences because they significantly influence the life opportunities available to individual students and students from certain groups.

THEORETICAL FRAMEWORK

To set the stage for a study of how accountability testing fits into districts' strategies for promoting inclusive education for diverse learners, we first provide illustrations of how transparency helps promote social justice in a more general sense (i.e., by shedding light on egregious instances of oppression and inequity). We then examine theoretical work that explains why transparency sometimes functions to incite outrage and inspire reform.

Illustrations

In 2011, the infant mortality rate among African Americans in the United States was 11.5/1000 in contrast to the rate among non-Hispanic Whites of 5.1/1000 (Centers for Disease Control and Prevention, 2011)—more than twice as high. Even though the 2011 rate represents overall improvement across the decades, the race-based gap remains just as large today as it has been in the recent past (Loggins & Andrade, 2014).

Looking at these data and what they tell us about social injustice as the persistent state of social relations in the United States, we might become outraged at the continuing impact of slavery, racism, and economic inequity on the life chances for children of different races. We might even be appreciative of the efforts made by government agencies to keep track of and report such statistics. However much we might worry about excessive government surveillance, we still might not be inclined to view efforts to bring racial disparities to light *primarily* as a way to control the populace (but cf. Bregham, 2017; Dorn, 2014; Foucault, 1977 who claim that ostensibly benign institutions, such as universities and state education agencies, use their knowledge about individuals and groups to protect and expand the control of powerful organizations, such as large corporations).

As is the case with infant mortality rates, school achievement and outcome data offer startling insights about equity (and inequity) in the United States. Reardon (2011) notes, for example, that the achievement gap based on family income is now much larger than it was 25 years ago, possibly because of the widening gap between the rich and poor accompanied by the erosion of the middle class. In addition, pronounced gaps between races (especially between Whites, on the one hand, and African Americans, Mexican Americans, and American Indians, on the other) are still quite evident in terms of educational as well as economic and other quality-of-life outcomes (e.g., Barton & Coley, 2010; Covay-Minor, Desimone, Phillips, & Spencer, 2015; Killewald, 2013; Magnuson & Waldfogel, 2008; McKown, 2013; Valencia, 2015). Achievement- and outcome-gap data support concerns (and, for some, indignation) not only about the implications of greater income inequality, persistent racism, and the reluctance with which we allow non-English speakers to become full members of our society, but also about who gets identified as "disabled" and the educational treatment such individuals receive (Schulte & Stevens, 2015; Suzuki & Valencia, 1997; Telfer & Howley, 2014).

Notably, evidence of substantial achievement and outcome gaps between students with and without disabilities continues to be reported even though approximately 80–85% of students with disabilities do not have significant cognitive impairments (Thurlow, 2010; Thurlow, Quenemoen, & Lazarus, 2011). According to Chudowsky, Chudowsky, and Kober (2009), achievement gaps in reading and math, between students with disabilities and those without disabilities, remain extremely large—often as high as 30 points in the percentages of students from each group that perform at proficient or higher levels (U.S. Department of Education, 2013). Further, being African American or living in poverty predisposes students to being labeled as having a disability (e.g., Bowen & Rude, 2006). Data reported by the United States Commission on Civil Rights (2007) show that students from low-income homes are approximately 1.75 times more likely than other students to be classified as having a disability, and that students of African descent are approximately 1.5 times more likely than other students to be classified as having a disability.

Finally, being classified as having a disability often limits students' opportunities to learn. For example, Cosier, Causton-Theoharis, and Theoharis (2013) found that, all else equal, the more time students spent in special education programs, the lower their achievement. This circumstance may result from the lower expectations held for students once they are labeled as having a disability (e.g., Bowen & Rude, 2006; Peterson, 2010; Shifrer, 2013) or from the fact that segregation in special education classrooms keeps students from participating in the general education curriculum and interacting with a wide range of peers with different skills and interests (Rea, McLaughlin, & Walther-Thomas, 2002; Roach, Chilungu, La Salle, Talapatra, & Vignieri, 2009; Wang & Baker, 1985).

Whatever the cause or causes, the educational circumstances that confront most students with disabilities significantly limit their life chances. As with other injustices, the visibility of the issue is likely to be a necessary, though—by itself—insufficient condition for its remedy (e.g., Klugman, 2011; Valencia, 2015). But, even among educators who would agree that students with disabilities ought not to be unfairly disadvantaged (e.g., Pullin, 2005), perspectives differ about the wisdom of using visible indicators (such as those provided by standardized accountability tests) to monitor what school districts are doing on behalf of these students (e.g., Eccles & Swando, 2009; Yates, 2013).

Theoretical Considerations: Visibility, Moral Outrage, and Accountability

The moral dimensions of visibility (and the related construct, transparency) are by no means straightforward. Whereas visibility into the dealings of businesses and governments may provide some corrective to corruption (e.g., Menéndez-Viso, 2009), increasing efforts by businesses and governments to make *individuals* and *subgroups* visible may actually reduce those individuals' and subgroups' opportunities for self-determination as well as intrude on their privacy (e.g., Foucault, 1977; Scott, 1998). Moreover, visibility into the workings of organizations hardly guarantees their ethical behavior, and efforts to ensure visibility (e.g., audits, accountability testing) ironically may provoke dishonesty and other forms of corruption (Figlio & Getzler, 2002). Similarly, the external accountability practices that purport to reveal organizational behavior and performance often subvert truth-telling in ways that limit the public's actual knowledge of what is going on (e.g., Olsen, 2015).

Nevertheless, accountability is both an organizational and a democratic function (e.g., Gonzalez & Firestone, 2013), and this function typically relies on data to make certain conditions more visible than they otherwise would appear. Awareness of these conditions provides a basis for speculation about internal and external causes of poor and unequal performance. In a system that is attentive to accountability indicators, efforts to improve performance and reduce inequity result from changes in policy and practice that specifically address these root causes; the impetus for accountability can be internal, external, or some combination of the two (Knapp & Feldman, 2012).

In recent scholarship on schools and school districts that have made improvements, internal (rather than external) accountability comes to the forefront as a significant motivator of reform (Carnoy, Elmore, & Sisken, 2003; Fullan, Rincon-Gallardo, & Hargreaves, 2015; Gonzalez & Firestone, 2013; Knapp & Feldman, 2012). Business organizations also look to internal accountability as the way to counter corrupt practices long before they lead to dire outcomes (e.g., Bishara & Schipani, 2009). As Fullan and associates (2015) argue, internal accountability supplies the moral imperative for improvement, the force for mobilizing improvement, and the structural arrangements and strategic initiatives needed to make improvement happen. Internal accountability, however, may work best when it aligns with an external system of accountability that, among other functions, sets standards and monitors performance (Yi & Shin, 2018). In the absence of a reliable external basis for setting expectations and gauging outcomes, even well-meaning organizations are likely to become complacent (e.g., McLaughlin & Rhim, 2007).

LITERATURE REVIEW

This section provides context for our account of the MYN study and especially for our interpretation of its findings. First, we review literature that examines the meanings and impact of educational accountability. We then turn our attention to the results of several studies with similar research aims as ours, allowing us to report on schools and especially districts that altered their structures and practices in order to redress persistent achievement gaps between students with and without disabilities.

Political Amalgam and Contradictory Theories of Action

For the past 40 years, policy researchers have argued over the aims and consequences of educational accountability standards, testing, sanctions, and other related practices (Sleeter, 2007). Some scholars (e.g., Darling-Hammond, 2007; Skrla & Scheurich, 2004) devote attention to these debates among policy analysts, categorizing them, for example, by the analysts' perspective on what accountability means under different circumstances or in different national systems (e.g., Fullan et al., 2015; Müller & Hernández, 2010). As Denhardt and Denhardt (2007) suggest, however, proponents of the different positions—in their enthusiasm for rendering summary judgments about the value of the effort—sometimes oversimplify the concept of accountability and the political environment that calls for it. These oversimplified analyses purport to answer the question, "is accountability a good thing?"

More nuanced analyses exist, of course. While some of these situate current educational accountability efforts in their historical context (e.g., Ambrosio, 2013; Ydesen, 2013), others identify specific sources of controversy (e.g., Wang, Beckett, & Brown, 2006), describe the inherent contradictions of policies that call for accountability (e.g., Falabella, 2014; Gordon & Whitty, 1997), evaluate actual accountability systems against criteria of effectiveness (Heap, 2013), or distinguish between the practical and rhetorical import of accountability requirements (Sirotnik, 2004).

Oversimplifying the aims and consequences of accountability systems occurs when commentators seek either to support or condemn these systems on the basis of certain features, while at the same time ignoring other features. From the vantage point of policy analysis, this approach is perplexing because it discourages careful review of the very system features that the analysts endorse or dispute (Lavis, 2009; Throgmorton, 1991). Heap's (2013) analysis of a Canadian accountability system contrasts to the typical approach while serving as a useful example. Despite the prevalence of these simplistic critiques, however, change in accountability policy is more likely to occur if systems can respond to nuanced findings about how (and how well) particular provisions work to accomplish certain aims (e.g., Fullan et al., 2015).

Visibility and the Disaggregation of Data

One provision of much educational accountability legislation, especially the No Child Left Behind (NCLB) Act and its successor the Every Student Succeeds Act, requires states to disaggregate academic achievement data and publicly share the results as a way to monitor the equity of schooling outcomes (e.g., Poplin & Rivera, 2005; Williams, 2003). Gap data that enable comparisons across subgroups illuminate the extent to which education provided by schools, districts, and states contributes to more or less equitable outcomes (Thurlow & Wiley, 2006; Valencia, 2015).[1]

The theory of action supporting this approach posits that evidence of inequitable schooling outcomes will produce a moral imperative, motivating states, districts, and schools to improve practices on behalf of student groups that perform less well than other groups. A further assumption contends that subgroup differences can be accounted for primarily by considering the relative quality of education that these groups receive. This assumption leaves little room for alternative theories based on biological determinism (e.g., Rushton & Jensen, 2005), economic determinism (e.g., Berliner, 2010; Rothstein, 2005), or critical theory (e.g., Foster, 2011).

Arguably, however, no single set of circumstances fully accounts for achievement gaps (e.g., McKown, 2013). But since the "effective schools" movement began, its impetus has been the belief that schools should take responsibility for their contribution to achievement gaps (e.g., Lee, 2008). From this perspective, disaggregation of subgroup data ought to give educational agencies sufficient motive to redress past inequities and to interrupt practices that tend to sustain those inequities (cf. Park, Daly, & Guerra, 2013). According to some commentators (e.g., Ravitch, 2010), however, the gap data also provide vocal critics of public schools with a basis for demonizing schools for their ostensible "failures." These critics make it seem as if the public education system holds primary responsibility for causing, not just for redressing, achievement gaps—an interpretation that supports the efforts of policymakers and corporate leaders with a vested interest in privatizing the education system in the name of improvement (e.g., Aske, Connolly, & Corman, 2013).

Nevertheless, schools, districts, and states that use their achievement gap data to identify areas for increased equity and to monitor their progress in improving equity take a markedly different stance. Their aims are to identify and then to push against beliefs and practices that tend to restrict the achievement of some groups of students. Among the most damaging of these beliefs is the view that students from certain groups (e.g., students with disabilities, African American students) are unable to learn as rapidly or deeply as other students (Torff, 2014). As Ysseldyke and associates (2004) comment, reflecting on how to close achievement gaps between students with and without disabilities, "if you begin with high expectations, students will achieve more; this provides the underlying framework for greater access to the general education curriculum through enhanced awareness of appropriate accommodations to access that curriculum" (p. 81).

Punishing Schools

Along with its focus on equity, recent accountability legislation (especially NCLB) encouraged the development of incentive structures that mete out sanctions to schools that fail to make rapid improvements, while at the same time placing trust and resources in the hands of for-profit vendors (e.g., charter school management companies) whose capacity to provide high-quality education remains untested (Belfield & Levin, 2002; Betebenner, Howe, & Foster, 2005; Ravitch, 2010). As several scholars argue (e.g., Aske, Connolly, & Corman, 2013), NCLB also used data from accountability tests to encourage individual families to abandon local public schools in favor of charter school and private school alternatives (see also Betebenner et al., 2005). The underlying theory behind this policy approach positions the dynamics of the market, rather than the embarrassment and outrage of professional educators, as the best mechanism for forcing the education system to change (see also Hursh, 2005).

To date, however, empirical studies offer little evidence that market forces lead to improved educational outcomes (e.g., Belfield & Levin, 2002; Betebenner et al., 2005). Rather, some studies now show that accountability legislation (with its reliance on incentive structures that invoke shaming and punishment) produces certain unintended consequences that have the potential to harm students, especially those from the subgroups that the legislation purports to help (e.g., Amrein-Beardsley, Berliner, & Rideau, 2010; Stecher & Barron, 2001). Two of these consequences may be particularly damaging to students with disabilities: (a) the tendency of charter schools to "cherry pick" students and, as a result, to decrease inclusiveness (e.g., Frankenberg, Siegel-Hawley, & Wang, 2011; Gordon & Morton, 2008; Lange & Ysseldyke, 1998) and (b) the tendency of some educators to respond to the stress of high-stakes accountability by gaming the system or even tampering with data (e.g., Amrein-Beardsley et al., 2010; Cullen & Reback, 2006; Figlio & Getzler, 2002).

With respect to the inclusiveness of charter and private schools, Lange and Ysseldyke (1998) found that, although families of students with disabilities exercised their prerogatives, they did so by moving students from more inclusive schools to less inclusive alternatives. Similarly, Frankenberg and associates (2011) determined that, while white families were not alone in using choice options, these options nevertheless led to greater segregation. This situation resulted from the fact that some charter and private schools explicitly sought to attract white families while others sought to attract African American families. Frankenberg and her colleagues also found that, more affluent white and African American children left public schools for charter and private alternatives while less economically advantaged students of whatever race remained. Gordon and Morton (2008) reported similar dynamics among schools in New Zealand.

In terms of gaming the system, some studies point to situations in which educators have responded to the stress of high-stakes accountability by: altering curricula; explicitly "teaching to the test"; providing short-term remediation to students whose scores are "on the bubble," a practice that Jennings and Sohn (2014) refer to as "instructional triage"; and categorizing struggling students in ways that, school administrators hoped, would disguise their low scores (e.g., Au, 2009; Cimbricz, 2002; Cullen & Reback, 2006; Figlio & Getzler, 2002). In the most extreme cases, school district administrators have permitted (and even encouraged) dishonesty in reporting the scores of certain students, namely those whose scores are likely to lower district or school performance ratings (e.g., Bush & Smith, 2014; Samuels, 2011).

Other studies, by contrast, show how educators resist the temptation to narrow curricula because of their commitment to providing rigorous academic content and high-quality instruction (Grant, 2001; Neumann, 2013). One recent study (Jennings & Sohn, 2014) presents well-marshaled evidence demonstrating the differential effects of high- and low-stakes tests on students in differing achievement bands (e.g., advanced, proficient, below proficient, and so on). These authors conclude that accountability testing, whether of the low- or high-stakes variety, supports productive narratives in some cases and unproductive narratives in others. Their characterization is useful to consider before we turn our attention to those schools and districts that, according to the researchers who studied them, responded to the inequitable outcomes of students with and without disabilities by deploying moral outrage in the service of productive action.

> We suggest that at least two different narratives about educational inequality and the role of schools in addressing it can arise from apparent increases in proficiency rates and declines in the size of proficiency-based achievement gaps. The first narrative is a "beating the odds" narrative. The fact that test scores tell a story of decreasing gaps may spur and legitimate investment in disadvantaged children, given that such gaps have been difficult to close historically. The second narrative is a "mission accomplished" narrative. From this perspective, our current policies have been successful at reducing inequality, and we need not look for or invest in new education or social policy solutions. (Jennings & Sohn, 2014, p. 137)

Existence Proofs

Although gap-closing data for certain subgroups do support a "beating the odds" narrative in some policy circles, there is little aggregate evidence to show improvements being made on behalf of students with disabilities (Albus, Lazarus, & Thurlow, 2014; Chudowsky et al., 2009; Council of the Great City Schools, 2005–2012). In fact, some reports on gap closing (e.g., Togneri & Anderson, 2003) do not even report data comparing students with and without disabilities. The aggregate data are not, however, the only place to look for evidence. Arguably, "beating the odds" is something that first appears in local examples, and a few of these cases can be found in the education literature.

Perhaps most notable are the case studies conducted by Nagle and associates (2007a, 2007b, 2007c, 2007d) in four states over a five-year period. Together, these studies examine how state policy and practices, on the one hand, and district practices, on the other, interacted to create more inclusive schooling and accountability testing experiences for students with disabilities. Nevertheless, these case studies provide limited descriptions of practices that had, in the early days of their use, shown clear-cut evidence of effectiveness. For example, data collection in California (Nagle, McLaughlin, Nolet, & Malmgren, 2007a) identified both state-level commitment to closing achievement gaps on behalf of students with disabilities but also serious challenges and a tendency to "game the system," even in districts that were making progress toward greater inclusiveness. In the Maryland districts, the researchers report ongoing efforts to provide relevant professional development to teachers and to help principals learn how to function as instructional leaders (Nagle, McLaughlin, Nolet, & Malmgren, 2007b), but observe that resource limitations and challenges associated with instructional and leadership capacity slowed down the change process. Similar impediments confronted the districts in New York (Nagle, McLaughlin, Nolet, & Malmgren, 2007c). Additionally, of the districts participating in the NY case studies, the largest urban district was hampered in its ability to establish focus because its staff busily responded to the multiple and competing demands that stemmed from a variety of externally funded initiatives.

Some findings from the Texas case studies (Nagle, McLaughlin, Nolet, & Malmgren, 2007d), however, offer more encouragement than do those from the other states, showing clear evidence of district-level commitment to practices that support improving the performance of students with disabilities in more inclusive settings. In their description of one of the districts, the researchers note that the district discouraged labeling and that teachers attempted to hold high expectations for the learning of all students. The researchers also heard district educators discuss their belief that certain policies, which require students with disabilities to participate in accountability testing, caused them to hold higher expectations for the performance of those students. Furthermore, participating district educators talked about the improvements generated by aligning IEP goals and objectives with general education curriculum standards.

We could find few other systematic empirical studies with a focus on district-level strategies, though one report—on schools and districts that provide inclusive, high-quality education to students with disabilities— details effective practices in three districts (Cortiella & Burnette, 2008), practices that relate to the use of data-informed decision-making and the commitment to holding high expectations for students with disabilities. A report from a Louisiana parish (Guillot & Parker, 2010) offers similar insights and documents progress in closing achievement gaps between students with and without disabilities. Focusing on literacy, the district increased its use of inclusion, Response to Intervention, and data-driven planning to improve the performance of students with disabilities. Relying primarily on Response to Intervention, another district also offered evidence of similar progress toward closing achievement gaps (Kashi, 2008). Some studies describing efforts to close the achievement gap for students with disabilities are less relevant to our study because they focus on school-level practices only (e.g., Hehir, 2012) or because they seek to document the impact of one particular instructional program or practice (e.g., Hankes, Skoning, Fast, & Mason-Williams, 2013; Walsh, 2012).

METHODS

In this section, we first discuss district and participant selection. We then describe data collection via on-site and telephone interviews, followed by our data analysis procedures. The section concludes with a discussion of the study's limitations.

Selection of Districts

We used a qualitative reputational approach to identify the districts for this study (Cyrenne & Grant, 2009; Dahl, 1961; Seiler, 1975). Our goal in using this approach was to find positive outliers—districts recognized for their inclusive practices and success in reducing achievement gaps for students with disabilities.

A project advisory board that represented national, state, and local perspectives provided the initial nominations of districts for possible inclusion in the study. The research team contacted state directors of special education, local special education and general education administrators, and special education advocacy groups for additional nominations, expanding the initial list of districts. The researchers then analyzed trends in publicly available achievement-test data to confirm evidence of notable "gap-closing" in the nominated districts. Altogether, the team identified 20 districts using this approach.

The selection process also involved efforts to ensure diversity of the selected districts, specifically regarding size and demographics (locale, poverty level, and percent of minority students). To achieve this variability, the researchers consulted data from the *Common Core of Data* (National

Center for Education Statistics [NCES], 2014) for each district nominated for participation in the study. The team's review of demographic information about the districts indicated that they did indeed differ in ways that would reflect important demographic variability nationwide.

The lead researcher then contacted all districts in the pool of 20 nominees. She telephoned an individual identified as someone in the district with knowledge of its efforts to improve results for all students, including those receiving special education services. Despite having contact information for a knowledgeable representative in each district, the lead researcher still needed to place several calls to either connect with this person or to talk to other knowledgeable district personnel. She particularly hoped to find a key informant who could confirm the district's commitment to students with disabilities, the fact that the district had made substantial efforts to implement inclusive practices, and the district's willingness to participate in the study. Of the 20 districts in the original pool, 17 agreed to participate in the study; seven of these districts later withdrew (see Table 6.1).

The 10 remaining districts were located in nine states: California, Florida, Georgia, Illinois, Indiana, New Hampshire, Ohio (two districts), Oregon, and Wisconsin. They included rural, urban, and suburban districts, with student enrollments ranging from fewer than 1,000 to more than 160,000. The districts also varied in the diversity of their students (see Table 6.1).

Within participating districts, the lead researcher asked to interview key informants including district superintendents or deputy/associate superintendents, curriculum leaders and other central office staff, special education directors, and principals. Participants also included teachers and, in some districts, related services personnel and family and community members.

Visit and Interview Procedures

The lead researcher set up either visits or phone interviews in the districts that agreed to participate in the study, according to their preferences. Some districts ($n = 2$) preferred telephone interviews for data collection. In the remaining districts, the lead researcher conducted face-to-face interviews during her on-site visits to the district.

All interviews followed a structured interview guide developed by the research team and the project's advisory board. Interview questions drew from extant literature on inclusive educational practices and gap-reduction approaches. The team designed the interview guide (see Appendix A for a matrix summarizing the guide) to create sufficient structure for obtaining comparable information across districts, while also allowing enough latitude for participants to talk freely about the district, its characteristics, structures, and practices. The interview topics included: the district's vision,

Table 6.1.
Characteristics of Student Populations in 10 Districts

District	Total Enrollment	Percent Economically Disadvantaged	Percent Minority	Percent Special Education	Percent English Language Learners
1	883	45.9	0.4	11.6	0.0
2	1,950	46.0	15.0	22.0	5.0
3	3,231	18.5	26.6	13.0	5.4
4	3,333	21.8	10.6	10.1	2.0
5	3,748	53.3	13.5	17.6	0.5
6	12,400	38.0	37.0	11.0	12.0
7	12,500	45.0	15.7	13.9	11.0
8	19,700	80.0	94.0	9.0	24.0
9	72,538	43.2	32.6	17.2	2.3
10	162,589	53.0	68.4	11.0	15.0

including beliefs, values, and goals; the district's history of planning efforts designed to promote reform; the district's decision-making structures, student placement procedures, and prevailing instructional practices; the roles of central office personnel and principals; the use of resources across the district; and the district's current challenges and future prospects. Questions were open ended so that participants could use their own words to explain district initiatives and changes in district practices and outcomes.

The lead researcher conducted interviews with a variety of leaders and other stakeholders in each district. The study protocol did not require the interviewer to speak with people occupying the same set of specified roles in each district but rather asked her to interview those educators and stakeholders who were (or had been) most deeply engaged in the district's improvement efforts. The research team adopted this approach because each district's configuration differed slightly, with different personnel taking leadership in the district's reform efforts. By including multiple participants from each district, the research team could triangulate across respondents, thereby providing one mechanism for establishing the credibility of the information obtained through the interviews.

During each interview, the lead researcher took extensive notes and, following the interview, added to them (i.e., to her field notes) to ensure that they contained detailed records of everything that had occurred, and that the participant had said during the interview. The lead researcher recorded exact quotes to the extent possible, and, following the approach mentioned by Gibson and Brown (2009), recorded additional field notes as soon after each interview as possible. The study did not use audio recording and verbatim transcription. Arguably, note taking opens up the possibility of introducing the interviewer's subjective judgment into the data—decisions about what to record, when to record, and how to code recorded data may also introduce similar types of bias (see e.g., Psathas & Anderson, 1990).

Data Analysis

We began data analysis by reading and rereading the interview notes and field notes to identify categories into which the data fell and, eventually, to identify patterns in the narratives and observations recorded at each research site and, then, across sites. The lead researcher shared emerging generalizations (i.e., theoretical statements about categories and patterns) with the project advisory board, whose members asked questions about quotes from participants and the researcher's recorded observations as well as reviewing other information supplied by the lead researcher. We used this approach to analytic triangulation to help ensure that the initial categorization of data made sense, based on what district participants shared, and did not reflect biases. It also gave the advisory board members a voice in naming the emergent themes that reflected a preponderance of evidence in the data set.

Once she categorized the data and interpreted the advisory board members' input, the lead researcher identified a final set of emergent themes as well as characterized similarities and differences across districts. She also drafted a case report for each district, which she then shared with participants from the district to ensure that the draft report accurately captured the descriptions, stories, and explanations that the participants had shared (i.e., member checking). Finally, the researcher conducted an audit showing how the data (i.e., notes from interviews and field notes) supported each emergent theme.

Study Limitations

Through systematic data collection and analysis, triangulation, member checking, and the final audit, the research team gathered evidence to support two claims about the study's credibility: (a) that individual case study reports constituted credible representations of practices in the districts and participants' views about those practices and (b) that emergent themes represented clear patterns in the data. Limitations with the study's design and execution, however, may create possible threats to its credibility.

First, district selection relied on a reputational nomination process. This process identified positive outliers effectively, but it did not allow the research team to identify the most extreme positive outliers or to select at random from a list of districts with a similarly strong record of gap closing. Second, visits to the districts were relatively short and involved just one researcher who conducted all interviews and recorded information from informal observations. The data set for each district was therefore limited, comprising interviews with a small number of participants at each site. This approach proved more serious in the larger districts because the researcher could not interview all (or even most) of the personnel involved with district reforms. In these cases, she could speak only with a small subset of the total population of district administrators, building administrators, and other stakeholders.

The decision to disclose the names of interviewees and their districts may constitute an additional limitation. Although the research team obtained all necessary permissions for such disclosures, the team could not control the extent to which this decision caused participants to become guarded about what they shared. For example, participants may have been more likely to put a positive spin on (or even sanitize) what they reported. Knowing that their identities would be revealed, not only to the public at large but also to others in their districts, may have prevented some participants from being candid about their perspectives on district practices, stakeholders, and events in the improvement process.

FINDINGS

The findings section first presents a brief profile of each district. Then it turns to a discussion of the emergent themes resulting from qualitative data analysis.

District Profiles

The Bartholomew Consolidated School Corporation is a small city district in Indiana enrolling approximately 12,000 students. Data from the *Common Core of Data* (NCES, 2014)[2] show that a moderate proportion (45%) of the district's students are economically disadvantaged, 11% are English learners (ELs), approximately 14% have identified disabilities, and approximately 16% are non-White.

The smallest MYN district is Bloom Vernon Local, a rural district in the Appalachian part of Ohio enrolling fewer than 1,000 students. Its proportion of economically disadvantaged students is 46%, making it similar to Bartholomew's, but other demographics differ. Notably, the district has no ELs and almost no non-White students (0.4%). Its percentage of students identified as having disabilities is 11.6%.

The Brevard Public Schools in Florida serve a large suburban region with considerable diversity. The district's enrollment of approximately 72,000 students includes 33% non-white students and 43% economically disadvantaged students. ELs comprise 2.3% of the school population, and students with disabilities comprise slightly more than 17%.

With the largest enrollment of any *MYN* district (approximately 180,000 students currently—162,000 at the time of data collection), Gwinnett County Public is also the largest district in Georgia, serving a growing suburban enclave outside of Atlanta. Its student body at the time of the study (when the district served approximately 2,000 fewer students than it does today) included 53% on free or reduced lunch, 15% ELs, and more than 68% non-White. Approximately 11% were identified as students with disabilities.

Lake Villa School District in Illinois serves a less diverse and more affluent suburb than some of the other MYN districts. Its enrollment of approximately 3,200 students includes 18.5% who are economically disadvantaged, 5.4% who are ELs, 27% who are non-White, and 13% who are identified with disabilities.

Another relatively small district (around 1,800 students) with limited diversity, SAU 56 serves the suburbs in and around Somersworth, New Hampshire. Economically disadvantaged students comprise 46% of the study body, ELs comprise 5%, and non-White students comprise 15%. The district identifies 22% of its students as having disabilities.

Wisconsin's Stoughton Area School District is also relatively small (approximately 3,400 students) and serves a large suburban community. Its diversity percentages include 22% of students who are economically disadvantaged, 2% EL, 11% non-White, and 10% with disabilities.

The Tigard-Tualatin School District enrolls approximately 12,000 students and serves a large suburban area in Oregon. Its proportions of diverse students include 38% who are economically disadvantaged, 12% who are ELs, 37% who are non-White, and 11% who have been identified with disabilities.

More diverse than most of the other MYN districts, California's Val Verde Unified is categorized by NCES as suburban, though at the time of the study its classification was rural. The district serves approximately 20,000 students, 80% of whom are economically disadvantaged and 24% of whom are ELs. Most students in Val Verde (94% at the time of the study) are non-white. With just 9% of students identified as having disabilities, the district appears to be the most inclusive among those in the study's sample.

Serving the town of Wooster, Ohio and the surrounding rural areas, the Wooster City School District enrolls around 3,700 students, 53% of whom are economically disadvantaged. Few district students are ELs (0.5%) and a small proportion (approximately 14%) are non-White. The district identifies somewhat more that 17% of its students as having disabilities.

Themes

Qualitative data analysis identified several themes that describe commonalities across perspectives and practices in the 10 districts. At the same time, the data revealed contextual specificity, demonstrating the distinct and locally-specific usage of a general strategy—such as implementing a multitiered system of support or organizing teachers into data teams—in each district. These local adaptations addressed district-level needs in ways that fit with each district's cultural precepts and organizational capacities.

In reporting these findings, we first look at the leadership context that enabled systemic responses to perceived embarrassment and outrage—the fact that students with disabilities performed academically at levels far below their counterparts without disabilities. Then, we turn our attention to the commonalities, describing and providing evidence of the three most salient themes: (a) use of an improvement framework, (b) use of data to support improvement, and (c) increased commitment to high expectations. Finally, we conclude with a brief discussion of differences across the 10 districts.

Leadership Context

In each of the districts, the leadership (broadly defined to include the superintendent, central office leaders, building leaders, and teacher-leaders) used the increasing external demand for accountability on behalf of all students and student groups as a motive for changing the conversation and practices across the district. The leaders' attentiveness to a perceived moral crisis reduced fragmentation and isolation on the part of educators at various levels and in varied roles; and it increased the quality, consistency, and coherence of the instruction provided to all learners.

While the educators participating in the MYN study differed somewhat in their views about externally imposed accountability requirements, they all considered state assessment results as one relevant indicator of their progress toward equity. At the very least, these results supported efforts to bring unacceptable subgroup outcomes to the forefront. Michael McCormick, Assistant Superintendent of Educational Services for the Val Verde Unified School District (CA) recalled, "Seeing our state assessment results for the first time was an inherently emotional experience for all of us, but especially for teachers, because we wanted our students to do well; the data served as a catalyst for springing into action."

Similarly, in rural Bloom Vernon Local School District (OH), former Grades 7–12 principal Bob Johnson shared his profound feelings of embarrassment when state assessment results were first reported and students with disabilities did not meet adequate yearly progress: "that had a huge effect on me personally," he said. Heidi Holstein, special education teacher in Bloom Vernon, recalled, "NCLB set a clear call to action and made us realize that kids can do this (achieve at higher levels); we just weren't set up to teach them what they needed to do well."

In contrast, the staff of the Bartholomew Consolidated Schools (IN) accepted state assessment data as a necessary part of life, rather than as the primary impetus for the district's reform process. Instead of worrying too much about the external measures of their performance, district leaders drew on their own observations and insights to direct attention district wide to promoting high-level learning among all students. Accordingly, district leadership intentionally chose not to focus on or be deterred by state testing. Their Director of Special Education, George Van Horn, captured the prevailing district attitude toward external accountability:

> Obviously Indiana has a grading scale and we want to have good grades, but we continue to believe that the way to get there is to stay focused on our work. Our internal conversation is focused on student learning no matter what comes at us from the outside. If we stay focused, we'll figure out how to bring external factors into our work rather than let them distract us. Keeping our eye on the ball has helped us improve as a district and helped us improve student learning, and we're seeing evidence of that.

Regardless of the role that *external* accountability played in the initiation of the districts' reform efforts, all MYN districts established a strong *internal* accountability system to support continuous learning and improvement. McCormick described the evolution of Val Verde's culture into one where educators shared accountability for the success of all children:

> It started with external accountability, but led to the development of an internal accountability system. The superintendent would say, "Kids from Val Verde are just as important as kids from anywhere else." Since 2005, we've maintained our focus on making sure our kids, even though 84% of them are on free and reduced lunch, can compete with other kids from other locations in higher education and in the job market. It comes down to a

simple concept: why wouldn't we want all kids to have access to high-quality education based on an agreed upon understanding of standards? This is the essense of why we're in this business, and seeing groups of children left out only cemented our passion. In the early days, schools would compete by having a staff pep rally the day before the first day of school for the kids. They'd bring in banners and parade to celebrate improvements in their school's state test scores. As our focus shifted to internal accountability as a deep-rooted culture, we've moved beyond a school-by-school competition to a larger sense of community that celebrates our collective achievements as a district.

Commonalities Across Districts

At the core of the MYN districts' work, leaders provided visible support—through both what they said and how they deployed district resources—for the expectation that educators in the district would examine their own and each others' practice as a way to promote higher levels of learning across the board as well as for students in underperforming subgroups. District approaches to improvement illustrate powerful responses to disaggregated achievement-test data and data from related classroom assessments. These responses entailed (a) the adoption of an improvement framework, such as a multi-tier system of supports (MTSS) approach, as the foundation for all instruction; (b) the increased use of reliable and valid data to identify specific instructional needs, monitor adult implementation of a shared set of practices, and continually evaluate student performance; and (c) intentionally focusing the district's core work—work that required widespread efforts to interrupt the use of deficiency language and deficiency explanations—to cultivate all educators' commitment to high expectations for student performance.

Adoption of an Improvement Framework

An improvement framework is a conceptual model that links particular strategic actions and ongoing practices to desired outcomes. Many such models exist, and their effectiveness depends on the power of the practices they incorporate, the coherence of those practices, and the fidelity with which users adhere to those practices (e.g., Fullan, 2011). According to some reform advocates, the coherence of the framework is particularly important to the success of a reform initiative. As Dougherty and Rutherford (2009, p. 1) assert, educators tend to view the complex parts of a reform initiative as "interlocking puzzle pieces" that create a complete picture—"an incorrect fit, the insertion of a piece that simply does not belong, or the failure to redesign the entire puzzle if that is what is needed, can cause the separate pieces not to make their expected contribution" (p. 1). From their perspective, the inability to establish a "coherent, big-picture approach to improvement" accounts for the failure of many educational reforms (p. 1).

The improvement frameworks used by the MYN districts delineated their core beliefs and set boundaries for key areas of work. The frameworks described the interrelatedness of their constituent parts (e.g., processes, team structures, tools, decision rules, and so on), and they guided decision-making related to core organizational functions, such as the use of time, how to employ and assign personnel, the nature and use of professional development, the role and function of principals and central office personnel, and the ways in which district educators can invite the larger community into reform efforts. Moreover, as they used the frameworks and observed their functionality, district educators' confidence in them—as a mechanism for building the collective capacity of the system to make and sustain improvements in student, adult, and organizational learning—increased.

For example, the Bartholomew Consolidated School Corporation (IN) used Universal Design for Learning (UDL) as its improvement framework. Advocated by the Center for Applied Special Technology (CAST) as a framework to improve and optimize teaching and learning for all people, based on scientific insights about how humans learn, UDL provided a foundation enabling Bartholomew's leaders to organize all aspects of the district's work around a coherent set of practices related to the engagement of all learners through the expansion of opportunities for representation, action, and expression (Rose & Meyer, 2006). The Stoughton Area School District (WI) used a different improvement framework—Integrated Comprehensive Services (ICS). ICS is a social justice model built around four key components that serve to leverage proactive service delivery: (a) non-negotiable core principles focusing on equity, (b) the requirement to establish equitable structures, (c) the requirement to provide access to high-quality teaching and learning, and (d) the commitment to implement change (Frattura & Capper, 2007).

Other MYN districts used different improvement frameworks, including the MTSS and the Ohio Improvement Process (OIP). Some of the districts combined features of established models to produce unique variants that fit with the district's needs and culture. Many of these variants relied on tiered approaches for aligning instruction and instructional supports to the needs of particular students, even though the districts had not explicitly adopted MTSS or a Response to Intervention model. District and school improvement plans often articulated or reflected elements of the framework, delineating goals, strategies, and indicators, and increasing focus within and alignment across the specific plans in each of the district's schools. A principal in the Bartholomew Consolidated School Corporation (IN) noted, "We tried to squeeze everything into our school improvement plans before; [but] we learned the importance of having a framework."

Across the districts, leaders used the improvement framework (whatever it was) to bring all adults (i.e., certified and noncertified personnel) in the district together, sharing responsibility for and ownership of the success of every child. Districts intentionally engaged personnel from all levels in shaping and communicating the district's focus, ensuring that all schools in the district aligned their work with district-established goals and strategies, involving everyone in professional development that was directly aligned with the district's focused goals and priorities, and actively working with the school board and members of the community to establish strong linkages and leverage support. Bartholomew's Van Horn explained,

> UDL as our framework allowed us to focus. We described our work before UDL as a lot of random acts of improvement. We had really good things going on, but they weren't tied together. UDL helped us bring our work together and if we felt a particular activity was not aligned with UDL, we moved away from it.

Similarly, at the time of data collection, Lake Villa School District #41's (IL) superintendent, John Van Pelt, described the district's approach prior to the use of a unifying framework: "In 2006, each building had different goals and there was no overall strategy for making improvements. We were a confederation of schools, not a school district." Grounding reform in an improvement framework, Lake Villa leaders established aligned team structures at every level of the district. These aligned teams helped ensure that the district's goals would remain focused and that practices at the school level would align with broader district goals and strategies. These teams promoted shared leadership and thereby provided a mechanism for increasing the district-wide coherence of discourse and practice as well as helping district educators maintain clear links between discourse and practice.

The strategy of sharing leadership, exemplified through the use of collaborative learning teams (e.g., data teams, learning teams, teacher-based teams, professional learning communities), occurred not only in Lake Villa, but across the MYN districts. District leaders established such structures as a way to communicate their district's improvement framework and to ensure the fidelity of its use at each level of the system. In general, they reported that these structures played a major role in building the collective capacity of personnel across their district to deliver on, learn from, and continually improve the quality of instruction. In the Wooster City School District (OH), for example, aligned leadership teams at the district (district leadership team), school (building leadership team), and classroom (teacher-based teams) levels implemented and oversaw priority work. Other districts, such as Lake Villa and Brevard Public (FL), reported that using teacher teams (i.e., teams of teachers that use data to plan, deliver, evaluate, and make changes in instruction based on how well students are learning) resulted in improved capacity on the part of district educators to meet new learning challenges.

Use of Data to Support Improvement Efforts

Every district believed that it was paramount to focus their core work around the most essential priorities. They viewed the effective use of relevant data—including state assessment data—as a primary strategy (e.g., referred to as a "pillar" by one district and described as "revered" by another district) for gaining and maintaining focus around a limited number of actions necessary for improvement. For example, Rob Saxon, superintendent of the Tigard Tualatin School District (OR), communicated continually and consistently the district's key message that "nothing matters as much as teaching every child to read at grade level." This focus—based on district leaders' realization that they could predict with 80% probability that if a third-grade student did not meet the benchmark on the Oregon Reading Assessment, the child would also be Latino—led to a reexamination of both the system and the notion of radical differentiation (Neumeier, 2006) to ensure that the district would meet the instructional needs of each student in equitable ways. The district's former director of curriculum and instruction elaborated on the importance of data use to focus the district's work: "We took a hard line on the use of data and teaming—everyone had to do it—and the results were ridiculously good."

In Tigard Tualatin, efforts to focus principals' work on fewer instructional issues, by directing them to "clean out the plans," helped ensure that they could effectively monitor the implementation of key work and initiatives. The Director of Curriculum and Instruction, Rachel Stuckey, noted that "we continue to fine-tune the school improvement plan process so that SIPs [School Improvement Plans] are focused on the use of highly effective instructional strategies." Similarly, in Wooster, the role of the principal changed, its primary focus moving away from school management and toward leadership of collaborative learning teams. Like the principals in the study's other districts, Wooster principals reviewed not only their own school's data, but also district data related to instructional effectiveness and student achievement. According to the District Superintendent, Michael

Tefs, this approach contributed to shared accountability across the system and sense of "all-ness." Tefs elaborated that,

> The Ohio Improvement Process has helped us use a variety of formative and summative data to identify ambitious goals for all students, create a sense of urgency district-wide, and support the development of collective responsibility where all personnel understand that the whole is greater than the sum of its parts.... Our teacher-based teams consistently look at the instructional strategies being employed in the classroom and how they're addressing individual needs, the length and duration of instruction and when it's provided, and how agreed-on strategies are being implemented across all classrooms.

Tefs's comment alludes to a broad definition of data—a definition that acknowledges the value of using data for various purposes beyond straightforward progress monitoring. In Val Verde Unified, school leaders also saw data in this way. For example, Mike McCormick, Assistant Superintendent for Educational Services, routinely sought out and videotaped school and teacher exemplars whose practice aligned with district-identified strategies and then shared these videos with other schools and teams across the district. Using what he called a "motivate, not mandate" approach, McCormick recently reported that he now uses social media, such as Facebook and Twitter, to document and share effective practices across the district. "We need to get serious about breaking down barriers and not working in isolation; we're just starting to reap the benefits of what Twitter has to offer," McCormick said.

Expectations, Shared Commitment, and Culture

At the very heart of the districts' reform efforts lay the assumption that improving outcomes for children requires changes in adult beliefs, values, norms, and practices. Tigard Tualatin leadership noted in its district-wide equity plan (2010, p. 7), "we must change ourselves first because WE ARE THE SYSTEM." In the Brevard Public Schools, efforts to change beliefs both contributed to and were affected by changes in practice. Randy LaRusso, Alternate Assessment Coordinator at the time of data collection, explained that, as teachers and principals became more comfortable in meeting children's needs, they asked "why not bring this kid along too?" "We're changing what people think kids with significant cognitive disabilities can and should learn," LaRusso noted, "my job every day is to convince people to give it a try, give it a go, with kids."

Similarly, in Bloom Vernon Local, a district in rural Appalachia where almost half of the student body lives below the poverty line, leaders concluded that deficit views caused damage and needed to be replaced with beliefs supporting high expectations for all students' learning. Rick Carrington—superintendent at the time of data collection—observed, "Our greatest challenge involves eliminating the mindset that because we're poor and rural, kids can't achieve." Reporting on the progress the district had made, Heidi Holstein commented that "there is no whining here about what parents do or don't do for their kids. There are conditions that may present challenges, but they can't be used as an excuse for low expectations."

Although changes in the district culture helped the districts build staff capacity for using effective and inclusive practices, improvements in the collective capacity of staff also appeared to result in a culture shift. In other words, as educators got better at addressing the needs of diverse learners, their expectations for what children could achieve, and what they could do to support them, also changed. In SAU 56 (NH), for example, the phrase "it's not what we do, it's who we are" embodied the district's commitment to a universal and inclusive approach to educating every child and the responsibility felt by the district leadership to "make sure staff understand that our beliefs and our goals are interconnected." Similarly, staff across Val Verde Unified used the phrase "the Val Verde Way" to describe the district's refusal to allow any child to fail. According to McCormick:

> When I think about the Val Verde Way, I think about our commitment to do things differently and not be willing to put up with the status quo, but instead push people and the system to focus on the best decisions for kids. It goes back to our operational imperative to ensure that kids leave the system with the best opportunity to compete for positions and for college and university entrance; it's a kind of collective efficacy and we've been able to rally around it.[3]

Variability Across Districts

While we observed a unified and sustained focus on teaching and learning in each district, coupled with structures that promoted educators' collaborative learning, the processes used to improve student outcomes varied somewhat from district to district. This variance appeared across several interrelated dimensions, such as the chosen improvement framework, organizational hierarchy, the degree to which improvement plans were formalized across the district, the degree of autonomy at the school level, and the degree of flexibility in the use of selected practices.

As noted earlier, the improvement framework (e.g., UDL, OIP, ICS, MTSS) used by the *MYN* districts varied. Some frameworks were developed by national centers (e.g., CAST) or state education agencies (e.g., OIP) and adopted as designed, while others reflected what is widely accepted as effective practice (e.g., MTSS), but still allowed for a less prescriptive approach at the district level. Some districts used the improvement framework as the primary improvement strategy whereas others used it in combination with additional strategies (e.g., MTSS and data teams). Regardless of the nature of the selected frameworks, districts used them to establish a foundation for changing practice across the district and for improving outcomes for all groups of learners.

Organizational structures varied in terms of their hierarchical layering, with such variation in part reflecting the size of the district. For example, Bloom Vernon Local—a small rural district—employed a flat organizational structure with no central office staff other than the superintendent and treasurer. In contrast, Gwinnett County Public Schools (GA), with more than 162,000 children at the time of data collection, used a hierarchical structure typical of larger districts, with clearly defined but centralized departmental responsibilities (e.g., special education, assessment, curriculum, leadership development, and so on). Two districts—the Stoughton Area School District and Val Verde Unified—changed their organizational structures to embed what had been stand-alone departments of special education within larger offices (e.g., educational services), underscoring their responsibility to improve teaching and learning for every learner. This intentional shift set the stage for involving staff at all levels of the district structure in work to design and implement challenging high-quality curriculum and instruction for all students.

Goal Development

Each district took steps to identify priorities and communicate them to all staff. However, the ways in which districts developed goals for focusing their work, used terminology to describe their goals (sometimes referred to as strategic goals, objectives, or strategies), and included specifics in their goal statements varied. For example, the Wooster City School District identified three goals (e.g., "increase performance on state standardized reading assessment by three percent annually"), with no more than three strategies (e.g., "implement a district-wide approach to balanced literacy") per goal. These strategies included both adult implementation indicators (e.g., "100% of teachers will incorporate the district balanced literacy framework within instruction") and student achievement indicators (e.g., "100% of students will demonstrate improved achievement in reading and writing on common formative assessments"). Other districts, such as Brevard Public Schools, identified "operational expectations" and district-wide initiatives (e.g., implementation of the district's K–12 Literacy Plan), or, as in the Gwinnett County Public Schools, district goals and strategic priorities (e.g., accelerate instruction not only for students who excel, but also for those who are academically behind).

In Lake Villa, district and school personnel collaborated with community members to develop a comprehensive accountability plan that included a limited number of strategic goals and a coordinated set of district-wide, central office, and school indicators. The Stoughton Area School District developed three district goals (e.g., "developing/implementing a comprehensive professional development plan aligned with the district's approach") and a limited number of strategies aligned with each goal (e.g., "We will ensure that all students are high performing learners by engaging them in rigorous standards-based curriculum, assessment, and research-based instruction for the 21st century."). SAU 56 used a somewhat different approach to focus on "big ideas" (e.g., "all students are part of ONE proactive educational system") that aligned with the system's overriding focus on improving instruction and addressing the needs of all children by providing universal instruction to all learners.

Variability at the School Level

Not only were there differences in the ways that districts used their goals to align their core work, they differed in the amount of autonomy they gave to individual schools. Wooster, for example, used a very structured approach that involved a district leadership team identifying no more than three goals and a limited number of strategies for implementation by building leadership teams and teacher-based teams in each school. Schools were not permitted to develop additional goals or strategies; however, action steps associated with each strategy could vary at the school level based on the needs of the population served. Like Wooster, Lake Villa intentionally limited the discretion afforded to individual schools by requiring each building as well as the central office to use district goals and strategies. Lake Villa required schools to identify at least two indicators related to student achievement and at least one indicator aligned with other district goals. The district delineated all activities and action steps related to each goal, including timelines, roles and responsibilities, measures, and related resources.

Brevard Public Schools required every school in the district to use district-identified goals; however, individual schools could exercise discretion in adding goals and in developing plans for reaching them. Similarly, Gwinnett County Public Schools used district goals and strategic priorities to set the direction and expectations, but each school had wide latitude in developing its own school-level aligned goals. Although most districts embedded goals within a larger, formalized improvement or strategic planning process, the smallest MYN district—Bloom Vernon Local—used a more informal approach to identify and communicate priorities that aligned with its single goal (i.e., "All students will reach high standards, at a minimum attaining proficiency or better in core academic areas") and with its district strategies (e.g., "Collect and analyze data to identify patterns, pose hypotheses, design action steps, define evaluation criteria, conduct action research projects, drive decisions about practice, and commit to results"), relying more on frequent face-to-face conversations than on written communication.

All the districts committed to district-wide continuous improvement and viewed schools within the district as part of a larger system (e.g., described above by one superintendent as a *school system* as opposed to a *federation of schools*). Yet, in addition to variance in the degree to which districts allowed individual schools to move beyond or adapt district-identified goals, the amount of school-level autonomy with regard to instructional decision-making varied as well. The largest district (Gwinnett County Public Schools) allowed for greater autonomy at the school level than the moderate-sized districts (e.g., Tigard Tualatin School District). Accordingly, the degree of discretion in terms of instructional strategy usage was limited in most districts to agreed-upon priorities determined at the district level with allowances for variance in implementation (i.e., how to teach within the constraints of a particular strategy rather than what strategy to use). "We're very tight on the non-negotiables, such as ensuring 90 minutes of reading at the elementary level across all elementary schools; this is part of the culture and we have not veered from it," assured Stuckey.

DISCUSSION

Findings from this study show that U.S. districts in different locales and with different demographics used local adaptations of a relatively con-sistent set of practices to improve academic outcomes for students with disabilities and for those from other marginalized groups. These prac-tices entailed efforts to build a foundation for the sustainable growth of student learning by focusing on fewer, more relevant goals and strategies, supported by the continuous and effective use of data. These efforts went hand-in-hand with shifts in role for principals and central office person-nel. Districts clearly defined the role of central office personnel and school principals to emphasize practices directed toward the improvement of instruction and student learning. Central office responsibility evolved from serving primarily as a compliance function for controlling the work (what one district described as a *pedestal* function) to serving as a vehicle for supporting shared understanding and implementation of core work across the district. Futhermore, the districts sought to eliminate discourse that focused on deficiencies of students, families, or communities.

Common practices across the 10 *MYN* districts correspond to recommendations from recent empirical and theoretical literature on systemic change in education (see e.g., DuFour & Marzano, 2011; Hargreaves & Fullan, 2012; Leithwood & Louis, 2012; McNulty & Besser, 2011). In all MYN cases, the district's choice to use these practices resulted from district leaders' sober acknowledgement of evident achievement gaps as well as embarrassment and moral outrage about their persistence.

One approach to discussing these findings is to portray them as exemplars of what is possible. The MYN initiative frames the case studies in this way in the various publications on the project's website (http://movingyournumbers.org/). Other "existence proofs" (also known as "proof of concept" studies or "outlier" studies) have, over the years, taken this tack also. Critics, however, argue that outliers, almost by definition, are not exemplars that most others can emulate as workable models; they are more like exceptions that test the rule (e.g., Hoffman & Rutherford, 1984; Rowan, Bossert, & Dwyer, 1983). Still, some scholars push back against such critics, drawing attention to the moral insights that studies of outliers offer and suggesting that outliers teach us about the scope of *real* possibilities. Such studies represent a bridge between theoretical alternatives and typical practices. As Bullough (2012, p. 350) argues: "attending carefully to outliers can be helpful in anticipation of what is coming and in envisioning and planning for different and possible futures."

As well as demonstrating the possibility for momentous change, outliers also illustrate what it takes to make changes of significant scope and import. But they are not replicable models. As Bullough (2012) suggests, studies of outliers offer moral exemplars, not "best practices." Instead of telling us exactly what to do in order to achieve a desired improvement, they provoke us to discover what it takes on our own. In fact, the districts that the MYN study described—even though they used relatively similar change strategies—undertook the change process as a singular journey on behalf of the particular students they serve. We might think of their efforts not so much as quests for "what works," but more as committed actions to recalibrate the district's moral compass.

Outlier districts provoke us to consider whether or not educational practice in our own schools, districts, and states is "good enough." For this reason, we might benefit from a deeper understanding of the provocations that cause outlier districts to engage in moral recalibration. What characterizes the provocations that instigate moral improvement? Why does paying attention to infant mortality rates, for example, give us sufficient motive for fighting institutional racism in the health-care system? Why does public disclosure of achievement gaps require schools, districts, and even states to change?

One fruitful place to start is the literature that considers the impact of social emotions, such as shame and embarrassment, on organizational behavior (Covaleskie, 2013; Klaassen, 2001; Tangney, Stuewig, & Mashek, 2007; Warren & Smith-Crowe, 2008). This literature dovetails to some extent with work on external and internal accountability (e.g., Fullan et al., 2015), because both bodies of literature explore the impact of social norms on the actions of individuals in organizations, such as corporations and school districts.

The literature on the moral consequences of embarrassment, in particular, helps explain why educators might use evidence of achievement gaps as a reason to change their practice. As this literature suggests, embarrassment carries moral force when it alerts us to social norms of which we were largely unaware (Warren & Smith-Crowe, 2008). Shame functions differently from embarrassment as a moral emotion, because it reminds us of moral precepts of which we *are* already aware (e.g., Tangney et al., 2007). In other words, we already know our actions are not "good enough" when we feel shame. When we feel embarrassed in a moral sense, our embarrassment is what alerts us to the fact that our actions are not "good enough."

Furthermore, even though we often accept sanctions, even severe sanctions, as just retributions for something we did about which we feel ashamed, we do not react similarly with respect to actions that result in our feeling of moral embarrassment. In the case of moral embarrassment, we read severe sanctions as punitive, not helpful (Warren & Smith-Crowe, 2008). Because evidence of our wrongdoing is news to us—after all, we have just been made aware of our moral lapse—we believe we deserve a grace period. Both intellectually and emotionally, we conclude that fairness should confer adequate time for us to recalibrate our moral compass and embed our changed understandings in new commitments and practices.

An interpretation based on understanding how moral embarrassment functions might provide a foundation on which educators and policymakers can realize possibilities for the productive interplay between external and internal accountability. Such an interpretation also anticipates dysfunctions that are likely to occur when external accountability efforts overreach. Notably, external accountability can be effective in provoking district-level self-reflection that leads to the decision to change, but it can become dysfunctional when it attempts to require such change through humiliation or coercion, or when it fails to allow the district sufficient time to make the change (see e.g., Etzioni, 2011). In order for local agents (e.g., educators in a district) to pursue a change, rather than to resist or derail it, communal norms that constitute an internal form of accountability must take over after a new moral understanding becomes widespread. The district needs time: to absorb the news, to plan meaningful and effective change, to create structures that work to sustain improved practices, and to allow district educators to adjust to a new moral imperative.

Mandatory achievement testing coupled with public reporting of performance data provides a case in point. As a form of external accountability, it can lead (and has led) districts to change practices in ways that close achievement gaps for students with disabilities and for students from other marginalized groups. Accompanied by what districts perceive to be severe sanctions or unrealistic timetables, however, it often contributes to resistance, efforts to game the system, and self-deception on the part of district personnel. Mandatory achievement testing can provoke defensiveness rather than moral embarrassment. In fact, it may actually mobilize support for prevailing practices by encouraging local agents to reframe those practices as desiderata in a *different* moral debate, for example, the debate about teacher autonomy or the debate about how parents ought to raise their children.

We also see similar dynamics among many critics of accountability testing. Their reframing of the issue diverts attention away from the question of how the State should best exercise its responsibility to promote equity. These critics change the focus of the debate to local prerogatives or children's mental health or the consequences of coercion on school districts' practices. These issues are also important; but attending to them does not advance deliberation on the merits and likely consequences of different policy options for promoting durable improvements in the nation's system of public schooling—that is, improvements positioned to produce worthy outcomes and distribute them equitably.

NOTES

1. As Stiefel and associates (2007) note, however, racial segregation interferes with subgroup analysis by race, thereby contributing to underestimates of race-based achievement gaps.
2. Data in this section come from the NCES, *Common Core of Data*.
3. In 2012, Val Verde Unified received a second annual *AP District of the Year* award for significantly broadening the pool of students participating, and earning scores of 3 or higher, in advanced placement (AP) courses. For more information, see the *8th Annual AP Report to the Nation*, February 8, 2012, The College Board.

REFERENCES

Albus, D., Lazarus, S. S., & Thurlow, M. L. (2014). *2011–12 Publicly reported assessment results for students with disabilities and ELLs with disabilities* (Technical Report 69). Minneapolis, MN: University of Minnesota, National Center on Educational Outcomes.

Ambrosio, J. (2013). Changing the subject: Neoliberalism and accountability in public education. *Educational Studies, 49*, 316–333. doi:10.1080/00131946.2013.783835

Amrein-Beardsley, A., Berliner, D. C., & Rideau, S. (2010). Cheating in the first, second, and third degree: Educators' responses to high-stakes testing. *Educational Policy Analysis Archives, 18*(14), 1–36. Retrieved from http://epaa.asu.edu/ojs/article/view/714

Aske, D. R., Connolly, L. S., & Corman, R. R. (2013). Accessibility or accountability? The rhetoric and reality of No Child Left Behind. *Journal of Economics and Economic Education Research, 14*(3), 107–118.

Au, W. (2009). Social studies, social justice: W(h)ither the social studies in high-stakes testing? *Teacher Education Quarterly, 36*(1), 43–58.

Barton, P. E., & Coley, R. J. (2010). *The black-white achievement gap: When progress stopped*. Princeton, NJ: ETS.

Belfield, C. R., & Levin, H. M. (2002). The effects of competition between schools on educational outcomes: A review for the United States. *Review of Educational Research, 72*(2), 279–341. doi:10.3102/00346543072002279

Berliner D. (2010). Are teachers responsible for low achievement by poor students? *Education Digest, 75*(7), 4–8.

Betebenner, D. W., Howe, K. R., & Foster, S. S. (2005). On school choice and test-based accountability. *Education Policy Analysis Archives, 13*(41), 1–22. Retrieved from http://epaa.asu.edu/epaa/v13n41/

Bishara, N., & Schipani, C. (2009). Strengthening the ties that bind: Preventing corruption in the executive suite. *Journal of Business Ethics, 88*, 765–780. doi:10.1007/s10551-009-0325-4

Bowen, S. K., & Rude, H. A. (2006). Assessment and students with disabilities: Issues and challenges with educational reform. *Rural Special Education Quarterly, 25*(3), 24–30. doi:10.1177/875687050602500304

Bregham, D. (2017). The governmentality of teaching and learning: Acquiescence or resistance? *Critical Studies in Teaching and Learning, 5*(1), 18–35. doi:10.14426/cristal.v5i1.105

Bullough, R. V. (2012). Against best practice: Uncertainty, outliers and local studies in educational research. *Journal of Education for Teaching, 38*, 343–357. doi:10.1080/02607476.2012.668335

Bush, B., & Smith, J. R. (2014, August 14). Your schools: Columbus: Cheating helped secure bonuses. *The Columbus Dispatch*. Retrieved from http://www.dispatch.com/content/stories/local/2014/08/14/cheating-helped-secure-bonuses.html

Carnoy, M., Elmore, R., & Sisken, L. (2003). *The new accountability: High schools and high stakes testing*. New York, NY: RoutledgeFalmer.

Centers for Disease Control and Prevention. (2011). Multiple causes of death. In *2005–2011 data: Population Reference Bureau, analysis of data from the Centers for Disease Control and Prevention, National Center for Health Statistics* (Public Use Files for 2005–2011 CD-Rom and Births: VitalStats). Washington, DC: National Center for Health Statistics. Retrieved from http://www.cdc.gov/nchs/vitalstats.htm

Chudowsky, N., Chudowsky, V., & Kober, N. (2009). *State test score trends through 2007–08, part 4: Has progress been made in raising achievement for students with disabilities?* Washington, DC: Center on Education Policy. Retrieved from http://www.cep-dc.org/displayDocument.cfm?DocumentID=321

Cimbricz, S. (2002). State-mandated testing and teachers' beliefs and practices. *Education Policy Analysis Archives, 10*(2). doi:10.14507/epaa.v10n2.2002

Cortiella, C., & Burnette, J. (2008). *Challenging change: How schools and districts are improving the performance of special education students.* New York, NY: National Center for Learning Disabilities.

Cosier, M., Causton-Theoharis, J., & Theoharis, G. (2013). Does access matter? Time in general education and achievement for students with disabilities. *Remedial & Special Education, 34*, 323–332. doi:10.1177/0741932513485448

Council of the Great City Schools. (2005-2012). *Beating the odds archive.* Retrieved from http://www.cgcs.org/Page/112

Covaleskie, J. F. (2013). *Membership and moral formation: Shame as an educational and social emotion.* Charlotte, NC: Information Age.

Covay-Minor, E., Desimone, L. M., Phillips, K. R., & Spencer, K. (2015). A new look at the opportunity-to-learn gap across race and income. *American Journal of Education, 121*, 241–269. doi:10.1086/679392

Cullen, J. B., & Reback, R. (2006). *Tinkering toward accolades: School gaming under a performance accountability system.* Cambridge, MA: National Bureau of Economic Research. Retrieved from http://www.nber.org.proxy.library.ohiou.edu/papers/w12286

Cyrenne, P., & Grant, H. (2009). University decision making and prestige: An empirical study. *Economics of Education Review, 28*, 237–248. doi:10.1016/j.econedurev.2008.06.001

Dahl, R. A. (1961). *Who governs: Power and democracy in an American city.* New Haven, CT: Yale University Press.

Darling-Hammond, L. (2007). Standards, accountability, and school reform. In C. E. Sleeter (Ed.), *Facing accountability in education: Democracy and equity at risk* (pp. 78–111). New York, NY: Teachers College Press.

Denhardt, J. V., & Denhardt, R. B. (2007). *The new public service: Serving, not steering* (expanded ed.). Armonk, NY: M.E. Sharpe.

Dorn, S. (2014). Testing like William the Conqueror: Cultural and instrumental uses of examinations. *Education Policy Analysis Archives, 22*(119), 1–16. http://dx.doi.org/10.14507/epaa.v22.1684

Dougherty, C., & Rutherford, J. (2009). *The NCEA core practice framework: An organizing guide to sustained school improvement.* Austin, TX: National Center for Educational Achievement. Retrieved from http://files.eric.ed.gov/fulltext/ED516793.pdf

DuFour, R., & Marzano, R. (2011). *Leaders of learning*. Bloomington, IN: Solution Tree.

Eccles, S. E., & Swando, J. (2009). Special education subgroups under NCLB: Issues to consider. *Teachers College Record, 111*, 2479–2504.

Etzioni, A. (2011). On communitarian and global sources of legitimacy. *Review of Politics, 73*, 105–122. doi:10.1017/S0034670510000884

Falabella, A. (2014). The performing school: The effects of market and accountability policies. *Education Policy Analysis Archives, 22*(70–72), 1–29. doi:10.14507/epaa.v22n70.2014

Figlio, D. N., & Getzler, L. S. (2002). *Accountability, ability and disability: Gaming the system*. Cambridge, MA: National Bureau of Economic Research. Retrieved from http://www.nber.org.proxy.library.ohiou.edu/papers/w9307

Foster, J. B. (2011). Education and the structural crisis of capital: The U.S. case. *Monthly Review, 63*(3), 6–37. doi:10.14452/MR-063-03-2011-07_3

Foucault, M. (1977). *Discipline and punish: The birth of the prison*. New York, NY: Pantheon.

Frankenberg, E., Siegel-Hawley, G., & Wang, J. (2011). Choice without equity: Charter school segregation. *Educational Policy Analysis Archives, 19*(1), 1–96. doi:10.14507/epaa.v19n1.2011

Frattura, E. M., & Capper, C. A. (2007). *Leading for social justice: Transforming schools for all learners*. Thousand Oaks, CA: Corwin.

Fullan, M. (2011). *Choosing the wrong drivers for whole system reform*. East Melbourne, Victoria, Australia: Center for Strategic Education Seminar Series 204.

Fullan, M., Rincon-Gallardo, S., & Hargreaves, A. (2015). Professional capital as accountability. *Education Policy Analysis Archives, 23*(15), 1–22. doi:10.14507/epaa.v23.1998

Gibson, W. J., & Brown, A. (2009). *Working with qualitative data*. Thousand Oaks, CA: SAGE.

Gonzalez, R. A., & Firestone, W. A. (2013). Educational tug-of-war: Internal and external accountability of principals in varied contexts. *Journal of Educational Administration, 51*, 383–406. doi:10.1108/09578231311311528

Gordon, L., & Morton, M. (2008). Inclusive education and school choice: Democratic rights in a devolved system. In S. L. Gabel & S. Danforth (Eds.), *Disability and the politics of education: An international reader* (pp. 237–250). New York, NY: Peter Lang.

Gordon, L., & Whitty, G. (1997). Giving the "hidden hand" a helping hand?: The rhetoric and reality of neoliberal education reform in England and New Zealand. *Comparative Education, 33*, 453–467. doi:10.1080/03050069728460

Grant, S. G. (2001). An uncertain lever: Exploring the influence of state-level testing in New York State on teaching social studies. *Teachers College Record, 103*, 398–426. doi:10.1111/0161-4681.00120

Guillot, M. C., &. Parker, G. (2010). When we really believe: How Louisiana's St. Tammany Parish school system is reconciling IDEIA with the NCLB mandate. *Educational Horizons, 88*, 231–248.

Hankes, J., Skoning, S., Fast, G., & Mason-Williams, L. (2013). Closing the math gap of Native American students identified as learning disabled. *Investigations in Mathematics Learning, 5*(3), 44–59. doi:10.1080/24727466.2013.11790326

Hargreaves, A., & Fullan, M. (2012). *Professional capital: Transforming teaching in every school*. New York, NY: Teachers College Press.

Heap, J. (2013). Ontario's Quality Assurance Framework: A critical response. *Interchange, 44*, 203–218. doi:10.1007/s10780-014-9207-5

Hehir, T. (2012). *Effective inclusive schools: Designing successful schoolwide programs*. San Francisco, CA: John Wiley & Sons/Jossey-Bass.

Hoffman, J. V., & Rutherford, W. L. (1984). Effective reading programs: A critical review of outlier studies. *Reading Research Quarterly, 20*, 79–92.

Hursh, D. (2005). The growth of high-stakes testing in the USA: Accountability, markets and the decline in educational equality. *British Educational Research Journal, 31*, 605–622. doi:10.1080/01411920500240767

Jennings, J., & Sohn, H. (2014). Measure for measure: How proficiency-based accountability systems affect inequality in academic achievement. *Sociology of Education, 87*, 125–141. doi:10.1177/0038040714525787

Kashi, T. L. (2008). Response to intervention as a suggested generalized approach to improving minority AYP scores. *Rural Special Education Quarterly, 27*(4), 37–44. doi:10.1177/875687050802700406

Killewald, A. (2013). Return to *Being Black, Living in the Red*: A race gap in wealth that goes beyond social origins. *Demography, 50*, 1177–1195. doi:10.1007/s13524-012-0190-0

Klaassen, J. A. (2001). The taint of shame: Failure, self-distress, and moral growth. *Journal of Social Philosophy, 32*, 174–196. doi:10.1111/0047-2786.00087

Klugman, B. (2011). Effective social justice advocacy: A theory-of-change framework for assessing progress. *Reproductive Health Matters, 19*(38), 146–162. doi:10.1016/S0968-8080(11)38582-5

Knapp, M. S., & Feldman, S. B. (2012). Managing the intersection of internal and external accountability: Challenge for urban school leadership in the United States. *Journal of Educational Administration, 50*, 666–694. doi:10.1108/09578231211249862

Lange, C. M., & Ysseldyke, J. E. (1998). School choice policies and practices for students with disabilities. *Exceptional Children, 64*, 255–270. doi:10.1177/001440299806400208

Lavis, J. N. (2009). How can we support the use of systematic reviews in policymaking? *Plos Medicine, 6*(11), 1–6. doi:10.1371/journal.pmed.1000141

Lee, J. (2008). Is test-driven external accountability effective? Synthesizing the evidence from cross-state causal-comparative and correlational studies. *Review of Educational Research, 78*, 608–644. doi:10.3102/0034654308324427

Leithwood, K., & Louis, K. (2012). *Linking leadership to student learning*. San Francisco, CA: John Wiley & Sons.

Loggins, S., & Andrade, F. (2014). Despite an overall decline in U.S. infant mortality rates, the black/white disparity persists: Recent trends and future projections. *Journal of Community Health, 39*, 118–123. doi:10.1007/s10900-013-9747-0

Magnuson, K. A., & Waldfogel, J. (2008). *Steady gains and stalled progress: Inequality and the black-white test score gap*. New York, NY: Russell Sage.

McKown, C. (2013). Social equity theory and racial-ethnic achievement gaps. *Child Development, 84*, 1120–1136. doi:10.1111/cdev.12033

McLaughlin, M. J., & Rhim, L. M. (2007). Accountability frameworks and children with disabilities: A test of assumptions about improving public education for all students. *International Journal of Disability, Development & Education, 54*, 25–49. doi:10.1080/10349120601149698

McNulty, B. A., & Besser, L. (2011). *Leaders make it happen! An administrator's guide to data teams*. Englewood, CO: Lead + Learn Press.

Menéndez-Viso, A. (2009). Black and white transparency: Contradictions of a moral metaphor. *Ethics and Information Technology, 11*, 155–162. doi:10.1007/s10676-009-9194-x

Müller, J., & Hernández, F. (2010). On the geography of accountability: Comparative analysis of teachers' experiences across seven European countries. *Journal of Educational Change, 11*, 307–322. doi:10.1007/s10833-009-9126-x

Nagle, K. M., McLaughlin, M. J., Nolet, V., & Malmgren, K. (2007a). *Students with disabilities and accountability reform: Findings from the California case study*. College Park, MD: Educational Policy Reform Research Institute. Retrieved from http://files.eric.ed.gov/fulltext/ED509857.pdf

Nagle, K. M., McLaughlin, M. J., Nolet, V., & Malmgren, K. (2007b). *Students with disabilities and accountability reform: Findings from the Maryland case study*. College Park, MD: Educational Policy Reform Research Institute. Retrieved from http://files.eric.ed.gov/fulltext/ED509865.pdf

Nagle, K. M., McLaughlin, M. J., Nolet, V., & Malmgren, K. (2007c). *Students with disabilities and accountability reform: Findings from the New York case study*. College Park, MD: Educational Policy Reform Research Institute. Retrieved from http://files.eric.ed.gov/fulltext/ED509866.pdf

Nagle, K. M., McLaughlin, M. J., Nolet, V., & Malmgren, K. (2007d). *Students with disabilities and accountability reform: Findings from the Texas case study*. College Park, MD: Educational Policy Reform Research Institute. Retrieved from http://files.eric.ed.gov/fulltext/ED509867.pdf

National Center for Education Statistics. (2014). *Common core of data*. Washington, DC: U.S. Department of Education. Retrieved from http://nces.ed.gov/ccd/aboutCCD.asp

Neumann, J. (2013). Teaching to and beyond the test: The influence of mandated accountability testing in one social studies teacher's classroom. *Teachers College Record, 115*(6), 1–32.

Neumeier, M. (2006). *Zag: The #1 strategy of high-performance brands*. Berkeley, CA: Peachpit.

Olsen, J. P. (2015). Democratic order, autonomy, and accountability. *Governance, 28*, 425–440. doi:10.1111/gove.12158

Park, V., Daly, A. J., & Guerra, A. W. (2013). Strategic framing: How leaders craft the meaning of data use for equity and learning. *Educational Policy, 27*, 645–675. doi:10.1177/0895904811429295

Peterson, R. (2010). The persistence of low expectations in special education law viewed through the lens of therapeutic jurisprudence. *International Journal of Law and Psychiatry, 33*, 375–397. doi:10.1016/j.ijlp.2010.09.009

Poplin, M., & Rivera, J. (2005). Merging social justice and accountability: Educating qualified and effective teachers. *Theory into Practice, 44*, 27-37. doi:10.1207/s15430421tip4401_5

Psathas, G., & Anderson, T. (1990). The "practices" of transcription in conversation analysis. *Semiotica, 78*(1-2), 75–100. doi:10.1515/semi.1990.78.1-2.75

Pullin, D. (2005). When one size does not fit all – The special challenges of accountability testing for students with disabilities. *Yearbook of the National Society for the Study of Education, 104*, 199–222. doi:10.1111/j.1744-7984.2005.00031.x

Ravitch, D. (2010). *The death and life of the great American school system: How testing and choice are undermining education.* New York, NY: Basic Books.

Rea, P. J., McLaughlin, V. L., & Walther-Thomas, C. (2002). Mainstreaming programs: Design features and effects. *Exceptional Children, 68*, 203–222. doi:10.1177/002246698501900412

Reardon, S. F. (2011). The widening academic achievement gap between the rich and the poor: New evidence and possible explanations. In R. Murnane & G. Duncan (Eds.), *Whither opportunity? Rising inequality and the uncertain life chances of low-income children* (pp. 91–116). New York, NY: Russell Sage Foundation.

Roach, A. T., Chilungu, N., La Salle, T. P., Talapatra, D., & Vignieri, M. (2009). Opportunities and options for facilitating and evaluating access to the general curriculum for students with disabilities. *Peabody Journal of Education, 84*, 511–528. doi:10.1080/01619560903240954

Rose, D. H., & Meyer, A. (2006). *A practical reader in universal design for learning.* Cambridge, MA: Harvard Education Press.

Rothstein, R. (2005). The role of schools and society in closing the achievement gap. *Principal Leadership, 5*(7), 16–21.

Rowan, R., Bossert, S. T., & Dwyer, D. (1983). Research on effective schools: A cautionary note. *Educational Researcher, 12*(4), 24–31. doi:10.3102/0013189X012004024

Rushton, J. P., & Jensen, A. R. (2005). Thirty years of research on race differences in cognitive ability. *Psychology, Public Policy, and Law, 11*, 235–294.

Samuels, C. A. (2011). Test-tampering found rampant in Atlanta system. *Education Week, 30*(36), 1–22. Retrieved from http://www.edweek.org/ew/toc/2011/07/13/index.html

Schulte, A. C., & Stevens, J. J. (2015). Once, sometimes, or always in special education: Mathematics growth and achievement gaps. *Exceptional Children, 81*, 370–387. doi:10.1177/0014402914563695

Scott, J. C. (1998). *Seeing like a state: How certain schemes to improve the human condition have failed.* New Haven, CT: Yale University Press.

Seiler, L. H. (1975). Community power structures and methods' artifacts: A reinterpretation. *Sociological Quarterly, 16*, 272–276.

Shifrer, D. (2013). Stigma of a label: Educational expectations for high school students labeled with learning disabilities. *Journal of Health & Social Behavior, 54*, 462–480. doi:10.1177/0022146513503346

Sirotnik, K. A. (Ed.). (2004). *Holding accountability accountable: What ought to matter in public education.* New York, NY: Teachers College Press.

Skrla, L., & Scheurich, J. J. (Eds.). (2004). *Educational equity and accountability: Paradigms, policies, and politics.* New York, NY: Taylor & Francis.

Sleeter, C. E. (Ed.). (2007). *Facing accountability in education: Democracy and equity at risk.* New York, NY: Teachers College Press.

Stecher, B. M., & Barron, S. (2001). Unintended consequences of test-based accountability when testing in "milepost" grades. *Educational Assessment, 7,* 259–281. doi:10.1207/S15326977EA0704_02

Stiefel, L., Schwartz, A. E., & Chellman, C. C. (2007). So many children left behind: Segregation and the impact of subgroup reporting in No Child Left Behind on the racial test score gap. *Educational Policy, 21,* 527–550. doi:10.1177/0895904806289207

Suzuki, L. A., & Valencia, R. R. (1997). Race–ethnicity and measured intelligence: Educational implications. *American Psychologist, 52,* 1103–1114. doi:10.1037/0003-066X.52.10.1103

Tangney, J. P., Stuewig, J., & Mashek, D. J. (2007). Moral emotions and moral behavior. *Annual Review of Psychology, 58,* 345–372. doi:10.1146/annurev. psych.56.091103.070145

Telfer, M., & Howley, A. (2014). Rural schools positioned to promote the high achievement of students with disabilities. *Rural Special Education Quarterly, 33*(4), 3–13. doi:10.1177/875687051403300402

Throgmorton, J. A. (1991). The rhetorics of policy analysis. *Policy Sciences, 24,* 153–179.

Thurlow, M. L. (2010). *Written testimony to the U.S. Senate Health, Education, Labor and Pensions (H.E.L.P.) Committee.* Retrieved from http://www.cehd.umn.edu/ NCEO/Presentations/ThurlowTestimony2010.pdf

Thurlow, M. L., Quenemoen, R. F., & Lazarus, S. S. (2011). *Meeting the needs of special education students: Recommendations for the Race to the Top consortia and states.* Washington, DC: Arabella Advisors.

Thurlow, M. L., & Wiley, H. I. (2006). A baseline perspective on disability subgroup reporting. *The Journal of Special Education, 39,* 246–254. doi:10.1177/00224 669060390040501

Tigard Tualatin School District 23J. (2010). *District-wide equity transformation framework.* Tigard, OR: Author.

Togneri, W., & Anderson, S. (2003). *Beyond islands of excellence: What districts can do to improve instruction and achievement in all schools.* Baltimore, MD: Learning First Alliance, Association for Supervision and Curriculum Development. Retrieved from http://www.learningfirst.org/sites/default/files/assets/biefullreport.pdf

Torff, B. (2014). Folk belief theory, the rigor gap, and the achievement gap. *Educational Forum, 78,* 174–189. doi:10.1080/00131725.2013.878424

United States Commission on Civil Rights. (2007). *Minorities in special education.* Washington, DC: Author. Retrieved from http://www.usccr.gov/pubs/ MinoritiesinSpecialEducation.pdf

U.S. Department of Education. (2013). *National Assessment of Educational Progress (NAEP), various years, 1990–2013, mathematics and reading Assessments.* Washington, DC: Institute of Education Sciences, National Center for Education Statistics. Retrieved from http://www.nationsreportcard.gov/ reading_math_2013/#/student-groups

Valencia, R. R. (2015). *Students of color and the achievement gap: Systemic challenges, systemic transformations.* New York, NY: Routledge.

Walsh, J. M. (2012). Co-teaching as a school system strategy for continuous improvement. *Preventing School Failure, 56*, 29–36. doi:10.1080/10459 88X.2011.555792

Wang, L., Beckett, G. H., & Brown, L. (2006). Controversies of standardized assessment in school accountability reform: A critical synthesis of multidisciplinary research evidence. *Applied Measurement in Education, 19*, 305–328. doi:10.1207/s15324818ame1904_5

Wang, M. C., & Baker, E. T. (1985). Mainstreaming programs: Design features and effects. *The Journal of Special Education, 19*, 503–521. doi:10.1177/002246698501900412

Warren, D. E., & Smith-Crowe, K. (2008). Deciding what's right: The role of external sanctions and embarrassment in shaping moral judgments in the workplace. *Research in Organizational Behavior, 28*, 81–105. doi:10.1016/j.riob.2008.04.004

Williams, D. T. (2003). *Closing the achievement gap: Rural schools. CSR Connection.* Washington, DC: National Clearinghouse for Comprehensive School Reform. Retrieved from https://files.eric.ed.gov/fulltext/ED478574.pdf

Yates, L. (2013). Revisiting curriculum, the numbers game and the inequality problem. *Journal of Curriculum Studies, 45*, 39–51. doi:10.1080/00220272.2 012.754949

Ydesen, C. (2013). Educational testing as an accountability measure: Drawing on twentieth-century Danish history of education experiences. *Paedagogica Historica, 49*, 716–733. doi:10.1080/00309230.2013.815235

Yi, P., & Shin, I. (2018). Multilevel relations between external accountability, internal accountability, and math achievement: A cross-country analysis. *Problems of Education in the 21st Century, 76*, 318–332.

Ysseldyke, J., Nelson, J. R., Christenson, S., Johnson, D. R., Dennison, A., Triezenberg, H., Sharpe, M., & Hawes, M. (2004). What we know and need to know about the consequences of high-stakes testing for students with disabilities. *Exceptional Children, 71*, 75–95. doi:10.1177/001440290407100105

APPENDIX
Matrix Summarizing Interview Guide

Major Category	Subcategories	Illustrative Questions
Participant information	Name Role Title	• What is your name? • What is your role? • What is your title?
District information	District characteristics Community characteristics Community description	• What is the district locale? • What is the district enrollment? • What are trends that have taken place in the community over the last few years? • What are pressing community issues?
Beliefs, values, goals	Core values Goal settings District improvements	• If you could accomplish one thing as a district, what would it be? • How does the district define student success?
Planning	Focus Preparation for change (e.g., PD) Stakeholder engagement	• In what ways has the district engaged internal and external stakeholders in the process of making/sustaining improvements in teaching and learning?
Structures	Role of different structures (e.g., the central office) New structures associated with the improvement process.	• What structures have been established/used to improve instruction and achievement?
Practices	Curriculum Instructional practices Assessment practices	• Does the district require the district-wide use of an established curriculum? • What expectations does the district have for its principals with regard to instructional practice?
Challenges	What the challenges are How the district has addressed the challenges	• What have been the biggest challenges faced by the district in making changes needed to improve instruction and achievement for all students/student groups?
Future prospects	Most significant accomplishments to date Anticipated next steps	• What has been your biggest success as a district? • What are your next steps?

Source: Telfer and Howley (2014, p. 11).

CHAPTER 7

INCLUSIVE ASSESSMENT PRACTICES

Using Formative Instructional Practices to Support the Needs of All Students

Kristall J. Graham-Day
Ohio Dominican University

Carolyn Shemwell Kaplan
St. Charles Preparatory School

Cheryl Irish
Shawnee State University

Francis J. Troyan
The Ohio State University

INTRODUCTION

Effective instruction and inclusion begin with effective assessment (Cobb, 2003; Salvia, Ysseldyke, & Witmer, 2017; Spinelli, 2002; Stecker, Fuchs, & Fuchs, 2005). To provide instruction that maximizes learning for *all*

Inclusive Education: A Systematic Perspective, pp. 135–148
Copyright © 2020 by Information Age Publishing
All rights of reproduction in any form reserved.

students, educators must first gather and analyze a variety of evidence about students' learning—evidence enabling them to understand what students know and what they are still learning, in relation to the content standards and curriculum (Chappuis, 2015; Heritage, 2013). Special education has a rich history of data collection for monitoring student progress and informing instruction and intervention (e.g., Deno, Fuchs, Marston, & Shin, 2001; Fuchs & Fuchs, 2007; McLesky et al., 2017). Many of the assessment techniques used by special education professionals as part of the IEP process are also beneficial for monitoring all students' growth. Implementing a data-driven approach that draws from a variety of assessment sources increases inclusion for students with disabilities in general education settings (Conderman & Hedin, 2012; Lingo, Barton-Arwood, & Jolivette, 2011), including settings where they are traditionally underrepresented (e.g., world language classes).

In this chapter, we discuss the Formative Instructional Practices (FIP) framework (Ohio Department of Education & Battelle for Kids, 2017) as a model for inclusive assessment practice; we also provide an example of FIP's applicability to the Integrated Performance Assessments (Adair-Hauck, Glisan, & Troyan, 2013) used in world language education. Because current educational theory and practice place a heavy emphasis on supporting students with disabilities in core content areas—especially because of testing requirements (e.g., in reading and mathematics; Kleinert, Cloyd, Rego, & Gibson, 2007)—students with disabilities have fewer opportunities to access world language education (Wight, 2015). For this reason, the authors identified a need for more meaningful inclusion in world language settings, specifically because students with disabilities are often precluded from world language classes or they receive minimal specialized support in these classes. In our view, the inclusion of students with disabilities in world language education is a social justice issue; this belief inspired us to engage in transdisciplinary collaboration and discuss issues like best practices in assessment and preparing future educators to meet the needs of all students in an inclusive setting. While this chapter contextualizes FIP in the domain of world languages, FIP's core components can be applied to all content areas.

FORMATIVE INSTRUCTIONAL PRACTICES DEFINED

FIP consists of formal and informal ways that teachers and students collect and respond to information about student learning (Ohio Department of Education & Battelle for Kids, 2017) and which enable teachers to make instructional decisions. FIP goes beyond summative and formative assessments by structuring an engaging process through which teachers identify and address gaps in student learning. Additionally, the FIP framework facilitates active student involvement in the assessment process to promote student ownership of learning.

According to Chappuis (2015), effective formative assessment includes several components that are essential to implementing FIP (Ohio Department of Education & Battelle for Kids, 2017). First, educators should create and articulate clear **learning targets** based on content standards. Learning targets are operational statements delineating what students should know and be able to do by the end of a particular learning experience. Next, teachers must decide how to **collect and document evidence of student learning** in relation to the learning targets. Typically, teachers create a variety of instructional activities that range from informal to formal, and they use student responses to these activities as data to inform future instruction. Providing **effective feedback** is also foundational to implementing FIP. Feedback should be specific, related to the articulated learning target, focused on success, provided to students as quickly as possible (i.e., immediate), and related to new learning or previous performance on the target. Finally, it is essential to **plan for student involvement** in monitoring progress toward the specified learning targets. Student involvement in FIP may be accomplished through self-monitoring, self-evaluation, or the implementation of peer tutoring models (Chan, Graham-Day, Ressa, Peters, & Konrad, 2014). These foundational elements of FIP are not new to the world of special education (Graham-Day, Fishley, Konrad, Peters, & Ressa, 2014), and FIP's core components easily align with many traditionally lauded practices in special education. Additionally, FIP can provide support to all students in any content area, including world language classes.

THE INTEGRATED PERFORMANCE ASSESSMENT (IPA) IN WORLD LANGUAGE EDUCATION

The IPA exemplifies how FIP's core components, and the inclusive practices used within the FIP framework, align with best practices in assessment for a specific content area. The IPA, a framework for classroom-based performance assessment in world language education, measures students' progress in developing proficiency across three modes of communication (Adair-Hauck et al., 2013). These modes of communication, described in the *World-Readiness Standards for Language Learning* (W-RSLL; National Standards Collaborative Board, 2015), are interpersonal, interpretive, and presentational. Intending to promote authentic language use in the world language classroom, W-RSLL reframes the traditional language skills of reading, writing, speaking, and listening within these three modes of communication. Rather than performing the four skills in isolation, authentic communication using the three modes combines multiple skills.

For instance, interpersonal communication requires both listening and speaking while presentational communication could be spoken (e.g., a speech) or written (e.g., a story). The American Council on the Teaching of Foreign Languages developed the IPA to guide teachers in the design and implementation of classroom-based assessment of these three modes of communication (Adair-Hauck et al., 2013). The assessment leads students through three consecutive performance tasks unified by a common theme (e.g., healthy eating, conserving natural resources) and progressively builds knowledge about that theme as students move through the modes of communication. After each task, teachers provide students with descriptive feedback on their performance as a means of preparing for the next task and noting their current level of performance, demonstrating how they need to build upon what they already know in order to continue developing language proficiency (Adair-Hauck et al., 2013).

A backward design approach, such as *Understanding by Design* (Wiggins & McTighe, 2005) provides strategies that are integral for linking the IPA to instructional planning. Using backward design, teachers delineate essential standards and then deconstruct them prior to planning instructional events. Kaplan, Graham-Day, and Troyan (2017) note that during this process, before teachers can develop assessments and learning activities for an instructional unit, they need first to evaluate the discipline's content standards and then develop appropriate learning targets. After completing this step, teachers can then proceed to develop appropriate assessments and instructional activities that align to those targets.

Although teachers are encouraged to use backward design, research suggests (Kaplan, 2016) that they need further guidance on how to engage with the process of instructional design, or on tools to use during this process, especially in addressing the range of standards identified by state and national stakeholders. The components of FIP (Ohio Department of Education & Battelle for Kids, 2017) and the assessment practices traditionally used by special educators are, therefore, useful for providing planning methods and instructional strategies that world language teachers and teacher candidates can use. These strategies allow teachers to produce and use assessments across a wide range of standards and thus ensure that all students' needs are met. The following section illustrates how FIP's core components can be aligned to the IPA, which promotes and deepens inclusive approaches to world language classes.

RECOMMENDATIONS FOR USING THE FIP FRAMEWORK AS AN INCLUSIVE ASSESSMENT MODEL

The theory behind FIP and, indeed, our own experiences as educators demonstrate that effective instruction requires teachers in all content areas to deconstruct standards, collect and use evidence of learning, provide feedback, and encourage student involvement. These strategies are necessary as ways to maximize the inclusion of students with learning differences. The following subsections examine these strategies individually. In each subsection we begin by discussing historically proven approaches in special education. Then, we define and describe the core components of FIP. Finally, we illustrate how the components of FIP align with an example IPA in world language education.

Deconstructing Standards

Defining target behaviors and creating measurable objectives are central parts of the work to use assessment for student growth in special education settings (Alberto & Troutman, 2013). In order to effectively measure student performance and determine if students are making progress, teachers must clearly identify what they intend to measure (Bateman & Herr, 2006). Deconstructing standards is one way to operationalize definitions of what students should be able to know and do, based on the general education curriculum. In addition to supporting accurate measurement, deconstructing standards also provides opportunities for differentiation and scaffolding, which are also common practices for supporting students with learning differences. By breaking standards into varying levels of knowledge and performance, teachers provide meaningful instruction and individualized assessments for all students. Finally, deconstructing standards also supports teachers in identifying and creating a logical progression of learning events. Providing assessment opportunities throughout the instructional unit that gradually increase in difficulty increases student success and ensures mastery of the foundational skills required to perform higher-order tasks.

As part of FIP, Konrad and associates (2014) describe an approach for standards deconstruction using the Common Core Standards; Kaplan and associates (2017) demonstrate the approach's application to world language education using the W-RSLL (National Standards Collaborative Board, 2015). Konrad and associates (2014) advocate taking the following steps to break down learning standards in order to create effective learning targets. First, teachers identify the nouns and verbs within each standard to articulate the content that students need to know (nouns) and the skills and expected level of reasoning necessary for students to demonstrate mastery (verbs). Then, after identifying the nouns and verbs, teachers classify the standard's verbs into lower- and higher-level thinking skills, thus establishing the order for introducing these skills in an instructional unit (e.g., beginning with lower-level tasks that build fluency of knowledge and skills and gradually scaffolding to higher-order skills where students can apply what they have learned). After analyzing the standards for knowledge and skills, teachers develop learning targets that represent declarative knowledge (i.e., "what students need to 'know' or 'understand' ") and/ or procedural knowledge (i.e., "what students need to 'be able to do' "; Konrad et al., 2014, p. 79). Learning targets are statements of what students should know and be able to do by the end of the learning experience. Finally, targets can be broken down even further into four distinct types: knowledge, reasoning, skill, and product targets. Teachers then apply these deconstructed standards to the IPA design process to ensure that students receive assessment at a level appropriate to their knowledge or proficiency.

Figure 7.1 offers an example of how the standards deconstruction process outlined in Konrad and associates (2014) can be applied to a world language standard (Kaplan et al., 2017). In this example, the authors deconstructed the Relating Cultural Practice to Perspectives standard within the Cultures Goal Area (National Standards Collaborative Board, 2015). For the standard, the authors highlighted several verbs (investigate, explain, and reflect on), which represent actions that students should be able to do by the end of the learning segment. Additionally, the authors highlighted nouns and/or the subject of the standards statement (in this case, the relationship between the practices and perspectives of the culture) to become familiar with what content students should know by the end of the learning segment. The authors further analyzed the standard's breadth by continuing to highlight the nouns and verbs within the sample progress indicators for intermediate learners in Grades 6 through 12. By completing Stage 1, "Getting to Know the Standards," educators begin to conceptualize the knowledge and skills that students need in relation to the identified standard (see Figure 7.1).

In Stage 2, Konrad and associates (2014) advise educators to categorize the verbs from Stage 1 into convergent (lower-order) and divergent (higher-order) skills. In the example provided, the authors considered the verbs *investigate, explain, identify, engage, demonstrate, use, suggest,* and *connect* to be lower-order skills that students use, thus demonstrating learning related to the standard. Within the original standard and indicators, the authors categorized the verbs *reflect on, analyze, role-play, adjust,* and *acknowledge* as higher-order skills. During this stage, educators continue to take the nouns into account (what students should know) while beginning to think about workable learning targets and to generate activities students will engage in during instruction.

Finally, in Stage 3, educators formulate learning targets and tasks based on the deconstructed standard (Konrad et al., 2014). They translate the convergent verbs, such as *investigate* and *demonstrate,* into knowledge and skill targets with additional descriptors that capture the nouns (content) from the standard. They also convert the divergent verbs, such as *analyze*

Cultures: Relating Cultural Practices to Perspectives
Learners use the language to *investigate*, *explain*, and *reflect on* the relationship between the practices and perspectives of the culture studied.

Stage 1: Get to Know the Standards

Sample Progress Indicators - Intermediate Learners in Middle School and High School:
- *Identify* and *analyze* cultural practices from authentic materials such as videos and news articles.
- *Engage* in conversations with native speakers *demonstrating* an awareness of how to be culturally respectful.
- *Use* formal and informal forms of address appropriately in rehearsed situations.
- *Role play* culturally appropriate interactions with shopkeepers, ticket sellers, waiters, bus and taxi drivers, etc. in the target culture.
- Begin to *adjust* language and message to *acknowledge* audiences with different cultural backgrounds.
- *Suggest* cultural triangles with reasons *connecting* practices to associated products and perspectives.

Stage 2: Identify Level of Thinking Skills

Nouns (content)	Verbs (skills/"level of reasoning")	
Relationship between practices and perspective of culture studied, Cultural practices, Awareness of how to be culturally respectful, Formal/informal forms of address, Culturally appropriate interactions, Language, Message, Cultural triangles with reasons, Products, Perspectives.	Convergent (Lower Order): Investigate, Explain, Identify, Engage, Demonstrate, Use, Suggest, Connect	Divergent (Higher Order): Reflect on, Analyze, Role play, Adjust, Acknowledge

Stage 3: Develop Learning Targets

Sample Targets

Knowledge	Reasoning	Skill	Product
• Consult authentic materials to **investigate** practices and perspectives of the target culture, and their relationships. • **Identify** practices and perspectives and their relationships. • **Explain** practices and perspectives, and their relationships. • **Use** formal and informal forms of address appropriately in a skit.	• **Analyze** how cultural practices are described in an online news article. • **Reflect on** (in a conversation with a peer) the relationship of the practices and perspectives of the target culture. • **Suggest** (in writing) a cultural triangle with reasons **connecting** practices to products and perspectives.	• **Demonstrate** awareness of how to be culturally respectful when **engaging** in conversation with a native speaker (in a classroom in Mexico) about practices and perspectives in their country, and **adjust** language/message in a way that **acknowledges** the speaker's cultural background.	• **Role play** culturally appropriate interactions in a skit with peers.

Source: Adapted from "Starting at the end: Deconstructing standards as planning's first step," by C. S. Kaplan, K. J. Graham-Day, and F. J. Troyan, 2017, *The Language Educator*, 12, p. 39. Copyright 2017 by the American Council on the Teaching of Foreign Languages

Figure 7.1. Unpacking World-Readiness Standards for Learning Languages: Relating Cultural Practices to Perspectives Using the Sample Progress Indicators for Intermediate Learners in Middle and High School.

and *role-play*, into reasoning and product targets and include the nouns (content) from the standard. This stage produces four distinct levels of learning targets that assist educators in providing a continuum of access to the standard for all learners. By having a variety of options for standards-related targets and tasks, educators can more effectively differentiate learning and meet the varying needs of their students.

Collecting and Documenting Evidence

As a part of special education programming, ongoing progress-monitoring remains crucial for ensuring that students with disabilities make adequate progress toward reaching their IEP goals and objectives (McLeskey et al., 2017). By creating measurable targets through the standards deconstruction process, teachers can design multiple formative assessments that support the success of all students on summative assessments in the general education curriculum. The implementation of various formative assessments not only helps teachers and students monitor progress toward meeting the learning targets, it allows for students to engage in multiple practice opportunities with varied response requirements. Practicing targeted skills across various tasks is a common method for increasing generalization, which is an important component in effectively assessing and instructing students with learning differences. In sum, after deconstructing standards and identifying a range of targets, effectively creating and documenting evidence of student learning serves several important purposes in an inclusive classroom: (a) making expectations clear to students; (b) increasing collaboration amongst teachers through common assessments grounded in the curriculum; (c) supporting varied practice opportunities using diverse responses to increase generalization; and, most importantly, (d) setting the stage for effective formative assessment to increase success on summative assessments (Chappuis, 2015).

Within the FIP framework, teachers must decide how to collect and document evidence of student learning after articulating the learning targets and lesson objectives discussed in the previous subsection (Joseph et al., 2014). The process of developing assessments makes expectations clear to students and other teachers on the team. FIP relies on various evaluation methods and types of evidence to gauge student progress toward the learning targets. For example, teachers might create rubrics to evaluate products, collect observational data on students' learning behaviors, or have students complete a teacher-made test (Stiggins & Chappuis, 2008). Ultimately, within FIP, teachers select multiple ways to collect and document evidence of student learning as it is related to the identified target. In addition to these methods and assessments, various modes of responding across many performance levels provide a means for incorporating the principles of Universal Design for Learning (UDL; CAST, 2008).

Sample formative assessments for the identified world language standard (as described in Figure 7.1) can be found in Table 7.1. To prepare for a summative IPA, a world language educator employs several formative assessment strategies where s/he collects evidence of student learning in relation to the standard and the final assessment for the learning segment. For example, after reading an authentic text, students might respond to comprehension questions as a way to demonstrate learning. Comprehension questions include a variety of items that require students to use knowledge, reasoning, and skills. A world language educator then analyzes student responses to determine their current levels of performance, in relation to the continuum of targets identified in Figure 7.1. Other examples include having students complete either a condensed version of the summative IPA or brief entrance/exit slips; these allow the teacher to gather information about current levels of performance and, more importantly, to guide subsequent instruction prior to the summative evaluation.

Table 7.1.
Example Tasks Corresponding to FIP Core Components

FIP Core Component	Examples From Instructional Unit Leading to IPA
Collecting and documenting evidence	• Comprehension questions related to an interpretive reading of an authentic text (i.e., a text written by native speakers, for native speakers). • "Condensed IPA" Formative interpretive reading task focused on an authentic text. • Entrance slips, such as a contextualized cloze activity to verify students' understanding of grammatical concepts required to understand the text type used in the IPA tasks.
Providing feedback to students	• Using rubrics with descriptive levels of performance for interpretive reading tasks that focus on the language, content, and organizational features of the text type(s) in the IPA tasks. • Providing written feedback to students following completion of IPA tasks.
Implementing strategies to involve students in learning	• Teacher designs a unit based on an authentic scenario (i.e., how to spend a gap year between high school and college) and articulates the ultimate learning targets clearly to students. • Teacher shows students the "Can Do" statements from a lesson and asks them to complete an exit slip in which they circle the red, yellow, or green lights on a traffic signal to indicate "Stop (I'm totally confused); Proceed with caution (I could use more clarification on...); or Go (I'm ready to move on)." • Students engage in self-evaluation and peer review of instructional activities (e.g., using the summative rubrics to evaluate their work, and monitor progress).

Feedback

Giving effective feedback is an essential component of instruction for all students, and especially for students with learning differences (Hattie, 2012). Feedback is the information provided to a student or teacher about his or her performance with the goal of improving future performance (Chappuis, Stiggins, Chappuis, & Arter, 2012). A wealth of research demonstrates that giving effective performance feedback has a significant impact on student learning when such feedback includes critical components (Hattie & Timperley, 2007). In order to provide effective feedback, teachers must analyze student work samples and responses to determine what type of feedback would be meaningful. Common practices in special education—analyzing student work and collecting data—provide teachers with important information on how to support student learning. Error analysis, for example, yields valuable information with regard to common misconceptions, and identifying performance patterns for individuals and groups of students is a powerful assessment tool for informing the next instructional steps (McLeskey et al., 2017). Linking feedback to learning goals further reinforces a lesson's big ideas so that students maintain a clear understanding of the instruction's underlying purpose. Explicitly noting what students do well helps to motivate their ongoing learning and facilitates their continued success (Chappuis, 2015). In addition to discussing strengths, giving students steps for improvement also supports motivation and progress.

Another highly effective mechanism for giving feedback involves providing students with rubrics that include descriptive performance levels (Gallavan & Kottler, 2009; Joseph et al., 2014). Descriptive rubrics, for example, clearly define the important attributes of a skilled performance, and using these rubrics shows students the teacher's evaluation criteria and their performance in relation to those criteria. For the IPA, a world language educator uses the recommended IPA rubrics (Adair-Hauck et al., 2013) to describe student performance expectations in relation to language function, text type, communication strategies, comprehensibility, impact, and language control. When evaluating student work, a teacher uses the rubric to clearly designate individual students' strengths and areas for improvement based on these universal descriptors.

Student Involvement

As a field, special education has historically advocated for student involvement in the IEP process (Test et al., 2004), transition planning (Wehmeyer & Lawrence, 1995), and the commitment to self-determination skills (Wehmeyer, Agran, & Hughes, 1998). FIP extends student ownership of special education into more traditional content classroom settings by implementing strategies for student involvement in the assessment process. Ultimately, as educators, we want to prepare our students to be independent and self-determined adults, and this is a perspective we can model through inclusive assessment approaches such as FIP. As previously mentioned, Chan and associates (2014) discuss various evidence-based strategies for student ownership including self-monitoring, self-evaluation, and peer tutoring. Teachers can create supplemental materials to actively engage students in evaluating their own progress against specified learning targets (Stiggins & Chappuis, 2011). Students can also learn to use assessment data to set goals for improvement and monitor their own progress. Finally, as part of the new learning standards, FIP emphasizes teaching students how to collaborate. Student involvement in FIP is a logical way to teach students how to provide feedback to one another and foster collaboration skills.

Strategies for increasing student involvement in the world language IPA can be seen in Table 7.1. Increasing student involvement does not need to be a cumbersome activity for teachers. For example, using the standards deconstruction process described earlier in this chapter, teachers identify learning targets for the instructional unit. Simply articulating and posting these learning targets is one easy way to get students invested in learning course content (Konrad et al., 2014). In addition to stating and posting targets, teachers can ask students to evaluate their progress in relation to the targets using quick formative activities in which students rate their levels of understanding and comfort with the material. Finally, there is a push to engage students in collaborative activities that prepare them to work as part of a team in their future places of employment. Making time for peer collaboration and peer review activities not only increases student involvement in learning, but also reinforces the importance of collaboration skills. Using the IPA example, a teacher can devote class time for students to evaluate each other's work using the same rubric that the teacher uses for the summative assessment.

CONCLUSION

The components of FIP closely relate to many of the traditionally used evidence-based practices in special education. Within the IEP process, special education professionals identify measurable goals and objectives, determine how to collect evidence and monitor progress on those goals, provide feedback to support student growth toward their goals, and engage students in the IEP process to promote independence. The FIP framework includes all of these components, which can be applied to assessment practices in *all* content areas. The world language IPA example discussed here only scratches the surface of how FIP can enhance assessment practices at all levels in general education settings. By deconstructing standards and creating clear learning targets, collecting and documenting evidence of student learning, providing feedback, and involving students in the assessment process, educators can reach more students in the general education setting. Including more students in general education classes (e.g., world languages) addresses social justice issues within our schools and ultimately provides more equitable access for all students.

REFERENCES

Adair-Hauck, B., Glisan, E., & Troyan, F. (2013). *Implementing integrated performance assessment.* Alexandria, VA: American Council on the Teaching of Foreign Languages.

Alberto, P., & Troutman, A. (2017). *Applied behavior analysis for teachers* (9th ed.). Boston, MA: Pearson.

Bateman, B., & Herr, C. (2006). *Writing measurable IEP goals and objectives* (2nd ed.). Verona, WI: Attainment.

CAST. (2008). *Universal design for learning guidelines version 1.0.* Wakefield, MA: Author.

Chan, P. E., Graham-Day, K. J., Ressa, V. A., Peters, M. T., & Konrad, M. (2014a). Beyond involvement: Promoting student ownership of learning in classrooms. *Intervention in School and Clinic, 50,* 105–113. doi:10.1177/1053451214536039

Chappuis, J. (2015). *Seven strategies of assessments for learning* (2nd ed.). Boston, MA: Pearson.

Chappuis, J., Stiggins, R., Chappuis, S., & Arter, J. (2012). *Classroom assessment for student learning: Doing it right, using it well.* Boston, MA: Pearson.

Cobb, C. (2003). Effective instruction begins with purposeful assessment. *The Reading Teacher, 57,* 386–388.

Conderman, G., & Hedin, L. (2012). Purposeful assessment practices for co-teachers. *Teaching Exceptional Children, 44*(4), 18–27. doi:10.1177/004005991204400402

Deno, S. L., Fuchs, L. S., Marston, D. B., & Shin, J. (2001). Using curriculum-based measurement to develop growth standards for students with learning disabilities. *School Psychology Review, 30,* 507–524.

Fuchs, L. S., & Fuchs, D. (2007). A model for implementing responsiveness to intervention. *Teaching Exceptional Children, 39,* 14–20. doi:10.1177/004005990703900503

Gallavan, N. P., & Kottler, E. (2009). Constructing rubrics and assessing progress collaboratively with social studies students. *Social Studies, 100,* 154–159.

Graham-Day, K. J., Fishley, K. M., Konrad, M., Peters, M. T., & Ressa, V. A. (2014). Formative instructional practices: How core content teachers can borrow ideas from IDEA. *Intervention in School and Clinic, 50,* 69–75. doi:10.1177/1053451214536041

Hattie, J. (2012). *Visible learning for teachers*. New York, NY: Routledge.

Hattie, J., & Timperley, H. (2007). The power of feedback. *Review of Educational Research, 77*, 81–112. doi:10.3102/003465430298487

Heritage, M. (2013). Gathering evidence of student understanding. In J. H. McMillan (Ed.), *Handbook on classroom assessment* (pp. 179–196). Los Angeles, CA: SAGE.

Joseph, L. M., Kastein, L. A., Konrad, M., Chan, P. E., Peters, M. T., & Ressa, V. A. (2014). Collecting and documenting evidence: Methods for helping teachers improve instruction and promote academic success. *Intervention in School and Clinic, 50*, 86–95. doi:10.1177/1053451214536043

Kaplan, C. S. (2016). Alignment of world language standards and assessment: A multiple case study. *Foreign Language Annals, 49*, 502–529. doi:10.1111/flan.12220

Kaplan, C. S., Graham-Day, K. J., & Troyan, F. J. (2017). Starting at the end: Deconstructing standards as planning's first step. *The Language Educator, 12*, 38–41.

Kleinert, H. L., Cloyd, E., Rego, M., & Gibson, J. (2007). Students with disabilities: Yes, foreign language instruction is important. *Teaching Exceptional Children, 39*, 24–29. doi:10.1177/004005990703900304

Konrad, M., Keesey, S., Ressa, V. A., Alexeeff, M., Chan, P. E., & Peters, M. T. (2014). Setting clear learning targets to guide instruction for all students. *Intervention in School and Clinic, 50*, 76–85. doi:10.1177/1053451214536042

Lingo, A. S., Barton-Arwood, S. M., & Jolivette, K. (2011). Teachers working together: Improving learning outcomes in the inclusive classroom-practical strategies and examples. *Teaching Exceptional Children, 43*(3), 6–13. doi:10.1177/004005991104300301

McLeskey, J., Barringer, M-D., Billingsley, B., Brownell, M., Jackson, D., Kennedy, ... Ziegler, D. (2017). *High-leverage practices in special education*. Arlington, VA: Council for Exceptional Children & CEEDAR Center.

National Standards Collaborative Board. (2015). *World-readiness standards for learning languages* (4th ed.). Retrieved from https://www.actfl.org/sites/default/files/pdfs/World-ReadinessStandards forLearningLanguages.pdf

Ohio Department of Education & Battelle for Kids. (2013). *FIP your school*. Retrieved from http://portal.battelleforkids.org/FIPOhio/what-is-fip

Salvia, J., Ysseldyke, J. E., & Witmer, S. (2017). *Assessment in special and inclusive education* (13th ed.). Boston, MA: Cengage.

Spinelli, C. G. (2002). *Classroom assessment for students with special needs in inclusive settings*. Upper Saddle River, NJ: Merrill Prentice Hall.

Stecker, P. M., Fuchs, L. S., & Fuchs, D. (2005). Using curriculum-based measurement to improve student achievement: Review of research. *Psychology in the Schools, 42*, 795–819. doi:10.1002/pits.20113

Stiggins, R. J., & Chappuis, J. (2008). Enhancing student learning. *District Administration*, 43–44. Retrieved from https://www.districtadministration.com/article/enhancing-student-learning

Stiggins, R. J., & Chappuis, J. (2011). *An introduction to student-involved assessment for learning*. Boston, MA: Pearson.

Test, D. W., Mason, C., Hughes, C., Konrad, M., Neale, M., & Wood, W. M. (2004). Student involvement in individualized education program meetings. *Exceptional Children, 70*, 391–412. doi:10.1177/001440290407000401

Wehmeyer, M. L., Agran, M., & Hughes, C. (1998). *Teaching self-determination to students with disabilities: Basic skills for successful transition.* Baltimore, MD: Brookes.

Wehmeyer, M., & Lawrence, M. (1995). Whose future is it anyway? Promoting student involvement in transition planning. *Career Development and Transition for Exceptional Children, 18,* 69–83. doi:10.1177/088572889501800202

Wiggins, G., & McTighe, J. (2005). *Understanding by design* (expanded 2nd ed.). Alexandria, VA: Association for Supervision and Curriculum Development.

Wight, M. S. (2015). Students with learning disabilities in the foreign language learning environment and the practice of exemption. *Foreign Language Annals, 48*, 39–55. doi:10.1111/flan.12122

SECTION IV INTRODUCTION

INCLUSIVE SCHOOL LEADERSHIP

Schools have long been perceived as institutions that foster social cohesion in a democracy. They offer a common context for learning. This context, however, serves some students better than it serves others, in part because it is not as commonly shared as it should be. Nevertheless, students' school and classroom experiences can have a greater influence on their academic performance than such important family characteristics as economic status. Classroom instruction is one of the most significant influences on students' achievement, and school leadership also exerts a significant influence. The pivotal role of leadership in schools today is to improve the common context for the betterment of all students. Section IV underlines the characteristics of good leadership to this end.

Mary Heather Munger and Elena Andrei's "The Core Work of Educational Leadership: Using Formative Instructional Practices to Support the Needs of All Students" explores the implications of school improvement efforts toward inclusive education in their interview with Brian McNulty. Dr. McNulty discusses successful strategies used in districts and schools that are making a focused commitment to collaborative inquiry along with other improvement strategies aimed to improve instruction and, through improved instruction, outcomes for all students.

In "Building Capacity for All Learners at All Levels Through Inclusive Educational Practices," Chad Wyen and Krista Wagner examine Mad River Local Schools' interpretation of inclusive education practice to demonstrate the importance of changing the mindset of school leaders and other educators so that they see their work not in terms of individuals but as collaborative teams and networked communities of practice. Wyen and

Wagner emphasize the importance of providing PK–12 students a deeper, more focused educational experience with an emphasis on relevant skills, in part through addressing the challenges of shifting students' understanding of their learning abilities from a fixed mindset to a growth mindset.

In "Inclusive Education Leadership: Meeting the Needs of a Diverse Society," Roger Morris and Moses Rumano describe a restructured principal preparation program at Malone University. The restructured program aims to help educators become leaders who understand and support the use of inclusive practices. The authors explain the collaborative processes used to develop the restructured program and how professors, principals, superintendents, and students provided significant input into the redesign and creation of the restructured program.

CHAPTER 8

THE CORE WORK OF EDUCATIONAL LEADERSHIP

Using Formative Instructional Practices to Support the Needs of All Students

Mary Heather Munger
University of Findlay

Elena Andrei
Cleveland State University

A TEACHER OF LEADERS

Brian McNulty is currently a partner at Creative Leadership Solutions. He has served as the Vice President for Leadership Development at the Leadership and Learning Center and as the Vice President for Field Services at Mid-Continent Research for Education and Learning (McREL) International. He is the author of over 40 publications, such as *Leaders Make It Happen! An Administrator's Guide to Data Teams* (McNulty & Besser, 2011) and *School Leadership That Works* (Marzano, Waters, & McNulty, 2005).

Inclusive Education: A Systematic Perspective, pp. 151–164
Copyright © 2020 by Information Age Publishing
All rights of reproduction in any form reserved.

His interest in inclusive practices and leadership stems from his extensive work experience. McNulty began his career as a preschool special education teacher in Washington, DC. Early in his career, he also ran a fully inclusive preschool program at the National Children's Center, a demonstration center for inclusive practices. After working for George Washington University's Regional Resource Center, he moved to Colorado to be the state's first Early Childhood Special Education Coordinator and to continue to teach and model inclusive practices. McNulty continued to advance in his career, demonstrating best practices as a Special Education Director and Assistant Commissioner in the Colorado Department of Education, and as the Assistant Superintendent for the Commerce City schools in Colorado.

Brian McNulty's work in PK–12 environments has always involved leadership that promotes inclusive education and promotes students' success. His writings, as well as his work as a consultant to education projects, contribute to more inclusive and equitable education in PK–12 schools. McNulty emphasizes the need for school leaders to focus on the growth of all learners by (a) leading teacher learning and development (Robinson, 2011), (b) developing strategies for distributed leadership (Leithwood & Seashore Louis, 2012), and (c) combining classroom observations with coaching (Goddard, Goddard, Kim, & Miller, 2015; Leithwood & Seashore Louis, 2012).

McNulty's efforts to promote inclusive practice have involved collaborations with Deborah Telfer and Stephen Barr. One such project, with statewide scope and a relatively long duration, was the development of the Ohio Improvement Process (OIP). McNulty's role on the project was to provide relevant research to demonstrate the "why" behind the OIP as well as to support efforts to implement it. He also worked with the Buckeye Association of School Administrators to create the Leadership Framework of the Ohio Leadership Advisory Council (OLAC). This framework drew on systematic research and other significant evidence to define what leadership practices, rather than traits or attributes, should look like for district, school, and classroom leaders. For McNulty and the others who collaborated on this work, the OIP and the OLAC Framework are part of the same effort. McNulty, in fact, views the OIP as Ohio's approach to implementing the OLAC framework.

As the lead trainer for the Ohio Leadership for Inclusion, Implementation, & Instructional Improvement (OLi[4]) program,[1] a program that works with cohorts of principals across Ohio, McNulty reviews the research on inclusive leadership practices. These practices promote better and more equitable outcomes for all students. McNulty develops content based on this research and shares that content with participating principals as well as with the leadership coaches who are assigned to provide one-on-one support to the principals.

The OLi[4] project defines these practices in operational terms. Notably, effective leadership practices are conceptualized within two "buckets" of work: first, work with collaborative teams and, second, observation of and dialog with individual teachers. This work depends on using practices from the project's six leadership domains:

- Visioning. The principal uses district and school non-negotiables to set specific achievement targets for all students and ensures the consistent use of evidence-based instructional strategies in all classrooms in order to reach those targets. Visioning focuses on the "why" of the work and helps to foster a collaborative environment where all personnel are learners.
- Using data well. The principal, in league with the Building Leadership Team (BLT), uses data to make effective decisions and helps teachers do the same. The principal and BLT examine adult performance data in conjunction with student achievement data; they closely and continually monitor the impact of their actions via data-rich discussions in BLT and Teacher Based Team (TBTs) meetings.
- Using research and evidence to guide instruction. The principal and BLTs guide teachers in their selection and effective use of evidence-based instructional practices for diverse learners.
- Sharing leadership. The principal shares leadership with teachers based on their expertise. The principal engages teachers, through the TBT and BLT structures, in collaborative problem-solving and other types of collaborative learning; principal leadership is a necessary condition to develop teacher collaboration and improved student outcomes (Goddard et al., 2015).
- Coaching teaching. The principal monitors teaching to ensure its effectiveness. The principal calls into question teaching practices that seem ineffective; time spent directly coaching teachers is positively associated with achievement gains and school improvement (Grissom, Loeb, & Master, 2013).
- Reflecting on practice. The principal reflects on his or her own practice. The principal models and encourages self-reflection, active learning, and the application of that learning (McNulty, 2017).

Serving in multiple positions within the field of K–12 education and working as an educational leadership consultant over the years are experiences that have given Brian knowledge and insights that make him uniquely qualified to advise schools and districts about how to become more inclusive. McNulty describes doing "the right work." He continually asks, "Where do leaders get the most return for their efforts and, therefore, where should they be spending their time?" The interview presented here (see Interview with Brian McNulty below) explores eight topics related to best practices in inclusive education. These include: (a) priorities and vision for school improvement, grounded in research-based practice; (b) inclusive education that serves all students; (c) types of data and how to use them; (d) strategies for using research to drive action in schools; (e) shared or distributed school leadership; (f) coaching and co-teaching; (g) reflection; and (h) commitment to school improvement.

INTERVIEW WITH BRIAN MCNULTY[2]

Author 1: You define a specific set of priorities to shape school improvement. Can you talk a little about how these elements work together to form a cohesive foundation for school improvement with inclusive education as the goal? What was the vision behind the work, and how did research inform your vision and work?

> McNulty: Vision evolves. It evolves over time as it bumps up against reality. With OLAC, we started with a review of the research regarding what is known about leadership. We were trying to look at teacher leadership, principal (i.e., school-level) leadership, and district-level leadership. We brought all of the research that we could possibly find to the members of OLAC. We tried to approach it in terms of what practices are effective that result in better outcomes for all students.

> Another project I was privileged to worked on had an influence on my vision. I worked on this project, which was called Moving Your Numbers (MYN; Howley & Howley, 2013; Telfer, 2011) with Deb Telfer. She studied 10 districts around the country, all of which had made significant gains in performance for all of their students. This allowed us to examine the practices used to improve outcomes for all students, including those identified as having disabilities. My vision of what districts can do was influenced by seeing what these 10 districts had done.

Author 1: How is inclusive education visible in this work and what case can you make for the need for inclusive education to be at the forefront of educators' minds?

The push ever since the No Child Left Behind (NCLB) federal education law has been around [is for] measures of student performance. We can argue about the assessment measures, but there is always going to be some measure of student performance because of the need for accountability associated with the amount of money we spend in education. If there is going to be a measure of student performance, then, from day one, the issue has been, "What about subgroup performance?" This issue has risen in importance since subgroup performance has been measured, and that has been since NCLB came on the scene. When we looked at subgroup performance, the group of students that was always performing the lowest was students with disabilities. However, we know, again from the MYN research, and from other people's research, that there were districts all over the country that had increased the performance of students with disabilities. One of those districts that we worked with was Norfolk, Virginia. As a district, Norfolk had out-perform[ed] their suburban counterparts in terms of all of their students. Some schools in Norfolk were 100, 100, 100 schools: 100% minority, 100% free and reduced lunch, and 100% proficient. We sent people from Ohio's Educational Service Centers to Norfolk to observe their schools. Their primary improvement strategies were (a) using effective teacher teams and (b) focusing on all students—that was the key.

Author 1: Another priority you mention is using data well.

Data is at the core of the teacher team work. The teams get teachers to examine specific teaching practices closely by examining a practice's impact on student learning. Student work can be one of the best forms of data if it helps us to know what students do and don't understand. The second-best form of data is going to be some form of formative assessment, with formative meaning it gives more feedback to the teachers. We are trying to get teacher teams to collect data that give them more information about the impact of their teaching. Which teacher teams are being effective? What practices could they share that they have found to be effective…. It is important to share what works across the whole school and to share those practices across the district. Data are the foundation for all of that work.

Another piece of data is implementation data. This is sometimes poorly received because it is associated with monitoring. At McREL, we did a book called Classroom Instruction That Works (Marzano,

Pickering, & Pollock, 2001). Many people said they were using the practices in the book. Yet, we would go into schools and no one was using any of the practices. They knew them, they understood them, but they did not use them. There is a big difference between knowing and doing, and this is often referred to as the "knowing-doing gap."

All leadership teams need to monitor the implementation of the work in a way that is helpful to the teams and to the work. Monitoring should be seen as feedback to the system on how well people are implementing the work and what helps them to do it better. If we think of monitoring as feedback, and that the goal of the system is to help teachers and administrators get the supports they need to implement the work better and deeper, then monitoring-as-feedback is critically important. Monitoring-data are important because they provide a metric of how well we are implementing. If an implementation isn't going well, what do people need to do to change that? If they are given support, a check needs to be done to make sure that the assistance really helps them. And, if it does not, it is time to regroup and examine why. All of that is data.

In fact, one important rule of thumb is this: Do not expect changes in student performance data until you have better adult implementation data. People tend to begin by measuring the student performance data, but that is outcome data. There is also input data, which is how well a practice is being implemented. The first source of data should come from monitoring what the educators are doing. And those data should be used to provide support to educators to help them implement better. Implementation data is about the adult practices. The maxim is, "Don't expect changes in outcomes if you haven't changed adult practices."

Author 1: Research and evidence are other priorities that you list.

Everything should be grounded in the research; no one has to start from square one. At McREL, we did the first meta-analytics study that I knew of on teaching practices. When we worked on Classroom Instruction That Works (Marzano et al., 2001), we discovered nine practices that we found that worked well. Everybody loved it because it was simple. Of course, most people did not actually do it, but they understood. I have always started from the idea that we can learn a lot from the research. In his powerful *book Visible Learning* (2009), John Hattie presented an incredible plethora of meta-analytic, research-based practices (teaching practice, school level practices, and home practices.) He compiled 20 years of meta-analytic research. The problem is that people misuse the research. I worked with one district in the state of Ohio whose principal told the teachers to start at the top of Hattie's list, the one with the highest effect size, and then work their way down that list. This was a completely unreasonable request to make of teachers. Many of the practices that have the highest effect sizes are really multiple practices that have been grouped together and then studied as a single set of practices. They are really multiple practices, each contributing to the large effect size. Consequently, they are complex and difficult to learn and do. Schools should start instead with their biggest teaching and learning need. Then they should go to the research and find a practice that will address that need. Next, they should study and implement the practice deeply. The research should act as the foundation.

Now, having said all that, can you study teacher practices that teachers are using now and create your own research? The answer is yes. In effect, it is action research on the part of teacher teams. When teams begin, however, most teachers do not feel comfortable putting their own practices on the table because that is too threatening. Instead, teams can start with a simple list of three to five practices that all team members are going to learn and study. Begin with a practice, decide on the evidence that will be collected to demonstrate whether or not it is actually being implemented, and then decide on the right evidence in terms of measuring impact on student performance. Do you have benchmark assessments? Can you use them for this purpose? Would it be reasonable to assume that the teams that are making significant progress would see some changes on those benchmark assessments? These determinations should be made by the BLT.

We originally said principals and BLT members should go into teacher teams and use the TBT rubric to assess where they are and give the teams some feedback. Teachers said that having BLTs use the rubric felt too threatening. So, since the rubric outlines the five- step process, we changed our recommendation to suggest to BLT members that they just keep this process in their mind when observing the TBT. Ask the teams, "What is it that you need?" Responses to this question can be another form of evidence. If it looks like a teacher team is struggling with student work, ask, "What would help you analyze that student work?" Probing for what people actually need, then giving them whatever they need, and then observing them again and reflecting, "What's the evidence that what we provided them with actually made the team stronger?" Then go back and repeat the cycle again.

In OLi⁴, we are encouraging principals and BLTs to complete two of these cycles, in the first and second semesters, so that they know where their teams are. The BLT should accurately know where its teams are and what they need. They should know what supports they have been given and what actually helped them. All of these are forms of evidence that are useful for moving the work forward. You have to have changes in practice before you are going to see changes in student performance.

Author 2: How do you share leadership with all stakeholders and what are some strategies that you would share with others so they might replicate these efforts?

The work that we do in the OLi⁴ project operates from the premise that distributed or shared leadership matters more than any form of single leadership. This is a finding from Leithwood and Seashore Louis (2012) in *Linking Leadership to Student Learning*. We also reviewed work by Vivianne Robinson, who did a more recent meta-analytic study of principal leadership and wrote a book called *Student-Centered Leadership* (2011). This is a book we share with the principals and we highlight the biggest finding: The largest effect size for principal leadership was an effect size of 0.84. A 0.84 effect size for principal leadership impacting student achievement is a hugely high effect size. The principal leadership actions that had an effect size of 0.84 came from principals leading teacher learning and development. So, it is the principal visibly leading the learning alongside their teachers, which is essentially shared leadership. This means that the principal is leading the learning, demonstrating that they are learning themselves in front of their own staff, not that they have all the answers.

Principals can be the most charismatic incredible leaders in the world, but when they leave, the school is going to go back to where it was unless they developed the capacity of their staff to do the work themselves in teacher teams and BLTs. This means developing lots of leaders across the school who can lead the improvement work. The teacher teams are all about empowering teachers, and by using teacher teams we are actually saying we value and trust the knowledge of teachers. We believe that we have all of the answers to all of our problems in our schools, but we do not have good ways of accessing this knowledge. The teacher teams are meant to develop a process where they test teaching practices and see what they can learn from them, and then we want those teams to share these effective practices with other teams. We do that kind of school-wide sharing through the BLT.

To all this, we need to add parent involvement, which is a hugely important piece of the work. While school leadership teams are focused on school improvement and instructional practices, it certainly would be fine to have a few parents involved on that committee, but other ways to involve parents—lots more parents—are also critical, but they also involve more work. For example, I worked in the poorest district in the state of Colorado, where over half of the parents were non-English speakers. We had huge challenges in engaging our families and helping them with basic needs. In these situations, schools really need community wraparound services for their families. In the case of this district, we integrated mental health services and had health clinics in our schools. We embedded a variety of other community services into the schools because we felt that if we were going to meet the needs of our parents and families we could not just say, "Come to a parent meeting." Comprehensive community wraparound services require schools and other agencies to all work together to serve their families. One other thing that we did was to have all of our presentations to families done in English and Spanish, so families could participate more fully. The point I am trying to make here is that when working with low-income families, keep in mind that they need a variety of wraparound community supports. Schools need to be the hub of these supports.

Author 2: How was coaching teaching implemented and what is the difference between coaching teaching and co-teaching?

Co-teaching is a methodology for teaching, rather than a form of coaching. It can be a very effective form of teaching. However, the biggest dilemma with co-teaching is that it is often more like "parallel teaching." The general education teacher does one set of things and the special education teacher does another, but only with specific identified students, usually students with disabilities. It is not as integrated as it could or should be.

Coaching teachers (coaching teaching) is different. It involves meeting with a teacher to look at professional growth. For example, a coach (the principal) and the teacher can use the Ohio Teacher Evaluation System framework to identify what might be an area of growth for the year, then jointly develop a plan for how the teacher is going to develop in that area, and when the coach (the principal) is going to come in to provide feedback and coach the teacher. Coaching is about development, and it's not evaluative. I have a problem with many of tools we use for evaluation. They are fine on a broad level, and principals can usually remember the five or six areas they are supposed to focus on, but they have problems when they have to drill down to the specific observable behaviors. There are too many things to remember and it gets too complex for them to keep all these factors in their heads. Therefore, they use checklists, and measure whether they saw the behavior or not; this is what teachers resent. Teachers resent the checklist mentality because teaching is more complex than a simple checklist.

In fact, personnel evaluation in general does not work. If you read the research in business and industry, most organizations are moving away from a traditional evaluation paradigm. They are moving to coaching, which is frequent observation and feedback around focused development in a particular area. This is more like instructional coaching. This approach means that the principal needs to be much more involved in classroom observations and much more knowledgeable about what is going on in teaching and learning. Principals need to spend more time in classrooms. We encourage the principals in the OLi[4] project to spend time in their highest performing teachers' classrooms and learn what they can learn from observing these teachers. However, because most evaluation models focus predominantly on the lowest performing teachers, principals do not spend as much time in classrooms where teachers are doing phenomenal things with kids, so that they can learn more. Most principals tell us they could dedicate up to an hour a day on classroom observations and coaching. If they can do an hour a day, this translates into 20 classrooms a month. That is a lot of classrooms. The Leithwood (Leithwood, Seashore Louis, Anderson, & Wahlstrom, 2004) study found that highly effective principals were in a minimum of 20 classrooms, and highly effective principals were in up to 60 classrooms a month, which is a very high bar. That's approximately three hours a day. However, an hour a day is a reasonable bar to set for classroom observations and coaching.

Author 2: Can you talk about some models and some roles of coaching and co-teaching that you have seen in inclusive education settings?

I have seen instructional coaching happening in many schools and certainly co-teaching in some settings. Often, we have an instructional coach who wants to come in and demonstrate a particular practice that a teacher or several teachers can implement. Afterward, the instructional coach gives the teacher specific feedback on his or her use of the practice. I see that going on all the time in terms of more inclusive models. The Ohio Department of Education's State Personnel Development Grant looked at inclusive models of teaching, where teams were using Universal Design for Learning (UDL) as a framework for the development of shared lessons or units in their teacher teams. UDL is one approach to using teacher teams to co-plan and co-serve that can be highly effective. This approach utilizes the expertise of all team members to meet the needs of all students, not in a parallel way, but in an integrated way.

Author 2: How is reflection on practice implemented in your work and why do you feel it is important?

People can profess to understand a lot of things, but if we do not reflect on our own practice, if we do not see what actually works, then how do we know if what we are doing is really working? We all have blind spots and we all have biases. We all think we are doing what works best, and yet we repeat the same practices that get us the same outcomes. We say one thing, but we do another. Most of us are not good at changing our own practice. This is one of the reasons we went to the team concept in Ohio and the idea of starting with collective reflection. If we each implement a practice, and then we come back and we collectively reflect on how it worked, this leads to richer discussions together around the practice and our teaching. As a result, we learn more. Unfortunately, I think the only time that most people have for reflection is when they are riding home at the end of the day and that's only if they do not turn on the radio or distract themselves in other ways.

We all profess and want to be better at reflection, but it is difficult unless we structure time for it. This is as true for principals as it is for teachers. Principals tend to implement what worked last time, just like all of us. However, what worked last time is really no indication that it will work this time. What we have to do is to study what we implement and see what works. This needs to be a disciplined set of practices. We study, reflect, and improve, and then implement the cycle again. This is what we call "deliberate practice." It's practice with feedback; but practice with feedback from more people than just ourselves helps us understand more deeply than we would on our own. If you want people to change their practice, it is best to surround them with other people who are also trying to change their practice. This is seen as a more effective way to change now in the change literature. For example, if you want to lose weight, surround yourself with people who are going to go out for a walk every day. Most of us are not strong enough to change our own practices unless we're in a group that is working to change our practice.

Author 2: Please expand on the following statement of yours—"The only thing limiting progress is one's level of commitment to the improvement process."

You have to unpack what commitment to the improvement process means. If we can learn together as teams about what works for our children, then change happens. In bringing research to the table for educators, my question is always, "Do they believe the research?" It seems that research is not sufficient for people to change their beliefs or practices. The only thing that is powerful enough to change beliefs or practices is to have the educators see that children do better when they use certain practices, in other words—"believing is seeing." Commitment is one element, but we have to create structures that allow teachers and administrators to have (a) an experience of seeing that certain practices have better outcomes and (b) an opportunity to practice and master those powerful practices. Commitment matters first, but belief often comes from doing and seeing. In order for this to happen, principals have to be the epitome of that "lead learner" for the teachers to believe it is safe to learn here. If it is safe to learn, and we study and perfect effective practices, and get better and see the results for our students, schools do better. That is what I mean by the improvement process: it is that we study and get better together, because we know what works.

More specifically, OIP and OLi[4] are continuous improvement processes. Gains in performance do not happen overnight; it is modest gains that build over time, so you need to be persistent. As mentioned earlier, teams at all levels should be involved with ongoing cycles of focused inquiry. We choose a focused problem and select specific strategies to study and implement deeply. Over time we learn to use the strategies more effectively based on our collective experiences and feedback to each other (a form of "deliberate practice"). Then we identify a new problem and repeat the process. The recent work by Bryk and associates (2015), in the area of improvement science, is an example of this kind of work. This work ties into inclusive leadership because the OIP and OLi[4] work involves continuous improvement cycles.

CONCLUSION

We would like to thank Brian McNulty for sharing his thoughts and expertise with us in this interview. Readers might want to think about the key takeaways from our discussion with him. These actions can be used to implement the steps in a district or school's improvement plan:

- Identify what research says about successful teaching practices that lead to student improvement.
- Focus on all students in an inclusive education model.
- Collect and use data in continuous reflection cycles to inform practices and processes of implementing the practices.
- Create a culture of shared responsibility by having school leaders model that culture and by allowing teachers to work in teams to support all students.
- Use co-teaching and coaching as vehicles for reflection and improvement of practices.
- Be committed to the improvement plan and be aware that results are not immediate.

Inclusive education takes time, intentionality, teamwork, and commitment. These insights guide McNulty's direct work with schools and districts and reflect what he shares with school leaders in various professional development projects. His suggestions for establishing and sustaining inclusive education can help teachers and administrators achieve the goal of supporting and assisting all learners to make the most of their educational journeys.

NOTES

1. See https://www.oli-4.org for more information on OLI[4].
2. (B. McNulty, personal communication, December 5, 2017)

REFERENCES

Bryk, A. S., Gomez, L. M., Grunow, A., & LeMahieu, P. G. (2015). *Learning to improve: How America's schools can get better at getting better.* Cambridge MA: Harvard Education Press.

Goddard R., Goddard, Y., Kim, E. S., & Miller R. (2015). A theoretical and empirical analysis of the roles of instructional leadership, teacher collaboration, and collective efficacy beliefs in support of student learning. *American Journal of Education, 121,* 501–530. doi:10.1086/681925

Grissom, J., Loeb, S., & Master, B. (2013). Effective instructional time use for school leaders: Longitudinal evidence from observations of principals. *Educational Researcher, 42,* 433–444. doi:10.3102/0013189X13510020

Hattie, J. (2009). *Visible learning: A synthesis of meta-analysis relating to achievement* (1st ed.). New York, NY: Routledge.

Howley, M., & Howley, A. (2013). *Ten-district synthesis: Moving your numbers across the country.* Minneapolis, MN: University of Minnesota, National Center on Educational Outcomes.

Leithwood, K., & Seashore Louis, K. (2012). *Linking leadership to student learning.* San Francisco, CA: Jossey-Bass.

Leithwood, K., Seashore Louis, K., Anderson, S., & Wahlstrom, K. (2004). *How leadership influences student learning: A review of research for the Learning from Leadership Project.* New York, NY: The Wallace Foundation.

Marzano, R., Waters, T., & McNulty, B. (2005). *School leadership that works.* Aurora, CO: McREL.

Marzano, R., Pickering, D., & Pollock, J. (2001). *Classroom instruction that works.* Alexandria, VA: ASCD.

McNulty, B. (2017, February). *Inclusive leadership practices: What's most essential?* Presentation at the Ohio Dean's Compact on Exceptional Children, Columbus, OH.

McNulty, B., & Besser, L. (2011). *Leaders make it happen! An administrator's guide to data teams.* Englewood, CO: Lead and Learn Press.

Robinson, V. (2011). *Student-centered leadership* (1st ed.). San Francisco, CA: Jossey-Bass.

Telfer, D. M. (2011). *Moving your numbers: Five districts share how they used assessment and accountability to increase performance for students with disabilities as part of district-wide improvement.* Minneapolis, MN: University of Minnesota, National Center on Educational Outcomes.

CHAPTER 9

BUILDING CAPACITY FOR ALL LEARNERS AT ALL LEVELS THROUGH INCLUSIVE EDUCATIONAL PRACTICES

Chad Wyen and Krista Wagner
Mad River Schools

This chapter describes Mad River Local Schools' experience with work to increase teachers' use of inclusive instructional practices. It discusses the challenges associated with making a shift from a "fixed" to "growth" mindset; and it demonstrates the importance of pushing educators to embrace collaborative teams, committees, and communities. Throughout, the discussion highlights the importance of providing a deeper, more focused educational experience for students, with an emphasis on skills relevant to the 21st century workplace.

Mad River's adoption of an inclusive educational mindset began several years ago, following Ohio's shift from state standards to the Common Core standards for reading and math. To move beyond Malcolm Baldrige's "cookie cutter" improvement model—the approach used by Ohio at the time (Banister, 2001)—we engaged in district-level discussions about our purpose. These discussions pointed to the fact that leadership teams across

Inclusive Education: A Systematic Perspective, pp. 165–175
Copyright © 2020 by Information Age Publishing
All rights of reproduction in any form reserved.

the district had lost their focus. The district leadership team's (DLT's) data walks and conversations had become routine and revealed little, and our building leadership teams' (BLTs') focus rarely moved beyond data recorded on compliance checklists, even though BLT members recognized that what they were doing did not align with district goals. Furthermore, our teacher-based teams (TBTs) complained about the lack of resources for teaching the Common Core and insisted on purchasing "canned" programs to meet their needs. Buildings functioned in isolation, teachers did not collaborate, and staff generally were unable to engage in wholesale reform. Rather, they tended to apply "band-aid" solutions to structural problems. In short, it became easier to hide from the Common Core than to engage with it.

But hiding was no longer an option once a change in the district's ranking on the state report card provided a "wake-up call." After eight years of receiving an *Effective* designation on the report card, Mad River Schools received a lower overall ranking. Demoted, with component grades of "Ds" and "Fs," the district clearly faced acute challenges. At first, however, district personnel became defensive and blamed one another, complaining and engaging in recrimination. Apart from the defensive grumbling, district educators felt that the lower ranking was humbling. Eventually, in fact, the lower ranking galvanized improvement efforts in the district. One of our first insights was that nothing would change in the district until the leadership team defined its purpose.

The DLT then began extensive work reviewing data and questioning the district's core values and beliefs. Several factors complicated this effort. Most notably, the switch to a curriculum grounded in Common Core standards meant using new assessments. As a result, the team did not have enough new data to generate meaningful insights, and the historical trend data did not reveal root causes. As the team delved deeper into the data and reflected on district needs, however, we created a graphic organizer that captured three essential components of our improvement work: the *what*, *how*, and *why*. We modeled the graphic organizer on Simon Sinek's *Start with Why* (2009) and used it to help us clarify our purpose. That work required several leadership team meetings. We eventually articulated our *why*: "to provide educational experiences and diverse opportunities for all of our students." This aim became our mission statement: *"It is the mission of Mad River Local Schools to create successful educational experiences for all students we serve through diverse opportunities."* We used the mission statement to redefine and guide our subsequent work.

This work included setting new goals. Our previous goals for continuous improvement had incorporated unrealistic benchmarks (e.g., 100% of our students will be proficent in reading/math by a particular date). None of the past improvement plans, however, had acknowledged the need for any kind of *inclusive* practice. Rather, they listed amorphous, top-down, compliance-focused goals—that is, goals parroting state expectations and then packaged as if they were actually meaningful to the district. The recent work, by contrast, sought to align the district's mission and goals, while at the same time involving staff at all levels in the process. District leaders realized that the failure to create focus and to involve all stakeholders would limit the degree to which the district could make substantive change.

To facilitate their students' capacity to learn and achieve academically, while meeting Common Core standards and requirements, Mad River Local district leaders began by analyzing data relevant to this challenge, and then established teams to focus on instruction and graduation. These teams—subgroups of the district leadership team—sought to develop consistent and focused instructional practices and other ways to help all students graduate on time with their cohorts. Each of these teams worked with both the DLT and the BLTs to build capacity across all levels of the system. The DLT oversaw the integrity of this process as well as fidelity of implementation.

Teams turned to the five steps identified in the Ohio Improvement Process (OIP; Ohio Department of Education, 2018) to help guide and make informed decisions about practices that would be positioned to meet district goals. To maintain their focus on advancing the district's goals and monitoring progress, the teams met quarterly to discuss their results, as well as to share reflections on using the 5-Step Process.

The 5-Step Process involves:

1. collecting and charting data related to adult implementation and student performance in order to identify needs;
2. researching and selecting evidence-based strategies to address those needs;
3. planning for implementation by reviewing and refining action steps;
4. implementing and monitoring actions; and
5. analyzing and evaluating implementation, making adjustments, and planning next steps.

The teams also met at other times in addition to quarterly meetings to review data specific to their goals, and to work with the BLTs on supporting the focus areas at both the building and classroom levels.

In taking a closer look at the process of implementation, district leaders quickly realized that leadership teams across all levels of the system struggled with meeting the district-wide goal of improving instruction. Unexpectedly, bringing district-adopted strategies to bear on the goal of improved instruction turned out to be complex, and it became clear that a concerted study of inclusive leadership practices was called for. While the district continues to focus on its graduation goal, the concerted effort to improve leadership practice (as a way to improve instruction) has become central. In fact, it is the main strategy for facilitating and supporting the district's trajectory of growth and improvement.

The complexity of the goal related to instructional improvement, as well as the mandate to align it with the district's mission and to bring all stake-holders into the process, combined to make its effective implementation difficult. Embarking on a new approach to instruction required a larger change in practice than the district had ever undertaken. Although the district found that there were improvements related to its graduation goal—in attendance, and in a behavioral intervention and support system—the challenge of meeting the goal related to instructional improvement proved elusive. The district's approach to promoting the high-quality instruction that is key to students' success had long been to make minor adjustments to instructional practices, which had seemed reasonable so long as the district was receiving an *Effective* designation. District educators had always tried to stay abreast of current trends in education by reading, among other experts in the field, McNulty, Marzano, Schmoker, Reeves, and Hattie (e.g., Hattie, 2009; Marzano, Waters, McNulty, 2005; Reeves, 2006; Schmoker, 2001), to learn about improvement strategies and effective instructional practice. They conducted book studies and attended regional professional development events, and each school had the flexibility to implement its own research-based strategy. District leaders also assumed that as teachers and leaders became more familiar with changes in state standards, they would be able to produce gains in achievement. But despite their increased knowledge about effective instruction, district educators still seemed unable to make consequential changes in their practice.

Several factors confounded improvement efforts. First, district educators did not fully appreciate the magnitude of the changes implicated by Common Core standards. Second, the district's current students were facing greater environmental challenges than previous students had faced: students entering district schools were less prepared to begin kindergarten, and they were experiencing greater childhood adversity. Not only did pre-assessment scores decrease significantly, the district's economically disadvantaged population nearly doubled, from 35% in 2000 to 60% in 2017. STAR Early Literacy results, which are drawn from beginning-of-the-year assessments, underscored the magnitude of these changes (see Table 9.1). The district found itself in an instructional crisis with no obvious or immediate solution. There were too many areas that needed to improve, and the district was, at the same time, failing to make real progress in solving existing problems and struggling to find a way forward.

Table 9.1.
STAR Assessment Results

Years	Literacy
2013–2014	75% at grade level
2014–2015	53% at grade level
2015–2016	31% at grade level
2016–2017	29% at grade level
2017–2018	28% at grade level

Note: STAR early literacy administration for students entering kindergarten. Longitudinal cross-sectional report data from the fall window of each year.

District leaders eventually realized that Mad River's usual professional development methods and models could not cope with its mounting problems, and they decided the district was at an impasse. Its longstanding top-down approach—likened to paving a road and then allowing each of its eight schools to make its own way along that road—actually stood in the way of progress. The district also faced several issues related to inclusive practices. For instance, the way it served students with disabilities, as well as its Response to Intervention process for students identified with learning difficulties (Tier II) or special education needs (Tier III), involved many more instances of pulling those students out of the general classroom than of implementing inclusive classroom practices. Many staff members held the belief that students with disabilities and at-risk students typically did not have the capacity to meet the expectations implicit in Common Core standards. Moreover, increasing the number of intervention groups brought little to no change in outcomes. Even though educators across the district believed they were doing what was best for students with disabilities and other learning challenges, their instructional practices did not produce improved results. Frustrations continued to mount. Despite studying books on educational theory and practice and participating in professional development activities, educators continued to revert to what felt comfortable. It became evident that the district lacked, and needed, an effective system for providing high-quality instruction to students with disabilities as well as other struggling learners.

Administrators had no clear path forward, and teachers bemoaned the reactive approach to instructional change. Indeed, pervasive frustration led a middle-school teacher-leader—also a past DLT and BLT member—to meet with the district's curriculum director and share information on a research project that had piqued her interest. The project, funded by the Ohio Education Association, required release time for the teacher to connect with nonprofit organizations, such as Student Achievement

Partners (n.d.), that are dedicated to helping teachers and school leaders meet high-quality, college- and career-ready standards. Removing a teacher from the classroom to work on an external project amounted to uncharted territory for the administration; but district administrators opted to move forward, not knowing where it would lead. This leap of faith was a first step in effecting meaningful instructional change and centering instructional goals on inclusive educational practices.

The curriculum director and teacher-leader met regularly to discuss her research, and their conversations increasingly confirmed growing suspicions that a new professional development model was needed. Up until that time, the district had drawn upon Ohio Department of Education resources to support its transition to the new Common Core standards. District administrators also tended to believe that teachers would mutiny if they were left on their own to sort out and work with the ODE resources or to engage in another round of work to "unpack" standards. It became clear that any new PD model must incorporate new ways to develop teams into professional learning communities, including changes in collaborative structures and support mechanisms to empower teachers as they developed the most effective practices for their classrooms. Such a model would also spotlight those practices that worked to (a) keep learning communities functioning smoothly, (b) teach faculty about self-study through Teach-Measure-Learn-Repeat cycles, (c) offer coaching instruction, and (d) support teachers' efforts to change and grow professionally. The district needed to find its focus—one from which everyone might benefit.

Guided by the teacher-leader's research findings, district administrators invested in instructional coaches. For example, a Title I coach helped elementary teachers from different schools learn to use small-group instruction more effectively. The district found that it could avoid the need for additional hiring by creatively adjusting staffing assignments, and it deployed two coaches to support instructional improvement in early elementary grades and in grades 5–8. This move helped resolve ongoing communication problems by giving everyone a voice. Up until that point, the district had relied upon leadership teams to promote communication. Although teachers had also met periodically, the focus of their meetings was to discuss upcoming thematic units or adjust leveled reading groups. And although BLTs also met, their work merely involved checking off tasks requested by the DLT. DLT meetings had essentially functioned as "sit-and-get" presentations on the state of things rather than opportunities for collaborative discussion. To change this, the instructional coaches made a point of observing teachers' practices in the classroom, and then facilitating open discussion among teachers, students, and principals. These dialogues revealed that a good many teachers and principals were inadequately informed about what the new standards required, or meant, for the classroom. In clinging to the practice of providing different—often separate—modes of instruction to students with differing needs, the schools failed to hold all students to higher expectations. It became clear that the district was deficit-oriented; the system had been identifying deficits and implementing the necessary scaffolding, but the work had stopped there.

After drawing on the support of the two coaches for a year, the district concluded that its initial instructional improvement goal did not align with its demonstrated needs. The goal was, therefore, revised to refocus on students' success, and to allow students and teachers, rather than the DLT, to determine practice. District plans for the next three years include employing study, dialogue, and experimentation to improve literacy instruction. Its coaching team will need to expand, and not only will teachers receive PD, but all administrators will be required to participate in literacy coaching, engage in "learning through implementation," and review case study data. To ensure consistency, the district has adopted foundational literacy and reading and writing programs, and district leaders will promote reflective practice and self-study in order to sustain the district's new focus on inclusion. Furthermore, expectations have been reframed: no longer will teachers or administrators automatically assume that some students cannot achieve complex reading and writing outcomes at their grade level. The district is working to rebuild its basic approach to instructional practice, and it is making efforts to ensure that all students find their school experience engaging and of high quality.

The district has experienced some setbacks since adopting its revised goal. Change can be uncomfortable and disorienting. It is easy to become discouraged, complain, and assign blame when things do not go as expected, and complacency is also a too-common fallback position. Nonetheless, the district has moved forward, and Mad River teachers now teach differently (see Appendix for the Year 1 Instructional Plan). David and Meredith Liben, the literacy content specialists behind Student Achievement Partners, neatly encapsulated this approach (Liben, & Liben, 2017), noting a desire to provide

> solid grounding in the foundational reading skills, development of academic language (vocabulary and syntax), the steady growth of knowledge, experiences that lead to the thoughtful use of comprehension strategies, the ability to express thoughts and learning clearly through speaking and writing, and the capacity and motivation to sustain a volume of engaged reading providing a coherent experience for students. (p. 1)

In the past, received wisdom dictated that many students' performance would fall short of Common Core standards. In an effort to challenge this notion, the district's new approach promotes teachers' deeper understanding of their purpose as instructors and strives to provide teachers with the resources and support they need to hone their professional practice. Principals now serve as instructional leaders, and students are learning that they must take risks and, if they fail, learn from their mistakes. The Mad River Local school district is not yet where it would like to be, but it continues to promote and develop those inclusive leadership practices that improve instruction and build, at all levels, learners' capacity for success.

REFERENCES

Banister, S. I. (2001, April). *A question of quality: The Malcolm Baldrige criteria as applied to education.* Paper presented at the Annual Meeting of the American Educational Research Association, Seattle, WA.

Hattie, J. (2009). *Visible learning: A synthesis of meta-analysis relating to achievement.* New York. Routledge.

Liben, D., & Liben, M. (2017*). 'Both and' literacy instruction K–5: A proposed paradigm shift for the common core state standards ELA classroom.* Retrieved from Student Achievement Partners website https://achievethecore.org/content/upload/Both%20And%20Literacy%20Instruction%20K-5%20%20A%20Proposed%20Paradigm%20Shift%20for%20CCSS%20ELA%20and%20Literacy.pdf

Marzano, R., Waters, T., & McNulty, B. (2005). *School leadership that works.* Aurora, CO: McREL.

Ohio Department of Education. (2018). *Ohio improvement process.* Retrieved from http://education.ohio.gov/Topics/District-and-School-Continuous-Improvement/Ohio-Improvement-Process

Reeves, D. B. (2006). *The learning leader: How to focus school improvement for better results.* Alexandria, VA: Association for Supervision and Curriculum Development.

Schmoker, M. (2001). *The results fieldbook: Practical strategies from dramatically improved schools.* Alexandria, VA: Association for Supervision and Curriculum Development.

Sinek, S. (2009). *Start with why: How great leaders inspire everyone to take action.* New York, NY: Penguin Group.

Student Achievement Partners. (n.d.). Welcome to achieve the core. Retrieved from https://achievethecore.org

APPENDIX

The Instructional Plan

Mad River Local Schools Principals, Coaches, and Teacher Literacy Plan Year 1

K–8

Principals, Assistant Principals, and Coaches

- Attend and participate in 8 hours per month of instructional and literacy professional development (PD; separate from teacher PD)
- Identify and support in collaboration with the coach/Title teacher the grade level support needed during Foundations and/or Wit and Wisdom Implementation
- Teach Wit and Wisdom Lesson
  - o K–4: one per grade level (4 total lessons)
  - o 5–8: two per grade level (4 total lessons)
- Participate in bi-monthly reflective practitioner 365 discussions

Building Leadership Teams

- Monthly meetings to discussions "Learning through Implementation"
- Review of Case Study Data (beginning in October)

Teachers

- Implement Foundations and/or Wit and Wisdom with integrity
- Attend and participate in Waiver Days Wit and Wisdom PD
- Attend and participate in bimonthly team/dept. meetings led by coach and focused on Wit and Wisdom or Foundations
- Participate in bimonthly reflective practitioners 365 discussions
- Teachers will follow the master schedule.

9–12

Principals, Assistant Principals, and Curriculum Director

- Attend and participate in monthly instructional PD (separate from teacher PD)
- Wit and Wisdom Study with curriculum
- Restructure all building level teams to be aligned with the work of the BLT

Building Leadership Teams

- Book study: *Rigor, Relevance, and Relationships in Action (Innovative Leadership and Best Practices for Rapid School Improvement) by* Willard Daggett
- Teaming- clear vision and plan going into year 1 (Identify top three priorities for improvement in the building)
- Data collection on building culture/climate (survey April 7, 2017 waiver day) and get formative assessment on Literacy in the high school.
- Differentiate PD for departments on waiver day
- Identify building leadership teams and what their role will be to support the priorities in the building

Teachers

- Teacher implementation of literacy plan will begin year 2.
- English language arts (ELA) teachers classroom visits to see Wit and Wisdom in action
- Vertical meetings with 9th grade teachers and the 7th/8th grade teachers
- ELA teacher training on the shifts in ELA and how Wit and Wisdom is impacting their future students and teaching
- Use Waiver Days and early release days to develop teaming and have PD in the priority areas the building leadership teams has identified.
- ELA teachers need to see how Wit and Wisdom will impact their map

- Coach provided PD sessions for High School Instructional Team during two-hour early releases. Topics: What is foundational literacy? What types of literature are students exposed to in the program/how does that change high school literature? What genres of writing are done in the program? What strategies are consistently used that could carry over to the high school? Shifts: What are they?

CHAPTER 10

INCLUSIVE EDUCATIONAL LEADERSHIP

Meeting the Needs of a Diverse Society

Moses B. Rumano and Roger N. Morris
Malone University

The new millennium has witnessed a growing population of students from diverse backgrounds in public and private schools across the nation. Especially in consideration of growing diversity, school leaders should be prepared to lead, serve, and guide all students toward academic achievement and their active engagement as citizens in adult life. It is the authors' position that educational leaders have the potential and ability to reach out to students from diverse backgrounds and help them become active participants in building democracy, the cornerstone of economic prosperity and sustainable development. In order to build democracy, diversity needs to be viewed and celebrated as an advantage in a school environment that fosters togetherness, motivation to learn about different cultures, and creation of new ideas. The inherent challenges that are associated with dealing effectively with a diverse student body (e.g., different religious backgrounds and varied socioeconomic status) call for a change in school

Inclusive Education: A Systematic Perspective, pp. 177–186
Copyright © 2020 by Information Age Publishing
All rights of reproduction in any form reserved.

leadership practices, including engagement of all stakeholders in educational decision-making. This chapter describes an educational leadership preparation program that recognizes and supports the new reality of 21st century schools, which enroll a demographically diverse student population that finds common ground in the quest for a high-quality education.

EFFECTIVE SCHOOL LEADERSHIP

Effective school leadership seeks to empower all students to be active members of the learning community. Students from diverse backgrounds should feel welcome, appreciated, and embraced by their peers from the dominant culture. Intentional activities that attend to and respect the culture and background of all the students, engaging them in both social and academic spheres, help to form strong bonds among students. It is the responsibility of educational leaders to ensure that an environment conducive to caring and inclusion is created for all students, teachers, and parents. Of particular concern to the authors is the widening achievement gap and the disproportionate suspension and expulsion of African American and Hispanic students in public schools relative to their White counterparts.

In creating an environment for learning and growth that close the achievement gap, principals should bear in mind the following key strategies (Harvey, Holland, & Cummins, 2013, p. 4):

- Shaping a vision of academic success for all students;
- Creating a climate hospitable to education;
- Cultivating leadership in others;
- Improving instruction;
- Managing people, data, and processes to foster school improvement.

Inclusive leadership incorporates all these strategies, utilizing them not only to improve the school but also to maintain high student outcomes and achievement, measured via multimodal assessments, rubrics, and indicators.

Shaping a Vision of Academic Success for All Students

Promoting academic success in a diverse learning environment can be quite a challenge for educators and school leaders. A plausible and inclusive vision is a prerequisite for success among students, especially those from marginalized backgrounds. All students have the ability and the potential to succeed in their academic endeavors, which means school leadership must come up with effective strategies that recognize the inherent differences among their diverse students and forge the best way forward through advocacy and proper planning. Educational Leadership Meeting the Needs of Diverse Students (ELMINDS) is a model educational leadership program that involves all stakeholders—such as students, parents, school staff, and community members—in the decision-making process. The ELMINDS model incorporates tenets from visionary and servant leadership, which helps our principal candidates to be the best advocates for their students, teachers, and parents. The program recognizes that school leaders require training in shaping a school's vision (National Policy Board for Educational Administration, 2011). Such training increases the likelihood that principals will have the skills needed to work with school staff to develop a collaborative and inclusive leadership model that enhances a positive school climate and a clear vision that embrace all students as valuable members of the school community.

Gabriel and Farmer (2009) assert that developing a solid vision creates a climate enabling the achievement of common goals and objectives leading to a positive work environment and an instructionally sound school. Eliminating obstacles and creating a positive school climate are essential ingredients for the success of any school (Gabriel & Farmer, 2009). Nevertheless, in an increasingly diverse society, school leaders face the challenge of creating unity of purpose among different groups of students, faculty, and staff—all of whom may have different views and goals for education. Shaping the vision is a significant part of inclusive leadership. It involves all stakeholders in the development of the vision and efforts to sustain practices that enact the vision. For all intents and purposes, dialogue and open communication should be the hallmark for success of school leadership in a diverse environment.

Creating a Climate Hospitable to Education

Competent school leaders have the ability to create a welcoming and productive school climate that pays attention to issues of equity, equality, and social justice. Vibrant school communities aim for high levels of social cohesion, instructional effectiveness, and cultural competence. Meeting the needs of an increasingly diverse society is a central focus of any educational leadership program that strives to meet the needs of its constituents. Understandably, leadership preparation programs are encouraged to embed courses that help prospective principals address the needs of a diverse population of students and their families. To this end, ELMINDS leadership candidates are required to complete a course in the foundations of social and cultural diversity and to work with a diverse population as part of their field experience.

To foster an all-inclusive leadership vision, ELMINDS emphasizes continuous training in diversity, equity, servant leadership, and embracing all cultures. Inclusive leadership is defined as leadership that carefully considers all stakeholders in the community or organization (Rayner, 2009). Inclusion in this sense means having all stakeholders "at the table" at every level of the institution or organization and valuing all stakeholders as responsible for contributing to the ultimate result. Inclusive leadership creates an organizational culture that consistently strengthens all stakeholders (Rayner, 2009).

Clearly, one course on diversity is not sufficient to prepare principal candidates to practice inclusive leadership. That is why ELMINDS, like many other high-quality educational leadership preparation programs, provides inclusive leadership training throughout the curriculum in addition to the course on meeting the needs of diverse student populations. Included in the curriculum of ELMINDS, too, are experiences that align with all the national ELCC standards. Canole and Young (2013) identify at least four leadership models that should be examined as part of the ELCC standards: inclusive leadership, servant leadership, distributive leadership, and proactive leadership.

In inclusive leadership in particular, efforts focus on intentional and purposeful engagement of all the stakeholders. Principal candidates are intentionally placed in urban, rural, and suburban school districts during their internship so that they will become well-versed in all the various organizational dynamics in these types of communities. While completing their internships, moreover, principal candidates engage their communities in different projects. Some of ELMINDS' principal candidates have, for example, worked in school districts that were involved in school levy campaigns, which provided invaluable insights and lessons on school finance and funding.

As a model for other programs that seek to prepare visionary and inclusive leaders, another aspect of ELMINDS is the development and sustenance of high-quality partnerships with community stakeholders. Partnership with local school districts and related agencies is a critical component of the educational leadership program at our university modeling what a school leader needs to do to engage the community surrounding his or her school. Community engagement programs and partnerships based on the needs of the students, not solely on the needs identified by staff, are the true essence of a professional learning community. Epstein and Salinas (2004) state that community partnerships can "improve schools, strengthen families, invigorate community support, and increase student achievement and success" (p. 12). When the community is engaged in the school, leaders find that the needs of the students can be addressed.

Cultivating Leadership in Others

Demographic changes have taken place due, in part, to the migration and immigration trends that have drastically changed the population landscape of the United States, including Ohio. Cultivating leadership skills among diverse populations goes a long way toward building strong communities that can celebrate differences. An effective school leader demonstrates the characteristics of distributive leadership by empowering the school staff, students, and partners to provide guidance and engage in authentic decision making to determine the school's direction. In Ohio, there is an abundance of choices for the education of some students in grades prekindergarten through 12. Others are not given a choice based on a variety of factors, including the location of the home of the child. An urban community with a diverse population has diverse needs; therefore, schools are working to ensure that students in high poverty areas are receiving a high-quality education. Following is a brief description of an exemplary school that partners with ELMINDS and uses the restorative approach to educate diverse and high needs students in a caring environment that supports all students' academic progress.

The Restorative Approach at Youtz Leadership School

Since the early days of schools in America the idea of classroom management has, in some ways, been comparable to the justice system of crime and punishment. According to the U.S. Department of Education's Office of Civil Rights (2014), Black students are suspended and expelled much more frequently—at a rate three times higher—than White students. Additionally, the U.S. Department of Education's Office of Civil Rights report states that students with disabilities receive out-of-school suspensions at more than twice the rate of students without disabilities (13% of the former as compared to 6% of the latter in the 2013–2014 school year). The tension between student behavior and the increased accountability of teachers for student achievement has caused school districts to re-examine "zero tolerance" policies that have contributed to these disparities and look at alternative measures for classroom management that lead to high student performance as well as teaching excellence. Although many teachers, school leaders, and the public at large still tend to view school discipline through the lens of crime and punishment, the restorative justice approach to education seeks to bring about equity and acceptance of all individuals, especially historically oppressed and marginalized populations, including African American students and students with disabilities (Teasley, 2014). Before the implementation of restorative practice, a larger proportion of African American students were suspended and lost valuable class time through suspension at Youtz. Such students are benefiting from the introduction of restorative justice.

At the beginning of the process for implementing the restorative approach at Youtz Leadership School (see https://www.ccsdistrict.org/Youtz), five goals were set:

- Reduce suspensions;
- Reduce pull-out of special education students;
- Handle discipline issues in the classroom;
- Help change behaviors rather than focus on punishments;
- ALL means ALL, meaning having a more inclusive environment and school community.

The next step was to revise the school mission and develop a new vision statement. The new vision statement reads, "Every student will have the opportunity to experience success in a positive, forgiving, and inclusive environment where all students, parents, and staff treat one another with respect and empathy" (as cited by The Stark Education Partnership, 2017). Orientation to the new mission and vision required that the staff and community learn about and eventually embrace dispositions needed for inclusivity, forgiveness, empathy, and respect. In the early phase of the orientation process, members of the school community learned about the "school to prison" pipeline; evidence showing that suspension from school is not effective; the extensive research on the power of relationship-building and maintaining mutual respect between teachers and students as well as teachers and parents; ways to create a safe learning environment; and how to create and sustain a positive school culture. For teachers and policymakers, the idea of doing the groundwork to promote a conducive school culture before thinking about academic instruction was especially difficult because these community members had long experience (perhaps as long as 30 years) with a prevailing ethos that had communicated the opposite message.

Effects of the Restorative Approach at Youtz Leadership School

In the collaborative project to implement a restorative approach at Youtz Leadership School, some initial progress has been observed. The results of the progress of Youtz Leadership School are still being measured; but at the end of the second year of implementation, the number of out-of-school suspensions was down by 93% and student enrollment had increased due to parental requests for their children to attend the school. (The district has an open enrollment policy.) There were challenges that the school faced, such as teacher resistance and concerns by some community members that a school without punishment would communicate the wrong message to children. But, so far, the results are promising. As a relatively new educational model, the restorative justice program is bound to face some difficulties; but early results offer encouraging signs. Over the course of the next several years, longitudinal data about school discipline, academic performance, and parent/student satisfaction will be collected and analyzed to determine longer-term progress.

Improving Instruction

Because effective instruction is empirically linked to student performance, educational leaders need to be well-versed in the most current and reflective teaching approaches. Leithwood, Seashore Louis, Anderson, and Wahlstrom (2004) make two important claims: First, "leadership is second only to classroom instruction among all school-related factors that contribute to what students learn at school"; and second, "leadership effects are usually largest where and when they are needed most" (p. 7). Without a visionary and restorative-oriented leader, schools that are troubled are unlikely to make significant improvements. There should be intentional effort to improve instruction so that all students can benefit from the general education curriculum. This effort will enable a positive school environment to exert a salutary influence on how learners respond to instruction and how they form social bonds.

In addition to creating a positive vision for schools and developing partnerships, effective educational leaders recognize that practicing distributive leadership almost inevitably leads to improved instruction. Natsiopoulou and Giouroukakis (2010) assert that a distributed leadership approach in schools takes place when "the principal shares authority and power; teachers take leading roles, assume responsibility, and act independently as individuals or groups" (p. 158). As the leader of instruction in schools, principals must be trained to distribute leadership and model a vision and approach that puts instruction as a primary focus of the school, along with providing for the needs of all the students. Delegation of duties and responsibilities must be encouraged as it serves as a platform that engages and empowers all teachers, staff, and students to be a part of a positive culture and community.

The primary mission of the school is instruction. Effective teaching and learning in the classroom begin with the competence of the classroom teacher to manage student interactions in a manner that increases academic engagement (Emmer & Sabornie, 2015). However, in a diverse society, schools are constantly challenged by student needs that are anything but instructionally-related. Society has become dependent upon schools to provide more resources to students, without more financial resources to pay for them; and students come to school with a myriad of needs that are unmet in the community. Payne (2013) identifies a variety of needs students have that can be barriers to their learning at school; these may relate to finances, emotional development, cognitive performance, spiritual life, physical well-being, social interactions, behavior, and communication. Whereas schools cannot be expected to provide for all these needs, a school leader can wisely choose strategies that give all children the best chance. Improving instruction is one such strategy. Research notably shows that effective principals find ways to increase teachers' effectiveness (Leithwood, Patten, & Jantzi, 2010).

Managing Data to Foster School Improvement

School-based reform requires a more individualized program to meet the needs of diverse students (Lachat, 2001). Individualization to promote students' progress requires school leaders to develop collection mechanisms for various data sets for the school. Once the data are collected, principals must use the distributed leadership strategy to encourage teachers' and other stakeholders' involvement in analyzing the data and developing strategies for improving and maintaining a positive and successful school climate for students.

A school leader must be able to identify key indicators in order to guide efforts to improve schools. When educators first identify key types of data, test scores are always named as an important data source. However, most models for instructional improvement involve a variety of data sets. Besides the state-mandated performance assessments and teacher assessments, principals must be able to interpret and use a variety of data sets, such as those showing attendance rates, discipline rates, school climate indicators, and various outcomes (both aggregated and disaggregated). The ELMINDS program develops skills for making data-driven decisions through its use of case studies and other real-world examples.

Principal candidates must be prepared not only to analyze varied data but also to interpret and communicate those data in a way that stakeholders and community partners can understand. Communication networks must be well oiled so that essential information is shared among stakeholders.

Parents, guardians, teachers, students, and policy makers need to have access to the information that pertains to their schools. Staff must also learn to collect the most relevant data, such as those in the four spheres of school-based data identified by Learning Point Associates (2004) as valid, usable, and communicable: achievement data, demographic data, program data, and perception data.

ELMINDS incorporates study of appropriate research and the use of available data. Program faculty believe that principal candidates must be grounded in appropriate research methods in order to identify and interpret data, as well as to communicate to stakeholders about what the data show. Data, in fact, are not valuable in their own right. They are valuable, however, as communication tools for working with others to develop a vision, promote effective instruction, cultivate a positive school culture, and foster system-wide leadership.

CONCLUSION

What ELMINDS illustrates is that a leadership program can develop leaders who are well positioned to enable all students to be successful. Effective leadership has the power to bring diverse students together and motivate them to learn and grow. It does so by shaping the school's vision, engaging partners in meaningful ways, promoting differentiated and servant models of leadership manner, encouraging staff participation in decision-making, improving instruction, and using data to identify needs and monitor progress.

REFERENCES

Canole, M. & Young, M. (2013). *Standards for educational leaders: An analysis*. Washington, DC: Council of Chief State School Officers. Retrieved from http://ccsso.org/Documents/Analysis of Leadership Standards-final-070913-RGB.pdf

Emmer, E. T., & Sabornie, E. J. (Eds.). (2015). *Handbook of classroom management* (2nd ed.). New York, NY: Routledge, Taylor & Francis Group.

Epstein, J., & Salinas, K. C. (2004). Partnering with families and communities. *Educational Leadership, 61*(8), 12–18.

Gabriel, J. G., & Farmer, P. C. (2009). *How to help your school thrive without breaking the bank*. Alexandria, VA: Association for Supervision and Curriculum Development.

Harvey, J., Holland, H., & Cummins, H. (2013). *The school principal as leader: Guiding schools to better teaching and learning* (Exp. Ed.). New York, NY: The Wallace Foundation. Retrieved http://www.wallacefoundation.org/knowledge-center/

Pages/The-School-Principal-as-Leader-Guiding-Schools-to-Better-Teaching-and-Learning.aspx

Lachat, M. A. (2001). *Data-driven high school reform: The breaking ranks model.* Providence, RI: Brown University. Retrieved from https://www.brown.edu/academics/education-alliance/sites/brown.edu.academics.education-alliance/files/publications/datdrv_hsrfm.pdf

Learning Point Associates. (2004). Guide to using data in school improvement efforts: A compilation of knowledge from data retreats and data use at Learning Point Associates. Naperville, IL: Author. Retrieved from http://wvde.state.wv.us/schoolimprovement/documents/guidebook.pdf

Leithwood, K., Patten, S., & Jantzi, D. (2010). Testing a conception of how school leadership influences student learning. *Educational Administration Quarterly, 46*, 671–706. doi:10.1177/0013161x10377347

Leithwood, K., Seashore Louis, K., Anderson, S., & Wahlstrom, K. (2004). *How leadership influences student learning.* New York, NY: The Wallace Foundation. Retrieved from https://www.wallacefoundation.org/knowledge-center/Documents/How-Leadership-Influences-Student-Learning.pdf

Natsiopoulou, E., & Giouroukakis, V. (2010). When teachers run the school. *Educational Leadership, 67*, 2–5. Retrieved from http://www.ascd.org/publications/educational-leadership/apr10/vol67/num07/When-Teachers-Run-the-School.aspx

National Policy Board for Educational Administration. (2011). Educational leadership program recognition standards: Building level. Retrieved from http://npbea.org/wp-content/uploads/2018/01/ELCC-Building-Level-Standards-2011.pdf

Payne, R. K. (2013). *A framework for understanding poverty: A cognitive approach.* Highlands, TX: aha! Process, Inc.

Rayner, S. (2009). Educational diversity and learning leadership: A proposition, some principles and a model of inclusive leadership? *Educational Review, 6*, 433–447. doi:10.1080/00131910903404004

The Stark Education Partnership. (2017). Building a respectful school. Retrieved from http://www.edpartner.org/links/issues_09-15-17.html

Teasley, M. L. (2014). Shifting from zero tolerance to restorative justice in schools. *Children and Schools, 36*, 131–133. doi:10.1093/cs/cdu016

U.S. Department of Education Office of Civil Rights. (2014). *Data snapshot: School discipline* (Issue Brief No. 1). Retrieved from, http://ocrdata.ed.gov/Downloads/CRDC-School-Discipline-Snapshot.pdf

SECTION V INTRODUCTION

PREPARING TEACHERS
FOR INCLUSIVE CLASSROOMS

Education reform, including the reform of educator preparation programs, must be a collaborative enterprise. There are too many responsibilities, too many intervening factors, too many biases and blind spots in a single perspective. Each of the chapters in this section is written by multiple authors, implying the communal nature of the project of teacher preparation reform and restructuring. Entering into multidimensional communities of practice in this project are groups of educators (including the editors of this book) who share a concern, even a passion, for teaching and for learning how to improve their professional preparation and professional development programs through interacting regularly to dialog and reflect on common concerns.

Valuing collective competence, partners in higher education reform make the commitment to reach a common goal. Because the chapters in this section focus on reform partnerships in Ohio, they report on efforts that have the improvement of all Ohio students' educational experiences and outcomes as their ultimate aim. The fact that this section is the largest of the seven suggests the complexity of the work toward this reform goal in Ohio and the perspective-taking required to see it through the various stages of design and implementation. The following chapters present a range of implementation efforts, each illustrating somewhat different facets of the complex change process.

In, "Restructuring Teacher Education Programs for Inclusive Instructional Practice: A Study of Change Processes and Outcomes," Stephen Kroeger, Aimee Howley, Barbara Hansen, and Cassondra Faiella present

Inclusive Education: A Systematic Perspective, pp. 187–189

findings from a qualitative research study examining the relevant organizational dynamics at six institutions that developed dual-licensure teacher preparation programs in special education and general education. Paying particular attention to the curriculum change process, the study reports themes reflecting commonalities across the six institutions.

In "An Integrative Teacher Preparation Model to Prepare All Teacher Candidates for Diverse Inclusive Education," Bridgie Ford, Shernavaz Vakil, and Lynn Kline discuss the development and implementation of a restructured teacher preparation program at the University of Akron. The restructured program—with a particular focus on culturally responsive education—allows teacher candidates who are pursuing middle childhood licensure to become licensed as special educators as well. The program enables them to acquire the competencies and dispositions needed to teach effectively in inclusive settings serving traditionally marginalized learners.

In "Developing Integrated Inclusive Content and Pedagogy for a Dual License Middle Childhood Education Program," Christopher Atchison, Susan Gregson, Emilie Camp, Stephen Kroeger, and Holly Johnson discuss the change process as well as findings from mixed-methods action research that enabled them to uncover patterns in the process of curriculum reform. These patterns relate to identifying and merging content, developing curriculum materials, integrating curriculum content and field experiences, overcoming obstacles to progress, and gaining state approval for a dual-license program.

In "Preparing Middle School Educators to Work with All Students," Catherine Lawless Frank, Joni Baldwin, Connie Bowman, and Laura Kuebel discuss the methods required to increase teachers' knowledge base sufficiently to enable them to teach all middle childhood learners effectively. The chapter uses the middle childhood education/intervention specialist dual-licensure program developed by University of Dayton faculty as an exemplar for discussing how to prepare a new generation of teachers whom districts expect to teach in inclusive ways.

In "Preparing Early Childhood Educators for Inclusive Practice," Mary Murray and Tammy Wagner detail the curriculum design process, program initiatives, stakeholder impact, and lessons learned in the development of the Inclusive Early Childhood Education Program at Bowling Green University. Of particular interest in this chapter is the focus on co-teaching, parent partnerships, and preparation for using Universal Design for Learning.

In "Developing an Online Dual-Licensure Graduate Program to Enhance Inclusive Knowledge, Skills, and Dispositions of Early Childhood Educators," Jennifer Ottley, Sara Hartman, Clarissa Bunch Wade, Sara Helfrich, and Christian Grygas Coogle describe experiences with adult learning models such as the Read, Reflect, Display, and Do model for online instruction and bug-in-ear eCoaching to supervise teacher candidates completing field experiences in distant locations. Their chapter describes major collaborative steps taken in the design and implementation of an online program at Ohio University to develop advanced knowledge, skills, and dispositions for addressing the diverse needs of young children.

In "Conscientious Consolidation: Developing and Implementing a Dual-Licensure Program with Montessori Credentialing," Kathleen G. Winterman, Victoria Zascavage, and Julie Kugler-Ackley describe the process Xavier University faculty used to restructure early childhood teacher and early childhood intervention specialist preparation programs. Their Montessori approach is a unique feature of the new program, and their discussion devotes particular attention to the integration of Montessori principles of education within an inclusive, child-centered approach to the education of young children.

Finally, in "Inclusivity in the Development of a Dual-Licensure Program: A Report by Program Developers," Beverly Sande, Charles Kemp, Paul Madden, Ray Blevins, and Traci McKee describe the curriculum restructuring process used, as well as various stakeholder responses to the restructuring effort, at Shawnee State University. Their chapter highlights the importance of collaboration with internal and external partners, such as state education agencies and local school districts, in curriculum restructuring efforts.

CHAPTER 11

RESTRUCTURING TEACHER EDUCATION PROGRAMS FOR INCLUSIVE INSTRUCTIONAL PRACTICE

A Study of Change Processes and Outcomes

Stephen D. Kroeger
University of Cincinnati

Aimee Howley
WordFarmers Associates

Barbara Hansen
Muskingum University

Cassondra M. Faiella
University of Cincinnati

Inclusive Education: A Systematic Perspective, pp. 191–223
Copyright © 2020 by Information Age Publishing
All rights of reproduction in any form reserved.

Students enrolling in schools across the United States represent diverse characteristics and backgrounds (e.g., Teixeira, Frey, & Griffin, R. 2015). A common strategy for addressing increasing diversity among students has been to group them according to their apparent characteristics and presumed instructional needs (Frattura & Capper, 2007); however, a growing body of evidence finds this type of grouping to be counterproductive. Instead, better outcomes result from an inclusive approach, which is based on practices such as educating diverse students in heterogeneous classrooms, using effective core teaching methods, and basing curricula for all students on general education standards (e.g., Cosier, Causton-Theoharis, & Theoharis, 2013; Frattura & Capper, 2007; Salle & Johnson, 2010).

Notwithstanding the effectiveness of inclusive education, teachers often find they are unequipped to handle its challenges (e.g., Fullerton, Ruben, McBride, & Bert, 2011). Some evidence suggests that their preparation programs may not equip them well enough. Notably, most teachers continue to receive their preparation in programs that educate them to become specialists—elementary education teachers, special education teachers, or teachers of emerging bilingual students, for instance (Wolfberg, LePage, & Cook, 2009). Gaps in their preservice and in-service preparation leave many teachers feeling ill-prepared to address the needs of diverse learners (e.g., Hamman, Lechtenberger, Griffin-Shirley, & Zhou, 2012; see also, Keefe, Rossi, de Valenzuela, & Howarth, 2000).

Despite the increasing prevalence of initial licensure programs that prepare teachers to work with all learners, only a few systematic studies examine these inclusive programs. While more information continuously emerges about why and how some colleges of education are changing their programs to enable their graduates to become instructional general-ists, capable of working with a wide range of students (e.g., Hamman et al., 2013; Keefe et al., 2000; Wolfberg et al., 2009; Zion & Sobel, 2014), a number of these accounts are anecdotal in nature and offer minimal empirical support. Our study expands on this emerging body of literature by examining areas of convergence and divergence between six teacher preparation programs that developed dual-licensure curricula over a two-year period. The study addressed the following research questions:

- What processes did the teacher preparation faculties use to reframe their curricula as dual-licensure programs?
- What types of curriculum models did the six programs develop?
- How did the development of the six curriculum models contribute to faculty learning?

LITERATURE REVIEW

Although collaborative programs—combining preparation for general and special education teaching—have become more common over the past decade (Brownell, Griffin, Leko, & Stephens, 2011), awareness of the need for such programs is long established. Indeed, teacher educators frequently work to promote greater social justice by preparing teachers who are willing and able to transform schools into productive and equitable learning environments (e.g., Cochran-Smith, 2005). According to Blanton and Pugach (2011), collaborative programs can be categorized into two types. The first collaborative program type, referred to as a *merged program*, leads to dual licensure, or licensure in general education and licensure in special education. An *integrated program*, by contrast, provides general and special education candidates with some common experiences but does not lead to dual licensure unless candidates complete additional coursework.

This literature review focuses on what we know about these programs, including the challenges that program developers face and recommendations for making the programs successful. Nevertheless, the literature offers an incomplete picture because there are few systematic studies of inclusive teacher preparation programs. The extant literature consists primarily of theoretical discussions and program descriptions written by faculty members who have played some role in developing or delivering a merged or integrated program.

Early Efforts

Interest in preparing general education candidates to use inclusive practices spurred government-sponsored efforts in the 1970s and 1980s (Brigham, 1993). Notably, the Dean's Grant Program (an incentive grant) aimed to infuse special education concepts into general education curricula. These efforts were not well received (Brigham, 1993) and tended to reinforce the practice of adding one or two special education courses to teacher preparation curricula for general educators rather than undertaking the more difficult task of preparing all educators to work with all students.

Collaborative programs have become more common over the past decade and align more closely with the vision underlying the Dean's Grant initiative (Brownell et al., 2011). For example, a survey conducted by Harvey, Yssel, Bauserman, and Merbler (2010) found that many programs across the nation have been experimenting with different strategies for preparing educators to meet the needs of diverse learners.

Program Design

The belief that general and special educators' practices overlap considerably supports the development of integrated and merged preparation programs (e.g., Dingle, Falvey, Givner, & Haager, 2004). According to Brownell and colleagues (2005, 2011), such programs ought to base their content and field experiences on empirical findings about the competencies needed to educate students with varying needs. But there is limited research to inform a knowledge base that supports integrated and/or merged teacher preparation programs, or to help faculties understand curriculum changes implicated by the creation of such programs, as the ensuing discussion reveals.

Integrated Programs

Some teacher education programs work to familiarize all teacher candidates with a set of common instructional strategies (e.g., Brigham, 1993). For example, the Valparaiso University program experimented with two methods for delivering common content: (a) pairing a general education and special education faculty member to provide different units within a foundations course (i.e., "turn-teaching") and (b) pairing a general education and special education faculty member to collaborate in delivering an educational psychology course (i.e., true "team-teaching"; Brigham, 1993).

More recent reports of integrated programs documented collaborations that range from modest to extensive. Missouri State University faculty reported on a modest collaboration—a one-day seminar in which students from both general and special education programs role-played participation on intervention teams (Arthaud, Aram, Breck, Doelling, & Bushrow, 2007). A program at Kansas State University proved more extensive: it provided instruction in Universal Design for Learning to secondary-education majors, integrating special education and general education concepts as well as providing co-teaching seminars (Frey, Andres, McKeeman, & Lane, 2012). Faculty at the University of Colorado Denver developed an even more extensive integrated program, enabling but not requiring candidates to obtain dual licensure (Sobel, Iceman-Sands, & Basile, 2007).

Merged Programs

In contrast to integrated programs, merged programs result in dual licensure, typically within the same timeframe required for completion of either a general education licensure or a special education licensure program. A small number of merged programs have been described in the literature. Across the reports are a few that discuss graduate-only programs (e.g., Oyler, 2011), but most merged programs seem to be offered to undergraduates, and the majority combine elementary (or early childhood) education with special education (e.g., Cyr, McDiarmid, Halpin, Stratton, & Davis-Delano, 2012). Less common are programs that prepare candidates for licensure in both special education and an academic specialty at the middle school or high school level (Fullerton et al., 2011; Hamman et al., 2013).

Among the program reports was one from faculty at the University of Hawai'i at Mānoa documenting an initiative of long duration (Jenkins, Pateman, & Black, 2002). Notably, this institution has offered dual-licensure programs since the mid-1990s, starting with a merged elementary-special-education program and later adding a merged secondary-special education program.

The Dynamics of Curriculum Redesign

The related literature shows that efforts to merge special education and general education curricula require complex, iterative change processes. A host of challenges face faculty when they decide to pursue collaborative programs, particularly merged programs, and only a handful of strategies have been suggested for managing these challenges.

The Challenges

Program reports identified several significant challenges: (a) differences in the philosophical or theoretical grounding of general and special education faculties (York-Barr, Bacharach, Salk, Frank, & Benick, 2004); (b) difficulty deciding which content to emphasize and which content to downplay (York-Barr et al., 2004); (c) the expansion of faculty members' time commitments to additional curriculum work, instructional responsibilities, and coordination of field experiences (Keefe et al., 2000; Sobel et al., 2007; York-Barr et al., 2004); and (d) the physical and social separation of general education faculties from special education faculties (Young, 2011). Each of these challenges made demands on faculties that depended on (but also cultivated) significant buy-in for the redesign effort.

Faculties that designed merged programs also faced other challenges. Notably, these faculties discovered the difficulty of locating appropriate fieldwork placements in preschool through grade 12 settings because many districts did not encourage inclusion (e.g., Cyr et al., 2012; Keefe et al., 2000; Kozleski, Pugach, & Yinger, 2002). Furthermore, faculty found that placing candidates in noninclusive classrooms compromised the link between what candidates learned through course work and what they observed and practiced in the field (e.g., Keefe et al., 2000; Kozleski et al., 2002). According to faculty members who had addressed this challenge, the process of finding clinical experiences in inclusive settings for such candidates required a broad coalition of stakeholders, all of whom had significant investment in the program's success.

Recommended Strategies

Many of the program reports included information about the conditions that aided in efforts to integrate or merge general and special education programs. The most salient conditions for restructuring a successful program of either type were:

- Orientation to a shared vision of what an integrated or merged program can accomplish (Brownell et al., 2005; Cyr et al., 2012; Oyler, 2011);
- Systematic review of curricular content, often grounded in relevant standards (Dingle et al., 2004; Sands, Duffield, & Parsons, 2007);
- Support from department and college administrators (Blanton & Pugach, 2011; Cyr et al., 2012; Young, 2011);
- Ample and open discussion across faculties from general and special education departments (Brownell et al., 2005, 2011);
- Involvement of supportive faculty members only (York-Barr et al., 2004);
- Creation of governance structures that break down disciplinary silos (Kozleski et al., 2002);
- Involvement of a critical friend or external evaluator (Cyr et al., 2012); and
- Provision of resources to support faculty members' time for curriculum work and team teaching (Harvey et al., 2010; Keefe et al., 2000).

Among these practices, the creation of and continuing orientation to a shared vision helped faculties sustain what typically proved to be challenging curriculum work. Not surprisingly, however, programs differed in the visions they crafted. One program, for example, focused on culturally responsive pedagogy (Cyr et al., 2012) while another used a critique of mainstream educational practices as its organizing principle (Oyler, 2011).

Regardless of their vision's specific nature, the practice of orienting to it enabled faculties to make difficult decisions about the content and field experiences that would be most important to emphasize in their redesigned curricula.

Faculties also used their vision of a redesigned program as the basis for improving upon traditional strategies for preparing teachers (i.e., extensive course work in pedagogy interspersed with a limited number of field experiences). They streamlined required course work in pedagogy based on applicable standards (e.g., Dingle et al., 2004) and found ways to deploy field experiences more intentionally. These efforts involved careful sequencing of courses to promote certain learning outcomes at specific points across the trajectory of the preparation program. They also involved intentional alignment of activities in the field with key content taught in pedagogy courses (e.g., Fullerton et al., 2011; Hamman et al., 2013; Keefe et al., 2000; Wolfberg et al., 2009).

As the discussion thus far indicates, the extant literature presents relevant insights from programs that are working to combine general and special education content; yet gaps remain in our knowledge of the necessary conditions for restructuring programs in this way. We need a comprehensive knowledge base to support integrated and merged teacher preparation programs and to help faculties understand the curriculum changes implicated by the creation of such programs. This study contributes to that knowledge base.

METHODS

In this section of the chapter, we discuss the selection of institutions to study, the selection of participants at each institution, data collection procedures, data analysis methods, and validity concerns (including study limitations).

Selection of Institutions

The research team sought the participation of six teacher preparation programs situated within institutions of higher education (IHEs) in Ohio. These programs had been recipients of competitive Ohio Department of Education (ODE) incentive grants, awarded under the auspices of the Ohio Deans Compact. The Ohio Deans Compact also oversaw and supported the creation of the merged general and special education programs leading to dual licensure at these IHEs. The six teacher education programs that received awards included four at larger state universities—the Ohio State

University (OSU), Kent State University (KSU), the University of Akron (UA), and the University of Cincinnati (UC)—and two at smaller private institutions—University of Dayton (UD) and Xavier University (XU). All six teacher preparation programs agreed to participate in the study. With the exception of OSU's Master's level program, which combined world language education with K–12 special education, all the initiatives merged an undergraduate preparation program in either early- or middle-childhood education with an undergraduate preparation program in special education.

Participants

All participants were members of the design teams at one of the six teacher preparation programs. Participants consisted of faculty members who served as principal investigators (PIs), grant-funded external evaluators serving each institution, and other faculty members who played a significant role in the curriculum restructuring process. One external partner from a school district was among the participants who were interviewed. Table 11.1 provides a list of participants by category.

Data Collection

A member of the research team contacted PIs at each institution to determine the willingness of that person and other contributing members of the curriculum restructuring team to participate in one-on-one interviews. The intent was to interview all PIs, all external evaluators, and at least one other team member at each institution. Altogether the research team completed interviews with 23 participants—10 PIs, six external evaluators (from five institutions), six other faculty members, and one educator from a partnering school district. No fewer than two interviewees represented each institution.

Upon initial contact, a research team member asked all participants if they would participate in an hour-long interview and complete a consent form. After obtaining consent, they scheduled interviews.

Four researchers conducted interviews either via Skype or by telephone. There were two exceptions to this approach: one participant requested an in-person interview and two participants preferred to be interviewed simultaneously via phone. Interviews lasted between 40 and 90 minutes, approximately, with most lasting about an hour. Interviewers made digital audio recordings, which team members later transcribed verbatim.

Table 11.1.
Participant Type by Institution of Higher Education

Participant Type		Institution of Higher Education					Count by Participant Type
	Kent State University	Ohio State University	University of Dayton	University of Cincinnati	University of Akron	Xavier University	
Institution PIs/Co-PIs	3	1	1	2	2	1	10
Additional Institution Faculty			3			3	6
External Stakeholders	1						1
External Evaluators	1	1	2	1	1		6
Total	5	2	6	3	3	4	23

Note: Participant breakdown.

199

Interview Protocol

The researchers developed interview questions based on: (a) documentation from the Ohio Deans Compact regarding expectations for the work, (b) ideas put forward in the IHEs' first-year progress reports to the Ohio Deans Compact, and (c) relevant literature. The team developed two versions of the interview schedule, one for faculty and university staff participants and one for local project evaluators. To illustrate the nature of the interview questions, Appendix A presents the interview protocol for faculty and staff participants.

Data Analysis

The interview transcripts constituted the primary data source for the study. A secondary data source comprised the set of written year-one and two progress reports developed by each of the teams. The researchers used these reports to verify statements about the curriculum process as well as to test the salience of themes emerging from the analysis of interview data. The team triangulated its findings by comparing the information shared by different participants from the same institution.

The four researchers who conducted interviews also participated in the data analysis process. Rather than using an *a priori* conceptual framework as the basis for coding, the researchers used Corbin and Strauss's (2007) process of open coding. The researchers used two different methods for the initial coding of data and then compared results. The first method involved three researchers—each of whom completed open coding with a different subset of the data. Although all three read every transcript, each coded only a subset (i.e., eight interviews). Next, the three met to compare codes and reach consensus about the most salient code names and descriptions. Then, each individually revisited the subset of data that he or she coded originally and recoded those data using the revised codes. The second method involved another round of initial coding in which the fourth researcher independently coded all the transcripts, using DEDOOSE, a software program for qualitative data analysis.

After the team completed both independent methods, the researchers compared the codes that had been generated using the two methods. They discovered considerable overlap in the salient concepts that the two coding procedures revealed, although their names for similar codes often differed. The researchers added all salient concepts from both coding efforts and agreed upon a final set of code names. Then they organized the final codes into categories and reorganized the data one final time to subsume coded quotes into the categories with the most prominent representation.

Whereas the original efforts to use open coding were quite fine-grained, resulting in the development of approximately 250 codes, categorization was much broader. Categories included larger concepts such as "curriculum development," "process steps," and "inquiry and experimentation." Then, by making comparisons between the events and conditions that participants described, the team looked for theoretical linkages between categories. For example, the team used a grid to examine differences between what participants said about external influences and what they said about internal processes. They also used a grid to compare perspectives from different participant groups, such as the perspectives of PIs versus those of external evaluators.

Orienting to the research questions, the researchers identified themes that related to curriculum processes, on the one hand, and consequences of the processes, on the other. This approach resulted in the identification of three themes altogether: (a) "the curriculum work required a guiding coalition"; (b) "the curriculum work turned out to be a messy problem"; and (c) "the curriculum work depended on, and also supported, faculty learning."

One of the last steps in the data analysis process involved mapping themes back to the actual data to ensure that the themes were well represented in data from across the institutions and participants. The researchers also used various matrices and word clouds, which the qualitative data analysis program allowed them to generate, as a way to double check the salience of the three themes in comparison to other possible themes. See Table 11.2 for an outline of the analysis process.

Validity Concerns

The credibility of findings from a qualitative interview study depends on the degree of alignment between what the researchers hear from participants and how they represent what they hear. As numerous qualitative researchers suggest, a variety of techniques increase credibility. Noble and Smith (2015) provide a useful list:

- Attending to threats from personal bias,
- Attending to threats from bias in sampling,
- Offering self-critique of data collection and analysis methods,
- Keeping meticulous records about methodological decisions and emerging interpretations of data and reporting them clearly,
- Looking for similarities and differences in comparison cases,

- Reporting thick descriptions and illustrative quotes from participants,
- Triangulating data from different sources,
- Involving several researchers in data collection and analysis to reduce bias, and
- Asking participants to validate emerging findings (i.e., member checking).

Table 11.2.
Data Analysis Stages

Stage	Steps
Stage 1—Independent coding	• Two methods were used for initial data coding. • In the first coding method, three researchers read every transcript and open coded a different subset of the data. • In the second coding method, one researcher independently coded all of the transcripts using qualitative analysis software.
Stage 2—Rectification of codes and recoding to match rectified codes	• The three researchers compared codes and reached a consensus on salient code names and descriptions. • Each of the three researchers revisited their original subset of transcripts and recoded using the revised codes. • Then the four researchers compared and combined the codes identified using the two methods and agreed on a final set of code names.
Stage 3 – Categorization and identification of themes	• The final codes were organized into categories and the data was recoded into the most prominent categories. • Comparisons were made between participant described events and conditions to identify theoretical linkages between the categories. • The researchers identified three themes that related to the curriculum process and consequences of the process.
Stage 4 – Review of quotes to determine the extent to which the data fit the proposed themes	• The three themes were mapped back to the data to ensure they were well represented in the data.

The research team conducting this study used many of these techniques, especially the use of a team approach, data triangulation, and member checking.

Team Approach

The research team included four members, all of whom brought different expertise and experiences to the effort. For example, one team member was a faculty member in special education and two had worked both in teacher education and educational leadership. One team member was a graduate student completing a degree in psychology.

The team also convened frequent meetings that encouraged open discussion of research methods and emerging findings. In addition to meetings, the team shared written documents (e.g., categorized quotes, research memos, grids, and diagrams) electronically, and team members provided critical feedback to one another during the data analysis and writing phases of the work.

Data Triangulation

The team triangulated data within institutions to ensure that they accurately documented the curriculum reform events. At the same time, the researchers expected variability across participants, even those at the same institution. The researchers, therefore, found it helpful to distinguish between events and participants' interpretation of events. To double-check events about which confusion or differences in perspective emerged, the researchers used the written reports that each of the six PIs submitted to the Ohio Deans Compact as part of the institution's contractual obligation. They mapped differences in perspective by examining grids based on role (e.g., PI, evaluator, other participant) and institution.

Few significant differences appeared, but one case illustrates how the researchers resolved conflicting interpretations. In that case, the external evaluator offered a perspective on certain events that diverged considerably from the perspective shared by the PI and other project participants. Without dismissing the divergent perspective, the researchers confirmed the sequence of events and their outcomes by reviewing the institution's written report, which had been developed by the PI in concert with other team members, and by querying the PI about the nature and possible causes of the differences in perspective.

Member Checking

To verify the accuracy of the researchers' interpretation of the data, one researcher from the team contacted all participants to ask for their perspectives on the relevance of the emergent themes. The researcher provided participants with a report of the study's findings and asked them to address two issues: (a) whether the reported findings corresponded to the participant's experiences and (b) any ways in which the reported findings differed from the participant's experiences.

Eleven participants responded to the researcher's request, all of them agreeing that the findings reported by the research team corresponded to their experiences during the curriculum-change process. Interestingly, the faculty members who replied offered more definitive responses than the evaluators. The evaluators said they were not well equipped to respond because they had been observers of the curriculum-change process rather than participants in it. Nevertheless, none of the institutional team members questioned the accuracy of any of the study's three emergent themes.

Study Limitations

Several factors represented limitations of the study. First, the study included interviews and document review processes only; only one researcher attended curriculum meetings, and those were at an institution where he served as co-PI of the curriculum team. Second, because one of the research team members participated in curriculum change at one of the institutions, his own experiences might have biased his interpretation of the data. To limit the possibility of bias, the team made sure that the researcher did not interview anyone from his own institution. Furthermore, the collaborative approach to data collection and analysis exposed all emergent findings to on-going discussion and critique. The likelihood that one researcher's experiences could bias the overall results is very slim.

Finally, the research took place during the first and second years of the participating institutions' two-year engagement with curriculum reform. As a result, not all participants could report on the full range of events (i.e., those who participated in only some aspects of curriculum reform). Furthermore, because of the timing of data collection, participants were not well prepared to provide complete details about the curriculum models under development by their teams because curriculum adjustments were still being made at the time of the study (see Trial and Error is Messy below). To provide readers with a richer contextual understanding, the research team used the institutions' first- and second-year progress reports as the basis for briefly describing the six models as well as the commonalities and differences across the models (see Appendix B).

FINDINGS

Data analysis supported the identification of three emergent themes: (a) each institution's work depended on the commitment and direct actions of a *guiding coalition*, (b) each institution encountered the work as a *messy problem*, and (c) engagement with the messy problem at each institution led to *team learning*. Although the sequencing of these themes presents a chronological account of the curriculum work at the six institutions, the themes more importantly describe the character of the work—who did it, what the work entailed, and how the work fit into each faculty's understanding of its overarching mission to prepare teachers for schools that serve diverse learners.

Guiding Coalition

To accomplish the curriculum work, all the institutions started off with a core team, which served as the guiding coalition sponsoring the work. This guiding coalition provided the necessary moral and technical impetus for allowing the difficult work to move forward. Interview data supported insights about the membership of the institutions' guiding coalitions, the relevant skills and dispositions that coalition members brought to the work, what guiding coalition members experienced, and the actions taken by the guiding coalitions.

Members of the Guiding Coalitions

Guiding coalitions at all six institutions included two to five members with a minimum of one member from a special education discipline and one from a general education discipline. Sometimes those faculty members worked in the same department, but not always. In most cases one or more members of the guiding coalition had been responsible for writing the grant proposal—the step that marked the start of the incentive grant-sponsored dual-licensure efforts at their institutions. At several institutions, the team included a member who served a college-wide function (e.g., an accreditation coordinator). One institution that chose not to include such a person thought this gap made navigating change more challenging. In fact, one interviewee from that institution remarked,

> [In retrospect], I would put an administrator on that faculty leadership team, that central body that is doing the brunt of the work. I would put an administrator on that, maybe an associate dean for curriculum or something like that so that there are open channels of dissemination to faculty.

Without expressly stating it, a number of interviewees' comments suggested they agreed. One participant commented that "having the correct people around the table is so important."

Relevant Skills and Dispositions

Whatever their roles in their respective colleges of education, guiding coalition members committed to developing a successful dual-licensure program. They saw the work as necessary in order to improve their teacher preparation programs and therefore wanted the effort to succeed. According to one interviewee, "We wanted this to work. We wanted this to be beneficial."

Members of the guiding coalition brought their own disciplinary expertise to the work, but more important than expertise was their open-mindedness, willingness to learn from one another, and flexibility. These three qualities allowed them to operate from a perspective of mutual respect and to be forthright in confronting differences of opinion. They were also able to be resourceful in finding ways to bridge disciplinary boundaries. An open mindset also enabled each coalition to identify and pursue a shared scope of work. According to one of the evaluators, "they [faculty members] are trying to … become knowledgeable in each other's areas because if they are going to have dually certified teacher candidates then they also have to understand the importance and the need for both of those licensures."

In addition to their faculty expertise, members contributed other areas of expertise. In one college of education, the human-relations skills of two coalition members proved particularly helpful. In another, the "institutional memory" of one coalition member provided important insights for navigating required approval processes. Previous experience with other dual-licensure programs enabled an external evaluator at one of the IHEs to contribute especially relevant insights to discussions among members of the guiding coalition (e.g., ideas about developing marketing tools to assist with the recruitment of community partners).

What Coalition Members Experienced

Coalition members experienced and built on a sense of camaraderie. In some cases, they knew each other well and were familiar with one another's programs. As one participant put it, "there were no silos to break down." In other cases, coalition members learned about one another's programs as part of the dual-licensure curriculum work. According to one participant,

I think we have [become] more collaborative because of it. Because we had
to sit in a room with the doors locked (no they weren't; I am kidding), but
we needed to work it out, and we have become closer. I don't know if that
is the right word, but we understand each other's program better and we
work better now together.

In the words of another interviewee, the learning processes in which
coalition members participated relied on having many "hard conversations" within a protected setting. Their commitment to the process led
them to stick with the effort—irrespective of the challenges they encountered—from beginning to end.

The Guiding Coalitions' Actions

Members of the guiding coalition took three important kinds of actions:
leading the discourse, managing structures, and managing boundaries. In
terms of discourse, guiding coalition members built support for the work by
first advocating and "translating" it to wider groups of faculty and partners.
Advocacy involved framing explanations in ways that enabled others to
participate in, and understand the importance and feasibility of, the work.
Translation involved helping faculty from one discipline understand the
perspectives of another discipline. According to some participants, faculty
members who were outside of the guiding coalition looked to members of
the coalition to provide clarity and support.

Members of the guiding coalition also spoke up in meetings and
provided intellectual leadership. According to one participant, their intellectual leadership led to a deeper understanding, among all college faculty
members, of program overlaps and differences and to greater program
coherence overall. One interviewee believed that the intellectual leadership provided by the guiding coalition "has built a tighter community for
the students as they come into this program, you know I think we have
learned, you know the values of each program, in terms of expectations and
the values that we carry in our programs, and who we want our students
to be."

The guiding coalitions also structured the work by: (a) organizing
meetings, (b) inviting a wider group of faculty members and institutional
partners to the table, (c) sequencing steps, (d) orchestrating efforts to draw
on relevant expertise, (e) dividing a wider group of faculty and partners
into work groups, (f) setting timelines, (g) employing helpers and coordinating their tasks, (h) pulling together written materials, and (i) completing
myriad other tasks. One member stated, "I feel like I am a chess player
and I just keep moving pieces around...." Structuring the work involved

continual attention to organization. As one participant reported, the work involved "getting all the required information that people may need to do this curriculum revamping and [getting] it up on that Blackboard site so everyone has access and so that common communication strategy and coming up with how they are going to organize all of that."

Members of the guiding coalition met frequently to consider processes that would likely advance the work as well as to track the progress of the curriculum work itself. They also determined which professional development the members of the wider group of program stakeholders needed. In several cases, the guiding coalition organized events at which stakeholders learned more about inclusive education and dual-licensure teacher preparation programs. In other cases, helping stakeholders learn teaming skills became important. Structuring also involved defining the nature of the products that would represent the completed work as well as intermediate products that would show progress toward eventual completion of the work. Coordination of products involved more than simply compiling the pieces, some members of the guiding coalitions edited and often rewrote documents that others had submitted. They also created documents when they struggled to get drafts from the wider group of faculty and partners.

In addition to advocating and structuring, the guiding coalitions managed boundaries in support of their work. For example, they involved widening groups of faculty members in the work and met with administrators to ensure that college leaders stayed informed of progress and understood the support needed from them. Members of the guiding coalitions were also the ones to liaise with evaluators, involving those individuals directly in the work as well as sharing the evaluators' insights with the wider group of stakeholders. As the work progressed—"from the broad down to the more specific," as one participant put it—the guiding coalitions continued to widen the circle of participants and supporters. The guiding coalition became the "hub of the wheel." One participant commented that "[the coalition needed to] … expand outwards to begin to address all of the other issues that were involved and enlist other people's support." According to one interviewee, managing boundaries required members of the guiding coalition to navigate across the different cultures of departments and other groupings of faculty.

A Messy Problem[1]

At each institution, the guiding coalition and a wider group of stakeholders confronted the curriculum work as a set of challenges. The complexity involved was not apparent at first. As each team moved forward, it gained a deeper understanding of the work's requirements—a process that led the teams to view challenges as more extensive and entangled than they originally had imagined. One participant compared the work to "peeling an onion. Dual licensure is like layers and with each layer you realize there is another you have to work through."

The set of expectations communicated by the ODE and the Ohio Deans Compact, as the funders and monitors of the work, constituted one challenge facing the IHE teams. Notably, each dual-licensure program needed to address all applicable professional standards, create a curriculum of approximately the same length as other teacher preparation curricula at their institution, and provide field experiences at three developmental levels (i.e., early, middle, and adolescent-young adult). These expectations inevitably required institutions to identify and include only courses and field experiences that were *most important* for preparing teachers with the skills needed to work with diverse learners. As one interviewee stated, "Along the way everyone had to give up something to get the larger dual-licensure program."

Another challenge for program restructuring was that it required faculty members and other partners to work in a non-traditional way. Notably, the program's focus on inclusive education breeched (with the hope of bridging) traditional barriers, both within PK–12 schools and university preparation programs. As one participant remarked, "We are putting together a whole new program, a whole new orientation that is built on inclusion of everybody." This new orientation required guiding coalitions to navigate philosophical differences undergirding the curricula for preparing general educators and the curricula for preparing special educators. They not only needed to surface these fundamental differences (e.g., the difference between a constructivist and behaviorist perspectives), they also needed to determine how to develop a pedagogy curriculum that accounted for both perspectives.

Trial and Error Is Messy

To accomplish the work, each team tested various approaches, not fully certain which would work best. A number of variables contributed to the direction taken by each IHE, including the background of coalition members; their work styles, readiness for the work, and levels of relevant knowledge; and their interpretation of the grantor's expectations. Tracking progress proved difficult because coalitions began work at different points; there was no distinct "starting point." Progress sometimes seemed to halt, and some coalitions later rethought decisions they had made early in the process. For example, one guiding coalition realized that involving clinical supervisors from PK–12 schools much earlier would have facilitated their work. Their subsequent effort to involve clinical supervisors required a significant amount of backtracking.

Trial and error was not only a short-term approach, but characterized the work overall. Stakeholders at each institution needed to accept the importance of the dual-licensure effort without having conclusive evidence showing that a dual-licensure curriculum was (or would be) more effective than the traditional curriculum. In the words of one participant, "Three years from now we are going to know a lot more than what we know right now." According to another,

> If this plan doesn't work out, there may be a Plan B or Plan C. Let's give this a try, you know let's see what we end up with. The need will continue regardless of what we finish doing, that is, the biggest facilitator is acknowledgement across the board that we need to do better.

As this comment suggests, the experimental nature of the curriculum work contributed to its tenuousness. Not only did this circumstance require faculty members to wait for evidence that the new curriculum was at least as effective as those it would replace, but the experimental nature of the work also fueled some opposition to the effort at several institutions. In fact, at the time of this writing, one of the institutions has chosen not to move forward with the implementation of its dual-licensure curriculum; another failed to obtain approval from university administrators.

Negotiation Is Messy

Because the process involved stakeholders with different perspectives about what candidates in a dual-licensure program would need to learn, discussions about the evolving curriculum required negotiations across faculty groups. The fact that members of the guiding coalition acted as representatives of their disciplines (e.g., special education), although they could not really speak on behalf of the faculty in the program they represented, further complicated this situation. They, therefore, needed to share emerging curriculum ideas with their colleagues, gather their colleagues' perspectives, and share that input with other members of the guiding coalition. The process was labor-intensive and often described as frustrating. As one faculty member commented regarding one such situation, "[I told everyone] you know we really just need to walk away, you know, and come back another day and see if we can't figure this out."

Negotiations intensified when the guiding coalitions pulled together broader groups of stakeholders. These stakeholders did not necessarily have the same passion for the work or the same understandings about it as did members of the guiding coalition. Interestingly, meetings with broader assemblages of faculty members tended to be more intense and conflictual than those with teachers and administrators from PK–12 partner institutions. Some participants attributed this difference to the greater pragmatism of the PK–12 educators. As one faculty member put it,

> All of the [PK–12] folks in the room were [sure] that the program couldn't be designed as a just kind of pulling pieces from [general education] and pulling pieces from the special [education] programs and lumping them together. It had to be full integration around key principles that are happening in the [PK–12] environment.

Others attributed it to the PK–12 partners' cachet, because they were ultimately the people who hired program graduates: "We have another meeting with principals to talk about how they see this working in their schools ... what do they feel we need to make sure is in our syllabi .... These people are those who have hired our [intervention specialists]."

The work's difficulty did not deter any of the IHEs. In fact, interviews revealed that the challenges contributed to significant benefits for each IHE, such as the improvement of curriculum coherence, the engagement of faculty in an informal type of professional development (see Team Learning below), and the reaffirmation of stakeholder buy-in.

Team Learning

Efforts to navigate and reflect on the messy problem produced team learning at each of the institutions. In particular, teams used various types of expertise to navigate and reflect on the curriculum challenges that they confronted. Teams also acquired new knowledge and skills as a result of their efforts to restructure their curricula. Consideration of team learning in this section focuses on: (a) how they learned, (b) what they learned, and (c) the results of their learning.

How They Learned

Data analysis suggested that the intensity of the curriculum work instigated a significant effect for faculty members' learning (both individual and collective). In fact, the work proved foundational in the sense that faculty members viewed it as requiring them to examine and, to some extent, change the assumptions that supported their disciplinary and pedagogical expertise. Their learning, therefore, was an adaptive reaction to the intensity of the work.

The work's unyielding nature contributed to its intensity. For example, the short timetable was stressful for faculty members, and meetings were long (often full-day meetings or even longer retreats). Its collaborative nature also heightened the intensity. One participant commented,

> I have learned a lot of content related to special education that I didn't know before. ... I had no idea what a functional behavior assessment was, but I am starting to learn how that specific content should be embedded in our courses ... it really is desirable and possible to integrate special education and general education and learn that it really shouldn't be anything separate.

High stakes at almost all the IHEs further contributed to intensity. Faculty members at five of the six universities realized that the work to create the dual-licensure program was likely to influence all the programs in their colleges (or departments). In the program that decided not to move forward with implementation, the stakes seemed lower because the new curriculum was highly specialized and therefore unlikely to attract many students, alter the thinking of most faculty members in the college, or have broad implications for the college's programs overall.

Learning occurred via the extensive set of collaborative processes used at each of the IHEs. Faculty members met many times in full- and half-day sessions, persisting with the work until they produced a revised curriculum that fit with the funders' expectations, the standards of relevant accreditation bodies, and institutional beliefs and requirements. Their learning was, in fact, a by-product of the curriculum-change process.

What They Learned

The team members acquired important knowledge related to theoretical and pedagogical assumptions and related skillsets within the general education and special education disciplines. These assumptions concerned: effective theoretical grounding (e.g., constructivist theories versus behaviorist theories), instructional methods (e.g., the need to focus on large group instruction rather than small group and individual instruction), and differing conceptions of fairness in accommodating the diverse needs of students. Team members typically knew the curriculum standards, theoretical assumptions, knowledge base, and relevant practices of their own disciplines, but they possessed limited understanding of the conceptual underpinnings of the other discipline. Learning as a team showed them how the two conceptual frameworks (and sets of practices) differed, but also how they overlapped. According to one participant,

The first year was a lot of self-study, looking at courses that were involved in the program, looking at what we had, what the gaps were, what we might have been duplicating. I think [we focused on] getting our philosophies [into alignment], and what it means to graduate a special educator, what it means to graduate a general education teacher. It was preparing whoever goes through this program to address all learners.

Work to understand a broader conceptual framework (and the theoretical and pedagogical assumptions underlying it) required faculty members to examine and ultimately revise their core beliefs about what school systems should accomplish and what teaching should entail. Differences in core beliefs became obvious to faculty members as they engaged more deeply with the curriculum work. According to one interviewee, "Differences in culture exist in our special education and general education faculty, in the sense of what is at the center of their philosophy." Another participant remarked that

I think it forced me to look more closely at the teacher education research.... It has really got me focused on both the academic side of supporting diverse learners and also on teacher education and teacher preparation for special education, especially.

Nevertheless, understanding the differences in core beliefs did not prove sufficient for accomplishing the curriculum work. Faculties also needed to figure out how to *resolve* apparent conflicts between their core beliefs. In most cases, the resolution required faculty to reach two conclusions and then act on them: first, that an umbrella concept could subsume two or more different sets of core beliefs and, second, that a program's conceptual framework was less important than the effectiveness of the practices it taught candidates to use. The following quote from a participant embeds both ideas:

Our school of ed[ucation's] conceptual framework [focuses on the educator as a] reflective decision maker in a pluralistic society.... It ties in [teaching] and consulting and health services and all kinds of things.... We are still about training the best teacher candidates we can, performance-based kind of assessments, they understand what they need to do, we tie it to their field requirements.... We are just doing more of what we always said we valued.

For most faculty members, these conclusions were the outcome of the extensive inquiry process that the dual-licensure curriculum work entailed, not simply insights resulting from dialogue with colleagues from other departments or programs. As one participant explained,

> What we were looking for was: what do we know about ...what frameworks [schools] use for implementing and sustaining effective practices? And we found authoritative sources—research on what is the best knowledge that we have about those models and frameworks.

According to another, looking for evidence of the effectiveness of teaching practices enabled faculty members with different core beliefs to identify the most critical content for inclusion in the dual-licensure program. As she explained, "evidence-based practices: we had this like an umbrella term to guide where we wanted to go." Another faculty member captured a similar idea when she talked about the importance of focusing the curriculum work on skills that candidates would "walk away with."

Results of Their Learning

Through an intensive process that required inquiry and collaborative problem solving, faculty participants expanded their knowledge of educational aims, structures, and practices. For example, one faculty member explained how she shared principles of culturally responsive pedagogy with her colleagues on the curriculum team. Another talked about how his original perspective on ways to manage students' behavior was narrower than it should be. In his opinion, participation in the curriculum work allowed him to develop a broader view.

Faculty members who played a role in this curriculum work also learned to participate in a collaborative culture outside their specific program or discipline. For many of them, specialized doctoral studies coupled with compartmentalized organizational structures within their universities kept them from interacting routinely with faculty members from other disciplines. Involvement with the dual-licensure work, however, showed them an alternative that they intended to nurture for the future. As one of the local evaluators commented,

> They seem to have developed a really good working relationship, so that has reinforced my belief in collaboration. They are talking to each other like super colleagues; and this is [a general education program] and [a special education program]. These are two different worlds.

The three emergent themes—construction of a guiding coalition, facing the multiple facets of a messy problem, and the demand for team learning to address the challenges associated with curriculum change—defined the curriculum restructuring efforts at the six institutions. These themes were more descriptive than prescriptive, but, as we discuss next, they do lend credence to suggestions drawn from the literature on similar curriculum restructuring efforts at other IHEs.

DISCUSSION AND IMPLICATIONS

Findings from the study demonstrate that dual-licensure programs can be developed when the effort receives adequate support (in this case, external support) and when faculty members and their PK–12 partners are sufficiently open to making the necessary changes. Although curriculum restructuring is messy work, it offers significant rewards to the faculty members who participate and the programs they serve.

As suggested (see Findings above), this study points to an oft-cited insight: context matters. One common contextual feature facing the institutions we studied was the funding assistance provided by ODE and the oversight provided by the Ohio Deans Compact. Without that support and routine monitoring it would have been unlikely for the IHEs to complete the intensive work needed to produce a curriculum and gain state approval for a dual-licensure program.

The study also found that, despite local differences in composition and function, a guiding coalition proved necessary for instituting and sustaining the work. This coalition provided the moral and technical force that enabled the difficult work to progress. To support the effort, the coalition drew on a wide range of relevant skills and knowledge, brought together "the correct people" capable of mutual respect and camaraderie, led discourse across an increasingly broad group of stakeholders, and coordinated a complex set of tasks by managing organizational structures and navigating institutional boundaries.

The members of the guiding coalition at each institution quickly discovered that the process was messy. The requirements of the funder contributed to the messiness of the problem because these requirements could be addressed only through foundational, and not superficial, curriculum reform. The messy problem, moreover, demanded negotiation across both the conceptual and practical differences that characterized the special education and general education programs at each IHE. The guiding coalitions (along with a wider network of stakeholders) had to respect and accommodate differences in perspective and ultimately forge a new, broader perspective.

The institutions involved in this restructuring process had to manage how they learned, how they incorporated what they learned, and how their learning would become institutionalized in program content and supporting structures. Each team's willingness to entertain new ideas—to listen, challenge previous assumptions, and incorporate new knowledge—sat at the heart of its learning. The processes used across the institutions in our study and the challenges the teams encountered appear similar in many ways to what has been reported in earlier literature. Our findings clarified and elaborated on these dynamics revealed in earlier research.

- Similar to descriptions in the work of York-Barr and associates (2004), restructuring efforts at the six institutions we studied confronted differences between the conceptual frameworks that inform the curricula of teacher preparation programs for general educators and for special educators. Our study showed that commitment to a shared vision (see also Brownell et al., 2005; Cyr et al., 2012; Oyler, 2011) and adoption of an experimentalist stance allowed the two faculties at each institution to identify commonalities in their aims and practices and to come to agreement about the content of their dual-licensure curricula.
- Like other studies, ours also showed how demanding this type of curriculum work can be (e.g., Keefe et al., 2000; Sobel et al., 2007; York-Barr et al., 2004). The infusion of external support from the state, coupled with the explicit understanding that each grant recipient would be held accountable for producing a new curriculum model, seems to have helped each of the six teams mobilize to accomplish significant restructuring in a relatively short amount of time.
- Other features of the curriculum work described in the interviews we conducted were akin to efforts elsewhere. Notably, the institutions involved in the process conducted systematic reviews of curricular content, often grounded in relevant standards (Dingle et al., 2004; Sands et al., 2007). They received support from department and college administrators (Blanton & Pugach, 2011; Cyr et al., 2012; Harvey et al., 2010; Keefe et al., 2000; Young, 2011); there was ample and open discussion across faculties from general and special education departments (Brownell et al., 2005, 2011); and involvement of supportive faculty members appeared evident at each stage of the process (York-Barr et al., 2004).

The institutions in our study also used less frequently cited practices. In particular, they created governance structures (e.g., guiding coalitions and teams with a wider assemblage of partners) that broke down disciplinary silos (see also Kozleski et al., 2002), and they used critical friends and external evaluators to provide formative feedback and to help identify and overcome challenges (see also Cyr et al., 2012).

Perhaps the most important finding of our work was the value of external sponsorship for efforts to forge merged and integrated teacher education programs. Such sponsorship can provide an incentive to do the work, on-going support during the work, and accountability to a wider community of practice. It also can help faculties push against unproductive disciplinary silos—silos that tend to be more attentive to socially constructed differences among students (e.g., students with learning disabilities, English learners, gifted students) than to their shared needs, interests, and aspirations.

Recommendations

Even without external support, however, teacher education faculties can undertake the major curriculum work needed to develop merged or integrated programs. The experiences of the faculty members in the current study suggest that the following actions might prove useful:

- Establish a guiding coalition and a wider stakeholder group.
- Include PK–12 educators in the stakeholder group and possibly also in the guiding coalition.
- Ensure that the stakeholder group (or possibly the guiding coalition) includes college leaders or support staff with college-wide influence.
- Establish non-negotiables that help define the work (e.g., that the credit hours required by the merged or integrated program remain comparable to those required by the institution's other teacher preparation programs).
- Set timetables and benchmarks. Keep timetables relatively tight.
- Establish protocols for meetings, expectations for deliverables, and contingency plans for handling predictable challenges.
- Enlist the help of an external facilitator, critical friend, or evaluator.
- Use applicable state and national standards to create a vision of the critical knowledge and skills required by all program graduates. Design course work and field experiences to match this vision.
- Sequence course work and field experiences in a way that allows each to provide support to the other.
- Prepare to sustain collegiality with the knowledge that some curriculum conversations may become difficult or even contentious.
- Recognize that the curriculum work will involve trial and error; assume an inquiring (even experimentalist) stance.

NOTE

1. The complexity of the work, while posing a variety of challenges, did not overwhelm the effort at any of the IHEs. For this reason, we did not characterize the problem as "wicked" (e.g., Rittel & Webber, 1973), but rather as just "messy."

REFERENCES

Arthaud, T. J., Aram, R. J., Breck, S. E., Doelling, J. E., & Bushrow, K. M. (2007). Developing collaboration skills in pre-service teachers: A partnership between general and special education. *Teacher Education and Special Education, 30*, 1–12. doi:10.1177/088840640703000101

Blanton, L. P., & Pugach, M. C. (2011). Using a classification system to probe the meaning of dual licensure in general and special education. *Teacher Education & Special Education, 34*, 219–234. doi:10.1177/0888406411404569

Brigham, F. J. (1993, February). *Cross-training: Faculty-sharing between general and special teacher education programs.* Paper presented at the annual meeting of the Indiana Federation, Council for Exceptional Children, Indianapolis, IN.

Brownell, M. T., Griffin, C., Leko, M. M., & Stephens, J. (2011). Improving collaborative teacher education research: Creating tighter linkages. *Teacher Education & Special Education, 34*, 235–249. doi:10.1177/0888406411404570

Brownell, M. T., Ross, D. D., Colón, E. P., & McCallum, C. L. (2005). Critical features of special education teacher preparation: A comparison with general teacher education. *Journal of Special Education, 38*, 242–252. doi:10.1177/00224669 050380040601

Cochran-Smith, M. (2005). Teacher development and educational reform. In M. Fullan (Ed.), *Fundamental change: International handbook of educational change* (pp. 27–88). The Netherlands: Springer.

Corbin, J., & Strauss, A. (2007). *Basics of qualitative research: Techniques and procedures for developing grounded theory* (3rd ed.). Thousand Oaks, CA: SAGE.

Cosier, M., Causton-Theoharis, J., & Theoharis, G. (2013). Does access matter? Time in general education and achievement for students with disabilities. *Remedial & Special Education, 34*, 323–332. doi:10.1177/0741932513485448

Cyr, E., McDiarmid, P., Halpin, B., Stratton, J., & Davis-Delano, L. C. (2012). Creating a dual licensure program in elementary and special education that prepares culturally responsive teachers. *Interdisciplinary Journal of Teaching and Learning, 2*, 158–168.

Dingle, M., Falvey, M. A., Givner, C. C., & Haager, D. (2004). Essential special and general education teacher competencies for preparing teachers for inclusive settings. *Issues in Teacher Education, 13*(1), 35–50.

Frattura, E., & Capper, C. A. (2006). Segregated programs versus integrated comprehensive service delivery for all learners: Assessing the differences. *Remedial & Special Education, 27*, 355–364. doi:10.1177/074193250602700 60501

Frattura, E. M., & Capper, C. A. (2007). *Leading for social justice: Transforming schools for all learners.* Thousand Oaks, CA: Corwin.

Frey, T. J., Andres, D. K., McKeeman, L. A., & Lane, J. J. (2012). Collaboration by design: Integrating core pedagogical content and special education methods courses in a preservice secondary education program. *Teacher Educator, 47,* 45–66. doi:10.1080/08878730.2011.632473

Fullerton, A., Ruben, B. J., McBride, S., & Bert, S. (2011). Development and design of a merged secondary and special education teacher preparation program. *Teacher Education Quarterly, 38*(2), 27–44.

Hamman, D., Lechtenberger, D., Griffin-Shirley, N., & Zhou, L. (2013). Beyond exposure to collaboration: Preparing general-education teacher candidates for inclusive practice. *Teacher Educator, 48,* 244–256. doi:10.1080/08878730 .2013.796030

Harvey, M. W., Yssel, N., Bauserman, A. D., & Merbler, J. B. (2010). Preservice teacher preparation for inclusion: An exploration of higher education teacher-training institutions. *Remedial and Special Education, 31,* 24–33. doi:10.1177/0741932508324397

Jenkins, A. A., Pateman, B., & Black, R. S. (2002). Partnerships for dual preparation in elementary, secondary, and special education programs. *Remedial & Special Education, 23,* 359–371. doi:10.1177/07419325020230060601

Keefe, E. B., Rossi, P. J., De Valenzuela, J. S., & Howarth, S. (2000). Reconceptualizing teacher preparation for inclusive classrooms: A description of the Dual License Program at the University of New Mexico. *Journal of The Association for Persons with Severe Handicaps, 25*(2), 72–82. doi:10.2511/rpsd.25.2.72

Kozleski, E. B., Pugach, M., & Yinger, R. (2002). *Preparing Teachers to Work with Students with Disabilities: Possibilities and Challenges for Special and General Teacher Education* (White Paper). Washington, DC: American Association of Colleges for Teacher Education.

Noble, H., & Smith, J. (2015). Issues of validity and reliability in qualitative research. *Evidence-Based Nursing, 18,* 34–35. doi:10.1136/eb-2015-102054

Oyler, C. (2011). Teacher preparation for inclusive and critical (special) education. doi:10.1177/0888406411406745

Rittel, H. W. J., & Webber, M. W. (1973). Dilemmas in a general theory of planning. *Policy Sciences, 4,* 155–169. doi:10.1007/bf01405730.

Salle, R.S., & Johnson, R.A. (2010). *Data strategies to uncover and eliminate hidden inequities: The wallpaper effect.* Thousand Oaks, CA: Corwin.

Sands, D. I., Duffield, J. A., & Parsons, B. A. (2006). Evaluating infused content in a merged special education and general education teacher preparation program. *Action in Teacher Education, 28*(4), 92–103. doi:10.1080/01626620. 2007.10463432

Sobel, D. M., Iceman-Sands, D., & Basile, C. (2007). Merging general and special education teacher preparation programs to create an inclusive program for diverse learners. *New Educator, 3,* 241–262. doi:10.1080/15476880701484113

Teixeira, R., Frey, W. H., & Griffin, R. (2015). *States of change: The demographic evolution of the American electorate, 1974–2060.* Washington, DC: Center for American Progress, American Enterprise Institute, & Brookings Institution.

Wolfberg, P., LePage, P., & Cook, E. (2009). Innovations in inclusive education: Two teacher preparation programs at the San Francisco State University. *International Journal of Whole Schooling, 5*(2), 16–36.

York-Barr, J., Bacharach, N., Salk, J., Frank, J. H., & Benick, B. (2004). Team teaching in teacher education: General and special education faculty experiences and perspectives. *Issues in Teacher Education, 13*(1), 73–94.

Young, K. S. (2011). Institutional separation in schools of education: Understanding the functions of space in general and special education teacher preparation. *Teaching and Teacher Education, 27,* 483–493. doi:10.1016/j.tate.2010.10.001

Zion, S., & Sobel, D. M. (2014). Mapping the gaps: Redesigning a teacher education program to prepare teachers for inclusive, urban U.S. schools. *Journal of The International Association of Special Education, 15*(2), 63–73.

APPENDIX A

Faculty/Staff Interview Schedule

NOTE: The main questions are listed with possible prompts included in parentheses after some of the questions.

Individual Roles:

1. What role have you played in the curriculum work sponsored by the Incentive Grant (e.g., the tasks and responsibilities you were given to accomplish/assist with)?
2. In what ways did you interact/collaborate with the evaluator and other faculty and staff participants in the curriculum-development process?

Overview of the Process:

3. Please describe the process of developing and implementing the program thus far. (Describe the essential role of evidence-based practices in your restructuring work.)
4. How would you characterize the priorities of your restructuring efforts? (What were the objectives of the program? Characterize the major learning objectives of your grant work.)
5. Briefly describe the pedagogical approach embedded in the program restructuring? (Describe the essential role of evidence-based practices in your restructuring work.)

6. What steps in the change process still need to be accomplished?

Facilitators/Barriers to Progress:

7. What aspects and conditions of the restructuring process have facilitated the work towards its end goal (e.g., resources you have utilized that contributed significantly to progress)? (Describe ways in which the evaluator facilitated progress.)
8. What aspects and conditions of the restructuring process have posed barriers to your work towards the end goal (e.g., aspects that hindered progress)? (Describe ways in which the evaluator created barriers to progress.)

Impact:

9. How have the faculty and staff who are involved in the curriculum revision been affected by the process? (Describe behaviors and practices that have changed as a result of involvement in the restructuring process.)
10. How have university administrators influenced or been influenced by the curriculum work?
11. What have you learned as a result of your involvement with the curriculum change process?

Reflections:

12. What processes or steps in the process did you see as essential? What processes or steps in the process did you see as distracting to or interruptive of the overall work?
13. Is there any additional insight you would offer to a university that is trying to restructure their program to accomplish similar goals?
14. What else would you like to tell me about the curriculum restructuring process that you haven't yet had a chance to tell me?

APPENDIX B

Brief Review of Curricular Commonalities and Differences

Course Type	Course Summaries	Institutions
Technology	Courses designed to teach preservice teachers how to effectively use and incorporate technology into their classrooms as an instructional tool.	University of Cincinnati Xavier University Kent State University
Educational Psychology	Use psychological theories to aid preservice teachers with understanding the dynamic of the classroom and the students and how the dynamic may vary with exceptional students. The University of Akron's course emphasizes the development of students (e.g. cognitively) and introduces various learning theories/approaches to assist preservice teachers in managing, motivating, instructing and assessing students in the classroom.	University of Cincinnati University of Akron Kent State University
Introduction to Education and/or Teaching	Courses that provide preservice teachers with an introduction to the historical progression of schools and the education system, the diversity of students (e.g. cultural, linguistic and economic differences) and how education is connected to society. Encourage students not only to learn new content, but also to think reflectively about the education process and how to facilitate the learning of all students. Ohio State University's curriculum also includes a Foundations of Multilingual Education course in which preservice teachers learn about how schools have managed linguistic diversity.	University of Cincinnati Xavier University University of Akron Kent State University University of Dayton
Assessment/ Evaluation Courses	Courses that focus on preparing preservice teachers to select, administer, and interpret formal and informal assessments as a basis for instructional planning.	University of Cincinnati University of Akron University of Dayton Ohio State University Kent State University
Classroom Management	Courses that help preservice teachers develop strategies for implementing instructional and behavioral management plans for diverse learners.	University Cincinnati Xavier University University of Akron Kent State University

(Appendix continues on next page)

APPENDIX B (CONTINUED)

Course Type	Course Summaries	Institutions
Diversity Courses	Courses focusing on different aspects of diversity including cultural and socioeconomic, but all are intended to demonstrate how diversity impacts schooling and to help develop practices for reaching all learners.	University Cincinnati Xavier University University of Dayton Ohio State University
Literacy Core	Four courses that focus on phonics, teaching reading to diverse students, using literature effectively in a classroom, and comprehension.	University Cincinnati Xavier University University of Akron University of Dayton Kent State University Ohio State University
Content Methods/ Instructional Methods	Courses that teach pedagogical strategies for instructional planning and delivery of instruction.	University of Cincinnati Xavier University University of Dayton Ohio State University Kent State University
Collaboration	Courses presenting strategies for communicating with co-collaborators in the schools and families of the students no matter how diverse a home life they have.	Xavier University University of Akron Kent State University
Development	Courses that provide preservice teachers with an understanding of typical cognitive, social, and behavioral development of children.	University of Cincinnati Xavier University Kent State University
Exceptionalities	Courses presenting content about different types of learners, effective interventions for teaching all learners (including those with disabilities and special talents), IEPs, and ethical and legal requirements of working with students with disabilities.	University of Cincinnati Ohio State University University of Akron Kent State University Xavier University

CHAPTER 12

AN INTEGRATIVE TEACHER PREPARATION MODEL TO PREPARE ALL TEACHER CANDIDATES FOR DIVERSE INCLUSIVE EDUCATION

Bridgie A. Ford, Shernavaz Vakil, and Lynn S. Kline
University of Akron

Traditional teacher preparation programs have been slow to adopt as core practices the collaborative, interdisciplinary, sustained, learner-centered approach indicated as best practice for ensuring equitable and quality education for all learners (Blanton & Pugach, 2011; Diamond & Powell, 2011; Utley, 2009). This situation leaves students with mild-moderate disabilities as identified under the Individuals with Disabilities Education Act and students from other groups—such as English learners (EL) and those from marginalized ethnic groups—with inadequate educational options. As a result, these students may underachieve in core academic subjects and face more limited opportunities for employment and postsecondary educational programs (Cummins, 2009). To better serve the increasing number of diverse students in general education classrooms, teachers must

Inclusive Education: A Systematic Perspective, pp. 225–234
Copyright © 2020 by Information Age Publishing
All rights of reproduction in any form reserved.

be prepared to work in inclusive settings and collaborate across disciplines; they need to diversify their practices on behalf of the diverse students with whom they work. Content area teachers of literacy, language arts, mathematics, social studies, and science need a teacher-preparation curriculum that teaches culturally responsive practices as well as a variety of research-based teaching strategies to meet the needs of students with disabilities and those from other marginalized groups.

UNIVERSITY OF AKRON INTEGRATIVE TEACHER PREPARATION MODEL AS A VEHICLE OF CHANGE

To equip all University of Akron teacher candidates with the knowledge, skills, and dispositions to best serve all preschool through Grade 12 (P–12) students, a team of faculty members collaborated in the development of a sustainable, replicable, *evidence-based* teacher preparation model. The University of Akron's Integrative Teacher Preparation Model (UA-ITPM) deploys an integrative paradigm incorporating evidence-based content and pedagogy for inclusive settings into the coursework and the clinical and field experiences required of ALL teacher candidates. To accomplish the goal of restructuring the University of Akron's (UA's) stand-alone teacher licensure programs to prepare teachers for inclusive practice, the UA-ITPM team:

- Modified the teacher education core, literacy, and content specific courses taken by all teacher licensure candidates. The UA-ITPM accomplished this by constructing a logic model emphasizing the essential professional knowledge, skills, dispositions, clinical activities, field experiences, and action research activities that prepare candidates to effectively teach diverse learners (i.e., students with disabilities, English language learners, and learners from other traditionally marginalized groups) in P–12 inclusive settings.
- Developed products aligned with best practices including online modules, instructional materials, and readings embedded in the restructured core and content area courses (e.g., science, math, social studies, and language arts) to address the needs of diverse learners in inclusive settings.

The UA-ITPM team explored new ways of thinking about professional learning, collaboration, and the process needed to implement the transition to two dual-licensure programs that would replace the university's traditional single-licensure programs. A conceptual change became imperative. To this end, the UA-ITPM team applied principles embedded within a well-respected theory of change.

UA-ITPM'S ADOPTED THEORY OF CHANGE

According to the theory of conceptual change developed by Posner, Strike, Hewson, and Gertzog (1982), four conditions must be met in order for change to occur: (a) individuals must be dissatisfied with the current understanding; (b) individuals must have an available and intelligible alternative; (c) the alternative must seem plausible to the individuals; and (d) the alternative must seem doable to the individuals. In essence, the theory of change requires four evaluative criteria related to alternatives to the status quo. It requires that proposed alternatives be plausible, doable, testable, and meaningful. Connell and Klem (2012) elaborate on the relevance of using these four criteria in evaluating conceptual change in educational reform.

Using the Posner and associates' (1982) theory of change framework for the UA-ITPM model, these conditions meant that (a) faculty in our department of Curricular and Instructional Studies, which houses all licensure programs, must be concerned with the limitations of the stand-alone teacher education programs; (b) the dual-licensure programs presented a viable alternative to address the concerns; (c) the dual-licensure option was accepted as a credible and professional alternative by faculty; and (d) the dual-licensure programs were determined to be of likely benefit to the primary stakeholders: teacher candidates and P–12 students.

To meet the initial condition within the theory of change, the UA-ITPM team began formal discussions among department faculty to identify the shortcomings of the stand-alone programs. These discussions led to the recognition of the need for change within the department. This important first step resulted in the creation of the UA-ITPM logic model (see Appendix) to address the limitations of stand-alone programs and provide a framework to guide development of dual-licensure content and process and create viable (*plausible*) alternatives. Therefore, plausibility was also established, with buy-in from faculty, administration, and external stakeholders (school district partners) for the dual-licensure initiative. After reviewing the UA-ITPM logic model, department faculty agreed to accept it as *doable* and the team moved forward. After the UA-ITPM logic model was adopted by faculty, it was shared with external stakeholders. To address the next criterion (*testable*) in the proposed alternative program, a Qualtrics survey was designed to test school districts' and teacher candidates' interest in the dual-licensure programs.

The final criterion, that alternatives be *meaningful*, indicates that stakeholders see the outcomes as important and see the magnitude of change in these outcomes being pursued as worth the effort. The UA-ITPM adopted the Empowerment Evaluation (Fetterman, Rodríguez-Campos, Wandersman, & O'Sullivan, 2014), a performance monitoring and evaluation approach, as a means of assessing whether the alternative program is *meaningful*. The UA-ITPM team used this approach with partnering school districts to obtain input, as embedded within the theory of change is the recognition that all stakeholders become and remain involved.

UA-ITPM LOGIC MODEL

Today's teachers need to understand their students and employ the best practices and pedagogy to meet diverse needs in an inclusive classroom and to establish authentic networks with family and community members. Moreover, since general education teachers are often the ones who refer students for special education assessment, it is important for them to have knowledge that helps them distinguish disabilities from other learning challenges, such as different background knowledge and prior learning experiences as well as to address learning difficulties appropriately.

In providing culturally responsive instruction, the challenge for teachers is to teach content through different cultural lenses, presenting different perspectives through vignettes, scenarios, examples, and discussion topics that enhance students' understanding of principles, concepts, values, ideals, and generalizations behind the "facts" contained within the curriculum content (Gay, 2002). Integrating content with student experiences to scaffold instruction that promotes understanding of key concepts is vital to creating positive inclusive learning environments for all students, but especially for those whose cultural difference may be related to learning difficulties (Klinger & Gonzalez, 2009; Worrell, 2007). While the focus of the two dual-licensure programs is primarily to prepare teacher candidates to work with students with disabilities in inclusive settings, the importance of culturally responsive practices is essential and must be interwoven throughout the teacher preparation curriculum. The UA-ITPM logic model takes this need into consideration.

Designed to give the team and stakeholders a comprehensive perspective on the program content, process, and outcomes to guide the transition from single to dual licensure, the UA-ITPM logic model contains the following major features:

- **Framework**—focused on identifying evidence-based practice and professional standards guiding the restructuring process (e.g., content, skills, and dispositions);
- **Input**—centered on the UA-ITPM team identifying program faculty, establishing the internal and EACs, whose members provided input into the curriculum for the dual-licensure programs;
- **Implementation**—detailed procedures for implementing program restructuring and forming collaborative partnerships including roles and responsibilities of participating entities;
- **Outcomes/Impact**—delineated the modules, materials, and clinical activities to enable the restructured teacher licensure program to enhance the capacity of *all candidates* to instruct diverse learners effectively within P–12 settings in Ohio.

The inclusive curriculum addresses professional knowledge, skills, dispositions, clinical activities, field experiences, and action research activities that prepare candidates to teach diverse learners in today's inclusive classrooms across demographics (e.g., inner city schools, suburban schools, and rural schools). This integrated structure is implemented throughout all coursework in the new programs.

Internal Advisory Committee Involvement in the Change Process

The curriculum-development team consisted of the UA-ITPM team and an internal advisory committee (IAC) which included Special Education, teaching English to speakers of other languages, Early Childhood, Middle School, and Literacy faculty and administration. The primary role of the IAC was to analyze current curriculum and restructure it to create dual-licensure programs that align with the framework of the integrative logic model. The curriculum-development team integrated the knowledge, skills, and dispositions in the dual-licensure programs by embedding inclusive content, materials, and a variety of external resources designed to engage teacher candidates and move them from a basic knowledge to the ability to apply what they learn. Among the resources tapped for this purpose were the Center for Research on Education, Diversity, and Excellence; Ohio Leadership Advisory Committee modules; CAST: Universal Design for Learning; and Connecting with Culturally and Linguistically Diverse Communities (Ford, 2004).

External Advisory Committee Involvement in the Change Process

In addition to the IAC, the UA-ITPM team also established and collaborated with members of an external advisory committee (EAC), which included representatives from partnering school districts. The EAC served an important role, providing input about the needs of the districts in order to enhance the field- and student-teaching experiences aligned with the UA-ITPM model. After the department adopted the UA-ITPM logic model and tentatively planned content and field experiences, the Empowerment Evaluation (Fetterman, 2013) was conducted by the team in each of the partnering school districts, as mentioned earlier in the chapter.

The UA-ITPM team met with the school partners at their individual sites. At each meeting, interactive sessions were held to brainstorm responses to two open-ended questions: (a) "What are the knowledge, skills, dispositions you believe our teacher candidates should have as a result of dual licensure to impact outcomes in ALL learners?" and (b) "What components of the clinical field experience do you believe are important to enhance the dual-licensure candidate's knowledge, skills, and dispositions?" The UA-ITPM used recommendations from these partnering school districts to help guide the restructuring of the program and the clinical practice design.

During the initial implementation of the dual-licensure programs EAC input resulted in most of the field experiences being moved to clinical hubs (schools with multiple teacher candidates working in a single building), which allowed additional support from the dual-license teacher candidates to pupils needing one-on-one and small group interventions. In addition, EAC involvement ensured that many of the classes associated with the field experiences for the dual-licensure program would be conducted, on a once a week or a biweekly basis, in the schools themselves immediately after teacher candidates' field-experience activity. University faculty members, along with the teacher candidates, interact with the teachers in the schools and are immersed in school activities.

INITIAL EVALUATION—DUAL-LICENSURE PROGRAMS

To begin the process of evaluating the preparedness of candidates enrolled in the two dual-licensure programs, the UA-ITPM team obtained verbal input from cooperating teachers and administrators in the clinical hubs where methods courses are taught and students co-teach. University faculty members also attended end-of-the-semester meetings held in the schools. Anecdotal evidence coming from informal interactions with cooperating teachers shows a high level of satisfaction with the initial implementation of the program in our clinical hubs. Additionally, cooperating teachers in the clinical hubs are required to complete an evaluation form, based on a Likert scale, of candidates in their classroom. Most of the dual-licensure candidates' scores range from "4" to "5," the high end of the scale, representing "effective" and "most effective." The cooperating teachers' feedback suggests that the dual-licensure candidates they evaluated have the beginning level professional knowledge, skills, and dispositions to provide optimal learning environments and experiences to increase academic and social levels of performance of students in clinical settings inclusive of students with mild/moderate disabilities. These field-based data provide some initial evidence of the preparedness of candidates enrolled in the dual-licensure programs. As part of the College of Education's outcome assessment process, on-going, comprehensive evaluation will occur as teacher candidates move through the dual-licensure programs.

CONCLUSION

In engaging in this ambitious change process, the UA-ITPM team operated under the premise that the dominant, stand-alone teacher licensure approach created a professional disconnect between the knowledge, skills, and dispositions necessary in today's diverse inclusive classrooms. This chapter presented (a) a brief description of the creation of the UA-ITPM logic model and the change theory principles on which the model was based, and (b) how the UA-ITPM team used the model to guide the transition of single-licensure teacher preparation programs to two dual-licensure programs: Early Childhood/Early Childhood Intervention and Middle Level/Mild-Moderate Special Education (P–12).

Among the primary challenges the UA-ITPM team confronted were (a) the length of time taken for approval of the new curriculum at university and state level, and (b) integrating two very separate programs into one dual licensure program while maintaining the integrity of program content and keeping the dual licensure programs at acceptable credit hours.

Evidence to date suggests the effectiveness of the new programs, but further data collection is needed, as assessment is a critical and integral part of the continuous improvement of teaching and learning. The established University of Akron College of Education's outcome assessment framework will be used to provide more detailed, comprehensive, and ongoing evaluation of the dual-licensure programs. To that end, data will be collected from various sources (e.g., candidate work products, Ohio Assessments for Educators results, and student teaching evaluations) and analyzed annually.

As part of a program improvement cycle, an annual university Day of Development includes providing faculty with aggregated data by programs. The data are then reviewed by college administrators, department chairs, program leaders, program faculty, and professional community representatives to ensure quality and recommend improvements. In regard to teacher preparation, this evaluative effort includes data obtained from student teaching, candidates' exit surveys, key assessments including formal field assessments completed jointly by university instructors and cooperating teachers in schools. Collectively, these assessments will help provide a clearer profile of the strengths and possible areas of need within the dual-licensure programs.

REFERENCES

Blanton, L. P., & Pugach, M. C. (2011). Using a classification system to probe the meaning of dual licensure in general and special education. *Teacher Education and Special Education, 34*, 219–234. doi:10.1177/0888406411404569

Connell, J., & Klem, A. (2000). You can get there from here: Using a theory of change approach to plan urban education reform. *Journal of Educational and Psychological Consultation, 11*, 93–120. doi:10.1207/s1532768Xjepc1101_06

Cummins, J. (2009). Pedagogies of choice: Challenging coercive relations of power in classrooms and communities. *International Journal of Bilingual Education and Bilingualism, 12*, 261–271. doi:10.1080/13670050903003751

Diamond, K. E., & Powell, D. R. (2011). An iterative approach to the development of a professional development intervention for Head Start teachers. *Journal of Early Intervention, 33*, 75–93. doi:10.1177/1053815111400416

Fetterman, D. M. (2013). *Empowerment evaluation in the digital villages: Hewlett-Packard's $15 million race toward social justice.* Stanford, CA: Stanford University Press.

Fetterman, D., Rodríguez-Campos, L., Wandersman, A., & O'Sullivan, R. G. (2014). Collaborative, participatory, and empowerment evaluation: Building a strong conceptual foundation for stakeholder involvement approaches to evaluation (A response to Cousins, Whitmore, and Shulha, 2013). *American Journal of Evaluation, 35*, 144–148. doi:10.1177/1098214013509875

Ford, B. A., (2004). Preparing special educators for culturally responsive school-community partnerships. *Teacher Education and Special Education, 27*, 224–230. doi:10.1177/088840640402700302

Gay, G. (2002). Preparing for culturally responsive teaching. *Journal of Teacher Education, 53*(2), 106–116. doi:10.1177/0022487102053002003

Klinger, J., & Gonzalez, L. S. (2009). Culturally and linguistically responsive instruction for English language learners with learning disabilities, *Multiple Voices for Ethically Diverse Exceptional Learners, 12*(1), 5–20. doi:10.1177/0022219413476553

Posner, G. J., Strike, K. A., Hewson, P. W., & Gertzog, W. A. (1982). Accommodation of a scientific conception: Toward a theory of conceptual change. *Science Education, 66,* 211–227.

Utley, B. L. (2009). An analysis of the outcomes of a unified teacher preparation program. *Teacher Education and Special Education, 32,* 137–149. doi:10.1177/0888406409334204

Worrell, F. C. (2007). Ethnic identity, academic achievement, and global self-concept in four groups of academically talented adolescents. *Gifted Child Quarterly, 51,* 23–38. doi:10.1177/0016986206296655

UA-ITPM Logic Model

Framework	Input	Implementation			Outcomes-Impact	
		Activities	Participation	Short-Term	Intermediate	Long-Term
Research Foundation • Disposition • Teacher Expectation/Efficacy • Teacher Ethics (Jordan & Glenn, Forlin, Hoy and Miskel) • Knowledge & Application in Inclusive Settings • Needs of diverse learners (Diaz-Rico, Ortiz, McLaughlin, Cartledge, Artiles & Trent, Villa & Thousand) • Collaborative networks (Friend, Alvarez, McHatton, Daniel) • Evidenced-based Pedagogy (Cohen, Ford, Pugach, Onu-Wilborn) • Culturally responsive practices (Gay, Billings) • Classroom management (Brophy, Good, Harry) • RTI (Fuchs & Fuchs) • Strategies for engaging families and communities (Epstein, Ford) **Standards** • CEC Standards • OSTP Standards • CAEP Standards	• Faculty • Teacher preparation programs • Evidence based practices for educators in meeting diverse learning needs in inclusive classrooms • Professional standards for beginning educators (e.g., CEC, CAEP, and OSTP) • Recommendations from area school leaders	**What We Do** • Reconceptualization of the UA core for teacher preparation licensure program • Reconceptualize the UA Teacher Preparation Core to address inclusive practices for all preservice candidates • Reconceptualize specific courses within the mild moderate licensure program to align with the newly conceptualized UA Integrated Core Model • Reconceptualize literacy courses required for licensure to align with the UA Common Core Integrated Model • Conduct collaborative meetings to develop content specific modules for students with special needs, ELL, culturally responsive practices for infusion into middle and high school teacher preparation programs • Partner with agencies and service providers	**Who We Reach** • Preservice teachers (general and special educators) • School Agency Representatives • P-12 Learners • Parents • Stakeholders in education	• Develop On-line modules & materials focusing on best practices such as differentiated instruction, scaffolding, universal design for learning, and co-teaching for the diverse learner • Develop clinical activities and field experience materials-tool(s) to evaluate collaborative practices in inclusive settings. • Develop course and syllabi focusing on understanding the diverse learner and planning for instruction, culturally responsive classroom management & collaboration • Develop assessments focusing on learning outcomes that reform practice & are aligned to the professional	• Restructure the UA Teacher Preparation Core to address inclusive practices for all licensure candidates by reconceptualizing the current core to emphasize planning & assessment, classroom management and collaboration for the diverse learner • Restructure specific courses within the mild moderate licensure program to align with the newly conceptualized UA-ITPM to expedite dual licensure • Restructure literacy courses required for licensure to align with the UA-ITPM by including the language and literacy needs of students with disabilities, English language learners and other traditionally marginalized groups	• Candidates will have the professional framework to provide optimal learning environments and experiences to increase academic and social levels of performance of students with disabilities, ELLs & other traditionally marginalized groups within inclusive P-12 classroom settings

CHAPTER 13

DEVELOPING INTEGRATED INCLUSIVE CONTENT AND PEDAGOGY FOR A DUAL LICENSE MIDDLE CHILDHOOD EDUCATION PROGRAM

Christopher L. Atchison, Susan A. Gregson, Emilie M. Camp, Stephen D. Kroeger, and Holly Johnson
University of Cincinnati

INTRODUCTION

Preparing teacher candidates to address the needs of all students, especially those who often struggle in academic settings, is not a new idea. Educators concerned with equity have encouraged this approach for decades (e.g., Ladson Billings, 1994; Tomlinson, 2003). Alongside the increasing attention paid to the educational needs of students from diverse cultural, linguistic, and economic backgrounds, repeated reauthorization of federal legislation—such as the Individuals with Disabilities Education Act—has drawn attention to the needs of students with disabilities. This attention has resulted in growing numbers of students with exceptionalities receiving

Inclusive Education: A Systematic Perspective, pp. 235–253
Copyright © 2020 by Information Age Publishing

their instruction primarily in general education classrooms. In Ohio, 62% of students receiving special education and related services currently obtain most of their instruction (at least 80%) in a general education classroom (Ohio Department of Education, 2017). Yet, achievement data continue to demonstrate the need for improved educational support for these students (e.g., Kena et al., 2016).

This reality underscores the imperative for training all teacher candidates to become effective teachers of students with diverse needs. In response, education faculty at the University of Cincinnati (UC) collaborated—using a community of practice model (Wenger, 1998)—to redesign the UC Middle Childhood Program so that it would prepare general educators for dual licensure in both middle and special education. During the redesign, we also developed our own competencies in critical areas like universal design for learning (UDL), understanding by design (UbD) lesson planning, positive behavior intervention and supports (PBIS), and intercultural competency. The redesign infused the general education coursework with relevant knowledge, skills, and dispositions as well as with strategies to develop and sustain effective partnerships between educators working as intervention specialists and general educators. The redesign also incorporated a systematic focus on research-informed practices that attend to cultural, linguistic, racial, and disability/ability diversity. Moreover, we aligned the curriculum vertically with clinical experiences across four years of teacher preparation.

Historically, the UC Middle Childhood Education Program emphasized the importance of inclusive practice through informally-connected coursework and by giving general education candidates field placements in classrooms where they would experience teaching that met the needs of students whose cultural, linguistic, socio-economic, and/or ability/disability backgrounds differed from their own. Despite these efforts, our candidates did not always experience inclusive practice in the field. We recognized that many experienced educators—those who routinely mentored and served as cooperating teachers for our degree candidates—had not formally learned methods of inclusive practice. We further realized that our approaches to "teaching all students" had not been clearly coordinated around key practices with demonstrated and powerful effects. We believed that, by creating a coordinated and systematic process to prepare teachers for inclusive practice, we would take an essential first step toward addressing the needs of all students.

In this chapter, we discuss the process of realigning our teacher preparation program to enable the dual licensure of our middle education candidates. We begin with a description of who we are as a faculty and the conceptual framework that we adopted to guide our practice. We then discuss the goals and essential elements of our work at the program level in respect to common and content-focused coursework and field components (see Description of Goals and Essential Elements below). We conclude with a discussion of the implications of our work (see Implications of Realignment below).

BACKGROUND AND CONCEPTUAL FRAMEWORK

Prior to the call for proposals from the Ohio Deans Compact on Exceptional Children to develop dual-licensure programs in the state of Ohio, the special education and middle childhood education programs at UC existed in discrete silos. While faculty socialized across programs and occasionally worked together, essential knowledge and skills for meeting the increasing needs of all learners remained isolated within each program. This circumstance made it necessary for faculty from both programs to commit to sustained collaboration as a required strategy for restructuring the program. The overarching aim of our effort was to improve outcomes for all middle childhood students by improving general education teacher preparation with a program that models effective and inclusive practices. Our faculty began this process in 2013; collective resolve moved us beyond surface-level differences of opinion and initial conceptual conflicts to achieve a common goal: mastering key practices known to have powerful learning effects, especially for students from historically marginalized groups.

We agreed to resist additive restructuring and to use instead an integrative approach for curriculum revision that requires stakeholders to assume full ownership of new content throughout the required licensure courses (Blanton, Pugach, & Florian, 2011). From the outset, our team agreed to a framework for restructuring informed by a specific group of inclusive practices, including: culturally responsive pedagogy (CRP), positive behavior intervention and support (PBIS), response to intervention (RTI), research-informed content methods, supports for English language learners (ELL), and Universal Design For Learning (UDL). Individuals in our development group approached restructuring with various levels of experience with these practices. Indeed, the work of achieving buy-in, for example, or of bringing numerous inclusive practices into conversation with one another, made our integrative approach formidable. We asked faculty who were fully ensconced in their own disciplines to integrate high-impact learning strategies that would support a wide array of learner variation as they prepared teacher candidates for current middle school classrooms. Despite these challenges, we articulated and implemented an integrated plan after four years.

Program redesign involves continuous learning, and this focus remains a high priority as we implement our restructured program with fidelity. To support measurable implementation, faculty members continue to develop and model increasingly complex learning strategies in their content area curriculum, and as critical friends we support new knowledge acquisition through the development of measurable profiles of our practice (see Appendix). These profiles outline non-negotiable components as well as the expected and acceptable manifestations of our goals and objectives (Duda & Mumme, 2014). We invite each other into our classrooms to observe our instruction and to examine samples of candidate work, using it as emerging evidence of implementation. This coaching process encourages dialogue that breaks down existing silos of knowledge and allows our faculty to think and talk about inclusive practice in new ways.

DESCRIPTION OF GOALS AND ESSENTIAL ELEMENTS

We grounded program restructuring in several key goals and essential elements. First, authentic change at this scale required faculty engagement as well as changes in faculty behavior. While a grant funded the effort, motivated faculty were essential drivers of the process. A community of practice model with strong representation across departments guided the activities, and participants took on different roles throughout the process as they shared and developed their expertise.

One nonnegotiable element of the process was addressing professional standards for teacher preparation in two areas that, historically, have not been combined at the state or national level. The Association for Middle Level Education (AMLE) accredited our existing middle childhood program and the Council for Exceptional Children (CEC) accredited our existing special education program. Stakeholders committed to creating a new middle childhood program that fully integrated the CEC standards with the AMLE goals, not merely adding the CEC standards to the existing middle childhood program.

The need to integrate two sets of standards dovetailed with the expectation that middle childhood education be collaborative and interdisciplinary (AMLE, 2010). In Ohio, for example, teachers must be licensed in two content areas (e.g., science and math). Middle education candidates take common coursework, but they also take content and methods courses related to their two content areas. At UC, this arrangement results in six separate, but overlapping course plans—a circumstance requiring strong collaboration among middle childhood faculty to ensure that the courses meet standards across content combinations. Under the new structure, with the CEC standards integrated, this complexity not only remained, but increased. Thus, restructuring required a similar, if not stronger commitment to collaboration among middle level faculty as well as extended periods of collaboration with special education faculty.

Meaningfully integrating the six elements of our conceptual framework across coursework was another essential step. This approach required that teacher candidates be introduced to CRP, PBIS, RTI, EBP, supports for ELLs, and UDL, across multiple contexts, if these ideas were to inform their conceptualization of effective practice. Candidates would not only need to engage with these ideas at the introductory level, they would also need the opportunity to deepen and transfer their understanding of these practices across the four years of the program. Vertically aligning coursework made this extensive infusion of the practices possible, while signature assessments provided (and continue to provide) ongoing information about candidates' knowledge and their ability to appropriately incorporate framework concepts using course content.

Given our goals, we found that middle childhood faculty needed additional professional development (PD) in order to productively integrate and model the framework practices across their courses. Furthermore, this PD needed to be ongoing and integrated within the change process. Faculty members, individually and collectively, needed to identify the knowledge, skills, and instructional practices required for this effort. Additionally, because faculty learning implicated a continuous improvement process, material resources and engagement with outside experts were important assets.

CROSS-PROGRAM IMPLEMENTATION

To begin restructuring, we considered those experiences common to all middle level candidates in the existing program, and we developed new common coursework to meet the aims of dual licensure. By the time we submitted the program for state approval, these common courses included the 12 credit hours of literacy instruction mandated by the state of Ohio and 12 credit hours of middle and special education courses focusing on assessment, middle level organization and practice, special education law, and general practices of special education. Having an established set of core courses allowed faculty to distribute responsibility for introducing and developing the established frameworks. In addition, we used content specific courses (i.e., methods courses) as a vehicle for applying inclusive practices in the various content areas.

We focused all common coursework related to dual licensure on integration. But this was not an easy or quick process; creating and implementing this program involved many iterations, and some efforts are still ongoing.

From early planning meetings to sustained efforts at implementation with fidelity, faculty repeatedly reflected (and continue to reflect) on their curricula and on practices connected with the foundational goals and conceptual framework. They gather information, discuss how that information fits short- and long-term goals, and work to establish both a common language and concrete steps for moving the work forward. Differences in faculty roles, responsibilities, and prior knowledge require us to revisit seemingly familiar terrain multiple times with each new action, prompting the emergence of new questions and learning.

Early in the process, for example, faculty members collectively discussed how the existing versions of their courses aligned with elements of the conceptual framework. During this activity, faculty became more familiar with components of the framework—elements like UDL or CRP—but also realized that there was much more to learn. Later, as faculty collaboratively addressed how to evaluate program implementation, their discussion about what denotes high-quality UDL similarly spurred new learning and raised new questions, even for those faculty with the most knowledge of UDL.

At different stages of the process, we produced materials to facilitate our progress. Examples include crosswalks that helped participants integrate their understandings of the CEC and AMLE standards and syllabi featuring framework-related readings and assignments. Eventually, we created a common syllabus structure to help all stakeholders more easily identify connections across courses. We did not anticipate the need for such artifacts, but their development resulted from moving forward through the work.

Even now, restructuring at the cross-program level remains more than a quick technical process. Within the UC model, middle childhood faculty open their courses for observation and critique to ensure the integration of CEC and AMLE standards, thus aiding revision and promoting the implementation of revised courses with fidelity. Intensive support in special education content (e.g., UDL and PBIS) proved vital in revising common coursework effectively, and it continues to aid with implementation. Additionally, professional development remains ongoing for all of the framework elements (e.g., CRP, support for ELLs). This process challenged (and continues to challenge) middle childhood faculty to do more than collaborate on program decisions; it pushed them to accept the vulnerability associated with peer observation and critique. Peer coaching of this sort, however, allows faculty to examine their practice and thus engage deep learning.

Application in Specialized Content Methods

Content methods faculty participated in the change process just as other faculty members did, but their collaboration needed to be particularly judicious. This perspective permitted them to address the goals for courses that are not common to all candidates, in content-appropriate and mutually agreed-upon ways. In preparing to meet the requirements for offering a dual-licensure program, methods faculty needed support to improve their understanding of the needs of students with learning disabilities in specific content areas and to address other aspects of the inclusive practice framework from a content-focused perspective.

Developing a common language for teaching, through the Understanding by Design (UbD) unit planning process, supported the integration of the frameworks in methods courses. Within the UbD process, two stages of unit development address the frameworks: the assessment plan and the daily lesson plans. For example, we use a rubric to assess the common UbD template used in all methods courses. This rubric requires teacher candidates to address UDL, CRP, the needs of ELLs, and the needs of students who struggle with content. Teacher candidates must describe and justify the strategies that they use and make specific plans for meeting the needs of students identified with disabilities as well as those with other learning needs.

As noted earlier, candidates in the middle childhood program take different instructional methods courses depending on their chosen content area. The program offers one methods course in language arts, two courses for social studies and two for science, and three mathematics methods courses. For the purposes of this chapter, we focus only on the integration of frameworks in the math and science methods courses.

Mathematics Content Methods

Implementing changes to mathematics methods courses necessitated focused collaboration between special education and mathematics education faculty. For example, a math methods professor and a special educator with expertise in mathematics education met regularly during the early planning stages to compare approaches to mathematics instruction from their differing perspectives. Their work included watching teaching videos that reflected high quality instruction (from the mathematics educator's view) and then discussing them; these discussions included comments from the special educator about how different instructional strategies could be adapted to better meet the needs of students with learning difficulties. Through this process, the general educator gathered insight into the needs of students with learning difficulties in mathematics while gaining a more nuanced view of special education approaches such as explicit instruction. Furthermore, the mathematics educator fine-tuned her understanding of the supports that students with learning difficulties do and do not need to participate in research-informed mathematics instruction that uses approaches like teaching through problem solving.

Science Content Methods

Historically, students from the UC kindergarten through Grade 12 (K–12) special education program took one methods course in science with their general education peers. This practice continues and has been intentionally structured to serve the dual-licensure curriculum. For example, the program requires middle childhood and special education students to partner during in-class science demonstrations and activities and to work collaboratively during activity planning, lesson design, and micro-teaching course assessments. This teaming enables candidates from both groups to share their specialized expertise and perspectives on content and inclusion, facilitating the common goal of planning content-focused science activities that support the needs of all learners.

Field Experiences

Prior to restructuring, the program sought to provide candidates with diverse, inclusive, and developmentally appropriate field placements in two content areas. Given UC's location in an urban community as well as Ohio's urgent need for effective teachers in urban districts, the middle childhood program committed to providing candidates with at least one urban placement. The program already placed candidates where they would experience middle grades concepts like teaming, advisory, and interdisciplinary units—considerations that responded to accreditation requirements and to faculty preferences for this structure. And, like all middle childhood programs in Ohio, UC was required to provide candidates with experience across Grades 4 to 9. But finding this variety of placements has always been a challenge. Still, under the new dual-licensure plan, all of these placement criteria remain. But now, there is an additional need to provide all candidates with experience as an intervention specialist. Previously, the roles of intervention specialist and general educator were quite different. New field experiences would need to anticipate the closer alignment (indeed, integration) of the two roles.

Under the new program, while the criteria remain, the general structure and sequence of field placements changed. Candidates continue to complete their first practicum (Practicum I) in year one. They spend two mornings a week in an urban elementary school (Grades 4 to 6). In this placement, candidates experience some teaming and use of advisory activities—two essential aspects of an effective middle childhood program. They do not, however, experience interdisciplinary units, another key element of the middle school model. Nonetheless, the placement schools do have strong leadership, relatively low teacher turnover, and caring teachers. During their second year in the program, candidates complete an additional part-time practicum semester (Practicum II) and full-time student teaching semester, both in the same classroom. Students work in a variety of urban and suburban classrooms.

Because Ohio issues special education licenses for grades K–12, the new program requires candidates to engage in both secondary and early childhood experiences. The new program, therefore, limits Practicum II and student teaching to Grades 7 through 9, with some placements in high schools that include Grades 7 and 8 and others in middle schools that use a modified middle school model. To provide candidates with early childhood experiences, our phonics course now includes a field component in Grades K–3 early literacy.

In addition to these changes, we implemented a number of field-related tasks and assignments that specifically focus on students with exceptionalities and involve progress monitoring with a responsive teaching cycle. For example, in conjunction with Practicum I and the Middle School Evaluation and Assessment course, candidates now complete a targeted analysis of student work for a specific group and complete a modified teacher work sample. Together, these assignments document a candidate's capacity to engage in the responsive teaching cycle as he or she plans and implements differentiated instruction that targets a specific student's learning needs as revealed in the student's work samples. Another example of this type of targeted assignment is one in which candidates in Practicum I review and discuss IEPs with their mentor teacher and intervention specialist. Candidates reflect on the range of student needs documented in the IEPs and then specifically address those needs in their lesson planning and instruction.

IMPLICATIONS OF REALIGNMENT

The work of implementing our new practices with teacher candidates has several larger implications. Some revolve around the barriers and challenges that come with change, while others contribute to rewarding outcomes as well as to future learning opportunities. Our work has the potential to generate meaningful change in our communities as well as for the state of Ohio. This prospect for transformation excites us, so long as—through such transformation—we positively impact the education of all students.

Outcomes of the Work

Some outcomes of our work include a renewed sense that our practices with teacher candidates will prepare them to address the needs of all students. In essence, our middle childhood candidates will be eligible for two teaching licenses—a circumstance that affords them the opportunity and confidence to work with middle school students who struggle with learning, whether or not those students qualify for an IEP. Because of their preparation, moreover, our candidates will be more marketable as they enter the field because they have a broader sense of the context in which they will work and a more robust skillset.

In respect to programmatic outcomes, the establishment of a Dual-Licensure Implementation Team (DLIT) as well as a completed curriculum for creating better prepared beginning teachers provide faculty with a sense of accomplishment and excitement about moving forward with their work. At present, the DLIT meets regularly with members who are dedicated to curriculum alignment; consistent and effective implementation of our key frameworks; and efforts to facilitate the professional development of middle childhood faculty, new faculty, and adjuncts teaching within the program. Furthermore, the faculty acceptance of the process is extensive even as we recognize that the work never ends and, indeed, requires continuous effort from all involved. Our "students-first" disposition reinforces not only our community of practice, but also our willingness to be collaborative and open with one another.

A final outcome is also related to our dispositions as teacher educators. With the implementation of a more authentic curriculum, we recognize that implementation science frameworks (Duda, Fixsen, & Blase, 2013) will be helpful to us, and thus we acknowledge the ongoing nature of our own learning. We further realize that to remain relevant, our progress will need to be iterative. We must not only stay abreast of new knowledge, but we must also create ways to include this new knowledge in our coursework. At the same time, we must also remain true to the nonnegotiables that we documented and operationally defined. Addressing these goals requires grit, but we agree that doing so is essential to our work, and the work of all future teachers.

Challenges Going Forward

As we continue to work with one another on improvements to the Middle Childhood Program, we know that we will continue to wrestle with barriers and challenges to our work. And while we face opposition to change, we note that our candidates will also face obstacles as they enter the field.

As they proceed through the program, we must explicitly address such opposition with them and, indeed, when it comes from them. One of the most prevalent challenges that our teacher-candidates experience, even as they are being prepared for inclusive practice, is that they may not actively observe inclusive practice in the field. Our candidates become change agents within their school communities and need support to grow the necessary confidence for engaging their own agency, knowledge, and skills as beginning teachers.

The need to create such confident candidates compels us—as teacher educators, passionate about our disciplines—to continue addressing the challenges that *we* face. These include the challenge of making space for additional inclusive content when we feel passionately about the existing discipline-specific content within our individual courses. It can feel like we need to relinquish some of our autonomy as individual faculty members in order to realize the integration of knowledge across the program. We must, therefore, increase our own confidence in our knowledge and capability with respect to inclusivity, and we must continue to learn how to manage the integration of inclusivity with disciplinary knowledge in our content methods courses. Furthermore, as both general and special educators, we must increase our confidence in each other with respect to the diversity of knowledge that we bring to this project, diversity that strengthens our teacher candidates in both programs.

Only by remaining a community of practice that affords both diversity and communal understanding can we build this confidence in one another. This means questioning each other about disciplinary definitions, structures, and language as well as working together to bridge diverse disciplinary interpretations for and with our candidates. Furthermore, our community of practice must also allow for change, as knowledge continually changes; it must also face the challenges that will arise as we continue to improve our dual-licensure programs.

As we reflect upon the work that we completed and look forward to its ongoing implementation, we recognize that fomenting change takes time and that the push to continuously improve must remain at the forefront of our endeavor.

CONCLUSION

For six years we have worked together to create a program dedicated to addressing the needs of all learners. It has not been simple, requiring collaborative effort and sacrifice from both the special education and middle childhood programs. As we move forward, we acknowledge the recursive nature of our work and the need to reflect on our individual beliefs, the goals of the program, the needs of our local schools, and the hope for an educated citizenry that embraces the diversity and value of all children. We welcome the struggle of promoting academic justice for all.

NOTE

1. The template for this document is copyrighted © 2017, Dr. Michelle Duda, Implementation Scientists, LLC, www.behaviorhappens.

REFERENCES

Association for Middle Level Education (AMLE). (2010). *This we believe: Keys to educating young adolescents.* Westerville, OH: National Middle School Association. Retrieved from http://www.amle.org/AboutAMLE/ThisWeBelieve/tabid/121/Default.aspx

Blanton, L. P., Pugach, M. C., & Florian, L. (2011). *Preparing general education teachers to improve outcomes for students with disabilities.* Washington, DC: American Association of Colleges for Teacher Education; Washington, DC: National Center for Learning Disabilities. Retrieved from https://www.ncld.org/wp-content/uploads/2014/11/aacte_ncld_recommendation.pdf

Chappuis, J., & Stiggins, R. (2016). *An introduction to student-involved assessment FOR learning* (7th ed.). Boston, MA.

Duda, M. A., & Mumme, L. (2014). *Practice profile tool: Planning for implementation.* Retrieved from https://unc-fpg-cdi.adobeconnect.com/_a992899727/ai-lessonc4/

Duda, M. A., Fixsen, D. L., & Blase. K. A. (2013). Setting the stage for sustainability: Building the infrastructure for implementation capacity. In V. Buysse & E. Peisner-Feinberg (Eds.), *Handbook of response to intervention (RTI) in early childhood.* Baltimore, MD: Brooks.

Fisher, D., Frey, N., & Hattie, J. (2016). *Visible learning for literacy: Implementing the practices that work best to accelerate student learning grades K–12.* Thousand Oaks, CA: Corwin Literacy.

Hattie, J. (2009). *Visible learning: A synthesis of meta-analyses relating to achievement.* Abingdon, England: Routledge.

Ladson Billings, G. (1994). *The dreamkeepers: Successful teaching for African American students.* San Francisco, CA: Jossey-Bass.

Kena, G., Hussar W., McFarland J., de Brey C., Musu-Gillette, L., Wang, X., ... Dunlop Velez, E. (2016). *The condition of education 2016* (NCES 2016-144). Washington, DC: U.S. Department of Education, National Center for Education Statistics. Retrieved from http://nces.ed.gov/pubsearch

Ohio Department of Education, Office for Exceptional Children, Office of Data Quality and Governance. (2017). *Ohio implementation of special education and related services for children with disabilities.* Columbus, OH: Author. Retrieved from https://education.ohio.gov/getattachment/Topics/Special-Education/

Sections/Accountability-and-Funding/Special-Education-and-Related-Services-Legislative-Report.pdf.aspx

Tomlinson, C. (2003). Deciding to teach them all. *Educational Leadership 61*(2), 6–11.

UDL-IRN. (2011). *Critical elements of UDL in instruction* (Version 1.2). Lawrence, KS: Author. Retrieved from https://udl-irn.org/wp-content/uploads/2018/01/Critical-Elements.pdf

Wenger, E. (1998). *Communities of practice: Learning, meaning, and identity.* Cambridge, England: Cambridge University Press. doi:10.1017/CBO9780511803932

APPENDIX

Universal Design for Learning Practice Profile[1]

The UC Dual-Licensure Implementation Team (DLIT) defines *Universal Design for Learning (UDL)* as a process of deliberate planning to address learner variability and to remove barriers to learning. UDL includes 3 core components:

1. **Representation** [How do we present information (broadly) and content in different ways?]
2. **Engagement** [How do we stimulate interest and motivate the learner?]
3. **Action and Expression** [How can students express what they know in different ways?]

The team has also adopted critical elements of UDL as defined by UDL-IRN (2011) that are complementary or overlap across the three core components. These non-negotiable sub-components are:

1. **Clear Goals**
2. **Intentional Planning for Learner Variability**
3. **Flexible Methods and Materials**
4. **Progress Monitoring**
5. **Process-Based Feedback**

The following practice profile is designed to describe how the sub-components of UDL are applied in practice. The implementer behaviors described in this practice profile reflect UC faculty instruction and coaching.

Change Initiative: UDL Clear Goals

Critical Component (Nonnegotiable)	Contribution to the Outcome	Ideal/Expected Implementation	Acceptable Variation	Unacceptable Variation
Description of the component	*Description of why this component is critical to the outcome*	*Description of implementer behavior*	*Description of implementer behavior*	*Description of implementer behavior*
1.1 Goals and desired outcomes of the lesson/unit are aligned to the established content standards.	If goals do not align with the standards, the standards are not likely to be met.	Faculty member communicates AMLE and CEC standards and notes alignment to goals of lesson.	Faculty member writes goals that are aligned to AMLE and CEC standards but does not explicitly note the alignment.	Faculty member writes goals that are not aligned to AMLE or CEC standards.
1.2 Goals are clearly defined. Goals are separate from means. They allow multiple paths/options for achievement.	Clearly defining goals helps frame the content for both the teacher and students. Separating goals from means opens teachers to represent the material in ways that benefit a range of students.	Faculty member provides written goals, stated in clear language. The language of the goals aligns with the academic literacy norms of the content area, and also aligns with the standard(s) to be addressed.	Faculty member can state the goals, but may not have written them down, or the language of the goals may need to be refined to meet the norms of disciplinary language. These goals provide a partial description of what the students will be able to do after instruction.	Faculty member does not define the learning goals or the language of the goals is wordy, unclear, or out of alignment with the norms of disciplinary language. The goals do not provide a description of what students should be able to do after instruction.
1.3 Faculty member has a clear understanding of the goal(s) of the lesson and specific learner outcomes.	If faculty members do not understand the goals and learner outcomes, students are unlikely to meet those outcomes.	Faculty member states verbally or in writing how the goals align to specific learner outcomes that are observable and measurable These goals provide a description of what the students will be able to do after instruction. Teaching aligns with stated goals.	Teaching aligns with stated goals, but the faculty member cannot discuss how the goals align to learner outcomes that are observable and/or measurable. These goals partially describe what the students will be able to do after instruction.	Faculty member does not state verbally or in writing how the goals align to specific learner outcomes. Teaching does not align with stated goals.

(Table continues on next page)

Change Initiative: UDL Clear Goals (Continued)

Critical Component (Nonnegotiable)	Contribution to the Outcome	Ideal/Expected Implementation	Acceptable Variation	Unacceptable Variation
Description of the component	*Description of why this component is critical to the outcome*	*Description of implementer behavior*	*Description of implementer behavior*	*Description of implementer behavior*
1.4 Goals address the needs of every learner, are communicated in ways that are understandable to each learner, and can be expressed by them.	If students do not understand the purpose of instruction, and instruction does not address their needs, learners are less likely to engage.	Goals address the needs of every learner. Faculty member communicates goals in ways that are understandable to each learner. Students are given opportunities to express goals.	Goals could be interpreted to address the needs of all learners although this may not be explicit in the language. Faculty member communicates goals in understandable ways, but students might not have explicit opportunities to express goals.	Goals are written in such a way that they exclude some learners. Faculty does not communicate goals in an understandable way.
2.1 Intentional proactive planning that recognizes every learner is unique and that meeting the needs of learners in the margins—from challenged to most advanced—will likely benefit everyone.	If faculty do not plan to meet the needs of learners in the margins, those students will be less likely to access the content.	Faculty can communicate how the instructional plan intentionally addresses the needs of all learners.	Faculty member addresses learner needs and anticipates the need variation in methods, materials, and resources.	Faculty does not address the needs of the learner or does not anticipate the need for variation in methods materials and other resources.

(Table continues on next page)

Change Initiative: UDL Clear Goals (Continued)

Critical Component (Nonnegotiable)	Contribution to the Outcome	Ideal/Expected Implementation	Acceptable Variation	Unacceptable Variation
Description of the component	*Description of why this component is critical to the outcome*	*Description of implementer behavior*	*Description of implementer behavior*	*Description of implementer behavior*
		This may include: (a) addressing strengths and weaknesses, perceptual ability, language ability, background knowledge, cognitive strategies, and motivation; (b) anticipating the need for variation in methods, materials and other resources (e.g., student choice, personnel, scaffolding, reading materials, and grouping strategies); and (c) maintaining the cognitive load of the lesson for all learners by identifying and reducing barriers.	However, the faculty does not plan for maintaining the cognitive load of the task through the identification or removal of barriers.	Or, the faculty plans to reduce the cognitive load of the lesson (e.g., avoiding more challenging tasks, lowering expectations for some learners).

(Table continues on next page)

Change Initiative: UDL Clear Goals (Continued)

Critical Component (Nonnegotiable)	Contribution to the Outcome	Ideal/Expected Implementation	Acceptable Variation	Unacceptable Variation
Description of the component	*Description of why this component is critical to the outcome*	*Description of implementer behavior*	*Description of implementer behavior*	*Description of implementer behavior*
3.1 Faculty member uses a variety of media and methods to present information and content.	Multiple representations and methods: (a) ensure that information is comprehensible, accessible, and clear to all; (b) help all students to access prior knowledge; and (c) connect prior knowledge to current learning goals, and facilitate students' capacity for connecting and transferring knowledge to new contexts.	Faculty member switches among multiple activity types (e.g., small-group work, class discussion, teacher exposition) within and across related lessons. Faculty member differentiates the pacing within a class period. Faculty member uses a variety of representations through technology and physical materials.	Faculty member employs more than one type of activity within or across related lessons. Faculty member varies pacing at least once within a lesson. Faculty member uses more than one representation within a lesson.	Faculty member uses one activity type within and across related lessons. Faculty member uses the same pacing throughout a lesson. Faculty member uses only one representation within a lesson.
3.2 A variety of methods are used to engage learners and promote their ability to monitor their own learning	Both affect and student capacity to self-monitor are essential for learning. Because not all learners are engaged in the same ways, multiple methods and options for engagement are essential. Similarly, supporting all students to self-monitor requires a range of approaches.	Within & across related lessons, faculty member: (a) provides choice and addresses student interest in order to maintain engagement, and (b) provides opportunities for goal setting, self-assessment, and reflection (e.g., flipped classroom reflection, journaling, use of a rubric, collaborative decision making).	Faculty member either provides choice or addresses student interest in order to maintain engagement within or across related lessons. The faculty member provides opportunities for goal setting or self-assessment, or reflection across related lessons.	Faculty member neither offers choice nor addresses student interest to maintain engagement. Faculty member does not provide opportunities for goal setting, self-assessment, or reflection across related lessons.

(Table continues on next page)

Change Initiative: UDL Clear Goals (Continued)

Critical Component (Nonnegotiable)	Contribution to the Outcome	Ideal/Expected Implementation	Acceptable Variation	Unacceptable Variation
Description of the component	*Description of why this component is critical to the outcome*	*Description of implementer behavior*	*Description of implementer behavior*	*Description of implementer behavior*
3.3 Learners use a variety of media and methods to demonstrate their knowledge.	Because there is not one means of action and expression that will be optimal for all learners, providing options for action and expression are essential.	Over the duration of the course, faculty member offers a variety of options for students to use technology and physical materials for students to express their understanding.	Over the duration of the course, faculty member offers more than one option for students to express their understanding.	Over the duration of the course, faculty member only offers one option for students to express their knowledge.
4.1 Formative assessments are frequent and timely enough to plan/redirect instruction and support intended outcomes.	Effective feedback is timely, specific, understandable, and actionable. (Fisher, Frey, & Hattie, 2016, p. 66). Ongoing, formative assessment supports student self-assessment and should be used to guide next steps of instruction (Chappuis & Stiggins, 2016)	Faculty member uses frequent formative assessments in every class period (e.g., reflections prior to class, observations of small-group work, class polling). Faculty member adjusts instruction based on formative assessment outcomes (e.g., giving more time, reviewing a topic, using a different representation to convey meaning, exit slips, student survey, interactive feedback).	Faculty member uses at least one formative assessment in every class period. Faculty member adjusts instruction in a limited way based on formative assessment outcomes (e.g., does not respond to all of the data that indicate a need for change).	Formative assessments are not utilized, not timely, not understandable, nor are they useful. Faculty member conducts assessments but makes no adjustments, even when assessment results clearly call for some kind of a change.
4.2 A variety of formative and summative assessments are used by the learner to demonstrate knowledge and skill.	When feedback is provided to learners from a variety of assessments, achievement markedly improves (Effect size=0.73) (Hattie, 2009, pp. 173-178).	Over the duration of the course, faculty member offers a variety of assessment options (e.g., projects, oral presentations, 1-1 conferences, written tests) through a variety of media (e.g., paper and pencil, Google Forms, polling software, Blackboard).	Over the duration of the course, faculty member offers a limited variety of assessment options (e.g., only one in addition to the dominant mode) through a limited variety of media (e.g., only one in addition to the dominant mode).	Faculty member utilizes only one assessment mode throughout the course.

(Table continues on next page)

Change Initiative: UDL Clear Goals (Continued)

Critical Component (Non-negotiable)	Contribution to the Outcome	Ideal/Expected Implementation	Acceptable Variation	Unacceptable Variation
Description of the component	*Description of why this component is critical to the outcome*	*Description of implementer behavior*	*Description of implementer behavior*	*Description of implementer behavior*
4.3 Frequent opportunities exist for teacher reflection and new understandings.	Frequent reflection is required for changing complex practice.	Faculty member can share evidence of personal reflection at regular intervals throughout the course (e.g., journaling or note taking after class, debriefing in conversation, thinking ahead for course adjustments).	Faculty member can share limited evidence of personal reflection throughout the course (e.g., only when asked, not systematic or regular).	Faculty member is unable to demonstrate any reflective process, or if the reflective process is present, there is no evidence that the course undergoes any change or adjustments.
5.1 Learners understand that learning is a process that takes effort and they value relevant feedback. They see challenges as opportunities to learn and expand their knowledge.	Students who have a learner orientation are more willing to engage. They see the benefit of feedback as helping them grow. They learn more. A learner orientation can be developed through instruction.	Faculty member showcases the steps that lead to a final product (e.g., share editing drafts, mistakes in a math problem, or misunderstandings about content). Faculty member allows time for learners to discuss mistakes or mishaps they may have made through a variety of modes (e.g., peer and faculty collaboration in class, discussion boards through Blackboard).	Faculty member provides written description of expectations of the final product. Faculty member allows minimal opportunity (time or mode) for learners to discuss mistakes or mishaps they may have made.	Faculty member does not provide directions that lead to a final product. Faculty member does not require learners to discuss mistakes or mishaps they may have made.

CHAPTER 14

PREPARING MIDDLE SCHOOL EDUCATORS TO WORK WITH ALL STUDENTS

**Catherine Lawless Frank, Joni L. Baldwin,
Connie L. Bowman, and Laura Kuebel**
University of Dayton

According to the U.S. Department of Education (2017), approximately 11% of students in middle and high school are identified as students with disabilities. About 60% of these students receive instruction at least 80% of the time in the general education classroom; an additional 19% receive instruction there 40 to 79% of the time. Furthermore, approximately 80% of students with disabilities participate in state math and reading assessments in Grades 7–12. Nevertheless, only 7% of these students test as proficient in math and only 12% in reading (U.S. Department of Education, 2017). The high number of students with disabilities who receive most of their instruction in general education classrooms and the low number deemed proficient in math and reading indicate a problem. Possibly general education teachers are not well enough prepared to work with these students; perhaps they need better training about how to provide effective instruction to students with disabilities (Moreno-Rodriguez, Lopez, Carnicero, Garrote, & Sanchez, 2017).

Inclusive Education: A Systematic Perspective, pp. 255–264
Copyright © 2020 by Information Age Publishing

Some research supports these speculations. As DeSimone and Parmer (2010) reported, many teachers feel unprepared to teach in inclusive environments. Studies also have shown that training can improve teachers' confidence about working with students with disabilities. Sharma and Nuttal (2016) found that pre-service teachers became more positive in their "attitudes and efficacy" and their "concerns decreased significantly" (p. 142) after receiving training on inclusion. Other research indicates the positive impact preservice education can have on teachers' attitudes about and skills for working in inclusive classrooms (Ajuwon et al., 2012; Kraska & Boyle, 2014).

This chapter briefly presents some of the research that supported the University of Dayton's (UD) development of a dual licensure program to prepare teacher candidates to meet the needs of all middle childhood level students. It then describes, in greater detail, development of this preservice program.

CONTEXT AND RATIONALE

With the passage of the Education for all Handicapped Children Act in 1975, all children of school age were given the right to a free and appropriate public education. The law mandated that children with disabilities receive an education in the least restrictive environment. A reauthorization in 1990 renamed the law the Individuals with Disabilities Education Act (IDEA), added two disability categories—autism and traumatic brain injury—and included assistive technology and rehabilitative services as related services. Despite the directive to educate students with disabilities in the least restrictive environment, most were educated in self-contained classrooms or resource rooms until the second reauthorization in 1997. This second reauthorization pushed schools to provide the same curriculum to students with disabilities as that provided their peers. Schools were advised to serve all students in general education classrooms, providing the necessary supports to make the curriculum accessible. Since the reauthorization, most students with disabilities have been placed in general education classrooms for a substantial portion of the school day, but their teachers are often ill-prepared to provide them a quality education.

Many educators believe that inclusion classrooms are beneficial for all students (e.g., Yoon-Suk & Evans, 2011). Fuchs's (2010) study focused on general education teachers' perceptions of barriers to inclusion. The results indicated that educators from general classrooms perceived a lack of administrative support, lack of support from special educators and support staff, and lack of sufficient preparation in their preservice programs. The teachers in Fuchs's study unanimously agreed that the "one required course" in special education for general educators was "worthless" and contained "mostly terminology" (p. 34). They reported that the one required course did not teach them how to differentiate instruction, make accommodations in the classroom, or work with special education staff.

Mackey's (2014) qualitative study of three teachers who practiced inclusion in middle school classrooms found that teachers believed their undergraduate programs had not adequately prepared them to meet the needs of their students with disabilities. Mackey's results were similar to Fuchs's (2010) in that the general education teachers felt unprepared to work with students with disabilities and felt a lack of support from administration related to class size, collaboration, planning time, help in working with paraprofessionals, and in-service education.

Royster, Reglin, and Losike-Sedimo's (2014) study of middle school teachers who participated in professional development (PD) on inclusion found before PD, these teachers did not feel they had the knowledge to teach in an inclusive classroom, and they demonstrated negative attitudes toward inclusion. Following the PD, the teachers perceived themselves as competent to use best practices for inclusive teaching.

Sargeant and Berkner's (2015) study of teachers working in Seventh-Day Adventist schools found most teachers had positive perceptions of inclusive classroom teaching. These teachers felt their schools should address the needs of students with disabilities and give parents a choice of sending their children with disabilities to a faith-based school. They felt they could differentiate and make accommodations for students with mild disabilities, but not students with more intensive needs. As with other studies, these teachers reported needing more support and training.

These studies and others document how unprepared teachers feel with regard to teaching students with disabilities. In addition to lacking training on differentiation as well as sufficient administrative support for effective inclusion, teachers in these studies were concerned about maintaining academic rigor, as teachers are accountable for their students' performance. If they were to teach in inclusive classrooms, they knew they needed to be able to do so effectively, for the students' sake and their own professional status. Teachers in these studies would probably agree that

> Teacher preparation programs carry a significant responsibility to adequately educate future teachers so that they not only have the knowledge and skills, but also the classroom experiences to support successfully meeting the needs of all students in the general classroom setting. (Fuchs, 2010, p. 34)

Research demonstrates that general educators are willing to teach students in inclusive settings so long as they are adequately prepared for the challenge (Vaz et al., 2015). Downing and Peckham-Hardin (2007) found that 61% of general education teachers were willing to co-teach students with disabilities in inclusive settings, but they also reported needing proper training and the necessary tools to provide effective instruction to these students.

Dual licensure programs (i.e., merged general and special education programs) are one option for preparing teachers to work with students with disabilities alongside typically developing students. While there are many dual-licensure programs combining early childhood education (e.g., Grades K–3) and early intervention specialist preparation, there are few that combine middle childhood (e.g., Grades 4–9) and intervention specialist preparation. Through an Ohio Deans Compact Grant and a Collaboration for Effective Educator Development, Accountability and Reform grant, the UD has designed a four-year program in which middle childhood education majors earn a dual-licensure degree that prepares them to teach effectively in inclusive environments.

PROGRAM DEVELOPMENT

Blending two license areas (e.g., middle childhood and special education) into a program that was originally designed to accommodate a single license area within a four-year program, requires ensuring that candidates have the knowledge to meet the needs of all learners in both licensure areas. The development effort requires a university to examine the strengths and needs of both original licensure programs and then to revise the program to capitalize on strengths and address needs. Implicated in the curriculum assessment and restructuring process are professional standards, relationships with partner schools, and best practices for inclusive teaching.

UD began the process of blending the two licensure programs by examining the Association for Middle Level Education and the Council for Exceptional Children (CEC) professional standards. Faculty developed a crosswalk of the standards to determine the degree to which each standard was currently being addressed within the middle childhood single-licensure program. Based on the results of that crosswalk, courses and field experiences were reconfigured or added to ensure that candidates were adequately prepared to meet both sets of standards within a four-year program. The faculty determined that the CEC standards could be incorporated into a revision of the curriculum for middle childhood education by adding three courses and field experiences. The additional courses addressed topics such as special education law, multi-factored evaluations, individualized education programs (IEP), and specially designed instruction for K–12 students with disabilities.

The first of the additional courses was developed to teach candidates to differentiate instruction. This course emphasizes Universal Design for Learning (UDL) and other methods of planning and teaching that support all students' academic progress. Embedded within this course are field experiences that allow candidates to provide small group math instruction to elementary-school students. Examination of the program had determined that many candidates lacked experience providing both small group and math instruction. This embedded field experience was developed to address these needs and foster the use of UDL and data-driven instruction.

The second new course focuses on special education law and developing and writing IEPs. While special education law is addressed in other courses (e.g., a diversity course), the new course promotes deeper understanding of special education processes and procedural safeguards.

The third course addresses multifactored evaluations, formal and informal assessments, and progress monitoring. Emphasis is on administering assessments and interpreting results, communicating with parents, and developing tools to monitor student progress and guide instruction. These courses fill curricular gaps, as determined through program evaluation and dialog with educators from partner schools, while also capitalizing on existing areas of strength.

Ensuring that candidates are able to address the needs of all learners in a dual-licensure program requires assistance from and communication with partner schools. Partner schools can help determine a program's strengths and needs in terms of candidates' knowledge, skills, and dispositions as well as offer candidates a variety of experiences to ensure that they have adequate training in both licensure areas during field- and student-teaching experiences.

During the development phase of the dual-licensure program, the university solicited advice from the education advisory panel (including principals and both special and general educators) on program development, field- and student-teaching experiences, and current best practices implemented in their schools. The advisory panel, which meets annually, provides the university and district leaders an opportunity to share information and maintain dialog about shared interests and concerns.

Faculty members met with the advisory panel during the initial development of the dual-licensure program to ensure that such a program would fulfill a need within local schools and to discuss key components of the program. The advisory panel reported an ongoing need for teachers who were better prepared to provide instruction to all students and agreed that a dual-licensure program was a logical way to address that need. The university then asked the panel to identify the essential elements they thought should be included in such a program. While most of the elements identified aligned with the university's priorities (e.g., assessments, IEPs, UDL), the panel placed a greater emphasis on the legal components of special education than faculty had initially envisioned. Panel members stressed that candidates should be well versed in procedures and legal requirements under IDEA (e.g., timelines for referral, multi-factored evaluation, IEPs, and procedures for monitoring student progress towards IEP goals) which required the third new course discussed earlier in this chapter. The advisory panel continues to meet on a regular basis as a way to encourage ongoing communication and needs assessment.

Cooperating teachers (both general and special educators) in field placements and student-teaching sites were invited to participate in an online survey soliciting their opinions and ideas for implementing a middle childhood education program that had a strong emphasis on special education. The survey results indicated that, overall, cooperating teachers were in agreement that middle school candidates would benefit from additional knowledge about and experience with special education. The recommendations from cooperating teachers pointed to the need for practical classroom teaching methods such as making accommodations for students with disabilities, adjusting the curriculum to meet students' needs, and using effective behavior management practices.

The UD faculty was able to incorporate recommendations both from the advisory panel and the group of cooperating teachers who responded to the survey. The three new courses focused on making accommodations for individual students and adjusting curriculum. Other new content (e.g., legal aspects of IDEA and classroom procedures to provide effective instruction for all students) was either woven into syllabi throughout the candidates' four-year program or presented in the new courses. Behavior management was further emphasized in one of the courses in the middle childhood program.

The faculty also made use of on-going opportunities to connect with cooperating teachers. Notably, group meetings with cooperating teachers are conducted in both the spring and fall semesters and individual meetings throughout the student teaching experience. These meetings help ensure that expectations of both the university and the partner schools are clearly communicated and allow for direct communication to address any needs or concerns. During development of the dual-licensure program, cooperating teachers were also consulted as to how to develop rigorous field- and student-teaching placements that meet both middle childhood general education and special education requirements. Alternative ways to conduct field experiences were also discussed and implemented. A partnership was formed with an area school, and through courses in the junior and senior year, the dual-licensure candidates provided data-driven instruction to a small group of students in math (third graders) and language arts (first graders). These experiences simulate, to an extent, a resource-room teaching experience and provide candidates more experience working with students whose academic achievement falls short of middle-childhood expectations. These guided experiences also ensure that candidates receive support for developing and implementing individualized curricula for students with special learning needs.

At UD, candidates participate in some form of field experience every semester during their four-year program. They often register for field experience for a specific day and time of the week. These weekly visits to a single placement typically begin three or four weeks after the start of the semester. Round visits were incorporated to provide candidates one-time visits to different sites during the three to four weeks prior to their field experience. Candidates visit a different special education placement each week to learn about the diversity in special education classrooms (e.g., a first-grade classroom for students with moderate needs, a high school social skills classroom for students with autism, an elementary school resource room). They are required to reflect on what they see in each classroom in terms of environment, academic and behavioral supports and strategies, and teacher role and responsibilities.

After the faculty had examined professional standards, developed the curriculum crosswalk, and solicited feedback from the advisory panel and cooperating teachers, they conducted a review of current research. This process surfaced information about effective educational practices that could be infused into the curriculum. Practices such as a multi-tiered system of support, data driven instruction, UDL, and culturally responsive teaching were then integrated throughout the four-year program. This integration can be seen in the new syllabi, restructured student teaching and field experiences, new experiential learning opportunities (e.g., teaching experiences integrated and supported within courses, case studies, and guided reflections), and adjustments to the curriculum and assessments used in candidates' third and fourth years. The lesson plan format that candidates are required to use throughout their field- and student-teaching experiences was also redesigned to accommodate the requirements of UDL, data-driven instruction, and culturally responsive pedagogy.

A variety of assessments has been adopted department-wide to ensure that, not just the dual-license candidates, but all candidates are developing the skills to meet the demands of a diverse student population. The University of Dayton is now using the Intercultural Effectiveness Scale (IES), the Dispositions Attitudes Proficiencies (DAP) structured group interviews, and edTPA to obtain valid external assessments of teacher candidate competencies in terms of cultural responsiveness, dispositions for teaching, and readiness for teaching. The IES is designed to assess skills for interacting with people from different cultures. Candidates are assessed with the IES on admission to any UD teacher education program and re-assessed during student teaching to determine growth and continued areas of need in cultural competency. The DAP measures candidates' dispositions in terms of oral communication, human interaction, critical thinking, and leadership. This structured group interview is conducted at the beginning of candidates' program and again before student teaching. IES and DAP feedback is provided to candidates including suggestions for growth and development. The edTPA evaluates candidates' preparedness for the rigors of the classroom in terms of planning, instruction, and assessment. The edTPA is conducted during the student-teaching experience and offers an external evaluation of candidates' teaching ability. These assessments help ensure that candidates are provided with not just content knowledge but also with the necessary skills and dispositions to meet the diverse needs of all students.

CHALLENGES

Research shows that implementing a new inclusive education program always entails challenges (Heston, Raschke, Kliewer, Fitzgerald, & Edmiaston, 1998), including challenges in maintaining collaborative relationships with stakeholders (Keefe, Rossi, de Valenzula, & Howarth, 2000), team teaching and level of competence and confidence in inclusive settings (Lombardi & Hunka, 2001), and maintaining quality programs (Peterson & Beloin, 1998). At UD, these challenges were addressed by the advisory panel discussed earlier and by a steering committee of faculty with needed expertise. The steering committee held lunch meetings monthly and several day-long retreats. While these meeting times were used for program development, they also gave faculty the opportunity to build relationships and develop a sense of trust and community. Monthly meetings became the norm, fostering change in the dynamics of the group, open and frank conversations, compromise, and decision making in the best interest of teacher candidates and their future students.

A second challenge was to find ways to provide sufficient field experiences in both middle childhood education and special education. This challenge persists, but thus far faculty have been successful in their efforts to incorporate productive field experiences into the coursework that candidates complete in the early phases of the new program.

CONCLUSION

The impact of this new program has not been evaluated yet, as our first cohort is currently in its senior year. However, candidates express confidence in their knowledge of strategies to teach all children. Assessments to be used to determine the success of the program include state-required testing, as the candidates will now take the special education content knowledge exam in addition to those required for their middle childhood license. Performance on the Candidate Preservice Assessment of Student Teaching (C-PAST) form, the student-teaching evaluation, will also be reviewed to compare previous students' and current students' ability to differentiate instruction, engage in formative assessment, provide feedback to students, and accommodate individual needs. In addition, a survey will be developed to enable cooperating teachers to identify any changes they see in UD's teacher candidates.

In summary, the UD experience fits with research evidence suggesting that teacher preparation programs must change in order to prepare teachers for work in inclusive settings. These programs must prepare candidates not just to understand and communicate content but also to have the skills and dispositions to meet the varying needs of individual students. At UD, we found that collaboration among faculty members and with K–12 partners was essential to the program-development process. So too was our willingness to offer a program sufficiently rigorous to address the standards of both middle-childhood education and special education. We addressed these challenges with enthusiasm because we knew the result would be teacher candidates who are better prepared to teach all students in inclusive classrooms.

REFERENCES

Ajuwon, P. M., Lechtenberger, D., Griffin-Shirley, N., Sokolosky, S., Zhou, L., & Mullins, F. E. (2012). General education pre-service teachers' perceptions of including students with disabilities in their classrooms. *International Journal of Special Education, 27*, 100–107. doi:10.1177/088840640502800202

DeSimone, J. R., & Parmar, R. S. (2010). Issues and challenges for middle school mathematics teachers in inclusion classrooms. *School Science and Mathematics, 106*, 338–348. doi:10.1111/j.1949-8594.2006.tb17754.x

Downing, J. E., & Peckham-Hardin, K. D. (2007). Inclusive education: What makes it a good education for students with moderate to severe disabilities? *Research and Practice for Persons with Severe Disabilities, 32*, 16–30. doi:10.2511/rpsd.32.1.16

Fuchs, W. W. (2010). Examining teachers' perceived barriers associated with inclusion. *SRATE journal, 19*(1), 30-35.

Heston, M. L., Raschke, D., Kliewer, C., Fitzgerald, L. M., & Edmiaston, R. (1998). Transforming teacher preparation in early childhood education: Moving to inclusion. *Teacher Education and Special Education, 21*, 278–292. doi:10.1177/088840649802100404

Keefe, E. B., Rossi, P. J., de Valenzuela, J. S., & Howarth, S. (2000). Reconceptualizing teacher preparation for inclusive classrooms: A description of the dual license program at the University of New Mexico. *The Journal of the Association for Persons with Severe Handicaps, 25,* 72–82. doi:10.2511/rpsd.25.2.72

Kraska, J., & Boyle, C. (2014). Attitudes of preschool and primary school pre-service teachers towards inclusive education. *Asia-Pacific Journal of Teacher Education, 42,* 228–246. doi:10.1080/1359866X.2014.926307

Lombardi, T. P., & Hunka, N. J. (2001). Preparing general education teachers for inclusive classrooms: Assessing the process. *Teacher Education and Special Education, 24,* 183–197. doi:10.1177/088840640102400303

Mackey, M. (2014). Inclusive education in the United States: Middle school general education teachers' approaches to inclusion. *International Journal of Instruction, 7*(2), 5–20.

Moreno-Rodriguez, R., Lopez, J L., Carnicero, J. D., Garrote, I., & Sanchez S. (2017). Teachers' perception on the inclusion of students with disabilities in the regular education classroom in Ecuador. *Journal of Education and Training Studies, 5*(9), 45–53. doi:10.11114/jets.v5i9.2573

Peterson, M., & Beloin, K. S. (1998). Teaching the inclusive teacher: Restructuring the mainstream course in teacher education. *Teacher Education and Special Education, 21,* 306–318. doi:10.1177/088840649802100406

Royster, O., Reglin, G. L., & Losike-Sedimo, N. (2014). Inclusion professional development model and regular middle school educators. *Journal of At-Risk Issues, 18*(1), 1–10.

Sargeant, M. A., & Berkner, D. (2015). Seventh-day Adventist teachers' perceptions of inclusion classrooms and identification of challenges to their implementation. *Journal of Research on Christian Education, 24,* 224–251. doi: 10.1080/10656219.2015.1104269

Sharma, U., & Nuttal, A. (2016). The impact of training on pre-service teacher attitudes, concerns, and efficacy towards inclusion. *Asia-Pacific Journal of Teacher Education, 44,* 142–155. doi:10.1080/1359866X.2015.1081672

U. S. Department of Education (2017). *Executive Summary—39th Annual Report to Congress on the Implementation of the Individuals with Disabilities Education Act, 2017.* Washington, DC. Author. Retrieved from https://www2.ed.gov/about/reports/annual/osep/2017/parts-b-c/39th-arc-for-idea.pdf

Vaz, S., Wilson, N., Falker, M., Sim, A., Scott, M., Cordier, R., & Falkmer, T. (2015). Factors associated with primary school teachers' attitudes towards the inclusion of students with disabilities. *PLoS ONE, 10*(8), 1–12. doi:10.1371/journal.pone.0137002

Yoon-Suk, H., & Evans, D. (2011). Attitudes towards inclusion: Gaps between belief and practice. *International Journal of Special Education, 26*(1), 136–146.

CHAPTER 15

PREPARING EARLY CHILDHOOD EDUCATORS FOR INCLUSIVE PRACTICE

Mary Murray
Bowling Green State University

Tammy L. Elchert
Carey Exempted Village School

INTRODUCTION

All general and special education teachers should know how to meet the needs of all students, with and without exceptionalities (Turnbull, Turnbull, Erwin, Soodak, & Shogren, 2015). Nevertheless, recent research demonstrates that many preservice teacher graduates feel ill-prepared to work with students with disabilities across a range of settings (e.g., Friend & Cook, 2010; Murray, Handyside, Straka, & Arton-Titus, 2013; Murray & Mereoiu, 2013; Orr, 2009; Turnbull et al., 2015). Likewise, school districts do not feel sufficiently able to meet the needs of their students with disabilities. According to one study conducted by the National Association of State Directors of Special Education, some 98% of districts cite meeting the

Inclusive Education: A Systematic Perspective, pp. 265–278
Copyright © 2020 by Information Age Publishing
All rights of reproduction in any form reserved.

growing demand for special education teachers, especially those who are trained to work with students in inclusive environments, as a top priority (de Boer, Pijl, & Minnaert 2011; Harvey, Yssel, Bauserman, & Merbler, 2010). Beyond this growing demand and beyond the persistent issues related to preparing teachers for work in inclusive settings with diverse students is yet another reality: these issues take on heightened importance in early childhood settings (Collier, Keefe, & Hirrel, 2015).

These circumstances suggest that teacher preparation programs must find effective ways to train candidates to work with students with disabilities. They must prepare candidates not only by providing a rich knowledge-base but also by offering practical field experiences. This chapter examines one program's attempt to meet these challenges by developing a blended dual-licensure Early Childhood/Early Childhood Special Education program. The discussion looks at the program development process, including community advisory board collaboration, the various challenges, and the final outcomes.

THE BOWLING GREEN DUAL-LICENSURE PROGRAM

This section provides background information about the university and its PK–12 partners; it examines the program's conceptual framework and gives a high-level overview of the program.

University Details

Bowling Green State University (BGSU) is a large, public, primarily residential, research university in Ohio. Located in a midsized rural community with a population of 30,000 residents, including college students, BGSU is the largest producer of teachers in the state. But, in fall 2010, citing a surplus of early childhood teachers and subsequent shortage of jobs, the Ohio Board of Regents requested that BGSU significantly decrease the number of early childhood teachers that it produces. Rather than simply decrease the number of candidates admitted to its early childhood program, BGSU recognized the continuing need for early childhood special education teachers and developed a blended (or unified) program instead. The program's development responded to state and federal mandates; research on the most effective inclusive educational strategies; input from faculty, students, PK–12 teachers, and administrators; and the desire to make students marketable at local, state, and national levels. In order to provide inclusive fieldwork experiences, the program partnered with PK–12 school districts.

The chapter discusses one such partner district, located in a small midwestern community with 3,765 residents. The district , which is classified as a public exempted village district, serves a geographically small rural area of 40 square miles. Its one building, constructed in 2016, houses an elementary and high school. The elementary school enrolls 347 full time students and employs 27 teachers, four teacher aides, one secretary, and one principal. The district's student body is primarily White; 36% of the students qualify for free or reduced lunch and 13% have been identified with a disability. The elementary school also houses two preschool teachers and aides who work with an area educational consortium. Representative of much of northwest Ohio, the district offers an example of a typical prekindergarten through Grade 12 (PK–12) experience for students enrolling at BGSU. In the spring of 2014, partly in response to staff development on differentiation and a new teacher evaluation system, the school principal actively recruited teachers with five or more years of experience to mentor and engage in co-teaching with teacher candidates from the dual-licensure program; this work began the following academic year. Its aim was to provide additional support to classroom teachers and intervention specialists striving to meet the needs of all students; at the same time this collaboration aimed to deepen the dual-licensure candidates' learning. Table 15.1 shows the breakdown of candidate placements by level of instruction.

Table 15.1.
Number of Teacher Candidates at Partner School District

	2014–15	2015–16	2016–17	2017–18
Number of K–3 Elementary Teacher Candidates	1	6	6*	8*
Number of Teacher Candidates PreK	2	1	2	1

Note: *1 student with partial program

Conceptual Framework

Faculty at BGSU developed an innovative four-year degree program leading to two licenses (PK–3 Early Childhood and PK–3 Intervention Specialist) as well as a state education certificate, birth to age 3. Besides filling the shortage of special education teachers, the candidates in this program acquire the knowledge and skills to be more effective teachers in meeting the needs of all students (with and without disabilities) in their classrooms.

Interdisciplinary faculty teams together with their PK–12 partners developed the program. These interdisciplinary faculty teams embedded five essential components within the curriculum design: (a) research-supported practices; (b) justice, fairness, and equity for inclusive learning experiences; (c) respect for cultural and linguistic diversity; (d) family-centered practices; and (e) interdisciplinary collaboration.

During program development, leaders established an advisory board that included key stakeholders such as superintendents, principals, special education directors, parents, teachers, and faculty. Working together, the faculty interdisciplinary teams and board created an inclusive undergraduate program that blended the best practices from the domains of both early childhood and special education. This collaborative work created a curriculum that develops teachers, providing them with the skills to effectively meet the needs of every young child from birth through grade three. The first step for the faculty and advisory board was to craft the program's mission statement, vision statement, and program values (for details on the program see BGSU, n.d.).

The three statements that the development team created appear below:

Mission Statement

The mission of the Inclusive Early Childhood (IEC) Program is to prepare undergraduate teacher education candidates for employment in IEC learning environments. The inclusive program will address the knowledge, skills, and values necessary to meet the needs of every young child in settings that are inclusive and provide differentiated, evidence-based instruction. The program is committed to the development of partnerships and scholarly endeavors that reflect our professional values of justice, fairness, and equity.

Vision Statement

The vision of the program is to be a premier inclusive undergraduate program that blends the best practices from early childhood education with special education to develop teachers with the skills to effectively meet the needs of every young child in our diverse society, birth through grade three.

Program Values

- Justice, fairness, and equity for inclusive learning experience
- Respect for cultural and linguistic diversity
- Family-centered practices

- Interdisciplinary collaboration
- Research-supported practices

After determining the mission, vision, and program values, the development team brought in consultants from the University of North Carolina, Greensboro—where a similar inclusive program has been in place for over 15 years—to provide assistance with program development. Other teams working on this effort included a steering committee (charged with moving the new program forward), course design teams (interdisciplinary groups of faculty that developed initial course syllabi and sample assignments), course review teams (groups responsible for reviewing all of the course components), an assessment committee (responsible for designing program assessment and evaluation tools), and a field placement committee (comprised of both university faculty and practitioners and responsible for designing field experiences and the practicum).

The Inclusive Early Childhood Program

The IEC Education program resulted from three years of planning by university faculty, parents, and PK–12 partners. It was the first program of its kind in the state of Ohio and is still one of only a small number of U.S. programs designed to prepare undergraduate teacher education candidates for employment in IEC learning environments. Students graduate ready to develop strong parent-teacher partnerships; provide universal design for learning (UDL), differentiated instruction, and evidence-based instruction; as well as co-teach in both general education and special education environments and, most importantly, in inclusive environments.

Program developers used professional and content standards from the Council for Exceptional Children (CEC) and the National Association for the Education of Young Children (NAEYC). The CEC standards include concepts such as: foundations in special education, developmental knowledge of learners, individual learning difficulties, instructional strategies in general and special education curricula, creating learning environments, instructional planning, assessment, social interactions in the classroom, language development, professional and ethical practice, and collaboration with families. NAEYC standards include: promoting child development and learning; building family and community relationships; observing, documenting, and assessing young children; using developmentally appropriate approaches; using content knowledge to build curricula; and professional practice. Based on these, the development team created a crosswalk of standards and coursework tool to ensure that the course content reflected all relevant standards and to facilitate quality assessments that drive improvement and change.

Grounded in these standards, the IEC program consists of 134 to 136 credit hours across courses in general education and teaching methodology as well as two professional years of field-based experiences involving various types fieldwork and student teaching. Appendix A illustrates the program's plan of study. The IEC program especially prioritizes its field experiences. Appendix B underscores this emphasis by showing the program's Field Experience Plan. Each semester block focuses on a particular type of field experience. All content in the courses relates to the practical application of each semester's field experiences. The program also deploys a cohort model: students' progress with the same cohort of students through each designated block of courses.

IMPACT

The IEC program provides opportunities for learning and growth to several groups. This section highlights impacts on teacher candidates, mentor teachers, and students.

Teacher Candidates

The IEC program makes it possible for undergraduate teacher education candidates to obtain dual licensure in both general and special education. Since teachers' sense of self-efficacy has been consistently related to teacher behavior, student attitudes, and student achievement, one of the program's primary goals was to improve its candidates' capacity for entering the profession confident in their abilities to address the needs of all students, including students from marginalized groups (e.g., students will disabilities; Bandura, 1997; Tschannen-Moran & Hoy, 2007). The program's developers anticipated that teacher candidates would graduate with knowledge of inclusive pedagogical methods and structures. Their expectation was that teacher candidates would recognize pedagogy that limits opportunities for students and support strategies that promote equity (Gorski, 2014).

The university participated in a field study piloting a survey instrument given to program graduates. The survey included 28 items related to practices that are linked to increased achievement among students with disabilities and their classroom peers. The survey used a 4-point Likert scale and assumed that responses fit linear models, thus allowing for the use of parametric statistics. Researchers used Qualtrics as the collection tool due to its ease of distribution and analysis. To administer the survey, researchers sent a sample of 132 program graduates an email that linked to the survey; 111 individuals returned surveys (i.e., an 84.1% response rate). It took participants between four to five minutes to complete the survey. Respondents indicated that they felt most confident:

- Being able to build a sense of trust in students,
- Communicating with other professionals,
- Identifying students' academic strengths, and
- Collaborating with a co-teacher or team teacher (Bauer, 2016).

Conversely, respondents answered that they felt least confident:

- Proactively planning instruction using the principles of UDL,
- Addressing disruptive and noncompliant behaviors with evidence-based practices,
- Establishing positive home-school relations, and
- Using students' cultural background to help make learning meaningful (Bauer, 2016).

Cooperating Mentor Teachers

Anecdotal evidence offers some indication that the program positively impacts cooperating mentor teachers (CMTs). CMTs report that preschool and elementary students receive more teacher guidance through individualized and small group learning. One teacher shared that "many times we will work with high, middle, and low groups of students using differentiated materials. We work together to plan lessons using a variety of co-teaching strategies." Another teacher recounted that "just seeing the different ideas refreshes me. I can do more for the kids because I have that extra set of hands and make lessons more meaningful. I have more time to come up with ideas." A third CMT indicated that "it has been a wonderful experience. I love having the extra set of hands. For students who are struggling I can keep the lesson flowing while they get extra attention and one-on-one or small group work. This system works across all content areas."

Not only did having another teacher in the classroom offer additional coverage and open doors to co-teaching, it conferred other benefits, too. One teacher mentor noted that "the teachers' different personalities create new opportunities for interactive, meaningful relationships with learners." Similarly, one CMT reflected that "working with a teacher candidate has improved my communication skills. I have learned to articulate clear expectations at the onset, before I get frustrated. I am better at asserting my viewpoint with colleagues in professional conversations."

Student Growth Data

District growth data offer insight into student outcomes at the K–3 level resulting from participation in the program. The district measured student growth using the Northwest Evaluation Assessment MAP instrument (Northwest Evaluation Association, 2011). Students were tested in the fall and spring of each year to measure growth in reading and math. Tables 15.2 and 15.3 show an increase in students' mean RIT scores from fall to spring in both subject areas. Over a three-year period, observed growth data in all primary grades improved. The district's student growth exceeded projected growth norms. These growth data accounted for 50% of the CMTs' evaluations in the Ohio Teacher Evaluation System (OTES). For the purpose of this study, teachers not hosting teacher candidates are referred to as non-CMTs. OTES requires that teachers receive a numeric rating of 1 through 5, with 1 indicating "low student growth" and 5 indicating "high student growth." During spring 2015, CMTs received a mean rating of 4.87, compared to the 4.66 mean rating for non-CMTs (see Table 15.4). In the subsequent two years, aggregate data demonstrated that CMTs continued to receive a higher mean rating on OTES than their non-CMT colleagues.

CHALLENGES/BARRIERS

The development and implementation of the IEC program presented challenges and barriers, anticipated and unanticipated, which affected both the university and its partner schools. This section outlines several of these challenges.

University Level

From an institutional standpoint, developing an interdisciplinary program always proves challenging. Even though faculty from all units involved in the program remained committed to its conception and recognized the advantages for their own preservice teachers as well as for PK–12 students, many barriers still needed to be addressed. These included questions related to: faculty assignments and course load, how to count student credit hours, and which faculty from which programs would coordinate the new program. Additionally, the university committed to eliminating the single license early childhood program when the new

Table 15.2.
District Student Growth Math

	Fall 2014 Mean RIT	Spring 2015 Mean RIT	Fall 2015 Mean RIT	Spring 2016 Mean RIT	Fall 2016 Mean RIT	Spring 2017 Mean RIT
K	139.7	161.8	138.1	161.9	140.4	166.3
1	164.3	184.9	161.9	186.8	162.3	188.1
2	178.9	193.5	177.4	198.3	178.6	197.5
3	194.9	205.1	189.0	203.6	190.3	204.1

Table 15.3.
District Student Growth Reading

	Fall 2014 Mean RIT	Spring 2015 Mean RIT	Fall 2015 Mean RIT	Spring 2016 Mean RIT	Fall 2016 Mean RIT	Spring 2017 Mean RIT
K	141.4	159.9	139.7	163.1	142.8	167.3
1	164.1	183.8	163.3	185.4	161.6	186.3
2	176.3	193.8	177.6	199.0	175.2	196.8
3	193.2	201.5	189.9	202.7	187.4	204.5

Table 15.4.
Ohio Teacher Evaluation System Means for CMTs and non-CMTs

	Spring 2015	Spring 2016	Spring 2017
Cooperating Mentor Teachers	4.875	4.25	4.50
Noncooperating Mentor Teachers	4.66	3.875	4.3125

program began. Numerous faculty who had been teaching in the old program, often for many years, resisted its closure and also resisted the development of the new program. But, once program developers realized that some faculty mourned the impending loss of their program, they were able to address their colleagues' grief and work to secure "buy-in." This process was, nevertheless, arduous—a fact that should not be understated.

Another challenge that the university encountered related to the necessary professional development (PD) for faculty. Both general and special education faculty required significant PD to learn the latest inclusive practices. Since the program grew so fast, PD also included adjunct faculty. One solution for this challenge involved pairing a practitioner with a faculty member to co-teach courses. The program developers also implemented a general and special education faculty co-teaching pairing. This turned out to be one of the best PD experiences in which the faculty had ever participated.

Finally, the program struggled to place its students in inclusive field experiences. In Northwest Ohio alone, more than seven institutions of higher education compete for the same placements. Complicating this situation further, during the first two years of the program's implementation, the state unveiled a new teacher evaluation process that made teachers uncomfortable with inviting teacher candidates into their classrooms. Their concerns about hosting teacher candidates hinged on OTES's requirement that 50% of a teacher's total evaluation be based on student growth data. So, to allay concerns, the university implemented universal co-teaching training with districts and teacher candidates. Co-teaching with degree candidates afforded mentor teachers the opportunity to retain a measure of direction and control over classroom instruction while still providing a field experience for university teaching candidates. Nevertheless, several years passed before teachers regained full confidence that they would be able routinely to see positive student outcomes even when they co-taught with teacher candidates.

Partner School Level

The partner school district discussed in this chapter offers further evidence of the challenges involved with this work. One preschool mentor teacher shared two challenges: (a) the difficulty of hosting two teacher candidates at the same time and (b) the varied expectations that teacher candidates had for preschool students' work. The mentor indicated that, when hosting two teacher candidates simultaneously, it was important to monitor the teacher candidates during co-teaching in order to check for equal work distribution and collegial decision making. In one case of workload disparity, the mentor suggested that the two teacher candidates use either the one-teach, one-support model of co-teaching or individually deliver lessons. The preschool mentor teacher reported that co-teaching worked better when she hosted a single teacher candidate as it eliminated power struggles between candidates. Furthermore, the mentor indicated that a single teacher candidate enjoys more opportunities for engaging in instruction and taking the lead in the classroom, with regard to planning and implementing instructional ideas.

The mentor also noted that the preschool teacher candidates were in their junior year block experience and that this was their first opportunity to lead and teach. This fact may have contributed to their varied expectations of preschool learning. Specifically, some of the candidates expected preschoolers to complete work more suitable to the first-grade curriculum, while others entered their placement not acknowledging preschool students' current performance levels.

CONCLUSION

BGSU developed its IEC Program to meet needs at the local, state, and national level. This included decreasing the number of teachers trained in early childhood education, due to oversaturation in that area, and increasing the number of early childhood intervention specialists. BGSU accomplished this objective. Yet a more important reason for developing a program along these lines was to meet the needs of all children in the early childhood age range with and without exceptionalities. By preparing teachers in a blended general and special education pedagogy and providing inclusive internships each semester the program moves ever closer to meeting the needs of all typical and atypical children in inclusive settings.

Enrollment figures demonstrate the need for such a program. Each year enrollment increases, from 248 candidates in the first graduating class (2013) to 649 candidates in 2014–15 and 850 candidates in 2015–16. By 2016–17 the program enrolled 894 candidates and, for this past year (2017–18), 985 IEC teacher candidates matriculated. 2018 brought changing circumstances and, for the first time in years, Ohio will experience the beginnings of a teacher shortage. This situation brings new challenges, yet the program's enrollment continues to increase despite the fact that BGSU has discontinued all marketing efforts.

More important than enrollment, however, is the fact that the IEC program produces teacher candidates who feel that they are well prepared and able to meet the needs of all students, from birth to 3rd grade, in both general and special education environments (Bauer, 2016). Although *candidates* perceive that they are prepared to meet the needs of all students, future research will repeat the survey of practices with BGSU *graduates* after they have taught for a year or two.

REFERENCES

de Boer, A., Jan Pijl, S., & Minnaert, A. (2011). Regular primary schoolteachers' attitudes towards inclusive education: A review of the literature. *International Journal of Inclusive Education, 15*, 331–353. doi:10.1080/13603110903030089
Bandura, A. (1997). *Self-efficacy: The exercise of control.* New York, NY: Wadsworth.

Bauer, A. (2016). *Deans Compact Ohio student teacher survey: Bowling Green State University inclusive early childhood* (Unpublished manuscript). The University of Cincinnati, Cincinnati, OH.

Bowling Green State University. (n.d.). *Inclusive early childhood education.* Retrieved from https://www.bgsu.edu/education-and-human-development/school-of-teaching-and-learning/inclusive-early-childhood-education.html

Collier, M., Keefe, E., & Hirrel, A. (2015). Listening to parents' narratives: The value of authentic experienceswith children with disabilities and their families. *School Community Journal, 25*(2), 221–242.

Friend, M., & Cook. L. (2010). *Interactions: Collaboration skills for school professionals.* New York, NY: Longman.

Gorski, P. C. (2014). *Reaching and teaching students in poverty: Strategies for erasing the opportunity gap.* New York, NY: Teachers College Press.

Harvey, M., Yssel, N., Bauserman, A., & Merbler, J. (2010). Preservice teacher preparation for inclusion: An exploration of higher education teacher-training institutions. *Remedial and Special Education, 31*, 24–33. doi:10.1177/0741932508324397

Murray, M., & Mereoiu, M. (2013). Teacher-parent partnership: An authentic teacher education model to improve student outcomes. *Journal of Further and Higher Education, 40.* 276–292. doi:10.1080/0309877X.2014.971108

Murray, M., Handyside, L., Straka, L., & Arton-Titus, T. (2013). Parent empowerment: Connecting with preservice special education teachers. *School Community Journal, 23*(1), 145–168.

Northwest Evaluation Association. (2019). *MAP growth.* Retrieved from https://www.nwea.org/map-growth/

Orr, S. (2009). New special educators reflect about inclusion: Preparation and K–12 current practice. *Journal of Ethnographic & Qualitative Research, 3*, 228–239.

Tschannen-Moran, M., & Hoy, A. W. (2007). The differential antecedents of self-efficacy beliefs of novice and experienced teachers. *Teaching and Teacher Education, 23*, 944–956. doi:10.1016/j.tate.2006.05.003

Turnbull, A., Turnbull, H., Erwin, E., Soodak, L., & Shogren, K., (2015). *Families, professionals, and exceptionality: Positive outcomes through partnership and trust* (7th Ed.). Upper Saddle River, NJ: Pearson.

APPENDIX A

Inclusive Early Childhood Education 4-Year Plan

Freshman 1	Freshman 2

GSW 1100 or 1110: Writing (3-5)
EDTL 2010: Intro to Education (2)
BGP: Social & Behavioral Sciences (3)
BGP: Arts & Humanities (3)
Math 1150: Intro to Statistics (3)
BGP: Arts & Humanities (3)
 	
17
	GSW 1120: Writing (3)
	EDTL 2300: Intro to Educational
	  Technology (2)
	EIEC 1110: Continuum of Early
	  Childhood Development (3)
	BGP: Social & Behavioral Sciences (3)
	Math 2130: Math for Early Childhood
	  Teachers (3)
	BGP: Natural Sciences (3)
	
	17

Sophomore Block 1	Sophomore Block 2

EIEC 2100: Inclusive Perspectives on Early
  Childhood Classrooms (1)
EIEC 2110: Intro to Young Children with
  Exceptional Needs (3)
EIEC 2120: Foundations of Inclusive Early
  Childhood Education (2)
EDFI 3010: Educational Psychology:
  Applied to Early Childhood (3)
EIEC 2140: Communication Development
  in Young Children (3)
EIEC 2150: Creative & Expressive Arts &
  Movement for Inclusive Early Child (3)
Additional Courses:
ENG 3420: Children's Literature (3)
 	
18
	EIEC 2210: Cultural & Linguistic Diversity
	  in Early Childhood Education (3)
	EIEC 2220: Working with Families of
	  Young Children (3)
	EIED 2230: Infant & Toddlers in Natural
	  Environments (3)
	EIEC 2240: Curricula for Infant and
	  Toddler Early Care and Education (3)
	Additional Courses:
	BGP: Natural Sciences (3)
	BGP: Additional BG Perspective Courses
	  (3)
	
	18

Junior Methods Block (fall only)	Junior Student Teaching Block (spring only)

EIEC 3100: Inclusive Prekindergarten
  Field Experience (2)
EIEC 3110: Intentional Teaching for
  Young Children (3)
EIEC 3120: Phonics in Inclusive Early
  Childhood Classrooms (3)
EIEC 3130: Emergent & Beginning
  Reading (3)
EIEC 3140: Introduction to Assessment in
  Inclusive Early Childhood Settings (3)
EIEC 3150: Instructional & Assistive
  Technology (3)
 	
17
	EIEC 4110: Positive Behavior Supports for
	  Young Children (3)
	EIEC 4120: Advanced Assessment for
	  Program Planning (3)
	EIEC 4800: Inclusive Early Childhood
	  Student Teaching: Prekindergarten (8)
	EIEC 4810: Prekindergarten Student
	  Teaching Seminar (1)
	
	15

Senior Methods Block (fall only)	Senior Student Teaching Block (spring only)
EIEC 3300: Kindergarten—Grade 3 Practicum in Inclusive Classrooms (2)	**EIEC 4210:** Literacy Assessment for Instruction (3)
EIEC 3310: Reading and Writing Methods for Inclusive Early Childhood Classrooms (3)	**EIEC 4220:** Consultation, Collaboration, & Transitions (3)
EIEC 3320: Math Methods for Inclusive Early Childhood Classrooms (3)	**EIEC 4900:** Inclusive Early Childhood Student Teaching: Kindergarten—Grade 3 (8)
EIEC 3330: Social Studies for Inclusive Early Childhood Classrooms (3)	**EIEC 4910:** Kindergarten—Grade 3 Student Teaching Seminar (1)
EIEC 3340: Science Methods for Inclusive Early Childhood Classrooms (3)	15
EIEC 3350: Adapting and Accommodating Instruction in Inclusive Early Childhood Classrooms (3)	

17

APPENDIX B

Field Work-Up for Inclusive Early Childhood Program

Fall Semester	Spring Semester
Freshman 1—16-18 credits **EIEC 2010:** Intro to Education—20-hour field requirement	Freshman 2—18 credits No field hours required

Sophomore 1—18 credits
EIEC 2100: Inclusive Perspectives on Early Childhood Classrooms (1)—60-hour field requirement
    20 hours in **EIEC 2110:** Intro
    20 hours in **EIEC 2120:** Foundations
    20 hours in **EIEC 2130:** Ed Psych
	Sophomore 2—18 credits
	EIEC 2210: Cultural and Linguistic Diversity in Early Childhood Education—10-hour field requirement
	EIEC 2220: Working with Families of Young Children—10-hour field requirement
	EIEC 2230: Infant & Toddlers in Natural Environments—10-hour field component

Junior 1—18 credits **EIEC 3100:** Inclusive Prekindergarten Field Experience (2)—120-hour field requirement	Junior 2—18 credits EIEC 4800: Inclusive Early Childhood Student Teaching: Pre-Kindergarten (8)— 480-hour field requirement (10 weeks in field and 5 weeks campus)
Senior —17 credits **EIEC 3300:** Kindergarten–Grade 3 Practicum in Inclusive Classrooms (2)—210-hour field requirement	Senior 2 – 16 credits **EIEC 4900:** Inclusive Early Childhood Student Teaching: Kindergarten–Grade 3 (8)—480 hour field requirement (10 weeks in field and 5 weeks on campus)

CHAPTER 16

DEVELOPING AN ONLINE DUAL-LICENSURE GRADUATE PROGRAM TO ENHANCE INCLUSIVE KNOWLEDGE, SKILLS, AND DISPOSITIONS OF EARLY CHILDHOOD EDUCATORS

Jennifer R. Ottley
Ohio University

Sara L. Hartman
Ohio University

Clarissa Bunch Wade
George Mason University

Sara R. Helfrich
Ohio University

Christan Grygas Coogle
George Mason University

Inclusive Education: A Systematic Perspective, pp. 279–298
Copyright © 2020 by Information Age Publishing

Inclusive education in the United States often begins in early childhood. Half of all young students identified with disabilities participate in classroom settings alongside typically performing peers (National Center for Education Statistics, 2015). Decades of research demonstrate the efficacy and value of inclusive practices in early care and other educational settings (Odom, 2001). Children with special needs show increased positive learning outcomes when their early care and educational settings use inclusive practices (Justice, Logan, Lin, & Kaderavek, 2014). Additionally, typically performing and high-performing children who attend inclusive early care settings experience no negative learning impacts, are more likely to understand the challenges of living with a disability, show increased empathy, and are more accepting of children with disabilities (Justice et al., 2014). Despite these known benefits, many early childhood teachers lack skills for meeting the needs of all learners, in part because they are not dual-certified in early childhood and special education. This circumstance limits their ability to serve as lead teachers in inclusive early childhood classrooms and thereby limits children's access to high-quality inclusive programming (Barton & Smith, 2013).

In response to this circumstance, some advocates recommend recruiting more special education teachers, while others propose providing stronger supports to teachers already in the field as a way to reduce attrition (Brunsting, Sreckovic, & Lane, 2014; Sindelar, Brownell, & Billingsley, 2010). Following the latter strategy, a graduate licensure program can benefit education systems by reducing burnout and attrition; and it can benefit children in inclusive early childhood classrooms by increasing the efficacy of the teachers who work with them.

To meet the needs of educators and students alike, faculty members at Ohio University (OU) designed and implemented a dual-licensure graduate program in early childhood and special education. Given accessibility challenges faced by teachers in rural communities, the OU team designed the program to be fully online. This chapter discusses both the need for and value of this program, and it examines the process of developing such a program for master's degree candidates. Although not without challenges, developing the program represented a significant success for the Department of Teacher Education in OU's Patton College of Education (PCOE). Lessons learned from its creation and implementation are valuable to stakeholders in a variety of settings.

CONCEPTUAL FRAMEWORK

Early childhood development lays an important foundation for school readiness and later academic and social success (Diamond, Gerde, & Powell,

2008). For children with disabilities, early intervention can minimize delays and improve performance, thus lessening the possibilities of achievement gaps later in their school careers (Stanton-Chapman, Justice, Skibbe, & Grant, 2007). Unfortunately, young children with disabilities continue to perform below their peers without disabilities (Kelso, Fletcher, & Lee, 2007). In fact, three-fourths of all high-needs learners in Ohio enter kindergarten without the skills necessary to be successful (National Institute for Literacy, 2008). Moreover, some research even shows an increase in relatively recent years in the achievement gap between young children with and without disabilities (Rowe, Raudenbush, & Goldin-Meadow, 2012). These disturbing findings reinforce the need for all early childhood teachers to become better prepared to meet the diverse learning needs of all young children.

Nevertheless, Ohio (like other states across the United States) is experiencing chronic shortages of well-prepared early childhood teachers. And in early childhood classrooms, there is also great variability in instructional quality. In fact, according to Odom (2009), a majority of teachers provide instruction that is considered to be of low quality. A research-to-practice gap compounds these issues such that the instructional practices used by many teachers are not aligned with the latest research in early childhood development.

Consequently, in order to identify early learning delays and disabilities and to support the learning and development of all children, teachers working in inclusive early childhood environments need more comprehensive background knowledge and opportunities for practice. Teachers require specialized training and experience to gain the knowledge, skills, and dispositions necessary for working with children with disabilities and their families. It is, therefore, critical that teacher preparation programs base coursework and clinical experiences on the tenets of adult learning theory, online instruction, distance supervision, and leadership. Courses and field experiences grounded in these principles and practices are positioned to maximize the acquisition, maintenance, and generalizability of teachers' knowledge and skills and thereby to support their use of effective and inclusive instructional practices.

PROJECT GOALS, ESSENTIAL ELEMENTS, AND IMPACTS

We conducted all program development efforts with the project's goals and desired outcomes in clear view. To achieve these goals, we identified and implemented the elements of the program that faculty members in early childhood education and special education saw as essential.

Project Goals[1]

Our mission, in offering an online degree program grounded in current adult learning principles, is to increase the quantity and quality of dual-licensed early childhood education teachers and early childhood intervention specialists (i.e., special education teachers) across the state of Ohio. We believe this work will contribute to improvements in the services provided to children aged zero to eight and their families and, as a result, contribute to improved educational outcomes. The PCOE's newly developed program will achieve these outcomes by supporting teachers' engagement with advanced knowledge, skills, and dispositions. Such engagement will improve teachers' competence with practices focusing on the early identification of delays and disabilities as well as the implementation of reflective and responsive interventions (i.e., those that are child-centered and aligned with research and theory on young children with and without disabilities).

Based on shared commitments to inclusive practice, faculty members in the PCOE prepare degree candidates to be change agents. As the program's informational materials note, participating teachers complete coursework grounded in real-world contexts; and through these experiences, these teachers observe the impact of their teaching on student learning and use these observations to make data-driven decisions about what practices are best for students' education. Program completers share these data in respectful ways with the relevant stakeholders in children's lives (i.e., teachers and families), informing them about their student's progress and keeping them up-to-date about innovative evidence-based practices. According to the program's informational materials, the program also instills the value of lifelong learning so that, upon graduation, degree candidates continue to read empirical literature, seek out professional development opportunities, apply evidence-based practices in their classrooms, and reflect on the effectiveness of their teaching.

Program completers are also prepared to work with children and families from diverse backgrounds. Candidates (a) acquire the necessary knowledge and skills to support learning for children with mild to severe disabilities, (b) interact with families confronting varying circumstances, and (c) respect the various perspectives and beliefs of families and of their colleagues in early childhood education. The program, according to informational materials, empowers candidates to advocate for the needs of young children with disabilities and to disseminate information to relevant stakeholders, maximizing the quality of education received by all young children.

Alignment With Standards

One of the critical activities our program faculty completed was to align the curriculum with standards from multiple professional organizations—for example, the National Association for the Education of Young Children (NAEYC) and the Council for Exceptional Children (CEC). We created meaningful course outcomes and assessments for degree candidates by blending the content recommended by state and national organizations. This process required us to examine each standard individually and then to consider the similarities and differences between standards. Because we intentionally developed a one-year program to keep costs low for our candidates, our course objectives and program goals needed to be broad enough to encompass multiple standards, while still targeting the specific skills and dispositions our candidates need to be successful teaching children from diverse populations.

The first step of this process involved breaking down sets of standards into individual standards. We physically cut printouts of standards into individual strips of paper, each with one standard, and rearranged them into clusters. As we read the standards aloud, we flexibly moved them from one cluster to another to create groups of specific skills, dispositions, or content that would become the focus of specific courses. We found this method helpful because it gave us the opportunity to attach meaning to each of the emerging clusters. For example, we placed standards that emphasized professional and ethical practices for working with parents and families in a "Family Collaboration" cluster. These practices included collaboration, communication, and inclusion in the special education process. But, as we continued to examine the standards, we moved some of those in the original "Family Collaboration" cluster to a different cluster, one labeled "Teaming."

Next, we reviewed the clusters of standards and combined them to create broader groups, each of which thematically represented a course with related content. We recognized that, had we not used this method to cluster standards, we could have overlooked a large number of standards related to collaboration and teaming. Consequently, we might have placed all of the collaboration and teaming standards into one course, which would have made it difficult to address each standard appropriately. Instead, we created two courses—one that focuses on collaboration and one that focuses on teaming and leadership skills.

Once we identified courses, small groups of faculty members created objectives for each course, using the standards to develop the actual content and verbiage. The larger curriculum development team and the internal advisory board checked the alignment between standards and course objectives to ensure that the necessary content for licensure was embedded into each course. We used this same process of small group development paired with large group and advisory board review to develop activities, assignments, rubrics, and the topical outline for all courses in the program (see Table 16.1 in the Appendix for an example of an assessment rubric aligned with course standards).

Finally, the feedback process guided our creation of a standards matrix. During the initial stages of program development, this matrix allowed us to see any gaps between the actual standards and the content coverage within courses, making it easy for us to determine whether the standards were adequately covered or if they would benefit from further emphasis in another course. In the final stages of program development, the matrix contained several categories: the individual standards, the courses in the program that would cover those standards, and the formal assessments to measure candidates' mastery of the standards.

Collaboratively aligning standards across the entire program was a lengthy process. Small teams with interdisciplinary expertise ensured equal coverage of both early childhood and special education content within each course. Moreover, the feedback from the advisory board—whose members had interdisciplinary expertise across early childhood and special education, psychology, and community studies—proved invaluable for the development of an advanced graduate program that fit with the PCOE's overall mission and met Ohio's need for well-prepared teachers. This reflective, multi-step process integrated multiple perspectives and ensured that the program would address the interests of all stakeholders (see Figure 16.1).

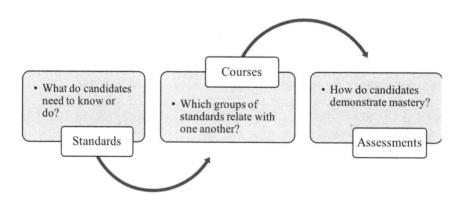

Figure 16.1.   The program development process.

Essential Elements

We identified three essential elements for our online dual-licensure program that guided our curriculum development efforts. First, we grounded our courses in research-based content. Second, we identified a meaningful format for sharing course content with degree candidates so they would acquire the desired knowledge, skills, and dispositions. Finally, we identified an evidence-based approach for remotely delivering performance feedback to candidates, thus preserving, in an online context, PCOE's clinical approach to teacher education.

Research-Based Content

We included research-based content in the curriculum for each course. Candidates complete readings and assignments focusing on practices whose effectiveness is supported strongly by the research evidence. Furthermore, by aligning our coursework with the research-based practices recommended by NAEYC and CEC, we ensure that our graduates can serve young children with and without disabilities using the most up-to-date knowledge, skills, and effective practices.

Research-Based Implementation of Course Delivery

We also use research-based practices to instruct our degree candidates. Historically, online programs have been criticized for being of lesser quality than face-to-face programs (Bonk & Zhang, 2006). Our model for online instruction—adapted from Bonk and Zhang's (2006) *Read, Reflect, Display, and Do* (R2D2) model—comprises four cyclical phases that support the diverse abilities and needs of adult learners. Phase 1 (Read) focuses on candidates' acquisition of knowledge. Phase 2 (Reflect) fosters a deeper understanding of course content through interactions with others and self-reflection. This phase is critical in expanding candidates' knowledge and shaping their beliefs by supporting reflective evaluation of their own ideas. Phase 3 (Display) pushes candidates to visually express their knowledge, which requires them to synthesize their learning in order to ensure accurate representation. Phase 4 (Do) requires candidates to apply what they know, make connections among the various concepts, and create artifacts to demonstrate their learning.

The R2D2 model fits with constructivist theories that view learning as a process of creating knowledge and understanding; it supports knowledge development by giving adult learners opportunities to reflect on their own individual experience as well as on shared social experiences (Driver, Asoko, Leach, Mortimer, & Scott, 1994). Individuals who have engaged in programs using R2D2 instruction report that they have found it to be effective in promoting their learning (Hanline, Hatoum, & Riggie, 2012). Using the R2D2 model, the course instructors facilitate learning experiences involving reflection and practical application that help candidates construct meaning and deepen understanding.

Research-Based Implementation of Candidate Supervision

To observe our degree candidates and provide remote performance feedback, we use several new technologies. All of our candidates have access to a tablet, Swivl robot, and Skype for Business. These tools enable candidates to video-record their teaching—a process that allows them to share recordings of their teaching and then receive feedback on their performance from peers and their university supervisors (Rock, Gregg, Gable, & Zigmond, 2009). Feedback providing specific information to candidates about their use of evidence-based practices in the classroom supports their translation of knowledge to practice (Scheeler, Bruno, Grubb, & Seavey, 2009). Feedback also minimizes the research-to-practice gap by assisting teachers with the acquisition, maintenance, and generalization of skills (Coogle, Rahn, & Ottley, 2015); emerging evidence shows that precise feedback improves teaching performance, which results in positive outcomes for young children with disabilities (Ottley, Ferron, & Hanline, 2016).

Anticipated Impact

This program recognizes our field's shift from recruiting new teachers to supporting current teachers (Brunsting et al., 2014; Sindelar et al., 2010); it addresses this shift by providing support to practicing teachers. Because of the ongoing support our program offers, we anticipate that our graduates will remain in the field of inclusive early childhood education for a longer duration than teachers who do not receive such support. And when well-prepared teachers stay in the field longer, more children (aged zero to eight and their families) end up having access to high-quality teachers with expertise in evidence-based practices that meet the needs of all learners. Consequently, we expect improved outcomes for all young children who are taught by our graduates—outcomes exceeding those attained by students receiving instruction from teachers who complete traditional single-licensure programs.

DEALING WITH CHALLENGES AND BARRIERS

During the curriculum development process, we encountered three challenges. These related to faculty commitment, the identification of appropriate standards, and the program's online nature.

Faculty Commitment to Program Development

In the first year, one member of the curriculum development team did not participate. Although this individual responded affirmatively to meeting invitations, he/she failed to attend any of the meetings. After three months, we invited a different faculty member (with similar expertise) to join the team. As a result of this change, our team moved forward productively in the second and third years. Fortunately, college and university leaders supported this change in team membership—which kept a potentially disruptive event from derailing the curriculum development process. One way for other institutions to prepare for a similar challenge would be to make their curriculum development teams purposefully larger than needed. Then, if a few members chose not to participate, the team would still retain the necessary expertise for program development activities.

Selection of the Appropriate Standards for Curriculum Alignment

A major challenge for curriculum development was in selecting the correct standards to guide a graduate degree program—one that works only with teachers already possessing a teaching license in either early childhood or special education. Because we were developing an advanced licensure program, according to the Council for the Accreditation of Education Professionals, we started our curriculum development work by considering the advanced licensure standards from CEC and NAEYC.

After our curriculum development team had created all course syllabi, materials, and assessments, however, we learned that the advanced standards were only applicable if all candidates possessed *both specializations* prior to enrolling in our program. Because this requirement would not be met by all candidates (i.e., some would be licensed in early childhood but not special education, and vice versa—so many candidates would be adding a new licensure to their existing license), we realized we should have used the sets of initial licensure standards. Consequently, we spent an additional two months comparing the advanced standards, which we had incorrectly used, with the initial licensure standards, which we should have used from the outset. We then took this information and aligned all new standards (at the initial licensure level) with the coursework and assessment objectives and outcomes. As needed, we added course requirements to cover content and skills outlined in the initial standards that had been left out in our first effort. Our program now meets all licensure requirements for CEC and NAEYC's initial standards. Other institutions can save valuable time and effort by learning from our misstep and starting all program development work with the initial licensure standards of their respective professional organizations.

Challenges With the Development of an Online Licensure Program

Developing an online program comes with unique challenges—for example, building a web-based learning platform. It is especially important that online course modules have a consistent layout and format to make the presentation of content easy to follow (Rivera & Rice, 2002). A strong online platform with an easily navigable interface keeps the focus on course content and thereby facilitates learning. Ohio University's Office of Instructional Innovation supported our development of such a platform by providing the services of an instructional design team. In league with this team, the faculty's work included the creation of "master" courses. When a new instructor is assigned to teach the course, he or she can use the "master" course template to guide his or her development of the course syllabus. The team also helped to develop a common format for all courses, ensuring consistency across the program's different instructors. Finally, the instructional design team helped us build an orientation module that introduces candidates to the program and its associated technologies. The Office of Instructional Innovation continues to provide technical assistance to our program's instructors, supporting their effective implementation of online instruction and their use of the University's web-based tools. Without these supports, the quality of our program would be greatly diminished.

We also found that some concepts are more challenging to explain in an online format than other concepts. Digital media offer solutions that help students comprehend these concepts. For example, we embedded demonstration videos on our course sites to illustrate difficult concepts. Some such videos show teachers modeling specific instructional strategies. Audiovisual content improves instruction in other ways, too. Courses frequently use field-based assignments that apply course content to the students' clinical settings. When this fieldwork is not possible, text and video case studies provide opportunities for students to think critically and use course concepts to problem-solve challenges they might actually encounter in their classrooms and schools. Both fieldwork and the case studies require candidates to demonstrate their learning and skills—demonstrations that enable faculty members to evaluate their performance.

CONCLUSION

Grouping students according to ability, heretofore a recommended practice, is not advocated today. Teachers can no longer avoid their responsibility to educate all students by arguing that certain groups of children "belong" to a specific type of teacher (Kim, 2011). Ideally, early childhood teachers and special education teachers should serve the same children. Preparing teachers to work in inclusive classrooms is, therefore, essential for the success of all children (Justice et al., 2014; Odom, 2001). Teachers need the knowledge, skills, and dispositions to support all children's success. Our online dual-licensure graduate program works to meet this need.

An online program helps us reach a larger audience in geographic terms, but also in terms of experience in the field. It accomplishes the latter by reducing structural barriers for participation, allowing novice and veteran teachers alike to continue their education without putting their careers on hold. The program fosters rich discussions among candidates and instructors, and it provides meaningful content and ongoing faculty support from experts in inclusive practice. Several challenges arose as we developed the program, but these were minor. Throughout, our focus remained on the children that our graduates will serve. We are confident that the teachers who complete our program will have the knowledge, skills, and dispositions necessary to teach all children in inclusive environments.

NOTE

1. This section both paraphrases and expands on the mission statement and program description found on the program's website (see Patton College of Education, n.d.).

REFERENCES

Barton, E. E., & Smith, B. J. (2015). Advancing high-quality preschool inclusion: A discussion and recommendations for the field. *Topics in Early Childhood Special Education, 35*, 69–78. doi:10.1177/0271121415583048

Bonk, C. J., & Zhang, K. (2006). Introducing the R2D2 model: Online learning for the diverse learners of this world. *Distance Education, 27*, 249–264. doi:10.1080/01587910600789670

Brunsting, N. C., Sreckovic, M. A., & Lane, K. L. (2014). Special education teacher burnout: A synthesis of research from 1979 to 2013. *Education and Treatment of Children, 37*, 681–711. doi:10.1353/etc.2014.0032

Coogle, C. G., Rahn, N. L., & Ottley, J. R. (2015). Pre-service teacher use of evidence-based communication strategies in inclusive preschool classrooms upon receiving bug in ear feedback. *Early Childhood Research Quarterly, 32*, 105–115. doi:10.1016/j.ecresq.2015.03.003

Diamond, K. E., Gerde, H. K., & Powell, D. R. (2008). Development in early literacy skills during the pre-kindergarten year in Head Start: Relations between growth in children's writing and understanding of letters. *Early Childhood Research Quarterly, 23*, 467–478. doi:10.1016/j.ecresq.2008.05.002

Driver, R., Asoko, H., Leach, J., Scott, P., & Mortimer, E. (1994). Constructing scientific knowledge in the classroom. *Educational Researcher, 23*, 5–12. doi:10.3102/0013189X023007005

Hanline, M. F., Hatoum, R. J., & Riggie, J. (2012). Impact of online coursework for teachers of students with severe disabilities: Utilization of knowledge and its relationship to teacher perception of competence. *Research & Practice for Persons with Severe Disabilities, 37*, 247–262. doi:10.2511/027494813805327269

Justice, L. M., Logan, J. A. R., Lin, T., & Kaderavek, J. N. (2014). Peer effects in early childhood education: Testing the assumptions of special-education inclusion. *Psychological Science, 29*, 1722–1729. doi:10.1177/0956797614538978

Kelso, K., Fletcher, J., & Lee, P. (2007). Reading comprehension in children with specific language impairment: An examination of two subgroups. *International Journal of Language and Communication Disorders, 42*, 39–57. doi:10.1080/13682820600693013

Kim, J. R. (2011). Influence of teacher preparation programmes on preservice teachers' attitudes toward inclusion. *International Journal of Inclusive Education, 15*, 355–377. doi:10.1080/13603110903030097

National Center for Education Statistics. (2015). *Digest of Education Statistics.* Retrieved from https://nces.ed.gov/programs/digest/d15/

National Institute for Literacy, National Early Literacy Panel. (2008). *Developing Early Literacy: Report of the National Early Literacy Panel.* Retrieved from https://lincs.ed.gov/publications/pdf/NELPReport09.pdf

Odom, S. L. (2001). Preschool inclusion: What we know and where we go from here. *Topics in Early Childhood Special Education, 20*, 20–27. doi:10.1177/027112140002000104

Odom, S. L. (2009). The tie that binds: Evidence-based practice, implementation science, and outcomes for children. *Topics in Early Childhood Special Education, 29*, 53–61. doi:10.1177/0271121408329171

Ottley, J. R., Ferron, J. M., & Hanline, M. F. (2016). Explaining variance and identifying predictors of children's communication via a multilevel model of single-case design research: Brief report. *Developmental Neurorehabilitation, 19*, 197–202. doi:10.3109/17518423.2015.1008149

Patton College of Education. (n.d.). *Dual early childhood and early childhood intervention specialist.* Retrieved from https://www.ohio.edu/education/academic-programs/online-programs/dualearlychildhood.cfm

Rivera, J. C., & Rice, M. L. (2002). A comparison of student outcomes and satisfaction between traditional and web based course offerings. *Online Journal of Distance Learning Administration, 5*, 151–179. Retrieved from https://pdfs. semanticscholar.org/63fd/b77f1bd2216e9734ca493452f66a92ebb094.pdf

Rock, M. L., Gregg, M., Gable, R. A., & Zigmond, N. P. (2009). Virtual coaching for novice teaching. *Phi Delta Kappan, 91*, 36–41. doi:10.1177/003172170909100209

Rowe, M. L., Raudenbush, S. W., & Goldin-Meadow, S. (2012). The pace of vocabulary growth helps predict later vocabulary skill. *Child Development, 83*, 508–525. doi:10.1111/j.1467-8624.2011.01710.x

Scheeler, M. C., Bruno, K., Grub, E., & Seavey, T. L. (2009). Generalizing teaching techniques from university to K-12 classrooms: Teaching preservice teachers to use what they learn. *Journal of Behavioral Education, 18*, 189–210. doi:10.1007/s10864-009-9088-3

Sindelar, P. T., Brownell, M. T., & Billingsley, B. (2010). Special education teacher education research: Current status and future directions. *Teacher Education and Special Education, 33*, 8–24. doi:10.1177/0888406409358593

Stanton-Chapman, T. L., Justice, L. M., Skibbe, L. E., & Grant, S. K. (2007). Social and behavioral characteristics of preschoolers with specific language impairment. *Topics in Early Childhood Special Education, 27*, 98–109. doi:10.1177/02711214070270020501

APPENDIX

Table 16.1.
Example Course Standards Aligned Rubric for the Four Stages of Assessment

Comprehensive Behavior Unit	Exceeds Standards (2)	Meets Standards (1)	Does Not Meet Standards (0)
Family & Colleague Collaboration			
Candidate includes the family in the assessment process by interviewing a family member of the target child with challenging behavior to identify family priorities, concerns, and the child's strengths and needs. (CEC-EC K4.1, S4.1, S4.2; NAEYC 2C; DEC-RP L12, A6, F4)	Candidate consistently includes the family in the assessment process by interviewing a family member to identify family priorities, concerns, and the child's strengths and needs.	Candidate includes the family in the assessment process by interviewing a family member to identify family priorities, concerns, and the child's strengths and needs.	Candidate includes the family's priorities, concerns, and the child's strengths and needs in the assessment process on a limited basis that does not reflect family-centered practices.
Candidate collaborates with the family to identify preferences and goals with respect to social-emotional development and behavioral outcomes. (CEC-EC S7.1, S7.2; CEC Ethics 5)	Candidate consistently collaborates with the family to identify preferences and goals with respect to social-emotional development and behavioral outcomes.	Candidate collaborates with the family to identify preferences and goals with respect to social-emotional development and behavioral outcomes.	Candidate minimally communicates with the family, identifying only 1 goal or preference.
Candidate interacts with families in supportive and respectful ways that demonstrate cultural competence. (CEC-EC S7.8; NAEYC 2B; PCOE D2.1)	Candidate consistently interacts with families in supportive and respectful ways that demonstrate cultural competence.	Candidate interacts with families in supportive and respectful ways that demonstrate cultural competence.	Candidate's interactions with families are limited in terms of their support and respect for diverse cultural competencies.

(Table continues on next page)

Table 16.1.

Example Course Standards Aligned Rubric for the Four Stages of Assessment (Continued)

Comprehensive Behavior Unit	Exceeds Standards (2)	Meets Standards (1)	Does Not Meet Standards (0)
Candidate interviews a colleague who teaches the target child and builds assessment partnerships with professional colleagues who can assist in early identification of children and in collecting assessment data. (DEC RP L12, L14; NAEYC 3D)	Candidate consistently communicates with a colleague who teaches the target child and collaborates in early identification of children and in the collection of assessment data.	Candidate builds assessment partnerships with professional colleagues by interviewing a colleague who teaches the target child.	Candidate's communication during the collaboration efforts minimally promotes positive partnerships with colleagues.
Conducting the Functional Behavior Assessment (FBA)			
Candidate selects a variety of appropriate assessments to conduct the FBA. (CEC-EC 4.0,4.1,S4.4,S4.5, S4.7; DEC-RP A6; OSTP 3.2; PCOE LE1.1)	Candidate selects 4 or more appropriate assessments to conduct the FBA.	Candidate selects 2-3 appropriate assessments to conduct the FBA.	Candidate uses 1 or no assessments to conduct the FBA.
Candidate uses a variety of valid and reliable assessment practices for the assessments' intended purposes in the gathering of data for the FBA to minimize bias. (CEC-EC 4.0,4.2,4.3, S4.4, S5.4; DEC-RP L14, INS3; NAEYC 3B; NAEYC Ethics I-1.6; OSTP 3.2; OLAC A-1 P.3; PCOE LE1.1)	Candidate uses 4 or more valid and reliable assessment practices for the assessments' intended purposes in the gathering of data for the FBA to minimize bias.	Candidate uses 2-3 valid and reliable assessment practices for the assessments' intended purposes in the gathering of data for the FBA to minimize bias.	Candidate uses only 1 or no valid and reliable assessment practices or does not verify the validity and reliability of assessments when gathering data for the FBA.
Candidate includes the use of technology in the documentation of data. (NAEYC 3B; PCOE CA3.2)	Candidate consistently includes the use of technology in the documentation of data.	Candidate includes the use of technology in the documentation of data.	Candidate uses all low-tech or no-tech mechanisms in the documentation of data.

(Table continues on next page)

Table 16.1.

Example Course Standards Aligned Rubric for the Four Stages of Assessment (Continued)

Comprehensive Behavior Unit	Exceeds Standards (2)	Meets Standards (1)	Does Not Meet Standards (0)
Candidate collects data across a variety of environments to measure child skill and performance across settings such as the home, school, and community. (CEC-EC 4.3, S4.3; DEC-RP A7, INS9; OLAC A-1 P.3; PCOE LE1.1)	Candidate collects data across a variety of environments.	Candidate collects data across more than 1 environment.	Candidate collects data in 1 environment.
Candidate includes families in the assessment process by surveying them about the behavior patterns of their child. (CEC-EC S4.5; DEC-RP A2, A6)	Candidate consistently includes families in the assessment process.	Candidate includes families in the assessment process.	Candidate minimally communicates with the family through the assessment process
Candidate encourages colleagues to participate in the data collection and assessment process and to utilize unbiased identification and assessment practices. (CEC-EC S4.8, S7.1; DEC-RP L12, L14, A2, A6; PCOE LE1.4)	Candidate consistently encourages colleagues to participate in the data collection and assessment process and to utilize unbiased identification and assessment practices.	Candidate encourages colleagues to participate in the data collection and assessment process and to utilize unbiased identification and assessment practices.	Candidate collects all data by him/herself without encouraging colleagues to participate in the assessment process.
Development of the FBA Report			
Candidate charts and analyzes data to document present levels of performance and plan for intervention. (CEC-EC S4.9, S4.10; OSTP 3.3; NAEYC Ethics I-1.7; OLAC A-1 P.3, A-1 P.4)	Candidate consistently charts and analyzes data to document present levels of performance and plan for intervention.	Candidate charts and analyzes data to document present levels of performance and plan for intervention.	Candidate analyzes data without charting or visual analysis of graphed data.

(Table continues on next page)

Table 16.1.

Example Course Standards Aligned Rubric for the Four Stages of Assessment (Continued)

Comprehensive Behavior Unit	Exceeds Standards (2)	Meets Standards (1)	Does Not Meet Standards (0)
Candidate writes the FBA report in a manner that is free from jargon and understandable to families, colleagues, and relevant community members. (DEC-RP A11; OSTP 3.4; PCOE LE1.6)	Candidate consistently writes the FBA report in a manner that is free from jargon and understandable to families, colleagues, and relevant community members.	Candidate writes the FBA report in a manner that is free from jargon and understandable to families, colleagues, and relevant community members.	Candidate uses jargon and/or technical language in the FBA report.
Candidate verbally shares the purpose of FBA with families along with the FBA's assessment results in a manner that is understandable and useful. (DEC-RP A11; OSTP 3.4; NAEYC Ethics P-2.7, I-2.7; PCOE LE1.6)	Candidate consistently verbally shares the purpose of FBA with families along with the FBA's assessment results in a manner that is understandable and useful.	Candidate verbally shares the purpose of FBA with families along with the FBA's assessment results in a manner that is understandable and useful.	Candidate uses technical language during communication with families and/or presents information that is not helpful to them.
Candidate demonstrates cultural competence in their communication of assessment results. (CEC-EC S7.8; NAEYC 2C; PCOE D2.3)	Candidate consistently demonstrates cultural competence in their communication of assessment results.	Candidate demonstrates cultural competence in their communication of assessment results.	Candidate uses monocultural practices that are limited in their cultural competence in their communication of assessment results.

(Table continues on next page)

Table 16.1.

Example Course Standards Aligned Rubric for the Four Stages of Assessment (Continued)

Comprehensive Behavior Unit	Exceeds Standards (2)	Meets Standards (1)	Does Not Meet Standards (0)
Candidate shares up-to-date information with families in a comprehensible manner that assists families in making informed choices and decisions. (DEC-RP F2; NAEYC Ethics I-2.7; PCOE LE1.6)	Candidate consistently shares up-to-date information with families in a comprehensible manner that assists families in making informed choices and decisions.	Candidate shares up-to-date information with families in a comprehensible manner that assists families in making informed choices and decisions.	Candidate shares dated or biased information with families.
Candidate collaborates with families and colleagues to identify resources and supports to achieve family identified goals/outcomes. (DEC-RP F7, TC4; NAEYC Ethics P-1.4, P-2.15; PCOE LE1.2, LE1.4, LE1.5, LE1.6)	Candidate consistently collaborates with families and colleagues to identify resources and supports to achieve family identified goals/ outcomes.	Candidate collaborates with families and colleagues to identify resources and supports to achieve family identified goals/ outcomes.	Candidate minimally communicates with families and colleagues, which is reflected in the generation of a limited set of resources and supports.
Candidate only shares the FBA Report with individuals involved in the child's life and ensures confidentiality of sensitive information, including documenting who should have access to the information. (NAEYC Ethics P-1.4, P-2.8, P-2.12)	Candidate only shares the FBA Report with individuals involved in the child's life and ensures confidentiality of sensitive information, including documenting who should have access to the information.	Candidate only shares the FBA Report with individuals involved in the child's life and ensures confidentiality of sensitive information.	Candidate does not protect the child's confidentiality when collecting and sharing data.

(Table continues on next page)

Table 16.1.

Example Course Standards Aligned Rubric for the Four Stages of Assessment (Continued)

Comprehensive Behavior Unit	Exceeds Standards (2)	Meets Standards (1)	Does Not Meet Standards (0)
Development of the Behavior Intervention Plan (BIP)			
Candidate collaborates with families and colleagues to develop the BIP and identifies resources to prevent and address challenging behavior. (CEC-EC S7.1, S7.2; DEC-RP L14, F4, F7; OLAC A-1 P.4; PCOE LE1.1, LE1.2, LE1.4, LE1.5, LE1.6)	Candidate consistently collaborates with families and colleagues to develop the BIP and identifies resources to prevent and address challenging behavior.	Candidate collaborates with families and colleagues to develop the BIP and identifies resources to prevent and address challenging behavior.	Candidate minimally communicates with families and colleagues to develop the BIP and identify resources to prevent and address challenging behavior.
Candidate implements culturally relevant intervention strategies including assistive technology to prevent and address challenging behavior. (CEC-EC 2.3, S5.5, S7.2; OSTP 3.5; PCOE CA3.4, D2.2, D2.3; PCOE LE1.3)	Candidate consistently implements culturally relevant intervention strategies including assistive technology to prevent and address challenging behavior.	Candidate implements culturally relevant intervention strategies including assistive technology to prevent and address challenging behavior.	Candidate minimally considers culturally relevant intervention strategies to prevent and address challenging behavior.
Candidate designs assessments to evaluate the effectiveness of practices in addressing children's behavioral needs. (PCOE LE1.7)	Candidate consistently designs assessments to evaluate the effectiveness of practices in addressing children's behavioral needs.	Candidate designs assessments to evaluate the effectiveness of practices in addressing children's behavioral needs.	Candidate uses only 1 assessment to evaluate the effectiveness of practices in addressing children's behavioral needs.

(Table continues on next page)

Table 16.1.

Example Course Standards Aligned Rubric for the Four Stages of Assessment (Continued)

Comprehensive Behavior Unit	Exceeds Standards (2)	Meets Standards (1)	Does Not Meet Standards (0)
Candidate selects assessment tools that are sensitive enough to document change in outcomes over a short period of time. (DEC-RP A11; PCOE LE1.7)	Candidate consistently selects assessment tools that are sensitive enough to document change in outcomes over a short period of time.	Candidate selects assessment tools that are sensitive enough to document change in outcomes over a short period of time.	Candidate selects assessment tools that are lacking in sensitivity to document change over a short period of time.
Candidate implements systematic, ongoing progress monitoring practices to evaluate the effectiveness of the intervention in addressing children's behavioral needs. (CEC-EC S4.11; DEC-RP A9; NAEYC 3B; OLAC A-3 P.6; PCOE LE1.7)	Candidate consistently implements systematic, ongoing progress monitoring practices to evaluate the effectiveness of the intervention in addressing children's behavioral needs.	Candidate implements systematic, ongoing progress monitoring practices to evaluate the effectiveness of the intervention in addressing children's behavioral needs.	Candidate implements progress monitoring practices to evaluate the effectiveness of the intervention for less than 3 occasions.
Candidate charts and analyzes assessment data to make decisions regarding the effectiveness of the intervention strategies and progress toward achieving individual, school, and district goals. (CEC-EC S7.9, S7.10; DEC-RP INS3, INS9; NAEYC 3C; OSTP 3.3; OLAC A-1 P.3, A-3 P.7; PCOE LL 4.3)	Candidate consistently charts and analyzes assessment data to make decisions regarding the effectiveness of the intervention strategies and progress toward goals.	Candidate charts and analyzes assessment data to make decisions regarding the effectiveness of the intervention strategies and progress toward goals. ;	Candidate provides a limited analysis of assessment data to make decisions regarding the effectiveness of the intervention strategies and progress toward goals.

CHAPTER 17

CONSCIENTIOUS CONSOLIDATION

Developing and Implementing a Dual-Licensure Program With Montessori Credentialing

Kathleen G. Winterman,
Victoria Zascavage, and Julie Kugler-Ackley
Xavier University

In 2015, the U.S. Department of Health and Human Services and the U.S. Department of Education issued a joint statement: "All young children with disabilities should have access to inclusive high-quality early childhood programs where they are provided with individualized and appropriate support in meeting high expectations." Despite that assertion, it is a fact that many students with disabilities do not have such access, and therefore may experience difficulty in meeting state educational standards and making progress. This situation may be due, in part, to ineffective teacher preparation. A statewide survey of preservice teachers ($n = 5,267$) revealed that most felt inadequately prepared to instruct students with disabilities;

Inclusive Education: A Systematic Perspective, pp. 299–308
Copyright © 2020 by Information Age Publishing
All rights of reproduction in any form reserved.

and a follow-up survey of in-service teachers with one to two years of experience showed that many of these educators felt even less well prepared than the preservice teachers (Rosas & Winterman, 2010). Such findings point to the possibility that, in failing to adequately prepare teachers who work with students with disabilities and other underperforming students, the education community may actually be contributing to students' marginalization and inhibiting their achievement. This chapter describes one university's efforts to address the situation by better preparing teachers to offer effective and appropriate classroom instruction to all their students.

PROGRAM BACKGROUND

Xavier University is a small, coeducational, liberal arts university in Ohio, and is the sixth-oldest Catholic, and fourth-oldest Jesuit, university in the nation. Its enrollment of 4,663 undergraduate and 2,165 graduate students reflects considerable diversity, with 23% of the students coming from ethnically diverse populations and 20% attending as first-generation college students.

The university's Early Childhood (EC) Education program leading to licensure is grounded in a holistic approach to pedagogy and learning that combines instruction in developmentally appropriate practice with intense reading in the field. Xavier also offers a Montessori course that complements the EC Education program by emphasizing the importance of carefully preparing learning environments to support development of the whole child. In addition, the university's Early Childhood Intervention Specialist (ECIS) program aligns with many Montessori principles, including individualized instruction, working with children at their current developmental levels, and providing needed support and services. The ECIS program also embraces a holistic approach based on the tenets of Universal Design for Learning (UDL; Center for Applied Special Technology, 2011), an instructional framework providing a learning environment supportive of all students' development.

The university made the decision to merge the EC and ECIS licensure programs with Montessori education, seeing this move as a natural step in improving and expanding its teacher preparation program, given those disciplines' similar philosophical foundations. The Montessori approach embraces the concept of individualized education within heterogeneous groups of students, and ECIS couples the basic principles of Montessori education with EC's focus on developmentally appropriate practice.

The construction of a curriculum combining all three disciplines (EC, ECIS, and Montessori) into a dual-licensure program required a team of professionals with extensive expertise. The team, which had informally been discussing ways to blend the three curricula, chose to embrace federal mandates and state initiatives in order to bolster their efforts and formalize the process. They recognized that dual licensure would increase teachers' capacity, as team members, to identify and assess young children with learning problems and enable them to intervene appropriately and effectively to help these students benefit from their schooling and, ultimately, go on to lead productive lives.

PROGRAM DEVELOPMENT

Recognizing the academic, behavioral, and social benefits of an early inclusive education (Howard, Williams, Miller, & Aiken, 2014), Xavier's new dual-licensure program has restructured its early childhood, early childhood intervention, and elementary school teacher preparation programs into a cohesive course of study that prepares those on educational teams to take on a variety of roles that maximize opportunities for young children (Zascavage & Keefe, 2004; Zascavage & Winterman, 2009). The new four-year undergraduate program's carefully selected foundational coursework draws on research-based, developmentally appropriate material. A double major of EC and ECIS prepares graduates to work with children from prekindergarten through Grade 3 (PK–3). And, though not the program's primary focus, the Montessori component complements it with theory and methods well suited for cultivating early-childhood educators. State standards are used to validate content proficiency, and program graduates must demonstrate content knowledge competency by passing the state tests required for licensure in EC, ECIS, and the Foundations of Reading (National Education Association, n.d.).

Program graduates also collaborate with families, education professionals, and professionals from related disciplines, to offer learning opportunities, in a variety of settings, to children with different capacities and requirements. Xavier's Montessori pedagogy, traditional EC programming, and ECIS program all stress the development of the whole child, informed by an understanding of how varied that developmental process can be. In earning their degrees, teacher candidates expand their capacity not only to teach effectively in general, but also to assess and meet the specific educational needs of all the young children in their care.

Montessori Education

Based upon Maria Montessori's vision of equity and opportunity for all children, Montessori education embraces the concept of individualized education within heterogeneous groupings (Montessori, 1967). EC Montessori coursework also embraces the same tenets of sound educational practices that are reflected in Ohio's Content Standards. The Montessori approach has proven effective for over 100 years. It remains faithful to its original intent: to teach academic, life, and social skills using a variety of materials, while emphasizing self-regulation in a culturally responsive environment (Cossentino, 2010; Montessori, 1967). Special education pedagogy for young children within a Montessori educational setting incorporates these principles (Cossentino, 2010).

Montessori EC classrooms use lessons and materials developed as the basis for continuous educational programming from ages 3 to 12. This continuity allows new learning to build on previously acquired skills and knowledge. Paying attention to the scope and sequence of curricula is essential for Montessori-trained educators, and children entering a Montessori early-childhood class choose from developmentally appropriate activities in areas such as practical living, math, language, art, music, drama, and physical movement and coordination (Scruggs & Mastropieri, 2017).

"Children with special needs are supported so that they benefit from Maria Montessori's program, a program designed to teach academic, life, and social skills to all children" (McKenzie & Zascavage, 2012, p. 38). This concept affirms a vision that does not allow any child in the classroom to be marginalized. In Montessori classrooms, social and academic classroom rules support students' success. Students are encouraged to develop their abilities to concentrate, to use self-discipline, and to respect others. Children with special needs especially benefit from the support of a structured environment where expectations for appropriate behavior are taught through example and peer interaction. Students learn the value of mutual respect as citizens of the classroom community (Cunningham, 2017). In inclusive public Montessori classrooms, special education intervention specialists traditionally work with Montessori-certified teachers.

ECIS Components

In the EC program and in ECIS coursework leading to licensure, teacher candidates are educated in evidence-based practices. And in the special education coursework, teacher candidates focus on the characteristics, issues, trends, assessment, and current best practices in accommodation and modification. Teacher candidates are instructed in the use of assistive technology, UDL strategies, evidence-based practices, and culturally responsive practices related to students with special needs. The EC and ECIS programs offer coursework in behavior management, social skills intervention, communication and collaboration, teaming, human development, reading theories and diagnostic approaches, learning theories, assessment methods, and effective use of instructional materials. ECIS candidates for licensure must meet the professional standards of the Council for Exceptional Children, as well as those of the Ohio Standards for the Teaching Profession.

In the practicum portion of their programs, dual-licensure candidates are placed in early-childhood Montessori schools, as well as in public elementary schools serving all children PK–3, including those with unique learning challenges. They complete student teaching in a variety of settings, including rural, urban, and suburban schools; and they are given the opportunity to work with children identified as having special needs, as well as those developing more typically. The dual-licensure program has partnered with the following types of schools to provide a diverse experience to preservice teachers:

- An urban public Montessori school, with a prekindergarten through sixth-grade student population that includes 51% from minority groups, 37% on free lunch, and 7% on reduced lunch;
- A rural public elementary school serving children from preschool through fifth grade, with a student population having 12.8% from minority groups and 43% eligible for free or reduced lunch;
- Educational Service Center preschool programs located in an urban area where the student population includes 86% students eligible for free or reduced lunch, 17% White students, 83% ethnically diverse students, and 21% students with identified disabilities.

Administrators and faculty from local school districts act as advisors in the development and implementation of Xavier's licensure and degree programs. They attend meetings with university faculty, and they conduct observations in the schools to help ensure that the program meets the needs of the community.

Curricular Mapping

The educators who developed the dual-licensure program applied curriculum mapping to the ECIS and EC program courses, to ensure that they aligned with Ohio Standards. All syllabi were reviewed for adherence to research-based practice. Newly developed courses were also examined according to the professional standards of the Council for Exceptional Children, American Montessori Standards, Montessori Accreditation Council for Teacher Education, and National Association for the Education of Young Children to determine where and how merged courses might meet professional expectations and lead to intended outcomes.

Curriculum mapping, curriculum review, and professional assessment provided extensive and frequent feedback on the curriculum, workshops, and modules to ensure development of a rigorous program. In addition, feedback from faculty participating in the workshops, and from students participating in the training and modules, enabled the team to assess progress and generate new ideas for further improvement. Evaluation methods have been planned for each phase of development and implementation, and the collection and review of data offer opportunities for continued improvement. The results of the data collection and curriculum adjustments will be shared with other programs through publications, the updating of curriculum materials, and workshops, as development and implementation move forward.

Faculty Training

The dual-licensure initiative's principal investigators hold degrees in their respective fields, with other team members holding doctoral or master's degrees along with advanced training in Special Education, EC, or Montessori Education. Principals, county education service center supervisors, and master teachers serve on our advisory council.

The initiative's developers have carefully selected and combined coursework from the three programs to create a unified curriculum highlighting each discipline's strengths. These courses will provide candidates with the knowledge and skills required to address the educational needs of a range of young children, including those with disabilities. Using principles of implementation science, the team has disseminated the program, sharing it with neighboring institutions for the betterment of all children in the community. We have strengthened our existing community relationships with local schools, and developed new ones, with the objective of benefitting future teaching candidates as well as our new undergraduate students.

In addition, the faculty from Special Education, EC, and Montessori Education are engaged in activities that help them expand their professional expertise. Notably, they participate in the workshop and module trainings that support the merged program, and they have either started to or will soon teach the new ("merged") courses. Feedback from these early efforts to teach the new courses will improve future iterations of these courses. Faculty "cross training" (i.e., giving faculty members the chance to learn about courses other than the ones they teach) is another promising approach that the program is using.

Reflections

An overarching strength of the dual-licensure development team was its collegial collaboration. The faculty from the three specialty fields used curriculum mapping to determine which courses would be merged, which would be redesigned, and which would remain the same. The outcome was a curriculum map and learning modules that meet required professional standards for all three specialty fields.

In the spirit of collaboration, and to ensure that all teaching faculty (full-time and adjuncts) possess the necessary background knowledge to instruct teacher candidates in the dual-licensure program, multiple full-day trainings were offered to faculty, staff, students, and community partners. Faculty representatives from each of the merged disciplines worked in partnership to prepare for the workshops and gave presentations on Montessori EC education with special education pedagogy. Feedback from faculty and adjunct participants made it clear that the workshops provided content essential to teaching the dual-licensure with Montessori course work. Participants' evaluations showed that they valued the opportunity to collaborate and share their views and insights on merging the three disciplines.

To ensure that the merged coursework met state licensure requirements, the faculty submitted the curriculum to internal and external review boards. The internal review boards approved the curriculum for implementation, and the external review board, the Ohio Board of Higher Education, approved the merged curriculum. Plans are now underway for evaluation activities that will assess (a) the preparation of teacher candidates who complete the merged program and (b) the extent to which the program is meeting its espoused goals.

CHALLENGES

Some of the procedural challenges we experienced resulted from institutional constraints that slowed down our efforts; and some resulted from procedural changes that occurred at the institution. Two substantive challenges were also significant. These related to clinical placements and the expertise of clinical supervisors.

Challenges Relating to Clinical Experiences

Graduates of the dual-licensure program will be candidates for EC and ECIS licensure with Montessori credentials. Therefore, the licensure team has worked hard on a rigorous plan to enable them to have opportunities during their preparation program to serve children, with or without disabilities, in Montessori EC environments. This plan requires candidates to undertake three major clinical experiences. In the first semester of the third year, candidates must participate in a 60-hour field experience in which they fulfill the PK–3 ECIS teacher role. In the first semester of their fourth year, candidates are required to participate in a half-day clinical experience fulfilling the role of an EC teacher using Montessori methods. In their final semester, the candidates complete a 15-week full-time placement in which, under the supervision of a cooperating teacher with a minimum of three years of experience, they gradually assume the dual role of the EC teacher and ECIS in either a preschool or K–3 placement.

Teacher candidates taking on this dual role will begin by observing and assisting students, during which time they will become familiar with student data and information from individualized education programs. As their experience progresses, the candidates will co-plan with the cooperating teacher, and present lessons to their students. These lessons will be based on formative and summative assessment data, and they will make use of various co-teaching models. Throughout the instructional day, candidates will employ Montessori, as well as special education strategies and materials, to respond to the needs of all students. As they progress, candidates will be expected to take the lead in planning, instruction, and classroom management. Candidates will participate in state and district assessments, as permitted, and conduct formative and summative assessments. They will also participate in individualized education program preparation and other activities, including developing and implementing data-collection systems, executing behavior plans, and modifying classroom work to accommodate situations.

Incorporating all of these different learning opportunities into one coherent set of clinical experiences is one significant challenge we face. To address this challenge, we need to find locations for placing students that support the program's philosophy and allow for a variety of learning opportunities, and we also need to structure clinical experiences carefully so they result in the outcomes we intend.

Challenges Relating to Supervisory Capacity

Another challenge the team faces has to do with the fact that most early childhood teachers and university supervisors do not hold EC, ECIS, and Montessori credentials. To address this capacity issue, the team developed a contingency plan that assigns each teacher candidate to two cooperating teachers, one holding EC licensure and the other holding ECIS licensure.

In this way, a candidate can be mentored by two experts in their respective fields. The university also provides two university supervisors for each placement, one fully licensed in EC with Montessori credentialing, and the other fully licensed in special education, with both supervisors having demonstrated previous successful experience in the classroom.

To fit with this approach, we designed a dual evaluation system to assess each teacher candidate's competency, both in ECIS and as an EC Montessori teacher. Every university supervisor will make three videos and conduct six on-site evaluations; the university supervisor licensed in special education will use a lesson implementation rubric, focused on differentiation. The EC university supervisor will complete two two-and-a-half-hour running records of each candidate's activities based on Montessori principles and Ohio Teaching Standards. The purpose of these assessment activities is to determine through observation whether the teacher candidate can implement instruction, based on Common Core standards, that meets the needs of all children, including those with disabilities or other learning challenges. As each candidate's student teaching experience draws to a close, his or her supervisor will complete a modified Ohio Teacher Evaluation System evaluation as a transition to employment. Teaching candidates will also participate in the edTPA assessment.

CONCLUSION

In creating a new way of thinking about philosophy, licensure, and student applications, we have challenged past ways of thinking. We believe our new merged (dual-licensure) program will prepare teachers with the knowledge and skills needed to work with all students—including those with disabilities and those from other marginalized group.

To build high visibility for the dual-licensure program, we worked with the student recruitment, website design, and marketing departments at Xavier. This effort required meeting with program directors from across campus to change current practices and devise new protocols (such as having a double major and not simply a major with a minor). University recruiters were provided with the new marketing materials and have targeted our partner schools across the country, specifically directing attention to other Jesuit schools.

In summary, the aim of Xavier University's dual-licensure program with Montessori credentials is to enhance teacher candidates' ability to meet the educational needs of all the children in their classrooms, including those students with disabilities or other learning difficulties. The program has the potential to increase the capacity of P–12 schools to staff early childhood programs with effective teachers who have the expertise to teach in inclusive classroom environments. Furthermore, it enables teacher candidates to meet state licensure requirements in EC and ECIS, as well as to obtain credentials in Montessori Education. Finally, the Xavier initiative incorporates a coherent professional learning system that combines a common early childhood curriculum with supportive training materials (e.g., curriculum maps, modules, evaluation plans). Our program serves as a model for other teacher preparation programs with an interest in merging early childhood and special education content, and we are enthusiastic about sharing our curriculum and associated materials with faculty across the state and nation.

REFERENCES

Center for Applied Special Technology. (2011). *Universal design for learning (UDL) guidelines: Full text representation* (version 2.0). Wakefield, MA: Author.

Cossentino, J. (2010). Following all the children: Early intervention and Montessori. *Montessori Life, 22*(4), 38–45.

Cunningham, J. (2017). From cosmic education to civic responsibility. *NAMTA Journal 42*(3), 19–28.

Howard, V. F., Williams, B. F., Miller, D., Aiken, E. (2014). *Very young children with special needs: A foundation for educators, families, and service providers* (5th ed.). Upper Saddle River, NJ: Pearson.

McKenzie, G. K., & Zascavage, V. (2012). A model for inclusion in early childhood classrooms and beyond. *Montessori Life, 24*(1), 32–38.

Montessori, M. (1967). *The discovery of the child.* New York, NY: Ballantine.

National Education Association. (n.d.). *Proposed alternative to highly qualified teachers.* Retrieved from https://www.nea.org/assets/docs/Backgrounder-HighlyQualifiedTeachers.pdf

Rosas, C. E., & Winterman, K. G. (2010). Teachers' perceptions on special education preparation: A descriptive study. *Journal of the American Academy of Special Education Professionals*, 118–128.

Scruggs, T. E., & Mastropieri, M. A. (2017). Making inclusion work with co-teaching. *Teaching Exceptional Children, 49*, 284–293. doi:10.1177/0040059916685065

U.S. Department of Health and Human Services and U.S. Department of Education. (2015). *Policy statement on inclusion of children with disabilities in early childhood programs.* Retrieved from https://ed.gov/policy/speced/guid/earlylearning/joint-statement-full-text.pdf

Zascavage, V., & Keefe, C. (2004). Students with severe speech and physical impairments: Opportunity barriers to literacy. *Focus on Autism and Other Developmental Disorders, 19*, 223–234. doi:10.1177/10883576040190040401

Zascavage, V., & Winterman, K. G. (2009). Assistive technology and universal design for learning: What does the middle school educator need to know? *The Middle School Journal, 4*(4), 46–52. doi:10.1080/00940771.2009.11461681

CHAPTER 18

INCLUSIVITY IN THE DEVELOPMENT OF A DUAL-LICENSURE PROGRAM

A Report by Program Developers

Beverly A. Sande
Prairie View Texas A&M University

Charles W. Kemp
Shawnee State University

Paul M. Madden
Shawnee State University

Ray Blevins
Ohio State Support Team 15

Traci McKee
Dawson Bryant Schools and Shawnee State University

Inclusive Education: A Systematic Perspective, pp. 309–326
Copyright © 2020 by Information Age Publishing
All rights of reproduction in any form reserved.

309

Substantial research has shown that the complexities of providing quality education require collaboration among stakeholders (Slater & Ravid, 2010). Ohio is one of a few states to have systematized collaborative practices; and the push for educators to collaborate at all levels of education (P–20) has created effective communication pathways across the state. Making use of these pathways, Shawnee State University (SSU) in Portsmouth, Ohio, worked with key stakeholders to develop a dual-licensure program for preparing early childhood and intervention specialist educators.

With support from the Ohio Deans Compact on Exceptional Children, SSU initiated curriculum revision through a program called Project Teachers for All Students (TeFAS). TeFAS was an initiative to develop a four-year teacher preparation program designed to enable graduates to obtain dual licensure in Early Childhood Education and Early Childhood Special Education (ECSE). Project TeFAS was also developed to serve as a model for other institutions of higher education seeking to develop, implement, and sustain a dual-licensure undergraduate degree program drawing on essential practices included in the Ohio Improvement Process (OIP) as defined by the Ohio Department of Education (ODE) and the Ohio Leadership Advisory Council (OLAC).

This chapter describes the rationale for developing a dual-licensure program, the curriculum restructuring process used, and various stakeholder responses to the restructuring effort. The chapter highlights key elements of collaborative practice among institutions of higher education and stakeholders from preschool through Grade 12 (P–12) schools, state support teams, and various state department offices, thus demonstrating how the successful development and implementation of this new program can be directly attributed to the collaborative approach used by the university and external partners.

RATIONALE FOR THE DUAL-LICENSURE PROGRAM

Both the Individuals with Disabilities Education Act (IDEA) of 1997 and the Elementary and Secondary Education Act of 2001 emphasize the importance of a an inclusive approach to education (Blanton, Pugach, & Florian, 2011). Preparing teachers according to categories of learners, such as students with disabilities or English language learners, reinforces the idea that different groups of teachers are needed for different types of learners. It also reinforces the mistaken view that the wide range of students' needs found in many of today's general education classrooms in the US cannot be met in the absence of such specialization (Blanton et al., 2011). Nevertheless, approximately 60% of U.S. students with disabilities spend at least 80% of their day in general education settings and about

95% of students with disabilities are included for at least a portion of their day; moreover, there are many students with learning needs who do not qualify for special education services to meet their needs (U.S. Department of Education, 2018).

A study by Ying Hu (2010) found that many general education teachers in early childhood education felt unprepared to deal with assessment, individual education plans, teaching strategies, and behavior management for students with disabilities despite the increasing popularity of inclusion models. Many teachers found that, when they used the intervention strategies with which they were familiar, they did not get the anticipated results (Ying Hu, 2010). This circumstance made it difficult for them to know how best to help the children.

Other reports also show that general education teachers are often ill-prepared to meet the demands of today's diverse classrooms (Kemp, 2015). They may lack the skills that their intervention specialist colleagues routinely use. Nevertheless, both groups of educators need to learn how to use evidence-based and high-leverage practices for conducting informal and formal assessments, providing differentiated instruction, and using direct (i.e., explicit) methods of presenting instructional content (Vakil, Welton, O'Connor, & Kline, 2009).

Single licensure programs, however, do not prepare new educators to use all of these practices. In contrast, dual-licensure programs have sufficient scope to prepare new educators to use a wider and more flexible set of teaching practices. According to some researchers, the preparation offered in dual-licensure programs benefits college students who are preparing to become educators (Blanton & Pugach, 2011) as well as the children they eventually teach.

PROJECT TeFAS

Project TeFAS was a response to the critical needs in southern Ohio for teachers qualified to work with all young children especially those who are struggling yet are not identified as needing special education services. This section highlights the conceptual framework that guided the change process at Shawnee State University leading from a traditional to a dual-licensure program.

Conceptual Framework

According to Voss and Bufkin (2011), a coherent program vision begins with common language and agreement on program philosophy. As part of the process of ongoing development and evaluation of the program, the TeFAS program development team reviewed the following practices identified in the Ohio Improvement Process—OIP (Ohio Department of Education, 2018) as effective for improving practices and performance to help in developing and sustaining this dual licensure program.

Seeing the Big Picture

The program developers envisioned a program to prepare highly qualified teachers (HQT) to work with young children including struggling learners and students with disabilities.

Establishing Leadership Teams

Many researchers advocate the use of team structures to facilitate shared learning for instructional improvement (DuFour & Marzano, 2011; Leithwood & Jantzi, 2008; McNulty & Besser, 2011; Seashore Louis, Leithwood, Wahlstrom, & Anderson, 2010). The literature also suggests that cooperation among state education agencies, institutions of higher education, school districts, and other organizations is key to providing teachers and leaders with the knowledge and skills needed to improve student achievement (Blanton & Pugach, 2011; Darling-Hammond, 2005). For these reasons, the Department of Teacher Education at SSU determined that two faculty members—one from each of the two programs (Early Childhood and Intervention Specialist) would take the lead roles to develop the program. These program developers then solicited internal and external partners to be part of the process of developing the dual-licensure program.

Identifying Critical Needs

The team's first action was to establish the need for teachers with dual licensure. To do this, the team sent out a survey to preschool and elementary principals and directors of special education in districts in the region of the state served by SSU. The survey results informed the team's decision to take on the project. According to respondents, there is a dire need for early childhood teachers. More importantly, according to the administrators, the region has a significant need for special education teachers (also known in Ohio as intervention specialists). With dual licensure, the SSU program developers concluded, teacher candidates would be well prepared to teach young children, including those who start school with greater needs than their typically developing peers.

Parents and others in the local community were also surveyed to identify their perceived needs. The parent survey developed by the team concentrated on gathering information regarding parents' best experiences, concerns, and communications with their child's school and teachers. The parents who responded expressed openness to collaboration with general and special education teachers and were interested in multiple means of communication with teachers: written correspondence, face-to-face meetings, emails, text messages, and phone calls. According to the parents, the characteristic they would most like to see in new teachers would be concern for addressing each child's individual needs and abilities. This perspective about what new teachers should be able to do supported the SSU team's goal of creating a dual-licensure program, because such a program would be better able than a traditional one to prepare new teachers to use differentiated instruction to address the needs of individual students.

Creating SMART Goals

Conzemius and O'Neill (2009) define SMART goals as ones that are specific, measurable, attainable, relevant, and timely. The program development team identified specific goals to guide their program development efforts. These goals and their descriptions can be found in the Project TeFAS Logic Model (see Appendix A). It was important that the goals as well as specific program objectives and outcomes be carefully aligned with the overall outcomes intended for SSU students. It was also important that the goals be achievable.

Developing Strategies and Indicators

The program developers implemented specific strategies and indicators to see this project through to its completion. These included selecting curriculum specialists and community advisory council members who would effectively collaborate in the development of the program. Furthermore, the team developed a crosswalk of state standards and specialized professional association standards to show the alignment between these benchmarks and the outcomes of courses in the traditional program and, then later on, in the newly developed dual-licensure program. The team also quantified timelines for specific activities to meet goals stipulated in its logic model.

The Project TeFAS logic model was designed to help the program developers systematically identify the factors impacting the program as well as detailing available resources and data useful for the work of program development. Included in the logic model were the circumstances that prompted the program proposal, program implementation plans and targets, and projected program outcomes. The team also specified the resources needed and the activities in which the program developers would engage in order to accomplish the projected outcomes.

Producing Actions and Tasks

The program development team identified actions and tasks specific to the development, implementation, and sustainability of the project. Each person participating in developing the program had particular actions to perform, and each activity had a clearly specified deadline.

Implementing the Plan Systemically and Systematically

To build capacity, the development team sought to gain departmental, university-wide, and community buy-in for the program. Systematically, the team conducted surveys, solicited the commitment of internal and external partners, and established groups to work on various aspects of the project. The systemic impact (beyond awareness and acceptance) will be realized during the implementation stage.

Designing a Monitoring System and Evaluating the Impact of the Plan and Process

The Ohio Department of Education's Office of Exceptional Children built in mechanisms to ensure monitoring of progress through the development stage. Noell, Brownell, Buzick, and Jones (2014) highlight specific indicators for student evaluation and present a synthesis of research on teacher preparation and effectiveness in three domains: student-learning outcomes; measures of classroom practice; and ratings of educator effectiveness by supervisors. In addition to these domains, the team will use value-added modeling to evaluate the new educational program (e.g., Gansle, Noell, & Burns, 2012; Goldhaber & Liddle, 2012; Mihaly, McCaffrey, Sass, & Lockwood, 2012; Noell, Porter, Patt, & Dahir, 2008). To support this effort, the selection of an external evaluator was necessary.

Revising the Plan

The team put contingency plans in place to deal with unforeseen circumstances. For example, in the event specific group members were unable to fulfill their roles, the team had a pool of additional committed individuals ready and willing to step in and advance the project.

Project Goals, Essential Elements, and Impacts

The development team identified six goals for completing the project. The goals were specific to making this a sustainable dual-licensure program.

Goal One: Dual Program Curriculum Development

The development team created a blended program addressing professional standards of the Council for Exceptional Children; National Association for the Education of Young Children; Ohio Standards for the Teaching Profession; International Dyslexia Association; Ohio's New Learning Standards; and Ohio's Value-Added Progress Dimensions. The plan was to review current syllabi, create new syllabi, and collaborate with faculty in other departments as well as external partners. This goal could be met only by increasing collaboration with faculty members from other departments across the university. Monthly meetings were held to review progress toward addressing the standards and to discuss any program changes needed to better address these standards.

Goal Two: Enhance recruitment Efforts

One of the Council for the Accreditation of Educator Preparation (2018) standards requires providers to document their efforts to recruit diverse candidates (e.g., candidates with disabilities or diversity based on race, ethnicity, or other factors), and they must demonstrate efforts to identify and address local community, state, national, or regional needs and shortages, including shortage of teachers qualified to serve students with disabilities. To this end, the dual-licensure program was heavily promoted in the SSU region. The marketing strategy included travel to individual high schools within the region, presentation of the dual-licensure program at various conferences (either through face-to-face presentations or poster sessions), and distribution of brochures and pamphlets.

Goal Three: Prepare HQTs

General and special education teacher education programs should be grounded in evidence and informed by multiple indicators of quality by (a) calling on specific criteria in the selection of candidates for teacher preparation and (b) using multiple indicators for monitoring candidate performance, including impact on P–12 learning of all students—students with disabilities included—and for measuring the quality of the program overall (Blanton, Pugach, & Boveda, 2014). The goal of preparing HQTs ties in well with the team's previous goals.

According to Noell, Brownell, Buzick, and Jones (2014), the evaluation of educator preparation programs should include well-defined performance measures and student outcomes linked to program completion. The program development team reviewed assessment approaches and instruments such as value-added models, Education Teacher Performance Assessments, My Instructional Learning Opportunities Guidance System, and Framework for Teaching as viable evaluation tools for teacher education programs and incorporated some of them into the new program.

Goal Four: Build Partnerships With Early Childhood/Special Education Agencies

A critical goal for the development team was to build stronger partnerships with early childhood and special education agencies in the region. To gain support for the proposal, the team reached out to agencies and educational organizations that had not previously been involved in SSU field experiences. Needs assessments were conducted with both new and established external partners coupled with brainstorming efforts to identify ways the curriculum and field experiences could meet partners' needs. As a result of expanding the scope of external partnerships, analyzing available data, and creating an advisory team to regularly review the program, the intention was to stay abreast of the needs within the school community and to increase the number of qualified educators to work with diverse young children.

The Ohio Leadership Advisory Council's (OLAC's) Ohio Leadership Development Framework provided another kind of support for the work. This resource promotes the use of collaborative structures to empower district level, building level, and teacher-based teams (Buckeye Association of School Administrators, 2013). The framework (and its associated structures) will be used by SSU's program developers to build their own capacity, and it will also be used by faculty to expand the capacity of the SSU teacher education department to create effective partnerships across other departments and with P–12 outside agencies. It is the team's belief that a robust curriculum can be developed only when all stakeholders have input into its development.

Goal Five: Provide Field Experiences in a Variety of Settings

Teacher education programs in general and special education should be anchored in practice and should draw on high-quality partnerships with schools to ensure that graduates understand (a) the realities of teachers' future work relating to students with disabilities and (b) the fact that professional learning occurs along a continuum from preservice preparation through ongoing development of expertise over the course of a career (Blanton et al., 2014). The development team planned to provide SSU students with field experiences in a variety of settings by partnering with professional agencies and organizations serving the needs of children and their families: preschool settings and settings serving students with special needs. Because the external partners would receive extensive training in best practices for co-teaching, the program-development team believed SSU preservice teachers would receive a more well-rounded and inclusive experience in their student teaching placements.

To meet this goal, the team used the premise identified by OLAC-OIP that, like all learning, teachers' learning of instructional practices depends on behavior change in response to precise, relevant feedback (Buckeye Association of School Administrators, 2013). Routine classroom monitoring and continuous evaluation providing teachers with feedback and support constitute the most powerful way to enable teachers to improve their instructional performance. For professional learning to occur, teachers must deeply engage in understanding and responding to such feedback and support, not simply try to comply with external requirements (Buckeye Association of School Administrators, 2013). It is the objective of the SSU team to develop courses and identify settings that provide teacher candidates with positive field experiences, enabling them to receive the necessary and relevant feedback that will enhance their professional growth.

Goal Six: Implementation of the Dual-Licensure Program

The success of the demanding effort put into developing the new program could only be realized in its implementation stage. This was the most important goal of the team. The development team created a timeline highlighting the development and implementation of the dual-licensure program and including in the timeline dates for when proposals were to be submitted to the SSU curriculum approval process for review and approval, dates for submission of the new program to the Ohio Department of Higher Education (ODHE) for approval, marketing and recruitment efforts, the projected start date for the program, and dates for completion of necessary documents (e.g., handbooks for clinical and field-based activities). Finally, included in the plan was the timeline for collecting necessary data and documentation of the progress of dual-licensure students.

Challenges/Barriers and Solutions

Any new program brings a set of challenges and barriers, any one of which could derail the program. The program development team addressed each challenge as it surfaced. The major challenges faced were developing collaboration, restructuring coursework; scheduling meeting times; identifying clinical sites; the theory to practice disconnect; and leadership and policy changes at the university level.

Developing Collaboration

Initially, the barrier of internal collaboration loomed as a potential threat to the effort. Discontinuing two licensure tracks—the early childhood and early childhood intervention specialist tracks—and implementing a merged program (Anderson, Smith, Olsen, & Algozzine, 2015; Blanton & Pugach, 2011) would not, we thought, take place without challenges from within. Nevertheless, our shared values kept this potential threat at bay. As Oyler (2011) noted, the work of merging two programs into one was "easy, not hard. Our philosophical, curricular, and pedagogical decisions were grounded in a shared commitment" (p. 12).

Restructuring Coursework

Faculty across departments of teacher education and academic content worked together to embrace the idea of a merged program. Part of the internal collaboration also involved administrative support for the program's restructuring efforts. To gain the support of deans, department chairs, and upper management, the program development team put forward the idea of "creating a 'niche program' that could be marketed" (Cyr, McDiarmid, Halpin, Stratton, & Davis-Delaney, 2012, p. 163) to prospective education majors. The team emphasized the potential value of the program to the institution's goal of increasing enrollment.

Scheduling Meeting Times

The work of the team involved weekend retreats and multiple meetings to determine course structure, key assessments for accreditation, and the field placements (Cyr et al., 2012; Kemp, 2015) to be aligned with university coursework. Scheduling time for all participants to meet was a challenge. Keeping minutes and audio recordings of meeting sessions helped keep all stakeholders informed, thereby helping the project move forward.

Identifying Clinical Sites

The value of collaboration between institutions of higher education and P–12 partners is well documented in the literature (Anderson et al., 2015; Blanton & Pugach, 2011; Oyler, 2011; Zeichner, 2010). Teacher preparation programs and P–12 schools need each other to further their respective work. Although the SSU teacher preparation program had already developed a clinical model in collaboration with a neighboring P–12 school, the focus of the original model was more traditional. One significant challenge was to refine field experiences in the partner school in ways that would allow candidates to integrate general and special education theory with general and special education practice by using co-teaching approaches in inclusive classrooms (National Council for Accreditation of Teacher Education, 2010). The decision to provide additional professional development (PD) around co-teaching models for prospective cooperating teachers helped the SSU team create more placement opportunities for teacher candidates (Fullerton, Ruben, McBride, & Bert, 2011). Further-more, these PD opportunities met the self-identified needs of educators at the P–12 partner school, thereby assisting the school in building its capacity for offering high-quality instruction in inclusive classrooms (Eargle, 2013; Strieker, Gillis, & Zong, 2013).

Theory to Practice

The concern for the theory-to-practice disconnect was felt by both sides of the partnership. The university was concerned that, within the new program, students have enough course work covering important academic content and pedagogical theory, while educators from the partnering school were concerned that candidates be able actually to implement what they learned in their course work (Zeichner, 2010). The PD on co-teaching actually helped both groups learn more about how course work and field experiences could work in tandem to promote high-quality professional learning among SSU's teacher candidates.

Leadership and Policy Changes

During the course of the program development work, there were faculty changes within the department, leadership changes across the university, changing roles among our P–12 partners, and changes in personnel at the state level. The SSU lab school's new director gladly became part of the program development team. SSU hired a new president after the first year of program development, and consequent changes included formation of a committee tasked with reviewing all new programs and making changes to the overall program approval process. As a result, the team had to restart its work to gain program approval. Some members of the advisory committee (P–12 partners) changed roles and could no longer serve on the program development team. Leadership and organizational structures also changed at the state level, including a change in the agency's name (from the Ohio Board of Regents to the Ohio Department of Higher Education).

Although these changes were significant, the development of the program was not significantly impacted. SSU's relatively small size made collaboration and communication with the university's leadership quicker and less cumbersome than it might have been at a larger university (Cyr et al., 2012).

Concrete Application and Potential for Replication

To develop an effective dual-licensure program requires systematic planning, successful collaboration, and evidence-based assessment methods. A close evaluation of the Cross Walk of Standards was performed as the courses were revised or formulated. The syllabi were scrutinized by a variety of faculty members within the department with relevant expertise. The department chair and faculty members edited brochures created to promote the program. More importantly, the external partners provided much needed support and expertise.

One of the specialists, for example, was a representative from the State Support Team (SST). The SST serves as a component of ODE's regional Multi-Tiered System of Support, and the team members are local and regional educators with expertise in school improvement, preschool education, and special education. The SST provides coordination and support to address common barriers to school improvement and services for low-performing or at-risk students. SST consultants, moreover, expand a district's leadership team to add specially trained experts who can help develop custom solutions using evidence-based practices to improve learning outcomes for all students. The SST serves as a regional technical resource for educators, districts, universities, and families.

The TeFAS project team member from the region's SST served on the advisory board for the dual-licensure program, providing feedback and consultation at each phase of the project. Because of the role this SST member played in the region, he was able to provide information with significant bearing on the TeFAS project. In particular, he was able to share details about the specific needs of each county for licensed Early Childhood Intervention Specialists; the system structures used for providing early childhood programming within each county and district; communication and system barriers that might impact program implementation; contracted service providers whose work might have some impact on the new program; community resources; and barriers related to the identification of appropriate preservice field placements.

The SST representative also served as a communication link between the project, the local districts, and Education Service Centers (ESC). With the assistance of each ESC Superintendent, the SST sought the input, feedback, and support of each district by meeting with groups of district superintendents to identify and prioritize needs as well as provide possible solutions related to the recruitment and preparation of dually licensed early childhood teachers. In addition to his direct interaction with district superintendents, the SST consultant provided an opportunity for the project coordinators to meet with the regional directors of special education services.

The identification of appropriate site locations for student teaching was a significant barrier identified in the project. The SST was able to help the project team navigate various barriers in different districts across the region as the team worked to expand local educators' capacity to use evidence-based co-teaching practices.

The SST consultant also assisted with systematic data-gathering efforts. These efforts, which included surveys and analyses of syllabi, informed the curriculum development work. They also allowed the teacher education faculty at SSU and educators in the partner districts to engage in work to promote simultaneous renewal, particularly around the use of co-teaching in inclusive settings.

Despite some challenges, the program development team was collaborative, cohesive, flexible, and willing to listen to suggestions and to entertain questions. The small size of the university and its strong and sustained partnership with the SST in the region helped the team overcome what might otherwise have turned into significant barriers to program development and implementation.

SUMMARY

In this chapter, the development of a dual-licensure program was presented with a discussion of the conceptual framework guiding the development of the program, challenges faced along the way, and the products resulting in and from the development of the program. Outcomes include an evidence-based dual licensure program systematically developed with structures in place for implementation and sustainability over time; improved collaboration with regional partners; and increased enrollment within the department due to the marketability of the new program.

Our experience suggests that programs to expand the use of inclusive practices can be supported by collaborations among stakeholders who share common visions and goals. A robust educator preparation program, developed collaboratively, helps cultivate new cadres of highly qualified educators who are prepared to work with all students in inclusive settings.

REFERENCES

Anderson, K., Smith, J., Olsen, J., & Algozzine, B. (2015). Systematic alignment of dual teacher preparation. *Rural Special Education Quarterly, 34*, 30–36. doi:10.1177/875687051503400107

Blanton, L. P., & Pugach, M. C. (2011). Using a classification system to probe the meaning of dual licensure in general and special education. *Teacher Education and Special Education, 34*, 219–234. doi:10.1177/0888406411404569

Blanton, L. P., Pugach, M. C., & Boveda, M. (2014). *Teacher education reform initiatives and special education: Convergence, divergence, and missed opportunities* (Document No. LS-3). Retrieved from University of Florida, Collaboration for Effective Educator, Development, Accountability, and Reform Center website: http://ceedar.education.ufl.edu/tools/literature-syntheses/

Blanton, L. P., Pugach, M. C., & Florian, L. (2011). *Preparing general education teachers to improve outcomes for students with disabilities.* Washington, DC: American Association of Colleges for Teacher Education and The National Center for Learning Disabilities. Retrieved from www.aacte.org

Buckeye Association of School Administrators. (2013). A report on the work of the Ohio Leadership Advisory Council from 2007 to 2013: Identifying and implementing essential leadership practices needed by superintendents, district leadership teams, building leadership teams, and teacher-based teams to make and sustain improvements in district-wide instructional practice and student learning. Columbus, OH: Author. Retrieved from http://www.ohioleadership.org/up_doc_cms/OLAC_LDF.pdf

Conzemius, A., & O'Neill, J. (2009). *The power of SMART goals: Using goals to improve student learning.* Bloomington, IN: Solution Tree.

Council for the Accreditation of Educator Preparation. (2018). CAEP 2018 K-6 Elementary Teacher Preparation Standards. Washington, DC: Author.

Retrieved from http://caepnet.org/~/media/Files/caep/standards/2018-caep-k-6-elementary-teacher-prepara.pdf?la=en

Cyr, E., McDiarmid, P., Halpin, B., Stratton, J., & Davis-Delano, L. C. (2012). Creating a dual licensure program in elementary and special education that prepares culturally responsive teachers. *Interdisciplinary Journal of Teaching and Learning*, 2, 158–168.

Darling-Hammond, L. (2005). Developing professional development schools: Early lessons, challenge, and promise. In L. Darling-Hammond (Ed.), *Professional development schools: Schools for developing a profession* (pp. 1-27). New York, NY: Teachers College Press.

DuFour, R., & Marzano, R. J. (2011). *Leaders of learning: How district, school and classroom improve student achievement.* Bloomington, IN: Solution Tree.

Eargle, J. C. (2013). "I'm not a bystander": Developing teacher leadership in a rural school-university collaboration. *The Rural Educator, 35*(1), 23–33.

Fullerton, A., Ruben, B. J., McBride, S., & Bert, S. (2011). Development and design of a merged secondary and special education teacher preparation program. *Teacher Education Quarterly, 38*(2), 27–44.

Gansle, K. A., Noell, G. H., & Burns, J. M., 2012. Do student achievement outcomes differ across teacher preparation programs? An analysis of teacher education in Louisiana. *Journal of Teacher Education, 63*(5), 304–317

Goldhaber, D., & Liddle, S. (2012, January). *The gateway to the profession: Assessing teacher preparation programs based on student achievement* (CALDER Working Paper No. 65). Retrieved from National Center for Analysis of Longitudinal Data in Education Research website: http://www.caldercenter.org/upload/Goldhaber-et-al.pdf

Individuals with Disability Education Act Amendments of 1997, 20 U.S.C., §1400 *et seq.* (1997). Retrieved from https://www.congress.gov/105/plaws/publ17/PLAW-105publ17.pdf

Individuals with Disability Education Act Amendments of 2001, 20 U.S.C., §6301 *et seq.* (2001). Retrieved from https://www2.ed.gov/policy/elsec/leg/esea02/107-110.pdf

Kemp, C. W. (2015). *Inclusive education for preschool-12th grade students with low incidence disabilities: A case study of state leaders' perceptions* (Doctoral dissertation, Liberty University). Retrieved from http://digitalcommons.liberty.edu/doctoral/1124

Leithwood, K., & Jantzi, D. (2008). Linking leadership to student learning: The role of collective efficacy. *Educational Administration Quarterly, 44*, 496–528. doi:10.1177/0013161X08321501

McNulty, B., & Besser, L., (2011). *Leaders Make it Happen. An Administrator's Guide to Data Teams.* Englewood: CO: Lead+Learn.

Mihaly, K., McCaffrey, D., Sass, T., & Lockwood, J. R. (2012). *Where you come from or where you go? Distinguishing between school quality and the effectiveness of teacher preparation program graduates* (Research Paper Series Working Paper 12-12). Retrieved from Andrew Young School of Policy Studies website: http://aysps.gsu.edu/sites/default/files/documents/uwrg/workingpapers/2012/12- 12%20SassMihalyMcCaffreyLockwood-Where You Come From.pdf

Noell, G. H., Brownell, M. T., Buzick, H. M., & Jones, N. D., (2014). *Literature synthesis. Using Educator Effectiveness Measures to Improve Educator Preparation Programs and Student Outcomes.* Retrieved from University of Florida, Collaboration for Effective Educator, Development, Accountability, and Reform Center website: http://ceedar.education.ufl.edu/wp-content/uploads/2014/09/LS-1_FINAL_08-27-14.pdf

Noell, G. H., Porter, B. A., Patt, R. M., & Dahir, A. (2008). *Value added assessment of teacher preparation in Louisiana: 2004–2007.* Retrieved from Louisiana Board of Regents website: http://regents.louisiana.gov/value-added-teacher-preparation-program-assessment-model/

Ohio Department of Education. (2018). *Ohio improvement process.* Retrieved from http://education.ohio.gov/Topics/District-and-School-Continuous-Improvement/Ohio-Improvement-Process

Oyler, C. (2011). Teacher preparation for inclusive and critical (special) education. *Teacher Education and Special Education: The Journal of the Teacher Education Division of the Council for Exceptional Children, 34,* 201–218. doi:10.1177/0888406411406745

National Council for Accreditation of Teacher Education. (2010). *Transforming teacher education through clinical practice: A national strategy to prepare effective teachers.* Washington, DC: Author. Retrieved from http://www.highered.nysed.gov/pdf/NCATECR.pdf

Slater, J. J., & Ravid, R. (Eds.). (2010). *Collaboration in education.* New York, NY: Routledge.

Strieker, T., Gillis, B., & Zong, G. (2013). Improving pre-service middle school teachers' confidence, competence, and commitment to co-teaching in inclusive classrooms. *Teacher Education Quarterly, 40*(4), 159–180.

U.S. Department of Education. (2018). *Thirty-eighth annual report to Congress on implementation of the Individuals with Disabilities Education Act.* Washington, DC: Office of Special Education Programs. Retrieved from https://www2.ed.gov/about/reports/annual/osep/2017/parts-b-c/39th-arc-for-idea.pdf

Vakil, S., Welton, E., O'Connor, B., & Kline, L. (2009). Inclusion means everyone! The role of the early childhood educator when including young children with autism in the classroom. *Early Childhood Education Journal, 36,* 321–326. doi:10.1007/s10643-008-0289-5

Voss, J. A., & Bufkin, L. J. (2011). Teaching all children: preparing early childhood preservice teachers in inclusive settings. *Journal of Early Childhood Teacher Education, 32,* 338–354. doi:10.1080/10901027.2011.622240

Seashore Louis, K., Leithwood, K., Wahlstrom, K. L., & Anderson, S. A. (2010). *Learning from leadership project: Investigating the links to improved student learning.* St. Paul, MN: Center for Applied Research and Educational Improvement.

Ying Hu, B. (2010). Training needs for implementing early childhood inclusion in China. *International Journal of Early Childhood Special Education, 2*(1), 12–30.

Zeichner, K. (2010). Rethinking the connections between campus courses and field experiences in college-and university-based teacher education. *Journal of teacher education, 61*(1–2), 89–99.

PROJECT LOGIC MODEL

Situation	Input	Output			Outcomes		
		Activities	Participation	Short-Term	Medium-Term	Long-Term	

Situation	Input	Activities	Participation	Short-Term	Medium-Term	Long-Term
• Need for HQT for EC and IS • Need for teachers who can work with students with disabilities • Need for teachers who can differentiate instruction • Lack of comprehensive knowledge in RTI, UDL, MTSS and inclusion • Need for early intervention for struggling students Assumptions: • Qualified personnel • Accredited programs • Need for teachers External factors: IHE External evaluators. • Periodic formative evaluation of project • End of year summative evaluation and project report	Human Capital: • DTE Faculty and Staff • Faculty in other departments • P-12 partners • IHE external evaluator • Advisory Council Funding: • Ohio Deans Compact Incentive Grant Resources: • Equipment • Building space • Technology • Research • Materials • Time	Goal 1: Dual Program Curriculum Development: Create blended program meeting SPA and accreditation standards • Revise current syllabi • Create new syllabi • Collaborate with faculty in other departments Goal 2: Enhance Recruitment Efforts • Develop a marketing plan Goal 3: Prepare Highly Qualified Teachers. • Prepare students to pass respective OAE tests • Present Integrated coursework • Test preparation review sessions Goal 4: Build partnerships with EC/IS Agencies • Conduct needs assessments • Create advisory council • Utilize resources from our external partners to plan field experiences	• IHE Faculty • P-12 Partners • External Evaluators • Staff & Student assistants • Extension agencies • Clinical faculty • Provost, Dean and Chair Goal 5: Provide field experiences in a variety of settings • Partner with external partners • Provide ongoing PD & support regarding the collaborative clinical model Goal 6: Implementation of the Early Childhood and Special Education Dual License Program; • Use developed course syllabi • Include courses in course sequence • Pilot first group of students • Collect data on program and student progress	• Identify specific needs for teachers in the schools we serve • Better understand the needs of all students in our schools • Identify CEC, NAEYC, OSTP, and OIP-OLAC standards for teacher preparation • Align CEC and NAEYC standards for dual license • Appreciate the inter and intra collaborations between P-16 institutions • Better awareness of research on inclusion, RTI, UDL, MTSS	• Increase the number of students enrolled in the Department of Education each year • Produce graduates with higher levels of satisfaction and a higher sense of preparedness as measured by surveys • Successful accreditation processes and increased university-wide collaboration • Produce students who consistently pass OAE tests, with scores equal to or higher than those in the separate EC and IS programs • Increased collaboration among SSU faculty and external partners • Greater inter-department collaboration and interaction • Continued P-16 collaboration • Develop course syllabi, assessments and curse sequencing	• Production of a workforce more prepared to address the diverse learning needs of young children • Increased awareness of the workforce, training, and PD needs surrounding our university • Maintenance of a sustainable program valued within the surrounding community • Increased research on inclusion, RTI, MTSS, and UDL • Professional development for P-12 schools • Continue to refine curriculum • Maintain a more comprehensive teacher preparation program • Provide training to external agents.

325

APPENDIX B

SPECIFIC LEARNING OUTCOMES

Specific learning outcomes were identified and included in the courses developed. The team also focused on including Evidence-Based Practices and High leverage Practices (McLeskey et al., 2017) in these courses. Below is a list of what was considered important.

- Students will be able to work with typical and atypical young children
- Students will be more employable with a more robust set of teaching skills and knowledge base
- Students will be able to administer formal and/or diagnostics assessments (standardized measures)
- Students will be able to implement evidence-based Behavior Management strategies including Applied Behavior Analysis (ABA) and Positive Behavior Intervention and Support (PBIS)
- Students will be able to work with students identified with dyslexia
- Students will use Universal Design for Learning (UDL) strategies
- Students will employ the use of instructional strategies that include differentiation
- Students will prioritize the use of gathered data to drive instructional decisions
- Students will be able to implement inclusive practices during collaboration—co-teaching (experienced during student teaching as a teacher candidate they can then perform in this role as a mentor teacher after completing their residency requirement).

SECTION VI INTRODUCTION

PREPARING PK–12 ADMINSTRATORS FOR INCLUSIVE SCHOOLS AND DISTRICTS

Although the term "principal" comes from two Latin terms, *primo* and *capas*, which taken together mean "holding first place" or, in some contexts, "ruler" or "prince," and the term still connotes the solo nature of a leader's role, educational leadership is experiencing a role shift. The shift is aligned with new evidence-based understandings about the functions of leadership, which turns out to be accomplished best through a sharing of those functions. The measure of effective student-centered leadership is its impact on students' learning. High-quality teaching ensures high-quality learning; and research in the past few decades has shown that high-quality teaching cannot be achieved through models of leadership that assume the singular nature of the role. Rather, a leader's sharing of decision-making about instruction and instructional programs appears to be a key element in high quality instruction in a school. As classroom instruction is too complex for one person, the task of supporting high quality teaching and learning in a school is too complex to be accomplished through the leadership of one person.

This section of the text, therefore, focuses on the distributed model of leadership. In "Inclusive School Leadership: Preparing Principals," Pamela VanHorn describes the Ohio Leadership for Inclusion, Implementation, and Instructional Improvement (OLi[4]) project, now in its sixth year. She explains how the project has been preparing principals to become inclusive instructional leaders through a unique professional development approach that features a curriculum that focuses on evidence-based instructional and instructional leadership practices and one-on-one coaching that provides ongoing support to participating principals.

Inclusive Education: A Systematic Perspective, pp. 327–328

In "Supporting and Promoting Inclusive Teaching Practices: An Administrator's Guide to Developing Tools," Dianne Gut and Pamela Beam describe the collaborative efforts higher education professionals at Ohio University and middle grade PK–12 partners used to develop tools for supporting, enhancing, and evaluating inclusive teaching practices. Their chapter provides descriptions of tools for team evaluation and self evaluation of inclusive practices as well as a discussion of barriers to inclusive practices identified by co-teaching dyads consisting of general education teachers and intervention specialists.

In "A Case Study on K–12 Inclusive Pedagogy," Joseph Hall and Jane Bogan provide an overview of a qualitative case study examining the inclusive instructional perspectives of classroom teachers and building administrators. The study made use of data collected via an online survey. Data analysis focused on the different definitions of inclusion that educators exhibited in their responses to open-ended survey questions as well as their different perspectives on barriers to the use of inclusive practice.

In "Enhancing Learner Access Through Invitational Inclusive Education: A Merger to Transform Perspectives and Practice," Barbara Hansen, Linda Morrow, and John Rocchi discuss the development and implementation of a new graduate course offered to teachers and administrators through Muskingum University. The course integrates invitational education with inclusive education in a professional development initiative designed to encourage an inclusive mindset within a building or district. Specifically, the course presents the tenets of invitational education as a foundation for supporting an inclusive classroom and school climate as well as educators' use of inclusive practices.

In "Reforming a Principal Preparation Program: Reconciling Equity-Oriented Leadership and the Accountability Era," Amy Farley examines the role of school leaders in creating and maintaining opportunity for all students and reflects on lessons from the process of restructuring the University of Cincinnati's principal preparation program to integrate a social justice focus as well as special education competencies and dispositions. As Farley notes, this process had important consequences for the structure of the principal preparation program and for the nature of its curriculum.

CHAPTER 19

INCLUSIVE SCHOOL LEADERSHIP

Preparing Principals

Pamela M. VanHorn
University of Cincinnati

The Ohio Leadership for Inclusion, Implementation and Instructional Improvement (OLi[4]) provides a two-year professional development (PD) program for practicing school principals, assistant principals, and other school leaders in Ohio. The program aims to develop these educators' competence as inclusive instructional leaders, defined in terms of six key practices. OLi[4] began with its first cohort, of 51 principals from 25 districts, in August 2014. Since then, two cohorts of principals have completed the two-year training; the program currently enrolls a further four cohorts. Thus far, the program has worked with over 300 principals from more than 75 districts across the state. The grant that initially supported the development of the program came from the Ohio Department of Education's (ODE) Office of Exceptional Children (OEC); current funding comes from the OEC and another office, the Office of Improvement and Innovation.

Inclusive Education: A Systematic Perspective, pp. 329–346
Copyright © 2020 by Information Age Publishing

Promoting instructional leadership for equity and social justice is OLi⁴'s chief purpose. As the discussion below shows, however, its grounding—in both mainstream and critical research on school leadership—supports an approach to instruction that welcomes diverse perspectives. Participants need not be devotees of any particular social justice model in order to feel welcome in the OLi⁴ community of practice. OLi⁴ uses PD methods that have strong research-grounded evidentiary support. Notably, it combines didactic instruction in centralized training sessions with small group discussion in regional cadre meetings and one-on-one leadership coaching sessions. In addition, the program asks participants to complete activities within their schools and districts and to use online tools to reflect on these experiences.

The discussion that follows examines OLi⁴'s theory of action, the research evidence supporting its curriculum, the six practices it fosters, and the two areas of work through which principals implement the six practices. Then the focus turns to the PD strategies that OLi⁴ uses and, finally, evidence of program impact to date.

THEORY OF ACTION

The educators who developed OLi⁴ aligned it with Ohio's improvement model—the Ohio Improvement Process (OIP).[1] This model engages educators in systemic work to improve the quality and equity of instruction for all students. Its primary innovation is a nested set of data teams at the district, school, and teacher-team levels. These teams support collegial dialog about instruction and undertake action research that tests the effectiveness of teachers' implementation of evidence-based instructional practices, schools' use of effective PD and support mechanisms, and districts' use of promising organizational structures and leadership strategies. As Barr (2012, p. 2) noted, the OIP focuses on "consistent structures," "a culture of shared accountability," and "a redefinition of leadership" as a set of essential practices that are supported consistently within a statewide system.

According to OLi⁴'s theory of action, when principals use a set of inclusive practices within OIP structures and alongside ongoing instructional discussions with teachers, their teacher teams will adopt instructional strategies that will lead to improved inclusiveness and student engagement as well as to improved student achievement. Figure 19.1 illustrates the theory of action.

The theory of action also posits that OLi⁴'s instructional improvement and social justice aims and practices complement one another. The program's emphasis on the inclusion of all students in general education classrooms, and the consistent use of effective strategies for instructing them, treats

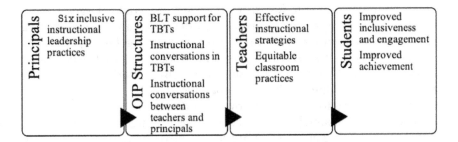

Figure 19.1.   OLi^4 theory of action.

social justice as a set of practices rather than as simple adherence to a certain set of beliefs. As the discussion below demonstrates, the OLi^4 program does not subscribe to any one perspective on instructional leadership or social justice; instead, it draws on insights from many research traditions that focus on leadership for school improvement and social justice.

RESEARCH UNDERGIRDING THE CURRICULUM

The first work in developing the OLi^4 curriculum was to identify intersecting practices in the theoretical and empirical literature on *instructional leadership* and *inclusive leadership*. Next, we organized the findings from the literature into a coherent framework. An important part of this process was to create a grid showing, on one side, domains of practice supported by the two bodies of literature and, on the other, the major theorists and researchers who contributed to our current understanding of the practices within each domain and the impact of those practices. The Appendix presents the final version of this grid.

A second step involved identifying researchers with a sufficiently broad conception of inclusive instructional leadership—the criterion we used to justify using their work as the foundation for the project's curriculum. Scholarship on school leaders as lead learners, improvement through collaborative inquiry, and inclusiveness as a social justice strategy proved particularly salient.

Leaders as Lead Learners

OLi^4 drew inspiration from Viviane Robinson's (2011) research on student-centered leadership. Her meta-analytic study identified the impact of principals' leadership practices on school outcomes, particularly student achievement. According to Robinson, the practices with the largest impact included (a) leading teacher learning and development, (b) establishing goals and expectations, and (c) ensuring quality teaching. OLi^4 operationalized these practices in two areas of principals' work: work with teacher-based teams (TBTs) and building leadership teams (BLTs) and work observing teaching and providing feedback. Through work in both areas, principals establish the vision for school improvement (framed as a set of "nonnegotiables," cultivate shared leadership, encourage the ongoing use of relevant data, support dialog about evidence-based instructional practices, coach teachers in the use of effective practices, and model reflectiveness.

Improvement Through Collaborative Inquiry

With the OIP as a central vector for educational improvement in the state, the OLi^4 development team also sought to ground the curriculum in literature on collaborative inquiry. Work by Seashore (2009) and Leithwood and Seashore-Louis (2012) proved especially germane. These researchers found that leaders in high-performing districts engaged school staff in collaborative inquiry about student learning and teacher performance. They also tailored the district's support for improvement to each school's specific needs. This view of collaborative inquiry fit with the OIP's strategy of using a combination of collaborative structures and processes to expand shared (or "distributed") leadership. With OIP, all educators are accountable to one another and, most importantly, to their students and families. This perspective reflects theoretical and empirical insights from the work of Michael Fullan (2002, 2006, 2011, 2013) and James Spillane (2006).

According to Fullan (2002, p. 20), "an organization cannot flourish—at least not for long—on the actions of the top leader alone. Schools and districts need many leaders at many levels. Learning in context helps produce such leaders." "Learning in context," moreover, builds "professional capital"—the expanding capacity of a school district and its schools for team learning, evidence-based instructional practice, and coherent organizational support (Fullan, 2013). OLi^4's curriculum team also drew on related ideas in the work of several other leadership experts (DuFour, 2004; Elmore, 2006; Leithwood & Jantzi, 2008; Marzano, Pickering, & Pollock, 2001; Marzano, Waters, & McNulty, 2005; McNulty & Besser, 2001; Reeves, 2000, 2006, 2008; Schmoke, 2001).

Inclusiveness as a Social Justice Strategy

One other body of literature provided important grounding for the OLi^4 program—literature on leadership for social justice. This literature documents the policies and practices used by districts and schools that have closed persistent opportunity and achievement gaps (Frattura & Capper, 2009; Telfer, 2011). According to Johnson and LaSalle (2010), these districts and schools close gaps by challenging conventional views of what is normal. For example, they plan strategic improvement efforts based on the view that all learners—including those from traditionally marginalized groups (e.g., students with disabilities, English learners, African American students)—should have access to high-quality instruction in the general education curriculum.

One major initiative that has influenced the work of OLi[4] is *Moving Your Numbers* (MYN), a research and development project sponsored by the National Center on Educational Outcomes (Telfer, 2011). The first MYN study investigated the practices of five school districts across the United States that successfully improved the academic achievement of students with disabilities. The study identified six strategies common to the five districts (Telfer, 2011):

- They used data strategically.
- They created and adhered to a focused set of goals.
- They selected and implemented a shared set of instructional practices.
- Their implementation of the shared instructional practices was deep and widespread.
- They monitored the implementation of the shared instructional practices and provided feedback and support to enable teachers to use the practices well.
- And they created organizational cultures in which inquiry and learning were highly valued.

A follow-up study with an additional five districts confirmed the salience of these practices (Tefs & Telfer, 2013). Other work on social justice leadership also provided similar insights (e.g., Frattura & Capper, 2007; Gorski, 2013; Theoharis, 2009).

TWO AREAS OF WORK AND
SIX INCLUSIVE LEADERSHIP PRACTICES

To focus participants' attention on these salient practices, the OLi[4] curriculum developers identified two areas of principals' work: guiding and supporting leadership teams and coaching instruction. The program refers to these two areas colloquially as "buckets." The first bucket of work involves principals' efforts to build the capacity of leadership teams at their schools. Within the OIP, each district uses a nested set of teams to examine data, set goals, identify promising strategies, implement shared strategies, and monitor the implementation and impact of those shared strategies. Figure 19.2 illustrates the connections between these teams.

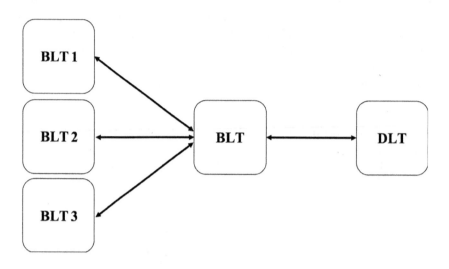

Source: Retrieved from https://ohioleadership.org.

Figure 19.2.   OIP connections between teams.

The second bucket of work focuses on principals' efforts to help educators learn about and use effective instructional practices in their schools. In this area, principals first engage in activities to help them learn about instruction by observing teachers in their buildings, and then they engage in activities that give them opportunities to practice skills needed for coaching teachers in the use of effective instructional practices. Their coaching of teachers involves asking questions to prompt teachers' reflection about their instructional practices—especially the practices that the principal observed.

Through work in these two areas, OLi⁴ intends for principals to improve their use of the following six leadership practices:

1. *Visioning*: The principal uses district and school nonnegotiables, including those focusing on equity, to set specific achievement targets for all classrooms and students.
2. *Using data well*: The principal uses data to make effective decisions.
3. *Using research and evidence to guide instruction*: The principal guides teachers in their selection of evidence-based instructional practices for diverse learners.

4. *Sharing leadership*: The principal shares leadership with teachers based on their expertise.
5. *Coaching teaching*: The principal monitors teaching for effectiveness.
6. *Reflecting on practice*: The principal reflects on his or her own practice.

The curriculum offers a variety of opportunities for principals to develop competence with the six practices, and a rubric helps them measure their progress. Principals access an interactive version of the rubric several times a year to document their growth and set goals for continued growth.

THE PD MODEL

The OLi[4] curriculum developers used principles of effective PD (e.g., Trivette, Dunst, Hamby, & O'Herin, 2009) to design job-embedded learning opportunities for participating principals. The resulting program combines four aligned types of PD: centralized training, regional training, coaching, and in-school activities accompanied by online reflection.

Centralized Training

During the two-year program, principals participate in six centralized training sessions (i.e., three sessions each year). Facilitators of the training are nationally recognized experts in fields such as school improvement, systems change, curriculum and instruction, and data-based decision making. Coaches also attend these sessions to guide small group discussions, and superintendents attend part of each session to learn alongside their principals and show support for the effort.

Each centralized training session provides between 8 and 12 hours of face-to-face training focused on one or two inclusive leadership practices. Over the course of each year, the centralized training sessions cover all of the OLi[4] practices in considerable depth. Facilitators present information and teach skills relating to each practice by using an informal lecture method coupled with pair sharing and small group discussion. These activities enable participants to process what they are learning and to begin applying it to problems of practice within their own schools.

Regional Cadre Sessions

Regional cadre sessions take place six times a year and offer participating principals opportunities for deeper exploration of (a) OLi[4] leadership practices, (b) the challenges associated with implementing these practices, and (c) the impact of the practices on improvement efforts underway at their schools. Each cadre includes principals from the same geographic region to reduce travel time to and from the meetings. A facilitator— typically a consultant from one of Ohio's State Support Teams—leads the regional meetings with assistance from the coaches who work with each cadre's principals. Training sessions are two and a half hours long. During winter months, some of these sessions are held virtually using an online conferencing platform.

During each regional session, the facilitator helps principals adapt and apply the ideas and skills presented in centralized training sessions to improvement work in schools. Facilitators also encourage the principals to reflect on and discuss changes in their leadership practices and to share insights relating to problems of practice that occur in their schools. Although facilitators use a common agenda across cadres, locally generated problems of practice make the regional sessions relevant to the concerns of the principals who attend.

Principal Coaching Sessions

The OLi[4] coaching component, based on Elle Allison's (2011) leadership performance model, provides support to participating principals on a monthly basis. Each principal works with a trained coach in 60- to 90-minute sessions that enable the principal and coach to discuss the principal's work in the two OLi[4] areas of focus (leadership teams and teacher observation with coaching) as well as to discuss the principal's emerging competence with inclusive instructional leadership practices. Providing support while ensuring confidentiality is the cornerstone of the principal-coach relationship.

Coaching sessions also focus on principals' reflections and responses to 12 sets of readings and in-school activities: principals complete one set of readings and activities prior to each regional training session. Principals record their reflections in an online "Principal-Coach Notebook," which tracks their progress toward mastering the program's six leadership practices. In three coaching sessions each year, principals also use an online rubric to rate their levels of mastery of these practices.

In-District Progress Checks

These meetings, which bring together participating principals, their coaches, and their superintendents, serve as an additional opportunity for superintendents to provide district-level support as principals learn to use

OLi[4]'s inclusive instructional leadership practices. Guided by a common agenda written by OLi[4]'s curriculum developers, each meeting focuses on the district-wide values ("nonnegotiables"), structures, and processes that support equity and inclusivity on behalf of all students. Items from a district equity audit—the MYN *District Self-Assessment Guide for Moving Our Numbers* (Telfer & Glasgow, 2012)—facilitate this discussion. Over the course of the two-year project, facilitators of centralized training sessions ask the principals and their superintendents to discuss the changes they have made to improve district-wide equity and inclusivity and then share these changes with the cohort as a whole.

Online Readings and In-School Activities

The fourth component of the OLi[4] program includes activities centered on guided readings, practical assignment in schools, and reflection prompts. Participants access these activities via the OLi[4] website. The program provides various ways for principals to reflect on these readings and activities: the online Principal-Coach Notebook, an online blog available to multiple cohorts, individual discussions with coaches, and small-group discussions in regional cadre meetings.

PROGRAM IMPACT

OLi[4] sets an ambitious agenda, especially considering the dramatic inequity of schooling provided in the United States (e.g., Glass, 2008; Riehl, 2000; Theoharis & Causton-Theoharis, 2008). In fact, the magnitude of the inequities (not to mention the structural and ideological forces keeping them in place) almost ensures that any social justice agenda will tend to overtax those PD efforts that hope to advance it (e.g., Erevelles, 2000; Miller & Martin, 2014; Rigby, 2014). A PD program that works to improve instruction and, through it, achievement—and which also embraces a social justice agenda (like OLi[4])—might seem so overtaxed as to be doomed to fail. Nevertheless, OLi[4] has shown some modest evidence of effectiveness. This is, perhaps, because it deploys several provisions that characterize excellent PD (e.g., Trivette et al., 2009), including:

- long term effort (two-year program),
- regular training,
- job-embedded training (coaching at the principals' schools), and
- rigorous evaluation.

Evaluation, moreover, is participant-oriented: the lead evaluator joins the OLi[4] planning team at its regular meetings, both to present formative evaluation reports and to discuss the implications of findings with the curriculum team. In other words, evaluation data and collaboration that draws on the experience and wisdom of team members inform any changes to the program.

Such features are positioned to improve program quality and, perhaps, the odds that the PD will produce the intended improvements. To date, three research-based efforts, all of which occurred (or continue to occur) under the auspices of program evaluation, provide data relevant to OLi[4]'s impact: (a) evaluations of participants' satisfaction with program features and their self-rated performance of the six leadership practices, (b) a quasi-experiment based on participants' self-reported data, and (c) a study of collective efficacy at the participants' schools, based on data from teachers. Brief discussions of each follow.

Participant Satisfaction and Self-Ratings of the Use of Inclusive Practices

OLi[4] administrators rely on an established survey form to evaluate the quality, relevance, and usefulness of every PD opportunity (including centralized trainings, regional trainings, coaching, in-school activities, and online reflection and discussion). Six Likert-scaled items, based on the work of Trivette and colleagues (2009), evaluate quality, while the relevance and usefulness portions of the survey each use three items. The evaluation gathers data during (or shortly after) each session. Results have been consistently high for each dimension, with small and irregular variations across the different PD opportunities as well as across cohorts. Notably, participants rate coaching near the top of the scale.

On the same survey form, participants also give self-ratings of their use of the six inclusive leadership practices that the program cultivates. Altogether, cohort members have three opportunities to rate themselves each year. Thus far, changes (i.e., improvement) following one year of PD have been recorded for three cohorts. Although the self-reported growth varied across practices and cohorts, all changes were in a positive direction.

Quasi-Experiment

Howley and colleagues (2018) conducted a quasi-experiment in 2017 using data from Cohort 2. The study included two dependent measures: data from (a) an instrument measuring attitudes toward inclusion and

(b) an instrument measuring OLi[4] practices. The study used propensity score matching to compare the ratings of 56 OLi[4] principals to a very similar group of 56 principals with no experience of OLi[4]. Findings favored the OLi[4] principals' attitudes ($d = .47$) and showed that OLi[4] principals believed themselves to be more effective at working collaboratively with teachers on instruction ($d = .38$). The other practice items showed non-significant differences. However, no scores at the item level—on either instrument—favored the comparison group, and all but one (which had no difference) favored the treatment group.

Collective Efficacy Study

Another study used collective efficacy to measure school faculties' belief in their own capacity to manage instruction. Using a collective efficacy instrument with 21 well-validated items (Goddard, Hoy, & Hoy, 2000), the study compared scores at both the start and end of Cohort 3's participation in OLi[4]. Evaluators designed this study as a trial effort to help guide subsequent use of the instrument with Cohorts 4 and 5 (in 2018–2019). According to a review of the relevant literature, the instrument had not been used previously to judge program effects. In fact, the literature described collective efficacy as a stable characteristic of schools; the measure is often used as an intervening variable. In the collective efficacy study, results proved to be statistically non-significant.

Impact Take-Aways

According to the routine evaluation work and the quasi-experiment, participants perceived an impact from OLi[4]. But, self-reported data may be a questionable indicator of program effects, especially given the possible influence of social desirability bias. For that reason, the program undertook its study of collective efficacy by surveying teachers who were under the supervision of OLi[4] principals. That research is ongoing, and the results from the trial collective efficacy study are being used to modify the iterations with Cohorts 4 and 5.

Overall the evidence is inconclusive, which is a common result according to the research literature on the effectiveness of PD for principals (Herman et al., 2017). In this case, with an instructional leadership PD program focused on social justice, one might prudently forecast limited aggregate impact. Effective instructional leadership proves rare enough (May & Supovitz, 2011; Urick & Bowers, 2014), and social justice efforts meet with on-going opposition in the United States (Rigby, 2014). Their combination in one program remains daunting. Nevertheless, some evidence from the OLi[4] program evaluation suggests that principals who are deeply engaged in the program learn more than their less-engaged counterparts; on-going efforts to study this phenomenon systematically are still underway.

SUMMARY AND CONCLUSIONS

This chapter described OLi[4]'s comprehensive two-year leadership development program, designed for principals and other school leaders. The discussion showed the program's grounding in the relevant literature on instructional leadership and inclusive practice (i.e., equity and social justice) and its use of evidence-based and job-embedded PD methods. So far, there is some evidence that the program effectively changes principals' attitudes toward inclusive practice, and efforts are underway to determine the program's impact on the collective efficacy of teachers in participating schools.

NOTE

1. The OIP is the framework that Ohio's State System of Support (SSoS) uses to promote improvement in school districts that perform inadequately, either in terms of low student achievement levels (in general) or because of low sub-group performance. In the 2001 No Child Left Behind Act, one of the requirements for each State Education Agency was to provide a SSoS for districts and their schools so they would be able to meet targets for Adequate Yearly Progress (Lloyd, McNulty, & Telfer, 2009). Confronting statewide achievement gaps in Ohio's schools, ODE, under the leadership of Superintendent Susan Zelman, established a team of educators to collaborate with the Great Lakes East Comprehensive Center to build Ohio's SSoS, which included the development of a leadership framework and a statewide school improvement process (Buckeye Association of School Administrators, 2013).

REFERENCES

Allison, E. (2011). *Leadership performance coaching*. Denver, CO: Lead & Learn Press.
Barr, S. L. (2012). *State education agencies: The critical role of SEAs in facilitating school district capacity to improve learning and achievement for students with disabilities*. Minneapolis, MN: University of Minnesota National Center on Educational Outcomes.
Buckeye Association of School Administrators. (2013). *A report on the work of the Ohio Leadership Council from 2007 to 2013: Identifying and implementing essential leadership practices needed by superintendents, district leadership teams, building*

leadership teams and teacher-based teams to make and sustain improvement in a districtwide instructional practice and student learning. Columbus, OH: Author.

DuFour, R. (2004). What is a professional learning community? *Educational Leadership, 61*, 6–11. Retrieved from http://www.ascd.org/publications/educational-leadership.aspx

Erevelles, N. (2000). Educating unruly bodies: Critical pedagogy, disability studies, and the politics of schooling. *Educational Theory, 50*, 25–47. doi:10.1111/j.1741-5446.2000.00025.x

Elmore, R. F (2006). *School reform from the inside out.* Cambridge, MA: Harvard Education.

Frattura, E., & Capper, C. (2007). *Leading for social justice: Transforming schools for all learners.* Thousand Oaks, CA: Corwin.

Frattura, E., & Capper, C. (2009). *Meeting the needs of students of all abilities* (2nd ed.). Thousand Oaks, CA: Corwin.

Fullan, M. (2002). Beyond instructional leadership. *Educational Leadership, 59*, 16–21. Retrieved from http://www.ascd.org/publications/educational-leadership.aspx

Fullan, M. (2006). *Turnaround leadership.* San Francisco, CA: Jossey-Bass.

Fullan, M. (2011). *Change leader: Learning to do what matters most.* San Francisco, CA: John Wiley and Sons.

Fullan, M. (2013). *Motion leadership in action.* Thousand Oak, CA: Corwin Press.

Glass, G. (2008). *Fertilizers, pills, and magnetic strips: The fate of public education in America.* Charlotte, NC: Information Age Publishing.

Goddard, R. D., Hoy, W. K., & Hoy, A. W. (2000). Collective teacher efficacy: Its meaning, measure, and impact on student achievement. *American Educational Research Journal, 37*, 479–507. doi:10.2307/1163531

Gorski, P. (2013). *Reaching and teaching students in poverty: Strategies for erasing the opportunity gap.* New York, NY: Teachers College Press.

Herman, R., Gates, S. M., Arifkhanova, A., Barrett, M., Bega, A., Chavez-Herrerias, E. R., ... Wrabel, S. L. (2017). *School leadership interventions under the Every Student Succeeds Act: Evidence review* (Research Report. RR-1550-3-WF). Santa Monica, CA: Rand Corporation. Retrieved from https://www.rand.org/pubs/research_reports/RR1550-3.html

Howley, C., Howley, A., Yahn, J., Van Horn, P., & Telfer, D. (2018). *Inclusive instructional leadership: A quasi-experimental study of a professional development program for principals.* Manuscript submitted for publication.

Johnson, R. S., & LaSalle, R. A. (2010). *Data strategies to uncover and eliminate hidden inequalities: The wallpaper effect.* Thousand Oaks, CA: Corwin Press.

Leithwood, K., & Jantzi, D. (2008). Linking leadership to student learning: The contribution of leader efficacy. *Educational Administration Quarterly, 44*, 496–528. doi:10.1177/0013161X08321501

Leithwood, K., & Seashore-Louis, K. (2012). *Linking leadership to student learning.* San Francisco, CA: John Wiley and Son.

Lloyd, J., McNulty, B. A., & Telfer, D. (2009). *A vehicle for enacting the work of the Ohio Leadership Advisory Council: The Ohio Improvement Process.* Retrieved from www.ohiolearning.org.

Marzano, R. J., Pickering, D., & Pollock, J. E. (2001). *Classroom instruction that works: Research-based strategies for increasing student achievement.* Alexandria, VA: Association for Supervision and Curriculum Development.

Marzano, R. J., Waters, T., & McNulty, B. A. (2005). *School leadership that works: From research to results.* Denver, CO: Mid-continent Research for Education and Learning.

May, H., & Supovitz, J. A. (2011). The scope of principal efforts to improve instruction. *Educational Administration Quarterly, 47,* 332–352. doi:10.1177/0013161X10383411

McNulty, B. A., & Besser, L. (2011). *Leaders make it happen! An administrator's guide to data teams.* Englewood, CO: The Leadership and Learning Center.

Miller, C.M., & Martin, B.N. (2014). Principal preparedness for leading in demographically changing schools: Where is the social justice training? *Educational Management, Administration, and Leadership, 43,* 129–151. doi:10.1177/1741143213513185

Reeves, D. B. (2000). *Accountability in action: A blueprint for learning organizations.* Englewood, CO: Lead and Learn.

Reeves, D. B. (2006). *The learning leader: How to focus school improvement for better results.* Alexandria, VA: Association for Supervision and Curriculum Development.

Reeves, D. B. (2008). *Reforming teacher leadership to reform your school.* Alexandria, VA: Association for Supervision and Curriculum Development.

Rigby, J. G. (2014). Three logics of instructional leadership. *Educational Administration Quarterly, 50,* 610–644. doi:10.1177/0013161X13509379

Riehl, C. J. (2000). The principal's role in creating inclusive schools for diverse students: A review of normative, empirical, and critical literature on the practice of educational administration. *Review of Educational Research, 70,* 55–81. doi:10.3102/00346543070001055

Robinson, V. M. (2011). *Student-centered leadership.* San Francisco, CA: Jossey-Bass.

Schmoker, M. (2001). *The results fieldbook: Practical strategies from dramatically improved schools.* Alexandria, VA: Association for Supervision and Curriculum Development.

Seashore, K. (2009). Leadership and change in schools: Personal reflections over the last 30 years. *Journal of Educational Change, 10,* 129–140. doi:10.1007/s10833-009-9111-4

Spillane, J. (2006). *Distributed leadership.* San Francisco, CA: Jossey-Bass.

Tefs, M., & Telfer, D. M. (2013). Behind the numbers: Redefining leadership to improve outcomes for all students. *Journal of Special Education Leadership, 26,* 43–52.

Telfer, D. M. (2011). *Moving your numbers: Five districts share how they used assessment and accountability to increase performance for students with disabilities as part of districtwide improvement.* Minneapolis, MN: University of Minnesota, National Center on Educational Outcomes.

Telfer, D. M., & Glasgow, A. (2012). *District self-assessment guide for moving our numbers: Using assessment and accountability to increase performance for students with disabilities as part of district-wide improvement.* Minneapolis, MN: University of Minnesota, National Center on Educational Outcomes. Retrieved from http://www.movingyournumbers.org/tools-and-resources/myn-downloadable-resources

Theoharis, G. (2009). *The school leaders our children deserve: Seven keys to equity, social justice, and school reform.* New York, NY: Teachers College Press.

Theoharis, G., & Causton-Theoharis, J. (2008). Oppressors or emancipators: Critical dispositions for preparing inclusive school leaders. *Equity and Excellence in Education, 41,* 230–246.

Trivette, C. M., Dunst, C. J., Hamby, D.W., & O'Herin, C. E. (2009). *Characteristics and consequences of adult learning methods and strategies* (Winterberry Research Synthesis, Vol. 2, No. 2). Asheville, NC: Winterberry Press.

Urick, A., & Bowers, A. J. (2014). What are the different types of principals across the United States: A latent class analysis of principal leadership. *Educational Administration Quarterly, 50,* 96–134. doi:10.1177/0013161X13489019

APPENDIX

Table 19.1.

OLi[4] How Principals Support Inclusive Instructional Practice: Knowledge Base to Inform a Practice Profile

Principal Practices Identified in the Literature	Research Base
Shaping the discourse about school *[Maintain Focus]*	
• Holding positive attitudes toward inclusive schooling • Articulating clear statements about the value of inclusiveness • Modeling inclusiveness in actions relating to matters such as employment of personnel, showcasing of student and staff accomplishments, and so on • Challenging assumptions • Speaking out against school practices that do not work on behalf of inclusiveness • Encouraging productive conflict and effective conflict resolution	Avissar, Reiter, & Leyser, 2003; Ball & Green, 2014; Guzman, 1997; Harpell & Andrews, 2010; Hoppey & McLeskey, 2013; Kugelmass, 2006; Kugelmass & Ainscow, 2004; Leo & Barton, 2006; Lindqvist & Nilholm, 2014; Little, 1990; Mamblin, 1999; Mayrowetz & Weinstein, 1999; McGlynn & London, 2013; McMaster, 2013; Muijs, Ainscow, Dyson, Raffo, Goldrick, Kerr, Lennie & Miles, 2010; Parker & Day, 1997; Pazey & Cole, 2012; Rice, 2006; Riehl, 2000; Ryan, 2010; Salisbury & McGregor, 2002; Sindelar, Shearer, Yendol-Hoppey, & Liebert, 2006; Sperandio & Klerks, 2007; Theoharis & O'Toole, 2011
Establishing and maintaining a clear focus on learning *[Cultivate Instructional Effectiveness; Maintain Focus]*	
• Communicating up-to-date knowledge about effective instructional strategies	Fink & Silverman, 2014; Gallimore, Ermeling, Saunders & Goldenberg, 2009; Hallinger, 2008; Hallinger & Murphy, 1987, 1986,1985; Hargreaves & Fullan, 2012; Louis, Leithwood, Wahlstrom & Anderson, 2010; Robinson, 2011, 2007; Wahlstrom, Seashore, Leithwood & Anderson, 2010; Robinson, Lloyd & Rowe, 2008
Encouraging and supporting professional learning communities (PLCs) *[Support Educator Teams]*	
• Fostering trust • Building and supporting norms of collaboration • Building collaborative teams • Promoting collaboration among teachers • Structuring time and resources to promote collaboration • Supporting peer coaching and other methods of teacher-to-teacher feedback and support • Monitoring teacher teams • Supporting teacher teams	Conrad & Brown, 2011; Guzman, 1997; Harpell & Andrews, 2010; Hoppey & McLeskey, 2013; Kugelmass, 2006; Kugelmass & Ainscow, 2004; Little, 1990; Mayrowetz & Weinstein, 1999; McGlynn & London, 2013; Parker & Day, 1997; Pazey & Cole, 2012; Salisbury & McGregor, 2002; Smith & Leonard, 2005; Sperandio & Klerks, 2007; Theoharis & O'Toole, 2011

(Table continues on next page)

Table 19.1.

OLi[4] How Principals Support Inclusive Instructional Practice: Knowledge Base to Inform a Practice Profile (Continued)

Principal Practices Identified in the Literature	Research Base
Distributing leadership *[Distribute Leadership; Foster Culture of Inquiry]*	
• Sharing responsibility • Fostering shared accountability • Treating leadership as a function, not a role • Expanding opportunities for instructional leadership	Angelides, 2011; Hoppey & McLeskey, 2013; Kugelmass & Ainscow, 2004; Mamblin, 1999; Mayrowetz & Weinstein, 1999; McGlynn & London, 2013; Muijs, Ainscow, Dyson, Raffo, Goldrick, Kerr, Lennie & Miles, 2010; Mullick, Deppeler, & Sharma, 2012; Rice, 2006; Ryan, 2010; Salisbury & McGregor, 2002; Theoharis & O'Toole, 2011
Connecting to parents and community members, even those who are from traditionally marginalized groups *[Connect to the Community]*	
• Empowering students and parents • Communicating effectively across multiple stakeholder groups • Engaging parents and community members in educational decision-making • Cultivating partnerships and coordinated services	Angelides, 2011; Fleming & Love, 2003; Guzman, 1997; Hoppey & McLeskey, 2013; Kugelmass & Ainscow, 2004; Muijs, Ainscow, Dyson, Raffo, Goldrick, Kerr, Lennie & Miles, 2010; Pazey & Cole, 2012; Rice, 2006; Riehl, 2000; Ryan, 2010; Theoharis & O'Toole, 2011
Managing school structures and resources on behalf of inclusive practice *[Ensure Implementation, Monitoring, and Evaluation]*	
• Directing resources to support inclusion • Encouraging innovation • Monitoring implementation of agreed-upon instructional strategies • Arranging teaching assignments in ways that promote inclusion (e.g., co-teaching, limited "clustering" of students with disabilities) • Seeking useful supports from district leaders	Guzman, 1997; Kugelmass, 2006; Leo & Barton, 2006; Lindqvist & Nilholm, 2014; Mayrowetz & Weinstein, 1999; Messinger-Willman & Marino, 2010; Parker & Day, 1997; Riehl, 2000; Salisbury & McGregor, 2002; Smith & Leonard, 2005; Sperandio & Klerks, 2007
Creating a culture of inquiry *[Foster Culture of Inquiry; Use Data Effectively]*	
• Using data effectively • Supporting collaborative problem-solving • Using data to identify inequitable circumstances and practices • Fostering evidence-based planning • Providing opportunities for problem-solving • Modeling and encouraging self-reflection	Kugelmass & Ainscow, 2004; Guzman, 1997; Hoppey & McLeskey, 2013; Leo & Barton, 2006; Lindqvist & Nilholm, 2014; Parker & Day, 1997; Pazey & Cole, 2012; Rice, 2006; Salisbury & McGregor, 2002; Theoharis & O'Toole, 2011

(Table continues on next page)

Table 19.1.

OLi[4] How Principals Support Inclusive Instructional Practice: Knowledge Base to Inform a Practice Profile (Continued)

Principal Practices Identified in the Literature	Research Base
Providing meaningful and job-embedded professional development to teachers and teacher teams *[Provide High-Quality PD]*	
• Providing relevant feedback to teachers	Conrad & Brown, 2011; Cruzeiro & Morgan, 2006; Harpell & Andrews, 2010; Hoppey & McLeskey, 2013; Kugelmass & Ainscow, 2004; Rice, 2006; Theoharis & O'Toole, 2011
Informing him or herself about learning difficulties and interventions *[Provide High-Quality PD]*	
• Participating in on-going and job-embedded professional development • Expanding knowledge relevant to the work of establishing and supporting inclusive practice • Modeling continuous improvement of professional skills	Ball & Green, 2014; Barnett & Monda-Amaya, 1998; Guzman, 1997; Kugelmass & Ainscow, 2004; Mamblin, 1999; Pazey & Cole, 2012
Protecting teachers from unnecessary pressures *[Maintain Focus]*	
• Brokering between commitment to inclusion and other external requirements and demands	Hoppey & McLeskey, 2013; Kugelmass & Ainscow, 2004; Mayrowetz & Weinstein, 1999; Smith & Leonard, 2005

CHAPTER 20

SUPPORTING AND PROMOTING INCLUSIVE TEACHING PRACTICES

An Administrator's Guide to Developing Tools

Dianne M. Gut
Ohio University

Pamela C. Beam
Retired from Ohio University

INTRODUCTION

This chapter describes the process and products of a collaborative two-year project: *Successfully Navigating Partnerships in Inclusive Teaching Settings* (*SNPiITS;* Beam, Gut, & Hartman, 2017). The project, designed to address identified needs related to inclusion in a local school district, involved working alongside teachers to create an online resource for assessing and enhancing inclusive teaching practices. A project partnership of education

Inclusive Education: A Systematic Perspective, pp. 347–361

preparation program faculty and teachers, including intervention specialists, from two local schools developed several tools intended to assist educators in (a) preassessing teachers' strengths, weaknesses, and professional development needs related to inclusive practice in the classroom; (b) evaluating individual and team performance in co-teaching in inclusive settings; (c) identifying barriers to inclusive teaching, developing solutions, and supporting the successful implementation of those solutions; and (d) learning about highly effective inclusive practices. Although we designed the project to meet the specific needs of our school district partners, the results of the project may be helpful to educators in other districts across the state and nation who seek to improve inclusive teaching practices.

BACKGROUND INFORMATION

This section outlines the district context under which SNPiITS was developed. First, we provide a description of district struggles; and then we discuss the initiatives undertaken to help leaders in the district support the education of all students under these circumstances.

Conversations with administrators of two prekindergarten through Grade 12 (PK–12) schools, an intermediate and middle school, from a local district revealed that the district struggles with instruction for students with disabilities and for the many students who are economically disadvantaged. All students in the district qualify for free or reduced lunch, and a slightly larger proportion of students is identified as having disabilities than in most Ohio school districts, according to data from the Ohio Report Card (Ohio Department of Education, 2018).

Given these circumstances, the district wanted to increase the extent to which its teachers made effective use of inclusive practices. The Ohio Improvement Process (OIP) and the Ohio Leadership for Inclusion, Implementation, and Instructional Improvement (OLi⁴) program briefly described here, as well as SNPiITS—the focus of the chapter—are three efforts implemented by the district to achieve this end.

First, the district implements the OIP (see Ohio Department of Education, 2018) using the 5-Step Process through its leadership teams, which include: teacher-based teams (TBTs), building leadership teams (BLTs), and a district leadership team (DLT; Ohio Leadership Advisory Council, 2018). The 5-Step Process involves: (a) collecting and charting data; (b) analyzing data; (c) establishing shared expectations for implementing specific changes; (d) implementing changes consistently; and (e) collecting, charting, and analyzing follow-up data (see Ohio Leadership Advisory Council, 2018). Each TBT in the district comprises all instructional personnel responsible for making decisions about teaching and learning for an assigned group of students. They collect, chart, and analyze student data; and teams use these data to track student progress and make instructional decisions (State Support Team 2, 2017). The BLT supports school-wide improvement through select instructional practices, helps establish school priorities, facilitates the use of data, and helps ensure accountability across the school and district (State Support Team 2, 2017). The DLT supports instruction through goal setting, professional development, and progress monitoring (State Support Team 2, 2017).

Second, the PK–12 administrative team also participates in the OLi[4] program, which supports the implementation of the OIP (see Chapter 19, "Inclusive School Leadership: Preparing Principals"). According to the district personnel who participated as partners in the project, the DLT concluded, through its analysis of districtwide data, that students are strong in skill acquisition but struggle with skill application. District data also appeared to show that the district's educators possess strong skills, but struggle with implementation of the 5-Step process.

Finally, in line with the importance OIP and the OLi[4] program place on using data to understand and implement consistently effective practices, the SNPiITS project sought to develop tools to help support the district's assessment of teachers' efficacy in educating all students. The remainder of this chapter will focus on the SNPiITS project and the development of these tools (see SNPiITS Project below). For further information on using data to support leadership change and supporting inclusive practice (see Chapter 8, "The Core Work of Educational Leadership: Interview with Brian McNulty."

SNPiITS PROJECT

In this section we will discuss the conceptual framework for the project, the goals of the project, the tool development process, the essential processes of the initiative, the impact of the SNPiITS Project, and challenges faced with the SNPiITS project.

Conceptual Framework

Drawing on our diverse experiences as educators and mentors, the conceptual framework for this project is grounded in theoretical principles relating to coaching and mentoring of teachers. The supporting literature is discussed here.

Mentoring.

In their meta-analysis, Ehrich, Hansford, and Tennent (2001) analyzed 151 studies of educational mentoring to determine the underlying theoretical frameworks that support current research. They concluded that, regardless of the theory, "reflection is an important activity in which professionals (i.e., mentors and mentees) should and do engage to help them come to new understandings of their practice ... [and] is a key element inherent in many developmental and learning oriented theories" (p. 8). Most relevant for our work is Vygotsky's (1978) sociocultural theory, which, as Ehrich and associates suggest, views learners as individuals in need of "support when encountering new and complex thoughts and actions" (Ehrich et al., 2001, p. 9). In situations where mentors and mentees engage in new learning, their interactions create opportunities for the growth and development of both mentor and mentee. In the context of Vygotsky's theory, mentors serve as "More Knowledgeable Others"—individuals who possess a higher skill level than the learners with regard to a particular task or concept (David, 2014).

Coaching

Coaching differs somewhat from mentoring. Wolpert-Gawron (2017), in fact, noted that coaching "is defined differently from location to location—and that's its biggest challenge and greatest asset" (p. 56). Taking a less relativistic perspective, Knight (2016) claimed,

> Coaches should position themselves as partners by respecting teachers' professional autonomy, seeing teachers as equals, offering many choices, giving teachers voice, taking a dialogical approach to interactions, encouraging reflection and real-life application, and seeing coaching as a reciprocal learning opportunity. (p. 27)

According to Wang (2017), coaching begins once mentees have mastered some teaching and leading skills and are therefore ready to set goals for growth (Wang, 2017). Carr, Holmes, and Flynn (2017) made the following contrast between mentoring and coaching:

> In mentoring, the seasoned teacher leads the evaluating and goal setting, but in coaching, the coachee has more command of the dialogue as the targets are set. The coaching process provides the protégé more control over the course of their growth as they accept more autonomy throughout the process. (p. 118)

As with mentoring, coaching is not meant to be used for evaluation (Carr et al., 2017; Knight, 2016; Wang, 2017). As a strategy, coaching typically occurs after the mentoring process solidifies a trusting relationship. Coaching moves beyond the mentor/apprentice relationship into one defined by reciprocity, although the coach still has more experience and a higher level of expertise (Knight, 2016; Wang, 2017). Wang (2017) claimed that "coaching allows teachers to receive professional development that is uniquely suited for them since coaching is based on individual teachers' needs" (p. 23). During this project, the research team employed both mentoring and coaching strategies when working with dyads (paired-teacher teams), based on their experience and comfort levels.

These principals of mentoring and coaching were applied to teachers' development of inclusive practices (e.g., co-teaching strategies) that ensure the growth of all students. Figure 20.1 illustrates this conceptual framework.

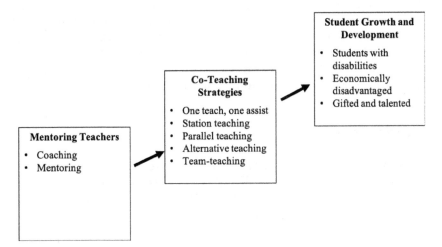

Figure 20.1.   The conceptual framework guiding the SNPiITS Project

Project Goals

The ultimate objective of the SNPiITS project was to generate tools to allow educators to analyze patterns and determine areas of strength and need as they relate to inclusive teaching practices. In consultation with school district personnel, the education preparation program faculty identified several desired outcomes for the SNPiITS project:

- Increase engagement of all students during instruction.
- Improve the ability of teachers to include all students in instruction, creating a more inclusive classroom climate.

- Change the vision for utilizing intervention specialists and sharing authority in an inclusive classroom.
- Increase teachers' shared capacity to support all students by increasing their knowledge and understanding of perceived barriers, skill deficiencies, conflict resolution, and effective strategies related to inclusive teaching environments.
- Increase teachers' ability to serve all students in inclusive classrooms, thereby increasing student success in the classroom.

The SNPiITS tools achieve these goals because the data generated by the use of the tools allow educators to analyze patterns and determine areas of strength and need as they relate to inclusive teaching practices. BLTs can use this feedback to determine the efficacy of inclusive teaching practices in their buildings and address any identified needs through targeted professional development. Finally, the use of the SNPiITS tools promotes increased reflection and introspection by individuals and inclusive teams. University and school-based partners co-designed all tools in the SNPiITS online module to better serve *all* students by making them comprehensive and user-friendly, especially in identifying strengths and areas for improvement related to inclusive teaching practices.

Essential Elements

Based on our experience during this process, we identified four essential elements that we believe contributed to the success of our work: establishing rapport, contextualizing the tools, implementing the tools, and assessing and evaluating outcomes.

Establishing Rapport

As outside consultants, it was essential for us to demonstrate our credibility. This was relatively easy given the team members' high degree of experience and expertise. Specifically, the team's three university partners represented three departments from a comprehensive college of education—educational administration, special education, and adolescent and young adult/secondary education—and together had more than 90 years of combined experience working in educational settings. We relied on this experience to demonstrate a strong capacity for facilitating the group's work. It was also critical that we build strong and trusting relationships with our school partners. To accomplish this, we scheduled meetings at times suggested by teachers or that were already scheduled during their regular day, and we were careful to limit additional demands on teacher time and closely followed announced schedules. Furthermore, teachers (unanimously) determined whether administrators participated in meetings and discussions, and teachers were also not required to participate in any activities if they did not feel comfortable (e.g., videotaping). Finally, communication was consistent and timely. Once we established rapport, we could begin our work as a cohesive team of education professionals.

Contextualizing the Tools

It was critical that the tools both represent the regional context of our teacher partners and remain applicable to teachers across the state and nation who want to improve inclusive teaching practices. We accomplished this by facilitating discussions that encouraged active engagement from all participants. Active participation ensured buy-in and ownership of the tools, and it established a shared vision. As a unified team, we used open and honest dialogue to problem-solve and identify both easy and more challenging responses and solutions to various barriers.

Designing the Tools

The SNPiITS project produced several tools designed to support the successful navigation of inclusive teaching partnerships. The set of tools and videos that comprise the *SNPiITS* online module provides inclusive teams with self-evaluation rubrics, a rating scale to determine readiness for inclusive teaching, a list of barriers to inclusive practice and potential solutions, and videos demonstrating implementation of the tools in a variety of inclusive teaching configurations (e.g., parallel teaching; station teaching; one teach, one assist). This section presents brief descriptions of the tools. As facilitators, we initially decided to develop the tools by holding separate meetings with each grade-level team, anticipating that the resulting tools might differ in significant ways. Teams organized by grade level created each tool separately, and these were then compiled into one comprehensive tool applicable across grade levels. Our initial meetings revealed that, before teams could begin generating solutions, they first needed to acknowledge their perceived barriers; this proved beneficial in helping us establish rapport. It was not only important to address the uniqueness of this particular district, but also to help district educators recognize that some of the barriers affecting them were in fact universal.

Consequently, the first tool we created (*Barriers to Inclusive Teaching*) listed these barriers along with potential solutions.

We next developed a checklist/observation protocol (*Inclusive Teaching and Observation Protocol*) with an accompanying rubric (*Collaborative Team Reflection Rubric for Inclusive Teaching*), designed to evaluate inclusive teaching practices at both the middle and intermediate levels. We developed the *Collaborative Team Reflection Rubric* and its accompanying *Observation Protocol* to assist teaching teams with reviewing, reflecting on, and evaluating their proficiency in all aspects of inclusive teaching practice. The *Observation Protocol* serves as a companion piece to the *Collaborative Team Reflection Rubric* by providing more detailed descriptions of the rubric elements. We designed this tool to be used immediately following an inclusive teaching session.

We created the final tool, *Self-Assessment of Readiness Skills for Inclusive Teaching*, for teachers to use as they reflect on their own readiness for inclusive teaching. Teachers should employ this tool at the beginning stages of their work and continue to use it periodically to monitor their growth and progress. This tool can also help teaching teams at the building or district level with setting goals. Once teachers complete the self-assessment, it can be used to identify areas of need and create targeted goals for improvement and personal growth; these needs and goals would support the development and assessment of teacher improvement plans. The self-assessment can also be used to assist in the co-teacher matching process by analyzing teacher strengths, needs, and preferences.

Implementing the Tools.

Equally important to our work was piloting the SNPiITS tools and then soliciting feedback to inform team-generated revisions; after modifying the tools, we implemented them in their final format. Inclusive teaching teams along with the research team piloted early versions of the tools in classroom settings. They determined the tools' effectiveness, decided on necessary modifications, and then made revisions to ensure that they fit within the context as well as to confirm their usefulness. Finally, the teams implemented the revised tools in the classroom to identify areas of strengths and needs. In response to one such identified need, that of universally designed instruction for learning (UDL), the research team worked with district administrators to provide relevant professional development to address this gap in knowledge and skills.

In addition to district implementation, we uploaded all final versions of the tools and videos to the Coalition of Rural and Appalachian Schools (CORAS) website (https://ohiocoras.com/snpiits-tools/). This avenue of distribution allows for the tools to be widely shared and easily accessed. The full list of online tools is below and each tool is described in further detail on the CORAS website.

- Self-Assessment of Readiness Skills for Inclusive Teaching tool
- Self-Assessment and Station Teaching video
- Responses and Solutions to Barriers tool
- Seventh Grade Math, One Teach-One Assist video
- Collaborative Reflection of Inclusive Teaching Checklist and Observation Protocol tools
- Seventh Grade Language Arts, Co-Taught with the Co-Teaching Model video
- Seventh Grade Math Station Teaching and Reflection video

Assessing/Evaluating Outcomes.

Throughout the project, we used formative and summative assessments to monitor outcomes (for details on the difference between formative and summative assessments see Garrison & Ehringhaus, n.d.). In formal and informal discussions with teacher partners, the research team gauged the teachers' overall satisfaction with the process. The co-development of all tools promoted teacher buy-in and satisfaction, and teacher partners reviewed drafts and offered their input, constructive feedback, and final approval. Piloting and revising each tool ensured its usefulness. In addition, by having established strong, yet confidential, rapport with our teacher partners, we improved the likelihood of receiving their open and honest feedback regarding both the tools and the development process. Additionally, because we worked to establish credibility at the beginning of the project, we believe that teachers recognized our commitment to producing quality products that would be useful and easy to implement, and that would produce positive outcomes for their students. As education professionals and equal partners in this work, we shared these common values and goals.

Impacts

Our project produced several positive outcomes. First, our experience demonstrates that our teacher partners were very positive and quickly bought into the project, despite an extremely short timeline during the first phase of work. Second, we developed the SNPiITS tools in an accessible format to be shared statewide, or even nationally; they are broad enough to be generalizable in contexts beyond our region. The tools are versatile and contain documents that can be printed for on-site use, and they are accompanied by short videos that demonstrate the skills or tools being addressed. Third, at the beginning of the project, several teachers recoiled at the prospect of being videotaped while demonstrating the use of the inclusive teaching models or SNPiITS tools. By the end, all but one teacher actively volunteered to be videotaped. We attribute this willingness to participate to their involvement in the development—and thus their ownership—of the products. Their growing confidence helped them to overcome their fears, and the teachers engaged in what would previously have been considered a risky and uncomfortable activity.

Most importantly, the SNPiITS tools helped teachers to determine their need for professional development targeting UDL. After piloting the tools and analyzing the data from year one, teachers recognized a need for skills in designing instruction that is accessible to all students. In response, they requested professional development focusing on UDL that would help them plan lessons appropriate for all students and which will be implemented in the project's second year.

One final outcome stemmed from the district administration's partnership on the project. The administrators freely gave the research team time during district-wide professional development days to work on the SNPiITS tools. They also supported and were instrumental in facilitating the UDL professional development for teachers. All teachers in the middle and intermediate buildings received professional development, which provided information on UDL to a larger audience of teachers than just those participating in the SNPiITS project.

Challenges/Barriers

We encountered several challenges during this project, including: teachers' limited training in the use of inclusive practices, administrator and teacher turnover, limited meeting time and administrative attention to teacher input, and issues of long-term commitment and accountability.

Limited Training

Our early discussions with school partners led us to conclude that lack of preparation for inclusive teaching was foremost amongst teachers' concerns. We also got the sense that they regarded inclusive education as one more initiative in a long line for which they received limited, insufficient, or no preparation. Although one professional development session had been provided on co-teaching models, none addressed teaming, UDL, how to accommodate diverse learners, or other forms of differentiation. As a result, teachers had varying levels of knowledge and skills based on their teacher preparation programs or self-study and no common vocabulary. They lacked a common understanding of basic principles, and no values had been directly communicated or developed around these issues. The lack of preparation meant that some teachers relied on very traditional views of general and special education roles. Some team members did not get along, acted disrespectfully at times, or were perceived as unsupportive in the inclusive teaching setting.

Based on identified needs, building administrators have the opportunity to set their professional development agenda for the year. One strategy they could implement would be to begin the year with team-building activities and training on how to deal with interpersonal conflict. If the administrators did not feel comfortable facilitating discussions to determine shared values and building-wide goals, they could seek outside facilitators. During the course of this project, university partners filled this role.

Turnover

Administrator and teacher turnover heavily impacted the project over its two years. One member of the research team was also a representative from the State Support Team (SST) doing focused work with the school district in the project's first year. In the second year, the district hired her to serve as its curriculum director and, although she continued her work with the project, her role changed somewhat from that of an outside consultant to an inside staff member. Additional changes included a new administrator in one of the schools and changes in teachers, with some leaving the district, switching grade levels or content areas, or taking maternity leave.

This is likely the most difficult issue for administrators to control, but it is a reality, and a plan should be put in place for how to bring new people on board and get them up to speed in a timely fashion. One potential solution would be to have TBTs involved in the interview and hiring process.

Meeting Time

In the project's first year, however, its greatest challenge proved to be the lack of adequate time to plan, implement, meet with, and observe classroom teachers. The project's grant funding, which constituted its financial base, was not awarded until very late in the academic year. As a result, the district had already set teacher schedules and professional development opportunities in place; this made available time extremely limited. The district superintendent and principals were, however, very supportive and flexible in arranging our time to meet with teachers. Our teacher partners also proved to be exceedingly cooperative and understanding of our time constraints, and they willingly gave up planning time and met with us after school when absolutely necessary. As noted, building administrators can have a large impact in facilitating new initiatives.

Attention to Teacher Input

The greatest obstacle during the second year stemmed from a perceived lack of attention to teacher input. Our open and honest discussion of barriers pushed our teacher partners to generate many potential solutions. While some of these possible solutions could be considered "wishful thinking," others proved insightful, innovative, creative, and achievable. When the administration did not fully implement several of their more reasonable solutions, some teachers became frustrated, less motivated, and disengaged. Specifically, the district largely ignored teachers' suggestions for how to deal with scheduling challenges in response to the lack of time for planning and actual co-teaching. Teachers also asked to focus on implementing existing initiatives, rather than adopting brand new ones each year. Again, the district did not grant this request, leaving teachers frustrated and feeling as if they had no voice; this led to an "us" versus "them" mentality between teachers and administrators. Using existing structures—for example, the DLT—building administrators are in the best position to address the issue of simultaneously implementing multiple initiatives. They can help prioritize the amount of time, energy, and resources allocated to initiatives and the order in which they are brought to full implementation.

We understood teachers to regard a lack of intervention specialists as a severe limitation on their capacity for co-teaching. In many cases, intervention specialists served in other roles during their planning time, or even during times scheduled for inclusive teaching. Unfortunately, in year one, inclusive teaching teams had been established with no input from teachers, which resulted in several mismatches in teaching partners. Additionally, schedules for teaming were inconsistent; we observed that this left teachers feeling that the district did not take their concerns seriously.

In response, administrators asked teachers to rank who they would like to be matched with before the start of the second academic year. In some cases, teaching partners who expressed dislike for their partner in year one, opted to continue in that partnership during the second year. It is unclear whether our discussions of barriers and potential solutions helped them to better facilitate a working relationship in their inclusive teaching partnership.

The building schedule is predominately the building administrator's responsibility. So, once again, they are in the best position to support such a significant initiative through scheduling. Unfortunately, when it comes to the need for additional personnel, a building administrator has little control. They do, however, have the ability to provide a voice for teachers' concerns. In addition, they can deploy existing personnel in unique and outside-the-box ways, for example by using community partners, volunteers, and retired teachers to fulfill some support needs that arise on a daily basis.

Long-Term Commitment and Accountability

Lastly, after completion of the project, we identified one long-term barrier: administrative support was not as strong as we had hoped. Although the administrators were cooperative and helpful, their long-term support of the initiative proved questionable. It was unclear whether the use of SNPiITS tools would continue after the project's completion, even though the materials were made available to all teacher partners and the entire district. Our teacher partners even developed recommendations for timelines and implementation checkpoints for the tools. Without administrative accountability and support, however, we fear it is unlikely that the district will adhere to the timelines and implementation checkpoints, despite their inclusion in district planning documents generated during the BLT and DLT planning process.

As part of the teacher evaluation system, it would be very easy for building administrators to require evidence of rubric use. They could also request that their classroom observations take place during inclusive teaching situations. This would allow administrators to dialogue with inclusive teaching teams about their proficiency with inclusive teaching practices, monitor the impact on all students in the classroom, and ensure the teaching teams' continued growth and development.

CONCLUSION

Throughout the chapter we noted the significant role that the building administration plays in any initiative for school improvement. This insight, of course, accords with much of the related literature about the leadership of improvement efforts (Robinson, 2011). If a school takes on a new initiative without full commitment from its building administrators, it is unlikely to succeed fully. The building administration possesses the necessary authority to address issues of time, coverage, and budget. If they are not "all-in," the initiative's success is questionable. Given that, having several simultaneous initiatives can be problematic, and it is important that building administrators prioritize initiatives, especially given limited resources. After prioritizing initiatives, administrators should conduct a needs assessment to determine training gaps. The building administrators can then use existing structures for professional development, ensuring that their staff has the necessary training to successfully implement the initiative.

As noted above, one significant contribution to the success of the project that our school-based administrative team partners made was their willingness to manipulate time and coverage to ensure that we had ample time to work as a team, developing and piloting the SNPiITS tools. This is another area where building administrators can ensure the success of a targeted initiative. Once a building administrator prioritizes an initiative, determines training needs, and allocates time to work on the initiative, then gathering teacher input and feedback becomes crucial to long-term success. Acknowledging teacher input and suggestions helps ensure continued buy-in and the active engagement of teaching professionals. This does not mean that administrators have to act on every suggestion, but they must actively consider and value all input. Teachers should be included in discussions about any suggestions that are discarded, allowing administrators to provide them with a rationale for why certain options are not viable. It is possible that some suggestions, through group discussions, could be reframed as potentially workable solutions.

One strategic way a building administrator can hold teachers accountable to using inclusive teaching practices is through the teacher evaluation system used by the school district. Requesting, collecting, and analyzing evidence of inclusive practices could become a routine part of a district's teacher evaluation process. Whereas this approach would demonstrate the district's commitment to inclusive practice, it might lose some of its power if teachers found the evaluation system aversive and therefore resisted change (Zimmerman, 2006).

REFERENCES

Beam, P. C., Gut, D. M., & Hartman, C. L. (2017). *Successfully navigating partnerships in inclusive teaching settings (SNPiITS)*. Retrieved from https://ohiocoras.com/snpiits-tools/ https://ohiocoras.com/snpiits-tools/

Carr, M. L., Holmes, W., & Flynn, K. (2017). Using mentoring, coaching, and self-mentoring to support public school educators. *The Clearing House: A Journal of Educational Strategies, Issues and Ideas*, *90*, 116–124. doi:10.1080/0009865 5.2017.1316624

David, L. (2014). Social development theory (Vygotsky). In *Learning Theories: In Plain English*. Retrieved from https://www.learning-theories.com/vygotskys-social-learning-theory.html

Ehrich, L. C., Hansford, B., & Tennent, L. (2001, December). *Closing the divide: Theory and practice in mentoring.* Paper presented at the Australian and New Zealand Academy of Management (ANZAM) Conference in Auckland, New Zealand. Retrieved from https://eprints.qut.edu.au/2261/

Garrison, C., & Ehringhaus, M. (n.d.). *Formative and summative assessments in the classroom.* Retrieved from https://www.amle.org/BrowsebyTopic/WhatsNew/WNDet/TabId/270/ArtMID/888/ArticleID/286/Formative-and-Summative-Assessments-in-the-Classroom.aspx

Knight, J. (2015). Teach to win: Seven success factors for instructional coaching programs. *Principal Leadership*, *15*(7), 24–27.

Ohio Department of Education. (2018). *Ohio improvement process.* Retrieved from http://education.ohio.gov/Topics/District-and-School-Continuous-Improvement/Ohio-Improvement-Process

Ohio Department of Education. (2018). *Ohio report cards.* Retrieved from https://reportcard.education.ohio.gov/district/detail/045021

Ohio Leadership Advisory Council. (2018). *Teacher-based teams in action.* Retrieved from https://ohioleadership.org/view.php?cms_nav_id=30

Robinson, V. (2011). *Student-centered leadership* (1st ed.). San Francisco, CA: Jossey-Bass.

State Support Team 2. (2017). *Ohio improvement process.* Retrieved from www.sstr2.org

Vygotsky, L. (1978). *Mind in society.* Cambridge, MA: Harvard University Press.

Wang, S. (2017). Teacher-centered coaching: An instructional coaching model. Retrieved from *Mid-Western Educational Researcher*, *29*, 20–39. http://www.mwera.org/MWER/archives/MWERv29n1.html

Wolpert-Gawron, H. (2017). The many roles of an instructional coach. *Educational Leadership*, *73*, 56-60. Retrieved from http://www.ascd.org/publications/educational-leadership/jun16/vol73/num09/The-Many-Roles-of-an-Instructional-Coach.aspx

Zimmerman, J. (2006). Why some teachers resist change and what principals can do about it. *NASSP Bulletin*, *90*, 238–249. doi:10.1177/0192636506291521

CHAPTER 21

A CASE STUDY ON K–12 INCLUSIVE PEDAGOGY

Joseph A. Hall and Jane E. Bogan
Wilmington College

A CASE STUDY ON K–12 INCLUSIVE PEDAGOGY

Since the passage of the Education for All Handicapped Children Act in 1975—with its guarantee of access to education—there has been a debate about where to provide the necessary services for students with disabilities (Zettel & Ballard, 1979). On one side of the debate is the argument that it is better to provide specially designed instruction and related services in a more isolated environment where students with disabilities can get more individualized instruction without fear of stigma. On the other side of the debate is the argument that it is better to include as many students with disabilities as possible in general education classrooms. The current iteration of that federal legislation, the Individuals with Disabilities Education Improvement Act of 2004 (U.S. Department of Education, n.d.-a), mandates the inclusion of children with disabilities in general education to the greatest extent possible. This legislation seems to come down on the side of inclusion.

Inclusive Education: A Systematic Perspective, pp. 363–382
Copyright © 2020 by Information Age Publishing

Nevertheless, the idea of inclusion raises concerns among many general education teachers. In a survey of general education teachers about inclusive classroom settings, for example, some viewed including students with disabilities as a privilege those students could earn once they proved they had the abilities needed to be successful in such a setting (Lalvani, 2013). Further, these teachers viewed inclusion in general education as a way for students with disabilities perhaps to receive instruction in academics but also to learn social skills. Still, they regarded the inclusive classroom as a less productive place for students with disabilities to be educated than the resource room, where students with disabilities could receive expert instruction from a special educator (Lalvani, 2013). In a review of research that focused on general educators' views of inclusive educational settings, de Boer, Pijl, and Minnaert (2011) found that most general education teachers had a negative or undecided view about inclusion and also lacked confidence in their abilities to provide instruction to students with disabilities.

The attitudes of general education teachers are not surprising. Unless those teachers had completed their preparation in dual-licensure programs, they were probably required to take only one or two classes focusing on ways to teach students with diverse learning needs. The thought of providing effective instruction to students with disabilities in addition to carrying out their other duties can seem daunting to a general education teacher. Special education teachers may feel equally intimidated by inclusive general education classrooms where they may be expected to co-teach the general education curricular content, work with typically developing students in addition to those with diverse learning needs, and provide specially designed instruction. Further, building administrators can struggle with how best to provide access to the general education curriculum to students with disabilities in such a way that all students benefit from the inclusive classroom while also ensuring that both special education and general education teachers remain satisfied with their jobs. In order to provide appropriate training and support to these three types of educators, it is important to understand their attitudes and beliefs, the barriers to inclusion they perceive, and their greatest fears about inclusion.

This chapter presents a case study exploring practitioners' definitions of inclusion, perceived barriers to inclusive best practices and co-teaching, and perceptions of how instructional delivery might be improved for all students. The main concern of the authors was to uncover the attitudes and beliefs of classroom teachers and building-level administrators related to serving students with and without disabilities in inclusive settings, including co-taught classrooms.

RESEARCH QUESTIONS, TERMS, AND METHODS

The primary participants in this case study were classroom teachers. In the context of the co-teaching framework referenced throughout this chapter, "classroom teachers" includes both special education teachers and general education teachers. Although classroom teachers were the primary study participants, the magnitude and level of instructional leadership required from building principals and assistant principals to shape school cultures cannot be ignored. Therefore, the research questions guiding this qualitative study required the participation of administrators as well:

- What are classroom teachers' and building administrators' definitions of inclusion? And what are similarities and differences between classroom teachers' and building administrators' definitions of inclusion?
- What are classroom teachers' and building administrators' perceived barriers to inclusive classrooms or schools?

Co-Teaching was defined in this study as one general education teacher and one special education teacher collaborating to deliver and assess instruction in a classroom of students with and without disabilities or more generally, as defined by Cook and Friend (1995), "Two or more professionals delivering substantive instruction to a diverse, or blended, group of students in a single physical space" (p. 2). A co-teaching framework was defined as an on-going strategy in which one general education teacher and one special education teacher routinely collaborate to design, deliver, and assess instruction in a shared classroom of students with and without disabilities.

A *Continuum of Special Education Services* was defined in accordance with Ohio Department of Education Operating Standards for Serving Children with Disabilities (2018), which require public institutions to provide a variety of placement options to satisfy students' need for instruction in the least restrictive environment. Such placements are based on each individual student's needs and may include but are not limited to: special education services provided within the general education classroom, special education resource room instruction supporting the general education curriculum, self-contained special education classroom with a modified curriculum, separate special education facility for more intense educational and/or behavioral needs.

Least Restrictive Environment (LRE) was defined per the U.S. Department of Education, Office of Special Education and Rehabilitation Services (n.d.-b) LRE means,

To the maximum extent appropriate, children with disabilities ... are edu-cated with children who are not disabled, and ... removal of children with disabilities from the regular educational environment occurs only when ... education in regular classes with the use of supplementary aids and services cannot be achieved satisfactorily. (Section 300.114/b/1)

Positionality was defined, within the context of action research, as referring to the roles in which individual study participants view themselves. Study participants' roles may include researcher, practitioner, study insider, study outsider, or any combination of these roles. Understanding and reflecting on positional constructs within action research is integral to interpreting study results (Herr & Anderson, 2014).

For this study, *practitioners* are classroom teachers (general or special educators) and building administrators. Practitioners engage in the craft of educating children, in varying capacities (Herr & Anderson, 2014).

Within the context of the school district and PK–8 research site, a *resource room* is a special education classroom, emphasizing a single academic subject area and/or providing instruction in behavior management tech-niques that support or are delivered in conjunction with general education classroom instruction.

A *study insider* is defined here as an individual participating in qualita-tive, quantitative, or mixed methods action research within an environment where she or he is employed, or otherwise routinely involved, and is therefore an internal stakeholder of the study's subsequent results (Herr & Anderson, 2014).

METHODS

This case study was conducted by a school district administrator to inform professional problem-solving and decision making. The study resembled action research in its effort to solve local problems by generating data rel-evant to local issues and concerns.

Study Site and Participants

The case study examined the perceptions of 160 ($n = 160$) special education teachers, general education teachers, and building administra-tors across a four-campus suburban school district in Southwest Ohio: a grade PK–2 primary building, a Grade 3–4 elementary building, Grades 5–6 intermediate school, and a middle school serving Grades 7–8. Table 21.1 disaggregates the study sample by building, teaching assignment, and administrative role.

Table 21.1.
Sample Size by School Building, Teaching Assignment, and Administrative Role

School Building	Special Ed Teachers	Gen Ed Teachers	Building Administrators	Total Responses
Primary (PK–Grade 2)	6	41	3	50
Elementary (Grade 3–4)	4	20	2	26
Intermediate (Grade 5–6)	9	32	2	43
Junior High (Grade 7–8)	10	28	3	41
Total Sample ($N =$)				160

The school district employing the educators who participated in the case study is historically high performing, with a total enrollment of approximately 6,000 students in Grades PK through 12, and per-pupil expenditures in the lowest 5% statewide. Approximately 10% of total student enrollment is composed of students with disabilities. Staff at the elementary school and junior high school, two of the four schools in this study, had extensive experience implementing co-teaching methodology. Due to recent turnover in building administration at the elementary school, however, co-teaching teams were no longer active at that school by the time of the study. Active co-teaching teams, therefore, existed only at the junior high school at the time of the study.

Data Collection

The researcher-designed survey consisted in part of the following: one open-ended question asking participants to provide their definition of inclusion; one survey item prompting participants to select from a list of eight common co-teaching barriers that they believed represented those most problematic to an inclusive classroom or school environment (with an optional "Other" requiring a description of the specific barrier be entered); and one dialog box requesting participants to provide feedback about how instructional delivery might be improved for all students. The researcher vetted the survey with others to ensure that items were easy to understand. After developing the survey and posting it using the SurveyMonkey utility, the researcher emailed a link to teachers and principals in the case-study schools. He requested that the educators complete the survey within one week.

Data Analysis

The researcher initially disaggregated data by school and met with each building-level administrative team to discuss study findings, highlight concerns that arose from identified themes, and discuss individual building action plans to address areas of professional development. This process also gave the researcher insights that informed further steps in the data analysis process.

Following the advice of Taylor-Powell and Renner (2003) and Taylor and Gibbs (2005), the researcher used predetermined codes. These authors recommend this approach for research involving qualitative inquiry, especially when data are gathered using survey questions framed within the context of professional experience. Additionally, codes used in this study were accompanied by brief definitions, to minimize possible miscommunication of study results (Taylor & Gibbs, 2005). Such predetermined coding as Level of Educational Experience (number of years in education), Secondary and Postsecondary Transition (impressions of level of high school and college and career readiness among students who have been exposed to co-teaching methodology), and Instructional Practice (pedagogical framework such as differentiated instruction, co-teaching strategies used, student discipline, level of co-teacher collaboration, co-teaching partner's subject matter expertise and the like) can establish the basis for a more deductive approach wherein, data are "analyzed according to an existing framework" (Patton & Patton, 2015, p. 453).

Export of data electronically from SurveyMonkey permitted the researcher to conduct various types of analysis using Excel (a popular spreadsheet program). For example, he was able to sort responses based on participants' different roles. Survey responses were also viewed individually, which proved helpful when interpreting findings in light of the self-reported data that respondents entered in the dialog box at the end of the survey.

The major approach to data analysis was to assign all data to the predetermined codes previously mentioned (level of educational experience, secondary and postsecondary transition, and instructional practice). Data entered in the additional comments field at the conclusion of the survey were analyzed in the same fashion. Then the researcher derived finer-grained codes based on a review of the data within each predetermined category.

The following subcategories within the category of Instructional Practice emerged:

- Purpose of Co-Teaching
- Responding to Academically Struggling Students

- Addressing IEP Goals and Objectives
- Extent to Which Co-Teachers Were Equals
- Most Significant Challenges
- Students with Emotional and Behavioral Challenges
- Students with No Previous Co-Teaching Exposure
- Perceived Impact on Student Achievement
- Lesson Planning, Instructional Delivery, and Assessment Roles

The researcher then used categories and subcategories of data to derive themes with relevance to each of the study's research questions.

RESULTS

The results of the study are reported below as answers to the study's two major research questions. The first question focused on definitions of inclusion (both across and within participant roles) and the second focused on perceived barriers to inclusion.

Definitions of Inclusion

As building administrators, general education teachers, and special education teachers articulated their interpretations of inclusion, two central themes emerged across all three groups of practitioners. First, both classroom teachers and building-level administrators associated inclusion only with students with disabilities. One administrator noted that inclusion involves providing necessary "accommodations and/or modifications, based on individual [student] needs." Another commented that the purpose of inclusion is to "access core curriculum" in the general education classroom. A general education teacher indicated that inclusion was simply, "Including students with an IEP in a general education classroom." Likewise, special education teachers shared the perspective that inclusion focuses solely on students with disabilities. One special educator, for example, asserted that inclusion was, "Including children with special needs into the general education classroom with support from an Intervention Specialist."

The second theme that emerged was that both classroom teachers and building administrators equated inclusion with the physical location in which instruction occurs; in this case, the general education classroom. For example, one administrator shared, "Inclusion is an education technique or method in which students who are identified as special ed. are educated in the general education classroom with the assistance of additional teachers and/or teaching techniques." Still another administrator posited that inclusion was, "Including all students into the regular education setting," while another administrator remarked, "Intervention specialists/ staff supporting [students with disabilities] within the [general education] setting." General education teachers were equally supportive of this perspective, with one noting that inclusion is, "Students that are on IEPs are in the classroom full time," and another citing that inclusion is, "Where students with disabilities spend most of their day in the same classroom with students without disabilities."

Both general education teachers and special education teachers addressed various levels of instructional support they believe students with disabilities require within the general education classroom, support typically provided by the special education teacher or paraprofessional. For example, general education teachers described two similar classroom scenarios: "Students with IEPs remaining in the classroom for regular education courses with the regular education teacher and resource teacher who makes modifications and provides support," and, "Special education and the general education [students are] combined in one classroom. Special Education teachers are used in the classroom for small group or alongside the general education teacher's instruction. Small groups are seldom pulled out of the classroom." A general education teacher shared, "When the special education teacher is in the regular education classroom supporting [her] own students," and another said, "Special education students participating in a regular education classroom with an intervention specialist or aide to assist them." Another general education teacher added, "All students are involved in the regular classroom environment. Special education inclusion students then receive additional support from the special educator [who] works with the regular education teachers in the general education classroom." Alternatively, still another general education teacher described a more collaborative approach:

> Students who receive educational support, both academically and for behavior, participate in the typical classroom. The classroom teacher and intervention specialist collaborate to provide supports and modifications necessary for all the students to be successful and grow academically and socially.

Special education teachers' characterizations revealed largely parallel viewpoints. "Including students with special needs/IEPs in classrooms with typical students. Special needs assistants are provided to assist the teacher with these students." Similarly another special education teacher noted:

> Students with special needs are mixed in with a variety of learners of middle to lower abilities.... They are included to gain social skills and con-

tent knowledge. Accommodations and modifications are provided by the regular education teacher and the intervention specialist.

Another special education teacher discussed her role as, "Providing students with disabilities the opportunity to be exposed to the general education curriculum with their same-aged peers. Helping [students with disabilities] access this curriculum through modifications and accommodations."

While not cited by general educators, some special educators and building administrators equated inclusion with the legal concept of LRE. For example, one special education teacher argued that inclusion meant, "Students who receive special education services get instruction in the general education classroom no less than 60% of the time with typical peers," while another noted that, "An inclusive classroom allows students to develop their 'full potential' in the least restrictive environment possible." Similarly, a building administrator shared a specific IEP team placement example, "Inclusion is when a student with specific needs gets a balance of a small group classroom environment for ELA and math but is included in general education classrooms for science and social studies." Another administrator approached the topic more broadly indicating, "Inclusion is when students are included into the least restrictive environment and given the necessary supports." The administrator added, "I think oftentimes this term [inclusion] is confused with co-teaching. In other words, students are included [in general education classrooms]; teachers meet the needs of this environment through co-teaching."

As previously stated, elementary and junior high school instructional staff were well acquainted with co-teaching, and the junior high still actively implemented co-teaching partnerships at the time this study was conducted. Consequently, various comments that came from classroom teachers from the elementary school and from the junior high administration conveyed a philosophical shift from inclusion as a means by which students with disabilities were educated in a general education setting exclusively to inclusion as the practice of offering differentiated instruction and co-teaching as a means of achieving more positive learning outcomes among diverse learners. For example, one administrator defined inclusion as, "Instruction that allows students of varying needs to access and succeed academically. Activities are differentiated to meet the needs of students."

Further building on this notion, general education teachers acknowledged the pivotal roles of their special education counterparts in delivering quality instruction with one general educator remarking, "The inclusion setting is one where all students are a part of the regular classroom setting and receive instruction from both the general education teacher as well as the intervention specialist." He went on to say, "[Inclusion] is basically … a shared classroom with shared responsibility between the gen. ed.

teacher and intervention specialist." Another general education teacher stated, "Inclusion is where the general education and intervention teacher work together to meet the needs of all students in the classroom." Still another simply identified inclusion as, "Co-teaching with the intervention specialist in the general education classroom." Other comments from general education teachers emphasized a commitment to rigorous and varied curricular expectations regardless of student ability: "Including and teaching all students in the classroom regardless of special needs or abilities"; "Including all types of learners in one single environment for the highest learning potential"; "Inclusion is having students of varying abilities in the same classroom. Accommodations can be made for any who need [them]"; "Instruction for students of all levels that is rigorous and challenging for everyone through differentiation."

Special education teachers, like their general education colleagues in the junior high and elementary school, viewed inclusion as synonymous with co-teaching. One noted that inclusion was "Co-teaching: two teachers equally sharing classroom responsibility; ALL students are both the general education teacher's and intervention specialist's responsibility." Another commented that inclusion is:

> A model in which general education teacher and intervention specialist deliver instruction to a diverse group of students in one setting. All students are included in instruction and accommodations and modifications are provided ... to help all students achieve success.

When not equating inclusion directly with co-teaching, special educators further explained that inclusion encompassed an educational philosophy that advocated for the needs of all students, with one teacher describing inclusion as, "An environment that is welcoming of students of all abilities. A team that understands that every child can learn but has different needs to be successful. The inclusive classroom is accommodating to make that happen for children." Similarly, another special education teacher articulated that inclusion is, "A classroom environment where all levels of students' needs are met through differentiation, accommodations/modifications, and specifically designed instruction."

Barriers to Inclusive School and Classroom Environments

The second research question addressed the barriers to inclusive classrooms or schools as perceived by the practitioners. As each site in this study demonstrated vastly different degrees of familiarity with and/or implementation of co-teaching methodology, perceived barriers to inclusive instructional practices were examined on a building-by-building basis. Table 21.2 summarizes the top barriers to an inclusive school or classroom for practitioners at the PK–2 primary school.

Table 21.2.
Barriers to an Inclusive School or Classroom Environment—
All Primary School Staff

Answer Options	Response Percent	Response Count
Lack of professional development	50.0%	25
Personality and/or philosophical differences among teaching partners	34.0%	17
Limited resources	52.0%	26
Scheduling issues	68.0%	34
Reluctance by co-teaching partners to relinquish classroom control	26.0%	13
Lack of time	48.0%	24
Lack of administrative support	12.0%	6
Apprehension about meeting the needs of students with disabilities	56.0%	28
	Answered question	50
	Skipped question	0

While one-fourth of special education teachers cited lack of professional development, more than half of general education teachers and all three building administrators thought this was a significant barrier to an inclusive classroom and/or school culture. Building administrators also cited scheduling issues and apprehension about meeting the needs of students with disabilities among the top three barriers to an inclusive school. Unlike teachers, however, only a single building administrator cited lack of resources; administrators did not cite limited time as a barrier to an inclusive school culture.

While the primary school had never adopted a co-teaching model, the elementary school that housed Grades 3 and 4 transitioned to co-teaching for several years. With a newer building principal and first-year assistant principal, oversight of co-teaching teams was no longer an administrative priority. Within this context, Table 21.3 outlines general education teachers' perceived barriers to an inclusive school and classroom.

Table 21.3.

Barriers to an Inclusive School or Classroom—Elementary General Education Teachers

Answer Options	Response Percent	Response Count
Lack of professional development	65.0%	13
Personality and/or philosophical differences among teaching partners	35.0%	7
Limited resources	65.0%	13
Scheduling issues	45.0%	9
Reluctance by co-teaching partners to relinquish classroom control	35.0%	7
Lack of time	50.0%	10
Lack of administrative support	20.0%	4
Apprehension about meeting the needs of students with disabilities	40.0%	8
	Answered question	20
	Skipped question	0

With the recent changes in administrative personnel, general education teachers claimed that lack of time, sufficient resources, and professional development were immediately impeding their ability to achieve greater inclusivity. Special education teachers, on the other hand, had little in common with their general education counterparts. Table 21.4 illustrates stark differences between the perceptions of general educators and special educators in the building, with the only areas of commonality being perceived lack of professional development and limited time. The two building-level administrators at the site did not participate in the study and were the only administrators in the entire school district who chose not to provide their input.

As previously mentioned, the intermediate school in the study serves students in Grades 5 and 6. Table 21.5 summarizes general educators' perceptions of barriers to inclusion. Like perceptions of general education teachers at the primary school, general educators in this building thought that a lack of professional development lessened their effectiveness as inclusive practitioners. However, like general education teachers at the elementary school, they thought that lack of time and limited resources were also major barriers to inclusion.

As with special education colleagues working at the elementary school, intermediate school special education teachers reported that a lack of professional development; limited resources; scheduling issues; a

Table 21.4.
Barriers to an Inclusive School or Classroom—
Elementary Special Education Teachers

Answer Options	Response Percent	Response Count
Lack of professional development	75.0%	3
Personality and/or philosophical differences among teaching partners	75.0%	3
Limited resources	75.0%	3
Scheduling issues	75.0%	3
Reluctance by co-teaching partners to relinquish classroom control	75.0%	3
Lack of time	50.0%	2
Lack of administrative support	25.0%	1
Apprehension about meeting the needs of students with disabilities	50.0%	2
	Answered question	4
	Skipped question	0

Table 21.5.
Barriers to an Inclusive School or Classroom—Intermediate General
Education

Answer Options	Response Percent	Response Count
Lack of professional development	41.9%	13
Personality and/or philosophical differences among teaching partners	48.4%	15
Limited resources	54.8%	17
Scheduling issues	51.6%	16
Reluctance by co-teaching partners to relinquish classroom control	32.3%	10
Lack of time	48.4%	15
Lack of administrative support	0.0%	0
Apprehension about meeting the needs of students with disabilities	45.2%	14
	Answered question	31
	Skipped question	1

reluctance by co-teaching partners to relinquish control; and personality or philosophical differences among teaching partners limited their ability to implement inclusive best practices. Table 21.6 outlines these perceptions. Comparisons between findings from the two groups (general and special educators) revealed notable differences.

Table 21.6.

Barriers to an Inclusive School or Classroom—Intermediate Special Education

Answer Options	Response Percent	Response Count
Lack of professional development	33.3%	3
Personality and/or philosophical differences among teaching partners	55.6%	5
Limited resources	44.4%	4
Scheduling issues	55.6%	5
Reluctance by co-teaching partners to relinquish classroom control	66.7%	6
Lack of time	55.6%	5
Lack of administrative support	0.0%	0
Apprehension about meeting the needs of students with disabilities	55.6%	5
	Answered question	9
	Skipped question	0

Interestingly Table 21.7 demonstrates congruence between perceptions of building-level administrators and special education staff regarding barriers to an inclusive school environment.

Junior high school personnel, as previously discussed, had implemented co-teaching building-wide as part of the continuum of services for students with disabilities. Most co-teaching teams had taught together for several years, and some teams facilitated professional development on the topic of co-teaching for personnel in neighboring school districts. However, at the time of this study, one special education educator was a first-year teacher. Given this context, Table 21.8 illustrates the perceived barriers to inclusion expressed by junior high general education teachers, perceptions incongruous with the perceptions of junior high school special education teachers and building administrators but shared at least in part by most of the other practitioners across the other buildings.

Table 21.7.
Barriers to an Inclusive School or Classroom—Intermediate Building Administrators

Answer Options	Response Percent	Response Count
Lack of professional development	66.7%	2
Personality and/or philosophical differences among teaching partners	0.0%	0
Limited resources	100.0%	3
Scheduling issues	33.3%	1
Reluctance by co-teaching partners to relinquish classroom control	66.7%	2
Lack of time	66.7%	2
Lack of administrative support	0.0%	0
Apprehension about meeting the needs of students with disabilities	66.7%	2
	Answered question	3
	Skipped question	0

Table 21.8.
Barriers to an Inclusive School or Classroom—Junior High General Education Teachers

Answer Options	Response Percent	Response Count
Lack of professional development	28.6%	8
Personality and/or philosophical differences among teaching partners	39.3%	11
Limited resources	57.1%	16
Scheduling issues	50.0%	14
Reluctance by co-teaching partners to relinquish classroom control	25.0%	7
Lack of time	35.7%	10
Lack of administrative support	7.1%	2
Apprehension about meeting the needs of students with disabilities	28.6%	8
	Answered question	28
	Skipped question	0

Junior high special education teachers' perceptions of barriers to inclusive practices were not unlike those of special education teachers at both the intermediate and elementary school. However, these special education teachers shared none of the perceptions of their junior high general education cohorts. Table 21.9 illustrates this. Interestingly, despite an experienced co-teaching staff, the majority of special education teachers expressed apprehension about meeting the needs of students with disabilities in an inclusive setting.

Table 21.9.
Barriers to an Inclusive School or Classroom—Junior High Special Education Teachers

Answer Options	Response Percent	Response Count
Lack of professional development	30.0%	3
Personality and/or philosophical differences among teaching partners	50.0%	5
Limited resources	20.0%	2
Scheduling issues	40.0%	4
Reluctance by co-teaching partners to relinquish classroom control	50.0%	5
Lack of time	50.0%	5
Lack of administrative support	20.0%	2
Apprehension about meeting the needs of students with disabilities	60.0%	6
	Answered question	10
	Skipped question	0

Table 21.10 summarizes perceptions of barriers to an inclusive school environment shared by junior high administrators. Barriers coincide with those expressed by special education teachers in the building; however, administrators also indicated a lack of professional development as a factor limiting successful inclusion, a perception held by virtually every other practitioner across all buildings. There are two possible factors contributing to this perception: (a) the presence of a first-year special education teacher in the building, and (b) the presence of a first-year building-level administrator (assistant principal).

Table 21.10.
Barriers to an Inclusive School or Classroom—Junior High Building Administrators

Answer Options	Response Percent	Response Count
Lack of professional development	66.7%	2
Personality and/or philosophical differences among teaching partners	100.0%	3
Limited resources	33.3%	1
Scheduling issues	33.3%	1
Reluctance by co-teaching partners to relinquish classroom control	100.0%	3
Lack of time	33.3%	1
Lack of administrative support	0.0%	0
Apprehension about meeting the needs of students with disabilities	66.7%	2
	Answered question	3
	Skipped question	0

DISCUSSION

Ensuring LRE clearly requires a more inclusive service delivery model. Various other studies have suggested that when students with and without disabilities were exposed to co-teaching methodology, not only did their performance on standardized tests improve, but they also benefited from intensified instruction and healthier peer socialization (Cook & Friend, 1995; Mastropieri et al., 2005; Walsh & Snyder, 1993; Vaughn, Elbaum, Schumm, & Hughes, 1998).

Many of the findings from the current study echo findings from other related studies. For example, the general education teachers and special education teachers held overwhelmingly positive views of the classroom environments in which they teach (Whitaker, 2011; Wiggins, 2012). Other examinations of teacher perceptions indicate special education teachers and general education teachers are typically more positive concerning inclusion of students with physical disabilities than of those with emotional or behavioral disabilities (Whitaker, 2011).

Austin (2000) offered that special education teachers co-teach more academic subjects than do their general education counterparts. While general education co-teachers tended to take a more active role in instruction than their special education counterparts, larger numbers of special educators felt more comfortable with their preparedness to co-teach than general educators (Austin, 2000). Similarly, because of their ability to implement more intense and varied instructional strategies, such as small group instruction and cooperative learning, most co-teachers regarded their co-teaching experiences positively and saw them as contributing to overall student growth (Austin, 2000). Co-teachers also expressed appreciation for improving their own professional growth via their collaborative classroom experiences (Austin, 2000).

According to research conducted by Goodin (2011, p. 3), special education teachers strongly supported "the concept of mainstreaming and/or progressive inclusion versus the full inclusion model." This finding suggests that special education teachers took a "balanced" view of including students with disabilities in general education classrooms: they favored serving students within a continuum of special education services, rather than including every student with a disability in a general education setting, regardless of the nature or severity of the student's disability. Goodin reiterated that perceived barriers to inclusive education persist. Among these barriers, according to the special education teachers in Goodin's study, were lack of appropriate communication, negative attitudes toward inclusion, lack of content-area expertise, and a school culture characterized by limited understanding or acceptance of students with disabilities.

Implications for Practice

Most practitioners across each of the four sites viewed inclusion solely from what might be termed a "special education perspective." They saw inclusion as primarily referring to a place—the general education classroom—and as primarily referring to an intervention for students with disabilities. A few practitioners offered comments with a broader focus— for instance, comments about the value of co-teaching as an instructional "best practice" for student in general. These more comprehensive ways of viewing inclusion were shared by the study participants from schools that either currently were implementing or previously had implemented co-teaching models. The more comprehensive view of inclusion emphasized the value of this practice as a method for realizing an instructional philosophy dedicated to improving educational outcomes for all students regardless of their abilities. In short, the participants recognized the value of placing two professionals together to co-teach, co-plan, and co-assess a heterogeneous group of students as advocated by Cook and Friend (1995).

Despite teachers' familiarity with this perspective on co-teaching, however, they often recommended a less inclusive approach. Across half the research sites, teachers advocated for a pullout model for students with disabilities. Consequently, based on the findings of this study, as well as open-ended feedback provided by practitioners after they completed the survey, we recommend three courses of action.

First, teachers and building administrators need sustained professional development relating to effective co-teaching methodology as a means of inclusion. Second, teachers require additional support in differentiating their instruction, as they remain apprehensive about meeting the needs of students with disabilities, particularly students with behavioral issues. Third, while most building administrators did not cite lack of resources as a barrier to an inclusive school environment, most teachers highlighted this barrier to an inclusive environment as a major concern. Given that implementation of effective co-teaching methodology is resource-intensive (Cook & Friend, 1995; Mastropieri et al., 2005; Murawski & Dieker, 2008), it remains critical that building administrators reassess the availability and accessibility of teaching staff to foster greater collaboration among teachers.

REFERENCES

Austin, V. L. (2000). *Co-teachers' perceptions of the collaborative instruction of elementary and secondary students with and without disabilities in inclusive classrooms* (Doctoral dissertation). Retrieved from ETD Collection for Fordham University. (AAI9960946)

de Boer, A., Pijl, S. J., & Minnaert, A. (2011). Regular primary schoolteachers' attitudes towards inclusive education: A review of the literature. *International Journal of Inclusive Education, 15*, 331–353. doi:10.1080/13603110903030089.

Cook, L., & Friend, M. (1995). Co-teaching: Guidelines for creating effective practices. *Focus on Exceptional Children, 28*(3), 1–16. doi:10.17161/foec. v28i3.6852

Education for All Handicapped Children Act, 20 USC § 1401 (1975).

Goodin, L. B. (2011). Perspectives of special education teachers on implementation of inclusion in four high schools in East Tennessee (Doctoral dissertation). Retrieved from Digital Commons @ East Tennessee State University (Paper 1371)

Herr, K., & Anderson, G. (2014). *The action research dissertation: A guide for students and faculty*. Thousand Oaks, CA: SAGE.

Lalvani, P. (2013). Privilege, compromise, or social justice: Teachers' conceptualizations of inclusive education. *Disability and Society, 28*, 14–27. doi:10.1080/09687599.2012.692028

Mastropieri, M. A., Scruggs, T. E., Graetz, J., Norland, J., Gardizi, W., & McDuffie, K. (2005). Case studies in co-teaching in the content areas: Successes, failures, and challenges. *Intervention in School and Clinic, 40*, 260–270. doi:10.1177/1 0534512050400050201

Murawski, W. W., & Dieker, L. (2008). 50 ways to keep your co-teacher: Strategies for before, during, and after co-teaching. *TEACHING Exceptional Children*, *40*(4), 40–48. doi:10.1177/004005990804000405

Ohio Department of Education. (2018). *Ohio Operating Standards for the Education of Children with Disabilities*. Retrieved from http://education.ohio.gov/GD/Templates/Pages/ODE/ODEDetail.aspx?page=3&TopicRelationID=968&ContentID=28143&Content=93404

Patton, M., & Patton, M. (2015). *Qualitative research and evaluation methods* (4th ed.). Thousand Oaks, CA: SAGE.

Taylor, C., & Gibbs, G. (2005). *How and what to code*. Retrieved from Online QDA website http://onlineqda.hud.ac.uk/Intro_QDA/how_what_to_code.php

Taylor-Powell, E., & Renner, M. (2003). *Analyzing qualitative data* (G3658-12). Madison, WI: University of Wisconsin- Extension Cooperative Extension. Retrieved from http://learningstore.uwex.edu/assets/pdfs/g3658-12.pdf

U.S. Department of Education. (n.d.-a). *Building the Legacy: IDEA 2004*. Retrieved from https://sites.ed.gov/idea/building-the-legacy-idea-2004/

U.S. Department of Education. (n.d.-b). *Sec. 300.114 LRE requirements*. Retrieved from https://sites.ed.gov/idea/regs/b/b/300.114

Vaughn, S., Elbaum, B. E., Schumm, J., & Hughes, M. (1998). Social outcomes for students with and without learning disabilities in inclusive classrooms. *Journal of Learning Disabilities*, *31*, 428–436. doi:10.1177/002221949803100502

Walsh, J. M., & Snyder, D. (1993, April). *Cooperative teaching: An effective model for all students*. Paper presented at the Annual Convention of the Council for Exceptional Children, San Antonio, TX.

Whitaker, K. L. (2011). *General education teachers' perceptions regarding inclusion* (Doctoral dissertation). Retrieved from Scholars Crossing (463). Retrieved from https://digitalcommons.liberty.edu/cgi/viewcontent.cgi?article=1499&context=doctoral

Wiggins, C. (2012). *High school teachers' perceptions of inclusion*. Retrieved from ProQuest LLC (UMI No. 3544866)

Zettel, J. J., & Ballard, J. (1979). The Education for All Handicapped Children Act of 1975 PL 94-142: Its history, origins, and concepts. *Journal of Education*, *161*, 5–22.

CHAPTER 22

ENHANCING LEARNER ACCESS THROUGH INVITATIONAL INCLUSIVE EDUCATION

A Merger to Transform Perspectives and Practice

Barbara Hansen, Linda E. Morrow, and John Rocchi
Muskingum University

Almost 25 years ago, the World Conference on Special Needs: Access and Quality adopted the Salamanca Statement and Framework for Action on Special Needs Education that included the following proclamation: "Schools with an inclusive orientation are the most effective means of combating discriminatory attitudes, creating welcoming communities, building an inclusive society, and achieving an education for all ... " (United Nations Educational, Scientific and Cultural Organization, 1994, p. ix). Access and quality are still far from being implemented fully in an increasingly diverse world with more and more students who have been marginalized or disad-

Inclusive Education: A Systematic Perspective, pp. 383–398
Copyright © 2020 by Information Age Publishing

vantaged. How do we combat discriminatory attitudes, create welcoming communities, build an inclusive society, and achieve a quality education for all? This chapter describes the conceptualization and development of a graduate course in which graduate students (licensed teachers) learned to successfully blend tenets of inclusive practice with tenets of Invitational Education (IE) resulting in a new concept, Invitational Inclusive Education (IIE). The blending of the two educational perspectives shows promise for deepening, extending, and enhancing the principles and practices of inclusive education, as evidenced in part by the development of a new tool, an invitational lens through which to view inclusive practice and increase the likelihood of its implementation, by students who participated in a section of the graduate course.

INTRODUCTION

Educators in kindergarten through Grade 12 (K–12) face the challenge of deciding what they believe is best for all students and how to deliver it effectively. Similarly, teacher preparation programs wrestle with building the capacity of their candidates to understand how to consider what is best for all students. Knowing what is best for students requires educators' first accepting that students are capable of learning, are valuable human beings, and are responsible as individuals. IE is a theory of practice that can assist educators in recognizing and appreciating the value of each student. "At its heart, [IE] is an imaginative act of hope that explains how human potential can be realized. It identifies and changes the forces that defeat and destroy people" (Purkey & Novak, 2016, p. vii). Shaw and Siegel (2010) described the theoretical underpinnings of IE as "a set of congruent suppositions about constructive human thinking and behavior that when applied across a multitude of human endeavors increases the probability for positive outcomes" (p. 106). Hansen and Morrow (2012) assert that IE's positive impact could increase significantly when applied reliably, consistently, and authentically" (p. 38).

According to Gershel's article entitled "Hazing of Suburban Middle School and High School Athletes" (as cited in Winter & O'Raw, 2010), the consistent application of effective strategies for all students certainly fits with both inclusive education and the legal requirement to provide a free and appropriate public education (FAPE) to students with disabilities. Furthermore, it acts on the moral requirement to extend FAPE to all student including those from traditionally marginalized groups. Prior to Gershel's work, revisions and amendments to Public Law 94-142, The Education for All Handicapped Children's Act, passed in 1975, brought more concentrated focus to minimizing the segregation of students with disabilities and providing them greater access to the general curriculum. According to federal mandate, to maximize students' potential, schools would need to give students with disabilities learning opportunities in the general education curriculum with specific supports included in their individual education programs (IEPs).

The graduate course merging the theory and practice of Invitational Education and the theory and practice of Inclusive Education, sought and continues to seek to offer a foundation for supporting teachers' efforts to ensure that their teaching cultivates the potential of all students in positive ways as well as countering any conditions or forces positioned to defeat or destroy students' initiative. Following the same organization as the conceptualized course content, the chapter first presents instruction in the basic tenets of IE followed by the foundational principles of inclusion, finally merging the two perspectives. It concludes with the candidates' serendipitous creation of a new tool to examine levels of support for inclusive practices. The tool organically emerged out of student learning and blends content from both IE and inclusive practice. Additionally, the chapter explains how, over time, the course transitioned from a face-to-face format to a fully online offering and concludes with a brief discussion of methods used in an examination of student and instructor learning.

DEVELOPMENT OF THE IIE COURSE

When a reorganization of graduate programs at Muskingum University was proposed, faculty saw and seized an opportunity to pilot a new graduate course to address the challenges of meeting the needs of all K–12 students. The Director of Graduate Studies asked two full-time university faculty members with relevant expertise and experience to work on the course. Both faculty members were the parents of children with exceptionalities and had been committed to enhancing inclusive practice across their entire careers (Hansen & Morrow, 2012). Furthermore, both faculty members had considerable experience in public schools, and both had been introduced to invitational theory and practice through professional development. They had learned to recognize the power of being invitational across settings and were able to identify both invitational and inclusive attitudes and behaviors in others, such as exhibiting trust, respect, and care for all students. They had found that when teachers exhibited such behaviors and the mindsets associated with them, students were engaged in learning and able to identify their unique strengths.

The new course, "Invitational Inclusive Education," took shape as the course creators blended concepts from invitational theory and practice with concepts from inclusive education. The faculty members viewed the two theories as not only aligned and compatible, but also as potentially synergistic. They accepted Purkey and Novak's (2016) definition of IE as a theory of practice "designed to create, maintain, and enhance human environments that cordially summon people to realize their potential in all areas of worthwhile human endeavor," and that "seeks to explain the nature of 'signal systems' that summon forth the realization of human potential, and to identify and change those forces that defeat and destroy potential" (p. vii).

When it was time to extend the instructional team to include other faculty, the search was short and successful since within the adjunct pool were two highly respected special educators who, through their own graduate studies, mentors, and experience teaching students with disabilities, had become state-wide proponents of inclusive practice. Their acknowledged expertise in special education was further enriched by their invitational traits of displaying optimistic approaches to problem solving and being professionally inviting with others through freely sharing their ideas, suggestions, and expertise.

The course creators called the merged perspective IIE, wondering all the while how others would respond. They knew that Muskingum's Educator Preparation Unit mission, "developing teacher leaders who encourage, equip, and empower all students" (Muskingum University, n.d., para. 1), would certainly support an exploration of these ideas, but would others embrace and value this new perspective? How would the course begin?

Believing the introduction of IE was foundational for the new course and could enhance the probability of increased teacher acceptance of inclusive practices, the professors planned for the introduction of IE at the beginning of the course. They theorized that if individuals in teaching or other leadership positions would embrace both IE and inclusive practice, there was potential for a powerful positive impact on student outcomes. The culmination of blending these perspectives would be the educator's internalization of principles and practices of the newly conceived course. Being invitational and inclusive would no longer simply define what one did, it would define who one was. The professors agreed that there was a need to present the foundations of both IE and inclusive practice because, in their experience, graduate students had varying levels of experience with these perspectives. They also agreed that teaching the perspectives separately was essential and that the IE foundation had to come first.

Tenets of IE

IE rests on the belief that education is an imaginative act of hope that explains how human potential can be realized and recognizes forces that negatively impact people (Purkey & Novak, 2016). Shaw and Siegel (2010) described the theoretical underpinnings of IE as "a set of congruent suppositions about constructive human thinking and behavior that when applied across a multitude of human endeavors increases the probability for positive outcomes" (p. 106). When such invitational practices are related to a school setting, the term IE is applied and, at the school and classroom level, may positively impact student confidence and ultimately improve learning and achievement.

Three interlocking foundations form the basis for IE: the democratic ethos, perceptual tradition, and self-concept theory. Purkey and Novak (1996) provided extensive explanations of these three foundations, which encourage a belief that all people matter and help educators build respect for all through shared activities. The first foundation, the democratic ethos, which relates to the engagement of all, is manifest where teachers and leaders consistently practice inclusive involvement, shared activities, and mutual respect.

The other two foundations are related more to the individual student than to the classroom climate. The perceptual tradition is based on the understanding that all human behavior is guided by how individuals interpret reality when they decide to act. Accepting this insight about others, particularly students, is helpful to teachers in understanding students' actions (Purkey & Novak, 2008). The third foundational element, self-concept, is described by Purkey and Novak (2008) as the internal picture people construct of who they are and how they fit into their perceived world. Integral to our relationships with others is our awareness of who they think they are. Through interactions with others, we begin to learn about them and their self-beliefs and actions. Understanding how students view themselves is integral to understanding what students may do and say and is therefore an essential foundation for teaching.

The IE framework includes five principles that are key to inviting and inclusive environments (Purkey & Novak, 2016):

1. People are able, valuable, and responsible and others should treat them accordingly.
2. Education is a cooperative, collaborative process where everyone matters.
3. The process is the product in the making.
4. People possess relatively boundless potential in all areas of worthwhile human endeavor.
5. Human potential is best realized by places, policies, programs and processes that are specifically designed to encourage human potential, and by people who are intentionally inviting with themselves and others, personally and professionally.

These five principles encourage an acceptance of all students and a belief that they can succeed when involved in a collaborative and cooperative environment with activities that honor process and seek to find and nurture the potential in each student.

Purkey and Novak's (2008) work further supports five domains wherein appropriate messages will enhance student potential. Table 22.1 defines the five domains of people, place, policy, program, and process, and provides a sample application.

Table 22.1.
The Five Ps of IE

Domain	Definition	Application
People	People in schools include students, teachers, administrators, food service staff, custodians, counselors, psychologists, librarians, bus drivers, parents, aides and volunteers.	Within a school there must be unconditional respect for all people, intentional caring and the honoring of diversity.
Place	The physical and visible environment is the setting in which relationships are built.	Within a school there must be critical attention paid to its appearance, cleanliness, and functional qualities. This upkeep is a message of care sent from adults in charge to peers and students.
Policy	Official mission statements, codes, rules, written and unwritten are the documents that regulate the school.	Policies considered fair and inclusive enable healthy relationships for student growth.
Program	School programs range from formal to informal and curricular to extra-curricular and are required to be inclusive, ensuring that all the programs must be for the benefit of everyone.	Healthy programs reflect inclusivity and encourage students to see themselves as lifelong learners. Small group programming can be of help to enable students to extend their work with others.
Process	Collaborative and cooperative processes, encourage networking which respects all people and honors relationships.	Effective processes prevent isolation, alienation, and bullying. Processes address people, place, policy and program in a way that engages those involved.

Purkey and Novak (1996) illustrate the interdependence of the 5 P's in the starfish image that serves as the logo for IE (see Figure 22.1).

Figure 22.1. Opportunities for enhancing inviting behavior can be found in the 5 P's of Invitational Education displayed here. This figure emphasizes the interconnectedness of all 5 P's by mapping them onto a starfish.

The 5 Ps Together

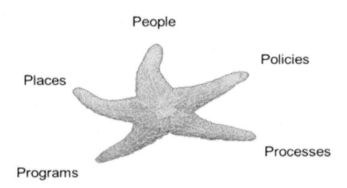

People

Policies

Places

Processes

Programs

Invitational Education® requires a holistic mentality that encompasses everybody and everything.

Figure 22.1. Opportunities for enhancing inviting behavior can be found in the 5 P's of Invitational Education displayed here. This figure emphasizes the interconnectedness of all 5 P's by mapping them onto a starfish.

I-CORT

Consistent with many processes and strategies focused on student success, IE is delivered, modeled, and encouraged through the student/teacher relationship. Purkey and Novak (2016) also described five behaviors one must exhibit to build a positive relationship and an inviting stance. The behaviors—intentionality, care, optimism, respect, and trust—collectively known as I-CORT, interact with each other and grow stronger when applied with consistency (see Table 22.2 for the I-CORT chart summarizing these behaviors). Intentionality is the one behavior that IE proponents believe is the most essential to an inviting climate.

When implementing IE, another crucial step is for the teacher to send invitations to learn. Shaw and Siegel (2010) define the "invitation" metaphor as an intentional and caring act of communication by which the sender seeks to enroll the receiver in a positive manner. The nature of the communication determines the quality of an invitation. For example, is the communication more or less inviting? Was what was communicated intentional or unintentional? Purkey and Novak (2008) represent the quality of an invitation to learn using four behavioral levels which build from being intentionally disinviting to being intentionally inviting (see Table 22.3).

Table 22.2.
IE Ladder

Behavior	Description
Intentionality	Teachers deliberately and consistently focus on promoting student potential through positive approaches with people, place, programs, policies, and processes.
Care	The most important of the inviting behaviors is an authentic interest in and the genuine desire to care about students.
Optimism	Teachers are optimistic when they hold the belief that student potential, though not always apparent, is always there, waiting to be discovered and invited forth.
Respect	Teachers must believe that students are valuable, able, and responsible and should be treated accordingly.
Trust	Teachers help students become trustworthy through activities that help them develop reliability, genuineness, truthfulness, intent, competence and knowledge.

Table 22.3.
IE Ladder

Level	Definition	Example
Intentionally Inviting	These interactions seek to consistently exhibit invitational beliefs, statements and actions.	These interactions are typical of people who strive to continually develop and exhibit positive behaviors and who encourage the same in others.
Unintentionally Inviting	Interactions in this category alternately work and/ or fail to enable an inviting approach.	This level of interaction could improve with an awareness of I-CORT.
Unintentionally Disinviting	Unintentionally disinviting behaviors are hurtful due to lack of direction and purpose.	These interactions are uncaring, condescending, and thoughtless in words and actions.
Intentionally Disinviting	Intentionally disinviting interactions are negative and near toxic levels.	Exhibiting these behaviors deliberately discourages, defeats and destroys others.

Why Inclusive Education

Following the introduction to IE, the course transitioned to an overview of inclusive education. Graduate students first explored early special education law (e.g., the Education for All Handicapped Children Act of 1975) and quickly recognized gaps between legal requirements and current practice. Most had personally experienced how even the most basic requirements of the law had not yielded the results anticipated by the law's passage and implementation (Boston-Kemple, 2012). The two basic principles, a FAPE and the least restrictive environment, were threaded through the discussion.

Teachers and administrators in the new IIE course easily recognized that schools still segregated many students with disabilities from their typically developing peers. Course participants agreed that these students often were placed in separate classrooms or even separate schools and provided with a watered-down curriculum and less rigorous instruction. Teachers shared how students with specific learning disabilities in basic reading skills still were sometimes segregated in special classes for content area instruction, used more basic texts and were more likely to have less exposure to complex concepts, as documented in research such as that conducted by Winter and O'Raw (2010).

Once again, graduate students recognized and/or had experienced the challenges of providing effective instruction to students with disabilities. Special education teachers' training prepared them to identify and meet the unique needs of students with disabilities. And yet, schools expected these same teachers to teach several subjects to students in multiple grade levels without the same level of content knowledge and credentials as required for the general education teacher. Another challenge occurred when teachers included students with disabilities in general education classrooms without providing necessary educational supports and then required the students to meet the same expectations as the rest of the class. Unfortunately, many students with disabilities reached neither the goal of receiving an education with typical peers nor the goal of receiving rigorous instruction with support.

The course then moved onto a discussion of how greater acceptance and advocacy for inclusive education had increased as teachers learned to use instructional practices with a strong evidence base (Boston-Kemple, 2012). When these practices yielded positive results, teachers began to use them more frequently.

For example, teachers and building leaders increasingly support co-teaching practices (Friend, 2013) where general and special educators co-teach students in general education settings. Students benefit from both the expertise in learning strategies that the special educators bring and the content expertise that the general educators bring when they teach together using a variety of co-teaching approaches.

As graduate students shared their challenges regarding the implementation of co-teaching and other inclusive practices for students with disabilities, they also recognized how other groups of students who were marginalized or disadvantaged in the general education classroom also faced barriers and limitations to meeting rigorous academic standards. Ruggs and Hebl (2012) noted similar perceptions on the part of students, stating that "students who come from stigmatized groups (e.g., groups that are the target of negative stereotypes, prejudice, and discrimination) still perceive barriers to education" (p. 1). Graduate students began to realize that more recent federal legislation, such as the Every Student Succeeds Act (2015), are, in part, designed to include, expand, and extend the foundational principles of the Individuals with Disabilities Education Act (IDEA) of 1997 to all students.

By this point in the course, most of the graduate students recognized that past and current obstacles to inclusive practice were also intentionally or unintentionally disinviting. In fact, many practices such as limited access, language barriers, segregated classrooms, lower expectations, and less rigorous curriculum and instruction failed to align even with the most basic premise of IE, that all children are able, valuable, and deserve respect. Likewise, because of these obstacles, teachers consistently were impeded in their efforts to show intentionality, care, optimism, respect, and trust (I-CORT). Teachers often did not make specific accommodations to meet individual learning needs, hold high expectations, or include students with disabilities in all school activities. Implementation of inclusive education therefore seemed to produce challenges whose potential solutions aligned with IE, and the tenets undergirding IE produced attitudes and beliefs that cultivated teachers' positive engagement with inclusive education.

What Is IIE?

With an introduction to IE, course participants now had an additional lens for analyzing student and classroom events and the impact of teaching on all students. They were able to explain and give examples and non-examples of both IE and inclusive practice and began to synthesize their new knowledge. By this point, most of the students were well aware of the premise of the course: if personnel in a school embraced IE, then inclusive practices and other services for students with disabilities could be more effectively implemented and supported. And since the IE mindset supports a foundation that fosters acceptance of the needs of all students, regardless of their ability, gender, race, ethnicity, language, care status, socioeconomic status, disability, sexuality, or religion, it could be possible to reach the ideal of embracing the unique needs of every individual.

Inclusive education provides accessible and meaningful learning experiences for all students with shared resources and in shared spaces. Inclusive education could further enhance student potential by embracing invitational theory and using such IE tools as the 5 P's, I-CORT, and the IE Ladder.

HOW WAS THE IIE COURSE IMPLEMENTED?

Since graduate students entered this course with a wide range of backgrounds and experiences with both invitational and inclusive education, the course began with a pre-assessment to adapt foundational teachings to their knowledge and experience. Students read *Fundamentals of Invitational Education* by Purkey and Novak (2008, 2016). The instructors practiced and modeled the tenets of IE, and the students shared a myriad of examples from personal settings which easily connected and supported the content of the text.

The second course text, *From Disability to Possibility*, by Schwarz (2006) shared brief case studies of children with exceptional needs and the strategies used by schools to respond to each child's needs. The graduate students discussed the cases in terms of how the application of IE principles could have been helpful to educators and enhanced student learning. Readings related to special education legislation over the decades also grounded class discussions about inclusive education.

The course instructors modeled a variety of co-teaching structures (Friend, 2013) including one-teach one-assist, one-teach one-observe, station teaching, parallel teaching, alternative teaching, and teaming (Friend, 2013). The graduate students also had the opportunity to consider their own practice in light of course learning through theory-into-practice projects.

As the course progressed to a consideration of ways to merge IE with inclusive practice, the graduate students quickly realized the potential synergy of these two perspectives and began to develop their own understandings of how such a merger could transform their mindsets and change their practice. Class participants, aware of the pilot nature of the IIE course content, enjoyed a high level of engagement, exploring and defining the learning activities for the course. Professors invited and encouraged reaction, reflection, and feedback for future conceptualization of the course.

Participants were particularly engaged in guiding their own reflection to complete a required group project that drew on their new learnings. Their engagement and in-depth discussion resulted in the creation of the IIE Ladder, which is a continuum to define degrees of teacher support for inclusive practice (see Table 22.4). In an epiphany, they blended their new IE learnings, their knowledge of inclusive practice, and their classroom experience by appropriately adapting the functional levels of the IE Ladder to relate to inclusive practice. The new IIE Ladder also included four levels of functioning, moving from the most negative and toxic way of considering how we involve individuals (intentionally exclusive) to the most beneficial way of considering how to involve students in ways consistent with their needs and desires (intentionally inclusive) across the Five P's (programs, policies, processes, places, and with other people).

Table 22.4.
IIE Ladder

Level	Definition	Examples
Intentionally Inclusive	These educators emphasize that everything is accessible to all students. They believe that inclusion is "the right thing to do." They believe that all students deserve their best effort.	The buildings have playgrounds with equipment that is wheelchair accessible and there are building-wide policies related to differentiated instruction. Teachers are very much focused and advocate quality learning environments for all.
Unintentionally Inclusive	These educators are the "lovables," who somehow make things work out. They are more inclusive by nature, somehow almost intuitively inclusive. They truly believe that the all students are the responsibility of all educators.	Just to be nice, teachers might read the written instructions to all students. They might offer extended time to all students. They can struggle with peers who are more exclusive than they are.
Unintentionally Exclusive	Unintentionally Exclusive educators are those who follow all adopted policies, rules, etc. regardless of the unintended and exclusive consequences that result. A rule is a rule is a rule.	They might see inequities but don't feel it is their role to advocate. They don't see themselves as exclusive and are insensitive to physical layout and adaptations that might be needed by some.
Intentionally Exclusive	Educators in this category use people, programs, processes, policies, and places, to purposely establish barriers to exclude students.	Teachers say they are not trained to help students with exceptionalities and so it is not their job. There is a teacher belief that students are incapable and should be in restricted settings. Some believe that students need to earn their right to be in the general education classroom.

After several initial offerings of the IIE course, two new instructors began co-teaching the course, using the same readings, resources, and assignments. Within two years, the course transitioned into a hybrid format taught by one instructor. In this format, the instructor blended online delivery of course content with at least three sessions requiring the students to travel to campus to meet face-to-face. As demand for online delivery increased, the university transitioned the course to a fully web-based platform. Although the instructor could no longer model co-teaching in a face-to-face environment, he could still teach its principles and practices and illustrate specific co-teaching approaches with video clips and other online resources. A newer edition of *Fundamentals of Invitational Education* (Purkey & Novak, 2016) replaced the older one. A second Schwarz text, *From Possibility to Success: Achieving Positive Student Outcomes in Inclusive Classrooms* (2013), provided examples of a greater range of inclusive practices.

Once the course moved to a fully web-based format, graduate students with an interest in its content had greater access to it. They could participate regardless of their location and schedules, and they had more flexibility to complete assignments. At the same time, the new format changed the nature of colleagues' interactions and eliminated face-to-face discussions, which created some challenges in personal interactions and the ability for the instructor to get to know the students as deeply as is possible with face-to-face instruction. The instructor found it more difficult to provide specific feedback in cases where web-based discussions progressed for a time without instructor involvement and to take advantage of what would have been a teachable moment in a face-to-face class. Another challenge was providing peer feedback for final projects submitted at the end of the course. It was also more difficult to get to know students sufficiently to provide credible employment references, a frequent request from students. In general, though, regardless of the course format, student responses from discussion boards, journal posts, course evaluations, and follow-up conversations revealed that the course has had and continues to have a transformative impact on educators' knowledge, skills, and attitudes.

HOW DID IIE TRANSFORM STUDENTS' PERSPECTIVES AND PRACTICES?

During class discussions, both face-to-face and online, students talked about understanding, accepting, and embracing all students, regardless of differences. They mentioned making their settings more inviting and wanting to encourage more success among all their students. In assignments and projects, they used the IE and inclusive terminology as if IIE were a new theory of practice.

Candidate reflections from nine years of course offerings (2009–2017) document substantive learnings and highlight the strength and confidence the course provided for them to move forward in advocating for their students. For the initial three years, comments from candidates showed that they grasped the merged concepts and saw their practical value. One student noted, "The course was a two-month step in the direction for me to become intentionally inviting. I can explain why things are effective and why they may not be. I am more confident to participate in school-wide discussions of various topics." Another student reported, "The text really aligned individual stories with the [IE] tenets which were meaningful to me. I really looked in depth at things that are so important, but sometimes overlooked. The tenets of IE really made me think about proper inclusion." A third student shared, "I found it really interesting to see how inviting and inclusive practice just seem to be so closely related. It seems like the more you foster one idea, the closer you can get to achieving the other."

Comments from the web-based platform indicated the development of a more inclusive mindset as well as collaborative steps taken with other staff and growth in advocacy: "My mindset has changed a lot regarding invitation and inclusive practices. I feel that I am more inclusive in my teaching practices. I want all students to feel welcome and accepted in my classroom." Focusing on the course's emphasis on collaboration, a general education teacher noted, "I am working with the special education teacher, gifted education teacher, and the speech pathologist to identify ways I can help all my students succeed."

The final comment is from a recent discussion with a graduate student enrolled in the earliest sections of the course who still adheres to the principles and practices of IIE:

> The book and course help galvanize the team approach to education in the modern world.... The biggest impact this text had was about six or seven years ago, when my school's special education department participated in a coordinator-led book study on the principles of IE ... this sparked significant discussion and resulted in the refinement of our IEP meeting procedures to ensure more parent participation and comfort during the meeting.

Instructor learnings have evolved during the stages of conceptualizing, packaging, delivering, evaluating, and repackaging the course. Ongoing refinement has resulted in a course that continues to reframe the principles and practices of inclusive education to respond to changes in student learning challenges. Course outcomes support developing skills to adopt, advocate for, and model an inclusive mindset and emphasize the importance of collaborating with colleagues, parents, and community members. Additionally, course outcomes indicate the possible need to conceptualize a more comprehensive approach to inclusive education by continually examining, connecting, and aligning it with other appropriate systems that emphasize relationship building (e.g., IE). The language, principles, and practices of IE promote a more expansive concept of inclusive education as it applies to all learners. Furthermore, educator preparation programs may want to consider embedding IIE principles into their programs.

CONCLUSION

The IIE course blended IE with inclusive practices and resulted in a synergy that has impacted candidates in their classroom practices, even after several years have passed. Simply said, the pilot IIE course presented the tenets of IE as a solid foundation for building a supportive culture for inclusion and serving as a precursor for increased teacher acceptance of inclusive practices and mindset. An unintended significantly positive result in the implementation of the course was graduate students' development of conceptualizations of IIE that extended beyond the instructors' initial intended outcomes (e.g., the IIE Ladder).

The course demonstrated that if educators make greater effort to focus on building culture around invitational and inclusive knowledge and practice, the impact upon services provided to students and families can transform our schools and communities. IIE is, indeed, bigger than the sum of its parts. Each new generation of educators must re-define and refine inclusive education, connecting it to other frameworks to continually meet the needs of all students in a global society. The importance of IIE is its potential as a bridge to school-wide reform that embraces inclusive practice. It could be used on a large scale to encourage acceptance beyond the classroom to the school and district (Winter & O'Raw, 2010).

REFERENCES

Boston-Kemple, T. E. (2012). *A conceptual analysis of key concepts in inclusive education* (Doctoral dissertation). Retrieved from The University of Iowa's Institutional Repository.

Education for All Handicapped Children Act of 1975, 20 USC § 1401 (1975).

Every Student Succeeds Act, 20 U.S.C. § 6301, *et seq.* (2015). Retrieved from https://www.congress.gov/114/plaws/publ95/PLAW-114publ95.pdf

Friend, M. (2013). *Co-Teaching! A handbook for creating and sustaining Effective classroom partnerships in inclusive schools* (2nd ed.). Washington, DC: Marilyn Friend.

Hansen, B. A., & Morrow, L. E. (2012). Invitational inclusive education: First steps on a journey to develop perspectives and practices. *Journal of Invitational Theory and Practice, 18,* 37–44.

Individuals with Disabilities Education Act Amendments of 1997, 20 U.S.C., §1400 *et seq.* (1997). Retrieved from https://www.congress.gov/105/plaws/publ17/PLAW-105publ17.pdf

Muskingum University. (n.d.). *Education*. Retrieved from https://www.muskingum.edu/academics/education

Purkey, W. W., & Novak, J. (1996). *Inviting school success: A self-concept approach to teaching, learning, and democratic practice* (3rd ed.). Cincinnati, OH: Wadsworth.

Purkey, W. W., & Novak, J. M. (2008). *Fundamentals of invitational education*. Kennesaw, GA: The International Alliance for Invitational Education.

Purkey, W. W., & Novak, J. M. (2016). *Fundamentals of invitational education* (2nd ed.). Kennesaw, GA: The International Alliance for Invitational Education.

Ruggs, E., & Hebl, M. (2012). Diversity, inclusion, and cultural awareness for classroom and outreach education. In B. Bogue & E. Cady (Eds.), *Apply research to practice (ARP) resources*. Society of Women Engineers—Assessing Women and Men Engineering Retrieved from http://www.engr.psu.edu/AWE/ARPResources.aspx

Shaw, D., & Siegel, B. L. (2010). Re-adjusting the kaleidoscope: The basic tenets of invitational theory and practice. *Journal of Invitational Theory and Practice, 16*, 106–113.

Schwarz, P. (2006). *From disability to possibility: The power of inclusive classrooms*. Portsmouth, NH: Heinemann.

Schwarz, P. (2013). *From possibility to success: Achieving positive student outcomes in inclusive classrooms*. Portsmouth, NH: Heinemann.

United Nations Educational, Scientific and Cultural Organization. (1994, June). *The Salamanca declaration and framework for action on special needs*. Paris, France: Author. Retrieved from http://www.unesco.org/education/pdf/SALAMA_E.PDF

Winter, E., & O'Raw, P. (2010). Literature review of the principles and practices relating to inclusive education for children with special needs. County Meath, Ireland: National Council for Special Education.

CHAPTER 23

REFORMING A PRINCIPAL PREPARATION PROGRAM

Reconciling Equity-Oriented Leadership and the Accountability Era

Amy N. Farley
University of Cincinnati

My first semester teaching in-service teachers who were enrolled in a principal preparation program was an eye-opening experience. Prior to that semester, I believed I understood the realities of teaching and the political pressures that our nation's teachers face. After all, I had spent time as an elementary and middle school teacher before earning my Doctor of Philosophy; and, before getting my first faculty job, I spent four years working closely with a state department of education and a wide array of districts—small and large, rural and urban, high-poverty and affluent—in implementing controversial education reform. I thought I already knew how educators grappled to make sense of various policies and systems, particularly those related to data, assessment, and student performance. That first semester, however, students in my two courses—one focused on instructional leadership and data systems and the other on social justice and equity-oriented leadership—engaged with the course materials in

Inclusive Education: A Systematic Perspective, pp. 399–420

completely different ways. This surprised me. In fact, although I saw issues of equity as inherently linked to instruction and curricular development, I struggled to make those connections for my students. My students did not naturally understand the relationship between inclusive education and the policy prescriptions that impact work in schools. Instead, I found that my students divorced the moral imperative to serve all students from their discussions of data and assessment, even when those conversations explicitly focused on serving all students. As Rigby and Tredway's (2015) research on urban school principals demonstrates, the principal candidates in our program likely addressed those issues from "a more mainstream frame of discussion. They moved away from an equity frame to one that is more typically used in schools, bureaucratic, and 'value-free.' Rather than connecting their daily, perhaps ordinary, work to a moral imperative, principals stayed close to the task at hand" (p. 341).

In the two years following that first semester, I worked—with support from my colleagues and funding from the Ohio Deans Compact for Exceptional Children (or Deans Compact)—to help students reconcile these ideas. I created intentional connections between those two courses, and we moved beyond abstraction and theory to practice-connected work. Now when I teach these courses, the students and I talk about the challenges inherent in connecting an equity lens with policies that sometimes do not seem grounded in the best practices of equity work. Like many others, for example, we apply state school report card data to improvement planning, but we also consider how these data might motivate additional inquiry and support school leaders in developing equity-oriented goals, all while foregrounding school context, student needs, and the value of community partnerships. Together, we think deeply about where policies advance an equity agenda and where they do not. In the chapter that follows, I describe our institution's best efforts to help make these connections for our students.

(Author vignette)

As schools and districts across the country respond to shifting expectations around accountability reform—including new demands regarding teacher and principal evaluation, standards-based instruction, and Common Core aligned assessments—school principals must accordingly shift the focus of their leadership to a broader set of responsibilities and skills. To be considered highly effective in today's climate, these leaders face a wide range of (sometimes competing) demands and expectations (Horng & Loeb, 2010; Perilla, 2014). No longer does the role of building manager or student disciplinarian suffice; we now expect principals to develop a strong mission and vision that guides their building and stakeholders, while also leading the development and implementation of rigorous instructional programs that meet the needs of all children and draw on the capacity of all teachers. School leaders increasingly act as instructional leaders, teacher coaches, district and state representatives, policy advocates, and community and family liaisons. This is a weighty set of responsibilities, and one for which many prospective leaders find themselves ill prepared.

While many of the preceding chapters in this edited volume focus on preparing teachers to become inclusive, responsive, and equity-oriented educators, this chapter examines the role of principals in creating and maintaining opportunity for all students, particularly those who are traditionally marginalized in the American education system. While teachers are the cornerstone of equitable schools, the role of supportive principals in effecting transformative change remains essential. In fact, research consistently demonstrates that principals play a critical role in the implementation of school and district reform and in setting expectations for change (Manna, 2015; McLeskey, Waldron, & Redd, 2014). At the same time, evidence suggests that most administrators are not prepared to meet the needs of students from diverse backgrounds or with disabilities nor to create school cultures focused on social justice (Billingsley & McLeskey, 2014; Cambron-McCabe & McCarthy, 2005; DiPaola & Walther-Thomas, 2003; Pazey & Cole, 2013).

This chapter broadly examines the role of principals in creating just and inclusive schools, and it summarizes the programmatic work undertaken by the faculty of one principal preparation program to prepare educational leaders to do just this. First, it reviews the relevant literature about the importance of school leaders in implementing reform and educational change (see Background below); then it summarizes a two-year collaboration between members of the educational leadership and special education faculties at the University of Cincinnati (UC) that integrated a more inclusive approach within the principal preparation program (see Principal Preparation Redesign at a Major University section below). This collaboration serves as an example of how educational leadership programs can and should prepare leaders to become inclusive educators and "equity-oriented change agents" (Maxwell, Locke, & Scheurich, 2013, p. 1). To conclude, this chapter contends that educational leadership programs must prepare candidates to reconcile the principles of equity and inclusion with the realities of accountability and reform, realities highlighted in the opening vignette. Only by navigating these competing pressures can school leaders truly support the creation of inclusive schools and instructional programs.

BACKGROUND

Over the last several decades, the scholarship on inclusive educational leadership expanded considerably. The following discussion summarizes the most relevant aspects of this literature, beginning with the role of school leaders in propagating educational change and influencing school reform and transformation. The discussion then draws on literature that addresses the current contexts in which many school leaders work—including literature on persistent inequities and the opportunity gap—to illustrate the demand for leaders who are prepared to meet the needs of all students and to create equitable and inclusive environments. This section concludes by addressing two persistent challenges in the creation of school leaders with a social justice orientation. First, the literature suggests that principals do not receive adequate preparation for this role and that, in general, educational leadership programs marginally address the necessary skills for transformational change. Second, the current accountability climate appears to deprioritize equity and inclusion, leaving many practicing school leaders struggling to reconcile these social justice aims with accountability.

Role of Principals in Educational Change

Research demonstrates that principals are key influencers of school outcomes, student success, and teacher satisfaction. In fact, the recent discourse on educational leadership suggests that principals are among the chief levers for improving education generally, particularly in high-needs schools (Manna, 2015). Principals influence the educational systems in which they work in two significant ways: they provide direction and they exercise influence (Perilla, 2014). Thus, principals must be prepared to direct various stakeholders while also collaborating with staff and creating working conditions that "allow teachers to make the most of their motivations, commitments and capacities" (Leithwood, Harris, & Hopkins, 2008, p. 30).

School leaders must also be prepared to influence the political and reform climate around them. As schools and districts respond to shifting expectations around accountability reform, school leaders need to understand the policies that drive their work, recognize the underlying values and vision for education, and plan for the intended and unintended consequences that stem from implementation of reforms. They must also recognize how various individual, social, political, and organizational structures impact each school and community differently (DeMatthews, 2015); and they must use that knowledge to anticipate effects within their own school contexts. These expectations are complex, strategic, and forward-thinking; and they require principals who are equipped with an understanding of school leadership, social justice, and inclusive practices. Principals must also be prepared to engage with and advocate for district and state policies that align with a commitment to high-quality instruction for all learners. Prospective school leaders should therefore understand these forces and contexts and be prepared to work within these systems to enact positive change.

Persistent Inequalities and Opportunity Gaps in American Schools

Given the widespread and deep-seated inequalities within our public schools—considered by some to be the "the civil rights issue of our generation" (Confirmation of Arne Duncan, 2009, p. 9)—the contemporary field of educational leadership focuses extensively on principles of social justice (Furman, 2012; Theoharis, 2007). Chronic underfunding and the dearth of resources are tough realities affecting schools that serve marginalized populations (Darling-Hammond, 2013); meanwhile, White students and affluent students outperform students of color and low-income students on almost every state and national assessment and on measures of later life outcomes (e.g., high school graduation, college enrollment and completion, and employment and salary; Welner & Farley, 2010).

The gravity of this achievement gap has prompted many scholars to reconceptualize it as an opportunity gap, beginning long before any measured performance of student achievement (Darling-Hammond, 2013; Welner & Carter, 2013). The opportunity gap constitutes the unequal distribution of "key educational resources that support learning at home and at school: expert teachers, personalized attention, high-quality curriculum opportunities, good educational materials, and plentiful information resources" (Darling-Hammond, 2013, p. 77). Ladson-Billings (2008) further advocates that we think of the achievement gap as a debt owed to marginalized students, rather than an apolitical "gap" in performance. She argues that the language of achievement implicitly places responsibility on students, families, teachers, and schools, whereas "the notion of education debt requires us to think about how all of us, as members of a democratic society, are implicated in creating these achievement disparities" (p. 236).

Despite these persistent challenges, educational leaders can create schools with socially just and equitable policies and practices (Skrla, McKenzie, & Scheurich, 2011). The biggest hurdle in accomplishing this may be overcoming the deficit perspective with which many educators and school leaders view low-income students and communities (Gorski, 2013). According to Gorski (2013), equitable educators adopt a resiliency perspective of marginalized students in lieu of a deficit perspective. These school leaders focus on addressing systemic injustices—Ladson-Billing's (2008) educational debt—rather than fixing disempowered students and their communities. While this kind of equitable leadership is possible, school leaders must be intentional in taking steps to change their schools with regard to equity and justice (Theoharis, 2007). Further, principals need to be well informed and prepared to address policies and practices that are traditionally and historically discriminatory or unjust.

Principal Readiness for Inclusive, Equitable Leadership

Despite the potential for school leaders to facilitate transformative change, many traditional and alternative preparation programs do not fully prepare prospective school leaders for their roles within the school (Quin, Deris, Bischoff, & Johnson, 2015) or for the contemporary realities of school reform and policy (Darling-Hammond, Meyerson, LaPointe, & Orr, 2010). The lack of preparation appears to be exacerbated in high-needs schools; findings from a large-scale study suggest that in-service principals in high-poverty and high-minority schools were comparatively less effective leaders and were less likely to share leadership with teachers and other stakeholders, even when controlling for school level and urbanicity (Louis, Leithwood, Wahlstrom, & Anderson, 2010).

Further, the literature suggests that school leaders in general tend to be unprepared to advance an agenda related to equity and inclusion (Billingsley & McLeskey, 2014; Cambron-McCabe & McCarthy, 2005; DiPaola & Walther-Thomas, 2003). For example, Pazey and Cole (2013) found that administrators often complete training or certification programs believing that they have the expertise necessary to avoid and even combat potential lawsuits or accusations of inappropriate services for students with disabilities. However, the research indicated that this is often not the case: "A discussion of children with disabilities is rarely an integral part of leadership preparation programs, and disability issues remain outside of the leadership discourse" (p. 245). This lack of preparedness extends beyond students with disabilities, and includes students of color, low-income students, LGBTQ students and gender non-conforming students, English learners (ELs), immigrants, and other traditionally marginalized students.

Ryan (2012, p. 9) argues that "leadership and inclusion are not natural bedfellows," noting that traditional approaches to educational leadership are generally inconsistent with a more inclusive, equity-oriented approach. He identifies a host of challenges related to instituting inclusive practices in educational leadership preparation programs, including: outdated and hierarchical approaches to management; existing policy frameworks that define school leaders as "heroes" who can singlehandedly "create fundamental change" (p. 11); and, worst of all, a general "reluctance to recognize, or acknowledge exclusive practices like racism, sexism, classism, homophobia, ableism" (p. 12). Ryan and Higginbottom (2017) elaborate:

> It is not easy, at the best of times, for educators to promote inclusion, equity, and social justice in contemporary institutions that continue to display racist, sexist, classist, and homophobic policies, cultures, traditions, and practices (Ryan, 2012; Theoharis, 2007). But changing these practices is complicated by the way in which education organizations work. Scholars have acknowledged that, like most other institutions, schools are political organizations (Eliott, 1959; Scribner, Aleman, & Maxcy, 2003). Leaders who wish to promote social justice need to know how to work within these political structures. (pp. 103–104)

In essence, school leaders must acknowledge how education politics and school reform exacerbate existing inequalities as well as inhibiting some educators from becoming social justice-minded leaders (Ryan & Higginbottom, 2017).

Intersection of Accountability Reform and Inclusive Leadership

In addition to concerns about administrators' preparedness for social justice leadership, some scholars believe the current accountability climate interferes with administrators' ability to prioritize inclusion and equity (Cambron-McCabe & McCarthy, 2005; Louis et al., 2010; Ryan, 2012), or, at the very least, principals perceive that it does. Although accountability reform is at least theoretically motivated by a desire to improve student performance, evidence for the impact of large-scale accountability reform is "thin and mixed" (Louis et al., 2010, p. 12). Even worse, some evidence suggests accountability may exacerbate existing inequalities by disproportionately impacting students of color and students with disabilities (Darling-Hammond, 2010)—while also perpetuating exclusionary ideologies (Ryan, 2012).

Research suggests, moreover, that accountability systems make it even more challenging for administrators to create inclusive schools because these systems tend to narrow administrators' focus or distract them from more pressing equity concerns. School leaders have reported that they feel "constrained by rules, regulations, and state controls" (Cambron-McCabe & McCarthy, 2005, p. 202). They also feel disempowered especially with respect to participation in discussions to determine what is important in schools and how best to ensure learning and progress toward goals with a social-justice focus (Cranston, 2013). As Anderson and colleagues note, school leaders often feel overburdened by external reporting requirements that inadvertently restrict their focus and divert attention from problem solving (Anderson, Leithwood, & Strauss, 2010). Adding to the demands of accountability, the "complex maze of legal requirements" becomes yet more complicated when considering students with disabilities or other underrepresented students, particularly in contexts with limited resources (Pazey & Cole, 2013, p. 246).

The Call for Change in Educational Leadership Preparation

In short, the literature on education for social justice calls for additional attention to the work of school leaders and the educational landscape they confront. It demonstrates, in fact, the considerable need for responsive principal preparation programs that elevate the leadership capacity of future principals, particularly with regard to inclusion, equity, and justice. Despite the limitations outlined above, however, some findings appear to justify cautious optimism; the literature suggests that principal preparation matters, and innovations and intervention in pre-service principal preparation programs appear to impact practice in the field (Darling-Hammond et al., 2010; Orr & Orphanos, 2011).

Recent research suggests that implementing a social justice curriculum can influence school leaders' understandings of and approaches toward equity (Allen, Harper, & Koschoreck, 2017). While all university faculty have a responsibility to raise awareness of complex social problems through critical pedagogy, dialogue, experiential learning, reflection, social critique, and a commitment to change (Hurtado, 2007), this is particularly true within education programs. Principal preparation programs not only serve their own candidates; they also—though indirectly—serve PK–12 students, teachers, other school personnel, and the wider community:

> It is time for those who educate the educators to ask what kind of schooling they wish to promote. If social justice is to be the driver of our educational policy and is to be turned into meaningful practice, then we need to engage in critical conversations that address the educational and social needs of every student. Educational administrators must be armed with what they need: the knowledge, skills, and attributes necessary for engaging in 'social justice leadership' for each student. (Pazey & Cole, 2013, pp. 263–264)

In short, higher education should not only be a place of learning, but also a place that counters oppression, combats social problems, and encourages self-determination (Moses, 2002).

PRINCIPAL PREPARATION REDESIGN
AT A MAJOR UNIVERSITY

The following section outlines the two-year collaborative effort made at one university in Ohio to address the concerns of educational leadership preparation programs with a focus on inclusion, equity, and social justice. The section outlines the conceptual approach and objectives of redesigning the principal preparation program.

Project Theory of Action

The University of Cincinnati (UC) is a large, urban, Research I university currently enrolling over 40,000 students. The mission of the Educational Leadership program, situated within the School of Education, is to prepare excellent leaders for excellent schools and to seek, generate, test, and share new knowledge for the transformation and improvement of the profession. The program seeks to embody the principles of social justice, caring, diversity, and collaboration in authentic and tangible ways in all aspects of our practice. The principal preparation program meets the requirements for licensure in the state of Ohio and is accredited by the Ohio Department of Education and the Council for the Accreditation of Educator Preparation; the program requires seven core courses for licensure, with additional electives offered to students seeking a Master of Education.

Committed to leadership for social justice and aligned with the research outlined above, the educational leadership and special education faculties at UC embarked on a two-year collaboration to overhaul the existing principal preparation program, centering it on the principles of inclusion and equity. Funded by the Deans Compact, UC's program revision work modified the existing course of study for prospective school principals by enhancing and integrating special education competencies throughout each of the seven core courses required for licensure. The work reflected an existing commitment to principles of social justice and diversity, highlighted in the program mission statement, and elevated those principles through practice. The intended outcome of the work was, at its heart, quite simple: creating graduates who are well prepared to lead schools and meet the instructional needs of all students, especially students with disabilities.

The idea that a redesigned curriculum can improve the quality of leadership, thereby increasing equity and opportunity for all students, motivated this work. Figure 23.1 presents a visual representation of the redesign work.

This model draws on the research cited above and other literature suggesting that school leaders can transform schools into places that counter oppression and create equitable and just communities (Theoharis, 2009). Similarly, UC's work centered on the core belief that principal preparation programs can better prepare school leaders to take on transformative work. Drawing on Skrla and associates' (2009) work, faculty members redesigned the program to prepare candidates who will serve as "equity-oriented change agents," or leaders who embody a social justice/equity stance in their work (Maxwell et al., 2013; Skrla et al., 2009).

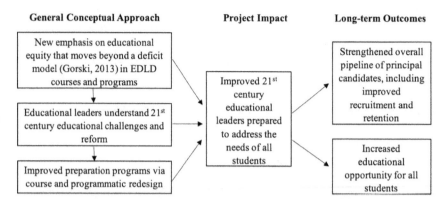

Figure 23.1. Simplified conceptual model, including project impacts and long-term outcomes.

Project Objectives

Three overarching project goals informed the work. First, the project sought to improve individual courses by increasing their focus on evidence-based practices and ensuring that syllabi and course content would address critical aspects of cultural, linguistic, racial, and disability/ability diversity. Second, it strove to refocus the principal preparation program's overall purpose by aligning curricular and clinical experiences and by integrating essential aspects of diversity across these. Finally, the project recognized that transformative change in educational leadership programs requires transformative change among educational leadership faculty. As part of course revision, UC faculty developed and grew using a community of practice model and, as a result, acquired new competencies in equity and inclusion.

Collaboration between the special education and educational leadership faculties was critically important in achieving these goals, particularly with regard to faculty growth. The redevelopment team—comprised of individuals from both faculties—knew that partnerships between and among programs could make or break their progress. In fact, some researchers view collaboration as a cornerstone of those educational reform efforts designed to improve teacher preparation and professional development (Rosenberg et al., 2009). Despite this recognition, the team also understood that successful partnerships are complex and difficult to foster; collaboration must be mutually beneficial and aligned with shared goals (Gardner, 2011). Faculty and staff in both programs began the work committed to the transformation of the educational leadership program, and they met monthly in extended retreats to work and think together, share feedback, analyze courses, and reflect upon the process of building a more inclusive principal preparation program.

To inform course and programmatic revisions, the team first aligned the Educational Leadership Constituent Council standards with the new Professional Standards for Educational Leaders (PSEL) and the Council for Exceptional Children (CEC) Leadership standards, in addition to Ohio's state standards for educators. The team then undertook a rigorous curriculum audit, with deep review work on each of the seven core courses in the program including the clinical internship. During the second year of the grant, the team met to review and analyze each course individually; team members brainstormed ways to improve and/or deepen course content, making it more inclusive and reflective of the diversity of students that prospective administrators would serve. The instructors for each course then undertook major course revisions, documenting their changes throughout.

PROJECT IMPACT

The project produced important outcomes with implications for the quality of both the program of study as a whole and individual courses. While project implementation is still in its early stages, preliminary trends appear quite positive. Programmatically, the educational leadership program of study at UC appears to have shifted toward a more inclusive and equity-oriented paradigm, one better aligned with the program's mission. Faculty impressions and student evaluations of individual courses suggest that they also appear to be significantly improved.

Programmatic Impact

The Deans Compact grant affected the program at UC in several ways. First, it helped refocus the program on its mission and vision. Second, it sparked critical conversations about the role of fieldwork, leading to immediate and longer-term revisions to the program's internship component. These developments have the potential to create meaningful change. Prior research demonstrates that programs with foregrounded instructional leadership and challenging fieldwork experiences prepare candidates who are more likely to indicate high levels of learning and to express more positivity about becoming a school leader (Darling-Hammond et al., 2010).

The work also inspired the faculty to adopt a strong predisposition toward continuous improvement and innovation. They recently applied for and received an innovation grant from the state of Ohio to extend the work described in this chapter, providing an opportunity for further mission revision and course redesign. While the initial work described here certainly influenced the program directly, it also highlighted the critical need to develop curricula and experiences (for principal candidates) that reflect the many aspects of diversity in our schools. Adopting a wider view of inclusivity—one that recognizes many marginalized groups, not only students with disabilities—is a critical next step inspired by the first round of work described here.

The commitment to equity work represents a significant shift for the faculty and demonstrates progress toward the third project goal—to develop faculty and build new competencies in equity and inclusion. Faculty at UC shifted and evolved their practice, embracing a core belief that the transformation of school leaders cannot occur without transformation within educational leadership programs. By modeling the principles of inclusion and equity within course design and instruction, UC's program is better prepared to create school principals who will lead inclusive, equity-oriented schools.

Impact on Individual Courses

Shifting the learning orientation of an entire program of study is a colossal task. While UC experienced some improvements to the program overall, those changes are still nascent. Promisingly, however, the impacts within individual courses are much more established. Although faculty have taught the redesigned courses for one year only, the project appears to have generated a significant impact on course design, pedagogical approach, and student perceptions of efficacy and value. Descriptions of these changes in two different courses—one that underwent critical review by the collaborative team and one that did not—can be found below. As a required course for principal licensure, Curriculum Development and Data Analysis was one of seven such courses reformed within the program. Leadership for Social Justice, on the other hand, is an elective taken by the majority of students pursuing a master's degree. Despite only one course receiving a formal review, the lessons learned from the review of the curriculum course appear to have permeated the elective as well. The program, therefore, brought about important and complementary effects in both courses, including for their broader pedagogical approaches and embedded theoretical orientations

Course Content Revision

The curriculum course—as part of a comprehensive approach to curriculum development, instructional design, and assessment—tackles issues related to the changing role of principals as instructional leaders and the integration of data-driven cycles of inquiry into instruction. Prior to redesign, it focused on high-quality instruction and progress monitoring of student achievement—two important facets of instructional leadership. The course, however, did not press students to challenge assumptions and misunderstandings about data and assessment. Now, in the reconceptualized course, prospective principals consider the many available sources of data that promote an understanding of student learning, and they begin to conceive of themselves as "critical consumers" of these data (Farley, Clayton, & Kaka, 2018). This "critical" approach does not involve dismissing or disparaging the data; on the contrary, students and the instructor work to understand that standardized assessment results provide important, but limited, information about content mastery across a school. These data are more useful for identifying trends and gaps in performance across student populations than in determining instructional approaches or determining overall performance (for individual students, teachers, or schools).

Although it did not undergo formal review, the social justice course also underwent significant revisions. It initially focused on identity politics and inequity in American schools, including how schools and educational systems contribute to and unwittingly perpetuate those inequities. This is important content, but it meant that the course primarily functioned as a vehicle for helping students acquire knowledge about social justice issues. Meaningful change in educational leadership requires principals who are equipped not only with knowledge, but also with the skills and tools needed to apply that knowledge in practical ways (Pazey & Cole, 2013). To move beyond the focus on expanding knowledge, the revised course now asks students to wrestle with the challenges and realities within schools and brainstorm strategies and approaches for how they can position themselves as equity-oriented change agents in their professional roles (Skrla et al., 2011). Students also engage with real-world case studies that highlight problems and dilemmas from the field, a pedagogical technique employed by several exemplary educational leadership programs (Darling-Hammond et al., 2010). Recent research (Allen et al., 2017) on social justice-oriented course revisions demonstrated that a revised social justice curriculum can influence students' understandings of and dispositions toward equity and justice, suggesting that these changes may not only impact the quality of the coursework, but the application of these commitments in the field.

Preliminary Outcomes From Revised Courses

It took a full year to complete the revisions of the two courses; these revised courses launched in summer 2017. As Figure 23.2 demonstrates, student course evaluations improved substantially following the revision process. The average instructor ratings also exceeded 4.8 out of 5.0, well above the university and program averages.

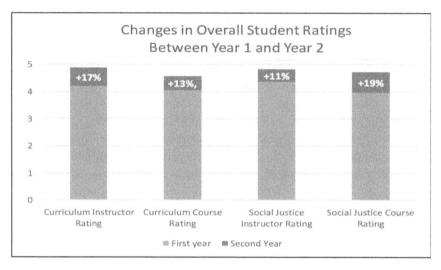

Figure 23.2.   Improvement in average instructor and course student ratings.

Furthermore, a faculty peer evaluator gave the revised curriculum course high praise, particularly highlighting the commitment to continuous improvement. In the review, a tenured faculty member at UC commended the revising faculty member's "openness to review," "determination to develop program-wide course work that was state of the art in terms of current practice," and an overall "commitment to map the program to best practices of the profession."

This evaluation and the student ratings together reflect the program's sincere commitment to evolving and improving its teaching practice and placing inclusion and equity at the center of its individual courses as well as its curriculum as a whole.

RECONCILING EQUITY IN THE ACCOUNTABILITY ERA

In addition to the changes described above, the team adapted both courses to foreground the ways that data and accountability systems can fit into an overarching social justice philosophy. This was, and continues to be, important work. As seen in the findings of the relevant literature (see Background section above), the prospective school leaders at UC also express a strong desire to adopt more inclusive and equity-oriented practices, but simultaneously struggle to understand how those practices fit into the current accountability cultures in their schools. To help them answer that question, both of the two revised courses explicitly focus on integrating a social justice orientation within a climate driven by data and accountability.

To prepare candidates to reconcile these competing forces—and to keep attention on equity when accountability sometimes pushes it off the agenda—educational leadership programs must provide candidates with opportunities to explore and discuss these issues. Faculty must intentionally raise these questions and encourage students to wrestle with them and develop strategies for navigating them in the real world. For example, in the revised curriculum course, students discuss the negative impact of assessment in today's schools and consider ways to advocate for policies that may better serve their schools and communities. They also engage in conversation about the tension between those groups that advocate for educational equity and those that advocate for high-stakes testing and accountability policies. Yet, the divisions between these groups are not as neat as popular discourse might suggest. In fact, in 2015, 12 of the country's most prominent civil rights groups came out in opposition to anti-testing efforts and in support of assessment as a tool for monitoring inequality (The Leadership Conference for Civil and Human Rights, 2015). They collectively argued that, "for the civil rights community, data provide the power to advocate for greater equality under the law" (para. 2) and that "abolishing the tests or sabotaging the validity of their results only makes it harder to identify and fix the deep-seated problems in our schools" (The Leadership Conference for Civil and Human Rights, 2015, para. 8). Fullan (2007) also argues that "data can be empowering or disabling," (The Leadership Conference for Civil and Human Rights, 2015, p. 60) while others note that data-driven improvement and accountability in schools "can lead to greater quality and integrity, or to deterioration of services and distraction from core purposes" (Hargreaves & Braun, 2013, p. 7). Whichever the case, the stakes are extraordinarily high, and it is imperative that school leaders be prepared to respond to policy and reform in ways that meet the needs of all students.

Certainly, the perspective advocated by civil rights groups advances the idea that data systems can fuel social justice work. Three paradigm shifts, drawn from educational leadership and accountability theory, may further enable school leaders to reframe their perspectives and thereby reconcile the tension between equity and accountability. These shifts involve reconceptualizing (a) data-driven decision-making, (b) external accountability, and (c) policy implementation. While each represents a major conceptual reorientation, each also has the potential to bridge the existing divide between a theoretical commitment to social justice and the practical realities of the accountability climate.

Data-Driven Decision Making

Several scholars (Anderson et al., 2010; Hargreaves & Braun, 2013) have either directly or indirectly advocated for a reconceptualization of data-driven decision making. Anderson and associates (2010) argue that the term "decision-making" is problematic because it "implies that the improvement challenge for schools is to choose among a set of known solutions for their readily understood improvement problems" (p. 323). In reality, of course, the work is much more complex. Nevertheless, an explicit decision-making orientation may also lead to a focus on account-ability *judgments* at the expense of *improvement* (Hargreaves & Braun, 2013).

For these reasons, Anderson and associates (2010) question whether reconceptualizing data-driven decision making as data-driven problem solving might be more appropriate. As school leaders consider the problems facing education today—persistent inequalities in resources and outcomes, unequal access and opportunity gaps, and a national discourse that superficially focuses on only some of the largest problems—attention to problem solving (as opposed to decision making) will lead to improvement. UC addresses this concern directly in the revised curriculum course. Whereas the course once asked students to identify problems or review state accountability data to build school improvement plans, it now pushes them to consider multiple sources of data, how those data speak to the most pressing questions facing contemporary education, and how school leaders could use preliminary results as a tool to pose new questions and promote further inquiry.

External Accountability

It is also critical for school leaders to understand that data analysis must move "beyond the identification of problem areas to an investigation of the specific nature of and factors contributing to the problem" (Anderson et al., 2010). The power of this work lies not in using data to understand a problem, but in the resulting actions that better a situation. Too often, however, school leaders, teachers, and other stakeholders use accountability data "to comply with external\ accountability reporting requirements" instead of pursuing an intervention or solution to address underlying concerns (Anderson et al., 2010, p. 315).

Cranston (2013) contends that the field of education should move away from externally-directed accountability reform and toward reform that foregrounds *professional responsibility*, a more powerful notion that shifts "the agenda of action in schools from an externally determined one, to one that is internal and contextualized" (p. 136). Similarly, scholars have long argued that external accountability measures fail when they are not accompanied by capacity building exercises and stakeholder buy-in; this realization has increasingly led educational leadership scholars to call for a shift from external accountability to internal accountability, where individual responsibility, collective expectations, and accountability data align (Elmore, 2004; Fullan, 2007; Fullan, Rincon-Gallardo, & Hargreaves, 2015).

Empirical research suggests that school leaders can shift their orientation to one of internal accountability, with positive results. In a multi-case study of 15 schools in four urban school districts, Knapp and Feldman (2012) found evidence that "internal accountability systems were in place that asserted a strong and reinforced sense of collective responsibility for the school's performance ... though often with adjustments to the accountability messages from the larger system, to make them fit with the school's own learning improvement agenda" (p. 689). In other words, school leaders in these cases reshaped accountability policies to align with internal values and systems, including inclusion and social justice.

Letter-of-the-Law Policy Implementation

This reshaping of accountability policy invokes the third reconceptualization advocated here: that principals should focus on "spirit-of-the-law" rather than "letter-of-the-law" policy implementation (Mavrogordato & White, 2017), particularly when meeting the mandates and expectations of accountability systems. The accountability era does not inherently disallow the prioritization of problem solving and improvement or the alignment of systems with internal values, but these practices are sometimes left behind. This may be because some leaders focus too closely on the "technical aspects of implementation" and narrowly tailor their work "to literal, strict implementation of what is formally written, irrespective of mitigating contextual factors" (Mavrogordato & White, 2017, p. 283). In these cases, school leaders let a preoccupation with letter-of-law implementation cloud their judgment and shift their attention from the general purpose and overarching goals and objectives—an approach that tends to interfere with the overall quality of implementation (Mavrogordato &

White, 2017). For example, in their research on EL reclassification policies in Texas, Mavrogordato and White (2017) found that district language policy committees charged with reviewing and monitoring reclassification policies heavily influenced the implementation of the required policies. While some schools understood the spirit of the policy and advocated for the "best instructional program for their students" (p. 305), others focused on administrative tasks and letter-of-the-law prescriptions. Furthermore, although the implementation of policy varied considerably, committee members consistently claimed that they had not interpreted policy at all. Mavrogordato and White argued, however, that these actors must have engaged in interpretation of policy because their implementation strategies varied to a considerable degree and clearly led to different outcomes.

All this suggests that it is important "to help policy implementers deepen their understanding of the policy" (Mavrogordato & White, 2017, p. 305), particularly when it allows for added flexibility or an enriched appreciation for the key purposes of laws and procedural guidelines. Given the limitations that accountability policies seem to place on inclusive, equitable school leadership—despite some stated equity goals and support from the civil rights community—it is time for school leaders to recognize their role in interpreting policy. There may be more flexibility within current evaluation and accountability systems than some educators realize, and school leaders must be more fully prepared to work within systems to reinterpret, revise, and push back against challenging aspects of policy while also maintaining the spirit of the law and focusing on growth and improvement.

CONCLUSION

Looking forward, there is certainly work that remains to be done: some principal candidates struggle to acknowledge and combat their deficit views of the diverse students and families who populate their school buildings and communities. The fact that UC continues to teach a distinct social justice course, outside the core program, also serves as a reminder of the work that remains in integrating inclusive principles and equity-oriented approaches into the core of its educational leadership program. Nevertheless, collaborating with colleagues from diverse disciplines to strengthen the curriculum and integrate principles of equity and inclusion throughout offers promise. By engaging students in difficult conversations and exploring the tensions that exist in practice, we can not only prepare school leaders to become equity-oriented change agents, but we can also scaffold their development and prepare them to reconcile a focus on equity and inclusion with accountability pressures and reform.

The next generation of educational leadership programs must train candidates to focus on assets, not only within the students and families they serve, but also within the teachers they lead, the mission and vision of their school building, and even in the spirit of those accountability policies that ask them to use data to improve services for all students. Hargreaves and Braun (2013) provide a compelling reminder of what is at stake:

> In the end, some of our most challenging educational and social problems will not mainly be solved by more or better data, just as they will not be solved by more technology or by any other silver bullet. More and better data can help us make more efficient educational decisions and judgments, but they will not, of themselves, help us make wiser or more humane ones. Often, what we need to alleviate children's suffering and lack of opportunity is not more data or better metrics, but more attention, and more support. (p. 6)

At first glance, equity and accountability may seem incompatible, and much of the relevant literature suggests that accountability policies can and often do exacerbate inequalities and distract from the most important conversations about justice in schools. But recognizing how the spirit of those policies can serve a more inclusive and equitable vision may be one of the most critical elements of becoming an equity-oriented change leader. Principal preparation programs must prepare candidates to acknowledge not only the varied sources of knowledge in our school communities (Moll, Amanti, Neff, & Gonzalez, 1992), but also the varied policies and laws that provide a backdrop to their important work as leaders. Only then will they be able to lead with a focus on inclusion, equity, and justice.

REFERENCES

Anderson, S., Leithwood, K., & Strauss, T. (2010). Leading data use in schools: Organizational conditions and practices at the school and district levels. *Leadership & Policy in Schools, 9*, 292–327. doi:10.1080/15700761003731492

Allen, J. G., Harper, R. E., & Koschoreck, J. W. (2017). Social justice and school leadership preparation: Can we shift beliefs, values, and commitments? *NCPEA International Journal of Educational Leadership Preparation, 12*(1), 33–52. Retrieved from http://www.ncpeapublications.org/index.php/volume-12-number-1-spring-2017

Billingsley, B., & McLeskey, J. (2014). What are roles of principals in inclusive schools? In J. McLeskey, N. L. Waldron, F. Spooner, & B. Algozzine (Eds.), *Handbook of effective inclusive schools: Research and practice* (pp. 67–79). New York: Routledge. doi:10.4324/9780203102930.ch6

Cambron-McCabe, N., & McCarthy, M. M. (2005). Educating school leaders for social justice. *Educational Policy, 19*, 201–222. doi:10.1177/0895904804271609

Cranston, N. (2013). School leaders leading: Professional responsibility not accountability as the key focus. *Educational Management Administration & Leadership, 41*, 129–142. doi:10.1177/1741143212468348

Darling-Hammond, L. (2010). *The flat world and education: How America's commitment to equity will determine our future.* New York, NY: Teachers College Press.

Darling-Hammond, L. (2013). Inequality and school resources: What it will take to close the opportunity gap. In P. L. Carter & K. G. Welner (Eds.), *Closing the opportunity gap: What America must do to give every child an even chance* (pp. 111–122). New York, NY: Oxford University Press. doi:10.1093/acprof:oso/9780199982981.003.0006

Darling-Hammond, L., Meyerson, D., LaPointe, M. M., & Orr, M. T. (2010). *Preparing principals for a changing world: Lessons from effective school leadership programs.* San Francisco, CA: Jossey-Bass. doi:10.1002/9781118269329

DeMatthews, D. (2015). Making sense of social justice leadership: A case study of a principal's experiences to create a more inclusive school. *Leadership and Policy in Schools, 14*, 139–166. doi:10.1080/15700763.2014.997939

DiPaola, M. F., & Walther-Thomas, C. (2003). *Principals and special education: The critical role of school leaders* (COPSSE Document No. IB-7E). Gainesville, FL: University of Florida, Center on Personnel Studies in Special Education. Retrieved from http://www.personnelcenter.org/pdf/copsse_principals.pdf

Confirmation of Arne Duncan: Hearing of the Committee on Health, Education, Labor, and Pensions, Senate, 111th Cong. 9 (2009) (testimony of Arne Duncan).

Eliot, T. H. (1959). Toward an understanding of public school politics. *The American Political Science Review, 52*, 1051. doi:10.2307/1952073

Elmore, R. F. (2004). *School reform from the inside out: Policy, practice, and performance.* Cambridge, MA: Harvard University Press.

Farley, A. N., Clayton, G., & Kaka, S. J. (2018). Linking teacher education to redesigned systems of accountability: A call for multiple measures in pre-service teacher effectiveness. *Education Policy Analysis Archives, 26*(12), 1–12. doi:10.14507/epaa.26.3441

Fullan, M. (2007). *The new meaning of education change* (4th ed.). New York, NY: Teachers College Press. doi:10.4324/9780203609071

Fullan, M., Rincon-Gallardo, S., & Hargreaves, A. (2015). Professional capital as accountability. *Education Policy Analysis Archives, 23*(15), 1–22. doi:10.14507/epaa.v23.1998

Furman, G. (2012). Social justice leadership as praxis: Developing capacities through preparation programs. *Educational Administration Quarterly, 48*, 191–229. doi:10.1177/0013161x11427394

Gardner, D. C. (2011). Characteristic collaborative processes in school-university partnerships. *Planning and Changing, 42*, 63–86.

Gorski, P. C. (2013). *Reaching and teaching students in poverty: Strategies for erasing the opportunity gap.* New York, NY: Teachers College Press.

Hargreaves, A., & Braun, H. (2013). *Data-driven improvement and accountability.* Boulder, CO: National Education Policy Center. Retrieved from http://nepc.colorado.edu/publication/data-driven-improvement-accountability/

Horng, E., & Loeb, S. (2010). New thinking about instructional leadership. *Phi Delta Kappan, 92*(3), 66–69. doi:10.1177/003172171009200319

Hurtado, S. (2007). Linking diversity with the educational and civic missions of higher education. *The Review of Higher Education, 30*, 185-196. doi:10.1353/rhe.2006.0070

Knapp, M. S., & Feldman, S. B. (2012). Managing the intersection of internal and external accountability: Challenge for urban school leadership in the United States. *Journal of Educational Administration, 50*, 666–694. doi:10.1108/09578231211249862

Ladson-Billings, G. (2008). A letter to our next president. *Journal of Teacher Education, 59*(3), 235–239. doi:10.1177/0022487108317466

The Leadership Conference on Civil and Human Rights. (2015, May 5). *Civil rights groups: "We oppose anti-testing efforts"* [Press release]. Retrieved from https://civilrights.org/civil-rights-groups-we-oppose-anti-testing-efforts/

Leithwood, K., Harris, A., & Hopkins, D. (2008). Seven strong claims about successful school leadership. *School Leadership and Management, 28*, 27–42. doi:10.1080/13632430701800060

Louis, S. L., Leithwood, K., Wahlstrom, K. L., & Anderson, S. E. (2010). *Investigating the links to improved student learning: Final report of research findings*. St. Paul, MN: University of Minnesota, Center for Applied Research and Educational Improvement. Retrieved from https://www.wallacefoundation.org/knowledge-center/Documents/Investigating-the-Links-to-Improved-Student-Learning.pdf

Manna, P. (2015). *Developing excellent school principals to advance teaching and learning: Considerations for state policy*. New York: Wallace Foundation. Retrieved from https://www.wallacefoundation.org/knowledge-center/Documents/Developing-Excellent-School-Principals.pdf

Mavrogordato, M., & White, R. S. (2017). Reclassification variation: How policy implementation guides the process of exiting students from English learner status. *Educational Evaluation and Policy Analysis, 39*, 281–310. doi:10.3102/0162373716687075

Maxwell, G. M., Locke, L. A., & Scheurich, J. J. (2013). Case study of three rural Texas superintendents as equity oriented change agents. *The Qualitative Report, 18*(11), 1–23. Retrieved from https://nsuworks.nova.edu/tqr/vol18/iss11/2

McLeskey, J., Waldron, N. L., & Redd, L. (2014). A case study of a highly effective, inclusive elementary school. *The Journal of Special Education, 48*, 59–70. doi:10.1177/0022466912440455

Moll, L. C., Amanti, C., Neff, D., & Gonzalez, N. (1992). Funds of knowledge for teaching: Using a qualitative approach to connect homes and classrooms. *Theory into Practice, 31*, 132–141. doi:10.1080/00405849209543534

Moses, M. S. (2002). *Embracing race: Why we need race-conscious education policy*. New York, NY: Teachers College Press.

Orr, M. T., & Orphanos, S. (2011). How graduate-level preparation influences the effectiveness of school leaders: A comparison of the outcomes of exemplary and conventional leadership preparation programs for principals. *Educational Administration Quarterly, 47*, 18–70. doi:10.1177/0011000010378610

Pazey, B., & Cole, H. (2013). The role of special education training in the development of socially just leaders: Building an equity consciousness in educational leadership programs. *Educational Administration Quarterly, 49*, 243–271. doi:10.1177/0013161X12463934

Perilla, N. (2014). Leading the future: Rethinking principal preparation and accountability frameworks. *Harvard Journal of Hispanic Policy, 26*, 59–69.

Quin, J., Deris, A., Bischoff, G., & Johnson, J. T. (2015). Comparison of transformational leadership practices: Implications for school districts and principal preparation programs. *Journal of Leadership Education, 14*(3), 71–85. doi:10.12806/v14/i3/r5

Rigby, J. G., & Tredway, L. (2015). Actions matter: How school leaders enact equity principles. In M. Khalifa, N. W. Arnold, A. F. Osanloo, & C. M. Grant (Eds.), *Handbook of Urban Educational Leadership* (pp. 329–348). Lanham, MD: Rowman & Littlefield.

Ryan, J. (2012). *Struggling for inclusion: Educational leadership in neoliberal times.* Greenwich, CT: Information Age.

Ryan, J., & Higginbottom, K. (2017). Politics, activism and leadership for social justice in education. In D. Waite & I. Bogotch (Eds.), *International handbook of leadership in education* (pp. 103–124), Hoboken, NJ: Wiley-Blackwell. doi:10.1002/9781118956717.ch6

Rosenberg, M. S., Brownell, M., McCray, E. D., deBettencourt, L. U., Leko, M., Long, S. (2009). *Development and sustainability of school-university partnerships in special education teacher preparation: A critical review of the literature* (NCIPP Document No. RS-3). Gainesville, FL: National Center to Inform Policy and Practice in Special Education Professional Development.

Scribner, J. D., Aleman, E., & Maxcy, B. (2003). Emergence of the politics of education field: Making sense of a messy center. *Educational Administration Quarterly, 39*, 10–40. doi:10.1177/0013161X02239759

Skrla, L., McKenzie, K. B., & Scheurich, J. J. (2011). Becoming an equity-oriented change agent. In A. M. Blankstein & P. D. Houston (Eds.), *Leadership for social justice and democracy in our schools* (pp. 45–58). Thousand Oaks, CA: Corwin. doi:10.4135/9781506335278.n3

Theoharis, G. (2007). Social justice educational leaders and resistance: Toward a theory of social justice leadership. *Educational Administration Quarterly, 43*, 221–258. doi:10.1177/0013161X06293717

Theoharis, G. (2009). *The school leaders our children deserve: Seven keys to equity, social justice, and school reform.* New York, NY: Teachers College Press.

Welner, K. G., & Carter, P. L. (2013). Achievement gaps arise from opportunity gaps. In P. Carter & K. Welner (Eds.), *Closing the opportunity gap: What America must do to give all children an even chance* (pp. 1–10). New York, NY: Oxford University Press. doi:10.1093/acprof:oso/9780199982981.003.0001

Welner, K., & Farley, A. N. (2010). *Confronting systemic inequity in education: High impact strategies for philanthropy.* Washington, DC: National Committee for Responsive Philanthropy. Retrieved from http://www.racialequitytools.org/resourcefiles/ncrp1.pdf

SECTION VII INTRODUCTION

STATE SUPPORT FOR INCLUSIVE PRACTICE

The role of the state in the enormously important project of public education is multifaceted and presents a confusing and contested array of functions and purposes. The dissemination of information across the state, development of legislation, granting of educator licenses, and the development of standards in keeping with those of the professional associations that provide national leadership in effective and ethical practice are critical. However, perhaps the essential purpose of the state department of education is to help educators across the state integrate services in the interest of making sure all students are provided equitable education programs.

In "State Support for Inclusive Practice: Perspectives from CEEDAR," Nancy Corbett, Lois Kimmel, and Paul Sindelar describe the CEEDAR Center's reform work, guided by the U.S. Office of Special Education Programs' 2012 initiative to establish a technical assistance center to support the development of effective educators to serve students with disabilities and to build capacity within and among educational systems by establishing collaborative teams of key stakeholders from state education agencies, institutions of higher education, and local education agencies. Orienting to the restructuring of teacher preparation, the authors explain program evaluation of relevant coursework and practice-based opportunities, the integration of high-leverage research-based practices, dissemination of practices that foster collaboration and sustainability, and identification of policy and practices that support reform of educator licensure standards.

In "History and Progress of the Ohio Deans Compact on Exceptional Children," Cassondra Faiella, drawing on her interview with Deborah Telfer and Aimee Howley, discusses the theoretical underpinnings of the

Inclusive Education: A Systematic Perspective, pp. 421–422

Ohio Deans Compact, a consortium of Ohio education professionals. This chapter describes the consortium's effort, its history and purpose, and the structures and practices that have given the Deans Compact an authoritative voice in statewide deliberations about education policy and the implementation of effective and inclusive education practices.

In "The Effect of State Policy on the Educational Environments of Students With Disabilities," Rebecca Watts discusses quantitative and qualitative analyses used to assess states' inclusive education policies. She explains the relationship of educator preparation policies, the credentialing structure, and the number of educators holding a dual license or an integrated license to the educational environments of learners with disabilities. The chapter concludes with recommendations for state policy design and implementation and credentialing structures.

In the final chapter, "Partnership for Statewide Improvement of Educator Preparation," Beverly Sande discusses the implications of collaboration between stakeholders and highlights the need for sustained efforts for replication in other states. Her chapter outlines key elements of collaborative practice such as documentation of shared values, formation of academic alliances, and emphasis on partnership grant programs between university stakeholders and stakeholders from P–12 schools, regional support teams, and the state department of education.

This section concludes our efforts to share work at Ohio institutions and at partner institutions elsewhere to promote equitable and inclusive education. Throughout all of the sections, we have explored the social justice underpinnings of inclusive education from a collaborative systems perspective. The internationally esteemed educator, Paulo Freire, saw education as a means of transforming systems through inquiry and dialog about practice; and our goal in publishing these accounts of the progress we have made so far, and what we have learned as we made progress is to encourage inquiry and dialog about practice in other educators' classrooms, schools, districts, universities, and state systems. We hope, too, that we have presented some possibilities for changes in practice that can be adapted to help advance inclusive education nationwide.

CHAPTER 24

STATE SUPPORT FOR INCLUSIVE PRACTICE

Perspectives From CEEDAR

Nancy L. Corbett
University of Florida

Lois Kimmel
American Institutes for Research

Paul Sindelar
University of Florida

The Collaboration for Effective Educator Development, Accountability, and Reform (CEEDAR) is a technical assistance (TA) center, funded by the U.S. Department of Education's Office of Special Education Programs (CEEDAR, 2015a). Housed at the University of Florida (UF; CEEDAR, 2015e), its partners include the American Institutes for Research (AIR) and the Council of Chief State School Officers (CEEDAR, 2015a). CEEDAR provides TA to states that have committed to reforming educator preparation policy and practice (CEEDAR, 2015a) so that students with disabilities meet college and career ready standards. In this chapter, we describe the strategies and resources that supported state efforts to restructure teacher preparation programs, and we report on CEEDAR's work in Ohio.

Inclusive Education: A Systematic Perspective, pp. 423–434
Copyright © 2020 by Information Age Publishing

Effective general and special education teachers are key to ensuring that students with disabilities develop the necessary skills to be college and career ready. Research focusing on both general and special education demonstrates that knowledgeable and skilled teachers play an essential role in student achievement (Bill & Melinda Gates Foundation, 2012; Brownell, Billingsley, McLeskey, & Sindelar, 2012; Leithwood, Seashore Louise, Anderson, & Wahlstrom, 2004). Despite such research, our systems for preparing, licensing, developing, and supporting teachers to provide effective instruction to students with disabilities remain insufficient (Sindelar, Brownell, & Billingsley, 2010). These systems fall short because they do not always draw on clearly articulated evidence-based instructional practices. They also fall short because they do not make consistent use of research-based approaches to teacher development or tie these approaches to actual implementation in schools and classrooms.

In 2012, the Office of Special Education Programs prioritized the funding and establishment of a TA center to support the development of effective educators for students with disabilities. The vision for the center was to assist state education agencies, institutions of higher education (IHEs), and local education agencies (LEAs) with the collaborative development of state systems (CEEDAR, 2015a) to ensure that teachers and educational leaders would possess the necessary knowledge and skills—grounded in research-based practices—successfully to meet the diverse needs of students with disabilities. Established in 2013, CEEDAR has worked with and offered TA to 20 states (see Figure 24.1) and more than 60 IHEs, building the capacity of personnel within state education agencies, preparation programs, and districts to ensure that teachers and leaders are well prepared to support a diverse range of learners.

TECHNICAL ASSISTANCE FOR EDUCATOR PREPARATION REFORM

The CEEDAR approach to TA rests on three principles found in the professional development literature (e.g., Desimone, 2009). First, systemic change depends on carefully designed learning supports that enable teacher educators to acquire the necessary knowledge and skills for reforming their curricula. Second, developing the knowledge and skills, and the ability to use that knowledge to solve problems, takes time. Third, a coherent and aligned policy structure—linking standards for student learning, licensure standards, a curriculum for enacting the standards, well designed professional development, and evaluation—is more likely than a less coherent approach to promote the desired change.

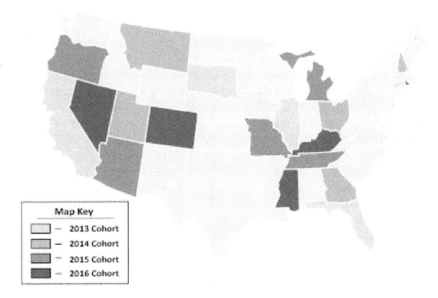

Source: Adapted from "CEEDAR State-by-State" by CEEDAR Center, 2015.
Retrieved from http://ceedar.education.ufl.edu/

Figure 24.1.   Map of CEEDAR state partners organized by cohort.

In order to be responsive to the various needs of educator preparation stakeholders, TA providers must find innovative ways to offer comprehensive services. CEEDAR provides TA at three levels of intensity: universal, targeted, and intensive (McCray, Kamman, Brownell, & Robinson, 2017). This format allows interested states to access products and services in ways that accommodate their unique needs, interests, and circumstances. To reform practice in teacher education while at the same time aligning state policies to support those reforms requires deliberate and intensive work. CEEDAR, therefore, ensures that all interested states have access to resources (e.g., CEEDAR, 2015d) through universal and targeted assistance, but prioritizes intensive TA and provides additional products and services to those states receiving intensive assistance. Through these formats, CEEDAR is able to provide widespread support for relevant changes in the curriculum and delivery of educator preparation programs across the nation.

Several tools support CEEDAR's intensive TA (e.g., CEEDAR, 2015b), allowing participants to analyze current practices and formulate a concrete understanding of what steps they might take to change their practice. For example, innovation configurations—rubrics that specify the essential evidence-based components of various practices that need to be infused in educator preparation curricula (e.g., writing instruction or culturally responsive teaching)—form the basis for much of the knowledge-building and design work (CEEDAR, 2015b). Innovation configurations have been used for over 30 years (Roy & Hord, 2004) and can be employed by teacher educators to determine the extent to which evidence-based practices are taught, observed, and applied in educator preparation programs. Using this resource, teacher educators can identify gaps and redundancies within their programs. This collaborative process involves: examining syllabi, texts, assignments, and field placements and discussing (a) the types of instruction and experiences that promote the use of evidence-based instructional practices, which teachers receive throughout their preparation and/or professional development, and (b) the extent to which teachers and teacher candidates are provided with an opportunity to apply these strategies with explicit feedback that ensures fidelity and leads to sustained implementation (see CEEDAR, 2015b).

Other related TA resources include the guidance document *High-Leverage Practices in Special Education* (McLeskey et al., 2017). The rationale for this document is the belief that teacher preparation programs need to focus on the essential content and instructional practices of effective teaching—"practices that can be used to leverage student learning across different content areas, grade levels, and student abilities and disabilities" (McLeskey et al., 2017, p. 9). In response to this need, the Council for Exceptional Children collaborated with CEEDAR to conduct a review of frequently used classroom practices that have been shown to improve student outcomes. These high-leverage practices are fundamentals of teaching, organized around four components of teacher practice: collaboration, assessment, social/emotional/behavioral practices, and instruction (McLeskey et al., 2017). High-leverage practices can be used by educator preparation programs to design a set of coherent and carefully sequenced opportunities for teacher candidates to apply their knowledge in practical settings and receive feedback about their practice (Leko, Sindelar, Brownell, & Kiely 2015).

One of CEEDAR's primary tasks involves assisting states to ensure that teachers receive the necessary preparation to provide evidence-based instruction to students with disabilities and to those who struggle with learning, so that all students will be prepared for college and a career. In order to ensure that students make gains in academic and behavioral learning, teacher educators, teachers, and administrators need to be able to identify and implement evidence-based practices with fidelity. From CEEDAR's perspective, therefore, it is essential that preparation programs and professional development providers offer quality instruction, well-crafted learning experiences, and sustained support—support that includes giving quality feedback to educators as they learn and implement these practices. To accomplish this task, CEEDAR offers professional learning modules that demonstrate how evidence-based practices can be used to support rigorous content instruction. CEEDAR's professional learning modules, designed for adult learners, include usable learning activities that promote authentic practice for educators. These resources are available on CEEDAR's website (www.ceedar.org).

Other CEEDAR efforts include work in various states to strengthen collaboration, coordination, and alignment among the state education agency (SEA), Local Education Agencies (LEAs), and Institutions of Higher Education (IHEs). This approach was used in Michigan to support Michigan's Top 10 in 10 Years and Every Student Succeeds initiatives. Through deepened collaborations, Michigan now prioritizes five High-Leverage Practices (HLPs) to implement across the preservice to in-service teacher continuum.

Similarly, TA work in Kentucky convinced the SEA, LEAs, and IHEs to commit to improving the quality of educator preparation in the state, ensuring that all teachers understand HLPs and the delivery of evidence-based practices. Using innovation configurations, Kentucky IHEs conducted syllabi and program reviews in order to determine course revisions to improve the quality of teacher preparation.

In the next section, we describe CEEDAR's efforts in Ohio. We describe how the three participating IHEs—the University of Dayton (UD), the University of Cincinnati (UC), and Kent State University (KSU)—used innovation configurations, professional learning modules, and high-leverage practices in the reforms they undertook.[1]

THE CEEDAR PARTNERSHIP WITH OHIO

The Ohio Deans Compact on Exceptional Children (or Deans Compact) is an advisory group to the Ohio Department of Education and the Ohio Department of Higher Education. Its membership includes representatives from the Ohio Department of Education (ODE), Ohio Department of Higher Education (ODHE), and LEAs, as well as deans, associate deans, and the heads of teacher education programs at four-year institutions.

In 2014, the Deans Compact applied for intensive TA from CEEDAR in order to improve Ohio's system of educator preparation and personnel development and more effectively prepare all educators to teach and support all learners. One of the Deans Compact's key initiatives included competitive grant awards for IHEs to incentivize the redesign of educator preparation program and other innovative restructuring efforts that lead to more inclusive teacher education and educational leadership models. The Deans Compact requested TA to support specific IHEs in redesigning their programs to develop dual-licensure educator preparation programs that integrate special and general education content (see Chapter 25, "Progress of the Work").

UC, UD, and KSU were among the first recipients of the Deans Compact Incentive Grants for developing dual-licensure programs in middle childhood and special education (i.e., intervention specialist) for mild/ moderate disabilities. The goals of dual-licensure reform include: (a) improving pre-service general and special education preparation; (b) infusing evidence-based practices into program content; (c) narrowing the knowledge gap that separates special education and general education faculty; and (d) increasing collaboration among key stakeholders, including public school partners. The incentive grants promoted collaborative inquiry between UC, UD, KSU, and other Ohio institutions and aimed to improve capacity in educator preparation programs in order to provide effective education for all students, including students with disabilities. In 2014, these three institutions also received a supplemental award of CEEDAR funds, via the Deans Compact, to facilitate substantial implementation of their incentive grant activities.

Each partner institution designed specific grant activities to accomplish the goals of dual-licensure reform. Information about the implementation and status of dual-licensure programs around the country was of particular interest to the partner IHEs as well as other Deans Compact members. In response to a TA request, CEEDAR staff developed a guide to secondary/special education dual-licensure programs (see CEEDAR, 2015c). The guide provides relevant information to those examining the essential components of dual-licensure programs, including program length, licensure area, cohort size, and descriptions of coursework and field placements. The partner institutions found it challenging to design field placements and practice-based opportunities that met course objectives, program approval requirements, and licensure standards; but the dual-licensure guide proved to be a useful resource to IHEs, helping them identify and meet with cross-state colleagues (both virtually and face-to-face) to discuss the development, coordination, and implementation of clinical and field experiences.

All of the CEEDAR/Ohio IHE partners extensively used innovation configurations to examine course syllabi and guide the revisions of their courses within the dual-licensure program. UC, UD, and KSU targeted evidence-based and high-leverage practices for integration in their middle grades/intervention specialist dual-licensure programs. UC targeted universal design for learning and culturally responsive pedagogy, UD focused on collaboration and co-teaching, and KSU pursued the use of instructional technology (i.e., TeachLivE™) to enhance clinical practice. Each institution used the additional CEEDAR funding to hire consultants who enhanced faculty knowledge and skills related to the targeted practices.

The anticipated result of incentive grant funding and the CEEDAR TA provided to UC, UD, and KSU is the implementation at each institution of an approved dual-licensure program. In 2015, the UD Middle Childhood/Intervention Specialist (MCIS) program received approval from UD and the Ohio Department of Higher Education; UD implemented the MCIS program in the fall of that year. UD faculty in the MCIS program will collect evaluation data as seniors begin to complete the program. UC has also received institutional approval as well as approval from the Ohio Department of Higher Education, and KSU is addressing questions raised by its institutional curriculum committee.

EVALUATION

Ohio IHEs figure prominently in the CEEDAR Center's ongoing evaluation efforts. Given the scope of Center's work—with 20 intensive states and upwards of 60 colleges and universities that prepare teachers and leaders (CEEDAR, 2015a)—evaluating the Center is a complex and multifaceted process. A team of scholars from the UF, AIR, and the Meadows Center at the University of Texas, Austin (UT) undertook this responsibility (CEEDAR, 2013). UF and AIR collaborate on formative evaluation activities and work with UT on the summative evaluation. Formative evaluation occurs annually to assess progress on performance measures for an annual performance report. The summative evaluation described here is more substantive and, therefore, more relevant for our purposes. Two Ohio universities, KSU and UC, have contributed substantially to this process.

The summative evaluation plan involves classroom observations and surveys that assess both the capacity that educator preparation programs develop for undertaking additional reforms and the impact of involvement with CEEDAR on programs' preparation policy and practice (CEEDAR, 2013). Initially, the evaluation team anticipated observing the classroom practices of the reformed teacher preparation programs' graduates and assessing their impact on student learning. The evaluation team intended to compare the performance of these graduates (and of the kindergarten through Grade 12 [K–12] students they taught) to the performance of the pre-reformed programs' graduates (and their K–12 students). We anticipated that such comparisons would reveal differences in practice and impact that could be attributed to the reforms undertaken by the participating IHEs. Unfortunately, we underestimated the time required for IHEs to redesign their programs and obtain institutional and state approval. In fact, only one institution implemented a reformed program during the Center's first five-year cycle—the Urban Dual Credential Program (UDCP) at Cal State, Long Beach.

Because the UDCP was a new program, and not the revision of an existing program, we could not compare pre- and post-reform graduates. Nevertheless, a similar effort is possible, and scholars from the Meadows Center are currently collecting classroom performance data for pre-merger graduates of the two individual programs that now make up the UDCP—in California, these are known as multiple subjects, elementary and education specialist (or special education)—as well as UDCP graduates. We hope to establish that UDCP graduates are as capable as the graduates of both the multiple subjects and education specialist programs. We have also gathered pre-reform data on Master of Arts in Teaching students at Central Connecticut State University, and post-reform data will also be collected. We had hoped to observe KSU and UC graduates, but the program approval process slowed implementation at these two institutions, with neither program implemented during CEEDAR's first cycle.

Along with Long Beach and Central Connecticut, however, KSU and UC did participate in the capacity survey. Generally speaking, this survey assessed faculty involvement in program reform and the capacity that the institution developed (as a result of participating in reform) to undertake additional initiatives. Because reforms and reform processes differed from institution to institution, the survey asked some differentiated questions regarding the nature of the reform process. Participants from all four IHEs, however, responded to questions about: communication; obstacles and facilitators of reform as they related to leadership, professional development, and data use; and interest and involvement in future reform efforts. The evaluation team prepared write-ups of the findings for and discussed them with each of the participating IHEs, and the team's final reports incorporated feedback from the IHEs.

Findings from the UC survey provide an example of the feedback that the survey supplied to CEEDAR and its evaluators. UC had been engaged in a long series of program reforms and restructuring work, beginning over a decade ago with its effort to reform special education preparation via a U. S. Department of Education grant. Subsequently, UC developed a dual-licensure program in middle grades and special education and participated in the professional development offered by CEEDAR. We surveyed 30 UC faculty members (not all of whom had been involved in these reforms) and found that, as a result of its own successful experience with reform, UC had developed not only a capacity but also an appetite for assisting colleagues at other IHEs who were undertaking reform and who were new to the reform process. This finding proved important because one goal for UC, written into the blueprint CEEDAR developed for Ohio's intensive TA, focused on supporting similar reform work at other institutions.

As we write this chapter, the CEEDAR Evaluation Team is embarking on the last phase of summative evaluation: the impact survey. This survey will be sent to leadership team members in all 20 intensive states to assess their perspectives of CEEDAR's impact on program reform and approval and candidate assessment. Taken together, these measures provide case-study portraits of four institutions that have undertaken significant programmatic reforms using CEEDAR TA. Thus, in our final report, we will describe the reforms undertaken at the participating institutions, the capacities that these institutions developed as a result of their participation, and the impact of those reforms on preparation policy and practice. For Central Connecticut and Long Beach, these findings will be complemented by comparative observations of teachers who completed traditional pre-reform programs and those who completed reformed programs. When published, this work will represent the most in-depth study of program reform yet to appear in the literature.

We learned from the evaluation (and from our own experience) that the redesign of teacher and leader preparation programs is, indeed, complex work. For example, developing dual-licensure educator preparation programs that integrate special and general education content and incorporate appropriate clinical experiences, requires more support and time than is needed to implement simpler, prescribed reforms (Damschroder et al., 2009). We also learned that, while stakeholders may share a commitment to improving student learning, they sometimes resist efforts to implement reforms that run counter to their views about which organizational and instructional practices are effective. This finding is similar to results reported from Denton and colleagues' study (Denton, Vaughan, & Fletcher, 2003). Finally, engaging with complex innovations like program reform can require great effort from stakeholders, and stakeholders may be reluctant to exert such effort if the benefits of doing so are not immediately realized (Greenhalgh, Robert, Macfarlane, Bate, & Kyriakidou, 2004).

NEXT STEPS

CEEDAR's first iteration accomplished important steps toward enhancing the capacity of teacher and leader preparation systems to prepare graduates to serve all students, including those with disabilities. Most notably, CEEDAR deepened collaboration within states, helped them align policy and practice, and improved educator preparation using research-based tools.

Several lessons learned over the past five years—supporting collaboration between states and IHEs to promote complex, sustainable change in teacher and leader preparation that improves outcomes for all students (including those with disabilities)—inform CEEDAR 2.0's TA approach (see CEEDAR, 2018). In CEEDAR 2.0, we plan to offer services in a more individualized and responsive manner, accompanied by repeated progress and needs assessments. Information from state leads, updated blueprints, and progress reports will be used in this collaborative process. CEEDAR 1.0 intensive states will be expected to emphasize efforts to sustain or scale up the reforms they achieved in the first cycle. We will add some new intensive states, but even they will participate in this more focused, efficient, and direct approach to intensive TA. This TA approach is fluid in that it responds to the current needs and priorities of the state. It relies on assessment to determine a state's readiness to undertake or continue educator preparation policy and practice reform, and to identify necessary TA supports and services.

CEEDAR will continue to provide multilevel TA. Universal TA, including access to the website, remains available to all interested stakeholders. The website continues to archive the previously described innovation configurations and professional learning modules. In addition, it provides access to policy briefs, public webinars, written TA responses, and connections with a national network of TA centers. Targeted TA is focused and designed to support states in either building or maintaining their momentum toward goals. States receiving targeted TA supports can participate in communities of practice, which CEEDAR refers to as cross-state learning groups. CEEDAR differentiates its cross-state learning groups according to states' readiness and needs. Through these cross-state learning groups, participants introduce and explore topics of interest related to CEEDAR's mission and state needs, engage in a deeper examination of selected topics related to blueprint goals, or participate in a focused inquiry on common topics of interest or problems of practice. Additionally, targeted states have the option to receive support from consultants with specific expertise in the reform of policy and practice. Finally, intensive TA involves a more deliberate and focused approach in order to provide individualized support to states as they develop or sustain momentum toward blueprint goals aligned to CEEDAR's mission.

SUMMARY

The desired outcomes for CEEDAR's TA seem ambitious: reformed teacher and leader education programs that incorporate high-leverage and evidence-based practices, improved capacity for evaluating teacher and leader education programs, scaling up teacher and leader education program reform statewide, and a coherent and aligned state policy structure that supports effective preparation program reforms for teachers and leaders. But in its first iteration, CEEDAR made strides toward achieving these goals by collaborating with states that were willing to tackle this complex work. Ohio, through the Deans Compact, set out to achieve the goal of statewide reform of educator preparation and worked to align its policy structure through its own support (in league with CEEDAR) of the Deans Compact. The Deans Compact serves as an example to other states seeking to establish structures that support the reform of educator preparation. The Deans Compact strategies with the greatest promise include a grant program incentivizing education program redesign, the establishment of a community of practice for representatives of funded incentive grant institutions, professional development opportunities embedded in quarterly meetings and an annual statewide conference.

NOTE

1. For additional information regarding any of the programs listed in this chapter, refer to the interactive map on the CEEDAR website home page (CEEDAR, 2015a).

REFERENCES

Bill & Melinda Gates Foundation. (2012). *Gathering feedback for teaching: Combining high-quality observations with student surveys and achievement gains.* Retrieved from http://www.metproject.org/downloads/MET_Gathering_Feedback_ Practioner_Brief.pdf

Brownell, M. T., Billingsley, B. S., McLeskey, J., & Sindelar, P. T. (2012). Teacher quality and effectiveness in an era of accountability: Challenges and solutions in special education? In J. B. B. Crockett, B. Billingsley, & M. L. Boscardin (Eds.), *Handbook of leadership for special education* (pp. 260–280). New York, NY: Taylor & Francis.

CEEDAR. (2013). *Collaboration for effective educator development, accountability, and reform center: Final center evaluation plan.* Retrieved from http://ceedar. education.ufl.edu/wp-content/uploads/2014/09/CEEDAR-Evaluation-Plan. pdf

CEEDAR. (2015a). *CEEDAR Center.* Retrieved from http://ceedar.education.ufl.edu

CEEDAR. (2015b). *Innovation configurations.* Retrieved from http://ceedar.education. ufl.edu/tools/innovation-configurations/

CEEDAR. (2015c). *Policy snapshot-dual-certification.* Retrieved from https://ceedar. education.ufl.edu/portfolio/policy-snapshot-dual-certification/

CEEDAR. (2015d). *Teacher and leader preparation resources.* Retrieved from http:// ceedar.education.ufl.edu/teacher-and-leader-preparation/

CEEDAR. (2015e). *University of Florida.* Retrieved from http://ceedar.education.ufl. edu/university-of-florida/

CEEDAR (2018). *The CEEDAR Center 2.0–Where we've been and where we're going.* Retrieved from https://ceedar.education.ufl.edu/portfolio/ceedar-2-0-where-weve-been-and-where-were-going/

Damschroder, L. J., Aron, D. C., Keith, R. E., Kirsh, S. R., Alexander, J. A., & Lowery, J. C. (2009). Fostering implementation of health services research findings into practice: A consolidated framework for advancing implementation science. *Implementation Science, 4*(1), 50. doi:10.1186/1748-5908-4-50

Denton, C. A., Vaughn, S., & Fletcher, J. M. (2003). Bringing research-based practice in reading intervention to scale. *Learning Disabilities Research and Practice, 18*, 201–211. doi:10.1111/1540-5826.00075

Desimone, L. M. (2009). Improving impact studies of teachers' professional development: Toward better conceptualizations and measures. *Educational Researcher, 38*, 181–199. doi:10.3102/0013189X08331140

Greenhalgh, T., Robert, G., Macfarlane, F., Bate, P., & Kyriakidou, O. (2004). Diffusion of innovations in service organizations: Systematic review and recommendations. *The Milbank Quarterly, 82*, 581–629. doi:10.1111/j.0887-378X.2004.00325.x

Leithwood, K., Seashore Louis, K., Anderson, S., Wahlstrom, K. (2004). *How leadership influences student learning. The Wallace Foundation.* Retrieved from http://www.wallacefoundation.org/knowledge-center/school-leadership/key-research/Pages/How-Leadership-Influences-Student-Learning.aspx

Leko, M. M., Brownell, M. T., Sindelar, P. T., & Kiely, M. T. (2015). Envisioning the future of special education personnel preparation in a standards-based era. *Exceptional Children, 82*, 25–43. doi:10.1177/0014402915598782

McCray, E. D., Kamman, M., Brownell, M. T., & Robinson, S. (2017). *High-leverage practices and evidence-based practices: A promising pair.* Gainsville, FL: CEEDAR Center. Retrieved from http://ceedar.education.ufl.edu/wp-content/uploads/2017/12/HLPs-and-EBPs-A-Promising-Pair.pdf

McLeskey, J., Barringer, M-D., Billingsley, B., Brownell, M., Jackson, D., Kennedy, M., … Ziegler, D. (2017). *High-leverage practices in special education.* Arlington, VA: Council for Exceptional Children & CEEDAR Center.

Roy, P., & Hord, S. M. (2004). Innovation configurations chart a measured course toward change. *Journal of Staff Development, 25*(2), 54–58.

Sindelar, P. T., Brownell, M. T., & Billingsley, B. S. (2010). Special education teacher education research: Current status and future directions. *Teacher Education and Special Education, 33*, 8–24. doi:10.1177/0888406409358593

CHAPTER 25

HISTORY AND PROGRESS OF THE OHIO DEANS COMPACT ON EXCEPTIONAL CHILDREN

Cassondra M. Faiella
The University of Cincinnati

INTRODUCTION

This chapter uses information from interviews with two of the founding members of the Ohio Deans Compact (also called the Deans Compact, or just the Compact) to discuss its establishment and accomplishments to date. In January 2018, I conducted individual phone interviews with Deborah Telfer, Director of the Systems Development & Improvement Center at the University of Cincinnati (D. Telfer, personal communication, January 17, 2018), and with Aimee Howley, Professor Emerita in Ohio University's Patton College of Education (A. Howley, personal communication, January 17, 2018). I transcribed the interviews and used the transcripts as the basis for this chapter. I extracted excerpts from the interviews for the purpose of illustrating the points that the interviewees made.

The Compact's overarching goal is to improve educator preparation in Ohio by bringing together a broad-based coalition to reform and

Inclusive Education: A Systematic Perspective, pp. 435–449
Copyright © 2020 by Information Age Publishing
435

restructure educator preparation programs so that graduating teachers and principals are able to meet the learning needs of *all* children, however diverse (The Ohio Deans Compact on Exceptional Children, 2018a). The Compact's primary strategy is to cultivate a networked community of practice—including Compact members and like-minded colleagues who share a commitment to equity and social justice—which will serve as the basis for expanding statewide use of inclusive educational practices (The Ohio Deans Compact on Exceptional Children, 2018b).

Creating the Deans Compact was the co-founders' response to three structural dynamics that they identified to be weakening Ohio's system of educator preparation. The first dynamic—and the one most central to the Compact's work—involves the division between special education and general education for both teachers and higher education faculty members. Such a division exists nationwide, of course, not just in Ohio (e.g., Frattura & Capper, 2007; Pugach, Blanton, & Correa, 2011). Telfer elaborated on this division:

> The big need we wanted to address was finding ways to move beyond this dichotomy of special education and general education sitting in their own boxes and challenge the long-standing assumptions that only people with a special education credential should ever teach a child with a disability. We wanted to get at that by looking at Ohio's system of preparation and ongoing personnel development, figuring out what strategic changes we could make, figuring out how we could affect the system in ways that everybody coming out of preparation programs—whether they were superintendents, principals, teachers, intervention specialists, or related services personnel—would understand that their job was to teach and support all children, no matter the label, and that they would be better prepared to do that.... It is trying to get adults to think differently about what they do instructionally to support kids, whether they are English learners, come from poverty, or whatever category they fall under.

The structures of both prekindergarten through 12th grade (PK–12) schools (Frattura & Capper, 2007) and educator preparation programs in institutions of higher education (IHEs; Pugach et al., 2011) reflect the underlying assumption that teaching typically developing children differs from teaching children with disabilities or children who have other types of learning needs (e.g., English learners) and that such teaching requires educators to have specialized skills for working with each type of student (McLeskey & Waldron, 2000). As a result, PK–12 schools often group and educate students based on perceived learning needs (e.g., segregating students with learning disabilities in special education classrooms; Frattura & Capper, 2007). Teacher preparation programs at colleges and universities tend to perpetuate this artificial division as well (Pugach et al., 2011).

Because teacher candidates at most universities must choose between special education and general education tracks, they often learn different practices. As Howley described it, "this thinking [is] not completely wrong, it just does not conceptualize the issue in a way that leads to inclusion. It conceptualizes the issue in a way that leads to exclusion." Given these structural silos, colleges and universities tend to produce new teachers who feel inadequate for the task of educating all students in their classrooms (e.g., Hamman, Lechtenberger, Griffin-Shirley, & Zhou, 2012). In fact, many new general education teachers are reluctant to assume responsibility for all students, especially those with unusual learning needs resulting from a disability, a first language other than English, or from experiencing economic or cultural marginalization. Similarly, structural divisions within IHEs keep principal preparation programs from graduating candidates with adequate capacity to support inclusive practices in their schools and districts (Cambron-McCabe & McCarthy, 2005).

The second dynamic concerns disconnects between PK–12 districts, teacher preparation programs, and the state education agency (in this case, the Ohio Department of Education or ODE). Disconnects between these three types of institutions occur nationally (e.g., Bartell, 2001; Stone, 2015); in Ohio (and perhaps elsewhere), they often limit the ability of PK–12 educators to engage with IHEs in curriculum reform work that supports state priorities. Difficulties arise, in part, because there are few incentives for IHEs to become involved. Since IHEs have a significant influence on educational practices, through their work to prepare new educators, their involvement in education reform initiatives is crucial. Reflecting this priority, Telfer described the Deans Compact as an initiative

> to get higher education in the room with the state, with district professional association partners, so that we were a community taking on this work together. Rather than forcing people, they would become invested in that mission and begin to work together and own it. It was a forum for doing that.

As a result of limited communication between the PK–12 system and state officials and policymakers (e.g., Levin & Van Hoorn, 2016), the third dynamic relates to gaps or lags in local awareness (at the PK–12 level) of statewide issues as well as in state-level awareness of local issues (e.g., issues in particular districts or regions). An example in Ohio concerns the shortage of qualified educators to work with students with low-incidence sensory disabilities (LISDs)—visual impairments, hearing impairments, and deaf blindness (Howley & Howley, 2016). PK–12 schools need qualified personnel to fill open positions, and the existing programs that prepare teachers to work with students with lLISDs produce too few teachers

(Howley & Howley, 2016; Howley, Howley, & Telfer, 2017). PK–12 schools, especially those in rural parts of the state, need a solution that will quickly provide high-quality teachers. The educators who started the Deans Compact saw the organization as a means for encouraging IHEs to respond rapidly to statewide needs—on the one hand, by interpreting local and regional needs to the ODE and, on the other hand, by translating ODE priorities to IHEs. Telfer further elaborated on the Compact's role as liaison:

> The Deans Compact could advise the state on issues as they arose. For example, we know we have huge shortages in certain areas, like low-incidence sensory disabilities; we have known it for years. So, determining what a group like this could do to change teacher preparation programs is a key piece of the work of the Compact. Operating in this way, the Compact can address state needs as they are identified.

HISTORY AND ORGANIZATION OF THE OHIO DEANS COMPACT

Once the educators who established the Deans Compact—notably Sue Zake (now retired from the ODE), Deborah Telfer, and Aimee Howley—unpacked these three dynamics (see Introduction above) they identified three ways of addressing them while staying true to the overarching goal and primary strategy of the Deans Compact. Specifically, they came to see the Compact as a means to improve the education of all children by developing a community of practice to (a) address differences in PK–12 students' learning needs from an inclusionary perspective, (b) involve higher education in the reform process, and (c) provide a forum for prekindergarten through undergraduate degree (PK–20) educators to discuss issues with state officials.

Establishing the Deans Compact

The idea for the Deans Compact stemmed partly from an initiative that began in the early 1980s: the Ohio Deans Task Force for Personnel Preparation for the Handicapped (Deans Task Force). The Deans Task Force was a deans-only collaborative chaired by Ellis Joseph, then dean of the University of Dayton School of Education, Frank New (the state director of the Division of Special Education at the time—today, the Office for Exceptional Children at the ODE), and Thomas M. Stephens (former department chair and associate dean for research in the College of Education and Human Ecology at The Ohio State University) cofounded the task force in response to the passage of Public Law 94-142, which upheld the right of all children with disabilities to a free and appropriate public education (Education for All Handicapped Children Act of 1975). The passage of the law created a need for more educators who could work with children with disabilities, and the initial purpose of the Deans Task Force was to create special education preparation programs to be overseen by special education faculties within various Ohio universities.

The group evolved over time and, in the 1990s, became the Special Education Personnel Development Advisory Committee (SEPDAC). Membership expanded to include Special Education Regional Resource Center (SERRC) directors and professional association representatives in addition to higher education faculty and administrators. SEPDAC focused on priorities like filling critical gaps in the number of educated special education personnel (e.g., teachers of students with sensory disabilities), but the group's relatively small size limited its effectiveness as a forum for engaging a broad set of higher education stakeholders. In the mid-2000s, the group disbanded and funding was discontinued.

In 2012, Deborah Telfer met with Aimee Howley and Sue Zake (as well as with other leaders from ODE's Office for Exceptional Children) to begin discussions about establishing a consortium to promote inclusive educator preparation. Early in their discussions, Telfer, Zake, and Howley developed a prospectus outlining the mission, proposed membership, and function of the Deans Compact. Telfer and Zake possessed a great deal of experience with interpreting state priorities and local district needs, state support structures, and key public education stakeholders. Howley brought deep knowledge of higher education requirements, such as accreditation and curriculum change processes. Howley described her involvement as a way to help the team

> get a feel for the higher education landscape—what was going on with teacher and leadership preparation programs. [Deborah Telfer] and I had been working together on other projects, and it seemed logical for her to get some information about what might be workable in higher education institutions by talking to me. Essentially, she wanted to discuss the merits, the likelihood for success, and the most effective ways to implement such a collaborative.

Membership

After the ODE agreed to fund the Deans Compact, the next step was to expand the group's membership. Early in the process, the leadership approached Rebecca Watts, then associate vice-chancellor of the Ohio Board of Regents (later to become the Ohio Department of Higher Education [ODHE]). According to Telfer, the ODHE's involvement was "critical in helping ... establish the group, get focus, get credibility, and move forward." The Compact invited representatives from teacher preparation programs in Ohio to participate as well as leaders from higher education and PK–12 professional associations. Additionally, involving the Collaboration for Effective Educator Development, Accountability and Reform (CEEDAR) Center one year into the work helped the Deans Compact gain statewide leverage as well as national visibility.

The Deans Compact as a Community of Practice

The Deans Compact was founded to promote a shared vision for a democratic, equitable, inclusive, and just system of education, and to connect educators who share a commitment to that vision (The Ohio Deans Compact on Exceptional Children, 2018a). Because the Deans Compact intended to advance this vision, and not just espouse a commitment to it, the Compact's founders organized it as a community of practice. According to Wenger-Trayner and Wenger-Trayner (2015, p. 1), "communities of practice are groups of people who share a concern or a passion for something they do and learn how to do it better as they interact regularly."

Telfer described the Deans Compact community of practice as

> a system where it is not them versus us, but one where we are in it together. I think we have structured the Deans Compact in ways that foster that kind of coming together by pushing people out of their boxes and identifying issues that sit above that separation to move forward in thinking about different, better ways to do the work that we all have a stake in.

Features of the Deans Compact community of practice include support from the ODE and ODHE, the collaborative involvement of higher education and PK–12 schools, and a focus on social justice and inclusive education for all students. Howley also noted the importance of another kind of support:

> The Deans Compact gets support from outside experts in the field when they come to share their ideas at the Deans Compact meetings and conferences. Even though their support is mostly just moral support, it is an important motivator when you are doing work that feels right to other colleagues nationally because it fits with their commitments and their work.

Another important feature of the Deans Compact community of practice is its capacity to recognize new needs as they arise and address them in real time. Howley provided an example:

The Deans Compact over time has surfaced important needs. For example, people did not really know that they had a need to collaborate in teacher preparation programs with one another, across the state, around social justice issues, but it turns out that they did. Before the Deans Compact, there was nothing pulling them together to talk about social justice issues, so the Deans Compact collaboration was helpful in terms of not producing the need exactly but addressing a newly recognized need. If you asked colleges of education if they needed to collaborate with other educators to talk about social justice education, or inclusive education, they may have said, "No, we have colleagues here." But actually, coming together around a set of meetings that involve professional development related to social justice is something attendees at the Deans Compact events value. So, it might not exactly be described as a "need," but it certainly is something that was missing in their experience before the Deans Compact came into existence.

PROGRESS OF THE WORK

The Deans Compact pursues its mission in four key ways: quarterly meetings, an incentive grant program, the LISDs initiative, and an annual statewide conference (The Ohio Deans Compact on Exceptional Children, 2018c).

Quarterly Meetings

In the early days of the Deans Compact, meetings were mostly organizational—agendas focused on establishing bylaws, discussing issues in teacher and leadership preparation programs, and drafting initiatives. The founding group had provided a preliminary outline of activities in their proposal for the ODE, but defining the Compact's purpose, mission, and core values was necessary work for the founding members. This collaborative process helped secure the buy-in required for enabling a diverse membership to work together toward shared goals. Once the Compact settled its early organizational issues, it pivoted toward more substantive matters such as establishing guidelines and criteria for incentive grant funding and creating a process for soliciting and vetting proposals.

Since those early days, the structure of the Deans Compact has changed significantly. Quarterly meetings now focus on opportunities for collaboration, networking, dialogue, professional development, shared learning, and collective action. Members discuss their institutions' work to reform educator preparation curricula, experts make presentations on topics of interest (e.g., social justice, equity, inclusive practice, implementation science), and committees meet to consider organizational and statewide issues as well as to frame relevant proposals.

Incentive Grant Program

The leaders of the Deans Compact see the incentive grant program as a vehicle for change because it requires award recipients to challenge their long-held identities and examine their organizational practices. At a philosophical level, grant recipients must think differently about instruction and leadership. Faculty members and their PK–12 partners must work to expand their self-conceptions as special educators or general educators and adopt a broader, more inclusive identity, seeing themselves as educators concerned with the instruction and support of all students.

The funding priorities for these incentive grants include: (a) the development of inclusive models of teacher preparation that lead to dual licensure with general education and intervention specialist (i.e., special education teacher) qualifications, (b) the development of inclusive administrator preparation programs, (c) the creation of coursework to improve special educators' competence in teaching and supporting children with low-incidence disabilities, and (d) simultaneous renewal efforts between educator preparation programs and their PK–12 partners (The Ohio Deans Compact on Exceptional Children, 2018d). The Deans Compact is currently on its fourth round of incentive grant funding.

Howley and Telfer agree that most faculty members responded well to this change in thinking. Telfer described the generally positive response of faculty and the few exceptions:

> I think, overall, faculty have responded very well.... In the end, people came together; there is excitement, there is more momentum around the work, and people are invested in it. As we get funded programs, [which] are then able to get a dual-licensure program approved through ODHE, that shows this [work] is possible. There have been a few exceptions where the faculty had this epiphany—that it is hard work and the current programs will be affected by this change—late in the game, and since then have been finding ways to rationalize why they are not moving forward.... But, overall, I think we have gotten a good response.

Dual Licensure Incentive Grants

The dual-licensure effort fosters the development of inclusive teacher preparation programs that offer their graduates licensure as both a general educator and special educator (called an "intervention specialist" in Ohio).

Faculty members in the funded programs examine the curricula and field placements of their existing general and special education programs and then merge them into a single, unified program that leads to dual licensure. So far, 10 institutions have obtained state approval for their redesigned merged programs, admitted students, and started to deliver the new curriculum. Seven additional dual-licensure initiatives, funded in 2017, are under development.

The majority of projects to date focused on merging early childhood education and intervention specialist programs, but a few merged middle childhood education and intervention specialist programs. The first round of incentive grants resulted in four reformed dual-licensure programs that then served as models for the incentive grant programs that followed. A number of the projects embed additional features that make their dual-licensure programs distinctive. For example, one university incorporated Montessori credentialing and another included the Teaching English to Speakers of Other Languages endorsement.

Leadership Preparation Incentive Grants

The Deans Compact has also worked to promote major changes in leadership preparation within university programs, but without as much success. Faculty members appear ready to make small changes to their programs but not to undertake a major overhaul. According to Howley, "with some very notable exceptions nationwide, leadership preparation programs are slow to change." She referenced an article suggesting that leadership preparation tends to cultivate leaders who sustain rather than push against current practices, including those that reproduce inequity (Breault, 2010). Howley remarked, "Donna Breault, the author of the article, was so right when she said that leadership preparation programs create 'keepers' of the status quo rather than change agents."

Support for Course Work Relating to Sensory Disabilities

The cofounders of the Deans Compact observed shortages in the number of personnel who are prepared to work with children with LISDs—children with visual impairments, hearing impairments, or both. In response, they determined that the Deans Compact should empanel a Low Incidence Committee to address this and other related needs. Among the Committee's first recommendations was to plan a cross-institutional incentive grant award for a collaborative of IHEs that would develop course work on sensory impairment. The course work would provide knowledge and skills that already-licensed intervention specialists could add to their repertoires, augmenting current skills with new competencies for working with students with sensory disabilities. Details on the work that resulted from this recommendation can be found later in the chapter (see Low-Incidence Sensory Disabilities Initiative below). Howley described several concerns that limited the speed of this effort:

> Another challenge deals with questions of what represents a high-quality program and what kind of preparation produces the expert who can teach students with sensory disabilities versus finding a compromise for providing them with better education without having a completely specialized program. I think the course work idea, developed through the Deans Compact, came out of an interest to meet a pressing need in a practical way that would improve education for a lot of students. It was seen as a definite improvement over the current state of things, especially in rural schools and districts.

Simultaneous Renewal Incentive Grants

The Deans Compact also funded (and continues to fund) higher education–school district partnerships leading to simultaneous renewal. The purpose of these "simultaneous renewal grants" is to provide teacher preparation faculty and PK–12 educators with opportunities to work together, fostering the use of inclusive educational practices in ways that benefit both the school district and the university preparation program. At the time of writing, the Deans Compact had funded 10 simultaneous renewal projects. These projects invested their award funds in the development of products (e.g., co-teaching modules) and the delivery of professional development on a variety of relevant topics (e.g., Universal Design for Learning, differentiation, inclusive assessment practices), with the goal of producing mutually beneficial PK–20 outcomes.

Low-Incidence Sensory Disabilities Initiative

In addition to funding incentive grants, the Deans Compact also funded a statewide initiative called the LISD Collaborative. The effort received support from both the ODHE and the ODE for creating an innovative model for LISD preparation that would begin in the area of visual impairment (VI) and then be replicated in other LISD areas (e.g., hearing impairment, orientation, and mobility). The LISD Collaborative designed its first component—the Teachers of the Visually Impaired (TVI) Consortium—to increase the number of educators who earn intervention specialist credentials for teaching students with visual impairments and enabling them to work in their local communities, particularly in rural areas of the state where there are severe teacher shortages.

The LISD Collaborative is a unique program under whose auspices five institutions of higher education came together to design and deliver a shared set of coursework and field experiences. The new multi-institution program received state approval in late July 2017, and the first cohort of 17 TVI Consortium students began taking coursework in August 2017. This post-baccalaureate, licensure-only program is administered through Shawnee State University, which serves as lead institution, but participants (individuals who hold a standard teaching credential and/or an intervention specialist license in any area other than VI) can enroll in the online program at their home institutions. A second cohort of students began taking course work in summer 2018.

Annual Statewide Conferences

The Deans Compact also hosts annual statewide conferences that, according to Howley, "pull together higher education faculty from educator preparation programs along with PK–12 faculty, staff, and administrators who are interested in inclusive education into a forum in which there is an exchange of ideas around issues pertinent to social justice education and inclusive education." The annual conferences draw a broad audience of Compact members, incentive grantees, PK–12 educators, regional providers, state officials, faculty in teacher preparation programs, preservice teachers, and other interested parties from across Ohio. A sampling of presentation titles from the conference's first five years underscore the Compact's commitment to equity and inclusion: "Understanding and Implementing Inclusive Practices," "Inclusive Practices across the P–20 Continuum," "One Profession: Defining Inclusive Educational Leadership," "Advancing the Learning of All Students through Systems Change Grounded in Equity and Social Justice," and "Preparing the Next Generation of Teachers for Inclusive Classrooms and Practices."

FUTURE PROJECTIONS AND FINAL THOUGHTS

Howley and Telfer foresee that the mindset of Deans Compact members together with the Compact's advocacy work will lead to the Compact's increasing influence, statewide and nationally. The key opportunities they see for growth involve funding more incentive grants, addressing teacher shortages, making changes at the PK–12 level, and involving other states in the Deans Compact's efforts.

According to both Howley and Telfer, there are a number of areas for increasing the scale of the work statewide. The first is simply to fund more dual-licensure incentive grants and to gain state approval for the programs. The Compact's objective is to continue funding the dual-licensure incentive grants until the majority of teacher preparation programs shift to focus on inclusive practices rather than siloed practices. Telfer noted, "we hope that having an inclusive teacher preparation program that leads to dual licensure is not the exception, but it becomes the norm and discrete programs are the exception."

Another way to scale up the Compact's work is to find solutions for teacher shortages in certain areas, including LISD, literacy, school psychology, and speech language pathology. Developing programs that balance a high-quality curriculum with the immediate need for professionals who can educate and provide other supports to students is an ongoing challenge. The LISD Collaborative began this work on behalf of students with sensory disabilities, but advancing the multi-institution collaborative model into other areas of licensure may be critically important as Ohio and other states face increasing teacher shortages.

A third way of increasing the scale of the work is to find ways to incentivize major changes in how schools operate. This effort might involve funding at least one successful inclusive leadership program to serve as a model for others and placing more emphasis on simultaneous renewal grants. Howley views this work as particularly important, because "nothing is going to change in education unless school districts' practices also change." Changes at the district level have to parallel the changes in educator preparation programs. Indeed, Howley described the ways in which teacher preparation program reform outpaces PK–12 reform:

> What I mean by this is that the number of new teachers that have been fused into the system is never large enough to alter the system. If three new teachers come into a district of 30 teachers, the 30 are going to overwhelm the three. If a school district finds kids with disabilities and puts them into special programs, then even if the educators have training, they will have to meld with the culture of the district or leave the position because there is a mismatch between their own values and the district's values. Now, new teachers infusing into a new culture of schooling—that is pretty powerful.

On a national scale, Howley and Telfer would like to see a network of inclusive educator preparation efforts similar to the Deans Compact. They believe that CEEDAR is an obvious candidate for moving the work forward, but the Deans Compact could serve as a model for how this type of intervention can be successful. One viable path toward a national agenda, therefore, is to continue conversations with CEEDAR regarding the intersection of its initiatives with those of the Deans Compact. Georgia and Florida have expressed interest in the Compact's work and are discussing similar initiatives. Lastly, another way that the Deans Compact opens conversations nationally is by making their work publicly accessible through conference presentations and publications.

CONCLUSION

For Howley and Telfer, in order to share the work more widely and cultivate a broad network of partners and allies, it is critically important to advance the Compact's work across Ohio and, indeed, nationally. The Deans Compact is a promising example of a statewide community of practice that other states could replicate or adapt. Its community of practice unites members in the shared mission of providing all PK–12 students with high-quality education in inclusive settings, and motivates those members to stay invested in and committed to the work. Based on its efforts thus far—most notably, the reformed dual-licensure teacher preparation programs, simultaneous renewal projects, and low-incidence disability teacher preparation programs—the Deans Compact offers an encouraging proof of concept. Along the way, its originators learned many lessons; these point to key practices for carrying this work forward:

- Establishing a community of practice that allows everyone involved to take ownership of the work.
- Involving persons from all aspects of the educational system, including personnel at the school, district, IHE, state, and national levels, in the community of practice.
- Uniting individuals under a shared vision.
- Providing opportunities and a comfortable environment for those involved to change their long-held educational beliefs and assumptions.
- Providing financial incentives for changing programs in ways that make them more inclusive.
- Providing individuals with opportunities to share their work and opportunities for professional development.
- Addressing diversity using an inclusive lens by focusing on the power of a shared core curriculum, the strengths that diverse individuals bring to a collective, and the importance of presuming the competence of all learners (including educators, support personnel, and other adults who work with children).

REFERENCES

Breault, D. A. (2010). Tethering one's self to the pole of utility: A Deweyan critique of recent shifts in leadership preparation. *Scholar-Practitioner Quarterly, 4,* 292–305. Retrieved from https://files.eric.ed.gov/fulltext/EJ942978.pdf

Bartell, C. A. (2001). Bridging the disconnect between policy and practice in teacher education. *Teacher Education Quarterly, 28,* 189–198. Retrieved from https://www.jstor.org/stable/23478343?seq=1#metadata_info_tab_contents

Cambron-McCabe, N., & McCarthy, M. M. (2005). Educating school leaders for social justice. *Educational Policy, 19,* 201–222. doi:10.1177/0895904804271609

Education for All Handicapped Children Act, 20 USC § 1401 (1975).

Frattura, E. M., & Capper, C. A. (2007). *Leading for social justice: Transforming schools for all leaners.* Thousand Oaks, CA: Corwin Press.

Hamman, D., Lechtenberger, D., Griffin-Shirley, N., & Zhou, L. (2013). Beyond exposure to collaboration: Preparing general-education teacher candidates for inclusive practice. *Teacher Educator, 48,* 244–256. doi:10.1080/08878730.2013.796030

Howley, C. B., & Howley, A. (2016). *Improving service to students with low-incidence sensory disabilities in Ohio: A mixed-methods study to examine national context and district* experience. Albany, OH: WordFarmers Associates. (ERIC Document Reproduction Service No. ED570178). Retrieved from https://files.eric.ed.gov/fulltext/ED570178.pdf

Howley, C., Howley, A., & Telfer, D. (2017). National provisions for certification and professional preparation in low-incidence sensory disabilities: A 50-state study. *American Annals of the Deaf, 162,* 277–294. doi:10.1353/aad.2017.0026

Levin, D. E., & Van Hoorn, J. (2016). *Teachers speak out: How school reforms are failing low-income young children.* Retrieved from https://www.deyproject.org/uploads/1/5/5/7/15571834/teachersspeakfinal_rgb.pdf

McLeskey, J., & Waldron, N. L. (2000). *Inclusive schools in action: Making differences ordinary.* Alexandria, VA: Association for Supervision and Curriculum Development.

Ohio Deans Compact on Exceptional Children. (2018a). *Incentivizing innovative practices.* Retrieved from https://www.ohiodeanscompact.org/our-work/incentivizing-innovative-practices

Ohio Deans Compact on Exceptional Children. (2018b). *Mission and goals.* Retrieved from https://www.ohiodeanscompact.org/our-purpose/mission-and-goals

Ohio Deans Compact on Exceptional Children. (2018c). *Priorities & focus.* Retrieved from https://www.ohiodeanscompact.org/our-purpose/our-purpos

Ohio Deans Compact on Exceptional Children. (2018d). *What we do.* Retrieved from https://www.ohiodeanscompact.org/our-work/what-we-do

Pugach, M. C., Blanton, L. P., & Correa, V. I. (2011). A historical perspective on the role of collaboration in teacher education reform: Making good on the promise of teaching all students. *Teacher Education and Special Education, 34,* 183–200. doi:10.1177/0888406411406141

Stone, J. E. (2015). *Misdirected teacher training has crippled education reform*. Retrieved from http://education-consumers.org/pdf/Misdirected-teacher-training.pdf

Wenger-Trayner, B., & Wenger-Trayner, E. (2015). *Introduction to communities of practice*. Retrieved from http://wenger-trayner.com/introduction-to-communities-of-practice

CHAPTER 26

THE EFFECT OF STATE POLICY ON THE EDUCATIONAL ENVIRONMENTS OF STUDENTS WITH DISABILITIES

Rebecca Watts
WGU Ohio

Authority (and responsibility) for education in the United States has been described as a three-layer cake with responsibilities at the federal, state, and local level. The middle and bottom layers of that metaphoric cake are very thick. In the United States, the establishment of schools; the credentialing, hiring, and deployment of professional educators; the development and delivery of curricula; and the determination of enrollment and graduation requirements are primarily a state and local responsibility. To emphasize the importance of the state and local roles, the United States Department of Education (USDOE) explicitly describes the federal role in education as a kind of "emergency response system," to fill the gaps in state and local support for education when critical national needs arise (USDOE, 2018a, para. 3).

This chapter focuses on the middle layer of responsibilities—state policies and their effects on the day-to-day educational experiences of

Inclusive Education: A Systematic Perspective, pp. 451–477
Copyright © 2020 by Information Age Publishing

students with disabilities. More specifically, this chapter provides a state-by-state examination of the percentage of time in each school day students with disabilities spend in the regular classroom. These data were analyzed against each state's educator preparation credentialing structure and policies, preparation program requirements, availability of innovative preparation programs, and financial commitments to kindergarten through Grade 12 (K–12) education.

What emerged from this study are indications that many state policies have little or no effect on student placement, whereas other policies and the state's support of the implementation of those policies have a measurable positive effect on the educational environments of students with disabilities. States that have created cultures of continuous improvement and sustainable innovation have gone beyond minimal requirements to foster the development of expert educational teams who take the student experience beyond just being in the same room with diverse learners to the more meaningful learning and development experiences of true inclusion. The gains these states have made warrant consideration by other states for replication.

GOALS, ELEMENTS, AND IMPACTS

Research has shown that students with disabilities achieve higher scores in reading and mathematics with more time spent in general education (Cosier, Causton-Theoharis, & Theoharis, 2013). Beyond those outcomes, students with disabilities benefit from authentically inclusive education settings by becoming more engaged in their learning, resulting in their knowledge and skills being more closely aligned with those of their peers who do not have disabilities (Kurth & Mastergeorge, 2012; Matzen, Ryndak, & Nakao, 2010).

The goal of this analysis was to determine which state policies, if any, correlate to the educational placements of students with disabilities. The study begins with a determination of which states are achieving the highest rates of placement in the "regular class" at least 80% of the school day. The study then examines the detail of each state's requirements in order to discern high-leverage state policies that result in students with disabilities being supported in an inclusive educational setting.

The study (a) identified state performance from 2012 through 2015 in placing students with disabilities in the "regular class" at least 80% of the school day, (b) identified state policies related to educator credentialing and preparation program requirements, (c) evaluated the measurable effect of individual policies and combinations of policies, (d) determined whether the policy effect is positive or negative, and (e) examined the magnitude of the effect size of state policies. Through this analysis the chapter identifies a small number of leading states for policy approaches that are having a measurable, persistent, and meaningful positive effect on student placements.

Data Sources

This exploration of relationships between state policies and direct services to students began with a compilation of each state's credentials for educators supporting students with disabilities and its requirements for professional educator preparation programs (EPPs). State policy factors examined in the study included: (a) the presence of a state agreement with the Council for the Accreditation of Educator Preparation (CAEP, 2018), (b) state requirements for educator preparation coursework and/or clinical experiences that stipulate candidate experiences related to students with disabilities, (c) a prerequisite or corequisite for a state license in general education to be eligible for special education license, (d) the availability of state approved dual-licensure/certification EPPs, and (e) the state's average per pupil expenditure (APPE).

The presence of a CAEP state agreement was included as a policy factor in the analysis, as some states stipulate adherence to CAEP Standard 1.3, which requires that educator preparation providers ensure that candidates demonstrate skills and commitments that afford all preschool through Grade 12 (P–12) students access to rigorous college- and career-ready standards, as well as CAEP Standard 2.3, which states that providers must work with partners to design clinical experiences to ensure that candidates demonstrate their effectiveness and positive impact on all students' learning and development (CAEP, n.d.).

This policy information was then compared to the percentage of all students with disabilities in each state who were placed in the general education classroom at least 80% of the school day each school year from 2012 through 2015. The student placement data were gathered from the Individuals with Disabilities Education Act Section 618 *Child Count and Educational Environments* reports from 2012 through 2015 (USDOE, 2018b). These data are detailed in the Appendix.

Data on each state's policies for educator preparation and licensure were gathered from state policy snapshots collected and reported by the Collaboration for Effective Educator Development, Accountability and Reform Center (CEEDAR, 2016) and verified by each state.

Data Analysis

The annual *Child Count and Educational Environments* report (USDOE, 2018b) provides a state-by-state listing of the total number of students by:

(a) state-defined disability category, (b) age, (c) ethnicity, and (d) limited English proficiency (LEP). The state-defined disability categories are: (a) autism, (b) deaf-blindness, (c) developmental delay, (d) emotional disturbance, (e) hearing impairment, (f) intellectual disability, (g) multiple disabilities, (h) orthopedic impairment, (i) other health impairment, (j) specific learning disability, (k) speech or language impairment, (l) traumatic brain injury, (m) visual impairment, and (n) all disabilities.

Student counts for each of these descriptors are then reported by educational environment as follows: (a) correctional facilities, (b) home, (c) homebound/hospital, (d) inside regular class 40% through 79% of the day, (e) inside regular class 80% or more of the day, (f) inside regular class less than 40% of the day, (g) parentally placed in private schools, (h) residential facility, (i) separate class, (j) separate school, (k) service provider location, (l) services in other location than regular early childhood program, and (m) services in regular early childhood program.

The *Child Count and Educational Environments* reports (USDOE, 2018b) include data for the following entities: all 50 states separately plus the District of Columbia (Washington, DC), American Samoa, the Bureau of Indian Affairs, the Federated States of Micronesia, Guam, Northern Marianas, Puerto Rico, the Republic of Palau, the Republic of the Marshall Islands, and the U.S. Virgin Islands. For purposes of this study, the data were analyzed solely for the all disabilities category, for all students age 6 through 21, for the educational environment inside regular class 80% or more of the day, and only for the 50 states and Washington, DC. The analysis did not disaggregate student placement data by disability, ethnicity, gender, or English proficiency.

Findings

Independent sample t-tests were conducted to compare the placement percentages of states with a particular policy or combination of policies against placement percentages of states which did not have the same policies. The results in Table 26.1 show significant differences (two-tailed) between the independent samples for the following policy conditions: (a) requiring all candidates for all licensure areas to complete coursework and/or clinical experiences specific to students with disabilities, (b) CAEP agreements combined with a requirement for all candidates for all licensure areas to complete coursework and/or clinical experiences specific to students with disabilities, and (c) providing coursework and/or clinical experiences specific to students with disabilities as well as having dual-certification/licensure programs available in the state.

Table 26.1.
Independent Samples T-Tests, State Policies 2012–2015, Using %
Percent in Placement Difference

State policy	M	SE	t(df)	p	95% CI LL	95% CI UL
State has CAEP agreement	-1.07%	1.33%	-0.80(197)	.42	-3.70%	1.56%
State requires all candidates for all licensure areas to complete coursework and/or clinical experiences specific to students with disabilities	-3.81%	1.20%	-3.16(201)	.002	-6.18%	-1.43%
State requires general education credential as prerequisite to special education license	-1.48%	1.89%	-0.78(201)	.44	-5.20%	2.25%
Dual certification/ licensure programs are available in the state	2.71%	1.47%	1.84(201)	.07	-0.19%	5.61%
State has CAEP agreement and requires all candidates for all licensure areas to complete coursework and/or clinical experiences specific to students with disabilities*	4.02%	1.61%	2.51(67.02)	.02	0.82%	7.23%
State has CAEP agreement and requires general education credential as prerequisite to special education license	0.42%	2.29%	0.18(197)	.86	-4.10%	4.94%
State has CAEP agreement and dual certification/ licensure programs are available in the state	-1.84%	1.91%	-0.96(197)	.34	-5.61%	1.92%

(Table continues on next page)

Table 26.1.
Independent Samples T-Tests, State Policies 2012–2015, Using %
Percent in Placement Difference (Continued)

State policy	M	SE	t(df)	p	95% CI	
					LL	UL
State requires all candidates for all licensure areas to complete coursework and/or clinical experiences specific to students with disabilities and requires general education credential as prerequisite to special education license*	-1.17%	0.63%	-1.85(192.79)	.07	-2.43%	0.08%
State requires all candidates for all licensure areas to complete coursework and/or clinical experiences specific to students with disabilities and dual certification/ licensure programs are available in the state	4.68%	1.86%	2.51(201)	.01	1.01%	8.36%
State requires general education credential as prerequisite to special education license and requires all candidates for all licensure areas to complete coursework and/or clinical experiences specific to students with disabilities	1.48%	1.89%	0.78(201)	.44	-2.25%	5.20%

(Table continues on next page)

Table 26.1.

Independent Samples T-Tests, State Policies 2012–2015, Using %
Percent in Placement Difference (Continued

					95% CI	
State policy	*M*	*SE*	*t(df)*	*p*	*LL*	*UL*
State requires general education credential as prerequisite to special education license and dual certification/ licensure programs are available in the state	-9.87%	3.06%	-3.22 (201)	.001	-15.91%	-3.83%

Note: CI = confidence interval; LL = lower limit; UL = upper limit. *Assumes unequal variances.

As detailed in the Appendix, states performing at or above the 90th percentile each year from 2012 through 2015 include: Alabama, Nebraska, North Dakota, and Vermont. To further evaluate these consistently top-performing states, a detailed analysis of the policy factors in place in these states is provided in Table 26.2. This analysis revealed that Alabama is the only state with a "collaborative special educator license," and North Dakota is the only state with a "special education strategist" license. Vermont has a special education endorsement, and the University of Vermont offers a special education dual-endorsement program. Nebraska and North Dakota do not offer any dual-licensure programs.

Alabama's state requirements for clinical experiences for candidates across all licensure areas include field experiences or internships that include students with exceptionalities and provide opportunities for candidates to develop and demonstrate knowledge, skills, and dispositions for helping all students learn. All baccalaureate programs in Alabama are required to provide a "survey of education" course.

Nebraska requires all candidates in all programs to participate in field experience or clinical practice that includes students with exceptionalities and to complete a three-semester-hour course in special education that provides knowledge of the educational needs of students with disabilities; the major characteristics of each disability; various alternatives for providing the least restrictive environment for children with disabilities; methods of teaching children with disabilities in the regular class; and pre-referral alternatives, referral systems, multidisciplinary team responsibilities, the individualized education plan process, and the placement process.

Table 26.2.
Policy Factors in Leading States Placing Students With Disabilities in Inclusive Settings

Year	State	# Students with Disabilities (SWD) Age 6 to 21	% of SWD Age 6 to 21 in Inclusive Setting	State Requires CAEP Accreditation for all Ed Prep Providers	State Requires Educators to Complete Coursework Related to SWD	State Requires a General Education Credential as a Prerequisite to a Special Education Credential	Dual Certification Programs Available in the State	State Offers Collaborative Special Education License	State Offers Special Education Strategist License	State Offers Special Education Endorsement
2012	Alabama	60,555	83.68%	✓	✓			✓		
	North Dakota	8,689	76.02%	✓		✓			✓	
	Nebraska	30,084	74.86%	✓	✓					
	Vermont	8,885	73.78%	✓	✓		✓			✓
2013	Alabama	61,671	83.83%	✓	✓			✓		
	North Dakota	8,689	75.32%	✓		✓			✓	
	Nebraska	31,035	74.59%	✓	✓					
	Vermont	8,991	74.15%	✓	✓		✓			✓
2014	Alabama	62,894	83.63%	✓	✓			✓		
	Nebraska	31,855	76.07%	✓	✓					
	Vermont	9,133	74.95%	✓	✓		✓			✓
	North Dakota	8,827	74.58%	✓		✓			✓	
2015	Alabama	64,268	83.56%	✓	✓		✓	✓		
	Vermont	9,189	75.76%	✓	✓					✓
	Nebraska	31,905	75.34%	✓	✓					
	North Dakota	8,875	74.08%	✓		✓			✓	

The consistently lowest-performing states, where less than half of students with disabilities were in the regular class at least 80% of the school day for all four years we studied, include Hawaii, Montana, and New Jersey. New Mexico's placement rates for students with disabilities in the "regular class" were below 50% in 2013 and 2015.

Yet, some of these lowest-performing states have policies in place to address the educational environments of students with disabilities. New Jersey and New Mexico have had dual-licensure programs available for many years. While limited English proficiency (LEP) was not analyzed as a factor in this study, the percentage of students with disabilities who also have LEP revealed low percentages for both the highest- and lowest-performing states. Detailed in Table 26.3, medium to large effect sizes for policy measures in place showed a negative effect in states for which there are dual-licensure programs available. The difference between states with and without this program availability is, however, not statistically significant.

Table 26.3.
Effect Sizes, Cohen's *d* and Hedge's *g*, State Policies, 2012–2015

State Requirements	No			Yes			Cohen's *d*	Hedge's *g*
	n	*M*	*SD*	*n*	*M*	*SD*		
CAEP Agreement	64	62.49	9.64	135	63.56	8.34	0.12	0.12
State requires all candidates for all licensure areas to complete coursework and/or clinical experiences specific to students with disabilities	115	61.59	8.44	88	65.39	8.58	0.45	0.45
State requires general education credential as prerequisite to special education license	179	63.06	8.56	24	64.54	9.68	0.16	0.17
Dual certification/ licensure programs are available in the state	159	63.82	85.08	44	61.11	9.09	-0.31	-0.31

(Table continues on next page)

Table 26.3.
Effect Sizes, Cohen's *d* and Hedge's *g*, State Policies, 2012–2015 (Continued)

State Requirements	No			Yes			Cohen's *d*	Hedge's *g*
	n	*M*	*SD*	*n*	*M*	*SD*		
State has CAEP agreement and requires general education credential as prerequisite to special education license	183	63.18	8.56	16	63.60	11.43	0.04	0.05
State has CAEP agreement and dual certification/licensure programs are available in the state	175	63.44	8.62	24	61.60	9.85	0.20	0.21
State requires all candidates for all licensure areas to complete coursework and/or clinical experiences specific to students with disabilities and requires general education credential as prerequisite to special education license	199	63.26	8.77	4	62.08	0.25	0.19	0.13
State requires all candidates for all licensure areas to complete coursework and/or clinical experiences specific to students with disabilities and dual certification/licensure programs are available in the state	179	62.68	8.85	24	67.36	6.09	0.62	0.54

(Table continues on next page)

Table 26.3.
Effect Sizes, Cohen's *d* and Hedge's *g*, State Policies, 2012–2015
(Continued)

	No			Yes			Cohen's	Hedge's
State Requirements	*n*	*M*	*SD*	*n*	*M*	*SD*	*d*	*g*
State requires general education credential as prerequisite to special education license and dual certification/ licensure programs available	195	63.62	8.48	8	53.75	8.92	1.13	1.16

To assess the relationship between state policies related to financial support for K–12 learning and the percentage of students with disabilities in that state placed in the inclusive setting at least 80% of the school day, a Pearson product-moment correlation coefficient was computed. There was a small (statistically non-significant) negative correlation between states' APPE and the percentage of students with disabilities in the regular classroom at least 80% of the school day ($r = -.127$, $n = 203$, $p = .070$), perhaps suggesting the possibility that increased investment in K–12 education might have a negative relationship with the percentage of students with disabilities placed in inclusive settings.

In addition to analyzing the data from a correlational perspective, a review of the data from 2012 through 2015 shows that the states averaging higher rates of per-pupil spending are not among the leaders in placing students with disabilities in inclusive settings. As shown in Table 26.4, of the top-performing states in the percentage of students with disabilities in inclusive placements at least 80% of the school day, only Vermont ranks in the top 10 states for APPE for the four years in the analysis.

So, at what level do the leading inclusion states fund K–12 education? As detailed in Table 26.5, from 2012 through 2015, Alabama, the state that consistently led the nation in student placement in inclusive settings, provided APPEs far below the majority of its peers across the country each year in the period. Nebraska and North Dakota rank in the top half of states, with only Vermont providing APPEs at rates that place them in the top 10 states in the nation.

In summary, multiple analyses of state policies and funding levels reveal that none of the state policies examined can be associated with high percentages of students with disabilities being placed in an inclusive

Table 26.4.
Top 10 States in Average Per Pupil Expenditure, 2012–2015

Year	Rank (Average Per Pupil Expenditure)	State	Average Per Pupil Expenditure
	1	New York	$ 20,290.00
	2	District of Columbia	$ 19,571.00
	3	Alaska	$ 18,550.00
	4	New Jersey	$ 17,547.00
2012	5	Connecticut	$ 17,057.00
	6	Vermont	$ 16,670.00
	7	Wyoming	$ 16,526.00
	8	Rhode Island	$ 15,838.00
	9	Massachusetts	$ 15,100.00
	10	Maryland	$ 14,346.00
	1	New York	$ 20,604.00
	2	District of Columbia	$ 19,741.00
	3	Alaska	$ 19,432.00
	4	New Jersey	$ 18,395.00
2013	5	Vermont	$ 17,556.00
	6	Connecticut	$ 17,447.00
	7	Wyoming	$ 16,537.00
	8	Massachusetts	$ 15,669.00
	9	Rhode Island	$ 14,686.00
	10	Maryland	$ 14,637.00
	1	New York	$ 21,504.00
	2	District of Columbia	$ 20,758.00
	3	Alaska	$ 19,699.00
	4	Connecticut	$ 18,652.00
2014	5	New Jersey	$ 18,632.00
	6	Vermont	$ 18,209.00
	7	Wyoming	$ 16,597.00
	8	Massachusetts	$ 16,162.00
	9	Rhode Island	$ 16,056.00
	10	Maryland	$ 14,744.00

(Table continues on next page)

Table 26.4.

Top 10 States in Average Per Pupil Expenditure, 2012–2015 (Continued)

Year	Rank (Average Per Pupil Expenditure)	State	Average Per Pupil Expenditure
	1	New York	$ 22,232.00
	2	Alaska	$ 21,610.00
	3	District of Columbia	$ 20,908.00
	4	Connecticut	$ 19,348.00
2015	5	Vermont	$ 19,127.00
	6	New Jersey	$ 18,945.00
	7	Massachusetts	$ 16,949.00
	8	Wyoming	$ 16,855.00
	9	Rhode Island	$ 16,481.00
	10	Maine	$ 15,275.00

Source: "National Public Education Financial Survey Data (Reports from 2012–2015)," by National Center for Education Statistics (n.d.).

Table 26.5.

Leading Inclusion States' Annual State Rank in Average Per Pupil Expenditure

Year	Rank Among All States: (Average Per Pupil Expenditure)	State	Average Per Pupil Expenditure	# Students Statewide
	45	Alabama	$ 8,172.00	744,621
2012	18	Nebraska	$ 11,418.00	288,389
	25	North Dakota	$ 10,587.00	97,646
	6	Vermont	$ 16,670.00	89,908
	39	Alabama	$ 8,685.00	744,637
2013	17	Nebraska	$ 11,596.00	303,505
	23	North Dakota	$ 11,065.00	101,111
	5	Vermont	$ 17,556.00	89,624
	41	Alabama	$ 8,767.00	746,204
2014	17	Nebraska	$ 11,720.00	307,677
	19	North Dakota	$ 11,595.00	103,947
	6	Vermont	$ 18,209.00	88,690
	42	Alabama	$ 8,926.00	744,164
2015	19	Nebraska	$ 12,038.00	312,635
	17	North Dakota	$ 12,585.00	106,586
	5	Vermont	$ 19,127.00	87,311

Source: "National Public Education Financial Survey Data (Reports from 2012–2015)," by National Center for Education Statistics, (n.d.).

classroom for at least 80% of the school day. This chapter next considers the path to high performance in the nation's leading inclusion state, Alabama.

A Closer Look at a Leading Inclusion State: Alabama

Alabama's focus on parameters for educator licensure and the work that supports implementation with fidelity are key to its outcomes. Key factors were the change management process the state employed in shifting licensure policy and the state department of education's subsequent commitment to providing school districts with an intensive system of support targeted on implementation with fidelity. Alabama's work presents a compelling case study to inform policymakers and practitioners across the country.

The state's transition several years ago to a collaborative special educator certificate was intentional and was led by the Alabama State Department of Education (ALSDE). ALSDE's Director of the Office of Teaching and Leading, Jayne Meyer (J. Meyer, personal communication, February 14, 2018), reports that prior to the advent of the collaborative special educator credential, Alabama had 12 different special education subspecialty certificates. The catalyst for the reducing the number of special educator credentials in the state was the result of ALSDE's analysis of student gains.

This analysis showed that a large number of subspecializations did not contribute to meeting the needs of students. After identifying the need for a fundamental policy change, the state convened special educators for their views on the issue and their recommendations on how best to reduce the number of special education subspecialization certificates.

This consultation with educators failed to yield recommendations for reduction in the number of credentials available and, in fact, resulted in the recommendation for the creation of an *additional* subspecialty certificate! ALSDE thanked the educators in the consultation for their recommendation and continued with the planned reduction in the number of special educator certificates and in the development of two collaborative teacher certificates, one for Grades K–6 and one for Grades 6–12, the former requiring knowledge of the state's entire elementary education curriculum.

The changes did, however, retain some certificates. Separate certificates continued in place for early childhood special education, gifted education, hearing impairment, visual impairment, and speech and language impairment.

To engage stakeholders in discussions about the newly proposed credentialing structure, ALSDE again held statewide meetings to discuss the changes and to detail the recommended approach. Meyer (J. Meyer, personal communication, February 14, 2018) reports that the changes met with resistance from multiple stakeholders. The reasons varied by stakeholder group but had a common theme. EPP faculty and special educators statewide felt threatened by the proposed change, as they had established strong professional and programmatic identities related to their subspecialty areas. Parents and advocacy groups opposed collapsing the areas of special educator certification, as they felt that each student should be served by an educator whose credential mirrored the child's specific diagnosis. Several State Board meetings hosted in regions across the state addressed the fears of parents, advocates, educators, and EPP faculty (J. Meyer, personal communication, February 14, 2018).

Once ALSDE won over the stakeholders statewide, it moved forward with implementation. The outcomes of the new model showed positive results for students. Specifically, Indicator 5 in Alabama's State Systemic Improvement Plan, a plan mandated by the USDOE Office of Special Education Programs, showed that the state was a national leader in its student outcomes. However, ALSDE wanted to be sure that educators statewide were receiving meaningful professional development in effective co-planning and co-teaching strategies to support implementation of the new collaborative model (C. Richardson, personal communication, February 14, 2018).

To this end ALSDE developed 11 demonstration sites in Alabama schools for ongoing in-service training and the use of instructional coaches assigned to the schools, predominantly middle schools. Teachers in the demonstration sites participated in ongoing professional development to ensure that they were effectively co-planning and co-teaching using the research-based Implementation Science framework (Fixsen, Naoom, Blasé, Friedman, & Wallace, 2005), co-teaching (Friend & Cook, 2013), co-planning (Ploessl, Rock, Schoenfeld, & Blanks, 2010), and instructional coaching (Knight, 2007). In addition to the co-planning and co-teaching professional development, all educators in the demonstration sites implemented positive behavior intervention and supports (PBIS).

Alabama's results further showed that students with disabilities in inclusive classrooms achieved academic gains at faster trajectories than their peers without disabilities in the same classroom. An additional positive outcome, potentially a correlational effect, coincided with the deployment of policy and implementation strategies. Data showed a decrease in the median number of unexcused absences per month in the demonstration sites from 156.41 days in fall 2015 to 128.02 days in fall 2016. In the same schools, the median number of incidents of student tardiness per month decreased from 262.94 in fall 2015 to 158.51 in fall 2016, and the median number of chronic absences per semester decreased from 65.14 to 41.00 in the same period (ALSDE, 2016).

From the EPP perspective Alabama providers have introduced some variability in their program offerings, with some providers structuring their undergraduate programs to prepare teachers for certification in both the K–6 collaborative teacher and the elementary education certificate. In this case, candidates meeting rigorous admissions selection criteria are challenged to meet the certification standards for both the collaborative special educator certificate and the elementary education certificate.

Alabama's progress has not gone unnoticed. In February 2018 the WestEd National Center for Systemic Improvement highlighted Alabama's successes. The highlighted performance indicators include 88% of students with disabilities in the demonstration sites showing gains on progress monitoring, and 48% of students with disabilities in the same schools posting gains on the ACT Aspire assessment, surpassing the benchmark goal of 40% (Hayes, Meinders, & Rosborough, 2018).

ALSDE leaders describe a philosophical shift at the agency: from being a purely regulatory agency towards one that provides facilitation and support to the state's schools and educators. This approach requires an ongoing commitment to funding professional development oriented to a collaborative teaching model in support of student success (J. Meyer, personal communication, February 14, 2018).

A Team-Led Learning Environment

Emerging from this study are indications that state policy combined with state-led facilitative, supportive action can effect positive change on local practices and the student outcomes they produce. These practices have a direct effect on the educational environments experienced by students with disabilities. At the same time, however, results did not show that any particular state policy or set of policies effect the kind of changes needed to ensure that students with disabilities have the supports they need in the "regular class."

Far more important than placement alongside peers is the concept of inclusion and the degree of collaboration and planning required to create authentically inclusive environments. Notably, two consistently top-performing states, Alabama and North Dakota, have specific licenses in place to address the communication and collaboration abilities and acumen needed to create truly inclusive environments. While educators, researchers, and policymakers have long agreed that students with disabilities benefit from inclusive education settings, meaningful inclusion requires support from highly collaborative, expert teams of education professionals who provide each student with the classroom supports needed.

CONCLUSION

It is not enough to keep students with disabilities in the "regular class" for the majority of the day if the professionals in the room are not equipped to work together to provide students with what they need. Spending hours each day in a learning environment that engenders frustration and a sense of failure is akin to the time a commuter sits in a traffic jam each morning. Just as the commuter is not nearing the goal destination, a student placed in a regular classroom without the support of a team of prepared professionals may be safe and warm but is not optimally progressing in learning and development.

All students grow and thrive best when supported by a team of professional educators who communicate, coordinate, and collaborate. Too many educators have not had the opportunity to develop and practice the fundamental skills and knowledge needed for co-planning and co-teaching. Many have not adopted the essential philosophical approach that the best educators are those whose *shared students* thrive and achieve. Perhaps too many times educators hold as their greatest source of pride the fact that they are *the best teacher in the school.* Teaching, however, should not be a competition among educators; it should be a collaboration with shared commitment, shared attention, and shared attribution.

Educator preparation providers must own some responsibility for the persistence of the prevalent mindset. To use a music analogy, for too long we have produced an education workforce of soloists, whereas what schools and students truly need are talented, well-practiced ensembles.

Schools themselves have responsibility for the current state, as well. Too few schools design educators' schedules and expectations to assure shared planning time, shared time for reflection, and shared data. Too few schools establish suitable expectations for all educators. What roles do art, music, and physical education teachers have in supporting student success for all students? How do speech pathologists, physical therapists, occupational therapists, and reading specialists engage the school librarian in meaningful collaboration to support individual student needs?

Future Research

This study calls for future research to learn more about the effects of state policy and support on students by specific disability, by LEP, by ethnicity, and by state characteristics of rurality or urbanicity. Additional research should be completed to evaluate variances between schools that deploy licensed collaborative special educators or special education strategists.

Recommendations for Action

As the percentage of students with disabilities who spend 80% or more of their school day in an inclusive classroom grows, the number of teachers adequately prepared to create and sustain that type of learning environment has failed to keep pace. Developing collaborative educators will provide students with opportunities to form strong personal relationships with more educators. A successful, integrated education model would provide more students with the kind of personalized expertise and support they need (Basile, 2018).

For policy leaders, a good beginning would be examination of the effect that licensure policies exert on the skills and competencies needed for collaboration in an inclusive setting. In many states, the pathways to a state teaching credential fail to include requirements that all educators gain knowledge and skill to support students with disabilities. Even worse, in some states the existing requirements *widen the chasm* that exists between general educators and special educators.

Once a state identifies optimal credentialing requirements, state leaders must demonstrate the courage and diligence to implement the needed changes. Based the experience of Alabama leaders, it seems essential to engage with stakeholders across the state including teachers, school district leaders, and parents, as well as EPP faculty and leaders. Meeting with groups statewide to build understanding and support for change is difficult, possibly frustrating, and time-consuming work. But the effort is fundamental to ensuring that the needed transformation will be fully implemented and supported with new practices in schools throughout the state.

Of course, as the Alabama experience suggests, multiple stakeholders may resist change in educator licensure structures and preparation processes. These groups include but are not limited to educators holding legacy credentials, parents, and school leaders. To prepare for and address this resistance, policy leaders must effectively use change management theory. Kotter (2012) describes an eight-step change management model that includes: (a) establishing a sense of urgency; (b) creating a guiding coalition; (c) developing a vision and strategy; (d) communicating the change vision; (e) empowering the broad-based coalition; (f) generating short-term wins; (g) consolidating gains and producing more change; and (h) anchoring new approaches in the culture.

Most states do not issue teaching credentials requiring knowledge and skills needed for a culture of collaboration. Therefore, taking up this work will be foundational and culture-changing. It will require schools, teachers, and EPPs to make major shifts away from their past practices. EPPs have historically provided preparation based on a silo-oriented approach in which the special educator addressed the needs of students with disabilities and general educators supported the learning of the general student population. Teachers and schools have used this same model.

While the work to effect these changes is arduous, it is past time to take meaningful action to equip all educators with the knowledge and skills they need to collaboratively meet the needs of all students. As demonstrated in Alabama, the types of educator credentials available in a state as well as the supports provided to those educators can have a positive effect on students. Local educators, educator preparation providers, and state policymakers should examine current policies and consider enhancements that foster the collaboration needed from educational teams to support student success.

The strong sense of urgency for these efforts is informed by the reality that it will take time for policy improvements to reach K–12 classrooms. As states establish collaborative educator credentials, EPPs will respond by creating programs leading to those licenses. Bolstered by a strong state system of support, school leaders will begin to implement collaborative approaches in their schools and will seek out and develop collaborative educators who will strengthen learning experiences for all students.

REFERENCES

Alabama State Department of Education (ALSDE). (2016). *State systemic improvement plan, phase III*. Retrieved from https://www.alsde.edu/sec/ses/Reports/FINAL%20SSIP,%20Phase%20III%20-%20Narrative,%20References,%20appendix.pdf

Basile, C. G. (2018). *Higher pay alone won't solve Arizona's teacher shortage*. Retrieved from: https://www.azcentral.com/story/opinion/op-ed/2018/01/19/solve-arizona-teacher-shortage-isnt-pay/1037234001/

Cosier, M., Causton-Theoharis, J., & Theoharis, G. (2013). Does access matter? Time in general education and achievement for students with disabilities. *Remedial and Special Education, 34*, 32-332. doi:10.1177/0741932513485448

Collaboration for Effective Educator Development, Accountability and Reform (CEEDAR). (2016). *Special education licensure policy snapshot*. Retrieved from http://ceedar.education.ufl.edu/portfolio/policy-snapshot-se-certification/

Council for the Accreditation of Educator Preparation (CAEP). (2018). *Program review options for CAEP accreditation by state agreement*. Retrieved from http://caepnet.org/~/media/Files/caep/program-review/program-review-options-by-state.pdf?la=en

Council for the Accreditation of Educator Preparation (CAEP). (n.d.). *State partnership agreements*. http://caepnet.org/working-together/state-partners

Fixsen, D., Naoom, S., Blasé, K., Friedman, R., & Wallace, F. (2005). *Implementation research: A synthesis of the literature*. Tampa, FL: University of South Florida, Louis de la Parte Florida Mental Health Institute, National Implementation Research Network.

Friend, M., & Cook, L. (2013). *Interactions: Collaboration skills for school professionals*. Boston, MA: Pearson.

Hayes, S., Meinders, D., & Rosborough, J. (2018). *State systems change spotlight: Alabama*. : San Fracisco, CA: WestEd, National Center for Systemic Improvement. Retrieved from https://ncsi-library.wested.org/system/resources/documents/000/000/213/original/2018-02-13_AL_Spotlight_final_508.pdf?1518643337

Knight, J. (2007). *Instructional coaching: A partnership approach to improving instruction*. Thousand Oaks, CA: Corwin.

Kotter, J. P. (2012). *Leading change*. Boston, MA: Harvard Business Review Press.

Kurth J. A., & Mastergeorge A. M. (2012). Impact of setting and instructional context for adolescents with autism. *The Journal of Special Education, 46*, 36–48. doi:10.1177/0022466910366480

Matzen K., Ryndak D., & Nakao T. (2010). Middle school teams increasing access to general education for students with significant disabilities: Issues encountered and activities observed across contexts. *Remedial and Special Education, 31*, 287–304. doi:10.1177/0741932508327457

National Center for Education Statistics. (n.d.). *National public education financial survey data*. Retrieved from: https://nces.ed.gov/ccd/stfis.asp

Ploessl, D., Rock, M., Schoenfeld, N., & Blanks, B. (2010). On the same page: Practical techniques to enhance co-teaching interactions. *Intervention in School and Clinic, 45*, 158–168. doi:10.1177/1053451209349529

United States Department of Education. (2018a). *The federal role in education*. Retrieved from https://www2.ed.gov/about/overview/fed/role.html

United States Department of Education. (2018b). *IDEA section 618 data products: State level data files*. Retrieved from https://www2.ed.gov/programs/osepidea/618-data/state-level-data-files/index.html

APPENDIX

Students with Disabilities Placement in Regular Class 80% or More of Day 2012-2015

Students with disabilities (SWD) inside regular class 80% or more of the day—2012

State	SWD Age 6–21 (N)	% of All SWD Age 6–21 in Regular Class >80% of Day	% of Limited English Proficient SWD Age 6–21 in Regular Class >80% of Day
Alabama	60,555	83.685%	2.16%
North Dakota	8,689	76.019%	2.69%
Nebraska	30,084	74.864%	3.91%
Vermont	8,885	73.783%	1.33%
New Hampshire	19,115	73.232%	2.26%
Oregon	52,387	72.628%	10.54%
Colorado	55,300	72.306%	15.22%
Kentucky	57,474	71.753%	1.84%
Rhode Island	15,219	71.602%	6.10%
Connecticut	42,849	69.442%	8.37%
Florida	219,521	69.275%	7.91%
Indiana	103,457	68.816%	4.10%
Maryland	61,421	67.968%	5.22%
South Dakota	10,607	67.746%	4.04%
Kansas	37,965	67.172%	3.78%
Mississippi	36,619	67.048%	0.95%
Texas	262,401	66.321%	15.06%
North Carolina	113,494	66.203%	7.69%
Delaware	10,962	64.787%	5.57%
Nevada	27,344	64.666%	18.59%
Georgia	108,046	64.450%	5.35%
Michigan	117,319	64.251%	4.18%
Iowa	37,633	64.031%	4.66%
West Virginia	24,940	63.942%	0.59%
Tennessee	72,399	63.319%	1.95%
Oklahoma	58,127	62.913%	3.92%

(Appendix continues on next page)

Wyoming	7,388	62.173%	3.53%
Pennsylvania	163,005	62.106%	2.18%
Minnesota	67,287	62.018%	6.94%
Wisconsin	66,224	61.914%	6.37%
Virginia	89,660	61.883%	8.22%
Arizona	69,600	61.650%	7.93%
Alaska	9,682	61.112%	14.76%
Louisiana	42,350	60.475%	1.26%
Idaho	14,366	60.354%	5.81%
Ohio	139,966	60.187%	1.55%
Massachusetts	88,057	58.762%	5.84%
Missouri	62,504	58.081%	1.84%
New York	221,910	57.525%	8.35%
South Carolina	50,951	57.310%	5.22%
Utah	38,421	56.187%	7.86%
Maine	15,816	55.688%	2.02%
Illinois	135,439	53.068%	4.91%
Arkansas	27,447	52.875%	6.60%
California	322,454	52.597%	29.82%
Washington	60,836	52.438%	9.86%
New Mexico	21,187	50.440%	22.09%
District of Columbia	5,461	49.488%	7.14%
Montana	6,972	47.258%	4.43%
New Jersey	96,304	44.926%	1.80%
Hawaii	6,141	35.824%	7.73%

Students with disabilities (SWD) inside regular class 80% or more of the day—2013

State	SWD Age 6–21 (N)	% of All SWD Age 6–21 in Regular Class >80% of Day	% of Limited English Proficient SWD Age 6–21 in Regular Class >80% of Day
Alabama	61,671	83.832%	2.38%
North Dakota	8,689	75.321%	2.53%
Nebraska	31,035	74.585%	3.95%
Vermont	8,991	74.153%	1.48%
Oregon	52,926	72.906%	10.84%
New Hampshire	18,822	72.846%	1.99%

(Appendix continues on next page)

Kentucky	57,946	72.310%	2.23%
Colorado	56,479	72.106%	15.28%
Rhode Island	14,500	70.746%	6.29%
Florida	223,330	70.041%	8.34%
Indiana	106,282	70.007%	4.53%
Kansas	39,386	68.608%	6.54%
Maryland	62,006	68.400%	5.60%
Connecticut	42,713	68.067%	8.52%
South Dakota	10,746	67.841%	0.75%
Mississippi	37,377	67.204%	1.18%
Delaware	11,358	67.199%	6.62%
North Carolina	115,472	66.252%	5.25%
Texas	265,178	66.171%	15.79%
Tennessee	77,830	66.067%	2.08%
Michigan	117,621	65.367%	4.54%
Georgia	112,283	64.881%	5.94%
Oklahoma	61,145	64.678%	4.16%
Iowa	37,526	64.511%	0.00%
Nevada	28,151	64.256%	20.18%
West Virginia	24,969	64.003%	0.44%
Wisconsin	67,658	63.536%	6.60%
Arizona	72,072	62.932%	8.77%
Virginia	90,749	62.689%	9.77%
Pennsylvania	164,676	62.428%	2.52%
Louisiana	42,963	62.371%	1.30%
Minnesota	67,917	62.120%	7.16%
Wyoming	7,417	61.844%	3.47%
Ohio	141,500	61.095%	1.77%
Massachusetts	91,075	60.676%	6.66%
Alaska	9,536	60.134%	14.92%
Idaho	14,628	60.118%	5.75%
New York	226,398	58.160%	8.35%
Missouri	62,305	58.096%	2.11%
South Carolina	51,367	57.585%	4.64%
Utah	37,442	56.806%	8.70%

(Appendix continues on next page)

Maine	15,863	55.666%	2.18%
District of Columbia	5,518	53.402%	7.70%
California	332,231	53.362%	29.48%
Illinois	135,842	52.936%	5.42%
Arkansas	27,844	52.898%	7.01%
Washington	61,679	52.569%	11.20%
New Mexico	21,357	49.741%	21.84%
Montana	7,020	47.187%	4.22%
New Jersey	96,746	45.846%	1.97%
Hawaii	6,175	36.714%	7.24%

Students with disabilities (SWD) inside regular class 80% or more of the day—2014

State	SWD Age 6–21 (N)	% of All SWD Age 6–21 in Regular Class >80% of Day	% of Limited English Proficient SWD Age 6–21 in Regular Class >80% of Day
Alabama	62,894	83.631%	2.51%
Alaska	12,386	77.466%	16.07%
Nebraska	31,855	76.070%	4.40%
Vermont	9,133	74.928%	1.26%
North Dakota	8,827	74.584%	2.76%
Florida	237,721	73.197%	8.76%
Kentucky	59,128	73.155%	2.40%
Oregon	53,394	72.923%	11.29%
Colorado	58,423	72.820%	17.41%
New Hampshire	18,552	72.339%	1.85%
Rhode Island	14,507	71.050%	4.69%
Indiana	107,606	70.546%	4.82%
Tennessee	82,818	70.065%	2.39%
Kansas	40,398	69.323%	0.00%
Maryland	62,682	68.858%	6.10%
Connecticut	44,540	68.669%	9.69%
South Dakota	11,229	68.440%	2.80%
Delaware	12,074	67.683%	7.45%
Texas	276,181	67.531%	16.55%

(Appendix continues on next page)

North Carolina	117,724	66.451%	7.94%
Michigan	117,109	65.897%	5.04%
Oklahoma	63,750	65.890%	3.39%
Wisconsin	68,088	65.101%	6.86%
Iowa	37,359	64.922%	0.00%
Georgia	115,368	64.696%	6.39%
Mississippi	36,729	64.269%	1.13%
West Virginia	25,210	63.883%	0.48%
Nevada	28,862	63.829%	20.25%
Arizona	74,106	63.650%	8.18%
Virginia	91,536	62.794%	9.57%
Pennsylvania	164,535	61.961%	2.73%
Massachusetts	92,743	61.385%	7.33%
Ohio	142,202	61.353%	1.99%
Louisiana	42,650	61.335%	1.39%
Idaho	15,340	60.849%	6.02%
Minnesota	66,652	60.515%	7.53%
South Carolina	52,513	58.264%	5.24%
Utah	39,421	58.110%	9.27%
New York	243,088	57.803%	8.52%
Missouri	62,293	57.650%	2.42%
Maine	16,062	56.407%	2.33%
District of Columbia	5,840	54.361%	11.90%
Washington	63,410	53.489%	12.04%
California	338,729	53.380%	29.20%
Illinois	136,390	53.005%	6.04%
Arkansas	28,219	52.510%	7.40%
New Mexico	21,974	50.608%	20.70%
Montana	7,217	46.827%	3.56%
New Jersey	96,295	44.934%	2.32%
Hawaii	6,168	36.897%	6.16%
Wyoming	–	–	–

(Appendix continues on next page)

Students with disabilities (SWD) inside regular class 80% or more of the day—2015

State	SWD Age 6–21 (N)	% of All SWD Age 6–21 in Regular Class >80% of Day	% of Limited English Proficient SWD Age 6–21 in Regular Class >80% of Day
Alabama	64,268	83.563%	2.61%
Vermont	9,189	75.761%	1.55%
Nebraska	31,905	75.536%	4.49%
North Dakota	8,875	74.076%	2.75%
Kentucky	60,633	73.728%	2.65%
Colorado	60,607	73.617%	17.63%
Oregon	54,396	73.366%	11.44%
New Hampshire	18,450	72.435%	1.59%
Florida	239,396	71.865%	8.87%
Indiana	109,473	71.402%	4.73%
Tennessee	82,073	70.460%	2.46%
Rhode Island	14,244	69.507%	10.14%
South Dakota	11,696	69.207%	3.11%
Maryland	63,413	68.952%	6.79%
Kansas	40,915	68.909%	9.04%
Texas	285,753	68.125%	17.51%
Connecticut	44,936	67.737%	9.69%
North Carolina	120,038	66.785%	7.74%
Oklahoma	66,380	66.757%	4.52%
Michigan	117,338	66.389%	5.37%
Delaware	12,414	66.342%	8.81%
Wisconsin	69,387	66.225%	7.03%
Iowa	37,801	65.631%	5.97%
Wyoming	8,003	65.379%	3.34%
Arizona	76,153	64.941%	7.50%
Georgia	119,120	64.699%	6.60%
West Virginia	25,974	64.463%	0.61%
Nevada	29,591	63.481%	22.38%
Alaska	10,316	63.386%	14.51%
Virginia	93,773	63.359%	9.76%

(Appendix continues on next page)

Mississippi	36,639	63.020%	1.41%
Massachusetts	94,388	62.345%	8.16%
Ohio	144,493	62.282%	2.19%
Pennsylvania	167,349	61.841%	2.86%
South Carolina	56,060	60.708%	5.25%
Idaho	15,978	60.553%	6.05%
Minnesota	67,931	60.450%	7.78%
Utah	42,268	60.448%	9.10%
Louisiana	44,032	59.671%	1.47%
New York	250,763	57.982%	8.54%
Missouri	62,890	57.589%	2.68%
Maine	16,451	56.690%	2.10%
District of Columbia	5,986	55.493%	12.46%
Washington	65,439	54.353%	12.44%
California	350,995	54.073%	28.94%
Arkansas	29,078	52.680%	7.74%
Illinois	136,310	52.648%	6.61%
New Mexico	22,620	49.800%	20.07%
Montana	7,418	46.964%	3.69%
New Jersey	98,287	45.987%	2.25%
Hawaii	6,180	36.832%	5.71%

CHAPTER 27

PARTNERSHIP FOR STATEWIDE IMPROVEMENT OF EDUCATOR PREPARATION

Beverly A. Sande
Prairie View A&M University

INTRODUCTION

This chapter showcases the collaborative practices used by the Ohio Deans Compact on Exceptional Children (also called the Deans Compact, or just the Compact) in Ohio to pursue a large-scale educational reform systematically and systemically. The Compact's goal was to promote inclusive practice in educator preparation and in schools: a big goal in the name of better service to all students and to the cause of educational equity. Collaboration was essential to the Compact, not only as consistent with its major goal, but also in its operation.

Evidence supports the use of cross-institution collaboration as a strategy for promoting educational improvement (Darling-Hammond, 2010; Davis, 2008; DuFour & Marzano, 2011; Gallimore, Ermeling, Saunders, Goldenberg, 2009; Leithwood, & Jantzi, 2008; McNulty & Besser, 2011; Schmoker, 2006; Seashore Louis, Leithwood, Wahlstrom, & Anderson,

Inclusive Education: A Systematic Perspective, pp. 479–495
Copyright © 2020 by Information Age Publishing

2010; Wahlstrom & Louis, 2008; Wahlstrom, Seashore, Leithwood, & Anderson, 2010). This strategy has the potential to enable partners to draw on existing collective capacity, share resources, provide one another with various types of support, and examine impact collaboratively. Because of the purported benefits of collaborative improvement, state education agencies and other funders encourage and incentivize these types of initiatives (Blanton & Pugach, 2007; Blanton, Pugach, & Boveda, 2014; Fixsen, Naoom, Blase, Friedman, & Wallace, 2005).

This chapter begins with a discussion of strategies that research shows support collaborative reform. Then it presents information about the Deans Compact—a collaborative initiative in Ohio that incentivized institutions of higher education to develop integrated educator preparation programs that would prepare teachers and school leaders to meet the needs of all students. Next, the chapter provides an assessment of how the Compact processes fit with characteristics of collaborative reform. The chapter concludes with a brief discussion of "lessons learned" from the work of the Compact.

Characteristics of Collaborative Improvement

Research about organizational improvement has come from several disciplines—business management, organizational sociology, communications, and education. Across these fields, much of the research involves case studies of effective organizations (e.g., Collins, 2001; Johnson, 1996). Review of these case studies suggests several commonalities among organizations that have been effective at making systemic improvement through the collaborative engagement of organization members and other stakeholders. Among these common practices are (a) promoting a shared vision, (b) orienting to a focused set of goals, (c) using evidence-based practices, (d) developing and maintaining strategic alliances, (e) fostering the ongong use of data, and (f) deploying a strategy for scaling-up the work.

Promoting a Shared Vision

According to a great deal of research on leadership and organizational dynamics, an organization's improvement depends on a clear vision of a desired future state (e.g., Nanus, 1992; Senge, 1990). Moreover, the organization's vision needs to be understood, and in the best case, shared by members of the organization and stakeholders that contribute to and depend on the organization. In fact, research on educational leadership suggests that the shared vision needs to be communicated to a wide set of stakeholders, even when doing so is problematic (e.g., Marsh & Hall, 2018). Sometimes sharing a vision involves efforts to develop a set of core values or organizational non-negotiables.

Orienting to a Focused Set of Goals

Goal setting is the process whereby targets and objectives are established (Posthuma & Al-Riyami, 2012). Specific goals, clearly defined at the outset of an intervention or change process, help to focus participants' attention, mobilize their efforts, and ultimately achieve higher performance (Locke & Latham, 1990). Collaborative educational reform that aims to better meet the needs of diverse students in a variety of contexts, with a range of participants and stakeholders, depends for its success on defining and focusing on shared values and cross-institution goals. Research literature on goal setting—applicable to collaborative groups as well as to individual entities—recommends that goals, whatever their scope, should include five characteristics, denoted by the acronym, SMART: they should be specific (focused), measurable (evidence-based), achievable (doable, though often challenging), relevant (appropriate to context and practice), and time-bound (timely assessment of success; Doran, 1981).

Using Evidence-Based Practices

Evidence-based practice (EBP)—also known as the "what works" agenda—involves using the best available evidence to bring about desired results or prevent undesirable ones (Kvernbekk, 2017). In education, "what works" means that educational researchers and practitioners come together to bring about results, guided by evidence of how well a proposed intervention or improvement strategy actually performs in a given context. For example, classroom-level EBPs might entail instructional techniques that, based on findings from rigorous research studies, show promise for improving student outcomes (Cook & Cook, 2013). Educator preparation programs can be evidence-based in two important ways: (a) the knowledge and skills they teach their candidates can be based on rigorous research and (b) the methods they use for preparing their candidates can be based on rigorous research.

Context is at center stage in EBP, and research and contextual evidence must be brought together for the use of any EBP to be a success (Bryk, Gomez, Grunow, & LeMahieu, 2015). The point is to gather evidence of what works and under what circumstances (Hargreaves, 1996). In education, researchers, practitioners, and faculty members who prepare educators not only can use EBP to address important questions about what and how to teach, but, according to Slavin (2002), they have a professional obligation to do so.

Developing and Maintaining Strategic Alliances

Meeting shared goals in collaborations aimed at educational reform requires that participating organizations build strategic alliances to ensure initial and continuing success in developing and implementing effective policies and practices. One advantage of such alliances is that they can take advantage of economies of scale (Westera, van den Herik, & van den Vrie, 2004) to assure the availability and distribution of funding; staff (teachers, administrators, faculty members, and other researchers); and expertise. For such alliances to be effective and stable, however, the glue holding them together must go beyond economic, personnel, and material benefits. Crucial to making inter-institutional and inter-departmental alliances work successfully are shared values and goals, such as an overarching commitment to providing equitable, quality educational opportunities to diverse student populations (Artiles & Koslesky, 2016).

Fostering the Ongoing Use of Data

The use of data to inform education practices is important in assessing the effectiveness of such practices (Abrams, Varier, & Jackson, 2016). It is also a necessary component in evaluating the success of innovations, strategies, practices, policies, and interventions in reform initiatives. Ongoing use of data undergirds data-driven decision making. According to Turner and Coburn (2012), the use of data is "one of the most central reform ideas in contemporary school policy and practice" (p. 3). Data gathered through routine assessments and observations as well as through rigorous survey and interview studies can be shared among participants within and across collaborating institutions to guide the educational reform process.

Deploying a Strategy for Scaling-Up the Work

"Scaling up" in education refers loosely to broadening the reach of evidence-based innovations (Bradach & Grindl, 2014; Coburn, 2003; Levin, 2013; Sutton, 2014). Coburn (2003) identified four dimensions of scaling up: depth (long-term changes in practice and belief), sustainability (continuation of intervention effects after implementation), spread (increased users), and a shift in reform ownership to employees across the organization or collaborative (as opposed to among only those constituting a guiding coalition). A strategy for scaling up the work would comprise: (a) continuing to build the evidence base for education practices; (b) translating research into policy and practice, (c) implementing what works; and (d) sharing findings and experiences among institutions, practitioners, and other stakeholders (DeWire, McKithen, & Carey, 2017).

THE OHIO DEANS COMPACT ON EXCEPTIONAL CHILDREN

The Deans Task Force originally formed in the 1980s as a result of the Education for All Handicapped Children Act of 1975 in order to establish the special education preparation programs at Ohio universities that would train the new personnel (i.e., special educators) needed as a result of the law. Despite expansion of the group's membership to include educators beyond institutes of higher education (IHEs) program deans and its evolution into the Special Education Personnel Development Advisory Committee, the reach of the organization remained limited and, by the mid-2000s, the organization had dissolved. The Deans Compact nonetheless grew out of these earlier efforts since the Compact's organizers had taken part in them.[1]

Organizing the Deans Compact

In 2012, Sue Zake, Deborah Telfer, Aimee Howley, and others (e.g., leaders from the Ohio Department of Education [ODE] and the Ohio Department of Higher Education [ODHE]) rekindled the initiative to create a collaborative organization that promotes inclusive education. Their efforts produced the Deans Compact, which confronts several issues surrounding Ohio's system of educator preparation and personnel development. These issues include: (a) the division between general and special educators, present amongst teachers as well as IHE faculty members; (b) a disconnect between school districts, educator preparation programs, and the state education agency that prevents these parties from working together on education reform work; and, finally, (c) an awareness gap between local and state officials, such that whereas district-level actors remain unaware of ODE priorities, state policymakers simultaneously fail to address local concerns.

To target these issues, the Deans Compact promotes inclusive educational practices (i.e., practices for educating all learners, regardless of their needs, status, or background), works to bring together expertise from higher education and PK–12 education to support wide-ranging educational reform, and provides a forum for policymakers to communicate with educators and faculty in higher education programs that prepare educators. As such, the Compact functions as an advisory group to state-level policymakers on issues related to educator preparation programs and continuing professional development, with a concerted focus on inclusive education that gives high-quality access to the general education curriculum to students from marginalized groups (e.g., ethnic minorities, students from impoverished communities, students with disabilities).

The Compact serves, more specifically, as an advisory group to state leaders from Ohio Department of Education's Office for Exceptional Children and ODHE (Ohio Deans Compact on Exceptional Children, 2015). A shared mission of the Deans Compact, ODE, and ODHE is to restructure and revamp teacher preparation and personnel development in Ohio (Ohio Deans Compact on Exceptional Children, 2015). An articulated common objective helps stakeholders identify fundamental targets and work toward them.

A Community of Practice

The founders organized the Compact along the lines of *a community of practice*, which is a "[group] of people who share a concern or a passion for something they do and learn how to do it better as they interact regularly" (Wenger-Trayner & Wenger-Trayner, 2015, p. 1). This format enables the Compact's diverse members (including state officials and policymakers, university deans and faculty, professional association representatives, school district leaders, and external stakeholders) to share views and expertise; connect theory to practice; and foster a collaborative environment for learning, inquiry, and dissemination of EBPs. The Compact also partners with organizations nationally (e.g., the Collaboration for Effective Educator Development, Accountability and Reform—CEEDAR—based in Florida; CEEDAR, 2015); several universities outside of Ohio (e.g., Teachers College, Columbia University; Portland State University; Rowan University; the University of Minnesota; and the University of Wisconsin; among others); and a number of school districts (e.g., California's Val Verde Unified School District, Indiana's Bartholomew Consolidated School Corporation; Ohio's Wooster City School District).

Collaboration also characterizes the Compact's quarterly meetings, where members have opportunities to engage in discussion, listen to presentations from outside experts on important topics, and participate on various ad hoc committees that address pressing issues in Ohio. Likewise, the Compact organizes an annual statewide conference (in its sixth iteration in 2019) that brings together diverse stakeholders for collaboration and discussion of important topics related to equity and inclusion. The Compact also spearheads several major funding initiatives, including various incentive grants (IGs) to support important statewide reform.

Projects and Activities

The fourth iteration of the Compact's IG program is currently underway. These IGs target four key areas by developing: (a) inclusive teacher preparation programs that lead to dual licensure in general and special education, (b) inclusive principal preparation programs, (c) partnerships between educator preparation programs and PK–12 school districts, and (d) coursework to improve educators' ability to work with students with low incidence sensory disabilities. Grants supporting the development of dual licensure programs enable faculty in departments with separate general and special education programs to engage in self-study, conduct program and curriculum redesign work, and create blended preparation programs. In Ohio, 10 new blended programs have already received accreditation; a further seven programs, funded during the 2017 grant cycle, are currently under development. Funding for the development of inclusive principal preparation programs proceeds along similar lines, though this work is not yet so far along as the dual-licensure work.

Another type of IG funds IHE-school district partnerships. These "simultaneous renewal" grants foster communication between different types of educators, notably IHE faculty and school district faculty, with the aim of increasing their efforts to promote and use inclusive educational practices.

The Compact also seeks to address the shortage of educators who are trained to work with students with low-incidence sensory disabilities. This effort was supported through another type of IG with a focus on the development of preparation programs and other course work on sensory impairments to be offered collaboratively across a consortium of Ohio universities—the Low Incidence Sensory Disability (LISD) Collaborative. In its first major initiative, the Collaborative brought together five IHEs to design and implement a new licensure program that prepares educators to work with students with visual impairments. This initiative, known as the Teachers of the Visually Impaired (TVI) Consortium, resulted in the development of a post-baccalaureate licensure program designed to increase the number of educators credentialed to work with students with visual impairments, and especially to increase the number of those working in underserved communities (e.g., rural districts). The Consortium program admitted its first students during the summer of 2018. The Collaborative is now undertaking similar work to support teaching in other LISD areas (e.g., hearing impairment, orientation and mobility).

Further Reach

Faculty have worked across programs to develop robust dual license programs that attract future teachers. Similarly, stronger alliances between university faculty and P–12 partners have resulted in creation of rich clinical experiences for teacher candidates through year-long clinical models, professional development schools, and co-teaching experience developed and implemented through collaborative academic alliances.

Looking forward, the Compact plans to continue its work and, indeed, to grow its presence both statewide and nationally. In Ohio this involves the ongoing funding of dual licensure programs, until these programs replace individual programs at most institutions. The Compact will also work on the problem of teacher shortages, especially in areas like LISD. Funding inclusive leadership programs also remains critically important because equitable schooling requires leaders committed to the implementation of inclusive practices. At the national level, particularly organizations like the CEEDAR Center offer a promising way of scaling up the Compact's work.

HOW THE DEANS COMPACT USES COLLABORATIVE IMPROVEMENT

The Compact provides an illustration of the common principles described in the first section of this chapter. Compact founders were, in fact, familiar with these principles and had used them successfully in efforts with smaller organizational footprints (e.g., state efforts to support paraprofessionals, the state's center for deafblind education, and educator preparation programs for career-changers). Experience as well as research established, in their minds, the principles and practices—for the Ohio context in particular. Compact leaders believed that the application of these principles and practices would support the creation and nurture of a large-scale collaboration with the promise of supporting inclusive schooling statewide.

Promoting a Shared Vision of Inclusive Education

The Compact's mission begins with concern for students with disabilities but, unconventionally, its vision of inclusive education (and much of its work) encompasses both special and general education. Not only is the Compact committed to full inclusion (in general education) for the vast majority of students with disabilities, it does not confine "inclusion" to the silo of special education. It views good schooling for everyone in the general education curriculum as a foundational principle.

The shared vision is evident in partner selection, curricular development, research endeavors, and the greater good of training high quality teachers. The Compact promotes this vision widely via its quarterly meetings and annual conference, which draw substantial participation from across the state. Key invitees present in plenary and concurrent sessions. Many have national reputations as scholars or change-agents in either general or special education (or both). Past speakers include Stephen Barr, Jim Borland, Antonia Darder, Gene Glass, Paul Gorski, Etta Hollins, Srikala Naraian, Celia Oyler, Martha Thurlow, and Kevin Welner. Even more significantly, the Compact strongly promotes its vision via its choices about the policy and curriculum development work to pursue. The dual-licensure initiative, for instance, engages special and general educators in collaboration that has both a programmatic and policy payoff. Dual-licensure program graduates work in schools, with their preparation shaped by the Compact's vision of inclusive practice.

How the Compact Sustains Its Focused Goals

The Compact's prime focus is educator preparation and personnel development, and a carefully chosen portfolio of ongoing projects (see Projects and Activities above) cleave to that focus. Although the focus is clear, the scope of the work (i.e., the whole state of Ohio) is comparatively large. More daunting still, the Compact carries out its projects consistent with a commitment to inclusion, equity, and social justice—values that are certainly not shared by all of Ohio's political leaders. How can the Compact sustain the focus under such circumstances?

Subcommittees of the Compact take responsibility for the projects, with considerable support from Compact leaders. Indeed, the formal and informal leadership press the Compact toward productivity within the focus and consistent with the commitment to inclusive schooling. The efforts have yielded notable successes (e.g., the establishment of dual-licensure programs and new statewide programs in sensory disabilities). Moreover, its meetings and conferences deal not only with the operation of the Compact and progress on its projects but offer participants intellectually substantive interaction with national experts whose own work resonates with that of the Compact.

The Deans Compact has provided opportunities for IHEs and their partners to be privy to advice from numerous experts who have shared many research-based collaborative frameworks: Active Implementation Frameworks, the Global Implementation Specialist Model, and Scaling-up Evidence based Practices Frameworks (Duda & Wilson 2015; Fixsen, Duda, Blasé, & Horner 2009; Metz, Louison, Ward, & Burke, 2017; Warren et al., 2012). These opportunities are provided to all stakeholders during the quarterly meetings.

As a result of such efforts, the Compact cultivates, though its activities and vision, a wider circle of participants who grasp the importance of the focus, the commitments, and the work and who help carry it out, promote it, and sustain it. By acquiring support from different constituencies and facilitating their joint engagement in substantive learning, the work of the Deans Compact becomes meaningful, relevant and authentic to its members from both general and special education.

How the Compact Uses EBPs

All else equal, the Compact's higher-education context positions the organization within a culture of scholarship. Its leaders, organizational partners, and individual participants bring well-developed (and varied) engagements with evidence to the work of the Compact. Notably, Ohio's State-wide System of Support has deployed an inquiry model for more than 10 year to promote district improvement. Furthermore, the ODHE also makes use of data-based processes to help educator preparation programs improve.

The Deans Compact creates an enabling context (Fixsen, Duda, Blasé, & Horner, 2009) for implementation of EBPs. As noted in the description of the Compact, the vectors for EBP within the Compact's focus on educator preparation pertain to (a) the content of preparation programs and (b) methods of preparation programs. Dual licensure programs at grantee institutions are based, in each case, on proposers' interpretations of the relevant evidence. Initial proposals, moreover, are peer-reviewed by a Compact review panel. Program design addresses both content and methods. The same process pertains to the development of programs for sensory disabilities and inclusive leadership sponsored under the Compact's aegis.

The Compact has also contracted with a third-party evaluator to provide formative feedback as well as coordinating some of its activities with original research efforts in Ohio. In addition, it has sponsored research initiatives undertaken through its ongong Community of Practice.

How the Compact Conducts Strategic Alliances

The best characterization of the Compact might be that it *is* a strategic alliance. The founders, for instance, represented the ODE Office of Exceptional Children (Zake), a university center focusing on personnel preparation and outreach (Telfer), and higher education (Howley). Most significantly, the three were in agreement about the importance of inclusive practice as a broad construct uniting general and special education. The agreement included, for instance, the view that good instruction was a unified phenomenon not separable into special tools for students with disabilities and general tools for those without disabilities. All three understood the evidentiary base very well, and they appreciated the gap between best evidence and typical practice in teacher preparation. The Compact would, in their vision, become a vehicle for helping shrink the gap.

The Office for Exceptional Children subsequently funded the competitive grant-making process used to support changes in preparation programs. The Compact leadership was able to enlist the participation of a small group of allies at the ODE (notably in general education), the ODHE, some university programs, professional organizations (e.g., the Ohio Federation of Teacher, the Ohio Education Association, the Buckeye Association of School Administrators), and in regional agencies (e.g., State Support Teams). Shared values among the initial participants—and productive airing of perspectives—helped the Compact grow more robust and expand to include additional participants. Such preparation enabled the simultaneous adaptation of policy and program change, statewide.

Faculty have worked across departments within their universities to develop robust dual license programs that involve strong alliances between university faculty and P–12 partners. These partnerships have resulted in the creation of rich clinical experiences for teacher candidates through up-dated course work, intensive clinical models, co-teaching opportunities, and other innovations. In addition, "simultaneous renewal" projects have encouraged collaborative partnerships eliciting equal contributions from higher education faculty and PK–12 educators.

How the Compact Fosters the Ongoing Use of Data

The Deans Compact provides support for research, demonstrations, and evaluations of the IG projects. During regular quarterly meetings and conferences, IHEs and their partners are able to demonstrate products resulting from the funding provided. Research done on the simultaneous grant initiatives is used to increase knowledge and skills as well as for capacity building.

The Compact conducts routine formative evaluations of its own processes, the results of which are discussed in the Compact's working groups. Grantee institutions update Compact members at quarterly meetings. Compact leaders monitor the progress on program design and implementation, and, based on such data, have periodically reconfigured the Compact's award process.

The Compact's Community of Practice also provides counsel to grantee institutions as their design and implementation work proceeds. The Deans Compact provides support for research, demonstrations, and evaluations of the IG projects. As noted previously, the Compact has also hired a third-party evaluator to provide the perspective of an outsider. Given the scope of the Compact's ambitions, the scale of its involvements, and the very nature of the work, the use of data is embedded in the Compact's activities and culture.

How the Compact is a Strategy for Scaling-Up Change in Teacher Education

Fixsen and colleagues from the National Implementation Research Network apply a model of implementation science to address the problem of promoting programs that utilize EBPs for students with disabilities (Fixsen, Duda, Blasé, & Horner, 2009; Metz, Naoom, Halle, & Bartley, 2015). They emphasize the importance of building an infrastructure at the state level, and propose a framework that involves external support for systems change, the creation of an executive management team, a process for training and support that flows from policy to practice levels, and, of particular importance, a feedback loop that incorporates information from the practice level into ongoing planning to support implementation (Cook & Odem, 2013).

As a statewide effort, the Compact itself is a strategy for "scaling-up" the reform of educator preparation in Ohio. *How* the strategy has unfolded via the Compact, though, comprises an account of one version of large-footprint change (across an entire state). The particulars of the scale-up effort might be summarized as *steadily incremental*. For instance, successive grant cycles have funded programmatic changes in general and special education teacher preparation, with the participating knowledge and involvement of the ODE and the ODHE. As innovative program designs were completed, implementation was enabled by the approval of the ODHE. The success of programs was sufficient to interest additional grant applications. The change spread more widely.

Equally important, but seemingly less practical, the Compact's meetings and annual conferences have been designed to attract the participation of higher education faculty and thoughtful practitioners and policy makers. This decision underscores and in fact propagates and elaborates the Compact's central commitment to a broadly defined concept of inclusive practice. The intellectually substantive portions of the meetings can be understood as fostering the motivation for growing membership and interest in the Compact's agenda. In addition, special "convenings" have, through support from CEEDAR, allowed the Compact to share its work with a wider group of higher-education and PK–12 educators.

LESSONS LEARNED

What lessons has the Compact learned as an organization? These answers are high-inference conclusions:

- By their nature *compacts establish* commitments, intentions, culture, and procedures as an organization. Compacts (as distinguishable from temporary coalitions) establish a largely democratic organizational framework based on a focused set of values (commitments) and aspirations (intentions). Additionally, they cultivate certain collaborative and deliberative ways of operating. The Deans Compact, as an organization, demonstrates these features.
- Statewide education coalitions (as compacts) should clearly articulate key commitments (e.g., inclusive education) and enlist initial partners from organizations crucial to the change effort. Organizational durability is essential to work entailing large-scale changes in practice and policy. The founding principles and commitments should guide the evolving culture. As it has grown, the Deans Compact has succeeded in enlisting new partners attracted to its work (and its culture—including these principles and commitments).
- Compacts exist to facilitate active collaboration to the point of consensual action. That is, effective compacts must implement their fundamental commitments ("non-negotiables") as real-world engagements with the force of solidarity. Compacts govern their members' collaborative planning and real-world action. The sustainability of a compact on such a basis means that such planning and action enter the realm of action with an established organizational footprint. That footprint extends beyond compact members to the separate organizations they inhabit. The Deans Compact works through the activity of individual members in solidarity but also through the participation (to some extent) of the members' organizations.

- Higher education compacts in particular (e.g., the Ohio Deans Compact) seeking statewide change must address policy, practice, and intellectual substance simultaneously. Higher education compacts exist in a realm of intellectual work: inquiry, debate, and considered judgment. For the Deans Compact, this existence has included intellectually substantive programming for participating members, data-gathering and analysis cycles, and planning episodes that position efforts directed toward institutional change.

The Ohio Deans Compact for Exceptional Children is entering its seventh year of activity at this writing (January 2019). Its focus on collaborative improvement, statewide, has conceptualized, organized, and accomplished some of its intended goals. Its collaborative effort, though, is not characterized mostly by its goals, but by its culture and the solidarity of its members. The excellence of The Deans Compact rests largely on the shared values of its members and partners.

NOTE

1. This section (on the Deans Compact) paraphrases information found elsewhere in this volume (see Chapter 25, Establishing the Deans Compact) as well as on the Compact's website (Ohio Deans Compact for Exceptional Children, 2019).

REFERENCES

Abrams, L., Varier, D., & Jackson, L. (2016). Unpacking instructional alignment: The influence of teachers' use of assessment data on instruction. *Perspectives in Education 34*(4), 15–28.

Artiles, A. J., & Koslesky, E. B. (2016). Inclusive education's promises and trajectories: Critical notes about future research on a venerable idea. *Education Policy Analysis Archives 24*(43), 1–24. Retrieved from https://epaa.asu.edu/ojs/article/view/1919

Blanton, L. P., & Pugach, M. C. (2007). *Collaborative programs in general and special teacher education: An action guide for higher education and state policy makers.* Washington, DC: Council of Chief State School Officers.

Blanton, L. P., Pugach, M. C., & Boveda, M. (2014). *Teacher education reform initiatives and special education: Convergence, divergence, and missed opportunities* (Document No. LS-3). Retrieved from University of Florida, Collaboration for Effective Educator, Development, Accountability, and Reform Center website: http://ceedar.education.ufl.edu/tools/literature-syntheses/

Bradach, J., & Grindle, A. (2014). *Transformative scale: The future of growing what works.* Boston, MA: The Bridgespan Group.

Bryk, A. S., Gomez, L. M., Grunow, A., & LeMahieu, P. G. (2015). *Learning to improve: How America's schools can get better at getting better*. Cambridge, MA: Harvard Education Press.

Collins, J. (2001). *Good to great: Why some companies make the leap and others don't*. New York, NY: HarperCollins.

Cook, B. G., & Cook, S. C. (2013). Unraveling evidence-based practices in special education. *The Journal of Special Education, 47*, 71–82. doi:10.1177/0022466911420877

Cook, B. G., & Odom, S. L. (2013). Evidence-based practices and implementation science in special education. Exceptional Children, *79*, 135–144. doi:10.1177/001440291307900201

Coburn, C. E. (2003). Rethinking scale: Moving beyond the numbers to deep and lasting change. *Educational Researcher 32*(6), 3–12. doi:10.3102/0013189X032006003

Collaboration for Effective Educator Development, Accountability and Reform (CEEDAR) Center. (2015). *Reform Efforts*. Retrieved from http://ceedar. education.ufl.edu/ta-map/ohio-intensive-ta/

Darling-Hammond, L. (2010). *The flat world and education: How America's commitment to equity will determine our future*. NY: Teachers College Press.

Davis, S. H. (2008). *Research and practice in education: The search for common ground*. Lanham, MD: Rowman & Littlefield.

DeWire, T., McKithen, C., & Carey, R. (2017). *Scaling up evidence-based practices: Strategies from investing in innovation (i3)*. Washington, DC: U.S. Department of Education. Retrieved from: https://i3community.ed.gov/insights-discoveries/2207

Doran, G. T. (1981). There's a S.M.A.R.T. way to write management's goals and objectives. *Management Review, 70*(11), 33–36.

Duda, M., & Wilson, B. A., (2015). *Using Implementation Science to close the policy to practice gap*. A Literacy Nation white paper. Science Panel. Vol. Spring (2015). San Francisco, CA.

DuFour, R., & Marzano, R. J. (2011). *Leaders of learning: How district, school, and classroom leaders improve student achievement*. Bloomington, IN: Solution Tree.

Fixsen, D. L., Duda, M. A., Blase, K. A. & Horner, R. (2009). *State capacity assessment for scaling evidence-based practices* (v.23). Chapel Hill, NC: University of North Carolina Chapel Hill.

Fixsen, D. L., Naoom, S. F., Blase, K. A., Friedman, R. M., & Wallace, F. (2005). *Implementation research: A synthesis of the literature*. Retrieved from http://ctndisseminationlibrary.org/PDF/nirnmonograph.pdf

Gallimore, R., Ermeling, B., Saunders, W., & Goldenberg, C., (2009). Moving the learning of teaching closer to practice: Teacher education implications of school-based inquiry teams. *The Elementary School Journal, 109*, 1–17. doi:10.1086/597001

Hargreaves, D. (1996). Educational research and evidence-based educational practice: A response to critics. *Research Intelligence 58*, 12–16.

Johnson, S. M. (1996). *Leading to change: The challenge of the new superintendency*. San Francisco, CA: Jossey-Bass.

Kvernbekk, T. (2017). Evidence-based educational practices. In *Oxford Research Encyclopedia of Education*. doi:10.1093/acrefore/9780190264093.013.187

Leithwood, K., & Jantzi, D. (2008). Linking leadership to student learning: The contributions of leader efficacy. *Educational Administration Quarterly, 44*, 496–528. doi:10.1177/0013161X08321501

Levin, B. (2013). *What does it take to scale up innovations? An examination of Teach for America, the Harlem Children's Zone, and the Knowledge is Power Program.* Boulder, CO: National Education Policy Center. Retrieved from https://nepc.colorado.edu/publication/scaling-up-innovations

Locke, E. A., & Latham, G. P. (1990). *A theory of goal-setting and task performance.* Englewood Cliffs, NJ: Prentice Hall.

Marsh, J. A., & Hall, M. (2018). Challenges and choices: A multidistrict analysis of statewide mandated democratic engagement. *American Educational Research Journal, 55*, 243–286. doi:10.3102/0002831217734803

McNulty, B. A., & Besser, L. (2011). *Leaders make it happen! An administrator's guide to data teams.* Englewood CO: Lead & Learn.

Metz, A., Naoom, S., Halle, T., & Bartley, L. (2015). *An integrated stage-based framework for implementation of early childhood programs and systems.* Washington, DC: Office of Planning, Research, and Evaluation, U.S. Department of Health and Human Services

Metz, A. Louison, C., Ward, C., & Burke, K (2017). Global Implementation Specialist Practice Profile (GISPP): Skills and competencies for implementation practitioners. *National Implementation Research Network*. Retrieved from http://nirn.fpg.unc.edu/sites/nirn.fpg.unc.edu/files/resources/NIRN-ISPracticeProfile-06-05-2017.pdf

Nanus, B. (1992). *Visionary leadership: Creating a compelling sense of direction for your organization.* San Francisco, CA: Jossey-Bass.

Ohio Dean Compact on Exceptional Children. (2019). Retrieved from https://www.ohiodeanscompact.org/

Ohio Deans Compact on Exceptional Children. (2015). *Incentivizing Innovative Practices.* Retrieved from https://ohiodeanscompact.org/our-work/incentivizing-innovative-practices

Posthuma, R., & Al-Riyami, S. (2012). Leading teams of higher education administrators: Integrating goal setting, team role, and team life cycle theories. *Higher Education Studies 2*(3), 44–54. doi:10.5539/hes.v2n3p44

Schmoker, M. (2006). *Results NOW: How we can achieve unprecedented improvements in teaching and learning.* Alexandria, VA: ASCD.

Seashore Louis, K., Leithwood, K., Wahlstrom, K. L., & Anderson, S. E. (2010). *Investigating the links to improved student learning.* Minneapolis, MN: University of Minnesota, Center for Applied Research and Educational Improvement.

Senge, P. M. (1990). *The fifth discipline: The art and practice of the learning organization.* New York, NY: Currency Doubleday.

Slavin, R. E. (2002). Evidence-based education policies: Transforming educational practice and research. *Educational Researcher 31*(7), 15–21. doi:10.3102/0013189X031007015

Sutton, R. I. (2014). Eight essentials for scaling up without screwing up. *Harvard Business* Review. Retrieved from https://hbr.org/2014/02/eight-essentials-for-scaling-up-without-screwing-up

Turner, E. O., & Coburn, C. E. (2012). Interventions to promote data use: An introduction. *Teachers College Record 114*(11), 1-13. Retrieved from https://www.sesp.northwestern.edu/docs/publications/75575854257c9a4096b5c2.pdf

Wahlstrom, K. L., & Louis, K. S. (2008). How teachers experience principal leadership: The roles of professional community, trust, efficacy, and shared responsibility. *Educational Administration Quarterly, 44,* 458–495. doi:10.1177/0013161X08321502

Wahlstrom, K., Seashore, K., Leithwood, K., & Anderson, S. (2010). *Learning from leadership: Investigating the links to improved student learning* (Research Report Executive Summary). Minneapolis, MN: University of Minnesota, Center for Applied Research and Educational Improvement.

Warren, S., Thurlow, M., Lazarus, S., Christensen, L., Chartrand, A., & Rieke, R. (2012). *Forum on evaluating educator effectiveness: Critical considerations for including students with disabilities.* Minneapolis, MN: University of Minnesota, National Center on Educational Outcomes and Washington, DC: Council of Chief State School Officers, Assessing Special Education Students State Collaborative on Assessment and Student Standards.

Westera, W., van den Herik, J., & van den Vrie, E. (2004). Strategic alliances in education: The knowledge engineering web. *Innovations in Education and Teaching 41,* 317–328. doi:10.1080/14703290420001733267

Wenger-Trayner, B., & Wenger-Trayner, E. (2015). *Introduction to communities of practice.* Retrieved from http://wenger-trayner.com/introduction-to-communities-of-practice/

ABOUT THE AUTHORS

EDITOR BIOS

Cassondra Faiella is a research assistant for the Ohio Deans Compact. She completed her undergraduate degree at The Ohio State University—majoring in psychology and minoring in education—and is currently working on her master's degree in general/research psychology at The University of Dayton. She has experience with research and evaluation in numerous fields including investigational devices, orthopedic surgery, physiology, usability testing, social psychology, inclusive education practices, and cancer screening materials.

Barbara Hansen currently serves as the Dave Longaberger Endowed Chair in Teaching and Learning at Muskingum University, teaching graduate courses in educational leadership. She was the East Muskingum Local Superintendent for 10 years and taught high school English and classes for identified gifted students K–8. She has a deep interest in Invitational Education and serves as a national trustee in the International Alliance for Invitational Education.

Aimee Howley, President of WordFarmers Associates, has a broad background in educational research, evaluation, and policy studies. She is also professor emerita at Ohio University, where she served as a faculty member in the Educational Studies Department and Senior Associate Dean of the Patton College of Education. Aimee Howley's research explores the

497

intersection between social context and educational practice; and she has used both quantitative and qualitative methods to investigate a wide range of questions relating to education for diverse learners (including intellectually talented students), rural education, education reform, and school leadership.

Stephen Kroeger, an associate professor at University of Cincinnati, has been an integral partner in the development of the Middle Childhood Dual License develop at the University. He facilitates a Statewide Community of Practice with the Deans Compact for Exceptional Children. He taught in St. Lucia, West Indies, in Peru among the Quechua Indians of the Andean Highlands, and in a high school in Detroit, Michigan.

AUTHOR BIOS

Elena Andrei is an Assistant Professor of TESOL and TESOL Program Coordinator at Cleveland State University in Cleveland, OH. She holds an MA in English Language and Literature from the University of Bucharest, an MAEd from Wake Forest University, and an EdD in Curriculum and Instruction from the University of Virginia. Her research is classroom-based and focuses on second language literacy and multiliteracies, teacher education, and non-native English-speaking teachers.

Christopher Atchison is an associate professor of geoscience education in the School of Education and Department of Geology at the University of Cincinnati and Founder of the International Association for Geoscience Diversity. A geologist by training and a former middle school science teacher, his research and teaching focuses on engaging all students in the classroom and in the natural environment. He routinely leads accessible and inclusive geoscience field courses around the world for students with physical, sensory, intellectual and social-emotional disabilities.

Joni Baldwin is a faculty member of the Department of Teacher Education at the University of Dayton. She believes in improving the quality of education for all students through preservice and in-service training of general education teachers to address the diversity of students in their classrooms. Her research interests are in student engagement through hands-on, activity-based learning.

Anne Bauer is a professor of special education at the University of Cincinnati. She has been a teacher, head teacher, and training specialist working with teacher, parents, and students with severe behavioral disorders. Dr. Bauer is the author of more than twenty special education textbooks.

Pamela Beam is a recently retired Lecturer in the Adolescent-to-Young-Adult Program in the Department of Teacher Education at Ohio University. The courses she taught covered a wide range including general methods courses in planning, classroom management and assessment, reading in the content areas, and curriculum and instruction, at the undergraduate and graduate level. Her research interests include mentoring at all levels and clinical practice in the field of education.

Ray Blevins is a Special Education and School Improvement Consultant with State Support Team Region 15. He has more than 20 years of experience as a teacher, adjunct professor, administrator, instructional coach, transition specialist, and special education consultant in public and private settings. He currently provides professional development, technical assistance and consultation on various educational topics for schools, districts, local colleges, community and state agencies, parent support groups, and community organizations.

Jane Bogan is an associate professor and coordinator of accreditation and field placement in the Education Area of Wilmington College. She earned her BSEd at Bowling Green State University and her MEd, and PhD, at the University of Virginia. Her research interests include implementation and evaluation of academic interventions with students who are struggling learners and who are at risk for academic failure.

Connie Bowman is Chair of the Department of Teacher Education at the University of Dayton. She works to bridge the gap between general educators and intervention specialists to improve the learning for all students. Her research interest is in the area of preservice teacher education.

Sara Brannan is an associate professor of Education and the Coordinator of Academic Success at Wittenberg University. Her primary research area examines collaboration among special educators and related health service providers for students with disabilities. In addition, Dr. Brannan is an advocate for Arts Integration for students.

Clarissa Bunch Wade is a doctoral student in Early Childhood Special Education at George Mason University; as a Dean's Scholar she works with faculty as a graduate research assistant on projects related to improving teacher practice and program development. She holds the BS in Child Development & Family Studies from West Virginia University and MEd in Early Childhood Intervention Specialist from Ohio University. Her research interests focus on evidence-based interventions to improve behavioral and communication outcomes for all children and examining equity for students from culturally and linguistically diverse backgrounds.

Emilie Camp is an associate professor, educator at the University of Cincinnati. Her work in teacher preparation focuses on social justice education within social studies and inclusive practices. In addition to her eight years at the university, Emilie has worked in urban public schools in northern Kentucky and southern New Mexico.

Nancy Corbett, is an Assistant Scholar at the University of Florida in the School of Special Education, School Psychology, and Early Childhood Studies. Her research concentrates on literacy-related and social emotional learning interventions for students at risk of school failure and the professional development of teachers working with students in inclusive settings. She has served as investigator and project director on numerous federally funded projects and is currently the coinvestigator on a study funded by the Institute of Education Sciences (IES) to test the efficacy of a theoretically based social-emotional learning curriculum.

Tammy Elchert is an elementary principal for the Carey Exempted Village School District. She has over twenty years of experience in PreK–12 education. She also works in grant writing, federal programming, and professional development. Her research interests include staff development and program evaluation.

Amy Farley is an Assistant Professor of Educational Leadership & Policy Studies in the School of Education at University of Cincinnati. Her scholarly interests include the politics of education and how policy and reform impact students, teachers, and educational equity and opportunity. Her most recent research has explored school and university reform, high-stakes data use and measurement, and the disparate impact of education policies on minoritized student and educator populations.

Bridgie Ford is professor emerita, University of Akron, LeBron James Family Foundation College of Education. Dr. Ford's scholarly activities include cofounder and first editor of the *Council for Exceptional Children's* journal, *Multiple Voices for Ethnically Diverse Exceptional Learners*; coauthor of two books and author or coauthor of numerous publications in educational journals and books focusing on equitable, quality services to African American youth with disabilities and their families; and a past member of the CEC Executive Committee. Dr. Ford is the recipient of several grants in the areas of special education and health-related issues of African American youth.

Susan Gregson is an assistant professor, field service at the University of Cincinnati. Her work focuses on equitable classroom practice in mathematics education, and the preparation of mathematics teachers for effective instruction of marginalized students. She has coached teachers, and taught mathematics in rural and urban schools, both in the United States and abroad.

Christan Grygas Coogle is an Assistant Professor in the Early Childhood Education Program at George Mason University where she teaches courses in Early Childhood Special Education. She received her BS and MS in Special Education and the PhD in Curriculum & Instruction, all from Florida State University. Her research focuses on embedded interventions implemented in natural and inclusive early childhood environments and supporting early educators in their use of these practices.

Dianne Gut is a Professor in Special Education and currently serves as Assistant Department Chair of Teacher Education in the Patton College of Education at Ohio University. She teaches graduate and undergraduate courses in Special Education and Curriculum and Instruction. Her major research interests include mentoring of educators at all levels, clinical practice in teacher education, and inclusive teaching practices.

Joseph A. Hall is an assistant professor and Education area coordinator (department head) at Wilmington College. He earned his BA in Organizational Leadership from Wilmington College, his MA in Education from Mount Vernon Nazarene University, completed his post-graduate studies in mild/moderate special education at Miami University, and earned his EdD in School Leadership from Concordia University Chicago. He has worked as both a general education teacher, intervention specialist, and special education director in a variety of P–12 public school settings with research interests that include implementation and evaluation of co-teaching methodology and practitioner perceptions of co-teaching and inclusion.

Sara Hartman is an Assistant Professor in Early Childhood Education at Ohio University where she teaches courses in assessment and social studies methodology for early childhood teacher candidates and serves as the faculty coordinator for early childhood teacher. She holds the BS in Elementary Education from Ohio University. She also holds the MEd in Curriculum & Instruction and the PhD in Teaching, Curriculum, &

Learning, both from the University of Nebraska-Lincoln. Dr. Hartman situates her research within the themes of university-community-school partnerships, rural education, and clinically-based teacher preparation.

Sara Helfrich is an Associate Professor of Reading Education and Program Coordinator for the Literacy Program at Ohio University where she teaches courses on the foundations of reading development, reading methods, and reading instruction and assessment; she also serves as a Faculty Coordinator for early childhood teacher candidates. She holds the BA in Elementary Education and the MEd in Special Education from Boston College and holds the PhD in Reading Education from the University of Pittsburgh. Her major research interests include reading teacher preparation and teacher/teacher candidate self-efficacy to teach literacy.

Holly Johnson is a professor in the Literacy and Second Language Studies Program at the University of Cincinnati. She teaches courses on literature for middle school students, language arts methods, and literacy as a cultural tool. Her research centers on critical content analysis of literature for young people.

K. Ann Kaufman, an instructor in the Education Department at Marietta College, has served as a Co-Principal Investigator for the Ohio Deans Compact Incentive Grant for the development of the Middle Childhood Dual License at the College. She is currently working on her dissertation research with peer mentors in a postsecondary education program for students with intellectual disabilities, Marietta College's Pioneer Pipeline. She taught middle school special education in Vienna, West Virginia before coming to Marietta College.

Charles Kemp, serves as Assistant Professor at Shawnee State University. Kemp has more than 30 years of teaching and administrative experience (PK–12), having previously served as the supervisor of special education with Portsmouth City Schools (Ohio). His passion for inclusive education of all students, including higher education, supports his research interests in postsecondary transition education, self-help skill development, and independent living skills for students with IDD and ASD.

Lois Kimmel is Research Assistant at American Institutes for Research (AIR) in the Special Education and Tiered Systems of Support Practice Area. She provides technical assistance to projects related to instructional interventions, math disability, and educator preparation. Through the Collaboration for Effective Educator Development, Accountability, and Reform (CEEDAR) Center, Kimmel works with a team of researchers to coordinate targeted technical assistance that promotes aligned professional learning systems across the teacher and leader career continuum by facilitating collaboration between state education agencies, colleges and universities, and local school districts.

Lynn Kline, Associate Professor, Department of Curricular and Instructional Studies, College of Education. Dr. Kline has had over 40 years of teaching experience in a variety of educational settings. She holds a doctorate in Urban Education, a master's degree in Early Childhood Education and a bachelor's degree in Elementary Education. She has published and presented research in the areas of early childhood teacher preparation, performance assessment, professional development, and mentoring. She has served on professional review committees for the Ohio Department of Education and Ohio Department of Higher Learning. Dr. Kline has also served as president of the Ohio Association of Teacher Educators; Association of Teacher Educators Early Childhood Special Interest Group and is currently a member the ATE Advocacy and Legislative Committee.

Laura Kuebel is a school psychologist serving Montgomery County. Laura works with students and families to ensure quality education and special education services in the preschool setting. Her research interests include preschool students and social-emotional development.

Julie Kugler-Ackley is AMS (American Montessori Society) credentialed for both EI and EII, holds an Ohio license for K–8, and is a Clinical faculty member at the Xavier University Montessori Teacher Education Program. She has presented at regional, national, and international Montessori conferences, and has teaching experience at all levels of Montessori elementary levels. She has developed online coursework and currently teaches courses in the Xavier Montessori Teacher Education program and the online Montessori Master of Education degree programs.

Catherine Lawless Frank has worked in education for 25 years. She has taught both regular and special education and in elementary, middle and high schools. Catherine is currently teaching in the Intervention Specialist Department at the University of Dayton.

Paul Madden, is the Dean of the College of Professional Studies at Shawnee State University. He is in his 26th year serving in faculty and academic administrative positions. Dr. Madden has remained active throughout his career supporting high quality educator preparation and development that helps meet the needs of all learners.

Traci McKee is a member of the School of Education Advisory Council at Shawnee State University. She spent several years as correctional educator and now works in adult education. Her addition to the council comes from extensive research on various ways of assisting and supporting teachers in working with children with Autism Spectrum Disorder. As the parent liaison, she brings an alternative perspective on inclusive practices, and works with teachers and therapists to ensure the provision of high-quality education.

Roger Morris is a former assistant professor of education at Malone University in Canton, Ohio. Prior to becoming a professor, Dr. Morris spent 27 years in P–12 education as a teacher, administrator, and superintendent in Virginia. He specializes in curriculum and instruction, school law and ethics, and leadership.

Linda Morrow is a professor emeritus of Muskingum University where she served for 23 years in numerous professorial and administrative roles in teacher education. Her teaching and leadership in special education spearheaded state and federally funded grant projects that infused inclusive education, co-teaching, and behavioral support across Muskingum's undergraduate and graduate teacher education programs and P–12 schools throughout Southeastern Ohio. Her work to weave inclusive and invitational education together now extends beyond the classroom as she weaves the principles of Inclusive Invitational Education into ministry.

Mary Heather Munger is an assistant professor in the College of Education at the University of Findlay, where she teaches literacy courses. She holds a BS in Special Education from The Ohio State University, an MEd in Language Education from Indiana University, and a PhD in Curriculum and Instruction from the University of Toledo. Her research interests include dyslexia, content area reading, pedagogical practices, and parent-teacher partnerships.

Mary Murray is a professor and associate dean at Bowling Green State University (BGSU). She has over 30 years of experience as an Early Childhood Special Education teacher, supervisor and administrator. She was one of the developers of the BGSU Inclusive Early Childhood (dual licensure) Program that now serves nearly 900 students. She has numerous presentations and publications in the area of personnel preparation in inclusive early childhood special education settings.

Jennifer Ottley is an Associate Professor in Early Childhood Special Education and Program Coordinator for the Special Education program at

Ohio University where she teaches courses in early childhood development, adaptations, and assessment for learners with special needs in early childhood settings. She holds the BS in Multidisciplinary Studies and the MS in Elementary Education—both from West Virginia University—she holds the PhD in Special Education from Florida State University, and she completed a Postdoctoral Fellowship in Early Childhood Research and Policy from The Ohio State University. Her major research interests focus on supporting the development of young children with disabilities by enhancing the capacity of early childhood educators and families to meet their individualized needs.

Celia Oyler is a professor of inclusive education at Teachers College, Columbia University where she teaches courses on curriculum, pedagogy, and participatory research methods. She devoted 15 years to teaching in public schools, 10 of which were spent teaching in inclusive classrooms. Her research interests focus on social justice, equity, accessible pedagogy, and their applicability to the areas of teacher education and inclusive education.

John Rocchi is currently the Director of Special Education with the Indian Creek Local School District in Wintersville, Ohio. He has served as Superintendent of two school districts in Eastern Ohio. He has an extensive background working with students with disabilities and taught students with emotional disturbances for 10 years. He also served as Ohio State Support Team Region 12 Special Education Coordinator and has been an adjunct professor with Muskingum University since 2009.

Moses Rumano is currently an associate professor and chair of the Education Department and director of the Education Graduate Program at Malone University where his interests are teacher preparation, transformative leadership, and community engagement. Originally from Zimbabwe, Dr. Rumano served as a teacher, deputy headmaster and a headmaster before coming to the United States. He taught at Miami University of Ohio and the University of Cincinnati before joining Malone University.

Beverly Sande is an Assistant Professor (Special Education) Intervention at Prairie View A & M University in Texas and has over 20 years of teaching experience (K-20). Her areas of expertise are Co-Teaching, collaborative clinical practices for teacher candidates (Clinical Model Practices), inclusive practices, (UDL, MTSS, RtI, and PBiS), culturally responsive teaching, and behavior management strategies (ABA). Dr. Sande is the treasurer for the Co-Teaching TAG of AACTE where she collaborates across institutions and across states to collect and share data on the impact of co-teaching on EPPs, teacher candidates and school age students.

Paul Sindelar is a Distinguished Professor of Special Education at the University of Florida. His recent research has concentrated on the special education teacher labor market and its implications for policymakers and educators, and he has written extensively on teacher certification, especially alternative routes. As a CEEDAR Center affiliate, his work has focused on policy analysis, developing demographic state profiles, and project evaluation.

Deborah Telfer is Research Associate and Director of the Systems Development & Improvement Center at the University of Cincinnati College of Education, Criminal Justice, Human Services, & Information Technology. Prior to working in higher education, she served for 25 years in a variety of roles at the Ohio Department of Education, including as Executive Director of the Center for School Improvement and Associate and Interim Director of the Office for Exceptional Children. Telfer received doctoral, masters, and bachelor of science degrees from The Ohio State University.

Martha Thurlow is Director of the National Center on Educational Outcomes and Senior Research Associate in the University of Minnesota's Institute on Community Integration. Her research and technical assistance activities address contemporary U.S. policy and practice for students with disabilities, English learners, and other marginalized students. She has published extensively, been a co-editor of *Exceptional Children*, and has received awards from the University of Minnesota and The Council for Exceptional Children.

Shernavaz Vakil received her doctorate from the University of Memphis in 1994 and is currently a Professor of Education in the Department of Curricular and Instructional Studies at the University of Akron. She is the author of several publications and presentations as well as the recipient of several grants in the areas of inclusion and best practices in special education for the diverse learner. She is currently a PI on an approximately 2 million dollar federal grant: NE Ohio ACHIEVE: Access to Curriculum and High Quality Instruction for Educators Valuing English Language Learners.

Pamela VanHorn, is the OLi[4] Project Coordinator at the Systems Development & Improvement Center within the College of Education, Criminal Justice, Human Services, and Information Technology at the University of Cincinnati. Pamela has over 40 years of school improvement experience as a special education teacher, principal, Ohio Department of Education director, and an instructor at The Ohio State University. The OLi^4 project works with over 75 districts statewide to improve outcomes for all students through systems leadership development training and structures.

Krista Wagner is the current Assistant Superintendent of Mad River Local Schools, where she dedicates herself to helping others realize the power of inclusive leadership practices and their importance to the overall success of a district. She received her undergraduate certification in Elementary Education (K–8th Grade) from Bowling Green State University and Urbana University and completed her graduate work in Educational Administration and Supervision at the University of Toledo. Prior to becoming Assistant Superintendent, she spent seventeen years in various teaching and administrative roles including 4th and 8th grade general education teacher, instructional coach, Principal of Spinning Hills Middle School, Special Education and Curriculum Supervisor, and Curriculum and Student Services Director.

Rebecca Watts, serves as Chancellor of WGU Ohio, a partnership between the state of Ohio and nationally recognized Western Governors University. Watts previously served as Executive Director for the University of Wyoming Trustees Education Initiative and as Associate Vice Chancellor for P–16 Initiatives at the Ohio Department of Higher Education. She holds a doctorate in higher education leadership from Ohio University, a master's degree from the University of Illinois at Springfield, a bachelor's degree from Sangamon State University, and an associate degree from Lincoln Land Community College.

Kathleen Winterman has over 30 years of experience working in the field of special education. Her experience includes serving as an intervention specialist serving children ages 3–10 in inclusive settings, serving as an Elementary Principal, serving as an Associate Professor and Director of the School of Education at Xavier University, and holds seven licenses from the State of Ohio. She is a published author where her areas of research interests include teacher preparation, IEP preparation, early childhood special education, Autism, educational leadership, the use of instructional technology, and services for students with mental illnesses.

Chad Wyen completed his undergraduate work at Bowling Green State University in Communications and Theater, special education teaching license at Wright State University, and graduate work at the University of Dayton in the area of Educational Administration. Chad was a special education teacher for one year at a Dayton Charter School and four years in Mad River Local Schools, until which time he began his administrative career. Over the past 15 years, Chad has served in various administrative roles including Assistant High School Principal at Stebbins High School, Principal of Brantwood Elementary, Special Education and Curriculum Supervisor for Mad River Local Schools, and his current role as Superintendent of Mad River Local Schools. During his tenure as an educator and administrator, he has assisted with the advancement of inclusive leadership practices within the district and community.

Victoria Zascavage worked for 15 years in the public schools in West Virginia and Texas as an Intervention Specialist for students with emotional and behavior disabilities. Victoria earned her PhD at Texas Woman's University in Denton, Texas and took a position at Texas A&M as faculty in Special Education. Currently, she is an Associate Professor of Special Education at Xavier University in Cincinnati. Victoria has published over 25 articles in peer reviewed journals, presented at conferences, and serves on the editorial board for several journals.

CPSIA information can be obtained
at www.ICGtesting.com
Printed in the USA
JSHW021420250220
4436JS00001B/1